MONETARY POLICY AND THE FINANCIAL SYSTEM

Fifth Edition

Paul M. Horvitz

Judge James A. Elkins Professor
Banking and Finance
University of Houston

Richard A. Ward

Associate Professor of Finance
and Business Economics
University of Southern California

PRENTICE-HALL, INC., Englewood Cliffs, New Jersey 07632

Library of Congress Cataloging in Publication Data

Horvitz, Paul M.
  Monetary policy and the financial system.

  Includes bibliographies and index.
  1. Monetary policy—United States.
2. Finance—United States. I. Ward, Richard
Alexander (date). II. Title.
HG540.H67 1983   332.4'973   82-12313
ISBN 0-13-599936-7

Editorial/production supervision and interior design by Pamela Wilder
Cover design by Jayne Conte
Manufacturing buyer: Ed O'Dougherty

Printed in the United States of America

10   9   8   7   6   5   4   3   2

ISBN 0-13-599936-7

Prentice-Hall International, Inc., *London*
Prentice-Hall of Australia Pty. Limited, *Sydney*
Prentice-Hall Canada Inc., *Toronto*
Prentice-Hall of India Private Limited, *New Delhi*
Prentice-Hall of Japan, Inc., *Tokyo*
Prentice-Hall of Southeast Asia Pte. Ltd., *Singapore*
Whitehall Books Limited, *Wellington, New Zealand*

Contents

Preface

It has become a cliché to note that the financial system is changing at a rapid rate. But the financial system has been changing rapidly for a long time. What is particularly relevant about some recent changes is that they have affected the day-to-day lives of the general public to an extent that has not been true in the past. This includes not only the development of NOW accounts and IRAs but also the changes in the level and volatility of interest rates. Students are not only more aware of what is happening in financial markets, they are more interested than ever before.

Similarly, the difficulties of the economy and economic policy in recent years have been brought home directly to college students in the form of traditional concerns about the job market for college graduates and because of inflationary tuition costs and decreased availability of student loans.

The central concept of finance is the relationship between risk and return. Students appreciate that the high and volatile interest rates that have prevailed in the 1980s mean that financial institutions are operating in an environment of greater risk. That makes their problems all the more interesting.

It is important to take advantage of the students' increased awareness and interest. It has long been my view that this can be accomplished best by making the discussion of financial markets and financial institutions as realistic as possible. Students are interested in the problems of the thrift industry and in learning why such institutions are not anxious to make long-term, fixed-rate mortgages anymore, but it takes a fair amount of background in history and regulation (as well as economics and finance) to make that story understandable and accurate.

Past editions of this text have discussed the need for deregulation of the financial system and noted the slow progress toward elimination of unnecessary restrictions. While the pace of deregulation is still slower than many of us would like, the process is now in motion. Barriers are falling with respect to interest rate competition and the geographic scope of operation of financial institutions, and chinks have appeared in the walls separating the activities of commercial banks, other financial institutions, and nonfinancial businesses.

These changes underscore the effort of previous editions to discuss the historical, competitive, and regulatory background necessary for an understanding of how the financial system operates. This text attempts not only to describe the structure of financial institutions but also to give some taste of the problems faced by the managers of financial institutions. This approach makes it easier for the student to see why the financial system reacts to policy measures the way it does.

The book has always devoted considerable attention to monetary policy. That continues with this edition. Previous prefaces have been somewhat apologetic about the inability to present to the student an analysis of monetary policy that represented a consensus of professional thought. We are no better off today, and the problem is perhaps worsened by the increased discussion of monetary policy issues in the popular press. The student is certainly aware that there is such a concept as a money supply, measured weekly, but is exposed to conflicting and confusing analyses of whether an increase in that number presages an increase or a decrease in interest rates. He or she is also exposed to conflicting views on such basic questions as whether a tax cut reduces or increases federal tax revenue. And 1982 has seen some life-long fiscal conservatives argue that federal deficits don't matter. The approach taken here is still one of presenting, as fairly as possible, the conflicting views and analyses.

The intent has been to provide a book which is appropriate for use in a course in Financial Markets or Financial Institutions as well as the traditional Money and Banking course. Some suggestions for alternative course formats are provided in the Instructor's Manual.

It became clear fairly early in the process that these develop-ments required a substantial rewriting of the entire text. I thought that a fresh perspective would be very helpful if it could be achieved without losing the strengths of the previous editions. I sought as a co-author for this edition Professor Richard Ward of the University of Southern California, with whom I had worked closely some years earlier. I have been very pleased with the results of this collabora-tion. Professor Ward is responsible for most of the extensive revi-sion. He has built on the previous editions, and our discussions of numerous issues have strengthened the presentation.

We owe thanks to many people in the task of completing this revision. Comments on this and previous editions from my former colleagues, Sherman Shapiro, Bernard Shull, and Clint Johnson have been very helpful. David Hildebrand and his staff at Prentice-Hall, particularly our production editor, Pam Wilder, have been encouraging and helpful.

Paul M. Horvitz

I

MONEY
AND FINANCIAL
INSTITUTIONS

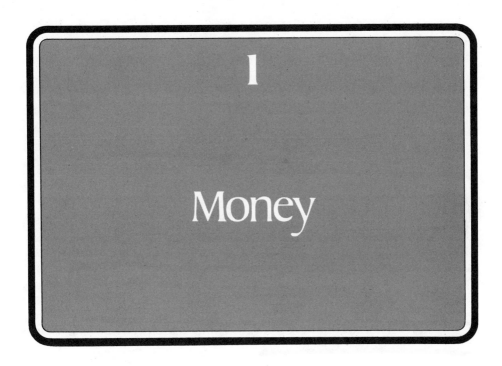

1

Money

In a book dealing with money, a definition of the subject matter and an explanation of why it is important may seem unnecessary. After all, everyone knows what money is and how important it is. In fact, if the man in the street is asked to name the most important economic factors determining his spending or other financial actions, he is likely to answer in terms of "how much money I am making," or "how much money I have." He would give much the same answer if asked how he would measure his economic well-being. Thirty years ago, professional economists would have rejected such answers as imprecise wording demonstrating confusion between *income* and *assets*, or between various forms of wealth.

The economist makes a sharp distinction between the *income* a person earns and the *money*—dollar bills or similar assets—that person holds. In the years following the absorption of John Maynard Keynes's *General Theory of Employment, Interest, and Money* into the mainstream of economic thought, the accepted view was that income was an extremely important determinant of spending decisions, but that money, strictly defined, was not very important.

In more recent years, many economists have come to the view that perhaps the man in the street is quite correct—that perhaps money is more important in economic decisions than the post-Keynesian economists appreciated. It is a principal task of this book to sort out the different senses in which the word *money* is used, and to trace the relationship between money and the other economic variables we are all interested in—prices, employment, wealth, and income. We can best approach this task by being more specific about the definition of money and its role in our society.

Dollar bills are a relatively recent development in historical terms, but money is not. Money, in one form or another, existed before recorded history. Virtually all societies developed money early in their existence. It has been in use for centuries.

But despite that fact, the concept of money is not easy to define. It will be helpful if we can pinpoint its essential characteristics. Money has been rather pompously defined as "the complex of those objects which . . . in a given economic system have as their normal purpose the facilitation of economic intercourse (for the transfer of values) between economic individuals."[1] Other economists have defined money as "property with which the owner can pay off a definite amount of debt—with certainty and without delay. . . ."[2] The heart of these definitions is simply that "money is what we use to pay for things."[3]

SPECIALIZATION, EXCHANGE, AND MONEY

Very early in the history of civilization, people discovered the advantages of division of labor and specialization. It was apparent even to primitive tribes that if some people devoted themselves to making weapons, others to hunting, and still others to farming, the tribe as a whole would end up with more weapons and more food than if everyone attempted to do everything for himself. The difficulty inherent in this specialization was that no one would specialize in making arrows unless he could exchange his arrow production for food. Provision for exchange is essential if specialization is to be successful.

The primary function of money is to facilitate the process of exchange. Of course, exchange could take place without money, but it would be extremely complicated. In primitive societies, direct bartering of goods for other goods is common, but there are obvious difficulties. A butcher who wants shoes must find a shoemaker who wants meat. If the shoemaker is a vegetarian, the butcher must

[1] Karl Helfferich, *Money*, trans. Louis Infield (New York: The Adelphi Company, 1927), p. 281.

[2] Albert G. Hart and Peter B. Kenen, *Money, Debt and Economic Activity*, 3rd ed. (Englewood Cliffs, N.J.: Prentice-Hall, 1961), p. 4.

[3] "Money," *Encyclopaedia Britannica* (1946), XV, p. 693.

either make a preliminary trade or go barefoot. The difficulty of finding the other party to a desired exchange would mean that little trading could actually take place.

Another shortcoming of a barter system is that no unit exists in which prices are expressed. Trade requires that everyone know the price of every good in terms of every other good. With money, all we have to know is the price in monetary terms.

The need for money to facilitate exchange indicates that money is desired not for its own sake but only for what it can buy. Robinson Crusoe had no use for money, because he had no opportunity to exchange goods or services for other goods. Even when he was joined by Friday, his necessary transactions could easily be handled by barter.

In colonial America, the family farm operated on a near-subsistence basis. Food and shelter, clothing and tools were all home-grown and homemade, with little need for money or markets. The small amount of trade conducted could be handled by barter. But as population and the opportunities for specialization grew and the standard of living rose, barter rapidly became too cumbersome. The 1960s and 1970s saw some people, dissatisfied with the complexities of modern life, seeking to return to the self-sufficiency of pioneer days. The communes of young people and the subsistence farm of the dropout advertising executive have not found it easy to completely eliminate the need for money.

Despite its disadvantages, barter persists, in some instances, even in advanced economies. In the majority of cases, the sale of a new car involves some element of barter; the customer exchanges his old car for a new one. This is not pure barter, of course, because the buyer must also make some money payment, and the transaction is expressed in terms of money.

THE FUNCTIONS OF MONEY

The preceding discussion of money has indicated two of its principal functions. Money serves both as a unit of value and as a medium of exchange. However, we can conceive of these as being two separable tasks. Money has other functions as well—it serves as a standard for deferred payments and as a store of value.

Unit of Value

Our unit of account is the dollar, whereas the British unit is the pound and the Russian is the ruble. The dollar (or pound or ruble) is simply the unit by which we express relative values, much as the inch (or centimeter) is the unit by which we express size. We can measure size in terms of inches even though the inch has no physical substance.

In our modern economy, we sometimes make use of measures of value that have no physical existence. Thus, we may say that a shoeshine costs "four bits" or a magazine "six bits," even though there is no such coin as the "bit." The British sometimes quote prices in "guineas," a monetary unit no longer in use.

We have seen that the principal reason for the existence of money is to make specialization and exchange feasible. By serving as the unit of value, or money makes it possible to express all values on a common basis.

Medium of Exchange

We have defined money in terms of its use as a means to pay for things. Thus, money serves as a means of exchange, and anything that will be accepted in payment for goods is money. In various societies, many different things have served as the medium of exchange—gold, stones, paper, teeth, goats, and accounts with a bank are only a small fraction of the complete list of things that have served as money. Even in our modern economy, to some extent store coupons serve as a means of payment.

In primitive economies, the medium of exchange is often something valuable for its own sake—arrowheads, for example. This type of money is called *full-bodied money*. Most monies in modern economies are examples of *credit money*, which includes all money that circulates at a value greater than the value of the material of which it consists. Prior to 1933, the United States had gold coins in circulation with a gold content equal in value to the face value of the coins. These coins would be classified as *full-bodied money*. Modern paper money is, of course, credit money. Thus, the money that serves as a medium of exchange in a modern economy is desired not for its own sake but because it will be widely accepted in exchange for goods and services.

Standard for Deferred Payments

The existence of a unit of value is important not only for current exchange but also for transactions involving future or deferred payment. In any modern economy, there are large amounts of money involved in contracts requiring future payment. These range from one-day loans to agreements whereby the borrower need not repay the loan for 50 years. They include the very common arrangement under which an employee begins work on Monday on the promise of payment on Friday. The total volume of contracts requiring future payment in the United States today, if they could be totaled, would be measured in the trillions of dollars. Because we express all these contracts in terms of the monetary unit, we say that money serves as the standard for deferred payments.

Such contracts can be written in terms of some specific commodity, but this has disadvantages. There is the serious risk that the commodity to be repaid may change considerably in value, causing a gain or loss to either party to the transaction. The price of wool is lower now than it was in 1952, and the price of steel is higher.

Because of this danger of fluctuation in the relative value of particular commodities, the parties to a contract would often be unable to agree on the particular commodity in which repayment is to be made. Moreover, when repayment is made, there might be disagreement over the quality of the goods repaid.[4] As a practical matter, contracts involving future payment would be extremely difficult to arrange without money.

Store of Value

Because money is widely accepted and represents, in effect, generalized purchasing power, it serves as a convenient store of value. The holder of money need not exchange his money for goods immediately—he can hold the money to spend when he desires.

Of course, money is not the only store of value. Any asset may serve more or less efficiently as a store of value. An asset that is likely to depreciate rapidly will not make a good store of purchasing power. A wheat farmer may keep some of his output as a means of storing purchasing power, but the fisherman is well advised not to use his product as a store of value.

Even money has some disadvantages as a store of value. If the owner of money keeps it in the form of currency, it will earn no

[4] An example of this difficulty is quoted by J. M. Keynes, *A Treatise on Money* (New York: Harcourt, Brace & World, Inc., 1930), p. 13: "A District Commissioner in Uganda today, where goats are the customary native standard, tells me that it is a part of his official duties to decide, in cases of dispute, whether a given goat is or is not too old or too scraggy to constitute a standard goat for the purposes of discharging a debt."

interest. Moreover, if prices of goods should rise, the value of a given amount of money will decline. Thus, the holder of money can suffer a loss in the purchasing power of his holdings even though its monetary value remains the same.

Consider the position of a person who carefully put $100 in his mattress in 1970. If he were to take that money out today, he would find that he still has $100, but that the sum will buy less than half what it would have bought in 1970. Because money may vary in value or purchasing power, it is not a perfect store of value.

Jewelry, stocks and bonds, land, and houses have all served as means of holding wealth. These may, at times, overcome the disadvantages of money as a store of value, but they involve other disadvantages. They may rise in value in terms of money, but they may also fall in value. They may, unlike money, earn a return in the form of dividends, interest, rent, or enjoyment, but sometimes they incur storage costs. Since only money serves as the medium of exchange, all other assets must be converted into money before they can be exchanged for other goods. If this must be done quickly, the holder of the asset could suffer a substantial loss. Thus, money has a great advantage over other assets for meeting unexpected expenses.

QUALITIES OF GOOD MONEY

We defined money in terms of its acceptance in payment for goods and services. Thus, general acceptability is an important quality if a money is to serve efficiently as a standard of value, medium of exchange, store of value, or standard for deferred payments. Other qualities are also important.

A commodity could conceivably serve as a medium of exchange or standard of value even if its value were not stable. However, it would not efficiently fulfill the other functions of money. If money varies in value through time, it will impose a burden on some people and provide others with windfall gains. Suppose Jones was considering buying a house in 1972 but instead lent his $60,000 to Smith for ten years. Jones expected that in 1982, when the loan was repaid with interest, he would be able to afford a better house than he could have bought in 1972. But since prices rose during the period, Jones finds that in 1982 he is not as well off as he was in 1972.

Suppose, on the other hand, that prices declined over the period of the loan. When Smith must repay the loan, he is returning more purchasing power than he borrowed. Because of the inequities caused by variations in the value of money, it is important that money be relatively stable in value.

Of even more importance than this inequity is the fact that if there is considerable uncertainty about the future value of money, Jones and Smith may refuse to enter into long-term arrangements that could be advantageous to both. We shall see that protecting the value of money is one of the most important objectives of monetary policy.

The commodity that is to serve as money should be easily divisible into fractional values. Metals such as gold or silver meet this requirement, but cattle or jewels do not. The monetary commodity—often referred to as the standard money—should also be one that is durable, easily recognizable, and portable. Portability implies high value per ounce. Iron has served in the past as money, but it is now so cheap that it would be difficult to use to settle a transaction of any size.

Gold has met most of these requirements better than any other single commodity, even though its value has been quite unstable. Paper money could, of course, meet all these tests, although it turns out that maintaining stability in the value of money takes deliberate management. Later on we will examine in detail what proper management of a monetary standard involves.

MONEY AND THE ECONOMY

Money is itself an important subject, but for many students it would not be worthwhile reading a book of this size if it were not for the fact that money has significant effects on the "real" side of the economy. We measure many economic variables in terms of dollar amounts—income, wages, production, and so on—but we are actually interested in the real things involved: goods and services. Although we may speak or think about our income as being so many *dollars*, we want dollars not for their own sake but for what they will buy. It is real income—income in terms of goods and services—that is of primary importance.

Economists are concerned about prices because of the inequitable effects of changes in the price level, but they are principally interested in real, or nonmonetary, factors: employment, production, real income, and so on. The classical economists of the nineteenth and early twentieth centuries tended to minimize the effects of money on the real side of the economy. These economists argued that money was simply a "veil behind which the action of real economic forces is concealed." They believed that if we removed this veil, we would see that the basis of exchange is the trading of goods

for goods, and not goods for money. As one of the clearest exponents
of this position put it:

> It must be evident, however, that the mere introduction of a particular mode of exchang-
> ing things for one another, by first exchanging a thing for money, and then exchanging
> the money for something else, makes no difference in the essential character of transac-
> tions. . . .
>
> There cannot, in short, be intrinsically a more insignificant thing, in the economy
> of society, than money; except in the character of a contrivance for sparing time and
> labour. It is a machine for doing quickly and commodiously what would be done, though
> less quickly and commodiously, without it: and like many other kinds of machinery, it
> only exerts a distinct and independent influence of its own when it gets out of order. . . .
>
> The reasons which make the temporary or market value of things depend on the
> demand and supply . . . are as applicable to a money system as to a system of barter.
> Things which by barter would exchange for one another, will, if sold for money, sell for
> an equal amount of it, and so will exchange for one another still, though the process of
> exchanging them will consist of two operations instead of only one. The relations of
> commodities to one another remain unaltered by money.[5]

This view of money was also inherent in the classical economists' argument that the economy always tended to operate at full
employment—that general overproduction or a "general glut of the
market" was impossible. This argument rested on *Say's Law*. According to J.B. Say, an early nineteenth-century French economist,
supply creates its own demand. When a producer of goods comes to
market with goods to trade, his supply is also his demand for other
goods.

This is obviously the case with barter: The baker cannot sell his
bread except by simultaneously buying something else—say, beer.
His supply of bread is equal to his demand for beer. If he cannot find
anyone willing to trade beer for bread, then production in the economy has not been optimal—there was too much bread baked and
not enough beer brewed—but there has not been general overproduction.

Money changes the picture. If the baker sells his bread for
money and uses the money to buy beer, money has merely facilitated the exchange of bread for beer—an exchange that could have
taken place with barter. But suppose instead that the baker sells his
bread for money and puts the money under his mattress. He has the
means of buying the beer, but chooses not to do so. How will the
brewer sell his beer? Will he be forced ot lay off workers? Money—
generalized purchasing power—has been withdrawn from the flow
of trade and has depressed the whole market system. It is possible
that a decline in all money prices may stimulate demand and rescue

[5] John Stuart Mill, *Principles of Political Economy* (New York: Appleton-
Century Crofts, Inc., 1923), Vol. II, Book III, Chap. 7 pp. 22–24.

Say's Law. This adds consideration of macroeconomic analysis to Say's microeconomic reasoning.

There is another possibility in a modern economy. If the baker is a reputable businessman, he may be able to borrow money from the bank and buy beer without providing any additional goods to the market. (We will have to wait until later to discuss how the bank can provide additional money to the baker.) Or the government may simply print more money in order to buy beer (or missiles) for its employees. This new money is an addition to the money already being used to buy goods. If there is no increase in the supply of goods available, all that this additional purchasing power can do is push prices up.

Once we accept the view that money can affect the economy, we are attracted to the possibility of influencing the economy by means of monetary policy. In fact, throughout history and to the present day, manipulation of money has appealed to some as a means of solving all the world's economic problems.

Modern economists generally take a middle course between these extremes. Virtually no one argues now that "money doesn't matter," nor is there much support for the view that "only money matters." After that is said, however, it must be conceded that economists differ greatly about the mechanism by which money affects the economy, the extent of such effects, and the time within which they operate. In recent years, economists have increased substantially their knowledge of monetary forces and of their effect on the economy, but considerable uncertainty still exists concerning these precise relationships and their implications for monetary policy.

Some issues have been in dispute for a long time, but it is important to keep this controversy in perspective. Even the classical economists did not argue that money has no effects on the economy. The statement by Mill quoted earlier refers to the effect of money on the *real* variables in the economy: the quantity and type of goods produced; the relation between the price of one good and the price of another; the distribution of income among workers, employers, and landlords. In the classical scheme, these variables were not affected by changes in the quantity of money in existence. The classical economists believed that only the overall level of prices was directly affected by the quantity of money; with respect to the real variables, money is neutral.

It was obvious to the classical economists that if people have more money, they spend more. Of course, there is not a perfect correspondence between the amount of money in the economy and the amount of spending. The classical economists were aware that some account must be taken of the *rate* at which money is spent. They called this rate the *velocity of money*, and held that it was fairly constant. Thus, the quantity of money is related (with the help of the velocity concept) to total spending—that is, to total demand in the economy.

If there is a rise in the quantity of money, the demand for goods increases. If we assume, as the classical economists did, that the quantity of goods available does not change as a result, it is obvious that prices must rise. In general, the classical economists argued that the price level would vary directly with the quantity of money in circulation. This has been called the *quantity theory of money*.

This conclusion rests on two assumptions: first, that velocity is stable; and second, that the quantity of goods produced does not change in response to a change in the money supply. The classical economists were interested in long-run tendencies in the economy, and perhaps these assumptions are valid in the long run (we will examine the evidence more closely later on), but they are less valid in the short run.

Modern economists focus more attention on the short run, where money often "gets out of order." Suppose the money supply is reduced; people's demand for goods will decline. The retailer may react not by simply cutting his prices but also by cutting his orders to suppliers. His suppliers in turn may lay off employees when they cannot cut wages. If his workers do agree to work for lower wages, they will cut their spending because of their lower incomes. So still other retailers will face a reduction in the demand for their goods. This approach recognizes that one person's spending is another 's income and focuses on the factors that affect income and spending in the economy.

This emphasis on income and spending (and their relation to employment) was stressed by John Maynard Keynes in the 1930s. In his analysis, changes in money have their most direct effects on interest rates. Changes in interest rates then have a series of effects on the economy.

In recent years, there has been growing interest in a modern reformulation of the quantity theory. The modern quantity theorists, or *monetarists*, accept the classical view that the velocity of money is more or less stable (or at least is a stable function of other variables), but reject the classical assumption of fixed output of goods and services. Some monetarists then come to the conclusion that change in the supply of money is the most potent means of managing the economy. It should be stressed that in their policy analyses, the monetarists are focusing on the short run. Most believe that in the long run, the classical conclusions about the neutrality of money are correct. That is, in the long run, the quantity of money determines the level of prices but does not affect the output of real goods and services. In Part VI we will consider both the quantity and the income-expenditure approaches to monetary theory.

It would certainly be neater for the student of monetary economics if we could present a single "true" version of the relationship between money and the economy. Even though some authorities are sure that their views are correct, it seems more appropriate for us to concede that the economics profession does not yet have the definitive answers to all questions on this subject. The approach in the rest of this book is not only to cover areas in which there is general agreement but also to point out those aspects of monetary theory on which economists differ.

SAVING, INVESTMENT, AND FINANCIAL INSTITUTIONS

The process of saving and investment are among the most important in any economy. These activities, and the relation between them, are crucial whether we are concerned with business fluctuations, the level of economic activity in a developed economy, or the process of economic growth in a less-developed economy. In a developed economy, saving and investment activities are undertaken separately by different individuals and business firms. They are facilitated by a variety of financial institutions and financial instruments interacting in a complex set of financial systems, but saving and investment go on in all economies, including the most primitive.

Saving and investment take place even in a Robinson Crusoe economy. In such an economy, saving and investment take place together; that is, the act of saving and the act of investing are one. The farmer who reserves some of his harvest to use as seed for the next year is simultaneously saving and investing. On a slightly more complex level, transactions among individuals can take place on a barter basis. The possibilities of borrowing and lending expand the opportunities for both saving and investment. The farmer seeking to expand his production can borrow seed from someone who has a surplus, with his investment thus aided by the lender's saving. Even interest can be part of this transaction. Presumably the borrower can afford to repay more than he borrowed, because the investment process is a productive one. In this situation, saving and investment, borrowing and lending take place without any financial institutions or, indeed, any financial instruments. We thus have a means of shifting resources—in this example, grain—from those units in the economy with a surplus to those with deficits. This is the role that in a developed economy will be played by financial institutions. Although such transactions can and do take place in primitive societies, such economic intercourse is facilitated by the use of money.

Money also becomes an additional asset for savers and an additional means of financing expenditures for investors. Savers may acquire real assets such as grain, land, and the like, or may accumulate cash balances. Investors may finance expenditures from current saving or by drawing down previously accumulated money holdings. With the introduction of money, the rigid link between saving and investment is broken and, even though all expenditures are financed within the economy, some flexibility has been introduced into the saving–investment process.

More complex and sophisticated financial systems extend the alternatives available to suppliers and demanders of loanable funds. By increasing the number and variety of savings media (uses of funds) and the techniques of raising funds (sources of funds), more sophisticated financial systems facilitate transfer of real resources from lenders (surplus units) to borrowers (deficit units).

A sophisticated financial system is an essential feature of a highly industrialized economy. The mass production and distribution of goods and services and the high degree of specialization involved are mirrored in the financial sector of the economy by a similar degree of complex interaction: An elaborate system of markets and institutions provides the mechanisms for bringing suppliers and demanders of funds together. The saving–investment process is facilitated by numerous institutions that offer savers a wider variety of substitutes for real goods or money, thus encouraging the flow and diversification of savings, and many methods of providing borrowers with funds to meet their requirements, thus promoting investment spending.

Saving and Investment

It is appropriate to pause here and ask why we are concerned with promotion of saving and investment. *Investment* is a confusing term, because we use it in two different senses. "Financial" investment refers to the acquisition of claims to wealth—typically, pieces of paper representing real assets or wealth. When I buy a corporate stock or bond, there is no change in the amount of wealth in the economy. An asset formerly owned by one person is simply transferred to another's ownership. This is not a trivial matter; facilitation of such transfers is important to the economy, and we will return to it in some detail later on. At this point, however, we are interested in "real" investment. Real investment is the process of capital formation, or adding to the economy's stock of "capital goods"—equipment, machinery, tools, construction material, inventories—in short, anything used in the production process.

Our capacity to produce more goods and services over time—growth in economic activity—results from supplying a larger, better-educated and trained labor force with more capital, or from utilizing more capital per unit of labor or output. Although there are clearly many physical, social, and psychological factors responsible for the differences in growth rates among countries, the ratio of capital to total national output seems empirically to be highly significant. Countries with high growth rates tend to save a high proportion of total income. An economy with capital-intensive production processes (that is, processes that use a large amount of capital goods) is likely to grow faster than other countries in terms of physical output. The development of a variety of financial instruments, institutions, and markets can provide encouragement to saving and facilitate investment.

In a developed economy, most investment is undertaken by business firms. Businesspeople order newly produced capital goods to use in producing consumer goods and other capital goods. Saving decisions, on the other hand, are made by consumers, who may spend less than their total income. The resulting savings may be used for *direct* investment, as, for example, when the sole owner of a business uses funds he has saved to add new equipment to his store; it may also be used for *financial* investment, in the purchase of financial assets such as stock or bonds; or it may simply be held in the form of additional money. Financial investment may go directly into loans and investments or may be channeled through financial intermediaries. Funds received by such institutions may be channeled into loans to business firms, purchase of government securities, or loans to consumers.

Financial Institutions and Intermediation

In any economy at any time, there will be some spending units that will be saving or accumulating surpluses. There will be other units in the economy that will be investing or otherwise spending more than their current income. If the investment process is to be facilitated, some means must be found to channel the funds from the surplus units to the deficit units. In a less-developed economy, most financing takes place directly from a surplus unit to deficit unit, but in a developed financial economy, institutions arise to serve as intermediaries in this process.

Some direct borrowing–lending transactions take place even in the most sophisticated financial system. Such a transaction requires some fortuitous coincidences: The borrower must find a lender who is willing and able to provide the appropriate amount of funds, and who is willing to accept repayment at the time desired by the lender. Typically, there will be little the lender can do to convert this direct debt into money if he should need his funds before the maturity of the contract with the borrower.

Figure 1-1 shows the transfer of funds from surplus units to deficit units. The diagram shows that some funds flow directly from ultimate lenders (surplus units) to ultimate borrowers (deficit units) in exchange for *primary securities*; that is, the obligations of the ultimate borrowers. Financial institutions serve as intermediaries to accommodate both the deficit and surplus sectors. Funds may flow from the surplus units to the financial institutions in exchange for *indirect financial assets*; that is, the obligations of the financial institutions. Funds flow from the financial institutions to the deficit spending units in exchange for their primary securities. Essentially, financial institutions gather the savings of individuals and lend those funds to business and consumers. This process is called *intermediation*.

Although one may start out with the view that transactions involving middlemen are less efficient than direct transactions, this is not so in the case of financial transactions. The process of intermediation, in fact, provides significant benefits both to the ultimate lenders and to the ultimate borrowers.

Let us look at this from the point of view of the saver: Instead of lending directly to an individual or business firm needing additional funds, the saver instead acquires an indirect financial asset issued by a financial institution. These indirect assets have different names and characteristics, such as *deposits* (in the case of banks), *shares* (in the case of some savings and loan associations or credit unions), or *insurance*. There are several advantages to the saver in this process. First is that the indirect securities have a wider range of maturities than those in which primary securities are typically issued. Financial institutions accept funds for as short as a day, or for as long as many years. These indirect securities come in a wide range of denominations. In particular, the saver can put very small amounts into a transaction with a financial institution, whereas this would not be practical in dealing directly with a business firm or other borrower. Second, and perhaps most important, the securities issued by financial institutions tend to have less risk

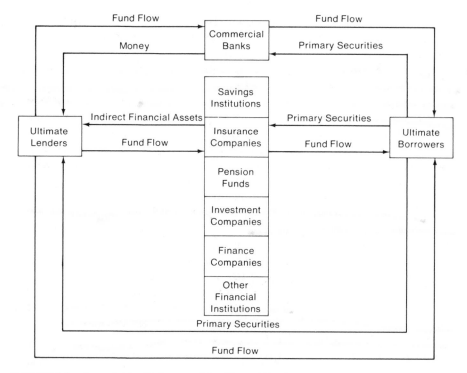

FIGURE 1-1 Financial Institutions and the Flow of Funds.

Source: Adapted from Charles N. Henning, William Piggot, and Robert H. Scott, *Financial Markets and the Economy.* Englewood Cliffs, N.J.: Prentice-Hall, Inc., 1980.

of default than primary securities. Intermediaries are able to re-duce risk by investing the funds received from money savers in a wide range of different primary securities. Diversification reduces risk, and the financial intermediary is much better able to obtain the desired diversification than the individual saver. Also, the financial institution is able to build up expertise as a result of spe-cializing in this type of business and is better able, therefore, to evaluate the creditworthiness of borrowers.

A third advantage, and to some customers of financial institu-tions the most important, is that the assets acquired by dealing with a financial institution typically have greater "liquidity" than most primary securities; that is, the instrument acquired from a finan-cial institution may be converted to cash with little or no risk of loss, either on demand or on short notice. (A more precise definition of this important concept must wait until the next chapter.) Financial institutions can afford to commit themselves to this because they know that not all of their many creditors will simultaneously seek to take advantage of it. Although there may be some penalties or loss involved in early conversion to cash, these are much less than would typically be the case in dealing with primary securities.

The net effect of these advantages is that the individual saver can generally obtain a higher true net return by investing in the obligations of financial intermediaries than by lending directly to an ultimate borrower. That is, after allowing for the differences in risk and liquidity, and saving on the costs of searching for an appropriate investment, the net return is generally higher. This is important, because it means that the individual in an economy with a well-developed financial system will have more incentive to save than the one in an economy without these options.

There are also advantages to borrowers in the economy from this process of intermediation. Financial institutions will buy primary securities from deficit spending units in a wider range of maturities than individual buyers will. Institutions make loans for as short a time as overnight, or for as long as many years. They will also buy securities or make loans in larger amounts than individual lenders typically could. The net effect is that the interest cost to the borrower, after allowing for the saving on searching for funds, is lower than if he were to seek lenders willing to lend directly. Again, the existence of financial intermediaries facilitates borrowing and hence encourages investment.

This discussion of financial institutions has been on a rather abstract level. A major purpose of the rest of this book is to flesh out the skeleton of financial intermediation depicted in Figure 1-1 and to explore the relevance of that theoretical framework to our real economy.

QUESTIONS

1 Can an economy operate efficiently without money?
2 What are the disadvantages of barter?
3 Why does barter become more common during very rapid inflations?
4 Would you be better or worse off if, other things being equal, you had more money? Is it possible for an economy to have too much money?
5 Is it possible for money to depreciate in value if it is backed 100% by gold?
6 How do financial institutions promote saving in the economy?
7 How do financial institutions promote real investment in the economy?

BIBLIOGRAPHICAL NOTE

At the end of each of the remaining chapters, the reader will find a short list of references for further reading. The references include alternative expositions of the basic points of the chapter, as well as differing points of view on policy issues and further discussion of some issues raised in the chapter.

In addition, the student should become acquainted with the professional journals in the fields of economics and banking. The leading economics journals, such as the *American Economic Review*, frequently include articles of interest to the student of money and banking. The *Journal of Finance* is devoted to articles concerned with financial institutions, monetary theory, and monetary policy. Although most of the articles in these publications are written for the professional economist, some are easily understandable to the interested layman. Moreover, it is helpful to the student of monetary economics to get some feel for the kind of research currently being done by specialists in the field. The *Journal of Money, Credit and Banking* and the *Journal of Bank Research*, contain a somewhat higher proportion of articles readable by the nonprofessional.

The student of monetary matters may be interested in current developments in the field. The financial pages of daily newspapers as well as such specialized newspapers as *The Wall Street Journal* provide news of monetary developments on a daily basis. The *Federal Reserve Bulletin* is published monthly and contains articles on monetary policy as well as a wealth of statistical data. Most of the monetary and banking statistics employed in this book appear regularly in the *Federal Reserve Bulletin*. All twelve Federal Reserve Banks have periodic publications that are available without charge.

Many large banks also publish periodic analyses of the business and financial situation. The *Monthly Letter* of the First National City Bank of New York is an excellent example of this type of publication. The *Annual Report* of the Board of Governors of the Federal Reserve System and that of the Federal Reserve Bank of New York include excellent summaries of the year's developments in the financial markets and in monetary policy.

The Federal Reserve Board publishes a loose-leaf *Federal Reserve Regulatory Service*, covering all Board regulations and related materials.

2
The United States Money and Financial System

We have indicated that the fundamental requirement of good money is that it be widely accepted. But what is it that makes a particular money widely accepted? I am willing to accept a dollar bill in payment of a debt because I know that everyone else will accept it. If I felt that it would be unacceptable to some, I would not want it either. This amounts to saying that the quality that makes money generally acceptable is its general acceptability!

In attempting to break this chain of circular reasoning, some have argued that money is acceptable because of its intrinsic value. Gold is a widely accepted money, they argue, because gold can be used for jewelry or teeth. Paper money that may be redeemed for gold is considered to be good money because it can be converted into widely acceptable gold. Those who uphold this view are generally suspicious of paper money that is *not* backed by, or redeemable in, gold or silver. On the other hand, others argue that much of the value of gold derives from the fact that it is acceptable as money.

In this chapter we will discuss alternative monetary standards and review briefly the experience of the United States with several of them. Our objective is to define and measure the U.S. money supply. In this country, as in all modern economies, the bulk of the actual money supply is furnished by financial institutions. We will therefore examine the role of certain financial institutions with respect to their contribution to the money supply.

MONETARY STANDARDS

At the present time, there is no real link between our domestic money system and the precious metals—gold or silver. For most of our history, however, there was some connection, and, in fact, much of our economic history can be traced in terms of a struggle between those who favored severing or loosening that connection and those who favored the greater discipline of a tight link between gold and the dollar.

Metallic Standards

A country may adopt either a *metallic* monetary standard, under which the circulating paper money may be converted into metal at a fixed rate, or an *inconvertible* standard, under which no promise of conversion is made. There are many possible variations on the metallic standard, with gold being the most frequently used. Silver has been used in the Orient as the monetary standard, and in the United States it has been used in combination with gold, as part of a *bimetallic* standard. Historically, however, silver has not been as universally acceptable as gold.

Even under the gold standard, there are a number of possible variations. In all cases under a gold standard, the monetary unit (say, the dollar) is defined in terms of a fixed number of grains of gold.[1] Under some systems, gold coins circulated, and in some, paper money could be converted to gold only in specified minimum amounts. The U.S. monetary system after 1934 was generally referred to as a gold standard (the dollar was defined in terms of gold), but paper money could not be converted into gold by Americans. In fact, until 1975, American citizens were not allowed to own gold.

Inconvertible Standards

A standard under which paper money cannot be converted into a metal is called an *inconvertible paper standard*. This means the government will maintain a parity among the different types of

[1] From 1934 to 1971, the dollar was defined as worth 13.714 grains of gold, so that an ounce (480 grains) of gold was worth 480/13.714, or $35.

money but not between paper money and gold or silver. Redemption of money under such a standard simply means exchanging one form of paper money for another.

Inconvertible standards are sometimes referred to as "managed" systems. This is somewhat misleading, because in modern times, all monetary systems—metallic or inconvertible—are highly managed. Under a pure metallic system, a country's money supply is determined by its stock of the monetary metal. We have seen that changes in the supply of money can have important effects on the economy. There is no automatic mechanism that assures that the stock of gold in a country at a particular time will be appropriate to the country's economic situation. There is no assurance that changes in the gold stock will be in the direction desired to maintain a stable economy. Since the money supply is important to the economy, it is not reasonable to allow it to be determined by the productivity of gold miners or the luck of prospectors. Thus, a country must manage its monetary system to some extent regardless of the type of standard under which it operates.

Even opponents of inconvertible standards generally concede that some monetary management is desirable. Their contention, however, is that having a currency that can be redeemed in metal provides a discipline for the money managers; that government authorities will be more cautious and prudent if they know they have an obligation to redeem paper money for gold.

Descriptions of rigid gold standards often imply that under a gold standard, the purchasing power of gold is constant. This is not true. Under a gold standard, the *money price* of an ounce of gold is fixed. The *purchasing power* of gold, however, can vary depending on the prices of other commodities. Fixing the money unit in terms of gold does not guarantee a constant purchasing power over goods; it merely means that the purchasing power of gold and the purchasing power of the monetary unit will vary together. There is no basis for the belief that a general rise in prices—inflation—is impossible under a gold standard. In later chapters we will consider the role of monetary policy in the economy, and we will then return to the question of monetary standards.

THE U.S. MONEY SYSTEM

During its relatively short history, the United States has had virtually every kind of monetary standard, from the simplest to the most sophisticated. The early American colonies had no monetary system of their own. They used various foreign currencies for money, and also commodities—from bullets to woodpecker scalps. Some colonies later did issue paper money of various qualities, none very good. The Continental Congress financed the Revolution by issuing paper money backed by the promise to pay coin. But since the Continental Congress had no coin, or any taxing power to get coin, the paper money rapidly became virtually worthless. In fact, it became the very epitome of worthlessness in the phrase, "not worth a continental."

This sad experience with inconvertible paper money led to the adoption of sound-money principles under the new Constitution. The Constitution gave Congress the power to "coin money, and regulate the value thereof." In 1792, Congress adopted a bimetallic standard, which set the relative value of an ounce of gold as equal to 15 ounces of silver. In terms of market prices and the monetary standards of other countries, this tended to overvalue silver. People thus tended to keep any gold they acquired (perhaps by converting their paper money) and to use silver to pay bills. In practice, then, we seemed to have a silver standard, since that was the only metal that circulated.[2]

The hard-money policies of the United States suffered during the Civil War. In 1862, Congress authorized the issuance of *United States notes*, which were not redeemable in gold or silver. These notes depreciated rapidly in terms of gold, but they increased in value after the war. The greenbacks, as they were called, were gradually retired in the postwar years, and in 1879, the remaining amount outstanding was made convertible into gold.

The resumption of specie payments in 1879 was in gold only, and this put the country, for all practical purposes, on a gold standard. Silver-mining interests fought bitterly for a more favorable status for silver, and they were joined by farmers and others who felt that any increase in the money supply (and in prices) would be to their benefit. As a result of such pressures, Congress enacted legislation, in 1878 and 1890, requiring the Treasury to buy specified amounts of silver.

Doubts about the Treasury's ability to maintain the convertibility of the dollar into gold led to a steady drain of gold. By 1893, the Treasury's gold reserves fell below the level that had been considered a safe minimum, and a full-scale financial panic developed. A special session of Congress was called by President Cleveland, and under strong pressure, it repealed the 1890 Silver Purchase Act

---

[2] This tendency for the overvalued money to drive the undervalued money out of circulation is called *Gresham's Law*. The idea that "bad money drives out good money" was known for centuries but was formulated most clearly by Sir Thomas Gresham.

in November 1893. It is unfair to lay the entire blame for the panic of 1893 on our silver policy, but certainly it made a serious situation a critical one.

The silver interests and their supporters did not give up easily. The election of 1896 was, to a considerable extent, a battle between silver and gold partisans. The Democratic candidate was William Jennings Bryan, and his Republican opponent was William McKinley. Bryan campaigned on a platform aimed at replacing the gold standard with free coinage of silver. He concluded his dramatic speech to the Democratic convention with the now-famous lines:

> We will answer their demand for a gold standard by saying to them: "You shall not press down upon the brow of labor this crown of thorns, you shall not crucify mankind upon a cross of gold."

McKinley lacked the oratorical talents of Bryan but succinctly revealed a great deal of his philosophy in his remark that "we cannot gamble with anything as sacred as money." McKinley campaigned, as many Republicans have since, as the defender of financial responsibility and sound money. Farm prosperity in late 1896 undermined farm support for Bryan, and McKinley won by a fair margin. In 1900, the victory of gold was solidified with passage of the Gold Standard Act, which recognized the gold dollar as the "standard unit of value."

From 1900 on, most economically developed nations adhered to one form or another of the gold standard. Although we might debate how well the gold standard worked on an international basis during the early years of the twentieth century, the Great Depression of the 1930s was more than the gold standard could handle. By 1933, about 40 countries (including the United States) had abandoned the gold standard in an attempt to protect themselves from the spreading depression.

Gold played a relatively minor role in the system that developed after 1934. Gold was the standard money in our economy, but it was not a medium of exchange. Gold could be imported or exported, but only jewelers, dentists, and the like could own gold. The Treasury bought all newly mined gold and all gold flowing into the country at $35 an ounce (minus a small service charge). The Treasury would also sell gold at $35 an ounce (plus a small service charge) to foreign governments or central banks. Actually, the most important function of gold was to act as a form of international reserve and a means of settling international balances. This role will be discussed in more detail in Chapter 31.

Following the experience of the depression, no country except the United States committed itself to maintain the convertibility of its currency into gold. The system worked relatively smoothly for a number of years after World War II. Then increasing doubts arose that the United States would be able to maintain convertibility of the dollar into gold at $35 an ounce. The price of gold in the free market rose well above $35 an ounce as speculators hoped to profit from an increase in the official U.S. price for gold. The United States and a group of European governments sought to maintain the $35 price by selling gold in the open market whenever its price tended to rise above $35.

These efforts to stem the speculative tide were successful for only a few years; in 1968, the monetary authorities abandoned the efforts to stabilize the price of gold in the free market. They determined to neither sell gold nor buy it from private sources. The result was the so-called "two-tier" gold market. One tier was the free market, where the price of gold could fluctuate from day to day in accord with supply and demand conditions. On the official tier, sales and purchases of the existing stock of monetary gold took place between the monetary authorities of participating countries at the agreed-upon price of $35 per ounce.

This system too lasted but a few years. Continued speculation and continued balance-of-payments deficits for the United States led ultimately to President Nixon's suspension of the gold convertibility of the dollar in 1971. By 1975, restrictions on the holding of gold by Americans were lifted, and gold became essentially a commodity like any other. It is actively traded on both the spot and futures markets. The dollar price of gold advanced rapidly, reaching as high as $875 an ounce in January 1980, but subject to wide price swings. By 1982, the price had dropped to under $315.

As the price of gold advanced, suggestions were made that, at the new price, it might be possible once again to return to the gold standard. Some have advocated this move as a means of curbing inflation, by limiting monetary issues to stocks of gold on hand. Others have suggested only the modified gold standard that prevailed from 1934 to 1971 for international purposes. We shall consider the modified gold standard more fully in Chapter 31. A full domestic gold standard would mean a return to the convertibility at a fixed price that prevailed from 1900 to 1933. President Reagan appointed a commission to study the matter, but it failed to recommend either a full or a modified gold standard in its 1982 report.

But many things have changed since the depression of the 1930s, and it is not at all clear what a "gold standard" would mean under current conditions. The pre-1933 gold standard meant that the monetary issues of government—its currency and coin—could be exchanged for gold at a fixed rate. But it did not mean that any asset denominated in dollars could be so exchanged. Many holders of dollar deposits in banks that failed found this out the hard way, if they did not already know it. But now, deposits in a wide variety of institutions are insured by government, and government policy is widely interpreted to mean that government is committed to provide its monetary issue, as needed, for conversion from deposits to currency. This would mean that ultimately deposits were convertible to gold, and these deposits run into hundreds of billions of dollars.

There is no easy way to return to the domestic gold standard while maintaining the same kind of financial system we have. Convertibility of currency to gold might be established, but perhaps at the expense of the convertibility of deposits to currency. If government does not limit the dollar assets that are gold convertible, then one can think of the gold standard as the government's fixing the worldwide dollar price of gold with no limitations on its sales or purchases. Whether this commitment could be kept for any prolonged period of time is doubtful, and it certainly could not be kept unless the dollar price of other goods were kept reasonably stable. The problems of maintaining price stability will receive considerable attention in this book, but at the outset it seems clear that a fixed price of one good—gold or any other—does not fix the price of the others.

U. S. Currency

Paper money and coin with a face value of $119 billion circulated in the economy in 1981. They included:

Federal Reserve notes. This is paper money issued by the Federal Reserve System, and now makes up the bulk of our circulating currency. These notes were not issued in a $1 denomination until 1963.

Silver certificates. Silver certificates were issued by the Treasury to match the cost of silver purchased, but are no longer issued. Their role in furnishing our $1 bills has been taken over by Federal Reserve notes.

United States notes. These are the "greenbacks" originally issued during the Civil War. By an act of Congress in 1878, the amount was fixed at $347 million, the amount then outstanding.

Other paper money. There are three other types of paper money outstanding, which are in the process of retirement. As these are turned in, no new currency is issued. These include Treasury notes of 1890 (originally issued under the Sherman Silver Act), national bank notes (originally issued by national banks but now a liability of the Treasury), and Federal Reserve Bank notes (now a liability of the Treasury).

Coins. Silver coins in circulation include silver dollars, half dollars, quarters, and dimes, although newly minted dimes, quarters and halves no longer contain silver. The Treasury also issues nickels and pennies. All these coins are obviously worth more as money than as bullion, although there have been times in the past when the value of the metal in certain silver coins was greater than their nominal value as money.

THE MONEY SUPPLY

The problems of defining gold convertibility provided a good introduction to the problem of delineating just what *money* is. The definitions of Chapter 1 must be applied, and those definitions rely on what people regard as money, not on how it is defined by government. As a British economist noted, ". . . money is the creation of the public that chooses to impute certain qualities to certain claims."[3]

Published government statistics recognize the uncertainties of the definition and provide no less than 17 different classes of assets from which a definition can be formulated. These assets make up what are called the "monetary aggregates." We present here one definition that is in wide use. Alternate definitions will be considered in Chapter 19, after the reader has been introduced to some of the complexities of the monetary system required for the discussion.

One criterion that is employed in defining money assets is to consider only those that are directly used in the purchase of goods and services. Two classes of assets clearly meet this test: One is the currency issued by the government as legal tender. The other is a deposit-type holding on an institution, provided the deposit can be transferred to third parties in making payments. These are called "transaction accounts" in official statistics. By this transaction definition, the money stock of the United States in December 1981 was $441 billion; its composition is shown in Table 2-1.

TABLE 2-1
Transaction Money Stock, December 1981
(in billions of dollars)

Currency and coin	123.1
Demand deposits at commercial banks	236.4
Other checkable deposits	81.3
Total	440.8

Source: Federal Reserve System.

[3] R.S. Sayers, "Monetary Thought and Monetary Policy in England," *Economic Journal*, December 1960, p. 721.

In commercial banks, the basic transaction account is the demand deposit. Savings and loan associations and mutual savings banks, as well as commercial banks, offer a transaction account called a NOW account (standing for Negotiable Order of Withdrawal). In credit unions, the transaction account is the share draft account. Included in the "other checkable deposits" category in the table, along with NOW and share draft accounts, is the Automatic Transfer Service (ATS), which is used in commercial banks and other thrift institutions. It is an arrangement by which funds can be automatically transferred from a savings account to a transaction account to cover checks that would otherwise "bounce."

A calculation of the money supply does not, unfortunately, consist of simply summing up all the demand deposits of commercial banks and other transaction accounts and all the currency and coin produced by government. There are certain adjustments that are usually made to produce a measure of the money supply that is useful in economic analysis. Currency held by commercial banks is not included in the money supply. If it were, a bank customer's deposit of $100 in currency into a checking account would lead to an increase in the money supply. (The depositor's holdings of currency would go down $100, matched by an increase in deposit assets. The bank's holdings of currency would go up by $100, resulting in a net increase in the money supply.) Clearly, a good definition of the money supply should not be subject to change as a result of a change in the form in which someone chooses to hold money. (A similar logic holds for the currency lodged in other depository institutions, but their transaction accounts are only a small portion of their liabilities.)

The check payment system can also lead to double counting. When a check is written, the recipient's demand deposit rises before the writer's is decreased, simply because the check-clearing system takes time. If we counted up the volume of demand deposits during this interval, both payer and payee would be counting what, in reality, belongs to only one. These checks, or *cash items in the process of collection*, are therefore deducted from the total demand deposits to arrive at an unduplicated figure for the money supply. For similar reasons, we do not count in the money supply deposits that one bank has with another.

We also exclude from the money supply all coin, currency, and demand deposits held by the Treasury and the Federal Reserve. This exclusion has nothing to do with double counting but goes to the reason for our concern with the money supply in the first place. We are interested in the money supply because of the view that the spending by people in the economic system is influenced by the amount of money they hold. It is not likely, however, that the U.S. government or the Federal Reserve Banks are greatly influenced in their spending decisions by the amount of their money holdings. This is due in part, as we shall see, to the fact that they are able to directly influence their money holdings. It is general practice, then, to exclude the money held by the Treasury and the Federal Reserve from the money supply, but not all authorities agree that this is appropriate. Some argue that more meaningful economic analysis results when demand deposits held by the federal government are included in the money supply.

All this country's paper money and coin has full legal-tender powers. *Legal tender* is a characteristic of some types of money granted by law. It means simply that the designated money is valid payment for all debts unless there is a specific agreement to the contrary. All our paper money carries the statement, "This note is legal tender for all debts, public and private." Although demand deposits do not have legal-tender power, the banks have a legal obligation to pay a depositor on demand in legal-tender money. Lack of confidence in the "moneyness" of demand deposits may arise only when there is doubt as to the ability of the banks to redeem their deposits for legal-tender money.

Alternative definitions of money that might be employed consider various types of assets that serve some of the money function but cannot immediately be used to make payments—in particular, savings deposits at thrift institutions. The choice may depend not only on the user's analytical predilections but also on data availability. Data on some assets are available more quickly and more frequently than on others. For historical development, different series might be required. For example, if we wanted to trace the historical growth of money, we would run into the problem that for years prior to 1914 there are figures available for bank deposits in total but not for demand and time deposits separately. Thus, in order to have a consistent series back to the nineteenth century, it is convenient to include time deposits in the money supply.

Money is defined because it is believed that there is a close relationship between the economy and some distinct class of assets that meets the concepts discussed in Chapter 1. For this reason, government conducts "monetary policy," influencing if not absolutely controlling certain types of assets. Since not all money-type assets are issued by the government itself, this control is not absolute. Major measures were taken in 1980 to strengthen monetary control with enactment of the Depository Institutions Deregulation and Monetary Control Act. Title I of the act, which is concerned most with monetary control, will be referred to frequently in this book as the 1980 Monetary Control Act. Other titles deal mainly with regulatory matters and will be referred to as the 1980 Deregulation Act.

LIQUIDITY

Inherent in the distinctions we have made as to the "moneyness" of different types of assets is *liquidity*. Liquidity is a rather complex concept, although we all have some general idea of it. We know, for example, that a time deposit is more liquid than common stock, and common stocks in turn are more liquid than real estate. Let us see why these statements are true.

Liquidity is the quality an asset has of being convertible into cash promptly without risk of loss to the holder. A savings deposit is almost perfectly liquid; that is, it can be converted into cash with virtually no risk of loss. There are several elements involved in the quality of liquidity.

First of all, the asset must be *marketable*, or transferable. Common stocks listed on a major stock exchange are highly marketable. With a phone call to a broker, such stocks can often be sold in a matter of minutes. U.S. savings bonds, although not traded in the open market, can be converted to cash easily and promptly. Some countries, on the other hand, have bonds outstanding that are not marketable and that cannot be redeemed prior to maturity. Such securities are highly illiquid, regardless of how safe they may ultimately prove to be.

Another quality of a highly liquid asset is *price stability*. The value of a time deposit is perfectly fixed in terms of dollars, as are U.S. savings bonds. Most other assets can vary somewhat in price. We will see later that, other things being equal, a short-term security will change less in price than one with a distant maturity. Shares of common stock may fluctuate considerably in value. Real estate and fixed assets may vary even more.

The ability of a holder of an asset to recover its cost in reselling it has been called *reversibility*. The holder of shares of common stock can always sell them promptly, but the price may be far lower than what was originally paid for the stock. Thus, common stock is not considered a highly liquid asset despite its ready marketability. A truly liquid asset must have both marketability and reversibility.

These considerations help explain why people choose to hold currency or demand deposits on which they earn no interest. All other assets must be converted into money, the only perfectly liquid asset, before they can be used to pay for goods and services. This conversion generally involves some cost or inconvenience. We will return in Part VI to the desires of people and business firms to hold money, but the reader should keep in mind that changes in the desire to hold money can affect the economy as a whole. If people's desire to hold money increases, this means that their desire to spend it is reduced; in other words, there is a reduction in velocity.

FINANCIAL INSTITUTIONS

The U.S. financial system is a structure comprising many different types of institutions. Each institution differs from the others in many characteristics: the legal form of its organization, the source of its charter, the degree and type of regulation it is subject to, its structure, the source of its funds, and the use to which it puts funds.

Some financial institutions are corporations, organized like other private business firms with stockholders owning the firm. Many institutions are mutual, meaning that they have no stockholders but are "owned" by their depositors or policyholders. All commercial banks and some savings and loan associations are stockholder-owned. All credit unions, all mutual savings banks, most savings and loan associations, and many insurance companies are mutual institutions.

Most corporations operate under a charter issued by the state in which they are organized. Several types of financial institutions may obtain charters from the federal government as well as from a state. This system of "dual chartering" is strongly upheld by the institutions involved, but it has led to problems as well as benefits from the point of view of the public interest. Commercial banks, savings and loan associations, mutual savings banks, and credit unions may obtain charters from the federal government or from their states as they choose. Insurance companies can obtain charters only on the state level.

Regulation of the different types of institutions differs considerably. In general, state-chartered institutions are subject to regulation by their state- and federal-chartered institutions to regulation by a department or agency of the federal government. However, there is a substantial amount of federal regulation of state-chartered institutions, particularly in the banking industry, and also some regulation of federally chartered institutions by the various states.

There is a significant difference among financial institutions in the degree to which they specialize in certain products or services. The deposits of savings and loan associations, for example, consist largely of the savings of individuals. Commercial banks offer checking accounts as well as savings and time deposits, and receive deposits from business firms and government units as well as individuals. Savings and loan associations invest their funds almost entirely in residential mortgages, and credit unions use most of their funds to make loans to members for the purchase of automobiles and other consumer goods. Commercial banks use their funds in a broader variety of financial activities. They make loans to businesses, to consumers, to farmers, and to home buyers, as well as investing in securities of federal, state, and local governments. Until fairly recently, only commercial banks could offer checking accounts.

All types of institutions discussed so far are privately owned and operated. The American financial system also has some institutions that are, in whole or in part, public or government institutions, such as the Federal Deposit Insurance Corporation, the Federal Reserve System, and the Federal Home Loan Bank System.

This book will discuss to a greater or lesser extent all these institutions. The principal focus, however, will be on the commercial banks and the Federal Reserve System. There are several reasons for the emphasis on commercial banks. One, of course, is simply their number and size. There are about 15,000 commercial banks in the United States, with total assets of $1.5 trillion, more than any other type of financial institution. More important is the fact that the operations of commercial banks cover a wider range of activities than do those of any other type of institution. Commercial banks have been called "department stores of finance," as distinct from the specialized functions of most other institutions.

The most important reason for focusing on commercial banks, however, is the fact that they account for the bulk of our demand deposits. As we have seen, demand deposits of commercial banks make up the largest part of the money supply of the United States. Since there is widespread agreement that changes in money can affect the economy, study of the banking and financial system is obviously important in understanding the workings of the economy.

There is another aspect of this relationship. Changes in the financial system that affect the money supply have effects on the real side of the economy that are not random or haphazard. We have a *central bank,* or monetary authority, in the United States that has considerable power to affect the position of the depository institutions. The role of the Federal Reserve System in relation to the commercial banks and the rest of the system will be described in detail in sections V and VII, but it is important to note here that monetary policy works through the financial system, and thus we must understand the system in order to understand monetary policy.

QUESTIONS

1 What are the principal characteristics of the gold standard? Does the U.S. monetary system have these characteristics?
2 What are the disadvantages of the gold standard?
3 What would happen to a gold standard if very large new sources of gold were discovered?
4 What would happen to an inconvertible paper standard if a much cheaper means of manufacturing paper were discovered?
5 Do the dimes and quarters in your pocket contain silver? Explain recent changes in U.S. coinage in terms of Gresham's Law.
6 What did Bryan mean by the "cross of gold"?
7 Should savings deposits be included in the definition of the money supply? Should traveler's checks?

SELECTED READINGS

EINZIG, PAUL, *Primitive Money*. London: Eyre & Spottiswoode Ltd., 1948.
FRIEDMAN, MILTON, and ANNA SCHWARTZ, *A Monetary History of the United States, 1867–1960*. Princeton, N.J.: Princeton University Press, 1963.
LAIDLER, DAVID, "The Definition of Money," *Journal of Money, Credit, and Banking*, August 1969.
STUDENSKI, PAUL, and HERMAN KROOS, *Financial History of the United States*, 2nd ed. New York: McGraw-Hill, 1963.

3
Banks and the Payments System

The public uses the commercial-banking system for $80 trillion of transactions annually. The biggest share of payments in the economy, by value, are made through the debiting and crediting of bank demand deposits. Although other institutions have begun to offer checkable deposits, they have joined, rather than supplanted, the commercial-banking system in conducting the payments-media function of money.

DEMAND DEPOSITS

The total of transaction accounts in the money stock reached $307 billion in September 1981. Commercial banks held about 95 percent of the total. Effective January 1, 1981, the law allowed all institutions to pay interest on transaction accounts, but only to individuals and nonprofit entities. Commercial-bank demand deposits, by holder, are shown in Table 3-1.

Although we intend to focus on the liability side of bank balance sheets in this chapter, we must take brief note here of an important item on the asset side. Since banks are obligated to meet their customers' withdrawal requests on demand, they must hold some cash or other assets that can be easily converted to cash. We call these assets *reserves*. We will find that bank reserves play an

TABLE 3-1
Distribution of Commercial-Bank Demand Deposits,[a]
September 1981

	Billions of Dollars	Percent of Total
Financial business	28.2	10.2
Nonfinancial business	148.6	53.5
Consumer	82.1	29.6
Other	18.6	6.7
Total	277.5	100.0

[a] Gross demand deposits of individuals, partnerships, and corporations, including cash items in process of collection.

Source *Federal Reserve Bulletin.*

important role in the ability of the financial system to provide our nation's money supply, and also in the ability of the Federal Reserve System to conduct monetary policy. Not only banks but all depository institutions must keep a specified portion of their deposit liabilities in one or a combination of two forms: currency on the premises (*vault cash*) or deposits held in the Federal Reserve. These Federal Reserve deposits are the "demand deposits" held by banks—they can be converted to currency instantly and can be transferred to the accounts of other banks by check and by electronic means.

THE PAYMENTS SYSTEM: CHECK CLEARING

People and businesses establish demand deposits because they expect to write checks rather than using currency. The bank must provide the facilities for the clearing and collection of checks. The process of check clearing and collection has developed to such an extent that depositors no longer give any concern to it. When we write a check in payment of our telephone bill, we expect that in a very short time the check will be returned to our bank and our demand deposit reduced by the amount of the check. When we deposit a check drawn on another bank in our account, we take it for granted that our bank will collect the amount of the check from the bank on which it is drawn and credit the amount to our account.

Our expectations in these matters will not be disappointed, but the process can be an involved and expensive one. Banks employ many more people to work on check processing than they do to make and service loans. Banks generally charge their depositors something for these services, but the direct charges are not enough in most cases to cover the full costs of servicing demand-deposit accounts.

Until 1981, the Federal Reserve imposed no charge for the services it performed in clearing checks and effecting transfers among banks. The 1980 Deregulation Act mandated charges for these services, a wise move from the standpoint of economic efficiency. Free services are overused, and the public, with no incentive to economize in writing checks, was using checks as small change. Imposition of Federal Reserve charges, along with the payment of interest on demand deposits, is causing banks to gradually bring service charges more in line with the costs of maintaining and servicing these deposits.

There are four different types of check-collection situations that the bank must be prepared to handle. The simplest case is the deposit of a check in the same bank on which it is drawn. A more complicated case arises when the check is deposited in a different bank in the same city. Still more complex is the check-collection process when a check drawn on a bank in, say, Cleveland is deposited in a bank in a different city in the same Federal Reserve district—for example, Cincinnati. The most involved check-collection situation arises when a check is deposited in a bank in a different Federal Reserve district from the bank on which the check is drawn. We will consider how the check-collection procedure operates under each of these four situations.[1]

Intrabank Clearing

I receive a pay check each month from my employer, drawn on the National City Bank. Since I also have a checking account with the National City Bank, I deposit my check in the bank each month. When the bank receives the check, it adds the amount of the check to my account and subtracts the amount from my employer's account. The bank now owes me more money and owes my employer

---

[1] The terms "check collection" and "check clearing" are often used interchangeably. Collection of a check actually means that the check is presented to the bank on which it is drawn for payment in cash. Clearance of checks means, on the other hand, that reciprocal claims are offset against each other and only the residual difference or net claim must be settled in cash. Check clearance is obviously more desirable than check collection—less manpower is needed, and less cash is tied up in the collection process.

less. This transfer of deposit liabilities on the books of the bank is all there is to the matter.

Intracity Clearing

From time to time I may receive checks drawn on other banks in the same city. Suppose I receive a check for $100 drawn on the First National Bank. This check is, in fact, an order written by a depositor with an account at the First National Bank instructing his bank to pay me $100. I could go to the First National Bank and get the $100 due me. Since this is inconvenient, I have decided to deposit the check and, in effect, let my bank collect the $100 from the First National Bank.

My deposit of the check drawn on the First National is obviously not as simple as my deposit of a check drawn on the National City Bank. Now National City must collect the $100 from the First National. They could send a messenger to the First National with the check. The First National would give the messenger $100 in currency and reduce the deposit account of the person who wrote the check by that amount. The messenger would then bring the money back to the National City Bank, which would have its holdings of vault cash increased by $100 and its deposit liability to me increased by the same amount.

At one time, banks did collect checks in this manner. There were messengers running from one bank to another all day. With all these messengers crisscrossing the city, it was inevitable that one day, two messengers would meet and discover that they could save themselves a long walk by simply exchanging their checks on each other's bank and settling the difference. Clearinghouses were the natural outgrowth of these informal check-swapping operations.

A clearinghouse is simply a central meeting place where messengers of all the participating banks come at a specified time each day with their bundles of checks drawn on the other banks. Some banks will have more checks drawn on other banks than those others will have drawn on them. Certain others will have more checks drawn on them than they have drawn on other banks. The clearinghouse then settles the net positions of the banks by notifying the Federal Reserve to credit the account of any bank with a surplus and debit the account of a bank with a deficit.[2] In this way,

---

[2] In cities in which there is a Federal Reserve Bank, that bank itself will be a member of the clearinghouse.

individual banks gain and lose reserves in the check-clearing process.

Intercity Clearing

Although the clearinghouse device works well for banks in the same city, it is obviously not practical to have a clearinghouse for banks in different cities. Yet the need for an intercity clearing arrangement is obvious. Prior to 1914, the system of check collection was fantastically inefficient. Collection of out-of-town checks took too long and cost too much. In fact, one of the most important reasons for establishment of the Federal Reserve System was to create a more effective check-collection system. Despite many obstacles, the Fed has been extremely successful in this activity and has maintained a major role in the check-collection system.

Let us suppose that, residing in Houston, Texas, I receive a check drawn on a bank in San Antonio. It is obviously inconvenient for me to go to the bank on which it was drawn to demand my money. Instead, I simply deposit the check in my account at the National City Bank of Houston. National City will take my check, together with all other checks it receives drawn on out-of-town banks, and send it to the Federal Reserve Bank of Dallas. The Federal Reserve Bank will increase the deposit account of the National City Bank and decrease the deposit account of the San Antonio bank on which the check was drawn. Since both banks have deposit accounts with the Federal Reserve Bank of Dallas, this transaction, from the point of view of the Federal Reserve Bank, is exactly the same as my deposit in the National City Bank of the check written by my employer.

If I should deposit in my bank a check drawn on a bank in San Francisco, the process is somewhat more complicated, but it is easily handled. The National City Bank sends the check I have deposited to the Federal Reserve Bank of Dallas. The Federal Reserve Bank of Dallas sends the check to the Federal Reserve Bank of San Francisco.[3] The Federal Reserve Bank of Dallas credits the account of National City (after a stated waiting period), and the Federal Reserve Bank of San Francisco reduces the account of the bank on which the check was written.

One bookkeeping result of this procedure is that the Federal Reserve Bank of San Francisco owes the Federal Reserve Bank of

[3] If the National City Bank has a large volume of checks drawn on San Francisco banks, it may send the checks directly to the Federal Reserve Bank of San Francisco and merely notify the Federal Reserve Bank of Dallas of this action.

Dallas the amount of the check. Clearing of these claims is effected through the Interdistrict Settlement Fund, which is a sort of clearinghouse for the Federal Reserve banks. This clearing simply involves bookkeeping entries, and no physical transfer of cash is necessary.

Although all depository institutions are eligible to use the Federal Reserve's clearing facilities, not all choose to do so. In some cases, small banks send their checks for collection to a larger bank with which they maintain an account. These "correspondent" relationships are important to the American banking system because of its decentralized structure. In many cases, small banks feel that they get faster collection of items through use of a correspondent. In addition, they do not have to sort checks as they must if they clear through the Federal Reserve. The Federal Reserve System has encouraged various sorts of direct clearing mechanisms that shortcut the Fed when the check-collection process can be speeded up.

In some cases, use of the Federal Reserve's check-collection system has been impeded by the distance between the banks and the nearest Federal Reserve Bank or branch. Several years ago, the Fed began the establishment of *regional check-processing centers* throughout the country, so that now more than half the checks handled by the Federal Reserve can be credited in one day.

The Federal Reserve's predominant role in the check-clearing system has been achieved partly because its services were provided free to members of the system. Now the Fed must charge for its services, and this gives banks the opportunity to compete for this business with the Fed. It is likely that this competition will result in some loss of market share by the Federal Reserve.

THE PAYMENTS SYSTEM: EFTS

Over a long period of time, the number of checks written in the United States has increased enormously, and this increased volume has caused rather severe strains on the check-clearing and -collection mechanism. Bankers have become concerned about both the time it takes to collect checks and the cost. The large clerical staffs required have produced concern as to the continued availability of a sufficient work force to maintain the present system.

These concerns have led banks to seek means of automating the check-collection and bookkeeping processes. Banks are now among the largest users of large-scale computers and other electronic equipment. So far, they have used computers only as a means of doing more quickly and more accurately the same tasks that clerical personnel had performed for years in the check-collection process. Some bankers, however, look ahead to a time in which the physical transmission of checks will be eliminated and the whole payments mechanism will become an *electronic funds transfer system* (EFTS).

Over the last few years, we have made some significant strides toward achievement of an EFTS. Several projects have moved from experimental to operational status, and more are coming on-line almost every month. Developments are occurring along four separate lines: automated teller machines, automated clearing-houses, point-of-sale systems, and wire transfer systems.

Many banks have installed electronic equipment that can perform many of the functions of bank tellers. Unmanned facilities equipped with automatic teller machines can be established in airports, shopping centers, and other convenient locations, at less cost than traditional brick-and-mortar branches. Because they need no staffing, they can be operated around the clock, seven days a week. The bank customer who can obtain cash from such a machine electronically can avoid the need to write a check for cash and hence can reduce the burden on the check-collection system.

Teller machines are accessed by a magnetic stripe card[4] and a secret identification code for each customer. The transaction may be the acceptance of a deposit, withdrawal of cash, transfer of funds from checking account to savings (or vice versa), or any of several other functions, depending on the type of hardware used. Where the machine is connected on-line to the bank's computer, the customer's account is changed immediately to reflect the transaction.

Automated clearinghouses have the potential to make a significant dent in the paper-check system. A typical operation for an automated clearinghouse would be the receipt of magnetic tapes, prepared by large firms, containing payroll information relating to local employees. The clearinghouse would electronically sort the information on the tapes and send each of its member banks a tape containing information on its depositors. Their accounts would automatically be credited, and the payroll accounts of the employers appropriately debited. Differences among the banks would be settled as at present. Thus, instead of the employer's preparing a paper check for each employee to take to his bank, initiating the collection process described earlier in this chapter, the whole process can be handled electronically. The Federal Reserve plays an

----

[4] Since credit is not necessarily involved in such transactions, this is a "debit" card rather than a credit card.

important role in fostering the development of automated clearing-houses. Its charges for use of its automated clearinghouse facilities are less than its full cost so as to encourage the use of this device.

Point-of-sale systems (POS) may have an even greater effect on the flow of paper. Consider a POS terminal at the checkout counter of the supermarket. The consumer has a number of options: He can pay for his purchases by electronically transferring funds from his account to the account of the store; he can have the transaction charged to his credit card; he can use the occasion to withdraw additional cash from his account, or to make a deposit of cash to his account. These transactions not only reduce the costs associated with the paper-check system, but they also save merchants the losses associated with bad checks. The customer is given a receipt of the transaction and later is sent a monthly statement from his bank listing all such transactions.

There are also systems in which the bank customer can make transfers of funds from home, in some cases by use of a touch-tone phone. The customer will call the bank or, eventually, the bank's computer and give instructions for payments to be made. The computer contacted may then have to communicate with the payee's bank's computer to complete the transaction. Again, no checks would be involved, but each customer would receive a monthly statement listing information about all the debits and credits to her account. As use of home computers becomes more prevalent, they can be hooked into the payments system.

The technical feasibility for all such systems exists now, and economic feasibility—a satisfactory level of costs—exists now for some systems and soon will for many. But realization of the potential inherent in the technology requires more than a satisfactory level of costs. Progress on EFTS has been impeded by legal, political, and economic problems.

Not all bankers have been enthusiastic about the new technology and its application to their business. Many have feared that EFTS will mean a competitive advantage for the giant banks that can afford the expensive equipment.[5] Some have feared that it will be the means by which the giant banks become able to compete on a nationwide basis. In several states, the deployment of automated teller machines and POS terminals has been attacked as a violation of state restrictions on branch banking. This has led to litigation on

[5] Some small banks may find that use of such equipment can enable them to expand their market at a much lower cost than the conventional branch would. Thus it might be relatively more beneficial to the small bank that does not have the capability of expanding by opening a large number of conventional branches.

the question of whether an unmanned electronic machine is a "branch" under the law.

The concern of some bankers has been echoed in Congress, to the extent that Congress a few years ago considered declaring a moratorium on further EFTS developments until the legal issues were resolved. It decided instead to establish a commission to consider all the issues and make recommendations to Congress. In 1977, the National Commission on Electronic Funds Transfers made its report, which included the sensible recommendation that the rules governing EFTS terminals be separate and distinct from those covering the traditional brick-and-mortar branch.

More important in the long run than these legal and political problems, which really amount to little more than delaying tactics, are the economic barriers to rapid acceptance of EFTS. First is the cost picture. Most EFTS systems involve large fixed costs associated with the expensive computer hardware that is necessary, including terminals, communication links, and the computer. Development of the necessary computer programs is also expensive. Once the system is in existence, however, the marginal costs are quite low. The dilemma facing the banking industry in decisions regarding EFTS development is that at present the average cost of handling payments by means of paper checks is cheaper than the average cost of a payment by electronic means. In the long run, when most payments are handled electronically, the costs of an EFTS will be very much cheaper than a paper-check system. The problem is simply this: How do we get from the present system to the long run?

Obviously, an EFTS becomes economically attractive only if a substantial portion of the check users can be persuaded to use electronic means. Unfortunately, there is now little incentive for customers to change from checks to electronic systems. Reactionary as it must seem to the technically advanced computer experts, people like checks. This reflects, in part, the desire to have a hard-copy record of payments and the ability to "stop payment" in a dispute. Partly it reflects the sophisticated awareness that the check writer gains the use of *float* —the time between which the payment is made and the check is collected. In large part it also arises from the public's lack of confidence in computer-based systems. It is the rare person who has not had some unpleasant experience over the last few years of an error in a computerized billing system that was frustratingly difficult to correct. Until the confidence of consumers is gained, it will be difficult to sell them on a change from the old-fashioned but familiar and reliable paper-check system.

But probably the most important obstacle to consumer acceptance has been the absence of demonstrable benefit to the individual depositor. Banks have not charged the full cost of deposit servicing, with the result that depositors who write few checks are subsidizing heavy users of checking services. In time, banks will move to a more rational pricing structure as a result of the lifting of the prohibition on demand-deposit interest and the imposition of charges for Federal Reserve check-clearing functions. If the consumer must pay the full cost of the check payments system, he will become more interested in seeing costs of the system reduced. As electronic transfers then become cheaper to depositors, they will more readily opt for them.

One development in American commercial banking that has received considerable attention in relation to the search for a "checkless-banking" technique is the bank credit card. In the early years of experimentation, many thought that the bank credit card would be the path to reduction or elimination of the check as a means of payment. It is true, of course, that if I make 20 purchases during a month and use my credit card rather than write individual checks, the number of checks written will decline. I will pay my monthly bills with one check instead of 20. Unfortunately, that is not the end of the matter. Each of the 20 charge slips I signed must be sent to the bank, which must process them to prepare my bill. The number of checks written has decreased, but the number of pieces of paper that must be handled, read, totaled, credited, and debited has not decreased. The bank credit card may be a great advance in the technique of extending credit to consumers, but it is not a solution to the problems of the payment system.

This discussion of electronic payments systems has dealt with those aimed at the consumer. We have already achieved a high degree of sophistication in electronic payment systems for large corporate transfers of funds. Billions of dollars are moved around the country and the world each day on the basis of orders transmitted through several "wire" (electronic) systems. The Federal Reserve operates one such system (the "Fed Wire"), and a private group of banks operates another (the "Bank Wire"). In addition, there are other systems used primarily for international transfers of funds.

TIME DEPOSITS

Historically, demand deposits have been the most important source of funds for commercial banks, but by 1970, time and savings deposits were equal to demand deposits. In December 1981, demand deposits were down to 28 percent of total deposits. The rapid growth of time and savings deposits has been the most significant change in American banking since World War II.

Savings deposits are made and withdrawn at the will of the holder. Time certificates of deposit (CDs) have fixed maturity dates. Banks may require 14 days' notice for withdrawal of a savings deposit, but in practice they do not. Time certificates are classified as of large denomination ($100,000 and over) or small denomination. They are issued as negotiable or nonnegotiable, but in practice, a CD of under $1 million is not easily negotiated. CDs may be issued at fixed or floating rates. The floating rate is generally tied to the current market rate on some financial instrument.

The beginning of the rapid growth of time deposits can be dated rather precisely. In 1961, Citibank of New York announced that it would issue negotiable certificates of deposit in large denominations and that a major securities dealer had agreed to make a market in them. Other banks and dealers quickly followed suit. The certificate of deposit had been in existence for many years; Citibank's contribution was the negotiability feature, which made it possible for the holder of a CD to sell it before maturity.[6]

The negotiable CD was designed specifically to attract corporate deposits that might otherwise have been invested in open-market securities—Treasury bills, for example. Corporate treasurers, wishing to economize on holdings of idle cash, will invest temporarily available funds in instruments that can be sold when the money is needed for business purposes. Nonnegotiable CDs would not fill this need, since the corporate treasurer is well aware that business needs are difficult to predict and that he might buy a six-month CD only to find that he needed cash 30 days later. If the CD is marketable, he can sell it after 30 days, or whenever his need for cash arises.

Fluctuations in time and savings deposits have largely been determined by the maximum interest rates imposed upon them by law. No large-denomination CD of any maturity has been subject to control since 1973, but others remain subject to control until their complete elimination in 1986, under the terms of the 1980 Deregulation Act. The law provided for a special Depository Institutions Deregulation Committee to determine ceiling rates in the period 1981–1986.

---

[6] Actually, some CDs that had long been issued by banks were, in legal form, negotiable. They were not negotiable in practice because there was no market for them. Growth of CDs required both legal negotiability and the development of a market.

In 1978, the rise of market rates above the deposit interest
ceilings led the authorities to authorize time deposits at rates tied
to the Treasury-bill rate. The most favored of these instruments
was the six-month money-market certificate authorized for banks
and other depository institutions. A $10,000 minimum was set to
minimize shifts from lower-interest savings deposits to the new
certificates. Outstanding amounts of these and other savings and
time deposits are shown in Table 3-2.

TABLE 3-2
Time and Savings Deposits of Insured Commercial Banks
(millions of dollars)

	July 30, 1980	July 29, 1981
Savings	204,142	201,981
Time deposits, interest-bearing, less than $100,000:		
6-month money-market certificates	147,904	217,892
Variable-interest, 2½ years or more	21,666	35,884
Other	99,608	69,142
Time deposits, interest-bearing, $100,000 or more	205,377	272,174
Time deposits, non-interest-bearing	4,304	4,383
Club accounts (Christmas, etc.)	2,233	2,202
Total	685,234	803,658

Source: *Federal Reserve Bulletin*, October 1981.

As short-term rates remained high going into the 1980s, banks
and other depository institutions were facing increased competition
from the unregulated money-market funds, which paid the holders
high interest but still permitted liquidation on instant notice (see
Chapter 8). Banks were not permitted to establish such funds, and
the Federal Reserve ruled out of order a variety of plans dreamed
up by innovative banks to evade the regulations.

BANK CAPITAL

A corporate balance sheet lists on one side the assets—physical
property owned by the corporation and claims that it holds on
others. On June 30, 1981, all insured commercial banks had assets of
$1,584 billion, principally loans, securities, and the value of banks'
premises. On the other side of the balance sheet are the corporation's liabilities—debts due to others. The banks' liabilities—
principally deposits—totaled $1,470 billion. The difference between
assets and liabilities was $114 billion. This is called the *capital ac-
count*. The capital account is not a fixed sum; it varies with changes

in assets (as when borrowers pay interest) and in liabilities (as when depositors accrue interest).

The amount of the capital account of a bank has important implications for the safety of its deposits. If a bank has capital equal to 20 percent of its assets and these assets should decline in value by 20 percent—say, through a fall in the market price of securities, or loans' becoming uncollectable—there would still be sufficient funds to pay the depositors. But if a bank's assets should ever become less than its liabilities (deposits mainly), the bank would be insolvent. It might continue to operate for a while, but if it were forced to go out of business, the depositors would suffer a loss.

The various banking authorities give close attention to bank capital accounts in examinations. Various rules of thumb as well as elaborate formulas have been devised to determine whether a bank's capital is adequate, but since there is no general agreement on what the capital should be adequate for, these attempts have not been successful. Bank capital as a percentage of assets has shown a downward trend since 1900, as shown in Figure 3-1. This has been due to a greater growth rate in assets than in capital. Many bankers are disturbed about this situation, but others hold that because of deposit insurance, their depositors do not worry, and therefore they need not.

Most concern over the adequacy of bank capital has focused on the larger banks.[7] Their capital ratios have always been lower than those of smaller banks, but the difference has been growing in recent years. The typical bank with deposits of $20 million has capital equal to about 8 percent of assets, whereas the average billion-dollar-deposit bank has a capital–asset ratio of only 6.6 percent. There has been a rapid increase in deposits at the foreign branches of American banks, and all these branches belong to very large banks. This growth has been so rapid that most large banks have had to seek new funds from the market to bolster their capital accounts, since retained earnings were not nearly sufficient to maintain capital ratios. Unfortunately, for most of the 1970s and early 1980s, neither the stock market nor the bond market was very favorable for new issues of bank capital.

The size of bank capital accounts also has important implications for bank earnings. A commercial bank can earn a respectable

[7] It has been argued, however, that capital ratios for larger banks are not lower if comparisons are made for banks of the same "soundness," as determined by the composition of assets and liabilities. J. Mingo and B. Wolkowitz, "The Relationship between Bank Soundness and Bank Size," *Journal of Economics and Business*, Winter 1978.

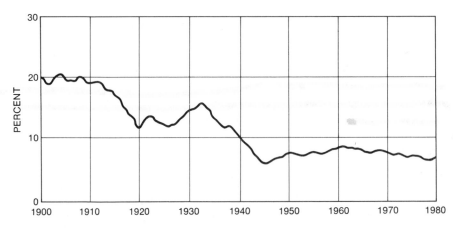

FIGURE 3-1 Capital to Asset Ratios, All Commercial Banks, 1900–1980

return on its invested capital even if earnings are quite small in relation to assets. For example, a bank with $20 million of assets and $1 million of capital will have a 20 percent return on capital if earnings on its assets exceed expenses by only one percentage point. This "leverage" factor allows commercial banks to operate profitably with lower interest rates charged on loans than would be feasible if banks had larger amounts of capital. As mentioned above, however, the thinner the "capital cushion," the greater the risk of bank failure.

Most increases in bank capital come from retained income. In the 1970s, the portion coming annually from retained income ranged from a high of 88 percent (1978) to 67 percent (1976).

At one time, bank capital accounts consisted solely of funds contributed by common stockholders and retained earnings on the common stock. Some banks did use preferred stock and debentures as sources of capital during the 1930s in order to maintain solvency. Perhaps as a result, these instruments fell into disfavor and, until the 1960s, were considered unsuitable for commercial banks. Debentures of commercial banks were virtually nonexistent in 1962 but in 1973 amounted to about $4 billion, and in 1981 totaled over $6 billion.

The use of preferred stock and debentures has real advantages to the common stockholders of banks, primarily through providing greater leverage.[8] Debentures may also be a profitable source of investment funds for a bank—there are no legal reserve requirements involved and no assessments for federal deposit insurance— if the interest rate is reasonable.

[8] For a good exposition of this point, see Stanley C. Silverberg, "Bank Borrowing: An Analysis of Recent Experience," *National Banking Review*, December 1964.

REGULATION AND CHARTERS

To maintain the safety of the public's deposits, depository institutions are heavily regulated and insured by government agencies. Establishment of a depository institution requires a special charter, which involves more than simple incorporation and obtaining of a business license. A charter may be obtained from either the federal government or the applicable state government. Insurance of deposits is optional for state-chartered institutions, but the great majority of institutions find insurance necessary for the conduct of their business. We conclude this chapter with a brief overview of the regulation of banking, which is discussed in more detail in Part IV. Chapter 7 discusses the regulation of other depository institutions.

The Comptroller of the Currency, an office of the Treasury Department, charters and regulates national banks. State banking commissioners regulate state banks. State laws and regulations vary in quality; some are more stringent than national regulations but many are less restrictive.

The nation had 14,700 domestically chartered commercial banks in 1981, and their combined assets were $1.5 trillion. National charters were held by only 31 percent of the banks, but these held 57 percent of the assets.

The Federal Deposit Insurance Corporation, established in 1933, provides deposit insurance for more than 97 percent of the commercial banks, and thereby puts almost every bank in the country under some degree of federal surveillance. Even noninsured banks come under Federal Reserve reserve-requirement regulations, but the Fed has chosen to exempt those institutions with less than $5 million in deposits.

(Part V will discuss in detail the Federal Reserve System. Membership in the Federal Reserve is mandatory for all national banks, but many state banks also belong.)

Banks vary greatly in size and in the scope of operations. Some emphasize service to business, some to consumers. Some of them have only one office; some have statewide branches. In all, there are over 38,000 branches. The two largest banks are located on opposite sides of the country. They are the Bank of America (California) and Citibank (New York), each with assets of around $100 billion. But on the whole, banking is conducted by a large number of relatively small institutions.

QUESTIONS

1 Organizing a new commercial bank requires the permission of a federal or state supervisory agency. Is this restriction on the individual's right to go into business warranted?
2 Why is it necessary to have government agencies examine banks but not oil companies?
3 Since it takes several days for a check to clear, is it possible to write checks on your account before making a deposit to cover the amount of the checks?
4 Why do banks have to maintain a minimum level of cash reserves against their deposits?
5 What would happen if all a bank's demand depositors exercised their right to withdraw their funds on the same day?
6 Are banks better off because of the lifting of the prohibition against demand-deposit interest?
7 What is the difference between demand deposits, savings deposits, and other time deposits from the point of view of the bank? from the point of view of the depositor?

SELECTED READINGS

EDWARD, FRANKLIN R., ed., *Issues in Financial Regulation.* New York: McGraw-Hill, 1979.

FLANNERY, MARK J., and DWIGHT M. JAFFEE, *The Economic Implications of an Electronic Monetary Transfer System.* Lexington, Mass.: D.C. Heath, 1973.

KNIGHT, ROBERT E., "The Impact of Changing Check Clearing Arrangements on the Correspondent Banking System" Federal Reserve Bank of Kansas City *Monthly Review,* December 1972.

MAYNE, LUCILLE S., "Impact of Federal Bank Supervisors on Bank Capital," *The Bulletin,* New York University Graduate School of Business Administration, September 1972.

MITCHELL, GEORGE W., "Effects of Automation on the Structure and Functions of Banking," *American Economic Review,* May 1966.

———, and RAYMOND F. HODGDON, "Federal Reserve and the Payments System," *Federal Reserve Bulletin,* February 1981.

National Commission on Electronic Funds Transfers, *EFT in the United States.* Washington: National Commission on EFT, 1977. The final report of the commission.

ORGLER, Y. E., and B. WOLKOWITZ, *Bank Capital.* New York: Van Nostrand Reinhold, 1976.

II

OPERATIONS
OF THE FINANCIAL
SYSTEM

4

The Financial Markets

THE STRUCTURE OF THE MARKETS

Every business is interested in the market for its product; in the case of financial institutions, the product is money or other financial claims. There is a market for such claims, and the purpose of this chapter is to examine the character and operations of the financial market.

Actually, the term *financial market* is something of a misnomer; there are actually many markets for financial assets. Many different types of securities are bought by investors and sold by issuers. Different lending institutions make a myriad of loans in terms designed to meet the needs of borrowers. We can make distinctions among all these different markets, but in many cases, the distinctions are rather fuzzy, since the boundaries of one market overlap others. For example, we usually make a distinction between securities and loans, even though buying a security is, in terms of economic function, exactly the same as making a loan. The distinction we make between them is simply that a "loan" is usually negotiated on a face-to-face basis, but the buyer and seller (or lender and borrower) of a "security" are generally unknown to one another.

A small part of the total business of the national financial markets takes place on organized exchanges, such as the New York

Stock Exchange. The bulk of the business takes place among a group of institutions and individuals, connected by telephone, computer or electronic links, and mail, carrying on the business of buying and selling money and credit. Although there are certain geographical areas or physical locations, such as the financial district of New York City, that we can pinpoint as financial markets, the markets are broader in scope than particular locations. The market for some types of loans is purely local, but the securities dealer in Portland, Oregon, and the commercial bank in Portland, Maine, are both part of the money and capital markets.

The financial market is a vast, complex mechanism because the financial needs of business and government are vast and complex. Billions of dollars' worth of goods move every day from manufacturer to wholesaler to retailer to consumer. Billions of dollars must change hands each day in this process. All this could perhaps be done without the need for a financial market except for one important point: Generally the retailers, wholesalers, brokers, and dealers who buy and sell goods do not have the billions of dollars necessary to pay for the purchases they make.

Since the financial market, as we have described it, covers such a diversity of transactions, it is helpful if we divide it into several sectors for the purposes of analysis, keeping in mind the fact that in the real world, the various sectors blend into and overlap one another. The principal distinction usually made is between short-term and long-term financing, or between the "money market" and the "capital market." Obviously, the dividing line between short term and long term is an arbitrary one, but we will adhere to the usual custom of considering money markets as those that deal in financial instruments with a maturity of under one year and the capital market as dealing in longer-term debt obligations and equities.

For various purposes, it is useful to make other distinctions among financial markets. An important distinction, for example, is between the market for newly issued securities, or *primary market*, and the trading of securities that are already outstanding in the *secondary market*. We have already discussed the concept of liquidity. Active secondary markets are necessary if financial assets are to have liquidity. This liquidity provides an important link between the primary and secondary markets. That is, an investor is more willing to buy a primary security (or is willing to pay a higher price for it) if there is an active secondary market so that he can resell the security if he should need cash.

We can also distinguish between the market for *debt* instruments, such as bonds or loans, and *equity* instruments, involving ownership of a business corporation or financial institution, such as common or preferred stock. From time to time, we will also make use of other classification schemes, based on whether the issuer is a business firm or a government unit, or whether the interest received on the financial asset is subject to normal taxes or is tax-exempt.

These classification systems are useful to potential purchasers of financial instruments because they enable them to analyze those attributes of the asset in question that are of most direct concern to them—the return they expect to derive from purchasing the security or making the loan, and the risk they are taking that they will not receive what they expect. The return is simply the interest paid on the instrument plus any increase (or less any decrease) in the market price of the asset while it is held. The risk in financial assets comes from several different sources. First of all, the borrower or issuer of the security may not meet its obligations with respect to interest or repayment of principal. We can call this *credit* risk or *default* risk. If we sell the security before maturity, the price we receive may be different from our cost. We can call this *market* risk (and since, as we shall see, an important factor making for changes in market price is a change in interest rates, it is also an *interest-rate* risk). Finally, even if we are repaid exactly as we anticipated, a change in the price level may make that return more or less than we expected in real terms. We can call this an *inflation* or *price-level* risk. Obviously, an investor contemplating the riskiness of alternative investment decisions is primarily concerned with the risk of an adverse result—ending up with less than he or she anticipates. It is useful in some analyses of investment decisions to consider the risk in terms of both favorable and unfavorable variability in returns. Much of the effort of portfolio analysis is an attempt to reduce this risk through diversification or through selection of combinations of assets that will result in less risk than that of any single asset.

Before we turn to an analysis of the financial markets, it is necessary to gain familiarity with some tools to assist in this analysis. In this chapter, we will discuss flow-of-funds analysis and explore the intricacies of the relation between interest rates and the price and maturity of financial instruments.

THE FLOW OF FUNDS

The flow-of-funds accounts developed by the Federal Reserve System are statements of sources and uses of funds for the economy, broken down for this purpose into several sectors and the flow of funds among these sectors examined. The flow-of-funds accounts allow us to discover where business firms get their funds, and what financial institutions do with the funds they receive.

In most presentations of flow-of-funds data, the economy is divided into six sectors: households (or consumers), business, state and local government, federal government, financial institutions, and the rest of the world. Because our principal interest in flow-of-funds analyses is the study of financial relationships and markets, it is customary to subdivide the financial sector into several subsectors, usually distinguishing at least among the monetary authorities (Federal Reserve and Treasury), commercial banks, and other (nonbank) financial institutions.[1]

The flow-of-funds accounts consist of "sources and uses of funds statements" for each sector. This is an accounting statement that combines the income statement and the balance sheet. Its starting point is a balance sheet that would look like the following for any sector:

Assets	Liabilities and Net Worth
Real assets	Liabilities
Financial assets:	Net worth
Money	
Other financial assets	

Total assets = Total liabilities + Net worth

Since this is a balance sheet, it must balance—total assets must equal total liabilities plus net worth—for each and every sector. The basic distinction in this balance-sheet presentation is between real assets and financial assets. We have discussed this distinction before, but now we can note that a real asset is one that appears only on the balance sheet of its owner. Such assets are houses, cars, plant and equipment, clothing, and toothpaste. A financial asset is a claim against some other individual or institution, and hence must appear on two balance sheets: that of its owner (where it appears on the asset side), and that of whomever the claim is against (where it appears as a liability). If I own a house, that is a real asset that appears only on my balance sheet; if I have bor-

---

[1] The presentation of flow-of-funds concepts in this chapter is based on the comprehensive and lucid discussion by Lawrence S. Ritter, "The Flow of Funds Accounts: A Framework for Financial Analysis," *The Bulletin*, New York University Graduate School of Business Administration Institute of Finance, August 1968.

rowed money to finance that house, the loan appears on my balance sheet as a liability and on the balance sheet of the lender as a financial asset. If I have a deposit in a bank, that is a financial asset on my balance sheet and a liability on the bank's balance sheet. If I hold dollar bills, that is a financial asset on my balance sheet and a liability of the Federal Reserve.

Stocks and Flows

A balance sheet, like the one constructed above, shows assets and liabilities as of a point in time. Our interest, however, is in the flow over a period of time rather than in the stock, or amount outstanding, at a particular moment. Stocks are essentially flows cumulated over time. This distinction between stocks and flows is an important one in economics, and we will encounter it several times. Some terms we have used may lead to confusion as to whether a stock or a flow is meant: "Savings" is a stock, while "saving" is a flow. Others are clearer: "Investment" is a flow, and "capital" is a stock; "borrowing" is a flow, and "liabilities" is a stock.

An income statement shows flows over a period of time, but the traditional income statement is limited to current transactions—that is, those relating to income and expenses for the period under consideration. We are more interested in capital transactions, or changes in the holdings of assets. To construct the kind of flow-of-funds statement we are interested in, we can compare two balance sheets for the same sector as of two different dates. If we note the *changes* in assets and liabilities between a balance sheet for December 31, 1981, and one for December 31, 1982, we can convert these stock statements into one of flows for the year 1982. We thus create the following statement:

Uses of Funds	Sources of Funds
$\triangle$ Real assets (RA)	$\triangle$ Liabilities (L)
$\triangle$ Financial assets:	$\triangle$ Net worth (NW)
$\triangle$ Money (M)	
$\triangle$ Other financial assets (FA)	

Total uses = Total sources

Now, instead of "assets" and "liabilities," we have uses and sources of funds. But since this statement is derived from changes in balance sheets, it must still balance. We can also give a different interpretation to the other items in the statement. An increase in liabilities to provide a source of funds is what we commonly call "borrowing." An increase in our holdings of financial assets is "lending." An increase in holdings of money is called "hoarding."

Net worth can increase over time only as a result of an excess of current income over current expenditures. This excess, or increase in net worth, is called "saving." The increase in real assets is equivalent to "investment." We can thus restate the sources and uses statement in the following way:

Uses	Sources
$\triangle RA$ (Investment)	$\triangle L$ (Borrowing)
$\triangle$ Financial assets:	$\triangle NW$ (Saving)
$\triangle M$ (Hoarding)	
$\triangle FA$ (Lending)	

The Flow-of-Funds Matrix

Since we have divided the economy into the appropriate sectors and have developed the necessary sources and uses of funds statements for each sector, we can now put them all together to form the flow-of-funds matrix. Figure 4-1 is a schematic sketch of the way the detailed flow-of-funds data are now published. The actual data are shown in Table 4-1.

We have already noted that financial assets and liabilities appear on two balance sheets, and hence, for the economy as a whole, total borrowing B must equal total lending L plus hoarding H. This allows us to say something about saving, S, and investment, I. We know that for each sector (and hence for the whole economy as well), $S + B = I + L + H$, or that total sources of funds equal total uses of funds. From these facts, we can deduce that for the economy as a whole, $S = I$. That is:

$$S + B = I + L + H$$

Since:

$$B = L + H$$

$$S = I$$

The conclusion that saving must equal investment for the economy as a whole does not apply to any given sector or economic unit. Any one sector may borrow more than it lends or save more than it invests. But for every surplus sector (one that saves more than it invests), there must be a deficit sector (one that invests

	Sector A		Sector B		Sector C		All Sectors	
	U	S	U	S	U	S	U	S
Saving ($\triangle$ NW)		s		s		s		S
Investment ($\triangle RA$)	i		i		i		I	
Borrowing ($\triangle$ L)		b		b		b		B
Lending ($\triangle FA$)	l		l		l		L +	
Hoarding ($\triangle M$)	h		h		h		H	
	U = S		U = S		U = S		U = S	

NOTE: The small letters within the matrix represent the data for sector saving (s), investment (i), borrowing (b), lending (l), and hoarding (h), and are placed in the appropriate space where such data would be entered. The large letters similarly represent the aggregate sum totals for the whole economy. Thus s + s + s = S. i + i + i = I, etc.

FIGURE 4-1 Flow-of-Funds Matrix for the Whole Economy

Source: Lawrence S. Ritter, "The Flow of Funds Accounts: A Framework for Financial Analysis." *The Bulletin.* New York University Graduate School of Business Administration Institute of Finance. August 1968. p. 22

more than it saves). As we noted in the very first chapter, it is the role of financial institutions to provide efficient channels through which the excess funds of surplus units can be transferred to the deficit units.

Flow-of-Funds Data

Table 4-1 presents a condensed flow-of-funds statement for the economy as a whole for 1981. For each sector, sources and uses balance, except for the statistical discrepancies in the actual data. Because it is difficult to obtain accurate figures on all these flows, the sources of funds do not always exactly equal the uses of funds by the same sector, as shown by the statistical discrepancies.

The sources for each sector are the sector's saving and increases in liabilities. Saving is for each sector the difference between receipts and expenditures. For the domestic private economy, receipts are net of taxes, and expenditure does not include capital spending, which is entered as a use. For the government and foreign sectors, "saving" is simply the difference between receipts and expenditures. The uses for each sector are capital expenditures and increases in financial assets.

As is typical, the 1981 data show that households increased their financial assets more than their financial liabilities, and businesses did the reverse. Thus, households were lenders to business, enabling business to acquire capital goods, and they were also lenders to government. By the nature of their activities, financial institutions have a rough balance between changes in financial assets and financial liabilities.

TABLE 4-1
U.S. Flow of Funds, 1981
(billions of dollars)

	Sources		Uses		
	Gross Saving	Increase in Liab.	Capital Expend.	Increase in Assets	Stat. Discrepancy
Households[a]	441.0	109.6	336.0	301.0	−86.5
Businesses (non-financial)	294.3	174.1	336.5	82.8	49.0
Commercial banking	13.1	123.5	10.8	130.3	−4.6
Nonbanking financial inst.[b]	0.5	296.9	5.7	291.7	0.1
Monetary authorities	.4	7.0	—	7.4	—
U.S. government	−65.9	97.9	—	22.3	9.7
State and local government	8.6	24.3	—	22.7	10.2
Foreign	−2.4	66.7	—	36.7	27.6

[a] Households, personal trusts, and nonprofit organizations.
[b] Savings and loans, mutual savings, credit unions, insurance companies, public and private retirement funds, finance companies, real estate investment trusts, open-end investment companies, money-market funds, and securities brokers and dealers.
Source: Federal Reserve Flow-of-Funds Accounts.

The condensed table is only a summary of a wealth of underlying data on financial assets and liabilities. (The quarterly flow-of-funds computer printout that the Federal Reserve releases to the public contains 55 pages of tables.) We shall be using this kind of data throughout the book, but we present in Table 4-2 for illustrative purposes one subsector, "Savings Institutions Combined," under one larger sector, "Private Nonbank Financial Institutions." This subsector encompasses savings and loans, mutual savings banks, and credit unions (each of which is also shown separately in Federal Reserve tables.)

For purposes of analyzing credit markets, flow-of-funds data are arranged to show total funds raised, according to the sectors borrowing, and funds supplied, according to the sectors lending. Table 4-3, for example, shows that in 1981, nonfinancial businesses lent $12 billion in the credit and equity markets and borrowed $153 billion. This kind of arrangement is particularly useful for forecast-

TABLE 4-2

Flow of Funds of Nonbank Depository Institutions
(four quarters 1981, millions of dollars)

	1981			
	I	*II*	*III*	*IV*
Current surplus	−790	−889	−1,300	−1,833
Net acquisition of financial assets	10,361	11,972	8,067	7,846
Demand deposits and currency	397	410	836	787
Time deposits	1,415	−809	−1,543	−227
Security RPs	2,119	913	1,105	−161
Corporate equities	−135	−109	−109	−27
Credit market instruments	7,076	11,097	4,866	4,901
U.S. govt. securities	862	−102	−731	6,115
State and local obligations	35	29	−21	−72
Corporate bonds	−59	−619	−147	−216
Mortgages	4,332	8,068	3,806	−942
Home mortgages	3,866	7,377	3,148	−751
Multifamily	50	−97	300	−90
Commercial	416	788	358	−101
Farm	—	—	—	—
Consumer installment credit	729	2,134	1,178	−525
Consumer noninstallment credit	329	470	2	−445
Open-market paper	848	1,117	779	96
Miscellaneous assets	−511	601	2,912	2,573
Net increase in liabilities	11,173	13,331	9,836	9,987
Deposits	10,931	1,091	640	7,296
Security RPs	−247	3,868	−1,726	4,000
Credit market instrument (savings and loan)	−1,127	7,337	9,062	−1,639
Profit taxes payable	−353	−396	−357	−430
Miscellaneous liabilities	1,969	1,431	2,217	760
Discrepancy	22	470	469	308

Source: Federal Reserve Flow-of-Funds Accounts.

ing purposes. Starting with the most recent period, projections can be made of expected changes in funds raised and supplied by each of the sectors. Governments establish budgets for future periods, and thus their activities can be projected with some certainty. Business firms make capital spending plans in advance, and surveys of their plans are published. A number of ongoing programs project national output and income, and from these forecasts, projections of household saving and income can be made. The Federal Reserve publishes its money targets in advance, so that the effects of mone-

TABLE 4-3
Net Funds Raised and Supplied in Credit and Equity Markets
(billions of dollars)

Sector	1978	1979	1980	1981
Net Funds Raised				
Total, all sectors	482	483	434	478
U.S. government	54	37	79	87
State and local government	24	16	21	23
Foreign	32	21	30	31
Private domestic nonfinancial	291	321	234	260
Business	128	156	133	153
Household	163	165	101	107
Domestic financial	81	88	70	78
Private intermediaries	40	36	23	34
Sponsored credit agencies	23	24	24	30
Mortgage pool securities	18	28	23	13
Net Funds Supplied				
Total, all sectors	482	484	435	478
U.S. government	20	23	26	25
State and local government	15	13	20	21
Foreign	40	−6	22	12
Private domestic nonfinancial	51	81	29	57
Business	−1	10	10	12
Household	52	71	19	45
Domestic financial	356	373	338	363
Private intermediaries	305	308	285	310
Commercial banking	129	121	104	103
Thrift institutions	76	56	57	28
Insurance and pension funds	84	90	98	84
Other[a]	16	41	26	95
Sponsored credit agencies	26	29	25	31
Mortgage pool securities	18	28	23	14
Federal Reserve System	7	8	5	9

[a] Includes finance companies, money-market funds, real estate investment trusts, open-end investment companies, and securities brokers and dealers.

Source Federal Reserve Flow-of-Funds Accounts.

tary policy on total credit flows can also be incorporated in the projections. From the resulting projections of demand and supply of funds, the direction of interest-rate changes is forecast.

We are going to apply these flow-of-funds concepts to the analysis of financial markets, financial institutions, and interest-rate movements. Before we do that, however, it will be necessary to be more precise in our concepts of interest rates and yields on investments.

INTEREST RATES AND YIELDS

When an investor buys a security, one of the most important considerations in the decision to do so is the return, or yield, on the investment. There are four different types of yields that may be calculated on bonds: the coupon rate, the current yield, the yield to maturity, and the yield to maturity after taxes.

The first of these, the coupon rate, is simply the nominal yield stated on the face of the bond. It is the income promised per $100 of par value. A $100 bond promising to pay interest of $5 per year has a coupon rate of 5 percent. But the coupon rate will equal the true rate of return to the investor only if the bond is selling at its par value. Thus, the coupon rate is not a significant measure of yield itself and is really used only as a means of identification. We may want to refer to an issue of U.S. Treasury bonds maturing in 1993. Since the Treasury has two issues maturing in 1993, it is convenient to refer to the "6¾s '93." These few figures identify an issue of bonds maturing in 1993 and paying interest at the rate of $6.75 per $100 of par value. Since these bonds are not necessarily selling in the market at their par value, 6¾ percent is not a significant measure of the return to an investor considering purchase of the bonds.

Current yield is of more significance to the investor than coupon rate. It is computed simply by dividing the annual dollar amount of interest by the market price of the bond. If a bond has a coupon rate of 6¾ percent and a market price of 95, its current yield is 6.75/95, or 7.11 percent. If the price were 105, the current yield would be 6.43 percent.

Frequently people are concerned over the fact that bonds, even U.S. government bonds, may sell in the market at less than par. It has even been argued that the Federal Reserve should use its powers to support government-bond prices at par because it is a reflection on the credit standing of the United States to have its bonds selling below par. Actually, credit standing is not involved— no one doubts that the United States will pay interest as due on its obligations and will redeem them for cash on maturity.

Why, then, do bonds sometimes sell at less than their par value? Conditions in the money market change from day to day and from month to month. The Treasury may sell an issue of bonds at par with a coupon rate of 12 percent today. Next month, the Treasury may have to sell a new issue of securities, and conditions in the money market may be such that it will have to offer a coupon rate of 14 percent in order to attract buyers. This will have an effect on the price of the outstanding 12 percent bonds.[2] No one would buy 12 percent bonds at par if he could get bonds paying 14 percent on the same terms. Investors will be willing to buy the 12 percent bonds only at a discount from their par value. This will make the current yield higher than 12 percent. Also, since the bond is going to be redeemed at par at some time in the future, the investor will receive some increase in the value of the bond as well as the annual interest payments. This latter point brings us to consideration of the third type of yield—yield to maturity.

The current yield is the "true" yield on a security when there is no maturity; but when the bond is going to be redeemed at par at some time in the future, the current yield is not the best measure of the return to the investor. The current yield does not take into account the difference between the price paid for a bond and the amount that will be received at maturity. The investor who buys a bond at less than par is going to have a profit equal to the amount of the discount. The yield-to-maturity concept includes this profit in measuring the average net return per year if the bond is held to maturity. It seems reasonable to include part of the discount each year as a return on the investment even though it is not received in cash until maturity.

A precise measure of the yield to maturity must take into account the fact that the par value to be paid at maturity will not be received until some time in the future. Interest payments will be received at specified dates until maturity. It is necessary to consider the present value of that future payment, which involves consideration of the force of compound interest. One thousand dollars to be received in ten years has a value today, or a present value, of $614, if the interest rate is 5 percent. At a higher interest rate, the present value is lower. That is, at 6 percent, $558 will accumulate to $1,000 in ten years, so $558 is the present value of $1,000 ten years hence at an interest rate of 6 percent. The formula for the relationship among maturity, present value, and the interest rate is as follows:

$$PV = \frac{R_1}{(1 + i)} + \frac{R_2}{(1 + i)^2} + \ldots + \frac{R_n}{(1 + i)^n} + \frac{P}{(1 + i)^n}$$

where PV represents the present value, R represents the interest payment to be received in dollars (the subscripts indicating the number of years in the future at which the payments will be made),

---

[2] Actually, the conditions that force the Treasury to pay 14 percent on its new issue will already have tended to push the price of the 12s down.

i is the interest rate, n is the number of years to maturity, and P is the par value of the bond.

Take, for example, a two-year bond with a par value of $1,000 and a coupon rate of 5 percent. If the going market rate is also 5 percent, the bond will sell at par:

$$\$1,000 = \frac{\$50}{1 + .05} + \frac{\$50}{(1 + .05)^2} + \frac{\$1,000}{(1 + .05)^2}$$

$$1,000 = \$47.62 + \$45.35 + \$907.03$$

If the market interest rate changes so that the bond now sells at a price of $981.67, what is the yield to maturity of the bond?

$$\$981.67 = \frac{\$50}{1 + i} + \frac{\$50}{(1 + i)^2} + \frac{\$1,000}{(1 + i)^2}$$

If the interest rate is 6 percent:

$$\$981.67 = \$47.17 + \$44.50 + \$890.00 = \$981.67$$

Solving the equation to determine the yield is rather difficult, although now many electronic calculators are programmed to solve this type of problem. Even without such assistance, we can come close to the true figure by rather simple means. Let us consider American Widget Corporation 5 percent bonds, due in 20 years. Assume that these bonds have a current market price of 94. Since they will have a value of 100 in 20 years, we can assume that the average accrued price of the bonds over the rest of their life is 97. Next, we divide the total discount of $6 by the number of years left until maturity—in this case, 20—giving a figure of $.30. This means that if we buy these bonds at 94, we can expect them to increase in value by $.30 per year. We can estimate the yield to maturity by adding this annual average discount to the annual interest payment and dividing by the average accrued value. This would be ($5 + .30)/$97, or 5.46 percent. This is quite close to the true yield to maturity calculated by more involved mathematical methods. (Actually, we never have to compute yields to maturity, because the results are available in convenient tables.)

Consideration of yield to maturity implicitly assumes that changes in the value of the bond are just as important to the investor as the interest payments received each year. This may be true for some investors, but it is misleading for others. The elderly widow living on income derived from bonds is much more concerned with the amount of her annual interest check than in the fact that in 40 years, when the bond matures, she will have a capital gain.

Other investors, because of the lower rate at which capital gains are taxed, will prefer to buy a bond with a low coupon rate at a discount than to buy a bond with a high current yield at a premium. To aid such investors in making decisions, the price lists issued by bond dealers include, in addition to a calculation of current yield and yield to maturity, a calculation of yield to maturity after taxes. This computation takes account of the different rates of taxation for ordinary interest income and capital gains. The after-tax yield to maturity is based on a tax rate of 46 percent, the rate at which banks and other corporations are taxed.

Bond Prices and Maturity

The preceding analysis has important implications for the relation between fluctuations in bond prices and the length of time until maturity of the bond. The market price of securities with a near-term maturity will fluctuate less than that of a bond of equal quality with a maturity many years in the future.

Let us consider two bonds with a coupon rate of 10 percent. Both bonds are selling at par, but one matures in one year and the other in 20 years. Now let us suppose that the market rate of interest on such securities rises to 12 percent. A rise in interest rates will tend to make bond prices fall. But the bond maturing next year cannot fall very far. If it should fall to, say, 98, a purchaser would receive, during the next year, $10 in interest plus $2 capital gain on an investment of $98. This would be a return higher than 12 percent. The bond, then, is not likely to fall even as far as 98. Thus, the holder of the short-term bond does not have much to fear from changes in interest rates.

The holder of the 20-year bond is not so secure, however. If market interest rates change to 12 percent, his bond will fall in price to about 85. That is, in order that a purchaser of the bond receive a yield to maturity of 12 percent, a bond with a 10 percent coupon rate and a 20-year term must sell at about $85.

If the interest rates rise, bond prices will fall, and if interest rates fall, bond prices will rise. However, the longer the period until the bond matures, the greater will be the price fluctuation in either case. It is for this reason that in Chapter 2 we indicated that short-term securities are generally considered more liquid than long-term.

The Pattern of Interest Rates

Economists often speak of "the" rate of interest, using one figure to represent the host of different interest rates that exist in the market at any one time. This is a convenience, but it is important to realize that it is an oversimplification and may be misleading because the many interest rates may not all move through time in the same manner.

There are several reasons why there are many different rates of interest. Different securities have different rates because of differences in the credit standing of the borrower, because of differences in maturity of the securities, and for various institutional reasons.

It is obvious that when the credit standing of borrowers differ, the rates they must pay for borrowed funds will differ. When a bank or other institution lends money to the Treasury, there is no doubt that the loan will be repaid. With any other borrower, there is always some element of credit risk—some chance that the borrower will be unable to repay the loan. The greater the risk, the greater the interest rate the lender will demand to compensate himself for incurring this risk.

Differences in maturity are also responsible for some differences in interest rates. We will consider the relation between long- and short-term rates in more detail later on in this chapter.

The liquidity of various securities differs, as we have seen. Short-term government bonds can be sold quickly at little cost. Other securities are difficult to convert into cash on short notice. It is obvious that most investors or institutions would demand a higher yield on an illiquid investment than on a highly liquid one.

Interest rates on various types of loans differ also because of differences in the costs of making and administering the loans. The relative cost of credit investigation and servicing a multimillion dollar loan to General Motors is certainly less than the cost of handling a $1,000 loan to finance a customer's purchase of a used Chevrolet.

Another institutional reason for differences in interest rates lies in differences in tax treatment of various securities. The most important example of this concerns state and local government bonds. Interest on these bonds is exempt from federal income taxes, and thus investors in relatively high income tax brackets (including some financial institutions) are willing to buy such securities at relatively low pretax yields. In fact, municipal bonds, on the average, sell at lower yields than U.S. government bonds, despite the fact that they are not as free from risk or as liquid.

Another important institutional factor is the fact that there are some rigidities in the flow of funds through the market. At a given moment there may be unusual demand for a particular type of loan, or an unusual supply of funds available for a specific purpose. For example, insurance companies generally invest in long-term securities. If insurance companies should have a large inflow of cash, they would use some of it to buy long-term securities. Other investors may then switch from longs to shorts in search of better yields. As borrowers and lenders adjust to the new supply-and-demand situation, the normal relationship among rates will tend to reestablish itself. The important point is simply that this adjustment takes time—at any given moment, the market pattern of interest rates may appear somewhat distorted, and the distortions may persist for some time.

The Term Structure of Interest Rates

If two securities are identical in every respect except maturity, it is likely that they will sell in the market at different prices (or yields). Generally, they will change in price in the same direction; that is, if the short-term security rises in price, the long-term issue will probably also rise in price. Investors generally hold both long- and short-term securities and are free to some extent to adjust their holdings, depending on the relative yields. For reasons noted earlier in this chapter, the long-term bond will tend to fluctuate more in price than the short-term, although its yield will probably not fluctuate as much. The relationship between yields on securities differing only as to maturity can be rather neatly summarized in a *yield curve*.

The yield curve is simply a graphic presentation of the yields on securities that are identical *except for maturity*. It thus shows what economists call *the term structure of interest rates*. It is easiest to draw a yield curve for U.S. government securities, because these are all of the same credit quality, and because there are enough different issues outstanding that a meaningful distribution of maturities can be plotted. Figures 4-2 and 4-3 illustrate the yield curve for Treasury securities as of two dates. The curve is constructed with maturity on the horizontal axis. Each issue of securities outstanding is plotted at the appropriate place in the diagram and a smooth curve fitted to the points. (The curve is fitted by eye rather than by mathematical formula.) Figure 4-2 illustrates the yield curve for Treasury securities as of May 30, 1980. Figure 4-3 is the yield curve that existed on February 27, 1981.

Until recent years, we have had more experience with upward-sloping yield curves than with downward-sloping curves. The basic reason for this is that there is a greater risk of loss if a long-term security must be sold before maturity than if a short-term security must be liquidated. Holders of short-term Treasury bills know they can sell, if necessary, with little risk of loss. The holders of 20-year Treasury bonds may take a loss of 10–20 percent or more if they have to sell before the 20 years are up. Investors are willing to accept this greater risk only if they are promised a higher return.

Although it may be normal for long-term rates to be higher than short-term rates, expectations of change in interest rates can distort the picture. Suppose, for example, that everyone expects interest rates to fall in the near future. This may be a widely held opinion when interest rates are very high. The business firm that wants to raise $5 million for a new plant expansion would not want to borrow on a long-term basis at currently high interest rates when it expects that lower rates will prevail in the near future. The firm may borrow on a short-term basis and plan to refinance the loan on more favorable terms in the future. If many firms analyze the situation in the same way, the demand for short-term funds may push the short-term rate above the long-term rate.

Let us look at the same situation from the point of view of a lender or investor. If he thinks that the current short-term rate of, say, 14 percent is going to fall, he may prefer to commit his funds on a long-term basis at, say, 10 percent, rather than invest now at 14 percent and face the need to reinvest shortly at perhaps 8 percent. In other words, from the investor's point of view, being sure of 10 percent for 20 years may be better than earning 14 percent this year and perhaps 8–9 percent for the next 19 years.

Another distortion of the normal pattern may result from the institutional rigidities discussed earlier. Lenders and borrowers, by tradition and by law, tend to be restricted to certain markets. Some depository institutions tend to limit their investment operations to short-term securities. In particular, if commercial banks have ample funds, short-term rates will be low in relation to long-term rates. If they are short of funds, then short-term rates will be high.

The yield curve gives us a way to judge how the market views the likely course of interest rates. A downward slope is associated with expectations of lower rates in the future. The same kind of information is available from interest-rate futures markets, which came into operation in 1976. In these markets, securities are bought and sold for delivery in the future. If prices are higher for longer-term delivery than for near-term, then the market expects interest

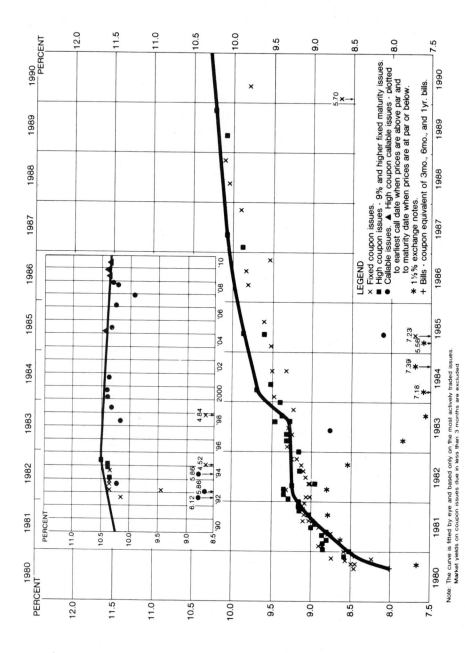

FIGURE 4-2 Yields of Treasury Securities, May 30, 1980 (Based on closing bid quotations) *Source: Treasury Bulletin.*

FIGURE 4-3 Yields of Treasury Securities, February 27, 1981 (Based on closing bid quotations) Source: *Treasury Bulletin*

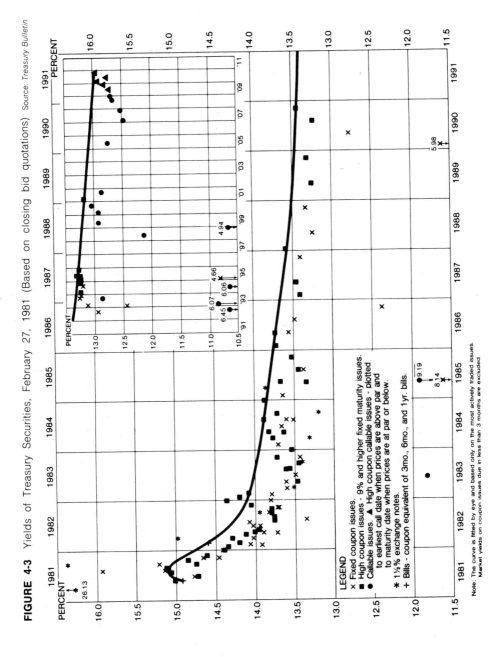

LEGEND
× Fixed coupon issues.
■ High coupon issues - 9% and higher fixed maturity issues.
● Callable issues. ▲ High coupon callable issues - plotted
   to earliest call date when prices are above par and
   to maturity date when prices are at par or below.
∗ 1½% exchange notes.
+ Bills - coupon equivalent of 3mo., 6mo., and 1yr. bills.

Note: The curve is fitted by eye and based only on the most actively traded issues.
Market yields on coupon issues due in less than 3 months are excluded.

rates to fall. Buyers are willing to take delivery in the future at higher prices because they expect security prices to move up (interest rates to fall) and they can resell with a gain. We shall discuss interest-rate futures markets in more detail in the chapters on housing finance and government finance. Generally, interest futures markets and the yield curve have shown consistent results with respect to the market's expectation of future interest-rate movements.

QUESTIONS

1 Economists often define risk in terms of *variability of returns*. Is this what most investors mean by *risk?*
2 What is meant by *interest-rate risk?*
3 What is meant by *over-the-counter markets?*
4 Why do long-term securities fluctuate more in price than short-term?
5 How can a 5% bond yield 6%?
6 There are some bonds outstanding with no maturity date (consols). Why are investors willing to buy such a bond when the issuer is not obligated to pay back his money?
7 Assume there are two bonds available that are exactly equivalent except for a difference in maturity date. What could account for the fact that these securities sell at different yields? Would you expect the longer-term issue to be selling at a higher or lower yield than the shorter-term?
8 Where would you find corporate retained earnings in the flow-of-funds accounts? the federal deficit?

SELECTED READINGS

Federal Reserve System, *Introduction to Flow of Funds*. Washington, D.C., 1980.
GOLDSMITH, RAYMOND W., *The Flow of Capital Funds in the Postwar Economy*. New York: National Bureau of Economic Research, 1965.
HOMER, SIDNEY, *A History of Interest Rates*, 2nd ed. New Brunswick, N.J.: Rutgers University Press, 1977.
RITTER, LAWRENCE S., "The Flow of Funds Accounts: A Framework for Financial Analysis," *The Bulletin*, New York University Graduate School of Business Administration Institute of Finance, August 1968.
ROBINSON, ROLAND I., *The Management of Bank Funds*, 2nd ed. New York: McGraw-Hill, 1962. Chapter 19 contains a clear analysis of some of the intricacies of yield curves.
VAN HORNE, JAMES C., *Financial Market Rates and Flows*. Englewood Cliffs, N.J.: Prentice-Hall, 1978.

5

The Money Market

Our emphasis in this book is on money and financial institutions in terms of their relation to monetary policy. Thus, in this chapter and in the rest of the book, we will be devoting more attention to the money market than to long-term borrowing and lending transactions. We will consider in some detail, however, some segments of the capital market, particularly the financing of housing. Our discussions of the financing of business firms and government will also consider their long-term financing needs. This chapter considers the money market from both the demand and the supply sides, and describes the most important financial instruments traded in the money market.

DEMAND FOR FUNDS

The U.S. government is one of the most important participants in the demand side of the money market. The total debt of the Treasury reached $1 trillion in 1981. About half of this amount matures within one year. Since tax revenues cannot be expected to provide enough cash to pay off these obligations when they come due, the obligations must be refinanced; that is, new issues of government securities must be sold to repay the holders of maturing securities.

Much of the federal debt is in the form of Treasury bills with original maturities of three months, six months, or one year. From time to time, Treasury notes and bonds come due and must be refinanced. The Treasury also borrows short-term funds at times to tide it over temporary shortages of cash or to avoid selling long-term securities when it is considered undesirable to do so. The major reason for these temporary cash needs is that tax receipts tend to be bunched around certain scheduled tax-payment dates, whereas federal expenditures are more evenly spaced through the year. Thus, even in a year with a balanced federal budget, there will be some months in which the Treasury has a need for funds.

Business firms are also important users of short-term credit. Their needs in this area are generally satisfied through negotiated loans from commercial banks or other financial institutions, but some firms seek funds in the open market. Some large, well-known firms of unquestioned credit standing issue short-term IOUs, known as *commercial paper*, which are sold on the open market, generally through commercial-paper dealers. This market has grown very rapidly during periods of tight money when banks have not had adequate funds to meet business loan demand.

Some of the large finance companies sell commercial paper directly to investors and use the funds obtained to finance business and consumers. This *finance-company paper* is now more important in dollar amount than the commercial-paper issues of nonfinancial corporations, although its growth in recent years has not been as rapid.

Firms engaged in *international trade* often require funds to finance the import and export of goods. Specialized financial instruments have been developed to meet this need.

Securities brokers and dealers need large amounts of short-term funds. A broker functions as a middleman, on a commission basis, between the buyer and seller of securities. Since the customers may not have the money available to pay cash for the securities they wish to buy, the broker needs money to relend to customers desiring to buy securities "on margin."

A dealer, on the other hand, buys securities for his own account that he hopes to resell at a profit. A securities dealer, like any merchant, must maintain an inventory. Since dealers in financial instruments such as government securities or commercial paper are turning over very large amounts of goods, they require large amounts of borrowed funds. Dealers operate on a very small margin per transaction, and success depends upon managing a highly leveraged position and finding access to borrowed funds as cheaply as possible.

State and local governments occasionally need short-term funds while awaiting receipt of periodic tax payments. Local governments receive most of their revenue from property taxes, which are paid only once or twice a year. These communities sometimes find it convenient or necessary to borrow in anticipation of these receipts by selling *tax-anticipation notes.* Most of the borrowing of state and local governments to finance capital expenditures—roads, hospitals, schools, sewers—is for relatively long periods of time and is more properly considered part of the capital market.

Depository institutions function on both the demand and supply sides of the market. They raise funds by sale of certificates of deposit, and they use the market to obtain reserves for maintaining legal requirements when they experience an unexpected deposit loss. Banks, in particular, function actively on the demand and supply sides of the money market, and thus they play an important role in bringing equilibrium to the market on a day-to-day basis.

SUPPLY OF FUNDS

Commercial banks are the most important suppliers of short-term credit. Their importance to the market lies not only in the size of their operations and their ability to operate on either the supply or demand side of the market, but also on the fact that their operations encompass the widest variety of financial instruments and types of financing. Of particular interest is the fact that banks operate in the open-market sector of the money market, buying and selling nearly all types of securities, and also in the face-to-face loan markets. Their ability to operate in both sectors tends to unify the market and ensures an appropriate relationship between the open market and the market for bank loans. If bank interest rates are "too high" in relation to open-market rates, those top-quality corporations that have access to the open market will raise funds in that way instead of borrowing from a bank. This reduction in the demand for bank loans will exert a downward pressure on the bank rates.[1]

Commercial-bank money-market operations are focused on short-term (one- or two-day) loans to other banks (called *Federal-*

---

[1] In fact, the relationship is a little more complex than this suggests. The bank loan rate may not be easily comparable with an open-market rate, because it may have other conditions attached—usually, the borrower must maintain a deposit with the bank that may be more than it would normally keep on deposit. On the other hand, a bank usually feels some responsibility to take care of a good customer even at times when funds are scarce. The open market has no such personal or business sentiments. Thus, some borrowers are willing to deal with a bank even if the rate is higher than comparable open-market rates.

funds transactions), similar-term loans to brokers and dealers in securities (through *call loans* and *repurchase agreements*), and short-term U.S. government securities. All these instruments allow the bank to earn interest on funds that may be needed on short notice. The commercial bank can be confident of being able to sell its holdings of Treasury bills on very short notice with little risk of loss. Commercial banks are also large investors in the tax-anticipation notes of state and local governments.

Other financial institutions supply large sums of money to the market. Most of these institutions—insurance companies, pension funds, savings banks, savings and loan associations—are primarily interested in longer-term investments. They do, however, maintain some part of their assets in short-term securities as a means of providing some liquidity. In addition, there may be times when the demand for long-term funds is inadequate, or when the long-term investment opportunities do not appear attractive; in such periods, these institutions may invest heavily in short-term securities to earn interest on what would otherwise be idle funds.

Business firms may temporarily have surplus funds that can be profitably invested in short-term securities. Many firms invest in Treasury bills the money they accrue to pay their federal tax liabilities. If a business firm has $1 million that it is not going to need for three months, it is clearly advantageous for the firm to buy Treasury bills (or CDs) rather than holding the money in a demand deposit. A million dollars' worth of bills may earn over $30,000 in three months. Business firms have been a major source of financing to other business firms through large purchases of commercial paper. In fact, business firms have been a major supplier of the funds needed to fuel the great growth of the commercial-paper market in recent years.

Foreigners have been accumulating dollars for over 30 years as our imports of goods and services and investment transactions have resulted in an outflow of funds from the United States. This was true even before the increase in oil prices made the petroleum-exporting countries holders of massive amounts of dollar claims. At one time, foreign holders of dollars could have converted them to gold, but now they have no choice but to continue to hold dollars. (Of course, any foreigner can sell his dollars to another for assets denominated in some other currency, but then the buyer has the dollar claim and the total amount is not changed.) We will devote considerable attention to the implications of our international financial transactions and policies, but for our purposes here, it is sufficient to note that foreign holders of dollars are large purchasers of short-term Treasury securities and, to a lesser extent, other, somewhat riskier money-market instruments.

Other suppliers of funds are sometimes important. State and local governments may occasionally be suppliers of funds. If a state sells a $10 million bond issue to finance construction of a new highway, it is not going to have to pay out the whole $10 million at once. Part of the proceeds of the bond sale may not be needed for months, and these funds may be invested in short-term securities.

Pension funds and trust funds are important suppliers of funds, and other suppliers participate in the money market from time to time. Labor unions accumulate substantial sums, which are generally invested in government securities so as to have maximum liquidity. College endowment funds also may invest in short-term securities temporarily.

Individuals have become more interested and more active in the money market in recent years, particularly in periods of high interest rates. Individuals with sufficient funds have invested directly in Treasury bills and other government securities, and have also become more significant purchasers of other money-market instruments. A particularly interesting development has been the growth of *money-market mutual funds* (see Chapter 8). These funds operate exactly like the traditional mutual fund except that their investments are entirely in money-market instruments—Treasury bills, commercial paper, and large certificates of deposit. They have become an efficient means by which the individual investor of moderate means can participate in the money market. Their birth in the 1970s was due in large part to the restriction of the interest rates that commercial banks could pay on small deposits.

The Federal Reserve, at times, may be the dominant factor in the money market. The Fed may operate either as a supplier or as an absorber of short-term funds, depending on economic and money-market conditions. We will consider the role of the Federal Reserve in detail in later chapters.

MONEY-MARKET INSTRUMENTS

Federal Funds

When an institution presents a check to its Federal Reserve Bank for credit to its account, the check is not added to its account immediately. The account is credited the next day or the day after, depending on the location of the institution on which the check is drawn. Therefore, funds represented by an ordinary check are not immediately available. This lag may not seem important, but to banks it is frequently crucial. A national market has grown up in funds that are immediately available at the Federal Reserve. Checks drawn on an institution's account at its Federal Reserve Bank are known as Federal funds (more commonly, Fed funds) and are *immediately* credited to the depositor's account.

At the level of short-term interest rates that has prevailed in recent years, the loss of even one day's interest in waiting for checks to clear is significant. The money market has shifted to Fed funds as the standard means of settling some transactions, particularly those involving money-market instruments. A separate market, however, has developed for Fed funds themselves, with most of the transactions taking place between banks.

Depository institutions are required to hold a specified percentage of their deposits as reserves, primarily in the form of deposits at their Federal Reserve Bank. On any given day, because of deposit fluctuations, some institutions may find that their reserves are in excess of their required amount, while others are deficient in reserves. The Fed-funds market essentially involves lending by institutions with excess reserves to the ones that are deficient.[2]

New York City is the center of the federal-funds market, with about one-third of the transactions originating in or moving through it. About 200 large banks participate regularly in the market, and a number of other depository institutions are in the market less frequently. The typical trading unit is $1 million, although many banks participate through correspondent relationships in amounts as small as $50,000.

A bank with excess reserves of, say, $5 million may lend its excess reserve for one day to a bank with a reserve deficiency. The arrangement may be made directly or through a Federal-funds broker.

Suppose a rate of 12 percent is agreed upon. The bank selling funds will wire or call, instructing its Federal Reserve Bank to debit its account and to credit the account of the buying bank with $5 million. The next day, the buying bank will call the Federal Reserve Bank and reverse the transfer. Interest on this loan amounts to $1,667 and is generally paid by a separate check or by crediting a correspondent account.

---

[2] Although the transaction is really *borrowing* and *lending*, we usually speak of *buying* and *selling* Federal funds.

This describes the most common type of Fed-funds transaction, but there are several variations on it. Some transactions involve the use of government securities as collateral. Some are for longer than the standard one-day period of most transactions.

The rate of interest paid on Federal funds varies from day to day and from hour to hour, depending upon money-market conditions. It is affected by the availability of funds—whether depository institutions in general have excess reserves or are short of meeting their requirements—and by the rate on alternative money-market instruments or sources of funds. The rate is also influenced by Federal Reserve actions. This is particularly important because, as we shall see, the effect of Federal Reserve operations is reflected promptly in the Fed-funds market, and, in fact, the Fed looks to the market to determine the basic "tightness" or "looseness" of the money market.

The rate on Federal funds and other money-market instruments is shown in Table 5-1. This should be referred to with consideration of each of the instruments discussed, particularly changes in the interest-rate relationships over time.

Repurchase Agreements

Only depository institutions and government agencies participate in the Federal-funds market, but the repurchase agreement serves a similar function with other customers. Under this arrangement, an asset manager—say, for a corporation or a municipal government—purchases a government security—say, from a commercial bank. Under the agreement, the bank will buy the security back the next day.[3] Thus, for that one day, the bank has additional reserves from the transaction. If the lender is one of the bank's own deposit customers, the bank's liabilities now include a repurchase agreement, which does not require reserves against it, rather than a deposit, which does. The "reverse repurchase agreement" is exactly the same transaction, but looked at from the standpoint of the lender. The repurchase-agreement interest rate is equal to or lower than the Federal-funds rate because it is a loan secured by government securities. The lender considers the repurchase agreement a highly liquid holding, since it is secured and will be reversed the next day, or shortly after. Some participants carry the transaction on their books as government securities holdings, rather than loans.

[3] Readers having occasion to use pawnbrokers will recognize this technique.

TABLE 5-1

Money-Market Interest Rates

Year	Short-Term Government Securities	Prime Commercial Paper	Banker's Acceptances	Federal Funds	Prime Rate on Business Loans
1929	4.42%	5.85%	5.03%	n.a.	5.5%
1933	.52	1.73	.63	n.a.	1.5
1946	.38	.81	.61	n.a.	1.5
1951	1.52	2.17	1.60	n.a.	3.0
1957	3.23	3.81	3.45	3.11	4.5
1961	2.36	2.97	2.81	1.96	4.5
1966	4.85	5.55	5.36	5.11	6.0
1969	6.67	7.83	7.61	8.21	8.5
1971	4.33	5.11	4.85	4.66	5.25
1973	7.04	8.15	8.08	8.74	8.31
1975	5.83	6.33	6.30	5.82	7.86
1977	5.27	5.60	5.59	5.54	6.80
1978	7.19	7.99	8.11	7.94	9.06
1979	10.07	10.91	11.04	11.20	12.71
1980	11.43	12.66	12.78	13.36	15.25
1981	14.03	15.32	15.32	16.38	18.87

Source: *Federal Reserve Bulletin.*

Government-securities dealers are active users of the repurchase agreement as a means of carrying their inventories. They have also become lenders through the reverse repurchase agreement, and thus they have emerged as intermediaries in this market for day-to-day money. At year-end 1980, securities brokers and dealers held $24 billion of security credit as assets and $32 billion of security credit as liabilities. Table 5-2 shows flows of both Federal funds and repurchase agreements.

Treasury Bills

The volume of Treasury bills outstanding was well over $200 billion by 1981. There are two segments of the market for Treasury bills—the sale of new issues, and trading in outstanding bills.[4]

New offerings of three-month and six-month bills are made weekly, and twelve-month bills are offered monthly. Generally the Treasury announces the amount to be offered on Thursday, with

[4] Treasury notes and bonds, issued with original maturities over one year, are part of the capital market rather than the money market. The dealers and the mechanics of trading are essentially the same as those for bills, and as they approach maturity, they become a part of the money market. These issues are considered further in Chapter 12.

bids for the new issue accepted by the Federal Reserve Banks until the following Monday.

Bills do not pay interest as such, but are sold, as are several money-market instruments, on a discount basis. That is, the bills are sold below their face or par value. An investor may buy for, say, $96 a Treasury bill that the Treasury promises to redeem for $100 in three months.[5] This $4 gain is the equivalent of an interest return of almost 17 percent per year.

The price of the bills is not set by the Treasury. It simply decides on the amount of new bills to be sold each week. Individuals and institutions submit bids, and the bills are awarded to the highest bidders. In addition, the Treasury accepts noncompetitive bids in amounts up to $500,000 per subscriber for which bills are awarded at the average price of the accepted competitive bids. Deciding what price to bid is a difficult problem for a participant in the weekly auction. He is faced with twin dangers: the risk of paying more than necessary for the bills, and the risk of not bidding enough to win the amount of bills desired.

There is a broad and active market for outstanding Treasury bills. Trading in Treasury bills takes place not on any organized

TABLE 5-2
Federal Funds and Security Repurchase Agreements
(millions of dollars)

	4th Qtr. 1980	1st Qtr. 1981	2d Qtr. 1981	3rd Qtr. 1981	4th Qtr. 1981
Net change in liabilities:					
Commercial banks	2,895	6,678	910	4,309	828
Savings and loans	1,875	− 247	3,868	−1,726	−4,000
Net change in assets:					
Nonfinancial corporations	1,165	1,850	−1,119	−2,899	226
State and local govts.	−1,504	2,387	726	− 554	68
Federally related agencies	1,277	921	− 195	2,391	168
Savings and loans	− 720	1,150	− 582	900	768
Mutual savings banks	−1,172	969	295	− 929	− 929
Money-market funds	2,735	− 650	2,557	2,564	4,415

Note: Asset and liability changes do not match because not all transactors are included.
Source: Federal Reserve Flow-of-Funds Accounts.

[5] Bond prices are always quoted in terms of the price of a $100 bond, even though the securities themselves are seldom sold in denominations of less than $1,000. A price quotation of $99 really means that a $1,000 bill has a price of $990. Prices on government bonds are quoted in thirty-seconds of a dollar, rather than cents. A price quotation of 99-8 or 99.8 means 99 8/32, or $992.50 for a bond with a face value of $1,000.

exchange but in the *over-the-counter* market maintained by a small number of firms specializing in government securities.

Most of the institutions discussed in the preceding section of this chapter are frequent participants in the Treasury-bill market. Commercial banks are the largest participants, and the Federal Reserve plays a crucial part in these dealings. Individuals started moving into this market in large numbers in 1966, when Treasury-bill rates exceeded the rates that could be paid to depositors by banks and savings institutions. The outflow of funds, particularly from savings and loan associations, caused considerable concern and led, in 1970, to the establishment of a $10,000 minimum size for Treasury bills. This effectively prices the small investor out of the Treasury-bill market.

The government-bond dealers play an important part in facilitating trading in the market. Their job is mainly that of bringing buyer and seller together, but the dealer, in contrast to a broker, buys and sells securities for his own account as well as simply executing orders for his customers. In the same way that the corner grocery store carries an inventory of potatoes and bread, the dealer maintains an inventory of securities that he stands ready to add to or sell from at stated prices. The grocer makes a profit by selling potatoes at a higher price than he pays for them; the bond dealer makes a profit by selling Treasury bills at a higher price—the "asked" price—than he pays for them—his "bid" price.

Certificates of Deposit

The major device used by financial institutions on the demand side of the money market is the negotiable certificate of deposit. At mid-year 1981, CDs outstanding were about $273 billion, exceeding even the public's holdings of short-term government securities (those due to mature within a year).

The borrowing institution issues the certificate at its maturity value. Institutions post interest rates, but they are subject to negotiation. No legal interest ceilings apply to large CDs. The maturity is set for 14 days or longer, and the instrument can then be traded on the secondary market. Yields on the secondary market are slightly higher than on the primary market. All CD yields are slightly higher than Treasury obligations of comparable maturity, since there is some risk of default by the borrowing institution, and deposit insurance is limited to $100,000. Some borrowing institutions must pay higher rates than others. Institutions issue both fixed- and variable-rate CDs. The variable rate changes every 90 days in accord with the borrower's issue rate on 90-day certificates.

In 1981, exchanges in New York and Chicago began trading in CD futures. The market participant buys or sells a CD of a selected bank. The price is determined at the time the contract is let, and delivery takes place at a specified time in the future. CDs of 90-day maturity are traded, and the minimum is $1 million. The trader can liquidate the transaction at any time by a reverse transaction.

Commercial Paper

Commercial paper consists of short-term, unsecured promissory notes of large firms. The commercial-paper market can be traced back to the early nineteenth century, but it developed into its present form only in the early twentieth century. Then, as now, a relatively small number of leading business firms tapped the market for short-term funds by selling their paper through commercial-paper dealers. The market has traditionally been used by manufacturers, wholesalers, and retailers to finance large seasonal inventories or accounts receivable.

A relatively recent development in the long history of commercial paper has been the use of the market by large finance companies and commercial-bank holding companies. These financial companies, instead of offering a stated amount of paper of various maturities, as do the industrial offerers of commercial paper, will quote rates on the different maturities and let the buyers take whatever quantities they want. Of course, the rates offered on the various maturities will significantly affect the buyers' choices. Most finance-company paper is sold directly to investors, rather than placed through dealers.

The volume of commercial paper placed through dealers reached a peak of over $1 billion in 1920 and fell after that date. It was not until 1960 that the figure again crossed the $1 billion mark. The market has grown rapidly since 1965, with the growth coming during those periods when banks were unable to meet the loan demands of industrial borrowers.

The volume of total commercial paper outstanding was $164 billion in October 1981.

Maturities on both types of commercial paper range from under one week to about nine months. Both are sold on a discount basis, like Treasury bills, and in large denominations. Although there is no active secondary market in commercial paper, many of the finance-company issuers will agree to buy back their paper prior to maturity.

During the early years, commercial banks were the major buyers of commercial paper. In recent years, there have been new suppliers of funds to the market, such as nonfinancial corporations (which now appear to be the largest holders of commercial paper), pension funds, insurance companies, and foreign investors. In many cases, these investors have been attracted to the market by rates higher than those available on other short-term investments and by the apparently riskless nature of the instrument.

It had traditionally been assumed that nearly all commercial paper outstanding was of very high credit quality. Thus, the collapse of the Penn Central, with $82 million of commercial paper outstanding, sent a major shock wave through the financial markets in general and the commercial-paper market in particular. Although the immediate effects of the Penn Central collapse were not as drastic as some feared at the time, there was a lasting impact on the commercial-paper market. Investors have become more quality-conscious, and the spread in rates between Treasury bills and commercial paper has increased, probably permanently, from what it was before investors realized that losses could occur on commercial paper.

From the point of view of potential purchasers of commercial paper, the relevant rate comparisons are between commercial paper and other money-market instruments (such as Treasury bills or bank CDs), but from the point of view of the issuers, the relevant comparison is with the lending rates of the commercial banks. A firm selling commercial paper has as an alternative borrowing from a commercial bank, and usually at the bank's lowest rate, since issuers of commercial paper are all top-quality firms. Most firms, unwilling to rely on the impersonal commercial-paper market as their major source of short-term financing, maintain borrowing relationships with commercial banks, even though the bank prime loan rate tends to be higher than the rate on commercial paper. In fact, the commercial-paper market reflects this situation, in that firms participating in the market must generally have well-established "backup" lines of credit with banks in order to assure the commercial-paper buyers that the firm has the ability to roll over or retire its paper at maturity. This was true even before the Penn Central collapse.

Banker's Acceptances

Banker's acceptances arise from the financing of international trade and result in a short-term obligation of a commercial bank. A typical transaction giving rise to a banker's acceptance occurs when an importer makes an arrangement with his bank whereby the bank agrees in writing (a "letter of credit") to accept bills drawn on it by the exporter up to a certain amount. The importer sends this letter of credit to the seller to assure him that the bank will pay on the specified basis. The seller can thus ship the goods without doubt as to the importer's ability to pay. The importer promises to pay his bank at or before the time the bank must pay the seller. The bank has not extended any credit under this arrangement. All it has done is to substitute its higher credit standing for that of its customer, and it charges the buyer an acceptance fee for this service. When the bank receives the draft or bill drawn on it by the seller, it signs or "accepts" the draft. Once accepted, the draft becomes a banker's acceptance, and a negotiable money-market instrument.

The accepting bank may hold the acceptance, or it may sell it in the market. A broad market has developed for such instruments, with New York as the central market and trading done by several large banks and a few dealers. Although the usual participants in the money market hold acceptances, the largest share is held by foreign investors. This reflects not only their greater familiarity and experience with the instrument, but also, and probably more important, the fact that earnings on foreign holdings of acceptances are exempt from U.S. income taxes.

Tax-Exempts

Although most financing of state and local governments is on a long-term basis, there has been a market in short-term tax-exempt obligations of such issuers. Some of the trading is in notes of local public housing agencies that are guaranteed by the federal government. Other than these securities, much of the short-term tax-exempt market has consisted of tax-anticipation or other short-term notes of large cities experiencing some financial difficulties. The problems of New York City, resulting in a default on such notes, have had a significant effect on the market.

YIELDS

For a comparison of yields, instruments of the same maturity should be used. Day-by-day money—that is, Federal funds and repurchase agreements—have no equivalent in the market for comparison. These yields fluctuate daily and are considered the most sensitive indicator of money-market conditions. For other in-

TABLE 5-3
Money-Market Investments

	Obligation	Marketability	Maturities	Denominations	Basis
United States Treasury bills	U.S. government obligation. U.S. Treasury auctions 3- and 6-mos. bills weekly. Also offers, through special auctions, one-year maturities and tax-anticipation bills.	Excellent secondary market.	Up to 1 year.	$10,000 to $1 million	Discounted. Actual days on a 360-day year.
Prime sales finance paper	Promissory notes of finance companies placed directly with the investor.	No secondary market. Companies under certain conditions will usually buy back paper prior to maturity. Most companies will adjust rate.	Issued to mature on any day from 3 to 270 days.	$1,000 to $5 million	Discounted or interest-bearing. Actual days on a 360-day year.
Dealer paper I. Finance	Promissory notes of finance companies sold through commercial-paper dealers.	Limited secondary market. Buy-back arrangement negotiated through the dealer.	Issued to mature on any day from 30 to 270 days.	$100,000 to $5 million	Discounted or interest-bearing. Actual days on a 360-day year.
Dealer paper II. Industrial	Promissory notes of leading industrial firms sold through commercial-paper dealers.	Limited secondary market.	Usually available on certain dates between 30 & 180 days.	$500,000 to $5 million	Discounted. Actual days on a 360-day year.

TABLE 5-3 (Cont.)
Money-Market Investments

	Obligation	Marketability	Maturities	Denominations	Basis
Prime banker's acceptances	Time draft drawn on and accepted by a banking institution, which in effect substitutes its credit for that of the importer or holder of merchandise.	Good secondary market. Bid usually ⅛ of 1% higher than offered side of market.	Up to 6 months.	$25,000 to $1 million	Discounted. Actual days on a 360-day year.
Negotiable time certificates of deposit	Certificate of a time deposit at a commercial bank.	Good secondary market.	Unlimited	$500,000 to $1 million	Yield basis. Actual days on a 360-day year. Interest at maturity.
Short-term tax-exempts	Tax- & bond-anticipation notes	Notes of states, municipalities, or political subdivisions	Good secondary market.	Various, usually 3 mos. to 1 year from issue.	$1,000 to $1 million	Yield basis. Usually 30 days on a 360-day year. Interest at maturity.

Source: Morgan Guaranty Trust Company.

struments, newly auctioned government bills usually carry the lowest yields, since they involve no risk and no transaction cost. Listed below, for comparison, are the yields on three-month instruments that prevailed on the average in January 1982, when the Fed-funds rate averaged 12.96 percent.

Treasury bills:	
Auction average	12.75
Secondary market	13.3
Certificates of deposit, secondary market	13.75
Commercial paper	13.75
Banker's acceptances	13.60

The purpose of this chapter has been to present an overview of the participants and instruments involved in the money market. A summary of the major money-market instruments and their characteristics is presented in Table 5-3. Subsequent chapters in this part and in Part III will consider the role of the important demanders and suppliers of funds in more detail. Parts V and VII deal with the role of the Federal Reserve and the link between monetary policy and the financial markets.

QUESTIONS

1 What are the principal institutions that need large amounts of short-term funds?
2 What institutions can provide these funds?
3 What are the differences between Treasury bills and bonds?
4 Items pertaining to bankers' acceptances appear on both the asset and liability sides of banks' balance sheets. What is the difference between these two items, and how do they arise?
5 Why do business firms borrow from banks if the interest rate on commercial paper is lower than bank rates?
6 Can banks sell Federal funds if they do not have excess reserves?
7 Would you expect yields on negotiable CDs in the secondary market to be higher or lower than yields offered by banks on new CDs?

SELECTED READINGS

BOWSHER, NORMAN, "Repurchase Agreements," Federal Reserve Bank of St. Louis *Review*, September 1979.
COOK, TIMOTHY Q., ed., *Instruments of the Money Market*. Federal Reserve Bank of Richmond, 1981.
DARST, D.M., *Handbook of the Bond and Money Markets*. New York: McGraw-Hill, 1981.

DOUGALL, HERBERT and JACK E. GAUMNITZ, *Capital Markets and Institutions*, 4th ed. Englewood Cliffs, N.J.: Prentice-Hall, 1980.

LINDOW, WESLEY, *Inside the Money Market*. New York: Random House, 1972.

McCURDY, CHRISTOPHER J., "The Dealer Market for United States Government Securities," Federal Reserve Bank of New York *Quarterly Review*, Winter 1977–78.

MELTON, WILLIAM C., "The Market for Large Negotiable CDs," Federal Reserve Bank of New York *Quarterly Review*, Winter 1977–78.

WOODWORTH, G. WALTER, *The Money Market and Monetary Management*. New York: Harper & Row, 1972.

6

Commercial-Bank Management

THE USE OF BANK FUNDS

The challenge facing commercial-bank portfolio management is to balance the need for safety and liquidity against the goal of earnings. Most of the liabilities of the bank are payable either on demand or at scheduled maturities in the near future. This liability structure calls for liquid assets, but the assets that are the most liquid generally have the lower yields. These considerations call for diversification of assets. A significant part of the banks' funds is held in the form of cash. Banks hold various types of securities and make many different types of loans. A relatively small part of bank assets is accounted for by fixed assets such as real estate, building, or equipment.

Reserves

One of the earliest types of bank regulation was the requirement that banks maintain cash reserves equal to a certain fraction of their deposits. New York, the first state to enact such regulation, in 1838 required banks to maintain a cash reserve equal to at least 12½ percent of their note liabilities. The National Banking Act also imposed standards for national banks.

The Federal Reserve Act gave the Federal Reserve System control over reserve requirements for member banks, and the 1980 Monetary Control Act extended this control to nonmember banks and other depository institutions. Reserves must be held either as deposits at the Federal Reserve Bank or as currency in the bank's vaults.

The purpose of reserve requirements was originally to compel banks to maintain a reasonable degree of liquidity in order to be able to meet demands for cash. With time, however, this conception has changed. Now these requirements are generally considered to be a control device through which the Federal Reserve can influence the monetary system. We will see later just how this mechanism works.

Since required reserves cannot be reduced below the legal minimum for any lengthy period, banks find it necessary, for normal operations and as protection against unforeseen large withdrawals, to maintain reserves in excess of their legal requirements. These working reserves are held in the form of vault cash in the bank, excess reserves with a Federal Reserve Bank, and deposits with other banks. (See Table 6-1.)

Vault cash makes up a third of banks' reserves. If a bank needs more cash, it can get it rather quickly from the Federal Reserve Bank or from another commercial bank. Only banks in isolated locations, far from these sources of currency, need proportionately larger amounts of vault cash.

The most important part of working reserves are those held as deposits with other commercial banks. Small banks in rural or suburban areas maintain deposits in banks in the nearest city. These city correspondent banks maintain deposits with banks in still larger cities, particularly New York and Chicago.

Correspondent banks compete for these deposits, since they provide the bank with funds to lend or invest. The correspondent

TABLE 6-1
Commercial-Bank[a] Cash Assets, December 31, 1981
(billions of dollars)

Currency and coin	22.0
Reserves with Federal Reserve Banks	28.0
Balances with depository institutions	54.5
Cash items in process of collection	68.6
Total cash assets	173.1

[a] Including domestically chartered commercial banks (14,713), but excluding U.S. branches of foreign banks.
Source: Federal Reserve Bulletin.

banks, however, are expected to perform various services for the smaller banks; for example, handling the clearing and collection of checks, and giving investment advice or help in handling a loan request too large for the smaller bank to make itself. Although banks do not earn interest on deposits left with correspondent banks, they are compensated through services.

Cash reserves now account for about 12 percent of total commercial-bank assets. The handling of this part of the bank's assets is an area in which efficient management can result in substantial improvement in the bank's earnings. We have noted that banks must generally maintain some reserves in excess of the legal requirements. At certain periods in the past, the volume of excess reserves has been very large. Bankers have now learned to operate with a very low level of excess reserves—in the past few years, excess reserves have averaged less than 1 percent of total reserves. This reduction has resulted from efforts of management that reflect a more aggressive attitude generally, with an extra incentive provided by the high interest rates that have prevailed in recent years. That is, when Treasury bills yield 3 percent, there is no great incentive to minimize holdings of cash. But when Treasury bills yield even as little as 6 percent, the bank can achieve a substantial increase in its earnings by reducing cash assets. In fact, the bank that reduces its cash assets, say, from 20 percent to 15 percent of total assets may generate a 25 percent increase in net profit.

Secondary Reserves

A bank could conceivably provide for all possible contingencies by maintaining a very large portion of its assets in the form of cash. This would generally be unwise, because it forces the bank to forgo earnings unnecessarily. Indeed, in the long run, it might be an unsafe policy. True long-run safety for a bank requires that it have adequate earnings. The term *secondary reserves* is applied to those assets that the bank holds to provide "(1) for likely and indeed almost forecastable cash needs, (2) for remote, unlikely, but possible cash needs."[1]

"Secondary reserves" is not a caption that appears on the bank's balance sheet. It is an analytical concept, and one that is very useful in examining portfolio policy. Secondary reserves are those assets of the bank that can quickly be converted into cash on very short notice without risk of loss.

[1] Roland Robinson, *The Management of Bank Funds*, 2nd ed. (New York: McGraw-Hill, 1962), p. 15.

We have seen that long-term securities fluctuate more in price than short-terms. Thus, only short-term securities are appropriate for inclusion in the secondary reserves of the commercial bank. Of course, not all short-term securities would be eligible for such inclusion. Some are not readily marketable, or involve a considerable amount of credit risk. Treasury bills are the securities most widely used by commercial banks for secondary-reserve purposes.

Treasury bills have an active, broad market, so the bank can sell even very large amounts with little difficulty. Because there is no risk of default and because they mature in a relatively short time, they fluctuate very little in price. If the bank buys Treasury bills today and finds that it must sell them next week, it is unlikely to suffer a significant loss. Commercial paper, banker's acceptances, Treasury certificates, and other government securities maturing within a year or so are also widely used for secondary-reserve purposes. Loans to brokers repayable on demand and secured by marketable securities meet all the requirements of a secondary-reserve asset. For many banks, the sale of Federal funds is the most important means for generating earnings on temporarily excess funds that may be needed without much warning.

The primary motive for holding secondary reserves is liquidity; yield on these assets is of far less importance. The bank does, however, expect some return on its secondary reserves, else it might just as well hold cash. At times, short-term securities may provide yields almost as high as or even higher than longer-term securities; that is, the yield curve may be flat or downward-sloping. At such a time, there is no difficulty in the bank's limiting itself to very short-term securities for secondary-reserve purposes. In other periods, there may be a very great difference between the yields available on, say, three-month Treasury bills and government securities maturing in, say, three years. During 1977, for example, three-month Treasury bills were yielding 4.77 percent while three-year Treasury securities yielded 6.45 percent. In such a case, many bankers feel tempted to stretch out the maturity of their secondary reserves. The question of how far it is safe to go is one that involves the exercise of considerable judgment. As in many areas of financial management, there is no easy answer to this basic conflict between the desire for profits and the need for adequate liquidity.

Commercial-Bank Loans

Once the banker has provided for adequate liquidity to meet any expected or unlikely need for cash, he can devote his funds to the primary business of the bank—making loans to business firms and individuals.

Bank lending operations have changed considerably over the years. For many years, the traditional type of bank lending activity was the "self-liquidating commercial loan." This is best exemplified by a short-term loan to a business firm to finance carrying its inventory. In the normal course of business, it was expected that the firm would sell the goods and this sale would generate the cash necessary to repay the loan. This traditional type of commercial-bank loan might be illustrated by a loan to a toy store in the fall so that the firm could build up its inventory of toys for Christmas. The store would buy toys in the fall, and its sales would be high in November and December. By the end of December, the store's inventory would be back to normal, and the sale of the goods bought earlier would have generated enough cash to repay the bank.

Over time, banks have broadened considerably the types of loans they make. During the nineteenth and early twentieth centuries, it was considered unsound for a bank to make loans with a maturity of over one year. The nineteenth-century banker would have been horrified at the thought of making three-year loans to finance the purchase of consumer goods. A distribution of the various types of bank loans is shown in Table 6-2.

TABLE 6-2
Loans of Insured Commercial Banks,
December 1981

	Millions of Dollars	Percent of Total
Commercial and industrial	358.5	36.8
Real estate loans	285.5	29.3
Loans to individuals	185.2	19.0
Security loans	21.9	2.2
Loans to nonbank financial institutions	30.3	3.1
Agricultural loans	33.0	3.4
Lease financing receivables	12.7	1.3
All other loans	47.8	4.9
Total	974.9	100.0

Source: *Federal Reserve Bulletin.*

We will consider bank lending activity in some detail in Chapters 9–13. At this point, it is sufficient to point out that making loans is the most profitable activity of commercial banks, the one that commercial banks can do better than any other financial institution. This comparison has been made, for example, between commercial banks and insurance companies:

Commercial banks are strategically located for lending. They know a great number of moderate-sized customers intimately; they can extend loan credit and collect it where other lenders could not. In the investment market they are not so strategically located. For example, face to face with insurance company competition, a commercial bank is vastly better equipped to make customer loans; working through loan agents and with few offices, the insurance companies just could not do so well. When it comes to open-market investment, insurance companies, greater in size and with more stable liabilities, have an advantage over most commercial banks.[2]

The role of loans in the balance sheets of commercial banks has changed over time. From the early days of banking in this country through the 1920s, loans accounted for most of the banks' assets. The Great Depression and is aftermath changed that, and we have only recently returned to what historically has been the more normal situation.

Bankers suffered vast losses on loans during the depression, which made them reluctant to extend loans afterward. Moreover, the depressed business conditions that prevailed throughout the 1930s meant that there was very little demand for loans. Commercial banks had loans averaging about 55 percent of assets during the 1920s, but this ratio fell to 30 percent during the mid-1930s, and even further during World War II. The recovery in bank lending activity was slow, but bankers are now operating with loan–asset ratios that would have made them very uncomfortable during the 1950s.

The change is due to more aggressive management, coupled with changed market conditions. In recent years, as compared with the period from 1930 to the mid-1950s, the demand for bank loans has been high, and bankers have been willing to meet this demand. Even the setbacks of the 1970s did not lead bankers to cut back on their desire for higher loan–asset ratios than those of the 1950s. Both banker willingness and adequate loan demand are necessary to reach high loan–asset ratios. If bank management were as conservative today as it was during the early 1950s, or if the demand for loans were as low as during the 1930s, loan–asset ratios would still be low.

Large corporate borrowers have access to borrowing at many banks throughout the country. The rate of interest to these borrowers is the prime rate posted by the banks, although a bank may make some loans at lower rates to customers who have a continuing relation with it. Also, when short-term rates are relatively high, longer-term loans may be made at less than the prime rate. Selected data on loans made the first week of August 1981 are shown in Table

[2] Robinson, *The Management of Bank Funds*, p. 17.

6-3. Three-fourths of longer-term loans were made with floating rates—rates that change with market interest rates.

Bank Investments

The bank's primary interest lies in making loans. If the demand for loans of acceptable quality is not great enough, the bank will use its extra funds for open-market investment.

Table 6-4 shows the proportion of interest-bearing securities in the total of interest-bearing assets. U.S. government bonds have the attraction of perfect safety from default and ready marketability. As the table shows, U.S. government obligations account for a large share of bank holdings of securities. Of course, many of these are held for secondary-reserve purposes rather than as part of a permanent investment portfolio.

Commercial banks are also large holders of obligations of state and local governments. These municipal securities vary in quality, but most have high credit standing. Their principal attraction is that interest on them is exempt from federal income taxes. For this reason, bank holdings of municipal securities are much larger than holdings of corporate bonds. A bank is better off earning 9 percent interest on a high-grade municipal bond than it would be earning 12 percent on a bond of a private corporation. The 9 percent is the bank's to keep; the 12 percent must be shared with Uncle Sam. For this reason, banks rarely hold sizable amounts of corporate bonds. When safety and liquidity are of paramount importance, U.S. governments are the first choice. Where additional risk can be taken in

TABLE 6-3
Terms of Lending at Commercial Banks,
August 3–8, 1981[a]

	Percent with Floating Rate	Weighted Average Maturity (Months)	Weighted Average Interest Rate
Short-term commercial and industrial	34.5	1.6	21.11
Long-term commercial and industrial	79.2	57.6	20.62
Construction and land-development loans	44.4	8.7	20.26
Agricultural loans	not available	5.0	19.57

[a] Prime rate was 20.50.

Source: *Federal Reserve Bulletin*, November 1981, p. A-24.

TABLE 6-4
Bank Portfolio and Liability Composition—
All Insured Banks, 1980

Item	All	Assets			
			$100 Million to $1 Billion	$1 Billion or More	
		Less Than $100 Million		Money Center	Others
		Balance sheet (as percent of average consolidated assets)			
Interest-earning assets	82.9	89.4	87.2	78.0	81.1
Loans	55.4	55.9	55.4	55.4	55.0
Securities	17.0	27.8	25.2	7.2	15.0
U.S. Treasury	5.3	9.2	7.9	2.2	4.5
U.S. government agencies	3.0	6.3	4.4	.9	2.3
State and local governments	7.8	11.8	12.3	2.8	7.7
Other bonds and stock	.8	.5	.6	1.4	.5
Gross federal funds sold and reverse RPs	3.7	5.5	5.4	1.6	3.6
Interest-bearing deposits	6.8	.2	1.3	13.7	7.4
Financial claims	89.1	89.8	90.7	87.8	89.1
Demand deposits	24.0	26.7	28.8	17.5	26.1
Interest-bearing claims	65.1	63.1	62.0	70.3	63.0
Time and savings deposits	55.5	61.4	55.2	57.8	49.7
Large time	12.8	9.5	14.4	11.1	15.7
In foreign offices	16.0	0	.2	40.3	11.4
Other domestic	26.7	52.0	40.6	6.4	22.6
Subordinated notes and debentures	.4	.2	.4	.2	.6
Other borrowings	2.3	.4	.9	4.2	2.4
Gross RPs and federal funds purchased	6.9	1.0	5.4	8.2	10.4

Source: *Federal Reserve Bulletin.*

the interests of higher earnings, tax-free municipals are the first choice.

Smaller banks hold a greater proportion of their assets in securities than do larger banks, because of smaller loan demand. Interest-earning assets as a whole make up a larger share of small banks' assets because of these banks' lower effective reserve requirement against total deposits.

In the rising interest rate period of the later 1970s and early 1980s, loan yields tended to rise more than securities yields, and banks reduced the proportion of securities in their portfolios. As interest rates rose, they experienced capital losses on their securities, and these realized losses reduced their tax liability.

LIABILITY MANAGEMENT

So far, this chapter has discussed only the asset side of the bank balance sheet. The liquidity needs of commercial banks have been treated as though they must be dealt with through proper management of the funds the bank has available to invest. Until only a few years ago, that was indeed the way bankers thought about the problem of liquidity—it was solely an asset-management problem. In recent years, however, more aggressive banks have taken an alternative approach to liquidity—liability management.

Since a large part of the deposits of a commercial bank are payable on demand, the bank must be able to generate a large amount of cash in a hurry. The traditional way of ensuring the ability to raise cash has been to hold *assets* that are cash or that can be turned into cash quickly and without sizable losses. It is also possible to generate cash quickly by use of *liabilities*—that is, to borrow it.

This seems particularly appropriate for the second need cited earlier for holding secondary reserves: "for remote, unlikely, but possible cash needs." Since these needs may never arise, it may be reasonable to handle this eventuality by borrowing when necessary rather than by a permanent commitment of funds. This requires, however, a sure source of funds when needed.

Banks have used many devices to assure themselves of a reliable source of cash when needed. Large, negotiable certificates of deposit are one important source of funds for liquidity purposes. The supply of funds offered for CDs is very sensitive to changes in offering rates posted by the banks. Thus, banks' ability to influence flows of time deposits could constitute an important source of liquidity. Both negotiable and nonnegotiable time deposits are issued at varying maturities, and the maturity structure is balanced by varying offering rates. These methods are more important for the larger banks, as shown in Table 6-4.

Borrowing at the Federal Reserve discount window is a means by which banks can obtain short-term funds. The Fed discourages frequent borrowing, however, and imposes a surcharge over the usual discount rate for large banks that borrow frequently. (See Chapter 20.) Overnight borrowing in the Federal-funds market and through repurchase agreements has also assumed increasing importance.[3] (See Chapter 5.) Banks doubled their nondeposit sources of funds (Federal Reserve discounting, Fed-funds borrowing, and others) between 1976 and 1980.

Banks have used several other devices to meet liquidity needs in recent years. Foreign banking offices, including branches of American banks, accept deposits denominated in U.S. dollars. American banks' borrowings of these "Eurodollars" constituted the largest nondeposit source of funds for American banks during some years of high interest rates. (See Chapter 13.)

Banks also raised funds for a time by issuing their own promissory notes. These notes were general obligations of the issuing bank but, at least for a time, were not subject to interest-rate ceilings imposed on deposits. More important in recent years has been the sale of commercial paper by banks through their holding companies.

Liability management is appropriately viewed as part of the general shift toward more aggressive banking since the early 1960s. Part of this movement has been reconsidered by bankers and supervisors, but none of the banking problems of the 1970s was reflected in inordinate liquidity pressures. Liability management did not do lasting harm to any of its responsible practitioners, and it, unlike some of the banking excesses of recent years, is to be a permanent part of banking operations.

BANK EARNINGS

The banking industry is characterized by a low profit margin on a large volume of business per dollar of equity capital. In 1980, for example, commercial banks reported net income after taxes of only .8 percent of their total assets. It is the great leverage factor of commercial banks that enables them to earn a respectable return on stockholder's investment with a very low return on assets. Thus, the commercial-bank net income mentioned above amounted to 13.7 percent of equity capital.

Over two-thirds of the banks' gross income in 1980 came from interest on loans. The remainder was from interest on securities

---

[3] Until 1965, it was generally assumed that the Federal Reserve rate on loans to member banks (the "discount rate") served as a ceiling on Fed-funds transactions. Why should banks pay a higher rate to borrow reserves from other banks than they pay to borrow from the Fed? The answer lies in the Fed's rather arbitrary administration of the discount window in recent years, and the finding that by paying a premium for Federal funds, banks were able to tap a large and reliable source of relatively permanent funds and liquidity.

and from various kinds of fees, such as from trust departments, deposit service charges, and credit cards. Income from foreign operations has become increasingly important for the very large banks, reaching $1.5 billion after taxes in 1979. A summary of bank income and expenses is shown in Table 6-5.

The largest expense item for commercial banks is interest on deposits. This now comes to almost one-half of gross income, more than double the proportion it made up in 1961. This change has resulted in part from the increase in the level of interest rates and in part from the increase in the relative proportion of time deposits as a source of funds for commercial banks.

Rises in interest rates increase both income and expenses of the banks, and the delicate balance between the two determines the operating result. Loans tend to be more interest-sensitive than securities, and during periods of business expansion, banks can shift toward loans. The move toward floating rates increased this sensitivity. When loan demand is down, bank earnings suffer, and particularly so if interest rates are rising, because banks' cost of funds continues to rise. Interest-sensitive deposits have risen as a

TABLE 6-5
Commercial-Bank Income and Expenses—
Insured Banks, 1980
(millions of dollars)

Income	
Interest on loans	126,663
Interest on securities	22,968
Other interest	24,785
Fees, including deposit service charges	7,525
Other income	8,168
Total	190,109
Expenses	
Interest on time and savings deposits	98,130
Interest on Fed funds and other borrowing	21,628
Payroll costs	24,565
Occupancy expense	7,325
Other expenses and loan loss provision	19,027
Total	170,675
Income before taxes	19,435
Net income [a]	13,950

[a] After income taxes, losses on securities, and other adjustments.
Source: *Federal Reserve Bulletin*, September 1981, p. 667.

proportion of the total, and they took a great upsurge beginning in 1978, when six-month money-market certificates were authorized. This move particularly affected small banks, which until then did not have interest-sensitive deposits.

The 1980 Deregulation Act increased the banks' interest expense, with the authorization of demand-deposit interest and the scheduled phaseout of all deposit interest ceilings. In the long run, of course, banks will adjust to the changed situation, presumably by charging the full costs of handling checking accounts (which now are provided free or at less than cost), or by not paying interest on accounts that are too small or too active to be profitable. In the short run, however, adjustment to interest on demand deposits and a system of explicit charges for services provided will be difficult for many banks and will have an adverse effect on bank earnings.

The costs of handling checking accounts make up a large fraction of total bank costs. Some bankers hope that a shift to electronic funds transfer systems will ultimately reduce costs. This is indeed likely in the long run, but again, in the short run, banks will be faced with the need to continue handling paper checks while they are also investing in the electronic equipment necessary for the new technology. Beginning in late 1981, as mandated by law, the Federal Reserve charged the full cost of check clearing. This further increases bank costs and adds to the necessary service charges for transaction accounts.

Losses on loans were a relatively negligible expense factor for most banks during the 1960s. Since then, however, loan losses have at times become significant in the aggregate and in relation to net income and to loans. Loan losses reached a record level in 1976, averaging over one-half of 1 percent of loans, then declined to less than one-third of 1 percent in both 1979 and 1980.

Banks have historically received rather favorable treatment with respect to federal taxation. Income taxes represented about 26 percent of bank income before taxes in 1980. In contrast, the effective tax rate for nonfinancial corporations was 34 percent. One of the advantages allowed banks is in the tax deduction for possible loan losses, and large banks also benefit from the investment tax credit and favorable treatment on their leasing and foreign operations.

The return on equity for recent years is shown in Table 6-6. The data indicate that small banks suffered no great disadvantages, but it is possible that protective government policies allowed them to maintain their position. These protections included deposit interest ceilings and lower effective reserve requirements.

TABLE 6-6
Profit Rates, All Insured Commercial Banks, 1973–80 (percent)

Return on Equity	1973	1975	1977	1978	1979	1980
	Net Income as a Percent of the Average of Beginning- and End-of-Year Equity Capital					
All banks	12.9	11.8	11.8	12.9	13.9	13.7
Less than $100 million	13.5	11.5	12.4	13.2	14.1	14.2
$100 million to $1 billion	12.6	11.1	12.0	13.2	13.9	13.7
$1 billion or more						
Money center	13.2	13.8	11.4	12.8	14.0	14.4
Others	12.0	11.2	11.2	12.5	13.5	12.7

Source: *Federal Reserve Bulletin*, various issues.

EXPANDED BANK SERVICES

In addition to deposit services and financing activities, banks provide some additional services to their customers. Some of these services have traditionally been associated with the banking business, such as trust services and the renting of safe-deposit boxes, and others have been more recent ventures into related financial activities, such as insurance and accounting. Nearly all the newer activities have been controversial, and even some of the traditional banking services have received critical scrutiny in recent years.

Some of the newer activities have been computer-based, relying on the high-priced equipment that banks must have to handle their check-clearing responsibilities. We have already described the role of automated clearinghouses in handling salary payments without the need for paper checks. It is a logical extension of this service for the bank to do the payroll bookkeeping for the firm, including the calculation of deductions and preparation of withholding statements. In fact, since the bank has a large-scale computer, it is probably cheaper for the bank to provide this service than it would be for the firm to do it itself.

Banks have also moved into the field of billing (and the associated accounting), handling these matters for doctors and other professionals as well as for some small businesses. All the services mentioned so far relate fairly closely to the traditional bank concern with efficient transfer of funds, but some banks have gone rather far afield (including, in some cases, calculation of golf handicaps for local country clubs). By moving in this direction, banks have incurred the ire of computer-service bureaus and accountants, who are unhappy about bank competition in what they consider their exclusive fields. In 1967, a group of computer-service firms brought suit against a Minnesota bank to stop it from using its computer for anything other than its own internal processing. This type of litigation has since become commonplace: Travel agents have sued to stop banks from providing travel services; insurance companies have (successfully) tried to stop banks from underwriting credit life insurance; leasing companies have tried to stop banks from leasing equipment; and investment bankers have sued (successfully) to stop banks from underwriting municipal revenue bonds. Businessmen are usually strong supporters of the benefits of increased competition, but they often seem to have objections when the increased competition affects them.

Banks have been active in the provision of fiduciary services for many years with relatively little controversy. Many banks have "Trust Company" as part of their names. In recent years, however, there has been increased concern about the possibility of conflicts of interest between the commercial, profit-making activities of the bank and its obligation to do what is best for its trust customers.

Debate over the proper scope of bank activities has been with us throughout our history. In recent years, it has focused on the appropriate activities for bank holding companies. We will consider that aspect of the problem in Chapter 16.

QUESTIONS

1 "When there is conflict between safety and profitability, it is better to err on the side of safety." Appraise this statement with regard to the investment policy of a commercial bank. Is the statement just as applicable to a savings and loan association? a life insurance company? an automobile manufacturer?

2 Why do banks sometimes hold excess reserves?

3 If a bank's deposits are payable on demand or on short notice, is it safe for the bank to make loans with a maturity of, say, five years? thirty years?

4 "Short-term business loans are more liquid assets for a bank than residential mortgage loans." Appraise.

5 What is the maximum loan–deposit ratio you would consider safe for a commercial bank?

6 Suppose a General Motors bond is available at a yield ¼ percent higher than a comparable-maturity U.S. Treasury bond. Is the additional yield worth the additional risk from the point of view of a commercial bank?

7 Why do commercial banks invest more heavily in municipal bonds than in corporate bonds?

8 How would you expect the investment policy of a bank with a large amount of time deposits to differ from that of a bank with only demand deposits?

SELECTED READINGS

CROSSE, HOWARD D., and GEORGE H. HEMPEL, *Management Policies for Commercial Banks,* 3rd ed. Englewood Cliffs, N.J.: Prentice-Hall, 1980.

GOLDBERG, L., and L. WHITE, eds., *The Deregulation of the Banking and Securities Industries.* Lexington, Mass.: Lexington Books, 1979.

HEMPEL, GEORGE H., and JESS B. YAWITZ, *Financial Management of Financial Institutions.* Englewood Cliffs, N.J.: Prentice-Hall, 1977.

LINDOW, WESLEY, *Inside the Money Market.* New York: Random House, 1972.

SAMETZ, ARNOLD, ed., *Securities Activities of Commercial Banks.* Lexington, Mass.: Lexington Books, 1981.

7

Nonbank Depository Institutions

The institutions whose operations come closest to those of commercial banks are savings and loan associations, mutual savings banks, and credit unions. The combined deposits of these institutions are slightly less than the time and savings deposits of the commercial-banking system. The flow of funds of these "Savings Institutions Combined" was shown in Table 4-2. This chapter first describes each of these three types of institutions and then discusses some common problems in their operations.

Table 7-1 shows the growth of these institutions in the 1970s. Although transaction accounts were not authorized for them on a nationwide basis until the 1980 Deregulation Act, institutions in some jurisdictions had already begun to offer them. The savings institutions as a group added about $8.6 billion of such accounts in 1981.

SAVINGS AND LOAN ASSOCIATIONS

The assets of $630 billion (year-end 1980) of savings and loan associations come to about half those of the commercial-banking system. The largest association, Home Savings and Loan (California), has $13 billion in assets, making it one-eighth the size of the largest

TABLE 7-1
Selected Savings Institutions' Assets, 1970–81
(billions of dollars)

	Savings and Loans	Mutual Savings Banks	Credit Unions
1970	176.2	79.7	18.0
1971	206.0	90.8	21.1
1972	243.1	102.3	24.6
1973	271.9	108.3	27.8
1974	295.5	110.3	31.1
1975	338.2	122.2	36.9
1976	391.9	136.4	43.3
1977	459.2	149.5	51.6
1978	523.6	161.2	58.4
1979	579.3	163.3	62.3
1980	629.8	171.6	70.8
1981	662.3	175.2	75.2

Source: Federal Reserve Flow-of-Funds Accounts.

commercial bank. There are about 4,700 associations, with average assets of close to $135 million.

The distinctive features of savings and loans (S&Ls) are that (1) their assets are primarily home mortgages, (2) their liabilities are primarily savings and time deposits, and (3) most are mutual institutions, rather than stockholder-owned. Associations are chartered, regulated, and insured by entirely different agencies from those governing commercial banks.

The original purpose of the savings and loan association can be seen in the case of a group of people, each wishing to buy a house. None has the cash available to buy the house himself. If all these people pool their funds, however, some of them will be able to use this money to buy the houses they desire. Interest on the money borrowed will recompense the other members of the arrangement for waiting. As the loans are repaid, other members can borrow the funds collected. This original concept of the savings and loan association has changed considerably in recent years, but the basic purpose is still the same—the facilitation of homeownership.

An association may obtain a charter from either the state or the federal government. Conversions between state and federal charter are possible, and the threat of conversions tends to keep some uniformity in the regulations under which the associations function.

All S&Ls are eligible for membership in the Federal Savings

and Loan Insurance Corporation (FSLIC), which insures each depositor up to $100,000. Insured associations account for 98 percent of the assets of all of them. An insured S&L pays a fee of 1/12 of 1 percent of its deposits (not just its insured deposits) annually, and this fee goes into a reserve fund. In addition to the reserve fund, the FSLIC can also protect deposits by borrowing from the Treasury. The ratio of the reserve fund to deposits declined throughout the 1970s, ending the decade at about 1.3 percent of the deposits of insured associations.

The federal supervising agency for savings and loans is the Federal Home Loan Bank Board.[1] Under the board is a system of regional banks, constituting the Federal Home Loan Bank System. The FSLIC is also a part of the system. Membership in the Federal Home Loan Bank System is voluntary for state-chartered associations, mandatory for federal associations. A federal association is supervised by its regional Home Loan Bank.

A little less than half the S&Ls have federal charters, but most are members of the Home Loan Bank System. Most S&Ls are mutual institutions, but some of the larger ones, particularly in California, are stockholder-owned, with the result that stock associations account for a fourth of all savings and loans' assets. Some stock associations are owned by holding companies that own a number of associations (such as Financial Federation, Inc., listed on the New York Stock Exchange) or that own other interests (Allstate Savings and Loan is a Sears, Roebuck subsidiary). A number of mergers have taken place in the past few years, many involving acquisition of S&Ls in danger of failing.

Aside from supervising federal associations, the most important economic function of the Federal Home Loan Bank System is as a source of liquidity to the member institutions. The regional Federal Home Loan Banks make loans to member associations, with mortgages pledged as security for the loans. This provides S&Ls with a source of liquidity and thereby enables them to invest a larger proportion of their assets in mortgages, which, in the absence of this arrangement, would be a rather illiquid asset. This lending function is viewed not as simply an emergency source of

---

[1] As distinct from most government supervisory agencies, the charter of the Federal Home Loan Bank Board requires it to "promote" the savings and loan industry. In many respects, the board functions as an effective lobbyist for the industry, much to the consternation of the commercial banks, which do not believe that their supervisors in Washington are as solicitous of the banks' welfare as the Home Loan Bank Board is with respect to its "constituents."

liquidity, but as a longer-run source of funds available to expand mortgage lending. The terms set by the Federal Home Loan Bank Board on such lending are varied, depending on the need for additional housing financing by the economy and on the rates the board must pay on its own borrowing, since it obtains its funds by the sale of securities on the capital markets. These "federally sponsored" agency issues carry lower rates than the associations would pay if they went directly to the capital markets. At year-end 1980, the Federal Home Loan Banks had $41 billion of debt outstanding.

Associations also have the right to use the Federal Reserve discount window. However, the Fed has ruled that they must first use the Federal Home Loan Bank's lending facilities. This ruling, along with the usual restrictive rules governing Federal Reserve discounting, minimizes the Fed as a source of funds for the associations.

Savings and loans obtain most of their funds from time deposits, as shown in Table 7-2. They issue the same types of savings and time deposits as issued by commercial banks (see Chapter 3). Most of their time certificates of deposit are of smaller denominations, with those over $100,000 making up less than 4 percent of the total. The 1980 Deregulation Act scheduled complete elimination of interest ceilings on deposits by 1986, and it established a committee to determine ceilings for all covered institutions in the interim. Effective January 1, 1981, the law authorized S&Ls to issue interest-bearing transaction accounts to individuals and nonprofit entities. Savings and loans began aggressive competition for these accounts, offering free services with lower balances than those required by commercial banks.

Increasingly in recent years, the associations have had to supplement their savings deposits with other sources of funds. Federal Home Loan Bank advances grew from $20 billion outstanding in 1977 to $62 billion in 1981. Many of the larger institutions issue special bonds backed by mortgages. The institution pledges as collateral mortgages in its portfolio equal to more than 100 percent of the value of the bond, but the mortgages remain as assets on its books. Bonds carry 5- to 10-year maturities and thus are a more stable source of funds than savings deposits.[2]

Associations have also been able to increase their mortgage lending activity by disposing of existing mortgages through the device of "pass-through securities." A pool of mortgages less than

[2] S&Ls usually pledge older mortgages that were issued at lower interest rates. In this way, they can obtain funds from these mortgages without selling them at losses.

TABLE 7-2

Assets and Liabilities of Savings and Loan Associations,
Year-End 1980
(billions of dollars)

Assets	629.8
Mortgages	502.8
Consumer credit	17.5
U.S. govt. and agency securities	46.7
State and local govt. securities	1.2
Open-market paper	4.9
Federal funds and repurchase agreements	10.8
Time deposits	7.8
Demand deposits and currency	3.6
Other	34.5
Liabilities and net worth	629.8
Savings deposits	511.0
Fed. Home Loan Bank advances	49.0
Bank loans	5.2
Repurchase agreements	8.5
Corporate bonds	3.7
Other liabilities	19.1
Net worth	33.3

Source: Federal Reserve System.

one year old is formed, and certificates representing a share of the pool are sold. These mortgages are no longer on the associations' books, but a fee continues to be earned from servicing them. Smaller S&Ls participate in this market through conduit companies, which put together packages of mortgages from 30 or more associations throughout the country. Savings and loan associations originate more than half the residential mortgages in the country, but because they sell some on the secondary market, their holdings are less—43 percent.

The principal assets of the associations, other than mortgages, are U.S. government securities (including the issues of government agencies). These, along with deposits and cash, meet the liquidity requirements imposed by the Federal Home Loan Bank Board. They are also subject to reserve requirements on their transaction accounts, in the form of currency or deposits at the Federal Reserve. Most of the consumer credit consists of passbook loans and credit that is housing-related, such as home-improvement loans and mobile-home loans.

The 1980 Deregulation Act broadened the investment powers of federally chartered associations. They may now hold up to one-fifth of their assets in consumer loans, commercial paper, and corporate debt securities, and the shares of open-end investment companies can be used to satisfy liquidity requirements. These funds must restrict their investments to the same instruments that savings and loans can hold directly. Up to 5 percent of an S&Ls assets may be in a combination of unsecured construction loans and loans for education and community development. Associations may issue credit cards and extend related credit, and they may establish trust departments. Over the years, S&Ls have built up a considerable expertise in mortgages, and they have been slow to exercise their new powers and broaden the scope of their lending.

Net worth in 1980 constituted only 5.3 percent of assets (Table 7-2). In the two preceding years, the ratio was 5.7 percent. Savings and loans have historically operated with lower capital ratios than commercial banks because of the less volatile nature of their deposits and the secured nature of their lending. But these conditions are changing, and there has been increasing concern over the adequacy of their capital as the industry suffered large losses in 1981. Net worth dropped below 5 percent of assets for the industry, and many S&Ls' net worth dropped into negative figures. The problems of the thrift institutions are discussed in more detail later in this chapter.

MUTUAL SAVINGS BANKS

Mutual savings banks were first established to provide a safe place for persons of modest means to keep their savings, and were basically philanthropic in nature. Groups of wealthy, public-spirited citizens contributed the capital funds necessary to start the institution, which then accepted deposits from poorer people who, at the time, had no safe means of holding their savings—commercial banks at the time were not interested in small accounts.

Savings banks were first established in this country in 1816 in Philadelphia, Boston, and New York. Their subsequent development has generally been restricted to the northeastern part of the country. Savings banks are currently operating in only seventeen states. Three states—New York, Massachusetts, and Connecticut—account for three-quarters of the savings banks. The number of mutual savings banks was relatively stable until very recently, declining from 515 in 1960 to 447 in early 1982. The record level of interest rates in 1981 put tremendous pressure on most savings institutions, and a number of mutual savings banks and savings and loan associations were merged into healthy institutions in order to prevent their failure.

Until recently all mutual savings banks operated with state charters. The Depository Institutions Deregulation Act of 1980 provided for federal charters for mutual savings banks in those states where savings banks already exist. A number of mutual savings banks have converted to federal charters. These institutions are supervised by the Federal Home Loan Bank Board and are insured by the Federal Savings and Loan Insurance Corporation (as are federal savings and loan associations). State-chartered mutual savings banks are supervised and insured on the federal level by the FDIC.

Mutual savings banks were the inventors of the NOW account, and most such institutions offered such accounts before the Deregulation Act gave such authority to savings and loan associations and commercial banks on a national basis. Mutual savings banks have traditionally served individuals rather than business customers, but they do have limited powers to accept corporate deposits and make business loans. The more aggressive savings banks are seeking expansion of these powers.

Because the original objective of the savings bank was safety for depositors, the investment policy of the banks traditionally stressed safety. Increasing competition among financial institutions for the saver's dollar, however, has forced many savings bankers to give more attention to the problem of securing a market return on the bank's funds.

The mortgage market has been the most important investment outlet for mutual savings banks throughout most of their history, although savings banks (as distinct from savings and loans associations) were not primarily organized as real estate lending institutions. Mortgage loans and securities now account for about 65 percent of the total assets of mutual savings banks, up considerably from the ratio that existed during the 1940s and 1950s, but well below that of the 1960s. The availability of mortgages guaranteed by the federal government has been an important factor in increasing the percentage of banks' funds invested in mortgages. Another contributing factor has been legislation allowing savings banks to invest in out-of-state mortgages.

The decline in the relative importance of mortgage loans in the portfolios of savings banks in recent years is a result of changes in interest yields on various financial market instruments. In the late 1960s good quality corporate bonds began to sell at yields higher than the going rate on conventional residential mortgage loans. Since corporate bonds are more liquid than mortgages and involve less servicing cost (no monthly payments to process, and so on), savings banks shifted toward portfolios with a higher proportion of corporate bonds. Actually it appears that savings bank managements felt some responsibility to continue to make mortgage funds available, because on a pure dollars-and-cents profit maximization basis, savings banks would have been better off to have shifted even further than they did to corporate bonds. Such an option was available to mutual savings banks, because they have traditionally had a broader range of powers than the more specialized savings and loan associations. Savings banks have long had installment loan powers, for example, which savings and loans have just recently acquired. The consolidated balance sheet of mutual savings banks in the United States is shown in Table 7.3

Cash amounts to less than 2 percent of the total assets of mutual savings banks and additional needs for liquidity are provided for by holdings of short-term United States government securities. Since the liquidity needs of savings banks are not nearly as great as those of the commercial banks, short-term securities account for only a small part of their total holdings of government securities. Another source of liquidity is loans from a commercial bank. The savings banks' tradition of not borrowing eroded substantially under the pressure of tight money during the late 1960s. Some mutual savings banks (both state-chartered and federal) have long been members of the Federal Home Loan Bank System and,

TABLE 7-3
Assets and Liabilities of Mutual Savings Banks, Year-End 1980
(billions of dollars)

Assets	*171.5*
Loans:	
Mortgage	99.8
Other	11.7
Securities:	
U.S. govt. (including agency)	8.7
State and local govt.	2.7
Corporate and other	39.6
Demand and time deposits and currency	4.3
Other assets	5.0
Liabilities	*171.5*
Deposits	
Ordinary savings	53.9
Time and other	95.9
Other liabilities	7.0
General reserve accounts	13.0

Source: *Federal Reserve Bulletin*, May 1981, p. A-27.

hence, eligible to borrow from the Federal Home Loan Banks. The Monetary Control Act of 1980 gave mutual savings banks (as well as savings and loan associations and credit unions) the right to borrow from the Federal Reserve System, thus providing them with a sure source of liquidity in a time of need.

CREDIT UNIONS

Credit unions are mutual thrift institutions, operating under either federal or state charter, with two basic functions: promoting savings among their members, and providing personal loans to their members at relatively low rates of interest.

Members of a credit union must have some common bond—belonging to the same church, lodge, or union; living in the same community; or, most commonly, working for the same firm. The common-bond concept plays an important role in the credit-union movement. On the one hand, it sets a serious restriction on the potential growth of the organization: Once a credit union has met the depository and credit needs of the employees or others it was originally set up to serve, its further growth can only be in accord with the growth of that group. No other financial institution faces this type of limitation. On the other hand, the common bond may generate a loyalty that shows up in a willingness to do volunteer work for the credit union, or perhaps in a greater feeling of responsibility to repay loans.

The common-bond concept also has economic implications resulting from the lack of diversification of customers. This is most clearly seen where the bond is occupational and a strike or poor year affects many members, leading to simultaneous savings outflows and increased loan demand. A good year can mean swollen deposit inflows but poor loan demand. In the extreme, a plant closing or relocation can mean the end of a credit union organized on such a basis. Over the years, there has been a steady trend toward loosening the common-bond requirements, for both federal and state credit-union charters; in many states, the requirements were looser to begin with.

Savings in a credit union are mostly in the form of "shares," which are, for all practical purposes, indistinguishable from deposits. There has been progress in recent years toward the issuance of a greater variety of savings instruments by credit unions, facilitated by the legalization of "share draft" accounts (transaction deposits) in the 1980 Deregulation Act.

Most credit unions are still quite small as financial institutions go, but growth has been very rapid for individual institutions and for the industry as a whole. There are now more credit unions in operation in the United States than there are commercial banks, mutual savings banks, and savings and loan associations combined. Total credit-union shares amounted to about $5 billion in 1960 and reached $65 billion by early 1981.

One factor in this rapid growth is the fact that credit unions have generally paid higher rates on savings than have competing institutions. When rates were restricted, the maximum rates were significantly higher than those allowed banks and other thrift institutions. As with other thrift institutions, the law provided for complete elimination of ceilings by 1986.

Federal credit unions account for more than half of credit-union assets, and they hold 58 percent of the more than 22,000 charters. The National Credit Union administration supervises federal credit unions, which are all covered by a federal insurance program on deposits. The program is similar to those for banks and savings and loans, with the same coverage limit ($100,000). State-chartered credit unions are eligible for insurance, provided they meet certain requirements, and about one-third are covered. Insurance has been important in the recent growth of credit unions and their competition with other savings institutions. The small size of credit unions and their lack of diversification might discourage the potential depositor who could not look to the federal insurance program for protection in case of failure.

The National Credit Union Administration also maintains a Central Liquidity Facility for short-term lending to credit unions. Credit unions must meet the same reserve requirements as other depository institutions, and they have Federal Reserve borrowing privileges as a secondary source behind the Liquidity Facility.

Consumer loans to members constitute more than 60 percent of credit-union assets (see Table 7-4). Credit unions have not been active mortgage lenders, but there have been recent liberalizations of credit-union lending powers that will enable them to play a more important role in this market in the future. Credit unions have been successful in competing for the business of those eligible to borrow largely because their rates have been lower than those of other lenders. The law limits the rate that federal credit unions can charge to 15 percent, although the National Credit Union Administration Board can set a higher interest limit on a temporary basis (not to exceed 18 months).

Since credit unions have generally paid higher rates on savings than their competitors, how do they manage to also charge less to borrowers?

Credit unions have several operating advantages over other financial institutions. Many credit unions have their overhead expenses subsidized or receive the benefit of volunteer labor. Frequently the employer provides free space for an employee credit union, and many also cover office supplies, telephone, and so on. Payroll deductions are widely used for both deposits and loan repayments, thus lowering operating costs. Because of the common bond, the costs of obtaining information about prospective borrowers, significant in most credit decisions, may be less for a credit union. Loan losses of credit unions on installment loans tend to be somewhat lower than for commercial banks, and very much lower than those of consumer finance companies. Another important factor is that credit unions are exempt from the federal income tax. This has been due to their cooperative nature, and perhaps their small size.

TABLE 7-4

Credit-Union Financial Assets and Liabilities, Year-End 1980
(billions of dollars)

Demand deposits and currency	1.7
Time deposits	2.0
Savings and loan deposits	5.2
U.S. government securities	13.6
Home mortgages	4.3
Consumer credit	44.0
Total financial assets	70.8
Credit-union shares	64.4

Source: Federal Reserve Flow-of-Funds Accounts.

The tax advantage has been under attack by their competitor institutions, and it is likely that, as credit unions grow and the common bond becomes loosened, they will tend to be treated as other institutions are. Mutual savings banks and mutual savings and loan associations are already subject to tax. Several of the other advantages noted above may also become less significant as credit unions grow. An employer is more likely to provide a modest amount of free space to a small credit union struggling to provide services to employees than it is to provide large amounts of space to a multimillion-dollar organization. The member is more willing to provide volunteer labor to the small institution that cannot afford paid clerical help than to spend evenings working for a more impersonal organization whose members he or she does not know.

Although the growth of credit unions has been spectacular, in the long run the success of the industry will depend on its ability to manage the transition from small institutions, providing limited services to a cohesive membership, to financial institutions providing more services to a broader set of customers. While some argue that continued growth depends upon expansion of powers, others are concerned that expansion of powers, like the liberalization of the common-bond principle, will tend to erode the traditional role of the credit union.

THRIFT INSTITUTION PROBLEMS

The three institutions examined in this chapter have faced some common, severe problems since the mid-1960s. In several periods, market interest rates have risen precipitously. These institutions have assets with fixed interest rates and long maturity. Their deposits have varying characteristics, and these have changed over time, but they are of much shorter maturity than the assets, and some are essentially payable on demand. Thus, as interest rates rise, the institutions' cost of funds has gone up more than their return on assets.

In some periods, the problem has manifested itself not so much in a rise in deposit interest payments, but in losses of deposits as funds were withdrawn for more attractive alternatives. Part of the problem has been the legal ceilings on interest which institutions can pay. The ceilings on the rates paid by thrift institutions provided an opportunity for the money-market mutual funds to draw funds from the thrifts by paying going market rates. In 1978, as the institutions faced mounting problems of deposit losses, the government authorized time certificates of deposit with the interest rate tied to the market-determined Treasury bill rate ("money-market certificates"). This move seemed to save the institutions from massive withdrawals, but at the same time it meant higher interest costs as their deposit structure became more interest-sensitive, with certificates making up 40 percent of deposits by 1980. In early 1982 certificate accounts tied to Treasury bill rates represented over 50 percent of mutual savings bank deposits. The 1980 Deregulation Act moved further toward increasing the interest-sensitivity of deposits by mandating the complete elimination of interest ceilings by 1986.

Because of their heavy concentration on long-term mortgages, the savings and loans and mutual savings banks have been more affected by rising interest rates than have the credit unions. Credit-union deposits, also, tend to be in smaller amounts and less likely to be converted to money-market certificates, which require a $10,000 minimum.

The problems of the institutions are not readily apparent by viewing aggregate data. Table 7-1, for example, shows continuous growth—at varying rates, to be sure, but growth nevertheless. But not all institutions necessarily have the same situation, and even those that grow are not necessarily free of financial difficulty. For one thing, we must inquire how the growth comes about. A part of the growth in deposit liabilities does not represent inflows of new funds. As interest accrues on accounts, liabilities rise. As interest accrues on loans and securities, assets rise.

In 1979 mutual savings bank deposits grew by only 2.4 percent, far less than would be expected by interest accruals alone. Some institutions found it necessary to discourage inflows of funds through money-market certificates because earnings could not justify the interest on them.[3] The following years were worse, with a one percent increase in 1980, and no change in deposits in 1981. As an institution's interest costs rise more than interest earnings, its net worth is affected, even if the institution is continuing to grow.

In 1981, savings and loan associations started the year with net worth of only 5.3 percent of assets, but 1981 was by far the worst year in the history of the thrift industry. Most savings banks and savings and loan associations suffered operating losses during the year, as interest rates soared to levels well above what they were earning on their mortgage portfolios. If the institutions did not pay market rates on their deposits and meet the competition of the money-market mutual funds, they would suffer large deposit outflows. Those outflows could only be met by selling assets, but low-yielding mortgages could only be sold at large losses. Thus they were forced to meet the rate competition and suffer operating losses that gradually eroded their net worth. Some actions were taken to alleviate the problem, including authorization of the "all-savers certificate," on which interest would be free of federal income tax (up to $1000 per taxpayer). The Federal Home Loan Bank Board adopted changes in accounting regulations, allowing savings and loans to defer recognition of losses incurred in the sale of mortgages, and also dropped its standard requirement that savings and loans maintain book net worth of at least 4 percent of assets.

Despite these actions, a number of thrift institutions were forced to close in 1981 and 1982, including several billion-dollar institutions. The insurance agencies, the FDIC, and the FSLIC generally managed to find merger partners for the failing institutions. All depositors were protected, though the cost to the insurance agencies was large.

[3] Part of the problem lay in the usury-law limits on mortgages in the northeastern states. The 1980 Deregulation Act overturned such interest limits. See H.K. Baker and S.R. Holmbert, "Money Market Certificates in Perspective," *Nebraska Journal of Economics and Business*, Summer 1980.

It is clear that the ultimate solution to this problem is more flexible portfolio management. Assets must be made more interest-sensitive by either shorter maturities or flexible rates, and the maturity structure of assets and liabilities (time certificates) must be more closely matched. The 1980 Deregulation Act provides an improved regulatory climate for this management by releasing some of the restrictions on assets and, ultimately, all the restrictions on deposit terms. Some economies of size may exist in this kind of portfolio management, and it is therefore likely that more and more mergers will take place. If the institutions are to grow, infusions of new capital are needed. The mutual form of organization may be an impediment to both mergers and capital buildup.

PROBLEMS OF MUTUAL INSTITUTIONS

The "mutual" form of organization of a financial institution means that it is owned by its creditors—depositors of depository institutions and policyholders of insurance companies. It is similar to a consumer cooperative, which is owned by its customers.

In savings and loan associations and credit unions, the depositor-shareholders elect a board of directors, which in turn chooses the operating officers of the institution. Mutual savings banks are somewhat different. Boards of trustees evolved on a self-perpetuating basis, with the trustees electing their own successors as the need arose. Although this is a rather unusual legal situation, in practice it does not differ very much in other mutual financial institutions: The existing board chooses nominees, and very few of the shareholders cast votes. The active participation of share-holders in some credit unions is the exception rather than the rule.

Although consumer cooperatives have long been part of our economy, and producer cooperatives are significant in some sectors, in no field other than financial institutions does the mutual form of organization play such an important role. It is a role that is difficult to analyze, because the traditional economic goal of profit maximization is not readily applicable to mutual institutions.[4]

In competition with stockholder-owned firms, mutuals have an important advantage, in that they do not have to pay dividends to

---

[4] Even for the ordinary corporation, the remoteness of the shareholder from management of the company renders questionable the assumption that the corporation is wholly oriented toward he shareholder's interests. See John Kenneth Galbraith, *The New Industrial State* (Boston: Houghton Mifflin, 1967).

stockholders.[5] This should allow them to pay higher rates to depositors or charge less to borrowers, or both. Aside from credit unions (with special circumstances, as discussed above), actual results do not support this presumption. Rates paid depositors have in the past been limited by regulation, and rates charged on loans do not seem to be systematically lower for mutual institutions. Part of the explanation seems to lie in higher operating costs and salaries for mutuals. After all, does the management of a mutual have an incentive to hold down such costs?

The stockholder-owned corporation is a much more flexible structure for mergers. A holding company cannot acquire a mutual by buying its stock as it can a shareholder-owned savings and loan. Officers of two separate mutuals have no incentive to merge and eliminate some positions, and there are no blocs of shareholders to force them to do so. The mass of depositors, each with a single vote—and few exercising them—is even less effective than a group of shareholders.

Mutuals are at a decided disadvantage as compared with stock corporations in raising capital. Their only source of new capital has been retained earnings, but the 1980 Deregulation Act did provide that federally chartered savings and loan mutuals could issue "mutual capital certificates" for inclusion in net worth. The problem of raising capital has provided an incentive toward conversion of mutual S&Ls to stock associations. It was not until the late 1970s that stock associations could obtain federal charters, and the Federal Home Loan Bank Board has developed rules for conversion from mutual to stock associations.

If a mutual association is allowed to convert to a stock association, who is to own the new stock? In particular, who owns the accumulated surplus or reserves of the association? Several alternative answers have been proposed. One approach is to view the surplus as arising from earnings on deposits that have not been paid out in full to past depositors. Hence, it is argued, the surplus really belongs to depositors and should be paid to them. Of course, the surplus has been built up over the years; the depositors of today are not necessarily the same ones responsible for the growth of the surplus. Others argue that since no one has a clear legal claim to the reserves, they really represent a community asset, and should be donated at the time of conversion for beneficial public purposes. The

---

[5] In some cases, mutual institutions have received much more favorable tax treatment. This is no longer the case for savings banks and savings and loan associations.

purpose of giving away the surplus is to avoid having a few fortunate depositors or insiders gain a windfall by the distribution of
a claim on the surplus accounts.

The board developed a scheme for conversion that provided for
sale of stock of the association to existing depositors at its full market value. Management of the association would be able to buy stock
only at full value and only if depositors did not exercise their rights
to buy. This approach seems both effective and equitable, although
a study of recent conversions indicates that in most cases, management does acquire control of the converted S&L.

It is clear that this opportunity to gain control is one of the
motives of existing management in seeking conversion, and this
raises the question of conflicts of interest. Many believe that that is
a more serious problem in mutual financial institutions than in
stock.[6] Consider why, for example, a group of capable businessmen
should devote time, energy, and money to establishing a mutual
savings and loan (rather than a stock association or a commercial
bank). It is possible that they are wholly civic-minded and believe
that a mutual will better serve the community. It is also possible
that they see some benefits to themselves: perhaps employment,
perhaps a source of borrowed funds, perhaps commissions on the
insurance sold on houses financed or legal fees for the title searches,
and so on, associated with housing finance. Some of these benefits
may be easier to achieve and maintain in a firm without stockholders. Stockholders have a vested interest in the efficiency with
which the association is run and in seeing that any earnings associated with the business accrue to the association rather than to
insiders.

Because of these considerations, it is by no means clear that
the public is better served by mutual institutions than by profit-
oriented stockholder-owned institutions. The best course for public
policy would seem therefore to lie with neutrality—nondiscrimina-
tory taxation and chartering.

QUESTIONS

1 What are the most important differences between savings and loan
   associations and commercial banks?

[6] For an excellent study of this problem, see Edward S. Herman, "Conflict of
Interest in the Savings and Loan Industry," in *Study of the Savings and Loan
Industry*, ed. Irwin Friend (Washington, D.C.: Federal Home Loan Bank Board,
1969).

2 If you have a deposit above the insured limit, do you prefer to have it in a credit union or a stockholder-owned savings and loan?
3 Would you rather own stock in a commercial bank or a stockholder savings and loan?
4 Are there any advantages to a mutual savings bank in converting to a mutual savings and loan?
5 Why have credit unions had such a rapid growth rate?
6 Will mortgage interest rates be affected by the increased asset powers of savings and loans?

SELECTED READINGS

HARLESS, DORIS E., *Nonbank Financial Institutions*. Federal Reserve Bank of Richmond, 1975.
HEMPEL, GEORGE H., and JESS B. YAWITZ, *Financial Management of Financial Institutions*. Englewood Cliffs, N.J.: Prentice-Hall, 1977.
Interagency Task Force on Thrift Institutions, *Report*. U.S. House of Representatives, Committee Print 96-14, July 1980.
SMITH, PAUL F., *Money and Financial Intermediation*. Englewood Cliffs, N.J.: Prentice-Hall, 1978.
U.S. League of Savings Associations, *Savings and Loan Fact Book*. Annual.

8

Nondepository
Intermediaries

Many institutions serve as intermediaries, issuing liabilities of one kind and acquiring assets of another. Their justification is economies of size. Small funds can be pooled to acquire assets that more nearly meet borrowers' needs. In this chapter we consider intermediaries whose liabilities are not of a deposit nature.

All the institutions discussed in the preceding chapter have highly liquid liabilities. Those of the first two types discussed in this chapter are also highly liquid. The remaining institutions have specialized, less liquid liabilities. The liability of the retirement fund is delayed till old age, of the life insurance company till death, and of the other insurance companies till catastrophe.

MONEY-MARKET MUTUAL FUNDS

Inflation, bureaucracy, and computers—these were the forces that gave rise to the money-market mutual fund. Inflation of prices and interest rates made it impossible for financial institutions to offer deposits with both rising rates and liquidation on demand. Bureaucracy compounded the problem with insufficiently flexible regulations on types of deposits and deposit-rate ceilings. But by means of the computer, investors can be offered instant transfers between deposits and assets with current money-market yields.

These conditions were emerging when the funds were created
in 1974, but then interest rates fell for the following three years. It
was not until 1978 that the real growth in the funds began, and they
topped the $100 billion mark in 1981 (Table 8-1), and reached $188
billion in early 1982.

TABLE 8-1
Money-Market Mutual Funds
(end of month outstanding, billions of dollars)

Dec. 1974	2.4
Dec. 1975	3.7
Dec. 1976	3.7
Dec. 1977	3.9
Dec. 1978	10.8
Dec. 1979	43.6
June 1980	74.6
Dec. 1980	75.8
June 1981	124.8
July 1981	137.8
Aug. 1981	148.2
Sept. 1981	160.0
Oct. 1981	169.4
Nov. 1981	180.0
Dec. 1981	182.2
Jan. 1982	187.7

Source: Federal Reserve System.

A money-market fund is organized by a sponsor, such as a
brokerage house or insurance company, as a trust or a corporation.[1]
The investor's claim is simply a share of the fund. Shareholders
elect a board, which legally directs the fund, but the sponsoring
company includes many of its own officers as nominees for the
board. The board then selects the sponsoring firm (in the case of a
brokerage house) as "investment advisor" to manage the fund.

As the public buys shares in the fund, the proceeds go into the
purchase of money-market instruments. Certificates of deposit are
usually heavily weighted in the portfolio because of their higher
yields. Commercial paper is also an important part of many fund
assets. Although some funds specialize in government securities,
most of them minimize such holdings because of their lower yields.
Interest earnings on the portfolio go immediately into the purchase
of more assets.

---

[1] Unlike a corporation, a trust does not have limited liability for its organizers,
and under some circumstances they might be held individually liable for claims
against the trust.

Redemption features vary somewhat among funds, but an important feature of all of them is speed and ease of liquidating shares. Some funds set up for each shareholder a checking deposit with a participating depository institution. The shareholder can write a check, which is then cleared by liquidation of shares. Most specify minimum amounts for checks. Shareholders can also arrange for liquidation of shares by wire, through the shareholder's own bank, to the fund headquarters. And some funds arrange for a charge card to be issued in association with shareholding. Through the card, purchases can be made or funds withdrawn up to the value of the holder's shares. The card is not thereby a source of credit for the holder, but it is a more readily usable instrument in many situations than is a personal check. With this device, the shareholder can liquidate on a moment's notice.

The value of the investor's shares in the fund fluctuates perhaps hourly, but it is computed once or twice a day. Aside from purchases and sales, holdings will fluctuate from interest earnings, changes in the market value of claims the fund holds, and expenses of the fund. If interest rates were to remain steady, then only interest accruals and expenses would be involved. Changes in market interest rates have an inverse effect on the market value of the instruments held by the fund.

The yield on money-market funds tends to fluctuate with the market but with something of a lag, since the fund already holds securities bought at previous yields. As interest rates rose in the recovery from the recession in 1980, this lag process caused net withdrawals from the funds at times when alternatives became more attractive (see Figure 8-1). Prices of securities also fall as interest rates rise, but the short maturities of the funds' holdings limit the magnitude of this effect.

Because the money-market funds compete with small time deposits, depository institutions have tried to convince the public that deposits are safer and over time not apt to greatly underperform the funds; but this was hard to accomplish in a regulatory environment that imposed interest ceilings and "penalties for early withdrawal." The money-market funds will be less of a problem for depository institutions in the regulatory posture that will ultimately result from the 1980 Deregulation Act.

The liquidity of the money-market funds renders them candidates for inclusion in the definition of what constitutes the nation's money supply. For this purpose, the Federal Reserve considers their shares in the same category as personal savings deposits (see Chapter 19).

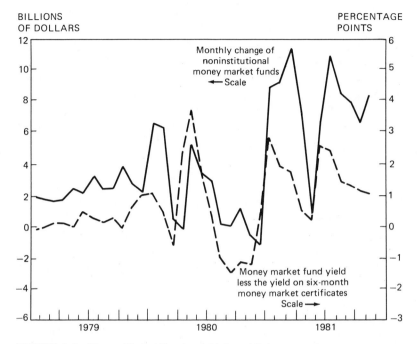

FIGURE 8-1 Money-Market Funds and Interest Rates

Source: Federal Reserve Bank of New York, *Quarterly Review*, Winter 1981–82, p. 12.

Investor Evaluation

The advantages of the money-market funds to the investor are convenience and yield. The convenience arises from the ease of purchase and withdrawals. Yields will remain high as long as money-market yields are high.

But there are disadvantages, and one of them is risk. Most of the assets of the funds are the liabilities of banks or business corporations. Because of the large size of the CDs, not even the bank liabilities are federally insured. Although the risk may be low, it is present, as we are reminded by the occasional failure of a large bank or business corporation.

Although the risk brings higher yields than could be earned from Treasury bills, the difference is partially drained off by the fund's expenses, primarily the investment management fee, and herein lies the benefit to the sponsoring investment house. These expenses can be expected to take perhaps 5 percent of the fund's income (depending upon the management-fee schedule that is set up). A $1,000 investment that would otherwise return 16 percent then returns only 15.2 percent ($160 less 5 percent of $160).

Some fund shareholders have filed lawsuits challenging the size of the investment management fees, and well they might. Negligible skill is required to advise the purchase of variable-rate CDs that float with the market, but advisors to a half-billion-dollar fund would receive $2½ million a year for doing so. The possibilities of such rewards have led to the aggressive promotion and growth of funds, which, in less than a decade, reached a size that exceeded the nation's credit unions.

INVESTMENT-COMPANY FUNDS

The money-market funds are only one of a wide variety of funds that sell shares to the public and use the proceeds to buy securities. The purchase of shares of an investment company allows an investor to gain the benefits of both diversification and professional management of investments. Investment companies may be organized in either of two ways:

Closed-end companies are set up in much the same way as ordinary corporations—they have a fixed amount of stock outstanding, which is traded on one of the stock exchanges or over the counter. A potential investor in a closed-end company, as with any stock, buys from someone who wants to sell.

Open-end companies, generally called *mutual funds* (such as the money-market funds), are operated on a somewhat different basis. The mutual fund has no specified amount of stock outstanding but is always ready to sell additional stock to new purchasers. Most mutual funds sell their stock at a price equal to the per-share value of the fund, plus a commission or "loading charge" (generally around 7 to 9 percent). A number of funds, whose record has been just as good on average, sell their shares without such a charge (the "no-load" funds). The funds also agree to repurchase their stock at its net asset value per share. These stocks are thus generally not bought and sold in the open market—the buyer or seller deals directly with the company.

There are many different types of investment companies, with different objectives and different methods of operation. There are, for example, companies specializing in bonds, in stocks, in "growth" stocks, in a particular industry, or in foreign securities.

In recent years we have seen the development of several new types of specialized mutual funds, responding to changes in law or economic conditions, designed to meet specific needs. Municipal-bond funds have grown very rapidly since a change in the tax law allowed them to pass on the tax-exempt nature of their income. Such a fund makes municipal bonds more accessible to the investor who otherwise would find the lack of liquidity of such investments undesirable.

Aside from money-market funds, mutual funds have had ups and downs, with essentially no growth in the 1970s and early 1980s. At year-end 1980, they totaled $56 billion, about the same as a decade earlier. The funds tend to fluctuate with stock prices and with investors' perception of the stock market, which has not been especially high since the 1960s.

One of the more dismal failures—dismal because it started with such great expectations—was the *real estate investment trust* (REIT). The size of REITs peaked at about $17 billion in 1973–1974, and they have declined since, to less than $6 billion at year-end 1980.

The REIT was established as a means of allowing the individual investor to participate in the real estate market in the same way the mutual fund facilitated the small investor's participation in the stock market. REITs grew very rapidly during the early 1970s, mostly investing their funds in loans on residential and commercial real estate loans. Bad judgment and bad luck combined to produce disastrous results for most of the REITs (although those that invested their funds directly in real estate rather than making loans did significantly better). Commercial banks shared heavily in the losses, since they lent large amounts of money to REITs. In many cases, commercial banks established REITs and served as advisors to them. Although the concept of a mutual fund for investment in real estate seems reasonable, the experience of the REIT industry is apt to make it very difficult for the concept to get a second chance.

Few mutual funds have had an investment performance as bad as that of the average REIT, but the record of the mutual-fund industry has not been one of great success. An investor who buys shares in a mutual fund is paying for professional management and expertise; yet in most years, the average mutual fund has not had performance equal to that of the investor who selects securities by throwing darts at the financial page of the newspaper. In recognition of this result, we have seen the recent development of "index funds," which invest their funds proportionally among the stocks that make up a standard stock-market index (such as the Dow Jones). In this way they can assure the investor that he will do no worse (and no better) than the average. There is a solid theoretical basis for this approach, since many students of the securities markets argue that in an efficient market like the New York Stock Exchange, in which many informed investors take account of all the information available about each security, no one can, in the long run, expect to earn higher-than-average returns.

In any case, the variety of mutual funds available allows the investor to select a company whose objectives and techniques fit his needs. Even if all a mutual fund provides is diversification, that is something that would be very expensive for the small investor to purchase on his own.

RETIREMENT FUNDS AND TRUSTS

The total of public and private *retirement funds* reached $480 billion by year-end 1980. The distribution of their assets is shown in Table 8-2. These pension funds are accumulated out of the contributions of employers and employees and are invested in securities to provide an income for the employees upon retirement.

Since payments to retired employees are on a definite contractual basis, the retirement funds have little need for liquidity. Most of the assets of such funds are invested in corporate bonds and stock. More than half the assets of the private funds are invested in stock, but only about one-quarter of the assets of the state and local government funds are so invested. Since retirement funds are not subject to federal income taxes, municipal securities have little investment appeal. As a result of political pressures, however, the state and local government retirement funds hold several billion dollars worth of state and local government securities. Such retirement systems in New York State hold sizable amounts of New York

TABLE 8-2
Pension- and Retirement-Fund Assets
(year-end 1980, billions of dollars)

	Private	State and Local
Corporate equities	168.2	54.3
Corporate bonds	58.1	98.0
Mortgages	3.7	10.9
Treasury issues	24.1	18.0
Government agency issues	6.7	18.0
State and local obligations	—	4.1
Other	18.4	4.6
Total	279.2	207.9

Source: Federal Reserve Flow-of-Funds Accounts.

City obligations. There was irony in the need for employee pension funds to bail out New York City, in that some believe that over-generous pension plans were partly responsible for the city's financial plight.

The most significant financial issues concerning pension funds in recent years have involved not investment policy, but rather the protection of the rights of employees covered by retirement systems and government regulation of pension funds. These concerns grew out of the failures of a number of retirement funds and the losses to employees who were covered by plans that did not provide for vesting. *Vesting* means a right to future retirement income even if the employee leaves his job before retirement. The Employee Retirement Income Security Act of 1974 (ERISA) established minimum standards for vesting and also minimum standards for funding of retirement programs by employers. The act also established the Pension Benefits Guaranty Corporation to provide federal insurance for employee retirement benefits.

Personal trust companies and the personal trust departments of commercial banks take possession of personal property and manage it for the benefit of the person establishing the trust or for someone that person designates. A businesswoman may turn over $300,000 to the trust department of her bank to invest for her, thus freeing her from this task. This is an example of a *living trust*. Or the businessman's will may turn over $300,000 to the trust department to handle in the interests of his widow. This latter would be a *testamentary trust*, but very often the two types of trusts are combined, so that the $300,000 would be paid into the trust before death, and income from it would be paid to the person establishing the trust while he lives and to his widow upon his death. Each trust is administered on an individual basis, with funds invested in a manner appropriate to the aims and needs of the individual beneficiary.[2] The amount of funds managed by trust departments is about $400 billion.

[2] Because the expenses involved in administering trust funds on a personal basis are rather large, it is unprofitable to handle small trusts. In fact, $200,000 may be a minimum practicable size for a trust. The so-called *common trust fund* was set up to get around this difficulty. Under this type of arrangement, the assets of several small trusts are merged into one investment pool. Although this does not have all the advantages of individual management, it does make the benefits of trust management available to the person with a small estate. Common trust funds of commercial banks (both national and state-chartered banks) are regulated by the Comptroller of the Currency.

LIFE INSURANCE COMPANIES

Most life insurance policies represent a combination of protection and savings. Because a large portion of annual insurance premiums represent savings, life insurance companies accumulate funds that must be invested so as to generate a return on the savings. The growth of the life insurance industry has been steady, but its share of the financial business of the country has tended to decline. Personal savings made through insurance companies represented over 2 percent of disposable personal income during the 1940s and is now under 1 percent. This trend reflects, on the one hand, the growing role of Social Security and private pension plans in the long-run financial planning of customers, and, on the other hand, the growing proportion of life insurance policies that are pure protection rather than including a savings element.

Insurance companies sell two basic types of life insurance contracts. Term insurance represents pure insurance with no savings aspects. The company agrees to pay the face value of the policy to the beneficiary if the insured dies within the term of the policy. If the insured lives through the term of the policy and still needs insurance protection, he may buy a new term policy (at higher rates, because he is now older and thus more likely to die in any given year). Most group insurance policies are term insurance, and term insurance accounts for about 30 percent of the ordinary (nongroup) life insurance in force in the United States. Group insurance has been the most rapidly growing sector of the business and now accounts for over 40 percent of all insurance in force.

Other types of insurance policies represent varying combinations of savings with insurance. Under term insurance, the insured must die in order that collection can be made from the company. With other forms of insurance, the policy is constantly building up a cash value that belongs to the insured, who can borrow against it or withdraw it as desired. Although such policies are obviously more expensive than term insurance because some of the annual payment represents savings, they have features that many people apparently find attractive.

Life insurance companies are chartered by the various states and may be either stock or mutual in form. Although over 90 percent of the 1,800 companies are stock companies, the mutuals are much larger, accounting for over 50 percent of the life insurance in force.[3]

[3] As with savings and loan associations, the actual operations of the companies are unaffected by the organizational structure. Policyholders of mutual life insur-

TABLE 8-3

Insurance-Company Assets

(year-end 1980, billions of dollars)

	Life	Other
Corporate equities	53.0	35.1
Corporate bonds	178.0	26.4
Mortgages	131.1	.7
Treasury issues	5.8	14.2
Government agency issues	11.1	7.3
State and local obligations	6.7	83.6
Other	83.4	17.7
Total	469.1	185.0

Source: Federal Reserve Flow-of-Funds Accounts.

The liquidity needs of life insurance companies are not very great. The companies know with a high degree of accuracy how much they will have to pay out in death benefits over the next year. As a result, they have only a small part of their $469 billion of assets in the form of cash and U.S. government securities, and most of the Treasury securities are long-terms.

Although liquidity needs are small, safety is extremely important to a life company. Capital and surplus are very small parts of total liabilities (about 8 percent), and thus even a relatively small loss on assets could make the insurance company insolvent. For this reason, most of the assets of life insurance companies are invested in bonds and mortgages, and only small amounts of common stock are held. Table 8-3 gives a breakdown of the assets of life insurance companies.

Life insurance companies would seem to be rather insulated from problems of inflation, given the fixed-money-value nature of their liabilities and the inability of the claimant to draw funds. But these companies too were beginning to feel the squeeze by 1980. High interest rates induced some policyholders to take out policy loans, on which the companies had contractual obligations to pro-

---

ance companies have a right to vote for trustees, but a study of these institutions showed that votes actually cast ranged from .02 percent to 2.5 percent of the eligible voters. A study of 30 mutual life insurance companies for the period 1954–73 found that eight had "excessive" policyholder surpluses at the end of 1973. "In his status as an owner, the mutual policyholder . . . has expected his insurer to declare adequate dividends since his financial interest in the going concern has not extended to retained earnings." Stephen Forbes, "Surplus Positions and Dividend Policies of Mutual Life Insurance Companies," *Journal of Economics and Business,* Spring/Summer 1978, p. 211.

vide low rates. The companies were apprehensive that this device would be recognized by an increasing number of policyholders. Perhaps more serious for the long run, companies have found it increasingly difficult to sell insurance, since the public has seen erosion in the real value of the death benefit. Companies have begun to draft new kinds of policies with benefits that can rise with inflation, and they have taken steps to reduce their reliance on fixed-income securities. For conventional policies, fees have come down because, with higher interest rates, smaller annual payments are required to reach a given fixed sum in the future.

> Pinched severely by the high interest rates recorded in 1980, the life insurance companies also sought ways to change their investment policies in order to reduce their vulnerability. More and more of the commercial mortgages that these companies are adding to their portfolios involve a flexible rate related to the prime rate or some other independent index, income participation in the properties, or call provisions entitling them to call back the loan before it matures and renegotiate the interest rate. There have been similar changes in their investments in directly placed corporate bonds. Increasingly, these bonds include a floating rate; income-participation features, such as warrants; and much shorter maturities than those prevailing in the past.[4]

FIRE AND CASUALTY INSURANCE COMPANIES

Nonlife insurance companies sell protection against loss of property from various disasters and from obligations incurred because of damage done by the insured to the property of a third party. We often refer to these companies as fire insurance companies, although they obviously include many other types of insurance business.

Property and casualty companies are not savings institutions in the same sense that life companies are. A fire insurance premium includes no savings aspects—it is a payment for protection only. But because premiums are generally paid in advance, the companies accumulate large sums of money, which may be invested until needed to settle claims.

There are more than 3,500 fire and casualty insurance companies in the United States, the majority of which are mutual companies. The situation is just the reverse of the life insurance industry, in that the stock companies, rather than the mutuals, are larger, accounting for over 75 percent of the total assets of property and casualty companies.

We have indicated that life insurance companies need little liquidity because their payments to policyholders can be fairly accurately predicted. The nonlife companies are not in such an enviable

---

[4] Federal Reserve Bank of New York *Annual Report 1980*, p. 13.

position. Although death is certain, fires, tornadoes, and hurricanes are not. The possibility of having to make large payments to policy-holders without warning necessitates holding large amounts of liquid assets. Not only are disasters unpredictable, but some rather predictable long-term trends are unfavorable to casualty under-writers. Inflation means that the cost of repair and replacement of property damaged in fires or automobile accidents tends to rise, as do losses due to personal injury. These rising costs have necessi-tated more frequent upward adjustments in insurance fees.

It is somewhat dangerous to generalize about property and casualty companies' investment policies, since there is a tremen-dous variation among companies. Companies specializing in fire insurance have different policies from companies specializing in automobile liability coverage. The data in Table 8-3 give only an overall view of the industry. Thus, some companies have cash and government securities equal to over 50 percent of total assets, whereas other companies can operate with much lower liquidity.

Many nonlife insurance companies have capital accounts that are considerably higher in relation to liabilities than is the case with the life insurance companies. This means that a sizable propor-tion of their assets can be invested in a less defensive manner. Common and preferred stocks are attractive to the fire and casualty companies not only because of the possibility of appreciation, but also because dividends receive favorable tax treatment. In fact, nonlife insurance companies are the largest holders of preferred stocks.

THE DIVERSITY OF INVESTMENT POLICIES

All financial institutions are faced with the problem of maximizing their profits subject to regulation and to their needs for liquidity and safety. As we have seen, one of the most important determi-nants of the needs of a financial institution is the character of its liabilities. Institutions whose liabilities are subject to payment on demand (commercial banks) or are payable in unpredictable amounts (fire insurance companies) must keep a higher proportion of their assets in highly liquid form than institutions that know the extent to which they will have to make payments in the future (life insurance companies and pension funds, for example).

The capital of a financial institution can be looked upon as a cushion or protection against depreciation or loss of assets. Thus, an institution with a high ratio of capital to total liabilities (fire insur-ance companies) can take more risks with investment than an institution that has only a thin equity cushion (commercial banks or life insurance companies).

Each financial institution has its own distinctive investment problems and has found different means of solving them. The operations of the financial institutions determine, and in part are determined by, the investment characteristics of their industry. All, however, are faced with the necessity to compromise between the dual needs of adequate liquidity and profits.

QUESTIONS

1 What explains the difference in investment policy between life insurance companies and fire insurance companies?
2 "With respect to financial institutions, differences in the type of asset held can be explained by reference to differences in the liability structure." Appraise.
3 In evaluating the soundness of a financial institution, which is more important: the character of the assets, or the amount of capital?
4 What do you predict will happen to money-market mutual funds in the next recession?
5 Why are money-market mutual funds considered for inclusion in money-stock definitions, whereas other investment companies are not?

SELECTED READINGS

CUMMINS, J.D. ed., *Investment Activities of Life Insurance Companies.* Homewood, Ill.: Richard D. Irwin, 1977.
HEMPEL, GEORGE H., and JESS B. YAWITZ, *Financial Management of Financial Institutions.* Englewood Cliffs, N.J.: Prentice-Hall, 1977.
Life Insurance Association of America, *Life Insurance Companies as Financial Institutions.* Library of the Commission on Money and Credit, Englewood Cliffs, N.J.: Prentice-Hall, 1962.
SMITH, PAUL F., *Money and Financial Intermediation.* Englewood Cliffs, N.J.: Prentice-Hall, 1978.

III

FINANCING
THE ECONOMY

9

Financing Business

In this chapter and the three that follow, we will examine the sources and uses of funds by the major sectors of the economy and in Chapter 13 extend the analysis to foreign transactions. The flow-of-funds accounts, introduced in Chapter 4, will be helpful in tracing the financial flows through the economy. This chapter will be focused on the financing of the country's industrial, commercial, and agricultural businesses.

EQUITY

Not all the funds of a business come from borrowing; what comes from the owners is called the *equity*. For unincorporated business, it is *proprietor's equity*, and for corporations it is *shareholders' equity*. The shareholders supply funds to the corporation when it sells new issues of stock, but funds "internally generated" by the firm are in a sense also supplied by shareholders, because the funds belong to them.

Internally generated funds regularly supply more funds to corporations than do external sources (which include sales of new shares). For analytical purposes, sources of funds are usually related to the firm's capital expenditures. As Table 9-1 shows, in 1981 corporations had capital expenditures of $244 billion, and 95 percent was financed by gross saving, or internally generated funds. In 1971 the ratio was 85 percent.

As you can see in the table, depreciation allowances provide for a very significant amount of the financing of gross capital expenditures (that is, acquisition of capital goods without considering depreciation of existing capital). As capital equipment is used, it generates revenue, and a part of this revenue is looked upon as compensation for wearing out of the capital. From the standpoint of the firm, one asset is replacing another—the stock of capital. As funds accumulate from these depreciation allowances, the capital stock can be replaced.

TABLE 9-1
Business Flow of Funds
(nonfinancial corporations, 1971 and 1981)

	Billions of Dollars	
	1971	1981
Gross saving:		
Retained earnings	15.3	58.6
Depreciation allowances	58.2	174.1
Capital expenditures:		
Fixed investment	82.1	239.4
Inventories	4.9	14.2
Net increase in financial assets:		
Liquid assets	9.3	12.2
Trade credit	14.6	36.9
Consumer credit	.5	2.4
Other (includes statistical discrep.)	21.2	81.9
Net increase in financial liabilities:		
Bonds	18.9	25.1
Stocks	11.4	− 6.9
Mortgages	10.9	19.9
Bank loans	3.8	44.6
Finance co. loans	.7	8.7
Commercial paper and banker's acceptances	− .6	16.8
Trade debt	12.2	33.6
Other	2.5	12.5

Source: Federal Reserve Flow-of-Funds Accounts.

There has been concern that in the inflation of the 1970s and 1980s, depreciation allowances are inadequate. If depreciation allowances are related to the purchase price of the capital, they will be inadequate because the cost of replacing the capital will rise with inflation. Income tax laws limit the amount of revenue that can be considered depreciation rather than income, and for tax purposes, depreciation is based on historical cost. The result is an overstatement of income for tax purposes, and the resulting tax liability limits the ability of the corporation to retain funds.[1]

A corporation obtains new equity funds externally when it sells new shares of stock. The stock of a corporation is often divided into two classes, with *preferred* stock given a right to a stipulated dividend and *common* stock given a right to earnings of the firm remaining after the preferred dividends. Generally, in the event of liquidation of the corporation, the preferred stockholder has a position superior to that of the common stockholder in sharing the assets of the firm.

The efficient channeling of funds from the investor to the corporation frequently involves the efforts of many financial institutions. In cases where small amounts of stock are to be sold, the existing stockholders or their friends and relatives may provide the funds required, and no institutional assistance may be needed. In many cases, however, the sale of stock involves such a large amount of money that no one institution or group of investors could handle it. The institutions and practices that have developed in the money and capital markets are extremely efficient in channeling large amounts of funds to large corporations.[2]

One of the most important participants in this process is the investment banker. Investment bankers are the chief intermediaries between the firms selling stock and the investing public. They are risk bearers, or underwriters, in that they buy the entire issue from the seller and then attempt to sell the securities to other dealers or to the public at a profit. They are more than securities jobbers, however. They serve as marketing experts, advising the issuing firm on terms of the issue, timing of its sale, legal details, price, and the like.

At one time, commercial banks were active in the investment-banking business. It is easy to see the possibilities for conflict of interest when one organization handles both functions.[3] Serious abuses developed during the 1920s, and the Banking Act of 1933

---

[1] It has been estimated that "when the inflation rate is 8 percent, a corporation is permitted to deduct only 53 percent of the 'true' depreciation on a thirty-year structure." Marcelle Arak, "Inflation and Stock Values: Is Our Tax Structure the Villain?" Federal Reserve Bank of New York *Quarterly Review*, Winter 1980–81, p. 5.

[2] Despite, or perhaps because of, the efficiency with which large issues can be handled in the market, the criticism has often been made that there are no adequate facilities available for channeling equity funds to small firms.

[3] The commercial banker–investment banker who finds it hard to resell an issue of securities may be tempted to push it on a small correspondent bank or, worse, sell it to a trust account handled by the bank.

separated commercial banking from investment banking. Now commercial banks are not allowed to underwrite corporate securities.

The stock exchanges and stockbrokers as such do not play a direct role in the sale of new stock by a corporation. Their indirect role is important, however. As we have seen in previous chapters, one of the factors that a potential investor will consider in contemplating a purchase of securities is liquidity, an important element of which is marketability. By providing facilities that improve the marketability of securities, the vast network of stock exchanges, securities dealers, and brokers makes feasible the original distribution of large issues of securities.

A stock exchange is an organized auction market for the purchase and sale of securities. Members of the exchange buy and sell on their customers' orders and charge a commission. Not all stocks are traded on a stock exchange. Stock exchanges will "list" or admit a stock to trading only after the company meets certain requirements. These requirements often include minimum size, publication of financial information, assurance of adequate facilities for transferring stock certificates, the guaranteeing of certain rights to stockholders, and so forth. Stocks not listed on an exchange are traded in the over-the-counter market.

Once a corporation's stock is outstanding, its price will fluctuate in accord with changes in expectations about future earnings of the firm. Unlike a bond, a share of stock has neither a fixed maturity value nor a fixed interest payment. The earnings per share and the price per share will therefore tend to move up and down together. Indexes of average stock prices, such as Dow Jones or Standard & Poor's, are widely published and interpreted by many analysts as barometers of business conditions. Low stock prices offer a deterrent to firms' raising funds by new stock issues.

The stock market performed rather poorly from the mid-1970s into the early 1980s. Although the Standard & Poor's Index of 500 had reached new highs at the beginning of this decade, if allowance is made for inflation, the index was about at the level of the late 1950s. And in view of the fact that the corporations had continually retained some earnings during all this period, ". . . the stock price per dollar of equity investment, which includes retained earnings, declined even more sharply than the real stock prices . . ."[4]

There is no consensus as to the cause of this performance, although again there is agreement that taxes are at least partially responsible, through the inadequacy of depreciation allowances in

[4] Arak, "Inflation and Stock Values," p. 4.

inflation. But inflation also benefits the corporate financial picture, in that it lowers the real value of its outstanding indebtedness. Some observers believe that investors do not adequately consider this effect.

Regardless of the reason, the behavior of stock prices has rather radically changed the makeup of the public's claims on corporations. In 1970, the market value of corporate shares was 2.4 times corporate debt. In 1980, shares were 1.5 times debt. In the issuance of new securities, corporations obtain more funds by bond issues than by stock issues, as shown in Table 9-2.

TABLE 9-2
New Security Issues of Corporations
(millions of dollars)

Type of issue	1978	1979	1980
All issues	47,230	51,533	72,886
Bonds	36,872	40,208	52,523
Public	19,815	25,814	41,545
Private placement	17,057	14,394	10,978
Stocks	10,358	11,325	20,363
Preferred	2,832	3,574	3,624
Common	7,526	7,751	16,739

Note: Issues of all corporations, including financial, over $100,000.

Source: *Federal Reserve Bulletin.*

DEBT

It is convenient, in discussing the sources of debt financing for business firms, to divide the sources into long-term and short-term lenders. There is, as we shall see, considerable overlapping, but the distinction remains a useful one. We shall consider the institutions advancing funds to business firms and the credit instruments involved.

Short-Term Debt

Trade Credit. For many firms, the most important source of short-term credit is another business firm rather than a lending institution. Practically all firms make some use of trade credit—credit extended to a buying firm by its supplier.

Trade credit may be advanced in the form of various credit instruments. A credit instrument is simply the evidence that debt exists. Frequently this involves a written contract, but a large volume of trade credit is advanced in the form of "book accounts." We order goods from our supplier. When he ships our order, he will send us a bill or invoice listing the items shipped, price, and terms of the sale. At the same time, he will enter the amount due him in his accounts-receivable ledger. We will enter the same amount in our accounts payable. We need not send to the supplier any formal acknowledgement of our debt to him. Large volumes of goods are bought and sold on the basis of this rather informal arrangement.

In some lines of business, it has become customary to extend trade credit in a form that involves a written acknowledgement of the debt. Trade credit in these cases may take the form of a promissory note or a trade acceptance. A draft or acceptance is in some respects the inverse of a promissory note: The basic message of a promissory note is, "I owe you," and the basic content of a draft is, "You owe me."[5]

When a person directed to pay signs or accepts the draft, it becomes known as a *trade acceptance*. A variation of this instrument occurs when the acceptor is a bank. The resulting instrument, known as a banker's acceptance, was described in Chapter 5. Banker's acceptances are principally used in financing international trade where the seller of goods may not know the buyer and may have no easy way of checking his credit standing.

In the aggregate, trade credit and trade debt come close to canceling out within the business sector, but this is not true for each individual firm. The unincorporated sector contains small firms relative to the corporate sector. In 1980, the unincorporated sector held $17.9 billion in trade credit but owed $19.4 billion in trade debt.

In addition to showing accounts by sector, the flow-of-funds statements are also organized by type of credit-market instrument. Trade credit is an interesting application of this organization, and trade credit flows for 1981 are shown in Table 9-3. As will be seen, all sectors of the economy are involved to some extent in trade credit as they make purchases from business firms. (The inclusion of nonprofit enterprises in the household sector explains this sector's participation.)

Bank Loans. The major business of commercial banks has traditionally been to provide short-term funds to business borrowers.

---

[5] Technically, a draft or "bill of exchange" is an "unconditional order in writing addressed by one person to another, signed by the person giving it, requiring the person to whom it is addressed to pay on demand or at a fixed or determinable future time a sum certain in money to order or to bearer." An ordinary bank check exactly fits this complicated-sounding definition.

TABLE 9-3

Trade Credit in the Flow of Funds, 1981
(billions of dollars)

Net change in liabilities:	
Households	1.5
Farm business	1.1
Noncorporate business	.5
Corporate business (nonfinancial)	33.6
State and local govt.	1.8
Foreign	.2
U.S. government	1.9
Net change in assets:	
Corporate business (nonfinancial)	36.9
Foreign	− .5
U.S. government	2.7
Nonlife insurance companies	2.0
Discrepancy	− .4

Source: Federal Reserve Flow-of-Funds Accounts.

We have seen that banks have broadened their lending activities to meet competition from other institutions and to adapt to the changing economic environment.

Some of firms' bank borrowing is indirect, through intermediaries. One firm may borrow from a bank and use the proceeds to extend trade credit to other firms. Certain specialized financial intermediaries borrow from banks and lend to business. The Federal Reserve has estimated that close to one-half of all business firms in the United States are frequent users of bank credit.

Banks have several advantages in extending credit to business firms. Banking's decentralized structure is indicative of decentralized authority to make decisions. Thus, decisions can often be made swiftly and on terms flexible enough to meet the varying needs of different types of borrowers.

The variety of terms under which banks lend is an indication of the banks' attempts to meet these varying needs. About half the dollar amount of business loans is unsecured. For loans on which collateral is required, the collateral may be a plant or other real estate, equipment, inventories, securities, accounts receivable, or almost any asset held by a business firm.

Many loans are made on a "one-shot" basis. Frequently, however, the borrower will arrange for a *line of credit*. This involves setting a maximum amount that the bank will be willing to lend the borrower, who is free to use up to that amount as needed. The borrower pays interest only on the amount actually borrowed, but often a fee will be charged on the unused part of the line to compensate the bank for keeping the credit available.

At any given time, interest rates on bank loans vary with the size of the loan, size of the borrower, industry of the borrower, location of the borrower and lender, and the degree of competition among banks in the borrower's market area. Of all the variables, however, the size of the loan is probably the most important. Rates on business loans of varying size and quality are scaled up from the *prime rate*, which is the rate charged on loans to the largest and most creditworthy business firms. Since these firms operate nationally, competitive pressures are usually sufficient to force all banks seeking such accounts to maintain a uniform prime rate, although differences of up to ¼ percent are not uncommon. Since interest rates on bank loans are sensitive to changes in monetary policy, these rates change considerably over time. Rates on small loans, although usually higher than those on larger loans, fluctuate considerably less from year to year. Because of this inflexibility, at times when the prime rate has gone to relatively high levels, larger loans have not always carried lower rates. As interest rates have risen, banks have turned to issuing loans with floating rates. About 50 percent of short-term and 75 percent of longer-term loans were issued with floating rates in 1981.

Most banks require a compensating balance from their borrowers. This means that the borrower must agree to maintain a deposit with the bank equal usually to between 10 and 20 percent of the line of credit extended. In some cases, the balance may be expressed as a minimum requirement, and in other cases, the requirement may apply to the firm's average balance. Unless the firm would maintain such a balance anyway, the effect of such requirements on a borrower is to increase the effective rate of interest he is paying on the loan. The strictness with which banks enforce their compensating-balance requirements seems to vary with money-market conditions. That is, when banks have plenty of funds available, they are less apt to strictly enforce compensating-balance requirements than when money is tight and loan demand is high.

Other Sources of Short-Term Credit. We mentioned earlier that business firms may obtain credit from certain specialized financial institutions. The most important of these are sales finance companies, commercial finance companies, and factors. We can define the business-financing specialty of these institutions easily, but the definitions will not neatly fit all firms in the field, because there is considerable overlapping of function. In fact, even some commercial banks may compete along all lines with these finance companies. The major business of commercial finance companies is granting loans based on the security of accounts receivable, but they will sometimes make loans on inventory or other assets. Factors specialize in the outright purchase of accounts receivable, although often they will lend on the security of receivables or inventory. Sales finance companies' chief business activity is the discounting of consumer installment paper. The large sales finance companies also provide all the services of the other finance companies.

One characteristic all these lenders have in common is that all their loans are secured — they demand that a borrower pledge some asset as security for a loan. This does not mean that the lender expects the borrower to default on the loan. If it anticipated that, it would not make the loan. The lender simply wants the security as added protection just in case anything should go wrong. This condition is accepted because the borrower cannot qualify for a loan on an unsecured basis. We should not be surprised to find that interest rates on secured loans are typically higher than rates on unsecured loans.

Accounts Receivable. Commercial finance companies, factors, and some commercial banks will make loans based on a pledge of accounts receivable. Typically, under a pledge of receivables, the borrower is responsible for collection of the accounts. That is, bad-debt losses are borne by the borrower, not the bank or finance company. Since collection responsibility remains with the borrower, his customers generally are not notified that their accounts have been pledged to secure a loan.

Different lenders will be willing to advance varying percentages of the receivables pledged, with commercial finance companies generally willing to go higher than commercial banks.

An alternative to this sort of accounts-receivable financing is outright sale of the receivables. *Old-line factors*, as distinct from commercial finance companies, deal exclusively in the business of buying accounts receivable. Two major services are provided by the factor. Perhaps the more important is the assumption of the credit and collection duties of the firm. The firm that factors its accounts will not need to maintain a credit department. This may be particularly advantageous to a firm in a seasonal business in which it would not be efficient to maintain a full-time department. In addition, factors often advance funds to the firm whose accounts are being factored in advance of actual collection.

Factoring is very important in the textile, furniture, and shoe industries. Because factors have become specialized in certain industries, they are probably better informed about the condition of these industries' customers, whose accounts they buy, than any one seller's credit department could be. Firms whose accounts payable have been sold to a factor are notified of the sale and instructed to make payment directly to the factor. The factor, of course, bears the credit risk on any accounts it has purchased.

Factoring charges are usually in two parts—a flat fee (expressed as a percentage of the face value of the receivables purchased) for services such as the assumption of credit risk, bookkeeping, and collection; and an interest charge when funds are advanced prior to the due date of the receivables.

The types of accounts-receivable financing described above are provided by banks, commercial finance companies, and factors to firms that sell to other business firms. Retailers that sell on credit to consumers generate accounts receivable of a different type— consumer installment paper. Sales finance companies specialize in buying consumer installment notes, and many commercial banks also buy such paper. Automobile dealers are, of course, the principal source of this paper, but appliance and furniture dealers also sell a significant volume of goods on installment terms.

In the typical case, a dealer sells an automobile, collecting part of the purchase price in cash and the rest in the form of a promissory note covering the schedule of monthly payments. The terms may run from 12 to 42 months. The dealer then sells the notes to a sales finance company or bank, which pays the dealer the balance of the purchase price (or more) and collects the monthly payments from the consumer. Sales may be made on a recourse or nonrecourse basis—*recourse* meaning that the dealer bears the risk of default by the customer, and *nonrecourse* meaning that the finance company takes the risk—but full nonrecourse is unusual.

Since the sales finance company becomes a creditor of a consumer rather than of a business firm, it is often classified as a consumer financing institution rather than as a source of business funds. The ability to sell installment paper to a sales finance company is of great help to the dealer, however. He makes what amounts to a cash sale—his investment in receivables is eliminated, and thus he finds it possible to carry on a larger-scale business with a limited amount of capital. This means that the manufacturer can expect to make a larger volume of sales. Because of this, some manufacturers have formed their own sales-finance-company affiliates. Firms that did so could formerly encourage their dealers to deal with the favored finance company. It was alleged that this encouragement sometimes took the form of shipping uncooperative dealers "black sedans in the summer and open cars in the winter." Such arrangements were ruled a violation of antitrust laws and have been eliminated. Now, sales finance companies compete on an equal footing with each other and with the banks for the dealers' business.

Inventory Financing.   Inventories are less attractive to lenders as collateral than accounts receivable are. Inventories vary in nature and in quality, it is expensive to maintain control over them, and a buyer must be found before inventories can be converted to cash. Thus, the business firm that must pledge its inventories as security for a loan must expect to pay a higher interest rate than a borrower that qualifies for unsecured financing or can offer receivables as collateral.

A common type of bank inventory financing is the *floor-plan* loan to automobile dealers. Under a floor-planning arrangement, the bank pays the manufacturer for the cars delivered to the dealer and retains title to them. The cars are held in trust for the bank by the dealer. The dealer must pay the bank in order to be able to convey title to a buyer. Frequently the dealer will pay the debt by turning over to the bank an installment note signed by the buyer. In fact, floor-plan loans on favorable terms are part of the lenders' competition for the consumer installment-loan business generated by the dealer.

Commercial Paper.   Commercial paper is an important source of short-term financing for large business firms and finance companies. The market for commercial paper was described in Chapter 5, but we can note here some aspects of the market from the point of view of the issuer of commercial paper.

There are several advantages to the borrower: The rate of interest is generally lower than the prime rate even when the commission that must be paid to the commercial-paper dealer is included; there is no need to maintain a compensating balance; and the bargaining position with its bank of a firm using commercial paper is improved. The principal disadvantage is that the market is completely impersonal—no lender feels any obligation to help a borrower out of a tight spot. The borrower must maintain lines of credit with banks in order to insure the availability of bank credit in an emergency.

Long-Term Debt

We have defined *long-term credit* as those funds available with a maturity of over one year. Frequently a classification called *intermediate-term credit* is used. This category generally comprises loans with a maturity of one to five years or one to ten years. For the sake of simplicity, we will include such loans with long-term financing.

Term Loans.   The majority of commercial banks in this country
are willing to make loans with a longer maturity than one year.
Called *term loans*, they were virtually nonexistent until the 1930s
but now constitute over one-third of all commercial-bank business
loans. For some larger banks, the proportion is over 50 percent.

During the 1930s, 1940s, and early 1950s, the demand for short-
term bank loans was relatively poor. In order to improve their earnings, many banks decided to extend the terms of their loans. Even
before term loans were extended on a formal basis, many banks
made short-term loans with the understanding that these loans
would be renewed again and again.

One reason that bankers originally hesitated to make term
loans was their feeling that liquidity was of extreme importance
because of potentially great fluctuations in deposits. The establishment of the Federal Deposit Insurance Corporation in 1934 lessened
the likelihood of "runs" and thus reduced the need for liquidity.
Moreover, term loans have somewhat more liquidity than their
maximum maturity would indicate, because such loans are almost
always repaid on an installment basis.

In order to protect themselves, banks generally insert certain
restrictive provisions in the loan agreement. A Federal Reserve
survey indicated that over 60 percent of all term loans, but only 44
percent of short-term loans, were secured. The borrower may be
required to maintain a minimum level of net working capital
(current assets less current liabilities). There may also be restrictions on dividends, officers' salaries, and/or purchases of fixed
assets.

There are several reasons for borrowers to seek term loans.
Term loans may be desirable to supplement working capital in industries where the production period is long. They may be desirable
to finance purchase of equipment when the expected cash flow—
earnings and depreciation—from the investment will not be sufficient to repay a short-term loan but will be rapid enough to make
very long-term borrowing unnecessary. Term loans may be a very
desirable sort of financing for the firm needing long-term credit but
too small to enter the capital market economically.

In any case, the primary advantage of a term loan to the borrower is its great flexibility.

> Negotiations can be conducted privately with a lender interested in promoting a sound
> long-run relationship. Maturities and conditions can be altered to fit shifts in the needs
> of the borrowing business or a change in its situations. Costs are often lower than those
> of alternative sources of such funds, funds are borrowed only when needed, and can
> usually be repaid in advance without penalty.[6]

[6] American Bankers Association, *The Commercial Banking Industry* (Englewood Cliffs, N.J.: Prentice-Hall, 1962), p. 149.

Interest rates on term loans are generally higher than on short-term loans of similar size. Although term loans are sometimes made on a fixed-rate basis, it has become much more common to float the rate in accord with movements of the prime rate. Thus, the interest rate on a term loan may be set at 1 percent above the prime rate.

Insurance companies also make term loans. Because of the long-term nature of their liabilities, insurance companies need not be greatly concerned with liquidity; safety and income are much more important. Thus, loans extended by insurance companies generally have a longer maturity than bank term loans. The longer maturity may be desirable to some borrowers, because it means that smaller annual payments on principal are needed to repay the loan. Frequently a bank and an insurance company will participate in a long-term loan, with the bank taking the short end of the loan and the insurance company the long end. Insurance companies' term loans tend also to be larger in amount than bank loans, because of the greater size of the average insurance company and because the bank's more intimate relationship with its customers gives it an advantage in handling smaller loans.

Equipment Financing. Commercial finance companies and some banks make long-term loans to finance purchase of equipment by business firms under arrangements very similar to those used in financing purchase of consumer durables. The typical maturity of equipment-financing contracts held by the finance companies most active in this business is three years or longer. The maturity is closely connected with the amount of down payment required—the finance company attempts to see that the resale value of the equipment will always be above the unpaid balance in case it should have to be repossessed. Because of differences in down payments, maturity, and type of equipment being financed, rates on equipment financing vary considerably from one contract to another.

An alternative method of acquiring equipment, which has become popular in recent years, is leasing. IBM and some other firms have long leased their products to customers, but now virtually any kind of equipment can be leased. The lease has several advantages over installment purchase for the user: For one thing, no down payment is required. In many cases, the lessor takes over responsibility for maintenance of the equipment. Since it owns the equipment, the lessor bears all risks of obsolescence. Also, the lease improves the appearance of the lessee's balance sheet.[7] The disad-

---

[7] Sound accounting practice does require mention of the terms of the lease in a footnote to the financial statements.

vantage of leasing is, of course, its cost. If the lessor is going to assume maintenance costs and the risk of obsolescence as well as the risk of incurring costs of repossessing and reselling the equipment in the event of a default on rental payment, it is going to insist on being paid for these services.

Since leasing is simply an alternative means of financing business firms on a secured basis, it would appear to be a logical area for commercial-bank participation. However, commercial banks were generally barred from this activity until the Comptroller of the Currency ruled in 1963 that national banks could own and lease machinery, equipment, fixtures, and other personal property. Since that ruling, the leasing of equipment by commercial banks has grown at a modest rate and amounted to about $13 billion in 1982.

Mortgage Loans. If a small firm is unable to qualify for an unsecured term loan, mortgage loans may be the only method by which the firm can obtain long-term funds. Real property of the small firm may be its best-quality asset (and often the only asset that can serve as collateral for a long-term loan). A Federal Reserve business-loan survey found that 38 percent of all secured loans were secured by plant or other real estate. The ratio was even higher for small firms. Both commercial banks and life insurance companies make this type of loan. Tables 9-1 and 9-4 indicate that such loans were a major source of funds for business firms in 1980.

Sale and Leaseback. Under a sale and leaseback, a businessman sells his property to an institutional investor[8] and then leases it back under a long-term lease. He pays rent for the property and continues to be responsible for insurance, maintenance, and taxes. At the termination of the lease, he may have an option to buy back at a predetermined price or, more commonly, the right to continue to lease at a reduced rental.

The advantages of sale and leaseback to the borrower as compared with a mortgage loan include an improved balance-sheet position, in that no long-term liability appears on the balance sheet. The careful reader of financial statements will recognize the obligation to make rental payments, however, since sound accounting practice requires that the arrangement be disclosed in a footnote to the financial statement, as in the case of equipment leasing, discussed above. Another advantage to the lessee is that this arrangement in effect provides 100 percent financing, whereas a mortgage loan would require some down payment.

---

[8] Insurance companies are now the most important owner-lessors, but this technique was pioneered by college endowment funds.

The firm may be able to achieve the tax-deferring effects of rapid depreciation if the term of the lease is shorter than the period over which the property must be depreciated. If this is offset by the need for earlier tax payments by the owner-lessor, there is no net tax gain on the transaction, and the apparent advantage to the tenant will be offset by higher rental charges. Actually, however, the owner-lessor is generally an institution that is tax-exempt (for example, a college endowment fund) or taxed at a low effective rate (an insurance company), so there probably is some net tax saving.

Bonds. The most important means by which business firms raise long-term external debt funds is through the sale of bonds. Basically, bonds are long-term promissory notes, but there are many variations in their form. Some bonds, called debentures, are unsecured; others may be secured by real estate (mortgage bonds), stocks and bonds (collateral trust bonds), or equipment (equipment trust certificates).

Bonds generally represent a firm obligation of the issuing company to pay interest at the stipulated rate, whether earned or not, and to repay the principal amount of the bond at maturity.[9] If the issuer of the bonds does not make payments as scheduled, the bondholders, like any other creditors, can take legal action against the firm.

The process of selling bonds, like the sale of stock, generally involves the services of the investment banker. The investment banker is consulted by industrial firms concerning interest rates, maturity, security provisions, and so forth, and then forms a syndicate to underwrite the bond issue. Railroads and utilities follow a somewhat different procedure. After settling the terms for the issue, perhaps with the advice of an investment-banking firm, they ask for sealed bids on the issue from investment bankers. These bids are frequently extremely close together; the difference between the bid of the winning firm and its competitors may be only fractions of a penny on a $1,000 bond. The general similarity in the business activity of different utilities and in the terms of various utility bonds makes competitive bidding more feasible than it would be for industrial firms.

When a large issue of bonds is to be sold, obviously a large number of buyers must be found. The investment bankers and their selling organizations provide an effective mechanism for finding the buyers. In some cases, however, the issue may be sold to one or

---

[9] Income bonds require payment of interest only if it is earned, and convertible bonds, instead of being held to maturity, may be exchanged, at the option of the holder, for common stock at a fixed rate.

a small group of institutional investors. The direct sale of large blocks of bonds to institutional investors is called a "private placement." As we saw in Table 9-2, about one-fifth are privately placed. Insurance companies have been the major buyers of securities through private placements, but pension funds and even commercial banks have participated in some. The chief advantage of such deals is a saving on the investment-banking costs and elimination of the delay, disclosure, and expense involved in registering a public issue with the Securities and Exchange Commission.

The total amount of bonds outstanding at the end of 1980 was $391 billion. Insurance companies and pension funds hold almost three-fourths.

SMALL-BUSINESS AND FARM FINANCE

Small businesses and farms do not have ready access to credit markets, and they rely heavily on secured credit, mainly mortgages. Table 9-4 shows the flow of funds for farm business and for the noncorporate sector, where small business resides. Bank loans to farms are somewhat more important than indicated by the 1981 flows. At year-end 1980, there were $32 billion of farm bank loans outstanding, and three times this amount of farm mortgages

TABLE 9-4
Farm and Noncorporate Flow of Funds, 1981
(billions of dollars)

	Noncorporate [a]	Farm [b]
Gross saving:		
Retained earnings	—	− .5
Depreciation		
Corporate	—	2.5
Noncorporate	44.8	18.2
Capital expenditures:		
Fixed investment	53.3	20.6
Inventories	.4	2.3
Net increase in financial assets	5.8	2.3
Net increase in liabilities		
Mortgages	5.3	9.8
Bank loans	1.8	1.5
Trade debt	.5	1.1
Proprietor net investment	− .9	−13.2
Other	7.9	5.9

[a] Nonfinancial firms only.
[b] Includes both corporate and noncorporate farms.
Source: Federal Reserve Flow-of-Funds Accounts.

outstanding. Farm bank loans tripled between 1969 and 1979. The growing use of equipment in farming increases the demand for loans to finance it.

Small businesses have difficulty in obtaining long-term funds; this is particularly serious for new companies. The sources of funds used by small businesses are similar to those tapped by large firms, but the smaller firms make relatively greater use of trade credit and bank loans.

A good part of the problem in securing long-term funds is that the officers of the small firm do not want to give up control of the corporation. As one authority pointed out, "They want venture capital on a loan basis." Moreover, in a great many cases, lending institutions are unwilling to grant the loans requested, because such companies lack good financial management.[10]

Since most small firms need relatively small loans, the rates charged on loans must be high. Lending costs are not proportionate to the size of the loans. In fact, the costs of credit analysis on a million-dollar loan to a national firm will probably be less than the costs of a credit check on a small local manufacturer, and the relative costs of public issues of securities are much higher for small issues than for large ones.

Perhaps because of the large number of small businesses in the country, there have been many government programs set up to help fill the financing needs of small firms that cannot obtain financing through regular private channels. These have run the gamut from direct loans of government funds by the Small Business Administration through simple Veterans Administration guarantees on loans made by private lenders to veterans. On the state level, "development credit corporations" have been established in several states to extend loans to firms unable to get financing from private sources.

Although the SBA's credit requirements may be less stringent, like private lenders it seeks to make sound business loans and expects to be repaid on schedule. In addition to making direct loans, the SBA may participate in a loan with another lender (usually a commercial bank), or may guarantee repayment (up to 90 percent) of a loan made by the private lender.

The Small Business Administration also assists the financing of small business through the device of "small business investment companies." The SBICs are private, profit-making corporations

---

[10] Lenders' caution is well advised. Up to a half-million new businesses are started annually. Out of every 100, half will fail within a year and 80 within three years.

established to supply loan funds and capital to small businesses. They are chartered by the various states, like any corporation, but they are licensed and supervised by the SBA, since they receive considerable federal aid in the form of tax benefits and SBA financing.

These government lending programs do not amount to very much in the overall financing picture, but in many cases they do serve as a last resort for firms that cannot obtain funds elsewhere. Their rates are generally lower than the market rate for the degree of risk involved, but because they accept applications only from firms that cannot qualify for loans from regular sources, a high proportion of applicants are rejected. The loans, when they are made, are almost always secured. Government programs to aid small business may be helpful in some cases, but they cannot be considered a cure-all for the financial problems of small firms.

It has frequently been charged that small businesses are particularly hard hit when a policy of monetary restraint is followed by the Federal Reserve. This issue has frequently been aired in the academic journals and in the halls of Congress, without being resolved in either place. We will discuss this issue in more detail later on, when we consider the effects of monetary-policy action.

QUESTIONS

1 Distinguish between internal and external sources of funds for business firms.
2 Is depreciation a source of funds?
3 What is the difference between an investment banker and a stockbroker? between an investment banker and a commercial banker?
4 Why do firms borrow from banks when they could raise funds at a lower interest rate by selling commercial paper?
5 What is a factor?
6 Do you favor special government programs to aid in financing small businesses?
7 "In periods of tight money, commercial banks discriminate against small businesses in making loans." Is this true? Is this bad?
8 Why does the volume of trade credit expand in periods of tight money?
9 Explain the commercial-bank policy of requiring "compensating balances" from borrowers.
10 Is trade credit or bank credit a more important source of funds to business as a whole? Explain.
11 How do stock-market prices affect sources of funds to firms?

SELECTED READINGS

Board of Governors of the Federal Reserve System, *Financing Small Business*. Report to the Committee on Banking and Currency, U.S. Congress, April 1958.

CORCORAN, PATRICK, "Inflation, Taxes and the Composition of Business Investment," Federal Reserve Bank of New York *Quarterly Review*, Autumn 1979.

HARRIS, MAURY, "Finance Companies as Business Lenders," Federal Reserve Bank of New York *Quarterly Review*, Summer 1979.

MAINS, NORMAN, "Recent Corporate Financing Patterns," *Federal Reserve Bulletin*, September 1980.

WESTON, J. FRED, and EUGENE F. BRIGHAM, *Managerial Finance*, 6th ed. Hinsdale, Ill.: Dryden Press, 1978.

10

Financing the Consumer

Consumer credit has had a long and checkered history. For thousands of years, prophets, popes, and politicians have advocated restrictions on consumer credit. The medieval church banned the charging of interest on loans of all types, but even when interest was considered proper on some types of credit transactions, interest on loans to consumers was often thought improper. This was probably due to the fact that the borrowers were generally in some sort of difficulty, and the feeling was that the lender was just exploiting this difficulty. Nevertheless, consumer loans have been made for centuries.

VOLUME OF CONSUMER CREDIT

Consumer credit had a period of rapid growth during the 1920s, reaching a peak in 1929. In the depression of the 1930s it declined, but as the economy picked up in the late 1930s, so did consumer credit. A decline occurred during World War II, owing mostly to shortages of consumer durable goods. The postwar period witnessed a great growth of consumer credit, interrupted periodically by cyclical downturns. Total consumer credit amounted to only about $5.7 billion at the end of 1945, but in three years it tripled. By year-end 1981, it stood at $411 billion.

Popular opinion seems to hold that America "lives beyond its means," buying virtually everything on credit. This is largely an illusion. If there is any delay between receipt of goods and payment, then some credit has been created. In any period there are large volumes of both extension of credit and repayments of old credit, and only the net increase constitutes consumer finance.

The largest net increase in consumer credit was in 1978, when it grew by $51 billion. But in that year, consumer spending was $1.35 trillion, so that less than 4 percent of consumer spending was on credit. Consumer credit typically falls during a recession, and this decrease was especially pronounced in 1980, when there was hardly any consumer credit at all ($2.3 billion) in comparison to consumer spending ($1.67 trillion). In addition to the recession, consumer credit in that year fell victim to policy actions aimed at inflation. Disturbed by the run-up in consumer credit in 1978, which continued at almost the same pace in 1979, President Carter imposed controls that reduced the return on certain types of consumer lending. (This action is discussed in more detail in Chapter 22). Although the controls were short-lived, they, along with the recession, seemed to have had a pronounced effect on the actions of lenders, or borrowers, or both.

A still further explanation, which may have been more important than the policy action, was rising interest rates for other kinds of loans. By custom, and in some cases by law, consumer lending rates are more inflexible than other rates, and at times, consumer-loan rates are lower than the rates being paid by large corporations. Lending institutions understandably become less interested in the consumer in these circumstances. In 1981 installment credit increased by a historically low rate of 6.3 percent, but this was far above the rise of less than 1 percent in 1980.

TYPES OF CONSUMER CREDIT

Consumer credit is reported as "installment" or "noninstallment" credit, but the division is rather arbitrary. Installment credit is an arrangement whereby the amount owed is gradually repaid at periodic intervals rather than in a single sum. But under current arrangements whereby consumers continually add to and repay accounts, the distinction is hard to make in practice. The Federal Reserve, which gathers the data, includes in its installment series consumer debt "scheduled to be repaid (or with the option of repayment) in two or more installments." By this broad definition, the series covers "most short- and intermediate-term [consumer] credit extended to individuals through regular business channels. . . ." By the official definition, a telephone bill is not installment credit because it is intended that it be paid on presentation. A bank credit card or a gasoline charge card gives rise to installment credit because the user has the option of extending payment, whether or not that option is exercised.

In 1945, noninstallment credit exceeded installment credit, but at the present time, installment credit accounts for 80 percent of consumer credit (see Table 10-1). The largest portion of noninstallment credit arises from single-pay charge accounts. The small, noncorporate businesses are more important providers of this form of credit than the larger, corporate retailers, which issue revolving accounts. Most of the remainder of noninstallment credit is issued by commercial banks, which are willing in some cases to make personal loans on a noninstallment basis to business and professional people. These loans are frequently secured loans, and often the people who qualify for them own stocks or bonds that serve as collateral. Service credit is the credit extended by telephone, electric, and gas companies, as well as by doctors and other professional people. This type of credit is often a convenience to the creditor as well as to the user of the credit—it is easier for the telephone company to send a monthly bill than to install and service a pay phone in every home.

The remaining credit classifications to be discussed are subdivisions of installment credit.

Automobile Financing

The most important use of consumer credit is in the purchase of automobiles. Consumer installment credit extended to finance automobile purchases amounted to nearly $126 billion by 1981, constituting over one-third of all installment credit. Nearly two-thirds of all new-car sales are financed on an installment basis, as are over one-half of all used-car sales.

Three important elements in an installment-credit contract— the down payment, the length of the contract, and the interest cost—determine the factor most important to the buyer, the monthly payment.

The car buyer will typically make an initial cash payment. If she makes a down payment of $2,000 on a car costing $4,250, she is borrowing $2,250. If she is charged $150 interest, her total debt is $2,400. Repayment in twelve monthly installments requires a monthly payment of $200. The monthly payment would be smaller

TABLE 10-1

Consumer-Credit Assets

(year-end 1981, billions of dollars)

	Installment Credit	Noninstallment Credit
Corporate business	16.3	16.4
Noncorporate business	1.9	19.0
Commercial banking	146.8	32.1
Savings and loans	11.6	9.3
Mutual savings banks	2.7	1.3
Credit unions	46.0	—
Finance companies	107.8	—
Totals	333.1	78.1

Source: Federal Reserve Flow-of-Funds Accounts.

if the down payment were larger or if the payments were to be spread out over two or three years rather than one.

Down payments are an important factor affecting the safety of the loan from the lender's point of view. The buyer who has considerable equity in the car is less likely to run the risk of having the car repossessed for nonpayment. And, in such a case, the large down payment reduces the risk of loss to the lender even if the car must be repossessed.

The interests of the lender, then, lie in relatively high down payments, but competitive factors may tend to lower down payments. During the 1950s, average down payments on new-car sales fell, and average maturity term lengthened. Liberalizing of credit terms continued at a slower pace during the 1960s and 1970s, so that 42 months has become the standard maturity available on an automobile installment loan, and 48 months is not uncommon. During the 1950s, 36 months would have been considered a relatively long maturity.

Low down payments and long maturities do inject an element of risk into the installment sale. If, for example, the buyer of a $6,000 car makes a down payment of $1,000 and agrees to pay off the remainder on a monthly basis over the next three years, the amount of the debt will decline steadily over the three-year period. The value of the car, which is the seller's security for the loan, will drop as soon as it is driven off the dealer's lot, and will continue to decline at a slower rate in the succeeding years. With normal depreciation of the automobile, for a considerable period of time into the second year, the buyer actually owes more on the car than it is worth.

During the first year, the buyer is apt to experience some pride of ownership that would encourage him to maintain payments despite this situation. However, later on, particularly if he should face some economic adversity, he may resent paying for a "dead horse" and may default on his obligations. The seller, of course, can repossess the automobile, but under the assumptions we have made, the value of the car is less than the amount owed on it.[1]

The low down-payment requirements and long maturities that are now prevalent mean that buyers' obligations frequently exceed the value of the items purchased. Despite this, however, the rate of loss on consumer credit has been extremely low. The loss experience of commercial banks, although probably lower than that of other lenders, is illustrative of the generally good record of consumers in fulfilling their installment obligations. The percentage of commercial-bank installment loans that are delinquent (having an installment past due by 30 days or more) has generally ranged between 1.5 and 2 percent. Loss ratios have generally been below .5 percent, which compares favorably with the recent bank-loss experience on business loans.

What these figures indicate is that a change has taken place in automobile lending, so that loans are now made on the basis of the buyer's income and credit standing rather than on the basis of the collateral. The lenders' low loss records indicate that this development has been justified.

Other Types of Installment Credit

Although automobile credit makes up the bulk of installment-sales credit, many other consumer goods are financed in this manner. For many years, furniture and appliances have been widely sold on installments, but the list of goods and services available on a "buy-now, pay-later" basis is unlimited. It is possible to buy dancing lessons, boats, trips around the world, swimming pools, a college education, and funerals on installments. In fact, some institutions make loans to consumers for the purpose of consolidating their installment obligations, thus allowing them, in effect, to pay their installments on an installment basis. It might also be noted that in the case of automobile credit, the car being financed provides some security for the loan. This is not the case in some of the other forms

---

[1] It should be noted that repossession does not eliminate the buyer's obligation to pay the agreed-upon amount. If the buyer in our example defaulted after paying $1,000 on the installment contract (leaving a balance due of $4,000) and the repossessed car is sold for $3,500, the buyer is still obligated to pay $500 even though he no longer has the car.

of installment credit. It is impossible to repossess dancing lessons or a funeral.

Purchases of consumer goods other than cars account for a sizable portion of all installment credit. In some cases, the consumer will buy the goods on an installment basis, and in other cases, the consumer will arrange in advance to borrow money from a financial institution and pay cash to the retailer. In many cases, the consumer will have used a *revolving credit* arrangement for the transaction.

Revolving credit had long been used for business lending before such plans were instituted for consumer lending. Under these plans, a bank will establish a line of credit for a customer that the customer can borrow against by simply writing a check. Most plans now are under credit cards.

There are several advantages to such plans. Credit is available to the borrower without the necessity of coming to the bank to arrange the loan (except, of course, for the initial establishment of the line of credit). Since the loan application is needed only once, the bank saves time and paperwork. This adds an element of risk, since the bank does not make a credit review with each extension of credit, but loss experience on such plans has been favorable. Rates charged are comparable to those on other forms of consumer credit.[2]

A smaller segment of the installment-credit picture is accounted for by installment loans for the purpose of repair and modernization of homes. This segment of the market grew rapidly during the 1950s with the aid of the federal government. Congress has authorized the Federal Housing Administration to insure loans made for such purposes. In recent years, home-improvement loans have grown somewhat more slowly than other sectors of the consumer-credit business.

About $18 billion of consumer credit is outstanding to finance the purchase of mobile homes. This represents an interesting combination of the problems involved in automobile financing and in home-mortgage financing: Because of the amounts involved, the loans must have a longer maturity than automobile loans; over time, mobile homes depreciate in value like cars, rather than appreciating like houses. The volume of such credit increased rapidly until 1974 and has changed little since then. Losses on such lending have been higher than those incurred in other forms of consumer installment lending.

[2] At one time, retailers did not impose interest charges on the users of their charge accounts, but as they have instituted more formalized revolving credit, they too levy interest (which they prefer to call a service charge). A common rate is 2 percent per month on accounts not paid within the billing month.

CONSUMER-CREDIT INSTITUTIONS

As we have seen, the extension of consumer credit is a profitable business. Thus, it is not surprising that many different institutions are anxious to share in the profits. Some institutions extend consumer credit in various forms, while other specialize in particular types of credit arrangements. The position of the various lenders in this market is shown in Tables 10-1 and 10-2.

Some consumer credit arises from loans made to consumers by financial institutions. In these cases, of course, the lending institution is the creditor. In other cases, credit arises through the sale of goods or services. The seller may hold the installment notes signed by the buyer, but often will transfer them to the firms that specialize in this business. Commercial banks and finance companies are the major institutions that discount or lend on security of consumer-credit receivables.

Commercial Banks

Commercial banks entered the consumer lending field relatively late; such activity was unheard of until the late 1920s. Now commercial banks are the largest institution in the consumer-credit field and participate in virtually all forms of consumer credit.

Automobile financing, the largest segment of bank consumer lending, is carried on in two ways: indirect loans made by the purchase of paper from automobile dealers, and direct loans to car buyers. Purchased paper accounts for nearly two-thirds of the total, although up to the early 1950s, direct loans accounted for the majority of bank activity in this field. A study by the American Bankers Association sheds some light on the reasons for this shift:

> This shift reflects deliberate efforts on the part of banks to attract this type of financing, which has advantages both for individual banks and for automobile dealers. Banks obtain automobile paper in volume at a lower cost than when each loan is handled individually for the prospective borrower and, in addition, get many of the preferred risks. Banks also use the dealer relationship involved as a step toward promoting a closer lending and deposit relationship with automobile dealers—an important consideration, as banks have become highly competitive in obtaining deposits to assure growth and capacity to meet the needs of their communities.
>
> From the point of view of the automobile dealer, the practice of selling a substantial part of his paper to a bank places him in a position to arrange financing more efficiently and promptly for individual customers as the need arises. This is extremely important in the highly competitive automobile market. The dealer also obtains financing for his inventory of cars and is in a better position to negotiate for other financing

TABLE 10-2

Consumer Installment Credit

(year-end 1981, billions of dollars)

Automobile	125.8
Commercial banks	58.5
Indirect paper	34.6
Direct loans	23.9
Credit unions	22.0
Finance companies	45.3
Revolving	65.4
Commercial banks	33.3
Retailers	26.7
Gasoline companies	5.4
Mobile home	18.5
Commercial banks	10.3
Finance companies	4.5
Savings and loans	3.2
Credit unions	.5
Other	
Commercial banks	44.7
Finance companies	40.0
Credit unions	23.5
Retailers	4.0
Savings and loans	8.4
Mutual savings banks	2.8
Total	333.1

Source: *Federal Reserve Bulletin.*

which may be needed. Furthermore, banks have followed the sales finance companies' practice of setting up part of the financing charge as a reserve for losses, and if the dealer's loss experience is good, part of this reserve reverts to him as profit.[3]

Banks also do a large volume of financing of other consumer goods, such as refrigerators, television sets, mobile homes, and boats. In most respects, the financing arrangements are similar to those used with auto financing, although the average size of a trailer loan is larger than a car loan and a loan on a television set is smaller. On the smaller loans, rates are generally higher than on auto loans. Loss experiences are not quite as favorable as on car financing. Losses on automobile paper have been extremely low—below .25 percent for both direct and purchased paper. Losses on financing of other consumer goods have been around .5 percent. Commercial banks are also the largest makers of repair and modernization loans (accounting for about 60 percent of the total).

[3] American Bankers Association, *The Commercial Banking Industry* (Englewood Cliffs, N.J.: Prentice-Hall, 1962), p. 176.

Credit Cards

The growth of bank credit-card plans has been one of the most significant developments in the consumer-credit field in recent years. The plans generally operate as follows: Retail stores arrange with the sponsoring bank to become members of the plan. Their customers who want to use the credit-card service fill out an application, which is forwarded to the bank. If the application is approved, the bank sends the customer a credit card good at any member store. The bank will also send cards to its customers and others who apply or who the bank considers satisfactory credit risks.[4] When a customer makes a purchase, the store sends the sales slip to the bank, which promptly credits the merchant's account with the amount of the sale (less a service charge that may be as high as 5 or 6 percent). The bank sends the customer one monthly statement covering all his transactions at all member stores during the month. Generally there is no charge to the customer if he pays promptly, but interest (typically at a rate of 1¾ percent per month) is charged on accounts not paid within a specified time.

Several banks attempted to enter the credit-card field in the 1950s and were generally unsuccessful. Banks stayed out of the field until the mid-1960s, when large numbers of them began to offer a wide variety of credit-card plans. Although only a handful of banks had credit cards as recently as 1965, the rate of entry since then has been very rapid. About 350 banks offered credit-card plans in late 1967, over 1,600 by 1972, and now most banks participate in one or more credit-card plans. Bank charge-card credit outstanding reached $30 billion in 1981.

Although the number of banks participating in credit-card plans has been increasing, the number of different plans has dropped since the late 1960s. Most banks have joined the national operations, Visa and MasterCard. Such plans offer the cardholder a wider range of businesses that accept the card and overcome the problem of the retailer who does not want to be affiliated with a large number of separate credit-card plans. These universal bank cards are beginning to be used as access cards to bank cash at a wide variety of outlets. Money-market funds issue them through coop-

---

[4] Because the success of the plan requires a large-scale operation, some banks attempted to acquire a large number of cardholders by more or less indiscriminate mailing of credit cards to potential users. Although this makes economic sense if the bank is large enough to absorb the losses that must inevitably result, even some large banks ran into larger losses than anticipated through use of this approach. There are now legal restrictions on the mailing of unsolicited credit cards.

erating banks to give shareholders instant access to cash from their accounts.

To the bank, the credit card is a source of income, both from the discounts charged the merchant and from the interest payments when the cardholder elects to pay the charge over a period of time longer than a month.[5] Equally important to the bank is the ability to make loans to people who are not depositors of the bank and perhaps attract their deposits.

The customer gains convenience in making purchases and also the opportunity to use credit on a regular basis without the need for a credit investigation each time. As has been pointed out, there is no charge to the customer if a bill is paid on time. The store gets the advantage of immediate use of money from its sales and no longer needs a credit department. The store may also gain sales from customers who could not pay cash. Many merchants oppose these plans, however, arguing that costs are too high and that they achieve better customer relations if they retain control over who gets credit at their stores, and how much.

Nonbank cards are the so-called "travel and entertainment" (T&E) cards issued by American Express, Diners Club, and Carte Blanche. One difference between them is that the bank cards, at least in the beginning, were oriented toward retail stores, whereas the T&E cards emphasized hotels, restaurants, and airlines. Now, however, many of these latter establishments accept bank cards, and the T&E firms have signed up a number of retail merchants.

Until 1980, a significant difference in the two cards was that bank cards were free while the major T&E operations charged an annual fee. When President Carter temporarily imposed controls, some banks seized the opportunity to begin imposing charges, although there are a wide variety of practices in this regard.

When charge cards were first issued, the sponsors forbade participating merchants from discriminating in their prices between card users and cash buyers. Congress subsequently outlawed this provision, but with regulations that still discouraged differential pricing. The discount offered to cash buyers had to be considered in informing card users of the interest rate that would apply to their purchases.[6] Federal Reserve Board member Nancy H. Teeters told Congress in 1981:

---

[5] Forty percent of bank credit-card debt is paid in full in the billing period.

[6] The cash discount was limited to 5 percent, and in a curious distinction, cash buyers could receive discounts but a surcharge could not be imposed on credit-card users.

. . . what we have not seen is merchants offering discounts—at least not to any appreciable degree . . . it may, once again, be a case of government regulation creating part of the problem—regulation that is grounded on a set of well-intended arguments but that introduces such friction into otherwise simple transactions that compliance is simply not worth the merchant's risk or effort.[7]

Finance Companies

Sales finance companies are second only to commercial banks in the volume of consumer credit extended. Sales finance companies have long specialized in financing the installment sales contracts of automobile dealers, and automobile paper now accounts for about 70 percent of the consumer credit extended by these companies. The sales finance companies have been losing ground relative to the commercial banks in recent years.

The funds advanced by the sales finance companies come from their own capital and borrowed money. The large companies borrow from commercial banks and sell large volumes of commercial paper in the open market (see Chapter 5). Because of their excellent credit standing, they are able to borrow at relatively low rates. The low cost of borrowed money to the sales finance companies, coupled with the rate charged on their loans, results in satisfactory profits for the companies despite the high costs involved in handling consumer loans. It might be noted that credit extended on purchases of automobiles is usually in fairly large amounts, and thus the costs on a per-dollar basis are not as great as they would be for smaller loans.

Consumer-finance or small-loan companies specialize in granting small loans to consumers, repayable on an installment basis. The development of the small-loan company is the result of efforts to eliminate the loan shark. It is difficult to outlaw extortionate lending practices when there is no legal alternative. The Uniform Small Loan Law, under which most consumer-finance companies operate, was designed to regulate such lending but to allow rates high enough to cover the high costs of doing business.

Small-loan companies are limited as to both the size of the loans they can make and the interest rate they can charge on their loans. The original Uniform Small Loan Law set a maximum loan limit of $300, but this has been raised in most states to as high as $5,000. An interest rate of 2 to 3 percent per month (24 to 36 percent per year) on the unpaid balance is now common.

[7] *Federal Reserve Bulletin*, February 1981, p. 143. The statement was made to the Subcommittee on Consumer Affairs of the House Committee on Banking, Finance and Urban Affairs.

Credit Unions

Credit unions have shown the most rapid growth of any consumer financing institution. In 1950, credit unions had loans out of only $500 million dollars. By 1960, the loans had reached nearly $4 billion, and in 1981, their consumer loans totaled $46 billion. Credit unions account for about 14 percent of all installment credit outstanding.

Because the basic purpose of credit unions is to make loans to members at rates as low as possible, and because of the nonprofit nature of credit unions, their rates on installment loans are lower than those charged by other lenders. Federal credit unions can charge only 15 percent. Many credit unions refund some of the interest payment to borrowers at the end of the year if earnings permit.

Other Consumer-Credit Institutions

Although the Uniform Small Loan Law was designed to put loan sharks (unlicensed lenders) out of business, there are still loan sharks operating and charging fantastic rates; rates of 20 to 40 percent per month are common. It should be noted that loan sharks do serve a real need by standing ready to make loans that other lenders will not. If a borrower cannot obtain better terms, and if he is willing to pay 300 percent interest on a loan, it is hard to object, on economic grounds, to a loan shark's making such a loan. Much of our objection to loan sharks is based on their collection methods rather than their loan terms, but of course, legal channels cannot be used to collect an illegal loan. It is legitimate to question whether loan sharks' activity is illegal because their methods are objectionable, or whether their methods are objectionable because the lending activity is illegal.

Pawnshops make small loans secured by the pledge of personal property. The majority of loans made by pawnbrokers are less than $200. Although the pawnshop has a long—and not always respectable—history, this type of financing is of small and shrinking importance.

Arthur Morris organized the first *industrial bank* in 1910 to make loans to workers at legal interest rates. The Morris Plan spread rapidly in the 1920s. Some industrial banks operate in a manner similar to the small-loan companies, but others are indistinguishable from commercial banks.

THE COST OF CONSUMER CREDIT

In 1968, Congress enacted the Truth in Lending Act to ensure that consumers are given accurate information as to the cost of the credit they obtain and to facilitate their shopping for the lowest-cost loans available. Before the passage of Truth in Lending, it was difficult for the average consumer to determine the actual interest rate on the loan he was negotiating, and the rate was usually higher than it appeared. Loan rates were quoted in such terms as "$6 per hundred," "5 percent discount," "2 percent per month," and some-times simply as "low bank rates," or "only pennies per day."

Although a rate of 2 percent per month is obviously 24 percent per year, some of the other methods of quoting rates were not so easy to interpret. An apparent 6 percent charge on an installment loan turns out to considerably understate the true rate. Suppose someone borrows $100 and agrees to repay in twelve monthly installments, with a $6 interest charge. Since he must repay $106, his monthly payment must be $106/12, or $8.83. After the first payment, he owes $97.17; after the second, $88.34; after ten months, $17.66. That is, he has not borrowed $100 for a year—he has the full $100 for only one month. In fact, for the last month of the year, he has use of only $8.83, yet he is paying at the rate of 6 percent for the use of $100. The average amount he has borrowed during the year as a whole is little more than $50, and the rate of interest he is paying on the money actually borrowed is around 11 percent, or nearly twice the stated rate.[8]

In some cases, the loan may be handled on a discount basis, so that the interest is deducted in advance. Thus, the borrower of $100

---

[8] The precise calculation of consumer-credit interest charges involves some rather complex mathematical techniques as well as some difficult definitional matters. Quite accurate results can be obtained from the following formula for virtually all consumer-credit interest problems:

$$APR = \frac{2mI}{P(n+1)}$$

where: APR = annual percentage rate (in decimal form)
I = dollar cost of the credit (interest)
m = number of payment periods per year (12 if monthly, 52 if weekly)
n = number of payments to be made
P = principal (net amount actually advanced)

The application of this formula to the example above is as follows:

$$R = \frac{2 \times 12 \times 6}{100\,(12+1)} = \frac{144}{1300} = 11.08 \text{ percent}$$

may actually get $94 but be obliged to repay $100 in monthly install-ments. The true rate paid under such arrangement is about 11.8 percent.[9]

Sometimes in the past, a reasonable-sounding interest charge was quoted, but the total repayment obligation included charges for credit investigation, insurance premiums, and other additions to the total bill. In some cases, no rates were quoted, and the borrower was merely told the amount of the monthly payments required. After all, it was argued, this is the only thing the borrower seems to be concerned about. The law now requires that the borrower be told the true rate of interest (or annual percentage rate—APR) on his transaction.

In addition to the requirements for disclosure to a borrower of all the terms of the borrowing transaction, the Truth in Lending Act authorized the Federal Reserve Board to prescribe rules for advertising consumer credit. Experience showed that it was diffi-cult to draft rules on advertising and disclosure that balanced ease of compliance with the intent of the law. The 1980 Deregulation Act permitted lenders greater tolerance (one-eight of 1 percent) in dis-closing the APR, and it exempted agricultural credit from the dis-closure requirement.

The Truth in Lending law also contains provisions for criminal and civil penalties for its violation. The Deregulation Act au-thorized the enforcing agency to require an institution to make reimbursement in case of inaccurate disclosure, but there is no civil liability for unintentional violations.

Usury Laws

The Truth in Lending Act is designed to afford consumers better information and is clearly in the interest of economic efficiency (though the disclosure requirements add to administrative costs). In this respect it stands in sharp contrast to the many state usury laws. Following seventeenth-century English law, Massachusetts enacted the first state usury law in 1641, and this became the pat-tern that many states subsequently followed.

The problems with usury laws are fairly straightforward. First, the costs and risks of lending small amounts to poor credit risks make such lending unremunerative at the statutory levels. Consequently, such borrowers will not be accommodated at all at the statutory rate. Secondly, the profit opportunities inherent in lending to such borrowers

[9]$APR = \dfrac{2 \times 12 \times 6}{94\,(12 + 1)} = 11.78$

at an unrestricted rate give rise to a variety of devices, legal and illegal, to circumvent the ceilings. Exceptions to the usury ceilings have proliferated, making a tangled web of the statutes governing lending in many states.

Finally, even usury ceilings that have appeared reasonable in normal times, in the sense of allowing lenders a modest but competitive rate of return, have become wholly unrealistic as market interest rates have risen sharply in recent years.[10]

States are gradually liberalizing usury laws through legislative and ballot processes, but many remain. Perhaps the chief beneficiaries of usury laws are the states that do not have them— drawing funds that would otherwise flow to the restrictive states.

Interstate banking operations have become one of the many ways usury laws are being avoided. In 1978, the U.S. Supreme Court ruled that national banks were bound only by the law of the home state in charging interest to out-of-state customers. In 1981, the Federal Reserve granted Citicorp, the New York bank holding company, permission to establish banking facilities in Sioux Falls, South Dakota, to use as a base for its nationwide credit-card activities. South Dakota does not regulate interest on bank consumer lending.

CONSUMER CREDIT AND CONSUMER PROTECTION

The Truth in Lending Act became law in 1968 after a lengthy legislative struggle; it was the forerunner of more recent consumer-protection legislation in the consumer-credit field.

The Fair Credit Reporting Act was passed in 1970 "to protect the consumer against arbitrary, erroneous and malicious credit information." Under this law, the consumer has the right to know when a credit report was the cause of his application for credit (or employment) being rejected, to have access to the contents of his credit file, and to have inaccurate information removed from his file. The act as passed represented a compromise between consumer groups, which wanted a stronger bill, and industry groups, which wanted none.

The Fair Credit Billing Act, which became effective in 1975, arose from the frustration almost everyone has experienced in receiving an erroneous bill prepared by a computer and being unable to find a human being to clear up the error. Typically, if the bill is not paid, service charges accrue, and threats to one's credit rating—computer-prepared—arrive regularly.

[10] "The Depository Institutions Deregulation and Monetary Control Act," Federal Reserve Bank of Chicago *Economic Perspectives*, September/October 1980, p. 17.

The act establishes a billing-error resolution procedure. Under the procedure, a creditor is prohibited from threatening a consumer with repossession of goods or a poor credit report while the billing dispute is being investigated. It sets a time limit for creditor response to inquiries about bills, during which time finance charges are controlled.

Although these provisions seem desirable from the point of view of the consumer, it must be stressed that not all laws aimed at some abuse or intended to protect consumers from greedy merchants or lenders are good public policy (or even in the best interests of consumers). There are areas where it is very difficult to find a reasonable middle ground between the rights of consumers and of creditors. The originally proposed Fair Credit Billing Act would have put severe restrictions on the use of "descriptive billing," the now common procedure where copies of sales slips are not sent to the credit-card or charge-account customer with the monthly bill. This provision reflected the concern that under descriptive billing, errors would be more frequent and would be more difficult to resolve. Of course, any provision that increases costs to creditors or makes lending riskier because collection is more difficult will result in an increase in costs to all consumers. Descriptive billing is a good example of this conflict—it is clearly desirable to reduce the enormous paper flow involved in small credit purchases, but the plight of the consumer faced with a bill for an item he does not remember purchasing must be considered.

Perhaps the clearest example of conflict between credit costs and consumer protection is the "holder-in-due-course" doctrine. Under that rule, a financial institution that, in the ordinary course of business, bought an installment sales contract from a merchant is not responsible for the merchandise that was financed. Until abolished by Congress in 1976, the holder-in-due-course doctrine was the rule in all but a few states. Suppose I bought a color television set on an installment basis when that rule prevailed. The dealer would probably sell my IOU to a bank or sales finance company. The bank is a holder in due course, and I would be obligated to pay all I owed, even if the television set turned out to be defective. The bank would tell me that my dispute is with the dealer or manufacturer and is of no concern to the bank. This would be true even if the dealer has defrauded me or gone out of business.

Under present law, all credit sales contracts must contain a provision permitting the purchaser of goods to assert against any subsequent holder of the contract the same claims and defenses that could have been asserted against the seller. At first glance, this elimination of the holder-in-due-course doctrine appears to be a clear gain to the consumer. But look at the transaction from the point of view of the bank. Under the holder-in-due-course doctrine, the bank can provide consumer credit without having to be concerned with the quality and service of television sets, furniture, or automobiles. If the bank knows that it is going to be held responsible for ensuring that merchandise performs as expected or that an auto dealer provides good service, it is going to require a higher interest rate on the credit transaction. That higher rate is going to be paid by the consumer. Opponents of the holder-in-due-course doctrine recognize this argument, but they argue that there is a problem only when fly-by-night or unethical merchants are involved. Bankers are in a better position to insist that merchants whose installment paper they are buying live up to their obligations than is the individual consumer.

The Equal Credit Opportunity Act was designed to eliminate discrimination on the basis of race, religion, sex, marital status, and the like in any credit transaction. Obviously, no one favors such discrimination in lending or unsavory collection tactics. The real issue, however, is one of assessing costs and benefits. In discussing any consumer-credit protection proposal, we should attempt to evaluate whether the benefits of eliminating a particular abuse outweigh the costs of administering, enforcing, and complying with the new law.

Other recent laws have dealt with problems in collecting outstanding debt. The Fair Collection Practices Act was designed to eliminate the abuses of some creditors and collection agencies in their efforts to collect debts.

Still more significant was the Bankruptcy Reform Act of 1979. Bankruptcy is a procedure by which a debtor in default turns his financial affairs over to the court for management. The advantage of the procedure to creditors is the liquidation of the debtor's assets and an equitable distribution among creditors. The advantage to the debtor is a final resolution of the debt.

The Bankruptcy Reform Act changed a number of procedures regarding the debtor's liability. The amount of property exempt from liquidation was increased, and changes were made in valuation of property that have been interpreted as beneficial to the debtor. Debtors' future income is not used in determining repayment—only their assets.

The National Consumer Finance Association, a trade group, estimated that creditors lost $3 billion from bankruptcies within a year after the act had become fully operative. Bankruptcy filings increased by 70 percent, to more than 400,000 in 1980.

Although the asset provisions of the new law may be too liberal, creditors wish to go much further and use debtors' future income for repayment. The uncertainties of this arrangement for the debtor would threaten bankruptcy's mutuality of benefits to debtor and creditor, which needs to be maintained.

QUESTIONS

1 Why do auto loans account for such a large share of total consumer credit?
2 "Interest rates of 18 percent or more, common on consumer loans, are immoral and should be prohibited." Do you agree?
3 If a lender is willing to make a loan to a poor credit risk at a very high interest rate (say, 150 percent) and the borrower is willing to pay that rate, should the law prohibit the making of such a loan?
4 Do credit cards represent a step toward "checkless banking"?
5 Why are automobile dealers sometimes willing to quote a lower price on a new car that is to be financed than on one paid for in cash?
6 Would the U.S. economy be very different if consumer credit did not exist? What would be the effect upon the automobile industry?
7 Have you made any use of the information disclosed under the Truth in Lending Act in shopping for credit? Do you think you would if you were to buy a new car?
8 Suppose the administrative costs of complying with each consumer-protection law resulted in a ¼ percent increase in the cost of credit. Which laws do you think are worthwhile on that basis?
9 What assets should a debtor keep in bankruptcy?

SELECTED READINGS

Board of Governors of the Federal Reserve, *Annual Percentage Rate Tables* (Truth in Lending, Regulation Z). 2 vols., 1969.
————, *1977 Consumer Credit Survey.* 1978.
JUSTER, F. THOMAS, and ROBERT P. SHAY, *Consumer Sensitivity to Finance Rates: An Empirical and Analytical Investigation.* New York: National Bureau of Economic Research, Occasional Paper 88, 1964.
National Commission on Consumer Finance, *Consumer Credit in the United States.* Washington, D.C.: U.S. Government Printing Office, 1973. The report of a committee appointed by the president and Congress.
National Consumer Finance Association, *The Consumer Finance Industry.* Library of the Commission on Money and Credit. Englewood Cliffs, N.J.: Prentice-Hall, 1962.
PALASH, CARL, "Household Debt Burden: How Heavy Is It?" Federal Reserve Bank of New York *Quarterly Review*, Summer 1979.

II

Financing Housing

Adequate housing for all has been an important social and economic goal in most countries. In the United States, this goal has taken the specific objective of promoting homeownership. Measures toward this end have been taken over the years at all levels of government, with the result that 65 percent of families now own their own homes. Some social critics have pointed out that this emphasis on individual homeownership has created problems: suburban sprawl and disruption of the environment, decay of inner cities, excessive energy consumption, and so on.

The typical home buyer is a heavy user of credit, and the monthly mortgage payment constitutes a significant portion of the budget. Much government intervention to aid the home buyer has been exerted through the credit markets. In some circumstances, government intervention tends to bring funds into the market (as with the guaranteeing of mortgages), but in others, it serves as an impediment (for instance, in the case of interest-rate ceilings).

As inflation gripped the economy in the late 1970s and the 1980s, the market price of housing rose rapidly, bringing heavy demands for mortgage financing, and by 1981, the value of outstanding mortgages on one- to four-family homes reached $1 trillion. Mortgage interest rates soared along with other interest rates, exceeding 17 percent in early 1980 and in 1981.

STRUCTURE OF THE MORTGAGE MARKET

Housing finance includes mortgages on units of various sizes, ranging from single-family homes to large, multiunit complexes. For reporting purposes, mortgages on structures of one to four units are grouped together, and these are the mortgages associated with owner occupancy. Mortgages on larger units are for business purposes.

Mortgage Lending Institutions

In 1981 financial institutions held $688 billion of the one-trillion-dollar total of one- to four-family mortgages outstanding. Savings and loan associations are by far the largest single source of mortgage credit, as shown in Table 11-1. These associations, as well as commercial and mutual savings banks, originate more loans for housing than they ultimately hold; the remainder are sold on the secondary market.

Other mortgages consist of $143 billion on multifamily residential properties, $278 billion on commercial property, and $102 billion of farm mortgage loans. The total amount of real estate mortgage loans outstanding was thus over $1.5 trillion. Life insurance companies are large mortgage lenders, but a large part of this lending is on commercial and industrial property. Mortgage lending by mutual savings banks is heavily concentrated on residential property, with a relatively high proportion of it on multifamily property. Commercial banks as a class are active in all phases of mortgage lending, but many individual banks do not devote much of

TABLE 11-1
Ownership of Mortgage Debt, 1- to 4-Family Houses, Year-End 1981
(billions of dollars)

Owner	Amount Outstanding	Percentage of Total
Savings and loan associations	432.7	42.5
Mutual savings banks	65.4	6.4
Commercial banks	172.5	17.0
Life insurance companies	17.8	1.7
Federal agencies	66.8	6.6
Mortgage pools	136.3	13.4
Individuals and others	126.5	12.4
Total	1,018.0	100.0

Source: Federal Reserve System.

their resources to mortgages. As we have seen, S&Ls devote nearly all their resources to mortgage lending (they had few legal options until recently), and mutual savings banks rank second in the percentage of assets invested in real estate loans. Life insurance companies and commercial banks, with much broader loan and investment powers, devote significantly smaller fractions of their assets to such loans.

Mortgage Bankers

Mortgage bankers are not significant mortgage holders, as can be seen in Table 11-1, because their chief function is in loan origination. Mortgage bankers have been in business for many years, but the industry became much more important during the postwar years when life insurance companies, mutual savings banks, and other investors became willing to buy mortgage loans made in other parts of the country. As loan originators, mortgage bankers find a borrower, complete the mortgage documents, and lay out cash to close the transaction and pay the seller of the property. The mortgages are then accumulated in large blocks and sold to institutional investors. Over the life of the mortgage, the mortgage company services the loan for the investor by collecting and accounting for the monthly payments, maintaining an escrow account for the payment of property taxes, seeing that insurance coverage is maintained, and so on. The mortgage banker's expertise in local real estate markets allows him to provide this service to investors at a lower cost than they would otherwise incur in making loans in an unfamiliar area. Some commercial banks are active in mortgage banking, and several large bank holding companies have mortgage-banking subsidiaries.

Mortgage bankers obviously need large amounts of funds to enable them to extend mortgage loans and then to hold them until they have accumulated a salable package and found a buyer. They obtain funds by borrowing from commercial banks, with their holdings of mortgages as security for the loans. This practice is called "warehousing" of mortgages.

The role of the mortgage banker is an important one in facilitating the interregional flow of mortgage credit in the United States. The development of a truly national mortgage market in this country is rather recent. Consider the problem: If mortgage loans are made primarily by local institutions operating locally, how can we be sure that the supply of funds in a given locality will be sufficient to satisfy local needs? Until rather recently, there was no adequate mechanism to move funds to where the need was greatest. Traditionally, interest rates on mortgage loans were relatively high in the western United States, where population growth was rapid and a large stock of local savings had not been built up. The Northeast, on the other hand, had lower demand for mortgage funds but large holdings of savings in financial institutions, and mortgage rates were relatively low. To some extent, the flow of savings helped meet this need, and the mortgage banker is a most important participant in the process. The arrangement whereby the mortgage banker originates the loan and sells it to the institution with surplus funds is an efficient one, and it is largely responsible for the fact that the difference in mortgage rates between the Sunbelt areas with excess demand for funds and the older areas with excess supply is now much lower than it was 30 or 40 years ago.

Mortgage Guarantees

A significant way in which government facilitates the flow of funds into the mortgage market is through the guarantee of mortgages. Veterans may receive guarantees through the Veterans Administration and others through the Federal Housing Administration. Guaranteed mortgages are more easily sold on the secondary market and are a means by which lenders, such as insurance companies, that may be remote from the borrower can participate in mortgage investment. The maximum interest rate on guaranteed mortgages is set by the agencies. On the frequent occasions when market rates exceed these maximums, guaranteed mortgages become unattractive to the lenders. Construction standards and uncertainty over property appraisals by the agencies also tend to discourage these loans, which account for about 20 percent of home mortgages.

Following the lead of government, private insurance against default, financed through an insurance fee (as are FHA loans), is now available and widely used. Although none of these insurance firms has the resources or credit standing of the federal government, their backing of mortgage loans has improved lenders' assessments of the risks involved in mortgage lending. That is, a financial institution that might insist on a 20 percent down payment on a conventional (noninsured) mortgage loan may be willing to accept a 10 percent or 5 percent down payment if the mortgage is insured by the FHA or a private mortgage insurance firm. Although there are differences in the policies of different lending institutions, there is no question but that mortgage insurance has broadened the mortgage market and improved the marketability of such loans.

Savings and loan associations deal almost exclusively in conventional mortgages rather than those backed by the FHA or VA. That is because they tend to make loans directly to borrowers in their immediate area, so they are able to evaluate both the property being financed and the borrower. Life insurance companies, on the other hand, lack the network of local offices to make such mortgage loans. Instead, they buy mortgage loans from mortgage bankers, who are in the business of originating loans and selling them to institutional investors. Since the insurance company never sees either the property or the borrower, it prefers to deal in government-backed mortgages.

Mutual savings banks combine the two practices, generally making conventional mortgage loans in their local area, and buying FHA and VA loans from out of the area. Commercial banks operate primarily in local mortgage markets and tend to emphasize conventional loans.

Mortgage Pools

The mortgage is a rather awkward instrument for most investors. For all investors, there are problems of monthly servicing; for small investors, most mortgages are too large; for the larger investing institutions, single mortgages are too small. For these reasons, the mortgage market has been dominated by certain financial institutions. In more recent years, there has been a rapid increase in sales of securities backed by pools of mortgages. The securities can be sold in amounts and terms suited to larger investors. There are two general types of such issues. In "pass-through" securities, the purchaser simply acquires a share of the mortgage pool and receives a pro rata share of its interest receipts and repayments. The other type of securities, mortgage-backed bonds, are issued with stated maturities and interest, and the mortgages generate the revenue for these bonds.

The first issuer of bonds for the purpose of mortgage finance was the Federal National Mortgage Association (FNMA, or "Fannie Mae"), created by Congress in 1938. It was organized as a government agency with the function of providing a secondary market for government-backed mortgages. The existence of such a market was intended as an inducement to lenders to offer the then-revolutionary low-down-payment, long-term, federally insured mortgage. The existence of a secondary market means that a financial institution needing cash can sell some of its mortgage holdings to the FNMA. The availability of this option has probably led some institutions to invest a higher proportion of their assets in mortgages than they would have been willing to without this liquidity feature.

Over the years, Fannie Mae has operated not simply as a market maker, buying and selling on a balanced basis, but as a net buyer of mortgages in periods of tight money or when the housing market is depressed. It finances net additions to its inventory of mortgages by selling short-term notes or long-term debentures in the market.

Although Fannie Mae was established as a government agency, in 1968 it was restructured as a government-sponsored, privately owned corporation. FNMA now has stockholders (the stock is listed on the New York Stock Exchange), and seeks to make a profit in its secondary-market activities, but it still has some public obligations.

At the time Fannie Mae was restructured, a new federal agency was created to absorb some of the activities that were best left with a government body. The Government National Mortgage Corporation (GNMA, or "Ginnie Mae"), like FNMA, has several programs designed to absorb the flow of mortgages when the regular suppliers do not have sufficient funds. Its major program involves a guarantee of payment of principal and interest on securities backed by a pool of FHA or VA mortgages. The securities are issued by private lending institutions, and the buyer receives interest and principal as payments are made on the underlying mortgages. These guaranteed securities are more attractive to some investors (pension funds, for example) than are mortgage loans themselves, and hence this device can bring additional funds into the mortgage market. Some of the pass-through securities are issued by GNMA itself, based on mortgage loans it acquires, generally from mortgage bankers.

Although pass-through mortgage-backed securities have been a successful device, not all the funds invested in such securities are a net gain to the mortgage market. Savings and loan associations have been large buyers of the securities, investing funds that otherwise would have gone into direct mortgage loans. In the same way, not all the secondary-market acquisition of mortgages by FNMA represents additional funds to the mortgage market. Fannie Mae must raise the funds it needs to purchase mortgages by borrowing in the capital markets. Some of the funds it obtains might otherwise have gone into savings and loans and hence into the mortgage market.

FNMA and GNMA have dealt primarily in FHA and VA mortgage loans. In the past, these mortgages were considered more suitable for secondary-market trading, because the insurance reduces the risk of loss and the need for the buyer to assess the quality of the individual mortgages he is buying. Also, the use of standardized documents and terms facilitated secondary-market trading. In recent years, secondary-market trading in conventional mortgages has greatly increased, in large part as a result of the growth of private mortgage insurance. Development of the secondary market in conventional mortgages needed an institution to assume the role that FNMA and GNMA play in government-insured mortgages. That need has been met by the Federal Home Loan Mortgage Corporation (FHLMC, or "Freddy Mac"). Freddy Mac is a subsidiary of the Federal Home Loan Bank System and is an important means by which the Federal Home Loan Banks provide support for the mortgage market. These banks also grant direct loans to savings and loan associations. As noted above with respect to FNMA and GNMA, the Home Loan Banks obtain funds from the capital markets by selling bonds, and hence some of the funds advanced to the savings and loan industry are obtained by pulling from the market some funds that might otherwise have gone directly to the S&Ls.

Most funds for government-guaranteed mortgages now come from sales of mortgage-backed securities, and the pools have largely supplanted direct holdings of mortgages by some of the larger investing institutions. In 1968 life insurance and pension funds held 13 percent of home mortgages. In 1981 they held less than 2 percent, but pools more than compensated, holding 13 percent.

Among the growing users of the pool market are the mortgage lending institutions themselves. They sell bonds with their existing mortgages as collateral, and they use the proceeds to acquire more mortgages. The issuer pledges to maintain mortgage collateral at some ratio, say 1½ times the value of the bonds, which are marketed both publicly and through private placement.

Futures Markets

Mortgage commitments and actual mortgage deliveries inevitably take time. Builders have commitments long before housing is actually available for occupancy. Buyers give commitments before transactions actually close. Mortgage companies accumulate mortgages before selling them to final investors. Parties to these transactions are therefore exposed to a risk of fluctuations in interest rates, leading to development of various types of markets to protect against such risk. The FNMA purchases mortgages at auction for future delivery, and an over-the-counter market exists in which dealers enter into commitments to buy or sell up to six months prior to delivery.

A later development, starting in 1975, was trading in interest-rate futures in organized exchanges in New York and Chicago. The instrument traded is the GNMA mortgage-backed certificate. The biggest portion of positions in these contracts at any one time is held by individuals and firms engaging in speculation. In a 1979 survey, mortgage bankers held only 2.5 percent and savings and loans slightly more than 4 percent.

The participant in the market buys or sells a $100,000 certificate for future delivery, putting up a margin of $2,000 (which can be met by posting securities). Contracts are traded for as far in the future as 2½ years. The exchange guarantees delivery, and thus the contract is actually with the exchange. The buyer of a futures contract will gain if interest rates fall (securities prices rise) and lose if they rise. The opposite prevails for the seller. Most participants cancel contracts prior to delivery, by buying (or selling, as the case may be) an offsetting futures contract. Daily trading of mortgage-backed futures on the Chicago Board of Trade, the first to instigate such trading, exceeds $500 million.

CREDIT INSTRUMENTS AND TERMS

Home buyers obtain financing by using the home as security, and the instrument associated with this loan is the mortgage, or trust deed in some states. More than one mortgage on a home may be held at one time. The lender holding the "first" mortgage has the primary claim on the home if the borrower defaults. Holders of second and subsequent mortgages have secondary claims. The traditional first mortgage is issued with a long maturity, often 30 years, and the monthly payment is fixed for the life of the mortgage so that it will be sufficient to cover both interest and repayment of principal. A prepayment penalty may be assessed if the loan is repaid before maturity. The actual average life of a first mortgage is about twelve years.

Secondary financing is usually issued with much shorter maturities than first mortgages. "Seconds" also have fixed payments, but these are not necessarily set so that all is paid off over the life of the mortgage. The amount outstanding at maturity is known as the "balloon" payment. In many cases, interest-only payments are made during the life of the mortgage.

Still another variant that arose with the very high interest rates of the early 1980s was the "wraparound." In this method, formerly used only with commercial properties, a lender takes over the existing mortgages on a property and lends additional funds to the buyer, who makes payments only to the one lender, who in turn makes payments on the existing mortgage. The lender may be a home seller, who uses the technique to increase sales possibilities and to gain from the interest difference between the outstanding mortgages and the new loan at a higher interest rate. In California, the instrument created by a wraparound is called the "all-inclusive trust deed" (AITD). As interest rates rise, a mortgage issued at a low interest rate becomes an attractive feature in selling a house. Lenders would prefer that subsequent buyers not have the right to assume such a mortgage, but in some states, regulated institutions are required to allow such assumptions. When rates are rising, lenders prefer "due-on-sale" provisions that require the loan to be paid off or refinanced (at current market rates) when the property is sold.

The holder (lender) on a mortgage can also change if the mortgage is sold on the secondary market (not to be confused with second mortgages). Sellers of homes are often the original lenders for second mortgages, but then they sell the mortgages. Typically, seconds sell at a heavy discount, resulting in effective yields as high as 30 percent.

The Cost of Mortgage Credit

Interest rates on mortgage loans are quoted on a true interest basis and have varied in recent years from 10 to 18 percent.[1] Table 11.2 shows the relationship of interest rate, monthly payment, and maturity.

Once a loan has a maturity of, say, 20 years, lengthening the maturity further does not reduce the monthly payments very much. Changes in interest rates, which do not greatly affect the size of the monthly payment on an automobile loan, do significantly affect monthly payments on mortgage loans. An increase in the interest rate on a 25-year, $50,000 mortgage from 13 percent to 14 percent means a $38 increase in monthly payments. Over the 25-year period, this means an increase of $11,389 in the cost of the house.

People who bought homes 15 to 20 years ago and arranged mortgage financing at the then-prevailing rates of 5 to 6 percent got, as it has turned out, an excellent buy. Their good fortune (or good interest-rate forecasting) has been bad luck for the lending

[1] The effective interest rate on mortgages is confused by a practice known as "points," a one-time charge imposed on the borrower. A point is 1 percent of the mortgage and is deducted from the amount received by the borrower. Thus, a borrower of $100,000 at 1½ points actually receives only $98,500, thus effectively raising the annual percentage rate.

TABLE 11-2
Monthly Payments Required to Repay an Amortized Mortgage Loan of $10,000

Maturity	8%	10%	12%	14%	16%	18%
10 years	121	132	143	155	168	180
15 years	96	107	120	133	147	161
20 years	84	97	110	124	139	154
25 years	77	91	105	120	136	152
30 years	73	88	103	118	134	151
40 years	70	85	101	117	134	150

institutions, which have found these low-rate mortgages a drag on their earning power ever since the mid-1960s. It is important to note that under present arrangements, if interest rates had gone the other way (that is, declined substantially), the shoe would not quite be on the other foot. Under the terms of most mortgages, the lender cannot raise the rate or call the loan if he finds he has made a mistake in setting the rate originally. On the other hand, the borrower usually has the right to pay the mortgage off, in whole or in part, before maturity.

Given the upward drift of rates in recent years, little opportunity for this kind of refinancing by borrowers has arisen. The major impetus for refinancing comes from the rising market value of homes. This refinancing has been at higher rates, and institutions will usually waive the prepayment penalty if the new mortgage is with the same institution. But if there is no refinancing, the lender is locked into a rate lower than prevailing rates. With continuing rises in rates, lenders have become increasingly unwilling to offer long-term, fixed-rate mortgages, and some flexibility is rapidly becoming the norm. Variable-rate mortgages (VRMs) provide for a change in interest rate and monthly payment over the life of the loan. Generally, the rate is tied to some market rate.

Graduated-Payment Mortgages

Another change that has arisen in mortgage terms is the graduated-payment mortgage. Rather than being fixed, the monthly payments increase in amount over the life of the mortgage. Given expectations of inflation, this is a logical way to schedule payments, but even in the absence of inflation, it is a way of matching payments to the expected rises in real income of the younger buyer.

The graduated-payment mortgage allows the buyer to justify a higher ratio of loan to purchase price, since initial payments are more in line with current income than would be the case with fixed payments. In the earlier years of a graduated-payment loan, the monthly payment may not even meet the interest cost for the month. The unpaid interest is added to the principal, and thus there is a negative amortization of the mortgage.

Graduated payments offer unattractive features from the standpoint of the lender and might never have been developed except for successful experiments undertaken in the mid-1970s by the U.S. Department of Housing and Urban Development. By 1980, more than a fourth of new mortgages were of this type. The principal problem from the standpoint of the financial institutions is the reduced monthly flows from mortgage payments, reducing the institutions' capacity to make other mortgage commitments. The graduated-payments feature might, however, enable the institution to make mortgages at higher interest rates than would otherwise be possible. There is also some concern that such mortgages might have a higher default rate, particularly in the early years when the principal of the loan is actually increasing, reducing, in a sense, the owner's equity in the house. This is no problem in a period of rising house prices but may render the market more vulnerable if there is any decline in prices.

PROBLEMS OF THE MORTGAGE MARKET

Our discussion of the mortgage market so far would lead one to conclude that the marketplace has been efficient and successful in resolving the difficult problem of providing adequate financing to meet our housing needs. However, despite the high priority that has been accorded to housing goals, and the government programs and mortgage innovations that we have discussed, the housing market has had considerable problems in recent years. Part of the problem has been cyclical. Years of overbuilding, with rising vacancy rates and inventories of unsold units, have alternated with periods of severe tightness in the mortgage market and sharp reductions in housing construction. Part of the problem is secular, although related to the cyclical difficulties. That is, in the long run, will the alternating good years and bad years result in an appropriate number of housing units of appropriate quality to meet our housing goals? Is the cost of the single-family home increasing so rapidly as to be beyond the means of the average American? Since the housing market seems to be very sensitive to monetary policy, is the countercyclical use of monetary policy incompatible with meeting our housing goals? Answers to these questions are not easy, and they can be approached only after a closer look at the problems.

The Problem of Specialized Institutions

The major cyclical problem in financing housing is the mortgage market's reliance on specialized lending institutions, such as savings and loan associations. Past years of high interest rates have brought to light a serious problem faced by such institutions. They accept deposits that are, in practice, largely payable on demand, and they invest their funds mainly in long-term mortgage loans. When market interest rates rise, these institutions do not experience any significant increase in their interest earnings. Most of their income comes from mortgage loans made in earlier years at lower rates of interest.

Legal interest ceilings have been used in an attempt to keep interest costs in line with interest earnings, but deposit outflows necessitated allowing a more competitive rate in 1978 through the money-market certificates discussed in Chapter 7. Although the certificates undoubtedly helped institutions retain funds, the housing industry was no better off than in the period when institutions were less able to compete for money-market funds. Fluctuations in new housing units started have been more extreme in the 1970s and early 1980s than the 1960s. After a few years of housing starts above 2 million units per year, starts fell to under 1.2 million in 1975. The problem continued into the 1980s. The Federal Reserve Bank of New York noted in its annual report for 1980:

> . . . . as interest rates in general surged to record high levels, mortgage lending dried up almost completely, with the rate on new commitments climbing as high as 16 to 17 per cent. Housing starts plunged. By May, housing starts were down to only 900,000 at an annual rate, the lowest level since early 1975 when the economy was also enmeshed in a recession.

A number of steps have been taken to free housing credit from its cyclical instability. One of these was the removal of state usury laws as they applied to first-mortgage lending. The 1980 Deregulation Act abolished such laws unless the states specifically reinstitute them by April 1, 1983. Usury laws with unrealistic interest-rate ceilings had virtually halted mortgage lending in some states, such as New York. Other measures have been discussed in this and other chapters:

Nonbank financial institutions may now issue interest-bearing checking accounts.

Interest restrictions on deposits were scheduled for gradual phaseout under the 1980 Deregulation Act.

Reserve requirements have been removed on personal accounts that are not subject to transactions.

Financial institutions have been empowered to issue variable-rate mortgages.

Mortgage-backed securities have emerged as important sources of funds to the housing market, reducing the dependence on deposit sources.

Interest futures markets have been developed, increasing institutions' ability to protect themselves against swings in mortgage interest rates.

Nonbank financial institutions have been granted power to diversify their assets and reduce their dependence on mortgage income.

In general, these changes would seem to greatly strengthen the ability of the mortgage market to compete with others for available funds, with the possible exception of the diversification of financial-institution assets. Although broader investment powers may enhance the savings institutions' ability to compete with commercial banks in periods of high interest rates, they may do so at the expense of reducing their commitment of funds to the mortgage market. During periods of higher interest rates, it is the rates on short-term loans that rise the most, and institutions may give them preference. On the other hand, the mortgage market has a stake in the preservation of these institutions, and their very existence has been threatened when interest rates on their short-term liabilities rise and rates on their mortgages remain fixed. Clearly, some changes had to be forthcoming. In view of the significant reforms that have taken place, it does not appear that the mortgage market suffers special disadvantages. In fact, by 1980, questions were arising as to whether too much lending was flowing to the housing market.[2] Mortgage credit was financing inflating home prices while business fixed investment was actually declining in real terms.

Housing Costs

The problems of housing are part of the overall problem of inflation. When prices are expected to rise, there is a demand to purchase real assets as an inflation hedge, and the single-family home has become a favored vehicle for this purpose. One of the equilibrating mechanisms in this process is the interest rate. But high interest rates also reduce new construction, and thereby the supply of housing, further exacerbating the problem.

Like the inflation problem in general, rising house prices create problems of distribution of gains and losses, rather than real losses in the aggregate. To current homeowners, rising home prices are a gain. To those who purchase, the acquisition is part investment, part housing occupancy. Some analysts view that the "price"

[2] Randall Pozdena and William Burke, "Housing: Sacred Cow?" *Weekly Letter*, Federal Reserve Bank of San Francisco, November 28, 1980.

of housing to the homeowner must be viewed net of the rise in the market price of the house, and thus the "cost" of homeownership is less than the monthly payment.[3] This is yet another of the many manifestations of the distributional effect of inflation. With home-owners—and multiple-home owners—gaining at the expense of non-owners, this distribution is surely not in a socially desired direction.

The component of rising housing costs that is real in the aggregate is the rise in construction costs (to the extent that it exceeds general inflation). The rapid rise in construction costs is explained at least in part by falling productivity in this sector. Since 1967, output per worker in construction has actually declined by 2 percent per year, and the real costs of home construction have thus gone up.

If the inflation climate persists, it can be expected that increased pressure will be brought for more subsidies to housing. Regardless of their form, subsidies require some redistribution of income and wealth. Although some redistribution may well be justified, any program must seek to identify the gainers and losers so that the redistribution is in the desired direction. Loans at less than market rates are a poor form of redistribution. Those who are in the greater need are not necessarily the ones who benefit. The payers and receivers are poorly targeted and ill-defined, and any gains may very well be offset by the higher house prices that result from the easy credit.

QUESTIONS

1 Are home buyers' interests served by regulations that allow variable-rate mortgages?
2 Which institutions are devoting a smaller share of their assets to mortgage loans, and why?
3 Are mortgage pools likely at some time to become the primary source of funds for home mortgages?
4 Does the lifting of ceilings on deposit interest tend to affect mortgage interest rates?
5 Should public policy encourage ownership of the single-family home? If so, how?
6 How does the secondary market for mortgages tend to affect the primary market?

[3] Glenn H. Miller, "The Affordability of Home Ownership in the 1970's," *Economic Review*, Federal Reserve Bank of Kansas City, September–October 1980, pp. 17–23.

SELECTED READINGS

Federal Reserve Bank of Boston, *Housing and Monetary Policy.* Conference Series No. 4, 1970. An excellent collection of papers.

GREBLER, LEO, and FRANK MITTELBACH, *The Inflation of House Prices.* Lexington, Mass.: Lexington Books, 1979.

MELTON, WILLIAM C., "Graduated Payment Mortgages," *Quarterly Review,* Federal Reserve Bank of New York, Spring 1980, pp. 21–31.

SIVESIND, CHARLES, "Mortgage-Backed Securities: The Revolution in Real Estate Finance," *Quarterly Review,* Federal Reserve Bank of New York, Autumn 1979, pp. 1–12.

U.S. League of Savings Associations, *Savings and Loan Fact Book,* annually. A good source of data on consumer savings and home financing.

12

Financing Government

The total debt of the federal government in 1981 reached $1 trillion, about the same as home-mortgage debt. Beyond the magnitude, there are few similarities in these two types of debt. Households incur debt because the cost of a home exceeds their marketable assets. Why does the federal government borrow?

The government can finance its expenditures by taxation, by creation of money to make payments (noninterest debt), or by the sale of interest-bearing securities. Since the power to tax and to create money has no constitutional limit, the issuance of interest-bearing debt is a matter of economic policy rather than necessity. In any period, the government determines its spending and taxation in accord with the economic conditions of that period. Any residual—a government deficit or surplus—is a by-product of this decision. Tax receipts and government spending constitute the exercise of what is called "fiscal policy." A residual deficit can be financed by money creation or borrowing, and money creation is determined by monetary policy. The deficit not financed by money creation, which is not really planned directly, gives rise to the public debt, which is the province of "debt-management policy," conducted by the Treasury.

The objectives of all these policies are the same (to be discussed in detail in Part VII)—to promote the economic welfare of the population. Thus, unlike most borrowers, government seeks to serve the objectives of the lenders, at least to the extent that they are in agreement with the objectives of the population as a whole. Another distinctive feature of the government's debt is that it is a liability borne by no one in the economy. When a mortgage is created, there is a mortgage holder and a debtor who will begin making monthly payments, a fact that surely affects the family's economic behavior. When government debt arises, there is an asset holder, but no one assumes the liability. No portfolio manager in the country takes on some share of the public debt in the liability column. And this is logical, since the government could at any time pay off the public debt by creating an equivalent amount of legal-tender money. To transform this much interest-bearing debt into legal tender would doubtless have undesirable economic consequences, but unlike the case of a household, repayment of the debt would not in itself reduce the resources of the nation that owes that debt. Since the government can always issue money to repay its debt, government debt is riskless.

SIZE OF THE DEBT

The gross federal debt amounted to only $65 million in 1860. The Civil War, like all wars, required large expenditures, which increased the size of the debt to nearly $2.5 billion by 1870. The debt was gradually reduced in succeeding decades, and by 1910, it was only $1.1 billion. World War I required government borrowing at an unheard-of rate, and by 1919, the debt was over $26 billion. Again debt reduction took place in the postwar years, reducing the level to $16 billion in 1929. The depression of the 1930s was the first period of substantial increase in the debt not associated with a major war. The national debt increased during the decade to reach about $43 billion in 1940. World War II, of course, led to a tremendous increase in public debt, which reached $259 billion in 1946. The gross federal debt grew gradually over the next 20 years, to reach $321 billion by the end of 1965. The substantial expansion of Vietnam War expenditures, coupled with the reluctance of the administration to raise taxes to finance the war, produced a more rapid increase in the debt in the following years. Thus the gross federal debt, which had increased by only $62 billion between 1946 and 1965, increased by over $200 billion in the next ten years. The debt was significantly affected by the recessions of 1974–75, 1980, and 1981–1982.

Given the peculiar nature of the public debt, we clearly have no rules to go by as to how large it can become. When the debt reached $1 trillion, it constituted 40 percent of the value of the nation's output (gross national product). In relative terms, however, the debt was far less than it was two decades earlier; in 1960, it was 60 percent of national output. Inflation is one of the primary reasons for the decline. Once incurred, debt retains its money value, since debt outstanding does not rise with the price level. But national product does rise with rising prices, and thus the ratio of a given debt to the GNP will fall in a period of inflation.

Although the relative importance of the debt has declined since World War II, the decline has not been continuous. Changes in the debt are irregular, depending primarily upon the deficit (surplus) that results from the interaction of fiscal policy and the economy. Deficits tend to be larger in periods of economic recession, when tax revenues lag from sluggish incomes and government spending is maintained or increased. In the recession of 1980, the deficit was $83 billion, twice the size of the 1979 deficit and about 3 percent of national output—the same rate it reached during the Vietnam War (fiscal year 1967–68). The deficit for the 1982 fiscal year became a matter of widespread concern as it approached $100 billion, in the midst of economic recession.

Interest on the national debt in the early 1980s was around $90 billion annually, somewhat over 3 percent of the GNP, whereas two decades earlier, it constituted 1½–2 percent. The payment of interest represents no net cost to the public in a resource sense—it is a transfer of purchasing power from nonholders of government bonds to holders. Government debt tends to be short-term, and thus interest outlays have risen with rising interest rates.

Another way of viewing the significance of public debt is in the proportion of total funds raised in the credit and equity markets. In 1981, the federal government raised 18 percent of the funds on these markets. In 1975, another recession year, it raised 38 percent of the funds. In the more prosperous year of 1979, the government accounted for only 7½ percent.

Intragovernment Transactions

The total obligations of government are difficult to measure, because of transactions between government agencies and because of the variety of commitments the government has taken on. Some of the public debt—almost a third—is held by government agencies, such as the Social Security system, the FDIC, and the Federal Reserve. But these agencies in turn have some kind of liability to the public. The Federal Deposit Insurance Corporation has a liability to bank depositors. The Federal Reserve's holding of debt results in a money debt ultimately held by the public. The Social Security fund and federal-employee funds ultimately have some kind of liability to make payments to those covered by them.

The assets of the Social Security system, in fact, are far less than projected payments to people now covered by Social Security. The gap is not made up even if Social Security taxes, too, are projected. Thus, as a larger proportion of the population goes into retirement, those working must pay higher taxes to support those not working, if benefits are to be maintained. No financing mechanisms can obscure the basic fact that in any period, if one group receives more of output, another group must receive less. An individual can store for retirement by acquiring claims on others. The nation as a whole cannot do this; it has no one on which to acquire claims.

Another way in which government-agency transactions affect debt accounting is through the agencies' *issue* of debt. Some agencies borrow and use the proceeds for special purposes, although agency debt accounts for less than 7 percent of the public debt. These agencies make loans to specific sectors of the economy and acquire assets, such as mortgages in support of the home-mortgage market. Examples of these agencies are the Export-Import Bank (loans for the export of American goods), the Student Loan Marketing Association, and the Government National Mortgage Association. The direct issue of the agencies has declined since the creation of the Federal Financing Bank in 1973. The agencies can acquire funds from this bank, which acquires them from the Treasury, which acquires them from the sale of government securities. The Federal Financing Bank can and on occasion does acquire funds directly from the market by sale of its own securities.

The activities of the agencies offer a potential problem in overall economic policy. They shelter certain types of resource allocation outside the main chain of fiscal and monetary control. To the extent that certain types of loans are subsidized, resources will be directed toward these activities. This may be desirable, but the flow needs to be scrutinized regularly in the light of changing economic conditions, as are activities in the ordinary budget. This problem persists whether the agencies issue their own debt or obtain funds from the Federal Financing Bank.

A similar problem in resource allocation occurs with respect to government guarantees of private debt. Some programs, such as home-mortgage guarantees, are continuous. Some programs arise under special circumstances. The federal government, under special legislation, guaranteed certain obligations of New York City and then of the Chrysler Corporation. Although a guarantee involves perhaps no direct outlay by government, it does result in a diversion of resources from the way they would otherwise be directed by the private market. What one borrower gets, another potential borrower does not. Such programs may be desirable, but the method of subsidy by loan guarantees makes it difficult to judge their true cost in terms of resources foregone elsewhere.

MATURITY OF THE DEBT

As a borrower, the federal government would seem to be a perfect candidate for the issuance of very long-term debt. The government is the closest thing to a permanent institution that any lender could find. Its debt is perpetual; there is no foreseeable circumstance under which the government would cease becoming a borrower. But as it turns out, the government is a very short-term borrower. At any one time, about half its marketable debt is due to mature within a year! The short borrowing of government is criticized by almost every observer, including those from the Treasury.

Perhaps the major problem with short-term debt is the liquidity it imparts to the holder. The purchaser of a short-term security has acquired a claim on government that bears interest, has no risk of default, will mature in a short period of time, and can be readily sold on the market prior to maturity. The economic function of lending is to transfer real resources from lender to borrower. But if the lender has sufficient liquidity that there is no need to reduce purchases, then the total demand for goods will have to be brought down by some other means. If many institutions and individuals in the economy are highly liquid, spending by them could present dangerous problems in a period with inflationary tendencies.

Another undesirable result of a short-term debt structure is that the Treasury is forced into the market to refinance the debt at frequent intervals. This has complicated the task of the Federal Reserve in conducting monetary policy. Even in a period of credit restriction, the Fed must move cautiously when the Treasury is engaged in a refunding operation, to avoid jeopardizing the success of the Treasury's undertaking. With a short-term debt structure, these periods in which the Treasury is in the market come very frequently, and thus the Federal Reserve may often be forced to put off a particular policy action.

Some have gone so far as to suggest that the government should issue only perpetuities (British "consols").[1] Such instru-

[1] The word is short for *consolidated annuities*, first issued by the British government in 1751. *Webster's New Collegiate Dictionary* (Springfield, Mass.: G. & C. Merriam Co., 1977), p. 242.

ments have no maturity date. They merely specify that a given amount of interest will be paid periodically. The market determines the price of the instrument and hence the rate of interest it bears. If the government runs a surplus, it can always buy up its own debt on the open market, and thus perpetuities need not be perpetually outstanding. They could be held by individuals but would more likely be bought by financial institutions, which in turn would issue liabilities of the type and maturity the public chooses.

The problem with the issuance of long-term debt is that this is not the kind of claim the public wants, and financial institutions are not fully able to "intermediate" this problem away. Basically, lenders wish to lend short, borrowers to borrow long. This is the situation that prevails in the private economy, and if government issues long-term debt or perpetuities, it is merely compounding this problem. Government then is in direct competition with mortgage borrowers and corporations seeking funds for capital formation. Government could pay the required interest, but the real question is, How much should government borrowing interfere with capital formation? The political opposition from groups affected by long-term borrowing has tended to force the Treasury into short securities, which more nearly meet the desire of lenders. Congress has nudged this process still further by placing limits on the interest the Treasury can pay on longer-term obligations. The public can hold no more than $27 billion of marketable bonds issued at interest rates of more than 4¼ percent. Shorter-term securities (bills and notes) have no such limitation.

Because it meets the economy's needs, short-term government debt is rather easily marketed. Financial institutions, particularly commercial banks, use them to balance their portfolios because of their ready marketability. Corporations and others use them when they have liquidity positions that are short-term. A Treasury official responsible for the public debt stated:

> The market for Treasury securities is far more flexible and resilient than either we or the market itself had thought. . . . The Treasury has been able to finance enormous deficits with issues larger than anyone would have imagined possible and with a frequency of offering that would have seemed inconceivable only a short time ago.[2]

But not all sectors are spared if the Treasury issues short-term debt. Opposition comes from financial institutions. Treasury bills are a rather good substitute for deposits. To reduce its competitiveness with such institutions, the Treasury limits its sales of bills to

[2] Robert A. Gerard, speech before the Investment Analysts Society of Chicago, October 6, 1976.

those of $10,000 denomination (although notes can be purchased in smaller denominations). An individual can purchase new security issues directly from Federal Reserve Banks but must have some knowledge of the process or be quite persistent. The Treasury offers no encouragement.

HOLDERS OF TREASURY SECURITIES

The wide range of types of securities offered by the Treasury appeals to many types of investors. Table 12-1 shows the ownership of U.S. government securities at various dates. Table 12-2 shows a further breakdown in 1980 for financial institutions. Commercial banks were, for many years, the largest holders of such securities. In 1945, they held about one-third of all outstanding government securities, but they have reduced their holdings both relatively and absolutely over much of the postwar period as more attractive lending and investing opportunities arose. Also, as banks shifted to liability management during the 1960s, they needed fewer Treasury bills to serve as secondary reserves. Even during the postwar decline in commercial-bank holdings of government securities, periods of recession, when loan demand was slack, found banks adding to their holdings. Thus, commercial-bank ownership of government securities reached a post–World War II low of $55 billion in 1974, but weak loan demand and rapid deposit growth brought such holdings to $105 billion by 1976. Although this was larger than the 1945 figure, it represented a much smaller relative role for commercial banks as owners of government securities than they had in 1945.

At present, individual investors hold more government securities than any single type of financial institution. Most of the holdings of individual investors consist of savings bonds, but holdings of marketable issues have accounted for much of the variation in the role of individual investors in the government-securities market. Since the late 1960s, rates on government securities have been very attractive in relation to rates paid on savings accounts and time deposits by banks and other savings institutions. Despite the introduction of money-market certificates by depository institutions, holdings of marketable government securities by individuals tripled from 1975 to 1981, when they reached $72 billion.

Holdings of all types of government securities by foreign investors and institutions tripled between 1970 and 1974 and doubled between 1975 and 1980. This development has reflected changes in the international financial system, changes in the U.S. balance of payments, and rises in the price of imported oil. Some of these

TABLE 12-1

Ownership of U.S. Government Securities

(in billions of dollars)

Year-End	Total Gross Debt	United States Government	Federal Reserve Banks	Commercial Banks	Mutual Savings Banks	Insurance Companies	Other Corporations	State and Local Governments	Individuals	Foreigners	Other Investors
						Held by					
1941	64	10	2	21	4	8	4	1	14	—	1
1945	279	27	24	91	11	24	22	7	64	—	9
1950	257	39	21	62	11	19	21	9	67	—	10
1955	281	51	25	62	9	15	24	15	65	—	16
1960	290	55	27	62	6	12	20	18	66	—	24
1965	321	60	41	61	5	10	16	23	72	—	23
1970	389	97	62	63	3	7	9	25	92	21	19
1975	577	145	85	85	5	10	20	34	91	67	38
1976	654	150	94	104	6	13	27	42	101	78	41
1977	708	154	103	102	6	16	22	55	105	110	45
1978	789	170	116	95	5	16	20	64	111	138	58
1979	845	187	118	97	5	17	23	70	116	124	90
1980	930	193	121	116	5	20	26	79	129	128	107
1981 (Sept.)	998	208	124	112	6	21	38	86	140	136	127

Note: "Other Investors" includes savings and loan associations, dealers and brokers, pension funds, nonprofit institutions, and, until 1970, foreign accounts.

Source: Federal Reserve Bulletin.

TABLE 12-2

Nonbank Financial Institutions' Holdings of U.S. Government and Agency Securities
(year-end 1980, billions of dollars)

	Treasury Issues	Agency Issues
Savings and loan associations	5.5	41.2
Mutual savings banks	5.3	17.5
Credit unions	7.1	6.5
Life insurance companies	5.8	11.1
Private pension funds	24.1	6.7
Retirement funds, state and local government	18.0	18.0
Non-life insurance companies	14.2	7.3
Investment companies	1.9	0
Money-market funds	8.2	0
Securities brokers and dealers	5.2	0

Source: Federal Reserve Flow-of-Funds Accounts.

foreign holdings represent intergovernmental transactions. As a group, the foreign holdings represent somewhat different considerations from the domestic holdings, and these issues will be discussed in subsequent chapters.

THE MECHANICS OF FINANCING

The Treasury sells marketable debt to accommodate government deficits and to replace maturing securities. The price of securities (and thus the interest rate on them) is determined in the market. Once sold, securities continually turn over on the secondary market, and contracts for future delivery trade on interest futures markets.

The Primary Market

In offering securities on the primary market, the Treasury can follow two approaches: It may auction the issue, in which case the market determines the price, or it may set a rate, in which case the market may determine how much it takes at that rate. The auction method is always followed on Treasury bills, as discussed in Chapter 5, and increasingly it is the usual method used for other types of securities.

Marketable debt consists of bills, notes, and bonds. Bills are sold in minimum $10,000 denominations, with a maturity of one year or less. They carry no interest payments as such. The yield on the bill is the difference between its purchase price and its value at maturity. Notes have a maturity of one to ten years, and bonds may have any maturity. Other than maturities, there are no differences between bonds and notes. Both are issued with coupons, two for each year the bond will be outstanding. The coupon is redeemed for the semiannual interest payment and is set to the nearest eighth of a percent of the average issuing yield from bidding. The exact yield for any particular accepted bid is then effected by adjustment in the price of the security. The yield is calculated to hundredths of a percent. A buyer may submit a noncompetitive bid of up to $1 million and will acquire the security at the average of the competitive bids. The noncompetitive limit in a bill auction is $500,000.

About 40 percent of new issues are purchased by dealers in government securities, who largely purchase them for resale. There has always been some concern about the concentration of purchases among a relatively few bidders. There are some 40 government-securities dealers, and the top five account for about a third of the trading in these instruments. This is a considerable improvement over the situation two decades ago, when there were only 17 dealers and the top five accounted for half the trading activity.

The Secondary Market

Trading in the secondary market is over the counter, dominated by the dealers who report their activities to the Federal Reserve Bank of New York. During a typical day, dealers handle $20 billion of transactions on the secondary market. Designation as a dealer requires that the firm conduct business in all maturities, maintain inventories, take positions, and make markets (that is, buy and sell securities for its own account). Some of the firms designated as dealers are commercial banks.

About 95 percent of dealers' inventories are carried with borrowed money. Dealers actively seek funds all over the country to get the lowest possible interest rate. They attempt to earn more interest on their inventories than they pay on borrowed funds, and they sell securities at prices higher than they paid for them. These sources, rather than commissions, provide their income. Another group of firms—government-securities brokers—act as intermediaries, arranging transactions between dealers; brokers' importance has risen in recent years with the increase in number of dealers and in trading volume.

Prices on the secondary market are quoted in points (dollars) and 32nds of a point. Yields are quoted in percentages to hundredths of a percent. Differences in yields, such as movements in a day or differences between bid and asked, are often quoted in "basis points." A basis point is a hundredth of a percentage point.

There are no margin requirements specified by law on government securities, and it is possible for participants in the market to take large speculative positions. Wide swings in interest rates in recent years have increased the volume of trading as participants sought to gain from price movements.

Futures Markets

Contracts for future delivery of Treasury securities are traded on commodity exchanges in New York and Chicago. For bills, the contract is for $1 million par value. For bonds and notes, $100,000 units are traded. Margins are relatively low, no more than $2,500 per contract, depending upon the instrument and the duration of the contract. Different delivery months, up to two years in the future, are available. The contract calls for delivery at some specified time prior to the instrument's maturity. Most Treasury-bill contracts call for delivery of specific bills that at delivery will have 90–92 days to maturity. Traders expecting interest rates to fall will buy for future delivery. If the prediction is correct, securities prices will rise, and thus the purchased security can be resold at a higher price. The resale may be made at any time by an offsetting futures contract.

Trading in interest futures on organized exchanges began in 1976, and in five years, the daily trading had approached the daily volume on the spot market. Although speculation motivates most of the trading in the market, trading is also used by some to reduce risks. Financial institutions and securities dealers use the market to offset risks they may incur by holding a portfolio of securities.

The authorities are watching the futures market closely for its effect on securities prices. A Federal Reserve Bank of New York study noted:

> Both the enormous size of these futures markets and the nature of the participants are a matter of concern for the regulatory authorities. The Treasury and the Federal Reserve System have become aware of potential problems for the functioning of markets in Government securities; these problems include the possibility of corners or squeezes on certain Treasury issues and the disruption of orderly cash markets for Treasury securities. In addition, the regulatory authorities have become concerned that the substantial numbers of small investors participating in the markets may not be fully aware of the risks involved.[3]

---

[3] Marcelle Arak and Christopher J. McCurdy, "Interest Rate Futures," Federal Reserve Bank of New York *Quarterly Review*, Winter 1979–80, p. 33.

SAVINGS BONDS

Savings bonds are a special category of security available only to individuals; they constitute the largest share of individual holdings of government debt. The Treasury sells savings bonds to individuals directly or through financial institutions, at fixed interest rates. Small-denomination bonds (currently, Series EE) are sold at 50 percent of their maturity value. They pay no periodic interest, the return being the difference between the purchase price and the redemption value. Savings bonds that are not redeemed continue to rise in redemption value, the rise depending upon the prevailing rate on newly issued savings bonds. These automatic extensions of the bonds do not continue beyond 40 years, and thus World War II bonds came up for redemption or exchange during this decade.

Larger-denomination bonds (currently, series HH) are sold at their maturity value, and they make semiannual interest payments. None of the series can be sold on the open market, but a holder who wants cash may turn in the bond to the Treasury for redemption. No one person can purchase more than $15,000 worth of savings bonds in a year (based on purchase price). In World War II, the limit was $5,000.

Savings bonds were introduced in 1935. The purpose of the original issuance was to encourage thrift and to "democratize public finance." The real growth of savings bonds took place during World War II, when the Treasury aggressively promoted their sale. After the war, sales slackened and redemptions increased as holders cashed in their bonds to buy consumer goods that were unavailable during the war. By 1951, the Treasury was paying out more on redemptions than it took in from new sales. The value of savings bonds outstanding continued to increase, however, owing to the continued growth of accrued interest on the outstanding bonds, until it peaked in 1978. In 1981, $68 billion was outstanding.

Obviously, sales and redemptions of savings bonds are greatly affected by the relation between the rate paid on such bonds and rates paid on alternative means of holding savings. In setting rates, the Treasury is constrained by the problems posed for financial institutions if it attempts to aggressively compete with them for savings. Series EE bonds have some advantages over savings deposits, but these are relatively minor and apt to be outweighed by the disadvantages. The holder of a series EE savings bond need not pay tax on the interest on the bond until it is redeemed. Also, the discount basis on which such bonds are sold makes them attractive for gifts. How else can you give a $50 graduation present for only $25? A significant disadvantage of the savings bond is the fact that if it is redeemed early, there is a sizable interest penalty.

Savings-bond rates move up with market rates, but rather sluggishly. In 1957, the rate of interest paid on savings bonds was increased from 3 to 3¼ percent, and over the years, several other increases have brought the rate to its current 9 percent if held to maturity.

The sensitivity of sales to market interest rates poses some problems for the Treasury. It is in periods of tight money, when the Treasury is having its problems selling marketable securities, that sales fall off and redemptions increase. The Treasury's job would probably be more difficult if savings bonds were a bigger share of the total debt than they are now.

Purchasing-Power Bonds

The most sweeping proposal made regarding savings bonds is the suggested issuance of "purchasing-power bonds." These would be bonds whose maturity value was tied to some price index, such as the Consumer Price Index. The intent of such issuance would be that the bonds would maintain their *real* value in the face of rising prices. They would provide people with a means of saving that would be protected against the erosion of the value of the dollar. Noting the advantages to small savers, Richard Musgrave, an early proponent of such bonds, has commented:

> Given these advantages, it is difficult to see why such bonds have not been issued. Perhaps the explanation lies in the fact that it is difficult for the Treasury to admit uncertainties regarding the value of the dollar, or because it would generate pressure for similar escalation clauses in the rest of the economy.[4]

But is it proper or feasible for the government to guarantee some given amount of real goods in the future? Such future availability cannot be known. If supplies were to become extremely limited—say, by a major war—could or should such bonds be honored? Even in the absence of such a serious reversal, the bonds might still cause an undesirable distribution of available goods. Rising prices are one way that falling productivity manifests itself, and a purchasing-power bond seeks to override these changes in available goods.

A somewhat similar principle was introduced into the Social Security system when benefits were made to rise automatically with prices. As inflation rose at a greater rate than incomes, Social Security taxes had to be raised to cause a greater share of real income to be transferred from the work force to the retired.

---

[4] Richard Musgrave and Peggy Musgrave, *Public Finance in Theory and Practice*, 2d ed. (New York: McGraw-Hill, 1976), p. 599.

Given recent rates of inflation, it is difficult to conceive of the magnitude of demand for purchasing-power bonds. The amounts that any one person could purchase would probably have to be limited. With sufficiently small limits, the program might be manageable, but then its effect would be relatively slight.

The 1981 tax-reduction law introduced for the federal tax code price indexation of income taxes. Although this is a major move in the direction of indexation, it is still quite a different principle from that of purchasing-power bonds. Even though indexed, the tax rate still remains at the discretion of the government. Any automatic downward drift in rates can always be compensated for by a discretionary increase in all rates. A purchasing-power bond would be a one-time contract by government that it could not overturn.

STATE AND LOCAL GOVERNMENT FINANCING

State and local governments have financing problems that differ from those of the federal government. The federal debt is much larger than the debts of all the states and municipal governments combined, but the latter have been growing at a steady and rapid rate. In each of the years 1978 through 1980, state and local governments raised more than $40 billion in the securities markets. Table 12-3 shows a breakdown of the use of the proceeds of these issues. More than half the funds are used for two categories of expenditures: social welfare, and utilities and conservation.

Despite their rapid expansion of borrowing, there is still a backlog of unmet needs for additional capital spending by these government units. It is true that the slowing of population growth has reduced the need for new schools in some areas, but needs still exist for highways, sewers, urban renewal, and rapid-transit systems. Even with population growth slowing in the aggregate, shifts in population from rural to urban areas, or urban to suburban, or Snowbelt to Sunbelt, require large expenditures to provide necessary facilities for the increased population of those areas. The volume of state and local government debt is sure to continue to rise.

Tax Exemption

The unique aspect of financing by state and local governments is that interest on their securities is not subject to federal income taxes. Their bonds (known as *municipal bonds*) thus have a particular appeal to investors in high tax brackets. For an investor in a 50 percent marginal tax bracket, a 7 percent return on a municipal

TABLE 12-3
New Security Issues of State and Local Governments
(millions of dollars)

Type of Issue or Issuer, or Use	1978	1979	1980
All issues, new and refunding	48,607	43,490	48,462
Type of issue			
General obligation	17,854	12,109	14,100
Revenue	30,658	31,256	34,267
U.S. government loans	95	125	95
Type of issuer			
State	6,632	4,314	5,304
Special district and statutory authority	24,156	23,434	26,972
Municipalities, counties, townships, school districts	17,718	15,617	16,090
Issues for new capital, total	37,629	41,505	46,736
Use of proceeds			
Education	5,003	5,130	4,572
Transportation	3,460	2,441	2,621
Utilities and conservation	9,026	8,594	8,149
Social welfare	10,494	15,968	19,958
Industrial aid	3,526	3,836	3,974
Other purposes	6,120	5,536	7,462

Source: *Federal Reserve Bulletin*, April 1981.

bond is better than a 12 percent yield on a (fully taxable) corporate or U.S. government bond. This explains why commercial banks find municipal bonds attractive investments, whereas financial institutions not subject to full corporate tax rates, such as life insurance companies and pension funds, do not.

This tax-exemption feature originated when there was concern about the legality of the federal government's taxation of such interest. Now there is little doubt that the federal government can constitutionally impose taxes on the interest, but the provision remains. Critics of this provision consider it a tax loophole for the wealthy investor, but defenders argue that it is a form of indirect subsidy to state and local governments (without the tax exemption, these governments would have to pay considerably higher interest rates to sell their securities), and that this type of subsidy is desirable.

The subsidy argument has validity, but there have been many efforts to develop an approach to municipal finance that would retain the subsidy to states and municipalities while eliminating the windfall to wealthy investors. Legislation has been under consideration for several years that would allow municipalities to choose whether to issue taxable or nontaxable securities. If they chose to sell taxable securities, the federal government would subsidize a portion of the interest cost (one-third is the most common figure cited). Supporters of this proposal argue that the Treasury would come out ahead, because it would receive tax payments from the buyers of the securities, but critics (and some supporters) of the plan believe that the proposal would cost the Treasury more than it would gain. Some supporters believe elimination of what they consider to be an inequitable tax loophole is desirable even if it costs the Treasury some money to do it.

The "windfall" aspect of the tax exemption has increased as the volume of state and local debt has increased. At one time, the volume of such debt was small enough that it could be absorbed by investors in relatively high tax brackets, who would bid the yields down to low levels. Now the volume of tax-exempts is so large that selling them must tap investors in tax brackets below 50 percent. If an issue of municipal bonds is priced to appeal to an investor in a 40 percent tax bracket, it must generate a very high effective after-tax yield to an investor in a 50 percent bracket. Regardless of the fate of the legislation described above, it is likely that some manner of restricting the tax-exempt feature of municipal bonds will be enacted sometime in the future.

Selling Municipal Securities

Once a municipality decides that it must raise a specified amount of money through a bond issue of specified maximum maturity, the issue is typically sold via competitive bidding to investment-banking firms. The state or municipality advertises the issue in local and financial papers so that any bond house that might be interested in bidding for it is notified. Each interested bond dealer submits a sealed bid for the issue.

At the time and place specified in the newspaper notices, the bids are opened and the bonds awarded to the highest bidder. The municipality always has the right to reject all bids if it is felt that they are not high enough. The winning investment-banking firm or bank then tries to resell the bonds at a higher price to the public.

As Table 12-3 shows, bonds are classed as general-obligation bonds or revenue bonds. General-obligation (GO) bonds are backed by the "full faith and credit" of the issuing government, and revenue bonds are backed only by the earnings of a particular project or agency of the government. Revenue bonds are issued by, for example, local water departments, electric power departments, and toll-road or tollbridge authorities, and the state or local government involved is not responsible for any of these obligations. New issues of revenue bonds exceed those of GO bonds, and their relative importance has increased in recent years.

Most state and local bond issues have relatively long maturities, but the maturity is generally based on the life of the project being financed. The most common repayment provision on municipal securities involves *serial bonds*. With this technique, some of the bonds come due each year. Thus, of a $10-million bond issue, $500,000 of the bonds may come due each year for 20 years. This allows investors to choose the maturity that best fits their needs. Generally, the long-term maturities bear higher interest rates.

Traditionally, most state and local government debt issues have been long-term. However, many government units have always done some short-term borrowing. Many cities, particularly, receive the bulk of their tax revenues (mainly from real estate taxes) at one time of year. The city or town that receives most of its taxes in, say, October, may find itself running short of cash in September. In such a situation, the town may issue short-term *tax-anticipation* notes. Because of the general high quality and short maturity of such notes, as well as the tax exemption, commercial banks have been the traditional investors in such issues.

In recent years, there has been a very substantial increase in the volume of short-term financing by state and local governments. There have been a variety of reasons for this new trend, some of which may prove temporary. During periods of very high interest rates, a local government may be unwilling to borrow long-term and commit itself to paying high interest rates for many years to come. Some issuers of tax-exempt securities have found it profitable to borrow short-term and invest the proceeds in U.S. government securities paying higher rates (although the law now restricts the opportunities for such arbitrage). Another reason for the increase in short-term borrowing has been the inability of some cities to borrow long-term on terms that they consider acceptable.

A Crisis of the Cities?

Although defaults on municipal bonds have occurred from time to time, the default of the New York Urban Development Corporation in 1975 and the subsequent problems of New York City were a traumatic shock to the municipal market. As a study by the Joint Economic Committee put it:

> The emergence of the New York City crisis and related credit crises in New York State brought from the cellar of neglect the question of municipal bond credit quality. Since

the Great Depression, few analysts have devoted much time or effort to the financial health of State and local governments or their ability to support debt.[5]

The federal government ultimately alleviated the New York crisis by guaranteeing loans made to the city. But problems have arisen in other cities, and one effect on the whole municipal market has been an increase in yields relative to corporate or U.S. government securities.[6] Other large older cities, such as Boston, Newark, Philadelphia, and Detroit, experienced difficulty in selling securities in the aftermath of the New York default (and default it was, in economic if not in legal terms).

A survey by the Joint Economic Committee found that half the cities had deficits in both fiscal years 1979 and 1980. Neither expenditures nor revenues were keeping up with the rate of inflation, and pressure for more expenditures was coming from employee groups seeking cost-of-living increases. Large-scale unemployment in the Detroit automobile industry threatened that city's financial condition, and Boston schools were threatened with closure after voters enacted property-tax limitations. The "taxpayer revolt," which started with a property-tax-limitation ballot measure in California in 1978, is a continuing problem hanging over the market for municipal bonds, which derive their main support from real estate taxes.

The Market for State and Local Government Securities

The demand for state and local government securities is dominated, of course, by tax considerations. This has led high-tax-bracket individuals to play a major role in the market. Commercial banks, subject to taxation at full corporate rates, have long been the major financial institution in the market, whereas life insurance companies, for example, taxed at lower rates, have not had much interest in the market.

Two major changes in the market seem to have occurred in recent years. First, commercial banks found other means of reducing their tax burdens, and for a while in the 1970s did not add to their municipal-bond holdings in significant amounts. Fortunately, at about the same time, the second change occurred: The law al-

---

[5] *Changing Conditions in the Market for State and Local Government Debt* (Washington, D.C.: U.S. Government Printing Office, 1976), p. 23.

[6] One beneficial aspect of this experience has been an increased emphasis on, and the supplying of, better information on the financial condition of municipalities seeking to raise money in the financial markets.

lowed mutual funds to invest in tax-exempt securities and pass the tax exemption along to their stockholders. This change in the law led to the establishment of a large number of mutual funds designed to invest in state and local government securities. Investors in these funds are able to gain diversification in their municipal-bond investments, and also to hold a more liquid asset. Mutual-fund shares can be sold easily, whereas small holdings of most municipal bonds are not actively traded and hence are not very liquid.

As yields on municipal bonds rose in the latter half of the 1970s, commercial banks regained their interest, and in 1980 they added almost $14 billion to their holdings. Yields have also attracted non-life insurance companies, most of which give greater weight to tax considerations than do the mutual life companies. Nonlife companies now rank second, behind commercial banks, as holders of state and local government securities (see Table 12-4).

THE BORROWER'S PROBLEMS

We have seen, in Chapters 9 to 12, that all borrowers face problems in raising the money they need. The automobile buyer may feel that she is in a particularly disadvantageous position in financing her new car. The small businessman may feel that his financing problems are particularly acute. But all borrowers face some difficulties. Even the government of the United States has complained about the difficulty of raising long-term funds.

TABLE 12-4
Ownership of State and Local Government Securities, 1970 and 1980
(year-end data, billions of dollars)

	1970	1980
Households	46.0	69.7
Nonfinancial corporate business	2.2	3.4
State and local government		
General funds	2.4	8.8
Retirement funds	2.0	4.1
Commercial banking	70.2	149.2
Savings and loan associations	0.1	1.2
Mutual savings banks	0.2	2.4
Insurance companies		
Life	3.3	6.7
Nonlife	17.0	83.6
Brokers and dealers	0.9	1.1
Total	144.4	330.1

Source: Federal Reserve Flow-of-Funds Accounts.

The financial markets are pretty competitive. Bond buyers are a cold-blooded lot—emotions must be ignored if one is to be a successful investor in this area. Investors do not buy government bonds (other than in wartime) out of a spirit of patriotism; they buy them when they appear to be the best investment available.

The meaning of these considerations is clear: The borrower must make his securities attractive to the market, either by offering terms that are desired by investors or by paying the rates that the market considers compensation for the risks and costs of the investment. All borrowers face this same marketing problem, although, of course, to differing degrees.

QUESTIONS

1 Compare the growth of the federal debt with the total debt of American Telephone and Telegraph. Which has been growing more rapidly?
2 Is there any good reason for an individual to buy U.S. savings bonds?
3 How would government issuance of purchasing-power bonds affect financial institutions?
4 Is federal debt inflationary? Is state and local debt inflationary?
5 What is the role of bond dealers in Treasury financing?
6 What would be the effect on financial institutions if the entire government debt were paid off?
7 "The size of the federal debt is no problem, because we only owe it to ourselves." Appraise this statement.
8 "The federal debt is a huge burden that we are leaving to our grandchildren." Appraise this statement. Is this more or less correct than the preceding statement?
9 Should local government bonds be exempt from federal income tax?

SELECTED READINGS

DAVIE, BRUCE, and BRUCE DUNCOMBE, *Public Finance*. New York: Holt, Rinehart & Winston, 1972.

Financing State and Local Governments. Boston: Federal Reserve Bank of Boston, 1970.

LINDOW, WESLEY, *Inside the Money Market*, Chap. 8. New York: Random House, 1972.

POWERS, MARK, *Inside the Financial Futures Markets*. New York: John Wiley, 1981.

RESLER, DAVID, and RICHARD W. LANG, "Federal Agency Debt: Another Side of Federal Borrowing," Federal Reserve Bank of St. Louis *Review*, November 1979.

13

International Financing

Financing does not stop at national boundaries, but there is no distinct line separating inter- and intranational financing. Activities of multinational corporations are not easily assigned to any one geographical area. Americans lend abroad and they borrow abroad, and in the process, Americans borrow from Americans through international channels.

The American role in international finance is unique in the world, because the U.S. dollar serves as a type of international money. Dollars are the unit of accounting for many international transactions, and dollars are also the payments media, even for transactions in which the United States is not a direct party. The American dollar became the unchallenged international money following World War II. It was the only currency that governments could hold and convert to gold, but the cessation of gold convertibility in 1971 did not topple the dollar as an international money. The governor of the Bank of Greece told an international monetary meeting in 1979:

> One fact has clearly been established and repeatedly stated in this forum: The dollar is, and will continue in the coming years to be, the pillar of the international money system. This implies that, when the dollar is strong, the international money system is

in a stable state. Conversely, when the dollar is weak, the international monetary system is destabilized.[1]

A Federal Reserve Bank of New York review of the U.S. international position in the postwar years noted that two-thirds of international lending is still denominated in dollars. The continued dominance of the dollar was attributed to the freedom of access that the United States allows to its financial markets as compared to other countries, which were reluctant to give up controls used in the postwar recovery.

> Even those countries which were most devoted to market principles still maintained informal controls over foreign access to their financial markets. . . . Experience suggests, it is true, that such controls rarely succeed in attaining their full objectives. Nevertheless, they probably did divert a significant proportion of the demand for international capital to the huge and freely accessible dollar markets.[2]

Foreign borrowers consistently raise more funds in U.S. credit markets than do U.S. state and local governments. International monetary flows involving U.S. banks grew at an astounding rate in the last decade. In the period 1965–1969, U.S. banks increased their foreign claims each year by $100 million. In the years 1978 through 1980, these increases averaged $30 billion annually. U.S. banks (including their foreign branches) reported $382 billion of claims on foreigners in 1981, a gain of 90 percent over 1976.

OIL AND PETRODOLLARS

One of the strange by-products of the oil price rises of the 1970s was an enlarged role of the dollar and American banking, as oil-exporting countries reinvested their earnings in the importing countries. In 1980, all countries of the Organization of Petroleum Exporting Countries combined took in $110 billion more from their sales abroad than they spent on imported goods. In essence, the OPEC countries were lending that amount to the rest of the world to buy their oil.

At the time of the OPEC price increase, there were fears that the international financial system would not be able to stand the strain of these massive flows of funds. Concern was expressed that

---

[1] Xenophon Zolotas, "Inflation, the Dollar and the Foreign Exchange Markets," *Papers and Lectures 46* (Athens: Bank of Greece, 1981), p. 33.

[2] Stephen V.O. Clarke, "Perspective on the United States External Position since World War II," Federal Reserve Bank of New York *Quarterly Review*, Summer 1980, p. 29.

the huge amounts of "petrodollars"—dollars earned from the export of oil—held by the oil-exporting countries could be used to disrupt and even to destroy the banking systems of the Western world. Although the oil price increase did have substantial real effects, involving a reduction in real income in developed countries and particularly in the non-oil-producing LDCs, the financial effects do not seem to have created substantial problems. The banking systems of the world seem to have been able to handle the financial flows involved in "recycling" the oil revenues. Let us see how that has been done.

In discussing matters of this sort, we tend sometimes to be misled by the terminology. We speak, for example, of the huge dollar "outflows" involved in paying for oil imports. This conjures up images of neat stacks of dollar bills (or rather of hundred-dollar bills) placed in attaché cases and carried off to the desert by Arab sheiks. But it does not really happen that way. We pay for the imported oil by writing checks on American banks. The oil-exporting country now has ownership of this demand deposit in place of the previous American owner. What can the new owner do with this demand deposit? He can spend it, but that simply means that ownership of the demand deposit is now transferred to someone else. As we have seen earlier, the spending of a demand deposit does not affect either the reserves or the total deposits of the American financial system. It is true that the individual banks may experience significant gains or losses of deposits, but there will be no net change for the banking system as a whole. If the spending being done by the oil-exporting country is for American goods, then those additional U.S. exports are a help in restoring our balance-of-payments position.

What if the oil exporter distrusts the U.S. dollar and wants instead to hold gold? He can convert his dollar holdings into gold, but again our terminology is somewhat misleading. He cannot really find an alchemist who possesses the magical ability to change dollar bills into bars of gold. What can be done, of course, is to buy gold with the dollar deposit. But in that case, the seller of the gold now owns the demand deposit and, once again, the reserve and deposit position of the American banking system is unchanged. The same is true if the oil exporter wishes to convert his dollar holdings into some other currency. He is able to do so by buying Swiss francs or British pounds with his dollars, and the seller of the francs or pounds ends up owning the deposit account in the U.S. bank.

This discussion does not mean to imply that the gigantic payments by the United States to the oil-exporting countries is not a real problem, or that these payments do not represent a real cost. If the OPEC oil revenues are spent on U.S. goods, then we have given up additional real resources—goods and services that it took American labor and materials to produce—in exchange for the oil. If the oil exporter sells dollars to buy another currency, this has the effect of reducing the value of the dollar in foreign-exchange markets, thereby increasing the cost of all foreign goods we buy. We are certainly poorer as a result of the higher price of oil. But the mechanics of handling the financial flows can be, and have been, easily accommodated by our banking system.

A more serious problem of recycling petrodollars concerns the less-developed countries. The OPEC countries have a strong preference for reinvestment in developed countries. About half their surplus is put into the banking system and another fourth into securities in the industrial countries. The LDCs without oil have been hard hit by the increase in the price of oil. They have not been able to generate sufficient revenues from their own resources to pay their greatly increased oil bills, and have been forced to borrow. Some of the borrowing has been from the oil-exporting countries, some from international financial institutions, and some from the governments of the developed countries. But much has come from the commercial banks in the industrialized countries. There is reason for concern about the ability of the poor LDCs to repay this debt and, if they are not able or willing to do so, reason for concern about the effect on those banks that are heavily exposed in this type of lending activity. Of course, part of the reason this has become a problem is the smoothness and swiftness with which the world's commercial-banking system moved to make financing available to the LDCs. Without this type of accommodation, several countries would have experienced even more severely the consequences of the oil price increase. A major feature of this accommodation was a system of dollar deposits outside the United States, called "Eurodollars."

EURODOLLARS AND EUROCURRENCY

Banks outside the United States (including foreign branches of U.S. banks) issue deposits denominated in U.S. dollars. Regardless of the location of the bank, these deposits are called Eurodollars. The Eurodollar market is part of a Eurocurrency market, since other monetary units ("currencies") may also be used in the issue of deposits in other than the currency of the country in which the bank is located. About three-fourths of all Eurocurrency accounts are in dollars, with the remainder in German, Swiss, and Japanese currencies.

The Eurodollar is not a separate monetary unit from other dollars. Ultimately, it is claims on the Federal Reserve that are being traded. The mechanics of the market do not differ greatly from those of domestic transactions. It is a market in which dollars are borrowed short and lent long. The borrowing bank receives claims on the Federal Reserve and then lends these out, resulting in dollar assets matching its dollar liabilities. The deposit issued is a short-term time deposit. It may be as short as overnight, and almost all such deposits are less than six months to maturity. Eurodollar loans are short- and medium-term (three to five years). Dollars are not being "created" in this process any more than they are when a domestic institution issues time deposits and uses the proceeds to buy assets.

The Eurodollar certificate of deposit is slightly higher in yield than certificates bought in New York. For example, in November 1981, three-month certificates in New York carried an average rate of 12.60 percent, and those in the Euromarket 13.80 percent.

Banks also borrow and lend among themselves in the Euromarket, just as they do domestically in the Federal-funds market. The center of interbank transactions is London, and the interest rate on interbank lending, the London Interbank Offer Rate (LIBOR), is the basis on which banks compute their ultimate lending rate on dollar loans to customers. Lenders (depositors) on the Euromarket are primarily from industrial countries, but those from OPEC countries have greatly increased in importance. Only the banks involved in the transactions are identified. The ultimate lenders—the banks' customers—are not reported.

With respect to borrowers from the market, governments and various types of government bodies predominate, although there is also private-sector borrowing to finance trade. The larger medium-term loans are syndicated among a number of banks. As oil-importing countries borrow on the market, the effect is that the oil-exporting countries, unwilling to run trade credit with their buyers, are doing so indirectly by lending to the Eurodollar market.

The net size of the Eurocurrency market is difficult to measure because of extensive interbank transactions, but gross Eurocurrency liabilities outstanding are estimated at almost $1 trillion. U.S. banks have foreign branches that are very active in the Eurodollar market. At year-end 1980, these foreign branches held $300 billion of liabilities denominated in dollars. Some of the activity of the Eurodollar market is not truly international in character. Branches are used to effect transactions that would otherwise flow through the parent bank as domestic transactions. Imposition of reserve requirements on Eurodollar liabilities of domestic banks (and on

loans to U.S. customers) has prevented use of this device to evade
reserve requirements, but there are still other matters, such as
taxes, that motivate an international route of transmission.

Tax policies of the Bahamas have contributed toward making
Nassau a major Eurodollar center. The absence of time-zone differences, and other features of the market have made overnight
deposits at Caribbean branches so liquid that they have been included in some definitions of the U.S. domestic money supply, as
discussed in Chapter 19. Referring to Nassau, a Federal Reserve
Bank of New York study commented:

> The offshore Eurodollar market is dominated by United States money center banks, who
> in fact conduct ther business out of their headquarters in New York, Chicago, or Cali-
> fornia and simply book loans and deposits to their Caribbean branches—which are
> commonly shell branches rather than ordinary full-service ones.[3]

THE BALANCE OF PAYMENTS

The balance of payments of a country is a systematic record over a
period of all economic transactions completed between its residents
and the rest of the world. Each transaction is classed as a debit or
a credit. Exports are credits, for example, and imports are debits.
Table 13-1 shows selected U.S. balance-of-payments flows for 1980.

Although the balance of payments as a whole must balance,
various parts of it may not be in balance. The usual position of the
U.S. trade account has been surplus, which means that the nation
is lending abroad.[4] This is the only way that net lending can take
place. Without a goods flow, any lending is necessarily matched by
borrowing. Thus, a creditor nation is a surplus nation, a debtor
nation is a deficit nation. The rise in imported oil prices eroded the
U.S. position as a creditor nation, and now, when viewed over an
entire business cycle, the U.S. trade position is roughly in balance.

Our balance of payments includes *all* international economic
transactions, not just those involving exchange of goods and services. *Unilateral transfers* play an important role in the U.S. balance of payments. These include U.S. government grants to other
countries, pensions paid to people living abroad, private remit-
tances to family abroad, and private charitable contributions.

---

[3] Edward J. Frydl, "The Debate over Regulating the Eurocurrency Markets,"
Federal Reserve Bank of New York *Quarterly Review*, Winter 1979–80, p. 20.

[4] Also sometimes called a "favorable" trade balance. The use of this term goes
back to seventeenth-century economists and is not very meaningful. There is nothing necessarily desirable or favorable about the situation in which foreigners are
getting more of our goods than we are getting of theirs.

TABLE 13-1

Selected Balance-of-Payments Flows,
United States, 1980 (billions of dollars)

	Outflows	Inflows
Trade	340.6	365.6
Direct investment	13.1	14.3
Corporate equities	—	5.7
Bonds (excluding U.S. government)	5.3	4.7
Net interbank claims	—	3.0
U.S. official reserves[a]	3.3	—

[a] Gold, SDRs, and official foreign-exchange holdings.

Source: Federal Reserve Flow-of-Funds Accounts.

The portion of the balance of payments most relevant to the financial system is called the *capital account*. (This is where Eurodollar and other banking-system flows are entered.) The capital account consists of changes in claims on foreigners and liabilities to foreigners. An increase in claims is called a capital outflow. Look upon it in the same way you would an import; you can buy a Volkswagen abroad, or buy a German bond. An increase in liabilities to foreigners is a capital inflow. Look upon it as having the same effect from an accounting standpoint as an export; you can sell tractors to foreigners, or sell them shares of International Harvester.

Since all transactions are included in the accounting, and everything must be paid for in some way, the debits and credits cancel out. Suppose that in some short period, the only thing that occurs is the purchase of a Volkswagen, paid for from an American bank account. The VW is an import (debit), and the rise in deposit liabilities to foreigners is a credit. What about the balance if America gives wheat to India? The export is a credit. The debit is the offsetting entry, "unilateral transfers." Suppose we give away money? In this case, unilateral transfers are offset by a rise in money liabilities to foreigners.

In the capital account, a separation is made between "direct investment" and financial-type flows. In direct investment, Americans acquire assets that are used as part of American firms' operations or are a part of a controlling interest in a foreign company. An American firm's construction of a plant abroad is an obvious case of direct investment. As would be expected for a large industrial nation, the United States has had significantly more direct-investment outflows in the postwar period than it has had inflows. These outflows reached $24 billion in 1979, but fell off in the recession of 1980-81. Direct-investment inflows to the United States have been increasing at a greater rate than outflows, and 1981 was the first year in which they exceeded direct investment outflows (see Table 13.1). These inflows have been related to the increased pace of industrialization abroad and the expanding scale of operation of these foreign companies. Some fears have been raised about increased foreign ownership of American interests, but good data are hard to come by. The Agricultural Foreign Investment Disclosure Act of 1978 required foreign owners to report certain land holdings, and only ½ percent of American agricultural land was reported under foreign ownership.

Purchase of foreign securities by private U.S. residents is relatively small, averaging less than $5 billion annually, 1977–1980. Private foreigners' purchases of American securities have been slightly more, but there is a near balance. (As reported above, banking flows have been much larger and are not included in the data on securities.)

Governments are also involved in the capital account, but their flows, including the purchase of U.S. government securities, arise from different considerations from those in the private sector. Government involvement is directly associated with the foreign-exchange market.

THE FOREIGN-EXCHANGE MARKET

If I want to buy an English bicycle, I expect to pay in dollars—the only kind of money I have. The British manufacturer expects to be paid in pounds—the only kind of money he can use to pay his employees. If the transaction is to be successfully completed, there must be some mechanism by which my dollars can be converted into pounds sterling. This conversion process is carried out through the functioning of the foreign-exchange market.

If everyone were confident that the pound would always have the same dollar value and vice versa, this aspect of international trade would cause no more concern than the need to convert a dollar bill into change to operate a vending machine. The real problem of the foreign-exchange market is that no one can be absolutely certain how much the dollar will be worth, in terms of foreign currencies, from one day to the next. This will depend upon market forces at the time and upon government policy with respect to the exchange rate.

The price of one currency in terms of another is called the *rate of exchange*. If the number of Japanese yen required to buy $1 rises, then the American dollar is said to *appreciate*. If the number of Japanese yen per dollar falls, then the dollar *depreciates*. A country's rate of exchange plays a fundamental role in its overall economic equilibrium. There is a two-way relationship: Changes in the domestic economy affect the exchange rate, and changes in the exchange rate work back on the domestic economy. A rise in the foreign-exchange value of a country's money will, for example, tend to make its exports more expensive (in terms of foreign money) and its imports cheaper (in terms of domestic money). Some producers may be adversely affected by the fall in demand for exports and goods that compete with imports. As consumers, the population benefits by the improvement in the terms of trade—the real imports that can be obtained in exchange for a given amount of exports.

Prices of currencies are determined as currencies are bought and sold on the foreign-exchange market (see Figure 13-1). As the purchaser of an English bicycle, I want to obtain British pounds and am willing to sell dollars in order to do so. Why should anyone want to sell pounds for my dollars? One good prospect may be the American who has sold cotton to a British importer. He may be paid in pounds, which he cannot use to pay his expenses, and may be very

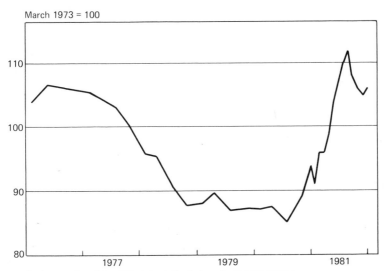

Exchange value of the U.S. dollar is the index of weighted-average exchange value of the U.S. dollar against currencies of other Group of Ten countries plus Switzerland using 1972-76 total trade weights.

FIGURE 13.1 Trade-weighted exchange value of the dollar

Source: Federal Reserve *Bulletin*, May 1981

willing to exchange his pounds for my dollars. As one authority has put it:

> In the course of their business, exporters collect foreign currency which they cannot use and therefore must exchange for domestic funds. Importers who start with a supply of domestic currency seek to acquire foreign currency in order to buy goods abroad. The unacceptability of foreign money for exports is the basis for a market in which foreign moneys are bought and sold. This is called the foreign exchange market.[5]

Commercial banks are the most important institutions operating in the foreign-exchange market. The large New York banks have a predominant role in this activity, and a small number of U.S. banks maintain deposits abroad to facilitate their foreign-exchange operations. In addition, there are many foreign banks maintaining branches or agencies in New York that deal in foreign exchange.

The New York banks are the link between the market and the ultimate supplier or demander of foreign exchange. On any given day, some of the customers of a large New York bank will ask for foreign currencies. These customers may be American importers who must pay for foreign goods, tourists who plan a trip abroad, or investors who want to purchase foreign securities. The bank will also find that some customers seek to convert holdings of foreign currency into dollars. If demand and supply of foreign currencies by the bank's customers should exactly balance, the bank does not have to engage in any transactions with other institutions. It has simply acted as a clearinghouse for its customers.

Such an exact balancing would, of course, be extremely rare. If the difference is small, the bank may be willing to end the day with slightly smaller or larger holdings of foreign exchange than those held at the beginning of the day. A bank facing an imbalance may seek to arrange purchases or sales of foreign currencies with other New York banks or with the foreign agencies.

All offers to buy or sell foreign currencies have an effect on the price of the foreign currency. Therefore, a bank must have contact with the market simply for the purpose of setting a price on a transaction with a customer. Since much of the business is conducted over the telephone, the customer has the opportunity to shop around among several banks to get the best price before arranging the deal. An official of the Federal Reserve Bank of New York has pointed out:

> It should not be thought . . . that trading in the New York market follows a neat and

---

[5] Charles P. Kindleberger, *International Economics*, rev. ed. (Homewood, Ill.: Richard D. Irwin, Inc., 1958), p. 44.

orderly pattern whereby New York banks first trade with their commercial customers, then utilize the interbank market to dispose of any net accumulation of exchange or to make up any deficiency, and finally have recourse to their foreign branches and correspondents if they are not successful in meeting their needs in New York. In actual practice, everything happens at once. Each bank trader is confronted by a constant flow of offers of, and bids for, foreign exchange not only from commercial interests, but also from other banks through the interbank market and by cable from foreign banks. As he sells exchange he must buy in order to make delivery, and as he buys he must sell in order not to accumulate balances. And through it all the exchange rate (the price of the commodity in which he deals) is being pushed first one way, then the other, by the changing balance of all the forces that make up supply and demand in the market.[6]

Thus, the private institutions operating the foreign-exchange market include the large commercial banks, foreign-exchange brokers, and foreign bank agencies, as well as exporters, importers, and investors. In addition, many government authorities are occasionally active in the market. In this country, the Treasury and the Federal Reserve engage in foreign-exchange operations, and many foreign central banks are quite active in the market for their currencies and for dollars.

There is, of course, no organized exchange on which trading takes place. The foreign-exchange market is an over-the-counter or over-the-telephone market. The smaller banks, which do not participate directly in the market, can carry out transactions for their customers through correspondent relationships with one or more of the large New York banks. Despite the absence of an organized physical exchange, it is logical to regard New York as the center of the foreign-exchange market, at least for the United States. London, Paris, Zurich, Frankfurt, and other financial centers are an important part of this market, and there is activity in some currencies in other U.S. cities, such as Boston, Chicago, Philadelphia, and San Francisco, which is particularly important in the trading of Oriental currencies.

These other cities cannot be considered as separate foreign-exchange markets. With the speed of modern communications, all the financial centers of the world are closely linked together. Probably more transactions of pounds for dollars take place in London than in New York, and more transactions in Canadian and U.S. dollars in Toronto. The prices in all international financial centers are virtually identical, however.

If, for example, the pound is selling for $2.20¼ in New York and for $2.20½ in London, one can make a profit by simultaneously

---

[6] Alan Holmes, *The New York Foreign Exchange Market* (New York: Federal Reserve Bank of New York, 1959), p. 13. This 54-page booklet presents an excellent description of the organization and operation of the market.

buying pounds in London and selling them in New York. This would tend to increase the demand for pounds (= supply of dollars) in London and to increase the supply of pounds (= demand for dollars) in New York. Both these effects would tend to push the prices in New York and London closer together. This transaction is called *arbitrage*. The arbitrageur is not a speculator—he takes no risk, except for a few moments, for he has no position in pounds. This profit is such a sure thing, in fact, that opportunities for it rarely exist, and the price of pounds in terms of dollars is always the same in New York, London, Paris, and Toronto.

Exchange Risk and Hedging

Suppose an aircraft manufacturer in Southern California is seeking a certain type of electronic equipment via competitive bidding. A Boston electronics firm decides that it can produce the required equipment at a reasonable profit, for $220,000. Assuming that the credit standing of the aircraft manufacturer is acceptable, the Boston firm can commit itself to a contract calling for payment of $220,000 on delivery of the equipment in three months. This type of transaction takes place every day in our economy.

If, on the other hand, the aircraft manufacturer is located in London and our Boston firm is competing for the order with British electronics firms, the Boston firm must submit its price quotation in pounds. What price should be quoted? Suppose that at the current rate of exchange, we could get approximately $220,000 for £100,000. We may be tempted, then, to quote a price of £100,000. But we know that the price of the pound fluctuates. Suppose that at the time of payment, the pound is being quoted at $2.24. If we could convert pounds into dollars at $2.24, we could afford to quote a price of £98,214. But we cannot be certain that the price of $2.24 will prevail three months from now when we will receive payment. Not only is there a danger of small fluctuations, there is also the slight but real possibility that the pound will be worth substantially less in three months, either as a result of economic forces or because of some official action of the British or U.S. government. A drop in the value of the pound to, say, $1.75, may convert an anticipated profit into an actual loss.

The foreign-exchange market provides a means of hedging against this risk by providing importers and exporters facilities for buying and selling "forward" exchange. The forward market is a close adjunct to the foreign-exchange market, just as the futures market is associated with trading in commodities. Banks handle forward contracts, but they are also traded on the Chicago Board of Trade.

Our electronics firm can sell the pounds we expect to receive in three months "forward," or in advance of their receipt. Suppose the three-month forward rate for the pound is $2.20. We can quote a price on our equipment of £100,000 and sell £100,000 forward at $2.20. At the time the forward transaction is made, no money changes hands; we merely promise to deliver £100,000 in three months, at which time we will receive $220,000, regardless of the price of the pound at that time. We have thus insulated ourselves from the fluctuations of the foreign-exchange market. Our electronics firm can concentrate on its business—electronics—without being concerned about the behavior of the market. This is advantageous from our point of view—we presumably know something about electronics, but we may have no knowledge about the workings of the foreign-exchange market.

The forward price of the pound, at the time we submit our price quotation, may be below $2.20—say, $2.16. We can submit a bid of £101,852 and sell that amount forward at $2.16, which would net us $220,000. If we decide to sell forward pounds at a discount from the current rate, we can look upon this as the price paid for insurance against depreciation of the pound.

Not everyone is interested in avoiding exchange risks. The existence of a forward exchange market makes it feasible for speculators to enter the market. A speculator in foreign exchange need have no business interests involving foreign exchange. He is interested solely in making a profit out of fluctuations in the exchange rate.

A forward market is not necessary for speculation, but it does make it more practicable. Speculators in the forward market avoid any immediate large outlay of funds. The "bull" on the Swedish krona may buy three-month forward exchange at, say 24 cents. The speculator makes no immediate outlay of dollars unless a margin is required. He is simply betting that in three months, the price of the Swedish krona will be above 24 cents. If he is right, and the price rises to, say, 26 cents, he can buy at 24 cents under his forward contract and immediately sell at a profit at the "spot" or going price. Likewise, the "bear" can sell forward krona and gains or loses depending upon whether the spot rate in three months is below or above the contractual price.

Speculation may serve a useful purpose in the functioning of the foreign-exchange market. Speculation is *stabilizing* if, in response to a depreciation, speculators begin to purchase the depreciating currency. Speculation is *destabilizing* if, in response to a depreciation, further sales of the currency are made. Stabilizing speculation tends to keep the price of a currency within narrow limits.

INTEREST ARBITRAGE

Speculative activity can take place on either the spot or forward markets. Actually, the forward market is not a separate market but a segment of the total foreign-exchange market. The forward rate cannot be independent of the spot rate, although of course the forward rate is especially sensitive to speculative influences and changes in sentiment. The linkage between the spot and forward rates is not direct but works through the relationship of interest rates in the two countries.

The theory of forward exchange holds that under normal conditions, the forward discount or premium on one currency in terms of another is directly related to the difference in interest rates in the two countries. The easiest way of analyzing this mechanism is by considering what would happen if there were no such relationship.

Suppose the spot and three-month forward rate for the Canadian dollar were both 99 cents. Assume, in addition, that three-month Treasury bills yield 12 percent in the United States and 15 percent in Canada. Americans could profit by selling U.S. Treasury bills, buying Canadian Treasury bills, and hedging the exchange risk by selling forward Canadian dollars. The American investor would now earn 15 percent on his investment instead of 12 percent. This type of transaction is called *interest arbitrage*.

It is important to realize that this is not a speculative operation. If I make such a transaction, I am not indicating any lack of confidence in the United States or any distrust in the dollar. I am simply taking advantage of the opportunity to buy Canadian government securities at a higher yield than American government securities provide. I am confident that the Canadian government will redeem the Treasury bill at maturity in Canadian dollars. (The Canadian government can create all the dollars it needs with the aid of the central bank.) I am hedging against the risk of a depreciation of the Canadian dollar by selling forward the Canadian dollars I expect to receive in three months. There is no risk involved.

If many Americans try to do this, there will be:

1 Upward pressure on U.S. interest rates as U.S. Treasury bills are sold
2 Upward pressure on the spot price of the Canadian dollar as Canadian dollars are needed to pay for Canadian Treasury bills

3 Downward pressure on Canadian interest rates as Canadian bills are bought
4 Downward pressure on the forward price of the Canadian dollar as Canadian dollars are sold forward for U.S. dollars

All these changes are in the direction of establishing a discount in the Canadian forward exchange rate equal to the difference between Canadian and U.S. interest rates.

As a result of these effects, it is possible that the forward price of the Canadian dollar might fall to 98.25 cents. At this point, there is no incentive for interest arbitrage. I will not be enticed to invest in Canadian bills by the additional 3 percent interest return, because as I seek to cover the exchange risk by hedging in the forward market (through the sale of three-month forward Canadian dollars), I will lose the same 3 percent (by being forced to sell forward Canadian dollars at 98.25 cents as compared with the 99 cents I paid to buy spot Canadian dollars). The forward rate of 98.25 cents is really a result of the spot rate and the relationship in interest rates in the United States and Canada, and thus the forward market is not really an independent market.

GOVERNMENT INFLUENCE

The rate of exchange prevailing at any time depends upon the forces of demand and supply for the currency in terms of other currencies. The basic forces behind a country's demand for foreign exchange are its desires for imports and for foreign investment. The supply of foreign exchange comes from its exports and inflow of investment. Speculative motives—purchase or sale of a currency because of expected exchange-rate movements—may at times be a dominant influence.

The exchange rate of a country is intimately related to its overall economic balance, and governments are concerned about exchange rates as a matter of economic policy. At present in most countries, exchange rates are free to fluctuate in the market but subject to government intervention. In the past, governments have been more rigid in their exchange-rate policies, and we will examine these policies in more detail in Chapter 31. The present system is sometimes called a "managed float," in that exchange rates are allowed to float on the market but not completely free of government influence. (Opponents of intervention call it a "dirty float.")

In order to nudge exchange rates one way or another, governments intervene in the foreign-exchange market as buyers or sellers of foreign currency. If a government buys foreign currency, it pays for it with its own money (created by government). Foreign-exchange purchases occur when a country's currency is tending to appreciate—there is an excess demand for it—and the government in question supplies the desired money. In doing so, it acquires foreign exchange.

International reserves are the stock of assets that countries hold for possible use in defending their currencies against depreciation. (see U.S. reserves in Table 13.1).[7] The actual asset used in such defense is the foreign currency in the form of a deposit in the currency in question. Pending such use, assets that can be converted to deposit are held. Many countries hold U.S. government securities for this purpose and they also hold gold. Gold accounts are not very active; they are left over from the time when gold was a part of the monetary systems. Governments have generally refrained from holding Eurocurrency deposits as reserves, except for the petrodollars discussed above.

Since an exchange rate involves two countries, either country can intervene to influence the rate. Obviously, some degree of coordination is highly desirable, and there are a number of both formal and informal channels where this takes place. Through such channels, countries provide reserves to each other through "swap" agreements in which each country acquires the right to obtain money claims on the other. The swap is a kind of reciprocal line of credit. When an actual drawing is made under a swap, interest is paid, based on rates in the lending country, while it is outstanding.

In addition to using its accumulated reserves, a country may also borrow for the purpose of intervening to stabilize exchange rates. The United States, for example, has issued for this purpose securities denominated in foreign currencies, and some countries borrow on the Eurocurrency market. Intergovernmental borrowing takes place through swaps and through the International Monetary Fund.

INTERNATIONAL FINANCIAL INSTITUTIONS

International Monetary Fund

The International Monetary Fund (IMF) is a multilateral organization established after World War II to foster international economic relations and currency stability. In addition to providing a mech-

---

[7] Note in Table 13-1 that an "outflow" in reserve assets means a rise in claims on the rest of the world, and thus an increase in reserves.

anism for various kinds of multilateral agreements, it is also a facility by which member countries may obtain funds for defense of their exchange rates. The IMF lends needed currencies to member countries, and it obtains the currencies from other members. Each country has a "quota" with the fund, which is an advance commitment to lend its currency up to a limit. The loan is in the form of a deposit claim on the country. In this way, countries whose currencies are strong become lenders to those whose currencies are weak.

Borrowing of a certain amount, based on a country's quota, is almost automatically available, and thus countries count as part of their reserves their "IMF positions." When a country is in debt to the IMF, its economic policies come under IMF scrutiny to determine if the country is taking measures to correct its "disequilibrium." The Eurocurrency market entails no such formal scrutiny, and some countries prefer it over the IMF for this reason.

In 1970, the IMF introduced a "Special Drawing Right" involving 16 of the member countries. A unit of account, the SDR, was created, with specified proportions of each of the countries' currencies in it. Participating countries are allocated SDRs, which can be used to purchase foreign exchange from the IMF, which in turn obtains the exchange from other participating countries, tapping those whose reserve positions are strongest. The United States has been allocated a $5.7 billion equivalent. The basis for valuation of the SDR is the weighted average of exchange rates of five major currencies. The SDR system is extremely complex, it has so far played a rather limited role in the international monetary system, and its structure is subject to further change.[8] For these reasons, we shall not attempt a full explanation of it and shall leave for Chapter 31 a discussion of the conditions that led to its creation.

The World Bank Group

The International Monetary Fund was designed to foster the development of a multilateral world payments system. The fund's resources were to be used to enable countries to sustain temporary balance-of-payments deficits without the need to involve exchange controls. In the long run, however, the development of a strong system of international trade requires economic development and

---

[8] The governor of the Bank of Greece noted, ". . . there has been a great deal of discussion and writing regarding the nature and characteristics of the SDR as a good numeraire and an attractive reserve asset. It is recognized that much remains to be done regarding its marketability and valuation." Zolotas, "Inflation," p. 18.

growth in many of the underdeveloped countries of the world. This is the function of three other international organizations, which are often referred to collectively as the World Bank Group.

The first is the International Bank for Reconstruction and Development (IBRD), which was created along with the IMF. Although the bank is a separate organization from the IMF, they are closely related. They have a common membership, with resources derived from contributions from the members made in accord with their economic strength. The IMF engages in short- and intermediate-term transactions, whereas the IBRD makes long-term loans.[9]

Economic development almost always requires some sort of international financial aid. Much of the machinery and equipment required for industrialization must be imported. Underdeveloped countries tend to import a large proportion of their consumer goods, and as incomes rise with progress in economic development, imports can be expected to rise as well. Even if an underdeveloped country does not import any consumer goods under normal conditions, when workers are diverted from production of consumer goods to work on investment projects, the need for imports will rise. To facilitate economic development, therefore, the country must be able to raise foreign exchange to pay for the necessary imports.

The IBRD is by no means a charitable institution. It makes loans on specific projects that are expected to pay for themselves. The borrowing country must repay the loan in "hard" currencies—that is, in foreign exchange rather than in local currency. The bank aims at supplementing rather than replacing private investment; in fact, the bank will grant loans only when the borrower cannot raise funds from private sources on reasonable terms. The bank charges all borrowers the same rate—a rate high enough, apparently, to cover fully the bank's costs. It may also aid the flow of private investment by guaranteeing loans made by private investors to borrowing countries. This type of operation does not require any direct outlay of funds by the bank. These guarantees are backed up by the fact that the bank has not required member countries to pay in their full quotas. These additional funds can be drawn upon if necessary. Much of the funds loaned by the bank has, in fact, been raised by the sale of bonds by the bank in world capital markets.

In addition to the need for an institution to make sound loans to countries trying to speed their rate of economic development,

---

[9] In this regard, it has been suggested that the fund operates as a bank and the bank operates as a fund.

there is also a need to provide funds for riskier projects. Several institutional arrangements have developed in recent years. The International Finance Corporation, which is associated with the IBRD, was established in 1956. It makes investments, including certain types of equity claims, to private business firms in under-developed countries. The loans of the IFC do not require guarantees from the government of the country in which the investment will be made. Rates and means of repayment are subject to negotiation and need not be as hard as those imposed by the IBRD.

The International Development Association was established in 1959 to grant loans to underdeveloped countries on easier terms than those of the IBRD. Loans made by the IDA carry low interest rates and long maturities, and may be repaid in local currency.

Other Institutions

The three organizations described above (IBRD, IFC, and IDA) share some manangement and financial resources, and their lending activities are carried on worldwide. In recent years, several regional international financial institutions have been established and have received some support from the United States and other developed countries.

The Inter-American Development Bank (IDB) was established in 1959 to assist the development of Latin American countries. Its lending terms tend to be "softer" than those of the IBRD, and in some cases allow repayments to be in local currencies. The United States may have some use for the local currency—for example, for embassy expenses or military expenditures in the country involved, or the travel expenses of junketing U.S. congressmen—but where there is no real use for the local currency, there is little difference between such a loan and a grant.

The Asian Development Bank was established in 1966 to foster economic development in Asia. Although the United States played a major role in the creation of the ADB (at the time, the United States was deeply involved in the affairs of Southeast Asia), today Japan is the largest contributor to the bank. The ADB has tended to have a more conservative lending policy than the other international financial institutions.

The African Development Fund (AFDF), established in 1973, provides soft loans to African nations. U.S. participation in the fund began in 1976, although contributions have so far been small.

Even though it is not an international financial institution, mention, should also be made at this point of the U.S. Export-

Import Bank. This is an institution basically designed to aid American export activities. An American firm may have the opportunity to sell goods to a foreign firm or government but cannot provide the credit terms that the buyer requires. Private lenders may be unwilling to undertake possible political risks—currency devaluation, expropriation of goods, or war. In some of these cases, the Export-Import Bank will guarantee loans by private lending institutions.

The Export-Import Bank's lending activities aid American firms in selling their goods and also aid the importing country, which might otherwise be unable to obtain the financing necessary to purchase the goods. The bank obtains its funds by borrowing from the Treasury and charges rates high enough to cover its expenses (including interest paid to the Treasury) and bad-debt losses (which have been small), with enough left over to pay dividends on the stock of the bank held by the Treasury.

The United States participates, although not as a full member, in the Bank for International Settlements. The BIS, based in Basel, Switzerland, is a sort of central bank for central banks. It has been involved in arranging currency swaps. The monthly meetings of the central bankers of the leading countries of the world have been the occasion for discussions and bilateral and multilateral arrangements designed to support the international financial system. The annual reports of the BIS, well-written and conservative, have been influential on government policy in many countries.

This chapter has focused on the financial aspect of international trade and our international monetary system. Our balance-of-payments situation has important implications for monetary policy as well. We will return to this issue in Chapter 31.

QUESTIONS

1 How does an arbitrageur operate in the foreign-exchange market? If the arbitrageur takes no risk and makes a sure profit, why do not other people enter this field?
2 What is the role of commercial banks in the foreign-exchange market?
3 Why does an American dollar exchange for more Canadian dollars and fewer Australian dollars?
4 Are Eurodollars in the U.S. balance of payments?
5 How can the IMF help a country with a depreciating exchange rate?
6 What are international reserves?
7 Will a persistent balance-of-trade deficit ultimately tend to correct itself?

8 Select a foreign currency and examine its price in terms of dollars over the last three years. How would you determine whether its fluctuations are the result of a "dirty" or a "clean" float?

SELECTED READINGS

CAVES, RICHARD, and RONALD JONES, *World Trade and Payments.* Boston: Little, Brown, 1977.

COOMBS, CHARLES A., *The Arena of International Finance.* New York: John Wiley, 1976.

KEMP, DONALD, "Balance-of-Payments Concepts—What Do They Really Mean?" Federal Reserve Bank of St. Louis *Review*, July 1975.

KUGARYCH, ROGER, *Foreign Exchange Markets in the United States.* Federal Reserve Bank of New York, 1978.

MACBEAN, A.I., and N. SNOWDEN, *International Institutions in Trade and Finance.* Winchester, Mass.: Allen & Unwin, 1981.

SOLOMON, ROBERT, *The International Monetary System 1945–1976: An Insider View.* New York: Harper & Row, 1977.

IV

BANKING
REGULATION
AND DEVELOPMENT

14

The Development of American Commercial Banking

BANKING BEFORE 1837

Although some banks were established in Europe during the seventeenth century, there were no real banks here during early Colonial days. A few *land banks* were established, one in Massachusetts as early as 1714. These banks issued paper money (bank notes) secured by real estate.[1] They did not last very long, because real estate, regardless of quality, does not have great liquidity, and the banks ultimately had trouble redeeming their notes or deposits for cash.

The first bank to begin operations in the modern manner in this country was the Bank of North America in 1782. The Bank of New York and the Bank of Massachusetts were established in 1784. All three of these banks were well managed, soundly financed, successful banking institutions and have survived, under different

---

[1] As we have seen, the major liability item of modern banks is deposits. These deposits arise from people bringing money to the bank and from banks crediting deposit accounts when they make loans. In the early days of banking, a loan was made in the form of bank notes rather than as a credit to the deposit account. Thus, for the early banks, notes were a larger liability item than deposits, but they were a similar type of liability, in that any depositor or noteholder could demand hard cash in return for a note or deposit.

names, to the present day. Other banks chartered by the various states around this time were not so fortunate. Banks at that time were given the right to engage in banking by special acts of their respective state legislatures.

The federal government entered the bank-chartering field in 1791 with the establishment of the Bank of the United States. This bank was intended to be national in character and opened eight branches in addition to its head office in Philadelphia. It had total capital of $10 million, $2 million of which was subscribed by the federal government. The government raised the $2 million by borrowing it from the bank.[2]

The bank functioned relatively well, but its charter, which ran for 20 years, was not renewed when it expired in 1811. There were several reasons for this. Some critics felt that Congress did not have the constitutional authority to charter a bank. The bank was also opposed by the state banks, whose freewheeling activities were hampered by its practice of demanding gold or silver in return for the notes of the state banks that it received. Agricultural sections also opposed the bank's insistence on sound credit policies. Perhaps more dangerous in the eyes of the people was the fact that nearly three-quarters of the bank's stock was held by foreigners. Although foreign stockholders could not vote their shares, the public was suspicious of anything that smacked of foreign control of American industry or finance. Then as now, nationalism was a powerful force in political affairs, and Congress by a narrow margin refused to renew the charter of the Bank of the United States.[3]

With the demise of the Bank of the United States, the state banks were required to carry the burden of providing the country with paper money. This they did, flooding the country with notes that depreciated rapidly. There were 88 state-chartered banks in 1811, and the number increased to 246 by 1816 despite a large number of failures. The War of 1812 added to the problems of the banking system, and, except for those in New England most banks were forced to suspend specie payments; that is, to stop redeeming their notes for gold or silver. Regulation of the banks by the states was inadequate and poorly enforced where it existed at all.

---

[2] This lesson in how to start a bank without any money was not lost on would-be bankers in the new country. Many banks were established following the unfortunate precedent set by the federal government. All a potential banker had to do after receiving a bank charter was to borrow from the bank the amount of his capital contribution. Thus, a bank might nominally have $1,000,000 capital but could open for business without a dollar in cash to its name.

[3] The vote was 65 to 64 against in the House of Representatives and 18 to 17 against in the Senate, with the vote of Vice-President Clinton breaking a 17-to-17 tie.

Second Bank of the United States

The situation was such that there was almost unanimous support for the creation of a Second Bank of the United States. The Second Bank was established in 1816 on terms similar to those of the First Bank. The federal government owned 20 percent of the capital stock, but the bank was primarily a private institution. Its capital was set at $35 million, considerably more than that of the First Bank, although it opened with cash nowhere near that amount. It was a branch-banking institution, with as many as 25 branches by 1825, at which time it held one-third of all bank assets in the country.

The Second Bank was not as successful as its predecessor, owing mainly to a lack of the sound management that had characterized the First Bank. In fact, officers of the Baltimore branch embezzled over $1 million. By 1823, however, when Nicholas Biddle became president of the bank, it was operating on a sound, businesslike basis. Unfortunately, that sound, businesslike basis incurred the wrath of the same forces that opposed the First Bank. Andrew Jackson, in a crusade against the bank, transferred government deposits from the Second Bank to various state banks—the so-called "pet banks." In 1832, a bill was passed to recharter the bank, but Jackson vetoed it.[4]

The federal charter expired in 1836, at which time the bank obtained a charter from the state of Pennsylvania[5] and continued operations as a state bank. Those operations were no better than those of other state banks, and it failed disastrously in 1841.

State Banking

Although the record of the early state banks left much to be desired from the point of view of depositors and note holders, it was not as bad as it has often been pictured. First of all, in many cases in which banks were forced to close their doors, the problem was one of inadequate liquidity to convert notes or deposits to specie and not a result of unwise loans or fraudulent behavior. Where the problem was one of liquidity, ultimate losses to depositors or note holders were small. Furthermore, even where too-easy extension of credit resulted in

---

[4] Jackson's veto message is a classic of political oratory and well worth reading. It is hard to think of a single pressure group, fear, or prejudice to which Jackson's message did not appeal; he missed motherhood, but came out strongly in favor of widows and orphans.

[5] Allegedly with the help of a $2.5-million bribe.

loans that could not be repaid, the net effect was not all bad. Easy money may have generated some economic growth; and some of the projects financed, uneconomic at the time, may later have proved useful as the economy grew. Finally, in several sections of the country, the banks operated effectively and safely.

Banking business was conducted on a sound basis in New England, for example, and in 1818, the Suffolk Bank of Boston started a system that further improved banking in that region. We can best understand the workings of the Suffolk system by looking at the conditions that prevailed before its introduction.

Notes of country banks circulated in Boston at discounts of 1 to 5 percent. These banks were generally in sound condition, but if a note holder wanted to redeem his notes for gold, he had to present the notes at the issuing bank. Since there was some expense or inconvenience involved in doing this, these notes circulated at a discount compared with the notes of the Boston banks, which could be redeemed easily.

This was not a very happy situation for the Boston banks. People tended to pay their bills with the notes of these country banks and presented the notes of the Boston banks for redemption when they wanted specie. Once again we see Gresham's Law in operation. With two types of money in circulation together, the poorer-quality money remains in circulation and the better money disappears.

The Suffolk Bank decided to do something about this unprofitable situation. It agreed to redeem at par the notes of any New England bank that would agree to keep with it a deposit large enough to meet the need. This was not very advantageous for the country banks, and they would have preferred to remain outside any such arrangement, but the Suffolk came up with a powerful counterweapon. In order to force the country banks to join the system, the Suffolk would accumulate the notes of nonmember banks and present them to the banks for payment in gold in awkwardly large amounts.

By 1825, almost all New England banks were in the system, giving New England the soundest currency system in the country.[6] Because of the constant threat of demand for redemption, no bank could afford to issue excessive amounts of notes. The system con-

---

[6] There was, of course, considerable discontent on the part of bankers more or less forced into the system. For a discussion of the opposition of contemporary bankers to the system, see N.S.B. Gras, *The Massachusetts First National Bank of Boston* (Cambridge, Mass.: Harvard University Press, 1937), pp. 102ff.

tinued in successful operation until it was made unnecessary by the National Banking System in 1863.

Although the Suffolk system achieved some of the results of a central or national banking system, it is important to note that the motives of the Suffolk Bank were not altruistic. It set up the system to make a profit, which it did, and fortunately, this worked out in the public interest. Profit-making schemes devised by early nineteenth-century bankers did not always have such desirable results.

Another interesting innovation in American banking was the New York Safety Fund, established in 1829. The Safety Fund law provided that each bank in the state make an annual payment to the fund equal to one-half of 1 percent of the bank's capital until its total contribution equalled 3 percent of its capital. The fund was to be used to pay creditors (note holders and depositors) of any failed bank.

A wave of bank failures beginning in 1840 depleted the fund, and the state advanced it a sizable sum, which the fund eventually repaid with interest. After 1842, the law was amended to provide protection for note holders only. Despite the fund's only partial success, it was a worthwhile experiment. The plan was a forerunner of the deposit insurance we now have.

FREE BANKING, 1837–1863

One of the most significant banking developments of the early nineteenth century was the introduction of "free banking" in Michigan in 1837. Prior to 1837, a charter to form a bank could be obtained only through a special act of the state legislature. State legislatures of the nineteenth century were no freer of corrupt elements than they are now, and the system led to many cases of favoritism, bribery, and other abuses.

The Michigan Act of 1837 established a system whereby anyone could get a bank charter by meeting certain requirements. New York passed a similar law the following year, and most other states followed suit soon after. The rush to take advantage of the new laws was fantastic. The number of banks increased from 500 in 1834 to 900 in 1840. Apparently, many people who did not have money felt that starting a bank was a good way of getting some.

Unfortunately, the requirements for establishment of a bank were not very stringent, and enforcement was lax. Banks opened with very little hard cash, and what they did have as often as not had been borrowed just prior to the appearance of the bank examiner.[7]

One clever device used by shrewd promoters was the establishment of banks in isolated locations, making it virtually impossible for a note holder to redeem his notes. This practice led to the use of the term *wildcat banking* to describe the situation—the locations in which many banks were opened were better suited to wildcats than to bank customers.

The situation got so bad, in fact, that the federal government refused to have anything to do with the banks, instead setting up an independent Treasury system whereby payments to and by the government were made in coin that was kept by the Treasury itself in a number of branches in various parts of the country. The Treasury maintained the system for nearly 20 years, until the burdens of financing the Civil War forced it to rely again upon the banks.

THE NATIONAL BANK ACT

The Civil War, like most wars, had significant effects on the banking system. As noted in Chapter 2, the government was forced to resort to the issuance of irredemable greenbacks to finance the war effort. The secretary of the Treasury, Salmon P. Chase,[8] devised a scheme to establish a system of national banks. He proposed that Congress charter banks that would be required to hold government bonds as security for their issuance of notes. It was hoped that this would be a means of increasing the sale of bonds to finance the war. Although there were many reasons for having a national banking system, it is unlikely that such legislation could have been enacted if it were not for the benefits it would have for the government war-financing effort.

Even with this justification, the plan did not meet with general support and barely passed Congress in February 1863. The bill was poorly constructed, and few banks were chartered under the act. It was thoroughly revised in 1864, but this made national bank charters only slightly more attractive. It was obvious that something was needed to make conversion to a national charter look inviting to the state banks.

---

[7] O. Henry has sketched an interesting picture of such banking operations in his short story, "Friends in San Rosario."

[8] Mr. Chase's face is probably familiar to those readers who have occasion to use $10,000 bills.

In 1865, Congress imposed a 10 percent tax on bank notes issued by state-chartered banks. This made issuance of notes unprofitable, and most state banks applied immediately for national charters. State banks were, in effect, to be taxed out of existence.

Provisions of the National Bank Act

Capital.   One advance of the National Banking System was the establishment of minimum capital requirements for the establishment of banks. Setting up a bank in a community with less than 6,000 inhabitants required a minimum of $50,000 capital. A bank in a community with a population of between 6,000 and 50,000 was required to have capital of at least $100,000. Establishing a bank in a city with over 50,000 inhabitants required a minimum of $200,000 capital. At least half the required capital had to be paid in before the bank could open for business, and the rest was due within five months. These do not appear to be seriously restrictive requirements (one would hardly open a retail store with less than $50,000 capital), but it was a considerable stiffening of the existing standards.

Assets.   Restrictions and limitations were put on the use of the bank's funds, many of them on the type and amount of loans that the bank could make. The act also set up minimum reserve requirements against the bank's liabilities (notes and deposits). The amount of reserves in cash that a national bank was required to maintain varied according to the location of the bank. National banks in New York, later Chicago, and, for a time, St. Louis, were classified as central reserve city banks. They were required to hold reserves equal to 25 percent of their notes and deposits. National banks in sixteen other cities were classified as reserve city banks and were also required to hold reserves equal to 25 percent, but part of this reserve could consist of deposits in central reserve city banks. The remaining banks, called country banks, were required to keep reserves of 15 percent, part of which could consist of deposits in reserve city banks. This classification of banks for reserve purposes continued, with some changes, until 1972.

Notes.   National bank notes were printed by the Treasury and sent to national banks to issue in an amount equal to the value of government bonds purchased by the bank and deposited with the Comptroller of the Currency. Each national bank was required to accept the notes of any other national bank at par. These notes were redeemable in lawful money at the issuing bank and at the Treasury. If a national bank was unable to redeem its notes, the Comptroller could sell the bonds deposited by the bank to pay the note holders. One of the most important results of the National Banking Act was the replacement of the hodgepodge of state bank notes with a uniform and safe paper money. But even though depositors were better protected under the National Banking System than they were previously, they could still suffer from bank failure.

Enforcement. Part of the trouble under the state banking systems was the existence of poor banking laws and the poor enforcement of the laws that did exist. Under the National Banking Act, the office of Comptroller of the Currency was established and made responsible for administration of the law. The Comptroller had a corps of bank examiners who were better trained and better paid than was the case under most state systems. Although the principle of free banking remained a part of national banking law, the Comptroller exercised considerable discretionary authority in approving or rejecting applications for national bank charters (even though no provision of the law gave him any such authority). As a result, the safety record of the national banks was a considerable improvement over what had gone before.

Rise of Deposit Banking

The imposition in 1865 of the 10 percent tax on state bank notes forced most of these banks out of business, since their major function was granting loans through note issuance.

The nineteenth century witnessed substantial changes in the character of economic life as business firms grew in size and transportation and communication facilities improved. The volume of transactions and the number of payments across local boundaries increased. Checks drawn on demand deposits became a more convenient payment mechanism than currency, so that extension of bank credit in the form of demand deposits rather than notes became the major operation of banks.

The National Banking Act was primarily concerned with note-issue banking. As banks found that they did not have to issue notes to operate profitably, the state banks began a strong comeback, since most state requirements were less stringent than those that applied to national banks. Deposit banking showed rapid growth in the 1870s, and by 1890, there were more state banks than national banks (see Table 14-1).

TABLE 14-1
Number of Commercial Banks

Year	National	State	Total
1800	—	28	28
1830	—	329	329
1860	—	1,529	1,529
1865	1,294	349	1,643
1875	2,076	586	2,662
1890	3,484	3,594	7,078
1900	3,731	8,696	12,427
1921	8,150	22,306	30,456
1933	4,897	9,310	14,207
1945	5,015	9,111	14,126
1953	4,874	9,131	14,005
1962	4,499	8,922	13,421
1965	4,815	8,989	13,804
1970	4,621	9,084	13,705
1973	4,661	9,533	14,194
1975	4,744	9,910	14,654
1977	4,655	10,085	14,740
1980	4,425	10,445	14,870
1981	4,471	10,248	14,719

Source: *Statistical Abstract of the U.S.*, 1970, 1972; FDIC; and Federal Reserve System.

Defects of the National Banking System

Although the National Banking System provided a substantial improvement over what had gone before, it had several shortcomings. One difficulty was caused by the legal pyramiding of deposits. As noted previously, country and reserve city banks could count deposits with other banks as part of their reserves. There was, of course, a great concentration of reserves in New York. The New York banks competed vigorously for these "correspondent" accounts of the interior banks. The country banks looked on these deposits as their reserves, and when faced with a need for cash, they drew from these accounts. This put pressure on the New York banks and frequently led to forced liquidation of loans and a financial crisis.

An aggravating factor in this situation was the setup established for issuance of notes by national banks. The amount of notes in circulation depended upon the number of government bonds outstanding and their prices. Notes could be issued up to the par value of the government bonds purchased by the banks. When government bonds sold at a premium above par, the issuance of bank notes became less attractive. The inelasticity of the supply of notes was not just an occasional problem; it arose every year, because there was no automatic mechanism or government authority to see that the amount of currency varied with the seasonal needs for currency.

This serious difficulty was itself aggravated by Treasury policy. The Treasury continued to maintain the independent Treasury system, although it was somewhat modified. This meant that when the Treasury tax collections were greater than Treasury disbursements, money was pulled out of the banking system. When the Treasury operated at a temporary deficit, the banks were flooded with money. These disturbances were irregular and violently disrupted the money market.

The real need under the National Banking System was for a central bank—a government or semiofficial banking institution to manage the overall operation of the banking system. The suffolk Bank of Boston had done this to some extent in earlier years in New England. What was needed was some institution to provide this general direction for the country as a whole. Under the Independent Treasury System, the Treasury had the opportunity and some of the powers necessary for this function, but performance proved to be irregular.

Proposals for reform were frequent, but in much of the country there was a deep-seated fear of just the sort of centralized control over the monetary system that was really needed. Thus, the economy endured financial crises about every ten years. There were serious panics in 1873, 1884, and 1893. A severe crisis in 1907 brought the problem to a head and overcame much of the public distaste for a central bank.

THE FEDERAL RESERVE ACT

The major provisions of the Federal Reserve Act will be discussed in Chapter 17. Its main feature was the creation of a much-needed central banking mechanism with the following objectives:

1 Generally strengthen reserves so that they might be more readily used to enable banks in any section of the country to meet their obligations instead of suspending cash payments. Concentration of reserves was also designed to organize and consolidate the strength of the financial community.
2 Furnish an elastic currency which would expand and contract with the needs of business. Abolish the rigid and inelastic bond-secured currency as issued by national banks.
3 Exercise the functions of a clearinghouse for its member banks in handling checks.
4 Provide general supervision of banking at the federal level and exercise broad functions in connection with the money supply, leaving to the highly competitive, privately

owned individual units the actual direction of the regular day-to-day business of banking, and to market forces and individual units the allocation of the money supply among
users. . . .[9]

The system established by the Federal Reserve Act consisted
of twelve regional Federal Reserve Banks and a coordinating Board
located in Washington. It was a rather decentralized central bank,
but it did provide for more overall control of the banking system
than had existed before. (However, some critics of Federal Reserve
policy have argued that this simply made bigger mistakes possible
than under the previously existing arrangements.)

The Federal Reserve was able to inject the needed elasticity
into the supply of bank reserves and currency. As a by-product, the
Federal Reserve Act created a system of credit control. We will
explore this in detail later.

The Federal Reserve Act did not change the principle of free
banking, and the number of banks continued to increase. By 1921,
there were more than 30,000 banks doing business in the country.
Bank failures were frequent—particularly among state-chartered
banks—all through the 1920s and culminated in the virtual breakdown of the banking system in the Great Depression of the 1930s.

REFORMS OF THE 1930s

The Banking Acts of 1933 and 1935, and many state laws passed
about the same time, were designed to curb the high rate of bank
failure that had characterized American banking history. A most
important provision was the end of free banking under the Banking
Act of 1935. Federal authorities were given greater discretionary
powers in the granting of bank charters. Now the organizers of a
prospective national bank must demonstrate to the Comptroller of
the Currency that there is a public need for a new bank and that the
new bank will be soundly managed and profitable without causing
serious losses to the existing banks. The Comptroller can turn down
a request for a new bank charter if he feels that these conditions will
not be fulfilled.

The banking legislation of the 1930s also imposed significant
new restrictions on the operations of commercial banks. The prohibition of interest payments on demand deposits was imposed at
least partly in the belief that banks sought risky assets in order to
earn enough to meet commitments to pay excessive interest on

[9]*Annual Report*, Federal Reserve Bank of Boston, 1958, p. 13. The fourth objective is a rather recent addition—the original framers of the Federal Reserve Act had
the first three objectives primarily in mind.

their deposits. Later research found no basis for that interpretation, and the 1980 Deregulation Act lifted the prohibition for household accounts (but it maintained a ceiling rate during a transition period). The prohibition still exists for corporate deposits.

Other restrictions applied to the portfolios and to other operations of the banks. A particularly significant change of the latter type was the attempt to separate commercial banking from investment banking (underwriting the distribution of new issues of securities). Many banks got into considerable difficulty during the 1920s as a result of their investment-banking activities, and apart from the risk aspects, there is a serious conflict-of-interest potential in the linking of commercial and investment banking. Now commercial banks may act as underwriters only of U.S. government securities and securities backed by the full faith and credit of state and local governments.

Some of the restrictions on commercial banks imposed by the banking legislation of the 1930s were an appropriate response to real dangers. But in many cases, they represented an overreaction to real or imagined problems, and medicine was prescribed on the basis of faulty diagnoses. Such restrictions are no longer necessary in a world in which the government has assumed responsibility for preventing economic disasters such as the Great Depression, and in which federal deposit insurance exists to protect depositors in those banks that do fail. In fact, many authorities consider the establishment of federal deposit insurance as the most significant of the reform legislation growing out of the Great Depression.

Federal Deposit Insurance Corporation

In addition to New York, several other states established deposit insurance systems in the early years of this century. All were unsuccessful before 1930 because of the large numbers of bank failures. Because of the relatively poor record, many felt that a federal system would also fail.

The Federal Deposit Insurance Corporation, established in 1933, was basically much stronger than any of the earlier state plans, and it avoided many of their weaknesses. Its original capital of $289 million was provided by the Treasury and the Federal Reserve Banks. Since the FDIC was a national organization, it had more diversification than was possible for the various state systems. In some cases, local agricultural depressions were enough to embarrass the state deposit insurance systems. In addition, the

FDIC has powers of supervision and examination that have helped maintain the strength of member institutions. An important part of FDIC activity is preventing bank failures, not simply repaying depositors after failure takes place.

Originally, deposits in a failed bank were insured up to a maximum of $2,500 per depositor. This has been increased several times, rising to $100,000 with the 1980 Deregulation Act. The deposit insurance reserves of the FDIC have also increased and now amount to about $11 billion. In addition, the FDIC has the right to borrow up to $3 billion from the Treasury if needed to protect depositors in failed banks. The deposit insurance fund has amounted to between 1 and 2 percent of insured deposits since its establishment.

Although the assets of the FDIC are small in relation to the deposits it insures, many people feel that the existence of the FDIC implies a moral commitment on the part of the government to bail it out if a wave of bank failures should deplete its funds. More important, however, the very fact that deposits are insured reduces the chance that there will be a run on banks or that financial difficulties will reach panic proportions. The reserves of the FDIC are not sufficient to handle a debacle like the 1930s, but bank failures of that magnitude are unlikely to occur again. In any case, prevention of another Great Depression is clearly the responsibility of the government and the Federal Reserve, not the FDIC.

Over the years, the issue has frequently risen as to whether deposits should be insured in full. This issue turns on what we see to be the purpose of deposit insurance. If deposit insurance is designed to protect small depositors from losses they could not be expected to avoid by selecting safer banks, then the $100,000 limit is appropriate to this objective. If we have deposit insurance in order to protect our money supply, full coverage would seem to be called for. Those who oppose 100 percent insurance argue that under the present system, large uninsured depositors put pressure on banks to operate in a safe, conservative manner. This continuous scrutiny by large depositors would have to be replaced by increased government supervision if deposits were insured in full. Otherwise, opponents of 100 percent insurance argue, banks would tend to operate in an excessively risky manner.

In practice, the FDIC attempts to handle bank failures by having a sound bank absorb the liabilities, including all deposits, of the failed bank. This approach is usually cheaper for the FDIC, and it does provide what is, in effect, 100 percent deposit insurance. Since the establishment of the FDIC, all large-bank failures have been handled in this way.

Large banks tend to oppose substantial increases in insurance coverage. With 100 percent insurance, large depositors would have less incentive to seek out the large banks with impeccable reputations; they would be equally safe with much smaller banks. Those who feel that banking resources in this country are too highly concentrated in the hands of a small number of very large banks would probably regard this as an advantage of 100 percent insurance.

RECENT DEVELOPMENTS

The cataclysm of the Great Depression left its impact on the banking business for many years. The generally depressed level of business activity continued through the 1930s. Demand for bank loans was very weak, and bank managers became very cautious. As a result, banks put most of their funds in government securities, maintaining balance sheets that looked like those of short-term investment funds rather than lending institutions.

The economy recovered with the outbreak of World War II, but the large government deficits that required financing, and the lack of consumer goods needing financing, kept bank balance sheets in the same pattern they had during the 1930s—large holdings of government securities and very low loan ratios.

The banking business did not begin to return to normal until the late 1940s. From then through the 1950s, we saw a gradual increase in bank lending activity. Bank loan–asset ratios moved up gradually on almost a year-by-year basis, although they still remained at low levels in comparison with the predepression years. The average loan–asset ratio was 41 percent in 1955, as compared with 16 percent in 1945 and 63 percent in 1925. The increase in lending activity was across the board, encompassing consumer loans, business loans, and home-mortgage loans.

During the 1960s, banking continued the trends of the 1950s but seemed to change in character. Banks in general, but especially the larger banks, became more aggressive in their competition, and more willing to take risks. The change was reflected in the standard measures of bank soundness—increases in the loan–asset ratio, declines in capital–asset ratios—and also in the movement of banks into new activities. During this period, many large banks greatly expanded their foreign operations, in terms of both financing activities and the establishment of branches abroad. They moved into other activities, related more or less to traditional banking services, and made use of the holding-company device to avoid legal restrictions on their activities. Banks also began to tap other sources of funds, beyond the traditional types of deposits. During the 1930s, 1940s, and early 1950s, banks had more funds than they had profitable uses for, and so it was not until loan demand caught up with this excess liquidity that they had any incentive to seek additional (and more expensive) sources of funds, such as the CDs described in Chapter 3.

The trends of the 1960s continued into the 1970s, but banks promptly ran into a changed set of economic circumstances. The 1970s and early 1980s brought record rates of inflation, record levels of interest rates, and the worst recession since the 1930s. These economic factors collided with the more aggressive, more risk-exposed posture of the banking industry coming into the 1970s. The result was a greater number of bank failures and increased concern about the soundness and safety of the banking system. During the 1960s, the trend was toward a relaxation of the regulatory constraints on the banking industry imposed in the aftermath of the depression experience of the 1930s. This changed in the 1970s, toward more emphasis on the need for stricter supervision of banks and bank activities in the light of the problems of financial markets and the economy. Concern about the soundness of banks and thrift institutions conflicts with the general trend toward deregulation in the financial system and the economy.

SOME SIGNIFICANT TRENDS AND CONTINUING PROBLEMS

The preceding discussion sketches the process by which our banking structure arrived at the position described in Chapters 3 and 6. This historical view is necessary for an understanding of how some of the illogical aspects of the American banking system began and continued to exist. Additional perspective may be gained by examining some important trends in the history of the commercial-banking system.

Central Control

Throughout this history, there has been an increasing trend toward more unification in banking and more government control. The First and Second Banks of the United States, the Suffolk system, the National Bank Act, the Federal Reserve Act, and the Banking Acts of 1933 and 1935 were all steps in this direction.

Most banks desire insurance, but in joining the Federal Deposit Insurance Corporation, they put themselves under the full weight of federal regulation. Thus, even state-chartered banks are subject to many of the same regulations that affect national banks. Part of the reason for the shift toward a greater role for the federal government has been the failure of many (but not all) states to meet their responsibilities for banking supervision and regulation under a normally dual banking system. Many states have underpaid supervisors and examination staffs who are very willing to turn the primary responsibility for chartering and examining their state banks over to the FDIC and the Federal Reserve. Although this trend toward more federal, rather than state, regulation of banking has been unintended, it has generally been a favorable development.

Safety

As we have noted, the safety record of American banking was dismal until after the Great Depression of the 1930s. Wildcat banking was completely irresponsible, and the system under the National Bank Act and the Federal Reserve Act during the 1920s was only slightly better. Since the breakdown of the 1930s, however, the commercial banking industry has enjoyed stable growth with few bank failures. Periods of poor business since the 1930s have been relatively short and mild. This may be due to sounder government economic policy or may simply be a matter of good luck. In any case, the banking system has not been subject to as severe a test since the 1930s, and we have reason to believe that it never will be again.

For most of our history, we have thought of bank failure as a small-bank problem. No bank with as much as $50 million of deposits failed in the 30 years following creation of the Federal Deposit Insurance Corporation. But, as we have noted, large banks became more aggressive during the 1960s. This increased willingness to take risks, combined with the economic stresses of the 1970s, including the worst recession since the 1930s, led to a significant increase in failures of larger banks. The ten largest bank failures in the history of the FDIC have all occurred since October 1973. These included three billion-dollar institutions: The Bank of the Commonwealth, Detroit; United States National Bank, San Diego; and Franklin National Bank, New York, which was the twentieth largest bank in the country at the time of its difficulties.

The economic problems of the 1970s created problems for smaller banks as well, so that the total number of bank failures during 1976 was 16, a record for our recent history. Despite this recent experience, there seems to remain a general view that failures are still an aberration and not the norm.

Certainly the institution of federal deposit insurance has been instrumental in reducing bank failures. It has improved public confidence in the banking system, and this in itself is an important factor. Perhaps more important is the fact that the banks' desire for federal deposit insurance has led to their more or less voluntary subjection to federal regulation. Some of the improvement in the stability of the banking system is certainly due to the reduced number of banks. If we had 30,000 banks today, as we did in 1921, it is probable that bank failures would be more common than they are. Most of the weaker banks were weeded out by the impact of the depression. Only strong banks survived, and the adoption of more stringent entry requirements has prevented weak banks from commencing operations.

Entry into Banking

One of the strongest influences shaping the development of American banking has been a deep-rooted fear of financial monopoly. This fear was involved in the debate over the First and Second Banks of the United States and in debate over the Federal Reserve Act. It led to the adoption of the free-banking principle. Farmers and small businessmen who depended upon bank credit were fiercely opposed to any policy that could mean monopoly control over their credit lifeline. This fear was reinforced by the performance of banking institutions chartered by special acts of the state legislatures.

The number of banks increased irregularly during the nineteenth century, set back occasionally by waves of bank failures. The first two decades of the twentieth century witnessed a tremendous growth in the number of banks and banking offices in the United States. These were years of rapid industrial and agricultural advance, accompanied by the development of the American West, and also a time of rising land and commodity prices. The increase in banking facilities was almost entirely in the form of new unit banks, and these were heavily concentrated in the agricultural states of the Midwest and Great Plains.

The 1920s and early 1930s were years of retrenchment for the banking system. Mergers and failures were responsible for the decline during the 1920s, and by 1929, the number of banking offices was down to about 25,000 from its peak of over 31,000 in 1922 (see Figure 14-1). These tendencies were intensified in the period from 1930 to the banking holiday of March 1933. During this three-year period, approximately 9,000 banks failed, and another 2,300, many of which were in financial difficulty, were absorbed by other banks.

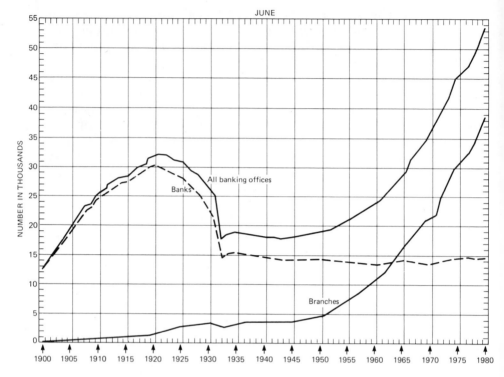

FIGURE 14-1 Commercial Banking Offices in the United States

The poor performance of the banking system under free banking led to the elimination of free banking in the Banking Act of 1935. There were several factors responsible for this poor performance during the 1920s. Many of the banks that opened from 1900 to 1920 were located in small agricultural communities. The weakness in the agricultural sector of the economy during the 1920s led to the failure of a number of these small, specialized institutions. The growth of the automobile was also a factor—transportation from one town to another became easier, and it was no longer necessary for every small community to have its own bank. Also, as the scale of industrial and commercial activity increased, so did the demand for services that only large banks could offer, and this led to the absorption of a number of smaller banks.

The reorganization of the banking structure forced by the depression was largely completed by the end of 1934. At that time, there were 15,353 commercial banks and 2,973 branches in operation. Structural changes were relatively slight during the next twelve years. The number of banks declined slowly but steadily to 14,044 at the end of 1946. The number of branches increased steadily, but at a rate not quite adequate to offset the decline in the number of banks, so that by 1946, the number of banking offices totaled 18,025.

This meant that despite the great economic growth of the war years, there were fewer banking offices in operation than at the depths of the depression. It was clear that the country required additional banking offices if the banking needs of the public were to be met fully and effectively. This was especially true in those urban and suburban areas that had experienced the greatest economic growth during the war.

The number of banking offices increased by nearly one-third between 1946 and 1960 and amounted to 23,716 by the latter year. This increase was accounted for by a rapid increase in branching activity, while the number of banks continued to fall (a decline due almost entirely to mergers rather than failures). The increase in banking facilities during this period, although substantial, failed to keep pace with the growth of the economy—real gross national product rose by over 50 percent between 1946 and 1960. It is fair to say that there was at least as great a need for additional banking facilities at the end of this period as at the beginning.

The early 1960s saw a significant change in the trend of the structural change in the banking system. From 1920 to 1961, there had been an almost uninterrupted decline in the number of banks and as nearly an uninterrupted increase in the number of branches. When James J. Saxon became Comptroller of the Currency in 1961, he recognized that the country needed not only additional banking offices but also the stimulus of new competition that only new banks could provide. The number of newly chartered banks increased sharply in 1962, and from 1963 through 1965, there was a net increase in the number of banks in operation as the new charters more than matched the continuing heavy attrition through merger.

Comptrollers of the Currency had rejected many applications for new national bank charters over the years, even though the legal authority to do so was not clear. In any case, the establishment of formal criteria for the granting of bank charters came only after we had antitrust legislation on the books that could help prevent abuses that might result from excessive concentration in banking owing to overrestrictive entry requirements.

We have already noted that the trends of the 1930s and 1940s left the banking structure in need of new banks. Nevertheless, Comptroller Saxon's move toward a more liberal entry policy during the 1960s generated considerable controversy and criticism. The chartering of a large number of new national banks required great political courage. Almost every new bank application brought forth protests from bankers not anxious to face new competition. Several of Saxon's most vociferous congressional critics were stockholders or directors of long-established banks faced with the threat of new competition. In retrospect, Saxon's chartering decisions hold up very well—very few of the more than 600 banks he chartered have failed. This appears to be a small price to pay for the stimulus the new competition gave to the banking industry.[10]

In response to the chartering activities of the Comptroller, the state banking authorities also took a more liberal view of charter applications. An increase in chartering activity by the states in the early 1970s led to a slow but steady increase in the number of banks. The present number, however, is still below that of the early 1930s. The number of banks and branches is shown in Figure 14-1.

Meanwhile, the almost uninterrupted increase in the number of branches in operation has not been without controversy. In fact, whether or not branch banking is desirable has been one of the most hotly debated issues in American banking. It is not simply an economic problem; political and social considerations have long been involved. There are numerous arguments on both sides, and we will consider these arguments in Chapter 16, along with a closely related development, the rise of bank holding companies.

QUESTIONS

1 Many early banks started with capital borrowed from the bank itself. Can that happen now? Can a new bank borrow its beginning capital from another bank?
2 Why were the First and Second Banks of the United States not rechartered? Was Jackson's veto of the recharter of the Second Bank a mistake?
3 Was the development of free banking a good thing? Does free banking exist now?
4 How did the growing use of deposits as a means of payment affect the United States banking structure?
5 What is meant by the term *inelastic currency*?
6 Appraise the reform legislation of the 1930s in terms of present-day banking practices and needs.
7 Why did the depression of the 1930s result in such a large number of bank failures?

---

[10] For a good discussion of the performance of the banks chartered in 1962, see David C. Motter, "Bank Formation and the Public Interest," *National Banking Review*, March 1965.

8 Could the FDIC protect depositors if we had a similar wave of bank failures today?
9 Would the banking system be safer if we had nationwide branch banking?

SELECTED READINGS

FRIEDMAN, MILTON, and ANNA SCHWARTZ, *A Monetary History of the United States, 1867–1960*. Princeton, N.J.: Princeton University Press, 1963.

HAINES, WALTER W., *Money, Prices and Policy*, 2nd ed. New York: McGraw-Hill, 1966.

HAMMOND, BRAY, *Banks and Politics in America from the Revolution to the Civil War*. Princeton, N.J.: Princeton University Press, 1957. Winner of a Pulitzer Prize in history.

HOLDSWORTH, JOHN T., *The First Bank of the United States*. Washington, D.C.: U.S. Government Printing Office, 1910. Publication of the National Monetary Commission.

ROBERTSON, ROSS, M., *The Comptroller and Bank Supervision*. Washington, D.C.: Office of the Comptroller of the Currency, 1968. A very readable history of bank supervision at the federal level.

STUDENSKI, PAUL, and HERMAN KROOS, *Financial History of the United States*, 2nd ed. New York: McGraw-Hill, 1963.

15

Regulation of Banking

Banking regulation appeared with the very beginnings of banking in the United States, but in its early days, regulation was quite limited.[1] Early types of banking regulations included requirements of periodic reports, examinations, and some restrictions on various types of activities or investments. Requirements were imposed by the various states, in part because the states were stockholders in many of the early banks. Before 1830, examinations were not made regularly by professional bank examiners but were ordinarily conducted in response to a questionable financial report or rumored insolvency, and often by prominent citizens or a committee appointed for the purpose by the governor or state legislature.

From very limited beginnings, banking supervision in this country has expanded to the point where there are now three federal and 50 state agencies supervising banks, and literally thousands of pages of banking laws and regulations applicable to the country's commercial banks. The growth of banking regulation has been sporadic rather than steady and has come about in response to

[1] Although this chapter deals specifically with regulation of banks, the considerations are identical for other depository institutions—savings and loan associations, credit unions, and mutual savings banks.

particular circumstances and to popularly accepted theories as to the causes of those circumstances.

Significant expansions in bank regulation arose from the financial crisis of the Civil War, the Panic of 1907, and the Great Depression of the 1930s. In response to these situations, there emerged the National Banking Act, the Federal Reserve Act, and the Banking Acts of 1933 and 1935. The Banking Acts of the 1930s included creation of the Federal Deposit Insurance Corporation; the Glass-Steagall Act, which separated commercial banking from investment banking; and authority for the Federal Reserve and the FDIC to regulate interest rates on deposits. This legislation represented the high-water mark of the tide of regulation aimed at making banking safer by restricting competition, although it was not until very recently that the tide began to turn. There were relatively few major pieces of banking legislation enacted in the next few decades, and much of that represented concern with preserving competition, as exemplified by the Bank Merger Act of 1960, the Bank Holding Company Act of 1956, and its 1970 amendments. This later legislation grew out of concern with the wave of bank mergers that took place during the 1950s and the expansion of bank holding companies into nonbanking activities in the 1960s. The Depository Institutions Deregulation Act of 1980 represented the first major move toward reversing the growth of regulation.

In view of the fact that the economy of the United States is based on a faith in the functioning of a competitive free-enterprise system, it is somewhat surprising that banking regulation has developed to the extent that it has. It has long been a belief in this country that although competition and free enterprise are desirable bases on which to build in the case of most industries, banking is different. There are several reasons for the view that we cannot rely on competitive forces to provide efficient allocation of resources in banking but must instead look to regulation. These reasons include some that form the basis of regulation of other industries as well as some based on unique aspects of the banking business.

THE THEORY OF REGULATION

Economists have long recognized that there are some situations in which total reliance on competitive forces is not sufficient to ensure that a good product will be produced at a fair price to all consumers. These situations are those in which "public goods" are involved, or in which "externalities" are important, or where there are "information deficiencies." "Public goods" traditionally include police protection and national defense, but we can also include money and the payments system. We might note that the Constitution specifically assigns to Congress the responsibility for regulating the value of currency.

"Externalities" exist where the production or use of a product involves costs to the community in addition to those borne by its producer or user. The costs resulting from pollution emanating from a factory are borne by society as a whole, or by neighbors of the plant, rather than by the firm's owners or customers. A nonsmoker may be made uncomfortable (or worse) as a result of a smoker's decision to use cigarettes. Note that the danger to the health of the smoker does not enter into this type of justification for regulation; the knowledgeable smoker takes the health risk into account in deciding to smoke. There are several externalities in banking. The failure of one unsound bank may lead to a run on other banks in the area that are operating soundly. This phenomenon has been used as a justification for regulation of the soundness of all banks. My use of a checking account is facilitated if other people have checking accounts so that I can make and receive payments by check. An efficient payments system is in the nature of a public good, and hence the externality is a justification for government action to encourage public use of and confidence in the checking system.

"Information deficiencies" represent the major reason for government regulation of the operations of banks. It is widely believed that consumers cannot distinguish a sound bank from an unsafe one. Since a mistake in choosing a bank is more serious than in choosing a brand of toothpaste or automobile, it is the government's responsibility to see that all banks meet a minimum standard of safety. This is similar to the basis for government regulation of airline or food and drug safety.[2]

Banks are regulated, then, because of concern that without regulation there would be an excessive rate of bank failures. Bank failures impede the government's obligation to provide a stable, dependable money supply and the maintenance of an efficient payments system. Regulation is also intended to protect consumers from making unwise choices that could lead to substantial losses if

---

[2] In the economic literature, "economies of scale" is another justification for regulation. If costs decline continuously as the size of the firm increases, eventually only one firm would survive, and the forces of competition would not protect consumers. This is the reason for regulation of electric utilities, but the evidence does not indicate that banking falls into this category.

their bank should fail. It is recognized that regulation can lead to inefficiencies, particularly when it takes the form of restricting competition, but it has been felt that these inefficiencies are outweighed by the social costs of bank failures.

Bank failures are somewhat different from failures of other businesses. In other industries, the costs of failure fall mainly on the owners of the business, whereas a bank failure imposes losses on depositors. The failure of a toothpaste manufacturer does not represent any significant loss to users of the toothpaste (although failure of an auto manufacturer can involve loss to customers relying on the manufacturer's warranty). The difference in banking is related to financial leverage. A business failure falls, for the most part, on the owners who have provided most of the firm's funds. But banks operate with capital of only 5 to 10 percent of their total assets. This may provide an incentive toward risk taking—a successful investment means substantial returns to stockholders, while bad luck means a loss borne in large part by depositors.

This suggests that even with honest, rational decision making on investment policy, officers of a thinly capitalized bank can make decisions that may result in failure. Many discussions of bank regulation are put in terms of the temptations to take undue risk when using "other people's money." Regulation is often justified on this basis, or on grounds that some bankers are likely to be incompetent or dishonest (especially when we have a system with 15,000 banks). It is important to note that bank failure can result from unlucky investment decisions that are made by rational, profit-maximizing businessmen. In fact, some of the most spectacular cases of banks' getting into serious difficulty in recent years have been of this sort. Overall, the most frequent cause of recent bank failures has been excessive loans by the bank to other business interests of those controlling the bank. In some cases, this has been in violation of law; in other cases, it has represented an abuse of a conflict-of-interest situation. In some cases, the intent of management has been to loot the bank to their benefit at the expense of depositors and minority shareholders. In other cases, however, the ultimate intent of the people responsible for the failure may not have been dishonest. Suppose, for example, that the president of the bank is also involved in a real estate development that he thinks is sound, but which others do not, with the result that no one will lend him the money needed to undertake it; he may be tempted to lend the bank's money to finance the project. This is a very difficult area in which to impose laws or regulations that will be effective against the abuses without stifling legitimate activities of all banks.

TYPES OF REGULATION

There are several forms of banking regulation in the United States, including restrictions on bank *entry, activities, balance sheets,* and *prices.* We have already noted that entry into the banking business is limited. A charter must be obtained from either federal or state authorities. In order to receive a charter, sponsors of the proposed bank must justify its existence by demonstrating to the chartering authority that the bank will serve the public convenience and will be profitable. Those are strange requirements. If I want to open a bowling alley directly across the street from an existing bowling alley, I do not have to demonstrate to any board or authority that the public will be benefited, nor do I have to demonstrate that my bowling alley will be profitable. As long as I think it will be successful, I am free to go ahead with my venture. But the chartering authorities want to be sure that the new bank will not fail and also that the competition engendered by the new entrant will not pose a threat to existing institutions. The tradeoff here is rather clear: Our system of regulation attempts to enhance bank safety by restricting competition.[3]

The allowable activities of commercial banks are also severely restricted, and this restriction also applies, with only minor modifications, to bank holding companies. In general, banks cannot operate nonfinancial businesses, and cannot even invest in common stock. A major reason for these restrictions is concern that non-banking activities involve an unacceptably high degree of risk.

Another form of banking regulation consists of setting standards for financial ratios or relationships among asset and liability items on the bank's balance sheet. The most prevalent are reserve requirements and capital standards. Depository institutions are required to hold liquid assets (cash or deposits with the Federal Reserve) equal to some fraction of their deposit liabilities. Originally, these requirements were related to concern about bank liquidity and safety, but now they are viewed primarily as a means of facilitating control of the money supply by the Federal Reserve.[4]

---

[3] Not only is entry by new banks restricted, but our system also restricts the establishment of additional branch offices of existing banks. The reasons for restricting branching are more complex than just concern for bank safety and will be explored in more detail in the following chapter.

[4] As a matter of fact, reserve requirements were made much more restrictive for thousands of institutions by the 1980 Monetary Control Act, which, in most of its other provisions, represented a step toward deregulation. The stiffening of reserve requirements was significant enough to lead some economists to refer to the legislation as the *Re*regulation Act.

Capital standards are less formal, but all supervisory agencies attempt to see that the institutions they supervise maintain some minimum ratio of capital to assets or deposits. Another important form of financial regulation is a limit on the maximum size of a loan that the bank can make to any one borrower. This ensures some diversification in the bank's loan portfolio. Generally the loan limit is set at 10 to 20 percent of the bank's capital.

Bank pricing is not subject to the same sort of government rate setting that prevails in the telephone or railroad business, but freedom to set prices is limited by ceiling rates on loans (usury laws) and ceilings on rates that can be paid on deposits. (Usury laws were discussed in Chapter 10.) Ceilings on deposits originally represented an attempt to prevent excessive competition among banks that might lead to bank failure. It has long been recognized that this involves a misinterpretation of the bank-failure experience of the 1920s. As we have noted, the persistence of interest-rate ceilings has been tied to concern over the competitive position of the thrift institutions rather than bank safety as such. The Deregulation Act has put us firmly on the path of eventual phaseout of such ceilings.

This discussion of bank regulation has been put in terms of concern about bank soundness. But other social and private purposes are served by the restrictions on banks. A major motive for restrictions on branch banking is the preservation of the local community bank and fear of a concentration of banking power. Similarly, restrictions on the allowable activities of banks are aimed at preventing them from amassing great power over the economy.

It is also misleading to view banking regulation as something forced on an industry that favors free competition. Speeches of bankers and other businesspeople criticizing excessive government regulation should be taken with a grain of salt. Restrictions on competition have been welcomed by banks already in the market. Interest-rate ceilings were long supported by many bankers because they protected bank profit margins (even though they weakened commercial-bank opportunity to compete for market share with thrift institutions and money-market mutual funds). And restrictions on allowable activities of banks protected them from being taken over by nonbank firms.

The justifications for government regulation of banking discussed above make a convincing case for *some* regulation; but it is easy to overstate the case. Professors Edwards and Scott have pointed out that a consumer mistake in choosing a bank that proves to be unsound is not as serious as a decision to fly on an unsafe airline, or to have surgery performed by an incompetent doctor. Moreover, in terms of broader economic impact, it can be argued that failure of the bank in a one-bank town is less serious than the failure of the mill in a one-mill town. It has gradually become recognized that our system of banking regulation has involved restrictions on competition that exceed the needs of bank soundness. The recent trend toward deregulation in the airline, trucking, and financial industries will convey more benefits than losses to consumers.

Deposit Insurance

In addition to seeking bank safety through government regulation, the United States has also provided protection to depositors through a system of federal deposit insurance. With coverage of deposits up to $100,000 and the FDIC and FSLIC policy of handling failures through mergers that provide protection to all depositors, it turns out that the principal party at risk in a bank failure is not the depositor, but rather the deposit insurance system.

Deposit insurance actually serves two purposes: It provides protection to the small (and not so small) depositor, guaranteeing that depositors cannot lose their life savings in a bank failure, as did occur during the Great Depression and even during the prosperous 1920s. But perhaps more important, it reduces the risk of bank failure by removing the incentive for a run on banks thought to be in danger. The failure of one bank no longer leads to a decline in bank deposits as depositors rush to withdraw their funds. Deposit insurance thus helps provide for stability of the money supply.

If bank depositors now rely on deposit insurance rather than regulation for protection, do we still need all the regulations that grew up in the days before deposit insurance? The insured bank depositor no longer need be concerned about bank safety, yet the deposit insurance system is now at risk and needs some protection. We still need sufficient regulation to protect the soundness of that system, but it turns out that that does not require the whole range of regulation and restriction on competition that has evolved over the years. It has been argued that a minimum capital requirement, combined with a system of bank examinations, is sufficient to protect the deposit insurance system.

Bank Examination

The bank examination is a rather unusual form of government regulation, involving as it does an on-site investigation by government officials with full access to all the books and records of the bank. One purpose of bank examination is to determine whether the bank is operating in accord with banking law and regulation. But although all firms must operate in accord with the law, only financial institutions seem to be subject to periodic examinations to determine their compliance. The primary purpose of the examination, however, is to determine whether the bank is in sound condition. Financial reports can be helpful in reaching this determination, but what is needed is not simply a tabulation of the bank's assets as shown in a financial statement, but an evaluation of their quality.

The most important part of the bank-examination process is the evaluation of the loan portfolio. Loan evaluation is most important both in terms of the amount of examiner time utilized and in its implications for the soundness of the bank. During the examination, the examiner reviews carefully every loan in excess of a minimum "cutoff" size. The examiner checks whether the loan is made in violation of any law or regulation (limits on loans to one borrower, or on loans to officers), and also whether there are adequate financial statements for business loans.

The examiner then considers the quality of the loan and classifies it in one of four categories. Loans that involve more than a normal risk, owing to the financial condition or unfavorable record of the debtor, insufficiency of security, or other factors, are classified as either "substandard," "doubtful," or "loss." Loans classified as "loss" are thought to be uncollectable, and the bank is expected to eliminate them from its reported assets (but not to stop trying to collect them). "Doubtful" loans are expected to result in some loss, although the amount may not be precisely determined. Loans classified as "substandard" have an element of risk that, if not corrected, is likely to result in some loss to the bank or forced sale or acquisition of the collateral by the bank.

Since loans represent generally five or ten times the amount of bank capital, substantial weakness in the loan portfolio means danger to the soundness of a bank. Evaluation of the loan portfolio has long been the heart of the bank-examination process.

In 1977, the General Accounting Office, an arm of Congress, reported on an intensive investigation of the examination procedures of the federal banking agencies. The report criticized the traditional practice of the agencies, which involved examining all banks at about the same frequency and with about the same intensity. It supported recent changes in the agencies in the direction of more flexibility in examination frequency, scope, and procedures. Rather than routinely examining each bank each year, it makes sense to examine banks with problems more frequently and more intensively. What is not so clear is the relative emphasis that should be given to large and small banks. It may be argued that small banks should receive more intensive supervision, since the record indicates that these are more likely to fail. On the other hand, the impact on the public is very much greater in the case (fortunately less frequent) of a large-bank failure.

STRUCTURE OF BANKING REGULATION

Throughout U.S. banking history, much attention has been devoted to the question of the structure of banking regulation. This concern has centered on two related but separable issues: first, the relationship between federal and state supervision of banking, and second, the division of responsibilities among the three federal banking agencies—the Comptroller of the Currency, the Federal Reserve, and the Federal Deposit Insurance Corporation.

Federal or State Regulation

The federal–state issue is the older one; it has been a virtually continuous source of controversy since the establishment of the First Bank of the United States in 1791. The earliest banks in the United States were chartered by the states and were subject to some regulation by them. This regulation included bank examinations of a sort and the required filing of periodic reports of condition. Federal regulation of banking, which began with the chartering of the First Bank of the United States, ended temporarily with the demise of the Second Bank of the United States in 1836. Thus, from 1791 to 1836, we had a period of dual banking. From 1836 to 1863 was a period of state banking exclusively, and since the establishment of the national bank system in 1863, we have again had a dual banking system.

It is clear that the legislation of 1863 and 1864 was not aimed at the establishment of a dual banking system. The intent was to create a system of national banks; the state-chartered banks could join it or go out of business. This was the purpose of the tax on notes of state-chartered banks imposed in 1865. The trend toward the national bank system ended as the state banks found that they did not need note issue to operate profitably. Thus we are left with a dual banking system; that is, state-chartered banks operating side by side with federally chartered banks, and with both the states and the federal government exercising supervisory responsibilities over them.

The rationale for federal control of banking is relatively simple. Commercial banks are the primary suppliers of money in our economy. This was true 100 years ago when bank notes were the major component of the money supply, and it is true today when checking accounts fill that role. The Constitution specifically grants to Congress the power to issue money and regulate the value thereof, thus providing explicit authority for federal regulation of banking.

This view of the constitutional issue was not always universally accepted. Many people, including James Madison and Thomas Jefferson, argued that chartering the First Bank of the United States was unconstitutional. It was not until the Supreme Court's decision in the case of *McCulloch* v. *Maryland* that the federal government's authority to charter banks was firmly established. Later Supreme Court rulings bore out the federal government's power to regulate banks, including, in some cases, the right to regulate state-chartered banks.

The case for state regulation of banking has been put very strongly by Frank Wille:

> In banking, as in many other areas of business regulation, there can be decided advantages to a system of state regulation as distinct from a system of federal regulation. It should be possible to shape the governing law, and the regulations which implement it, more precisely to the local or regional needs of a particular state than under a national system of regulation. . . . Moreover, under a system of state regulation, there can be a greater willingness to innovate and experiment because experience can be gained in limited areas and under controlled conditions.[5]

The dual banking system, despite its accidental birth, has become a cornerstone of the American banking structure. The basic argument in support of the dual system is that it ensures flexibility in meeting the banking needs of the country, fostering innovation by permitting either the state or the federal government to develop and experiment with new approaches.

Although this argument may have some merit, the principal reason for the widespread support in the banking community of the dual banking system lies in a resolution of the American Bankers

---

[5] Frank Wille, "State Banking: A Study in Dual Regulation," *Law and Contemporary Problems* (Durham, N.C.: Duke University, Autumn 1966), p. 734. Mr. Wille's experience covered both federal and state banking supervision, first as Superintendent of Banks in New York State and then as Chairman of the FDIC.

Association: "The checks and balances which are inherent in the dual banking system have served as a deterrent to inappropriate or unduly burdensome actions at either the state or national level."[6] What this means is that if banks have the freedom to convert from one system to another, the supervisors of both systems will be cautious about overregulation.

However, this argument concerning checks and balances has a converse. Some critics of the dual banking system have suggested that the existence of two systems with the banks free to choose between them can lead to a "competition in laxity." In the past, this was often put in terms of a lowering of national standards to meet those of some of the states. In recent years, it has been the Comptroller's Office that has been charged with the initial lowering of standards.

The existence of a dual banking system does create some real problems in banking supervision. One of these is dual examinations. All insured, state-chartered banks are subject to examination by a federal agency (FDIC or Federal Reserve) in addition to examinations by their state banking department. Such dual examinations can be duplicative and expensive, although the federal agencies have tried to work out programs with the states to minimize duplication. A second problem is that state-chartered banks are subject not only to regulations of the state but also to the sometimes more restrictive regulations of the federal agencies. Perhaps the most important of these problems is the need for dual approvals for branches and mergers.

The problems referred to here are not purely those of a dual banking system but the results of an overlay of federal regulations on top of state regulations. Some of these problems might be avoided if we had a truly dual system, in which banks chartered by the federal or state authorities would be supervised only by those authorities. Under this approach, state-chartered banks would be regulated by state authorities and national banks would be regulated by the federal government. State-chartered banks would be eligible for Federal Reserve membership or federal deposit insurance, but Federal Reserve membership or insured status would not involve any supervision by the Federal Reserve or FDIC.

The main problem with this idea, of course, is that the vast majority of states would have neither the resources, ability, nor inclination to do a thorough job of banking supervision if they were

[6] Quoted in *Conflicts of Federal and State Banking Laws*, Hearings before the Committee on Banking and Currency, House of Representatives, 88th Cong., 1st sess., April 30, May 1–3 and 6, 1963, p. 537.

not supported by the FDIC and the Federal Reserve. Of course, the present system provides no incentive for them ever to develop this capability. It may be that if more responsibility for banking supervision were turned over to the state authorities, they would improve in order to be able to meet these responsibilities.

There are some other problems caused by the overlapping of federal and state supervisory responsibilities. The laws on branch banking are an important example of a departure from a truly dual system. Under present law, national banks are subject to state restriction on branching. In a sense, the federal statutes are subordinate to the state laws in this respect. The issue of liberalizing federal branching law will be discussed in the following chapter.

Federal Regulation

In addition to the problems of conflicting and overlapping federal–state supervision, there are also problems within the sphere of federal law and regulation. Three federal agencies have supervisory responsibility for banks, and these responsibilities overlap and, at times, lead to conflicts.

All insured banks are subject to supervision by the FDIC. The state-chartered banks that choose to do so may become members of the Federal Reserve System and thereby also subject to supervision by that agency. All national banks are supervised by the Comptroller of the Currency but must also be members of the Federal Reserve System.

It has long been recognized that the structure of federal banking regulation in this country, consisting of three agencies with overlapping jurisdiction, is an illogical one. The practice is generally more reasonable than the law, however. The matter of bank examinations is a good example. Although national banks are members of the Federal Reserve and the FDIC, they are examined only by the Comptroller of the Currency. Likewise, state banks are examined by the Federal Reserve or the FDIC (but not both).

Although the system works fairly smoothly most of the time, there have been periods of conflict among the agencies. The most striking example occurred during the term of James Saxon as Comptroller of the Currency in the mid-1960s. Saxon issued a number of regulations and interpretations of statute that liberalized, in several areas, the ground rules under which national banks could operate. Bank supervisors are not famous for their receptivity to new ideas, and these actions by the Comptroller stirred up considerable controversy and conflict with the other supervisory agencies.

In most of these areas of conflict, the Comptroller's judgment was undoubtedly correct in terms of the economics of the situation, if not the law. His ruling that corporations could hold savings deposits, for example, certainly made economic sense, although the Federal Reserve adhered to its ruling against corporate savings accounts until 1976.

More recently, there have been disagreements among the federal agencies as to the proper handling of failing banks, and sharp differences as to policy on bank merger proposals. In some cases, banks have converted to a national charter so that a proposed merger would be ruled on by the Comptroller rather than by the Federal Reserve or FDIC.

Studies of the banking system over the years by committees, commissions, and Congress have come up with one proposal after another for improving the structure of regulation. The prestigious Commission on Money and Credit called for transferring all the powers of the Comptroller and the FDIC to the Federal Reserve. An advisory committee to the Comptroller in 1962 proposed putting all responsibility for banking supervision under the Secretary of the Treasury. The Commission on Financial Structure and Regulation in 1971 proposed a regulatory structure even more complicated than the existing one.

A more basic approach to the problem of unifying the banking agencies and the process of bank regulation has been taken by the former vice-chairman of the Board of Governors of the Federal Reserve System, J. L. Robertson:

> There should be established a *new* agency of government—perhaps to be called the Federal Banking Commission. . . . To it should be transferred all the bank and bank holding company supervisory powers presently vested in the Federal Reserve Board, the Comptroller of the Currency, and the Federal Deposit Insurance Corporation. The latter two would be completely absorbed into the new Commission. . . .
>
> The commission would have all the jurisdiction now exercised by the existing agencies over charters, branches, mergers, holding companies, fiduciary and foreign banking activities, as well as disciplinary actions such as termination of "insurance" or "membership," and removal of officers or directors. It would also promulgate all regulations which are now required or authorized to be issued by any of the three supervisory agencies, and it would otherwise administer and interpret the federal banking laws. . . .
>
> The Board of Governors of the Federal Reserve System should be permitted to devote all of its time and effort to the task [of making monetary policy], without diverting attention to bank supervisory matters that demand concentrated full-time attention by people especially qualified for the job.[7]

---

[7] J.L. Robertson, remarks before the 72nd Annual Convention of the Tennessee Bankers Association, Memphis, Tennessee, May 16, 1962. In addition to his service on the Board of Governors, Mr. Robertson has served in the office of the Comptroller of the Currency.

Although the House Banking and Currency Committee held full-scale hearings on Governor Robertson's proposal for a new banking agency, the issue faded from public view for a few years, and then reappeared during the 1970s in response to the increased number of bank failures. Heavy congressional criticism was aimed at the Comptroller of the Currency as a result of the failures of the United States National Bank and the Franklin National Bank, our two largest bank failures and both supervised by the Comptroller. Despite the publicity that these failures generated and the demand that something be done to ensure the stability of the banking system, no legislation was passed by Congress to change the regulatory structure.

Proposals for reform of the illogical structure of American banking supervision have been around for a long time. Opponents of change have conceded that the present structure looks strange on paper, but, they stress, it has worked pretty well. Open conflicts between the supervisory agencies have been rare, and the supervisors have generally been men of good will who have been able to resolve (or at least paper over) any differences that have arisen. This point of view was best expressed by Bert Lance, a banker and former high official of the Carter administration, in his comment, "If it ain't broke, don't fix it."

The inability to achieve agreement on any specific proposal to improve the present system leads many authorities to conclude that no change is likely in the absence of a real crisis. Actually, however, there are some economic forces in operation that may lead to change in the system. Recent changes in the powers of thrift institutions, making them more like commercial banks, suggest that it may be desirable to combine regulation of banks with that of the thrifts. In particular, the difficulties of the thrift industry in the 1980s have generated proposals for mergers among banks and thrifts, and for consolidation of the separate deposit insurance systems. A more important force is the development of interstate banking activity. As banks come to operate in several states, jurisdictional problems will arise. Should the Texas operations of a state-chartered Illinois bank be supervised by Texas or Illinois? Can Illinois afford to conduct supervisory activities in 50 states? Alternatively, would a bank be willing to be subject to supervision by each of the states in which it operates? These questions suggest that as bank interstate operations grow, the banks will opt for national charters. Over the long run, this will have a significant effect on the dual banking system and on the structure of federal regulation.

A third consideration will have a more immediate effect. All banks (and other depository institutions) are required to maintain reserves in the form of currency or deposits with the Federal Reserve, but this requirement only recently became law. Many banks had chosen state charters because, prior to enactment of the Monetary Control Act of 1980, they could choose not to belong to the Federal Reserve System and thereby avoid the Fed's onerous reserve requirements. But now they must reassess the advantages and disadvantages of state and national charters. There are significant advantages to the state charter in a number of states (principally in the form of more liberal limits on the size of loans). Nevertheless, the imposition of Federal Reserve reserve requirements on all banks removes a substantial reason for choosing the state charter. The advantage of dealing with only one supervisory agency, the Comptroller of the Currency, rather than with both a state and a federal agency, should lead more and more banks in the direction of choosing national charters. This will tend to weaken the dual banking system, enhancing the regulatory responsibilities of the Comptroller as compared with the FDIC or the Federal Reserve.

Inertia is a powerful force in banking and in government regulation. The changes discussed here will not come about overnight. But the forces that are in motion are also powerful, and it is likely that there will be much discussion in the years ahead as to the best means of organizing the regulatory agencies so as to meet the needs for bank regulation that will remain even after the deregulation process runs its course.

QUESTIONS

1 What are the advantages and disadvantages of a dual banking system?
2 What changes would you recommend in our regulatory structure?
3 How did the Monetary Control Act of 1980 affect the structure of banking regulation?
4 What is the purpose of bank examination? Do you believe it is really necessary today? Is it necessary to examine the large banks?
5 "Many of our banking regulations grew out of the depression of the 1930s and are not suitable for modern economic conditions." Do you agree? What changes would you favor?
6 If you were organizing a new bank, would you choose a national or a state charter?
7 How does its involvement in banking supervision help the Federal Reserve in its monetary-policy functions?

SELECTED READINGS

Advisory Committee on Banking to the Comptroller of the Currency, *National Banks and The Future*. Washington, D.C.: U.S. Government Printing Office, 1962.

Commission on Money and Credit, *Money and Credit*. Englewood Cliffs, N.J.: Prentice-Hall, 1961.

FRIEDMAN, MILTON, *A Program for Monetary Stability*. New York: Fordham University Press, 1959.

HORVITZ, PAUL M., "Failures of Large Banks: Implications for Banking Supervision and Deposit Insurance," *Journal of Financial and Quantitative Analysis*, November 1975.

———,"A Reconsideration of the Role of Bank Examination," *Journal of Money, Credit and Banking*, November 1980.

The Report of the President's Commission on Financial Structure and Regulation. Washington, D.C.: U.S. Government Printing Office, 1971.

ROBERTSON, ROSS M., *The Comptroller and Bank Supervision*. Washington, D.C.: Office of the Comptroller of the Currency, 1968.

U.S. Congress, Senate Committee on Banking, Housing and Urban Affairs, *Compendium of Major Issues in Bank Regulation*. Washington, D.C.: U.S. Government Printing Office, 1975.

16

Competition in the Financial-Services Business

The preceding chapter described the rationale for regulation of the banking business in the United States and the types of regulation in use. As a matter of social policy, the U.S. has long relied heavily on regulation to ensure appropriate performance by the banking industry; yet we have not abandoned traditional reliance on the forces of competition to provide an efficient allocation of resources and service to consumers. Banks are expected to compete vigorously for business and the profits that go with success, even though the extent of that competition is limited by the regulations we have discussed.

In banking as in other businesses, public policy to promote competition is reflected in laws designed to promote a competitive structure in the industry—a structure in which there are many firms competing and in which a few giant firms do not dominate. In most industries, the antitrust laws promote a competitive structure. The antitrust laws apply to banking too (with some modifications), but we also have other legal restrictions that affect the structure of the banking industry. These include restrictions on entry, on branching, and on bank holding-company operations. Some of these restrictions (those on entry, for example) impede competition; others have effects that both stimulate and restrict competition. We employ devices with mixed effects on structure, because our attitude toward competition is somewhat schizophrenic: We want a banking structure with a level of competition that will result in low prices to users of bank services, but that will not be so intense as to promote frequent bank failures.

So far, this discussion has been in terms of banks. But *commercial banking* no longer describes the extent of the competition that prevails in banking markets. Commercial banks provide a great many financial services, but in every one of them there are other firms competing for the business. Of course, other depository institutions have long been in direct competition for the savings deposits of the public, but now savings banks, savings and loans, and credit unions can provide checking accounts as well, and the money-market mutual funds have become a very potent force in the market for deposit-type instruments. The brokerage firms now offer accounts that combine a savings instrument with credit cards and credit lines attached, and that allow checks to be written against them. On the loan side, a variety of financial and nonfinancial institutions compete with banks in all types of lending activity. Sears and other retailers have millions of credit cards outstanding, and extend billions of dollars of credit to consumers.

In the remainder of this chapter, we will first discuss issues of structure and competition among commercial banks, and then consider the growing competition among banks and other financial institutions.

BANKING CONCENTRATION

Economic theory leads us to expect better performance (better in the sense of lower prices and greater output) in relatively unconcentrated markets that approach the ideal of perfect competition. There have been a number of empirical attempts in recent years to determine the effect of concentration on bank performance. The weight of the evidence is that concentration does matter—that is, bank performance is better in banking markets that are less concentrated.

There is no unambiguous way to measure the degree of concentration in American banking. There are nearly 15,000 banks in the United States, an enormous number by any standard. But the differences in the size of banks are such that the American banking system is less atomistic and competitive than that figure might suggest. The 100 largest banks and bank holding companies, for example, hold nearly one-half of all bank deposits in the country. To some, an industry in which 1 percent of the firms hold 50 percent of the assets is a highly concentrated one. (And to some, an industry in which it takes 100 firms to account for 50 percent of the industry is relatively unconcentrated.) We are also concerned about the trend of concentration, and here, despite the fears of some, developments over time have not been adverse. The 100 largest banks held 57 percent of bank deposits in 1940 and 48 percent in 1945, and their share has fluctuated in a very narrow range since then. The figure was 49 percent in 1960 and in 1980.

Most authorities would agree that these national data, interesting as they might be, do not provide a meaningful measure of the degree of concentration or competition in American banking. Banking for most of us is a local service, and what is relevant, even for most business firms, is the degree of concentration in local banking markets. Table 16-1 provides some measure of concentration on a state basis, and Table 16-2 shows similar data for selected metropolitan areas.

TABLE 16-1

Concentration of Commercial Bank Deposits, by State

	Percentage of State Deposits in Three Largest Banks or Holding Companies:	
	1960	1979
Alabama	31.2	38.5
Alaska	68.2	60.7
Arizona	95.8	85.2
Arkansas	17.3	13.1
California	65.7	57.6
Colorado	37.9	40.5
Connecticut	42.7	46.0
Delaware	79.8	73.5
Florida	17.9	25.6
Georgia	48.6	40.3
Hawaii	89.2	79.2
Idaho	74.5	75.0
Illinois	35.5	32.8
Indiana	23.8	17.2
Iowa	14.2	17.3
Kansas	14.3	10.1
Kentucky	27.6	23.1
Louisiana	29.3	15.2
Maine	34.7	48.4
Maryland	42.7	44.9
Massachusetts	49.3	46.1

TABLE 16-1 (continued)

	Percentage of State Deposits in Three Largest Banks or Holding Companies:	
	1960	1979
Michigan	40.8	35.4
Minnesota	58.6	52.5
Mississippi	24.9	27.6
Missouri	26.6	29.4
Montana	48.9	43.3
Nebraska	31.6	20.5
Nevada	93.5	83.5
New Hampshire	24.3	35.0
New Jersey	16.8	23.0
New Mexico	43.0	44.5
New York	40.0	37.2
North Carolina	46.8	50.9
North Dakota	46.6	39.1
Ohio	24.2	25.7
Oklahoma	32.6	19.6
Oregon	86.7	74.3
Pennsylvania	27.9	23.5
Rhode Island	92.8	87.4
South Carolina	42.4	44.5
South Dakota	37.5	43.7
Tennessee	28.7	27.9
Texas	21.1	24.7
Utah	65.6	61.5
Vermont	25.6	43.8
Virginia	20.2	33.1
Washington	61.1	62.3
West Virginia	17.3	8.7
Wisconsin	31.4	27.3
Wyoming	35.1	38.6

Source: Federal Deposit Insurance Corporation.

It is clear from these data that some states and cities do have high levels of concentration in banking. This is reason for concern, although the trend in recent years has been toward slightly lower levels of concentration in many states and metropolitan areas. This picture of the structure of banking in the United States should be kept in mind in reading the remaining sections of this chapter. Evaluation of branch banking and bank merger policy is closely connected with our ideas as to the appropriate banking structure for the country.

TABLE 16-2
Concentration of Commercial Bank Deposits, by SMSA
(June 30, 1980)

	Percentage of SMSA Deposits Held by the Largest Banks or Bank Holding Companies		
	Largest	Three Largest	Five Largest
Anaheim, Santa Ana, Garden Grove, CA	24.8	51.4	62.9
Atlanta	22.2	56.4	71.8
Baltimore	27.4	64.8	86.0
Boston	31.0	58.1	79.9
Chicago	22.6	45.2	52.7
Cincinnati	27.4	62.7	71.0
Cleveland	30.8	66.7	86.7
Dallas	20.6	47.1	59.5
Denver	19.3	49.8	66.6
Detroit	26.6	57.2	74.1
Houston	20.4	48.7	61.8
Indianapolis	26.2	72.2	76.2
Kansas City	12.2	34.9	45.9
Los Angeles-Long Beach	25.4	62.6	75.2
Miami	24.8	36.1	45.0
Milwaukee	28.0	57.4	67.4
Minneapolis-St. Paul	35.9	68.6	72.8
Nassau-Suffolk counties, NY	18.5	41.2	61.5
Newark	18.7	43.9	55.5
New Orleans	25.6	53.1	68.7
New York	15.5	39.4	58.7
Oklahoma City	20.9	46.0	52.0
Philadelphia	14.6	37.3	53.8
Phoenix	41.4	84.3	94.1
Pittsburgh	47.6	83.5	91.2
Portland, OR	25.4	60.1	73.9
St. Louis	13.9	33.7	42.6
San Diego	29.3	59.5	73.3
San Francisco	46.0	76.2	81.4
Seattle-Everett	41.9	69.1	80.1
Tampa-St. Petersburg	10.4	25.1	37.5
Washington	14.3	34.6	45.8

Source: Federal Deposit Insurance Corporation.

BRANCH BANKING

In most countries, banking systems consist of a relatively small number of banks, each with a large number of branch offices. There are only nine banks in Canada and fewer than 20 in England. The United States is the only major country to have a basically unit banking system—that is, a system in which most banks do not have branches. The reason for this probably lies in the fear of banking monopoly. Most states originally did not allow banks to establish branches, and as late as 1910, only twelve states allowed it.

The National Bank Act did not contain any provision regarding branches, and this lack of authorization was interpreted as a prohibition. In 1922, Comptroller of the Currency Crissinger ruled that national banks could operate additional offices in the same city as the head office to handle certain routine types of business. They were not authorized to grant loans independently of the head office. The Comptroller issued permits allowing national banks to establish branches only in cities where state banks were already operating branches. Over 200 such permits were issued in the next five years.

Congress formally legalized this procedure in the McFadden-Pepper Act of 1927. The Banking Act of 1933 liberalized these laws for national banks by allowing them to establish branches on the same terms as those applicable to state banks in the various areas. Thus, in a state allowing statewide branch banking, national banks can establish branches anywhere in the state; in a state where branching is restricted to the head-office city or county, national banks are subject to the same limitations. Although the number of commercial-bank branches has increased very rapidly in recent years, the issue of branch banking is still a very controversial one. Less than half the states allow statewide branching, and about another third of the states allow branching subject to some restrictions, generally limiting branches to the same city or county as the head office (see Table 16-3). Most of the remaining states allow branching on a very restricted basis, perhaps permitting only drive-in facilities close to the main office. Only a few states now prohibit branching completely.

The range of limitations in the "limited-branch-banking" states is very wide. Several states that allow branching do not allow branches to be established in the same city as the head office of another bank. These "home-office-protection" laws are clearly anti-competitive, but some states have tried a more extreme version—whereby banks can establish branches only by acquiring an existing bank.

Although these state laws are specifically applicable to state-chartered banks, the McFadden Act restricts national banks to the same limitations on branching that state banks are subjected to in the state in which they operate. Thus, in California, national banks can establish branches in any part of the state. In Massachusetts, national banks can establish branches only within the same county

TABLE 16-3

State Branch-Banking Laws

Statewide Branch Banking Allowed	Limited Branch Banking Allowed	Branch Banking Prohibited or Severely Restricted
Alaska	Alabama	Colorado
Arizona	Arkansas	Illinois
California	Georgia	Kansas
Connecticut	Indiana	Missouri
Delaware	Iowa	Montana
Florida	Kentucky	Nebraska
Hawaii	Louisiana	North Dakota
Idaho	Massachusetts	Oklahoma
Maine	Michigan	Texas
Maryland	Minnesota	West Virginia
Nevada	Mississippi	Wyoming
New Hampshire	New Mexico	
New Jersey	Ohio	
New York	Pennsylvania	
North Carolina	Tennessee	
Oregon	Wisconsin	
Rhode Island		
South Carolina		
South Dakota		
Utah		
Vermont		
Virginia		
Washington		

as their head office, because this is the limitation on branching for state banks. No state allows out-of-state banks to establish branches.

The McFadden Act became a live issue during the mid-1970s as some banks sought to move into the era of electronic banking by establishing unmanned, automated teller machines and cash-dispensing machines. If these machines were considered "branches," then the McFadden Act applied, and such facilities could be established only when state law allowed. The Comptroller of the Currency ruled that such "customer–bank communication terminals," or *CBCTs*, were not branches and could be operated by national banks in accord with regulations promulgated by the Comptroller.[1] Several lawsuits instituted by banks and state-bank

[1] The term was chosen to give the impression that the machines were mere communication devices, like a mailbox or a telephone, rather than something like a real branch.

supervisors challenged this interpretation, and they generally pre-vailed against the Comptroller. This issue is an important one, because it is likely that such automated facilities will be a major part of the system by which financial services are delivered to the consumer in the future. The costs of operating manned branches, housed in expensive real estate, have soared in recent years. The costs of computer capability have been falling, and consumer acceptance of automated devices has been increasing, overcoming initial resistance.[2] Both the National Commission on Electronic Funds Transfer Systems and the Carter administration study of the McFadden Act recommended that state laws against branch banking should not be allowed to slow the development of EFTS facilities.

The Branch-Banking Issue

There are many arguments involved in the branch-banking issue; the supporters of branch banking can list many advantages, but the opposition can list as many disadvantages. We shall attempt to analyze some of the more important issues.

Economic Efficiency. It is often argued that branch banking is more efficient, meaning that branches can be operated at lower cost than unit banks. This appears reasonable, since the branch does not need all the facilities and personnel of an independent bank. The branch need not be concerned with problems of investment in securities, for example, since this function is carried out at the head office. The bank with branches will generally be larger, and there should be some economies of large-scale operations in banking. Nevertheless, the argument is not clear-cut.

Proponents of branch banking speak of the economies of scale, meaning that a large bank is cheaper to run, relatively, than a small bank. The opponents of branch banking speak of the additional costs of the branch structure. It is true that a bank with $1 billion of deposits has lower average costs of operation than a $20-million bank. But it is also true that a $20-million unit bank has lower costs than a $20-million branch bank.

---

[2] Some of the most successful automated teller facilities have been on college campuses. It appears that although older bank customers prefer to deal with live tellers and feel insecure about dealing with a machine, college students do not share this reluctance. (Perhaps dealing with a college administration is like dealing with a computer.)

This distinction is an important one. Let us consider a small town with a population of 4,000. The most efficient banking service for this town could theoretically be provided by a billion-dollar unit bank, but clearly it would be impossible to establish such a bank in this community. The real choice for this town is between having a small unit bank or a branch of a large bank. The important question is which of these two alternatives can provide the most efficient service. The answer is not obvious, because the diseconomies of branch structure may be more important than the economies of scale.[3] Moreover, it appears that most of the potential economies are achieved at a relatively small size—say, $50 million.

Safety. Supporters of branch banking argue that it is safer than unit banking. Evidence for this is the fact that foreign countries that have well-developed nationwide branch banking have not experienced bank failures to the extent that the United States has. The reasons for expecting branch banks to be safer lie in the larger size of the branch banks and the greater degree of diversification in loans that a system covering a wide area is apt to have. It should be noted, however, that if a branch bank is limited to a small area, it may not obtain any more diversification than a unit bank.

When a bank is in danger of failing, the FDIC usually attempts to arrange for another bank to take it over, frequently with the financial assistance of the FDIC. It is easier to make such arrangements where branching is allowed. A healthy bank will probably not find it attractive to take over the business of a failing bank if it must close the office that it acquires. In such a case, it would promptly lose to other banks some of the business it has just bought. As a result, it is easier to protect the public from the losses associated with bank failure in states that allow branching, even if branch banking is not inherently safer than unit banking.

Service to Customers. One of the most serious arguments against branch banking is the alleged impersonal lending policy of branch banks. It is argued that branch managers must refer most loan applications to the head office to be decided by people who do not know the borrower personally, and thus loans are granted on purely mechanical standards. Character becomes a less important factor in the lending decision. Moreover, even when the branch manager has authority to make loans, he may not know the bor-

---

[3] For a discussion of this question, see Paul M. Horvitz, "Economies of Scale in Banking," in *Private Financial Institutions* (Englewood Cliffs, N.J.: Prentice-Hall, Inc., 1963); George J. Benston, "Economies of Scale of Financial Institutions," *Journal of Money, Credit and Banking*, May 1972; and William Longbrake, "Productive Efficiency in Commercial Banking," *Journal of Money, Credit and Banking*, August 1975.

rower well because of the policy of branch banks to shift managers from branch to branch to gain experience. The unit banker is presumably a long-time resident of his community and knows all potential borrowers well. In fact, it has been argued that the ability to give a prompt decision based on local knowledge is the chief advantage of the local bank.

The branch banks are, to some extent, guilty of a more impersonal lending policy than local unit banks, but this is not all bad. There have been many cases in which the local banker has made bad loans on the basis of personal knowledge of, and friendship with, the borrower when impersonal scrutiny of the borrower's balance sheet would result in refusal of the loan. Also, the branch bank may be able to provide more complete service to a community than the unit banks—trust services, credit-card plans, foreign-exchange facilities, and other services of the "department-store" bank. On the other hand, many communities do not need all these specialized services.

Facilities for Small Towns.   Perhaps the most important argument of branch-banking supporters is that branch banking can provide banking facilities for small towns better than unit banking can. Under any type of banking structure, there will be more or less adequate banking facilities in the large cities. The true test of the adequacy of a banking structure is how well it provides for banking facilities in small towns.

There are several reasons for believing that a system of branch banking would mean more banking facilities in small towns. In some cases, a branch can be operated at lower cost than an independent bank. Thus, in some cases a unit bank could not be operated profitably, but a branch could.

Although the logic of this argument appears convincing, the data on banking facilities in small towns are not so clear-cut. The evidence suggests that branch banking is apt to result in somewhat greater convenience of banking facilities in moderate- and large-sized nonmetropolitan areas. However, the number of additional facilities on the average is small in all but the largest such communities. The difference in the very small communities is negligible. It seems clear that in the larger cities, there are more banking offices where branching is allowed. Even though data on this issue do support a presumption in favor of branch banking, the case is not as strong as many supporters of branch banking have believed.[4]

[4] For a more complete analysis of the data on banking facilities, see Paul M. Horvitz and Bernard Shull, "The Impact of Branch Banking on Bank Performance," *National Banking Review*, December 1964.

Branch Banking and Competition

The key issue in the branch-banking debate is its effect on competition. Has the development of branch banking reduced the level of competition in banking? Would its further expansion mean further reduction in competition? If branch banking does lead to monopoly, its expansion is undesirable even though it may have other advantages.

Our concern with competition in banking is in regard to small borrowers. The large, nationally known firms will not find the banking situation very different if Minnesota, say, should authorize branch banking. General Motors can borrow from banks in New York, Chicago, or San Francisco as well as from Detroit banks. Even if a change in banking laws should result in a banking monopoly in Colorado, General Motors' ability to borrow money will not be weakened.

Small borrowers, on the other hand, generally have access only to the banks in their own town. In a town with only one bank, these borrowers may have no alternative source of supply, since they are not well enough known to seek a loan in the financial centers of the area. Their success in obtaining a loan depends upon a local banker's knowing enough of them or their business to be able to grant the loan.

The small-business borrower warrants special attention, because the local commercial bank is his or her major source of financing. The small firm can generally not borrow from insurance companies, or tap the commercial paper market, or sell long-term bonds in the open market. Although savings and loan associations and other depository institutions are important competitors of commercial banks with respect to many financial services, they are not yet significant sources of funds to small businesses.

There is some reason for believing that branch-bank lending policy is impersonal, in the sense of not taking account of the individual element in the lending process to the same extent as unit banks do. There is also some evidence that as far as interest rates are concerned, the small borrower is apt to be better treated by the small unit bank than by the large branch bank. A reasonable conclusion, then, is that small-business borrowers are harmed rather than helped when the unit bank in their community is replaced by a branch of a large bank. However, in many cases, the alternative to a unit bank may be not simply *a* branch, but two or more branches, or a unit bank and a branch (or branches). If the one bank in a town were replaced by a branch (through merger, for example), the position of small borrowers could be worsened. But if the coming

of branch banking allowed the town to be served by several competing branches, the level of competition would be substantially increased. This is a realistic possibility, since there are many towns
that can support only one unit bank but that could support more
than one branch of larger banks.

One reason for expecting more competition under branch
banking lies in the attitude of banking regulatory authorities. We
have already seen that avoiding bank failures is one important
factor in bank-chartering decisions. It is easy to understand why
bank supervisors would refuse to allow additional competition if
they felt that it would lead to bank failures. This explains why bank
supervisors have been quite liberal in granting permission for the
establishment of new branches when the new branches will compete with existing branches but not with existing unit banks. Competition between branches is most unlikely to lead to bank failures.
It is inconceivable that a large branch bank could fail because of
losses incurred by any one branch. That is, there are many areas
where the banking authorities may grant permission for the establishment of a branch of a large bank but would be forced to deny an
application for the establishment of a new unit bank.

We can summarize briefly the relationship of branch banking
to competition. Competition is a force making for efficiency in operations and lower prices for consumers. Large borrowers are not
seriously affected by the banking structure in any particular state,
but the existence of branch banking does have an effect on the level
of competition as far as small borrowers are concerned. If branch
banking simply means that small unit banks are replaced by
branches of larger banks, the position of small borrowers is likely to
deteriorate. If, on the other hand, branch banking means that communities formerly without banking facilities are going to have
branches of large banks, and that towns formerly served by only one
bank are going to have branches of several, then the position of the
small borrower will probably be improved. It is impossible to be
absolutely certain which tendency will predominate, but the latter
is more likely, and thus the extension of branch banking will probably increase competition in banking.

BANK HOLDING COMPANIES

As we have seen, the power of a bank to operate branches is restricted in many states. One way around these restrictions has been
the bank holding company. A bank holding company is a corporation
that controls, through stock ownership, one or more commercial

banks. In some states that prohibit or restrict branching, it is legal for a bank holding company to own and operate banks all over the state. A bank in Houston, Texas, cannot operate branches in Dallas or San Antonio, but there are bank holding companies in Texas that do own banks operating in all these cities and others.

The holding-company device is a means of legally achieving many of the benefits and advantages of branch banking; such functions as investment management and other staff services can be provided by the holding company for all the subsidiary banks. In practice, the degree of centralization varies; in some cases, the banks operate virtually as independent bank units, and in others, the controlled banks operate almost as branches of one bank.

Although some advocates of the holding-company device argue that *group banking*, as it is called, is actually more efficient and advantageous, most agree that branching is a superior means of providing and delivering banking services to the public. Most holding companies have switched to the branch-bank approach when that has been legal. Florida has long had an extensive system of bank holding companies, but when branching became legalized in the state in 1976, most of the holding companies merged their subsidiary banks so as to form branch banks. A similar process occurred earlier in New York. When state law was liberalized to a statewide basis, most of the large bank holding companies in the state promptly merged their subsidiaries into single banks with branches.

Holding companies that control at least two banks have been subject to regulation by the Federal Reserve Board since 1956 under the Bank Holding Company Act. That legislation severely restricted the activities of bank holding companies and required Federal Reserve approval for any acquisition of another bank by a holding company.

There were 53 such multibank holding companies registered with the Fed at the end of 1956. Their deposits accounted for about 8 percent of all commercial-bank deposits at that time. The number of holding companies fluctuated somewhat over the next few years, but their share of total deposits remained fairly steady until the mid-1960s, when changes in the law encouraged their somewhat more rapid growth.

Holding companies controlling only one bank were not subject to regulation under the 1956 act. Banks and multibank holding companies were generally limited to activities very closely related to banking. One-bank holding companies, on the other hand, were free to engage in literally any business activity. During the 1960s, many bankers became aware of this loophole, which fit in with their desires to diversify. Some of the bank ventures into allied fields of activity—providing data-processing services, for example—were being challenged as illegal by competing firms. Although banks might be able to defend data-processing services as part of the banking business, it was simpler to convert the bank's organization structure to that of a one-bank holding company. The holding company could then operate the bank as one subsidiary and the data-processing activity as another.

Many large banks converted to holding companies, and by 1970, they accounted for more than one-third of all commercial-bank deposits. The rapid growth led to calls for controls, and a lengthy congressional investigation and debate followed. It is worth examining some of the arguments involved, because they illuminate the general issues of competition and regulation in banking.

We have seen that the primary reason for most regulation of banking is concern for bank safety. Some critics of the bank-holding-company movement argued that as banks, through the one-bank holding-company device, moved into new (and riskier) activities, dangers of bank failure increased. This argument seems to overlook the essential nature of the holding-company device. The holding-company organization structure helps insulate the *bank* from nonbanking activities. That is, the bank is a corporate entity separate from the other subsidiaries of the holding company. If a subsidiary of a one-bank holding company were to go into a risky venture and fail, neither the holding company nor the bank would have any legal obligation to come to its rescue.

Actually, the argument on bank safety can be rephrased in a more sophisticated version. If an affiliate of a one-bank holding company does fail, won't management of the bank feel a moral obligation to come to the aid of the failing firm? Or may management mistakenly divert the bank's assets in an attempt to shore up the failing firm? Or may management feel the need to save the nonbank subsidiary in order to maintain confidence in the bank? In one case, a large California bank did pay off creditors of a foreign subsidiary of the bank even though it had no legal obligation to do so. One of our largest bank failures came about when the management of the parent holding company, concerned about the condition of an affiliated mortgage company, shifted a large volume of poor-quality loans from the mortgage company to the bank.

Perhaps the most important concern to many critics of the holding-company movement is the possibility that these institutions will be able to amass an undesirable amount of economic power. Our discussion of the history of banking in this country stressed the fear of concentrated economic power that has been a factor behind much of our banking legislation. This concern is partly an economic one and partly a political or emotional one, but it is real.

An additional factor in the debates over this issue was the concern of existing firms in various lines of business that they might be subject to increased competition from affiliates of commercial banks. Data-processing firms, insurance agencies, travel agencies, and others lobbied hard to restrict the allowable activities of the banks.

The lack of restrictions on one-bank holding companies meant not only that banks could organize holding companies and take over other firms, but also that other firms could take over existing banks. During the late 1960s, several industrial firms made tender offers for the stock of commercial banks. This posed a threat to the entrenched management of some banks, particularly those that had not been doing too well. It appears that a tender offer by a large computer-leasing firm for the stock of one of the largest New York banks led to strong effort by many banks to subject one-bank holding companies to regulation.

The result of all this was the 1970 amendments to the Bank Holding Company Act of 1956. These amendments made one-bank holding companies fully subject to the restrictions of the 1956 act. However, they also authorized the Federal Reserve Board to draw up a new list of allowable activities for holding companies that would represent some liberalization from the 1956 act. The new list of allowable activities (Table 16-4) applies to both one-bank and multibank holding companies.

The 1970 legislation was followed by a rapid expansion of multibank holding companies, since it liberalized the activities open to them. In 1965, bank holding companies (both one-bank and multibank) accounted for under 13 percent of total bank deposits in the country. By 1973, this figure had increased to over 65 percent and in 1977 reached 71 percent. Future expansion of multibank holding companies will depend on the continuation of limitations on branch banking. Liberalization of branch-banking laws in important holding-company states such as Colorado, Texas, and Virginia would lead to a reduction in the number of multibank holding companies. Recent legislation in Illinois, allowing multibank holding companies for the first time, will add to their numbers.

Bank holding companies have used the authority granted by the 1970 amendments to engage in nonbanking activities, but examination of Table 16-4 reveals that the list is a very limited one. Very few of these are activities that could not be engaged in directly by banks themselves. The restrictive posture taken by the Federal

TABLE 16-4
Status of Bank Holding Company Nonbanking Activities under Section 4(c)(8)

Activities Approved by the Board	Activities Denied by the Board
1. Dealer in bankers' acceptances[a]	1. Equity funding (combined sale of mutual funds & insurance)
2. Mortgage banking[a]	2. Underwriting general life insurance
3. Finance companies[a]	3. Real estate brokerage[a]
a. consumer	4. Land development
b. sales	5. Real estate syndication
c. commercial	6. General management consulting
4. Credit card issuance[a]	7. Property management
5. Factoring company[a]	8. Nonfull-payout leasing
6. Industrial banking	9. Commodity trading
7. Servicing loans[a]	10. Issuance and sale of short-term debt obligations ("thrift notes")
8. Trust company[a]	11. Travel agency[a]
9. Investment advising[a]	12. Savings and loan associations
10. General economic information[a]	
11. Porftolio investment advice[a]	
12. Full payout leasing[a]	
a. personal property	
b. real property	
13. Community welfare investments[a]	
14. Bookeeping & data processing services[a]	
15. Insurance agent or broker— credit extensions[a]	
16. Underwriting credit life & credit accident & health insurance	
17. Courier service[a]	
18. Management consulting to nonaffiliate banks[a]	
19. Issuance of travelers checks[a]	
20. Bullion broker[a]	
21. Land escrow services[a]	
22. Issuing money orders and variable denominated payment instruments[a]	

[a] Activities permissible to national banks.

Reserve reflects fear of criticism from businesses that do not want to face bank competition or takeovers. An extreme example is the failure of the Federal Reserve to include operation of a savings and loan association as an allowable activity for a bank holding company, even though banks can already do anything that an S&L can.

In one important respect, however, the 1970 Bank Holding Company Act represents a substantial liberalization of bank-holding-company operations. The law puts no geographical limitations on the operations of nonbank subsidiaries of bank holding companies. We have already noted that banks are not allowed to

establish branches outside their home states. Similarly, the Douglas Amendment to the Bank Holding Company Act prohibits bank
holding companies from establishing or acquiring *bank* subsidiaries
outside their home states.[5] In recent years, however, we have seen
a rapid expansion of interstate nonbanking activity by large bank
holding companies.

INTERSTATE BANKING

Although banks and bank holding companies cannot provide full
banking services across state lines, by a variety of devices they are
allowed to provide some financial services on an interstate or even
national basis. Some of these devices are new, but some have been
in existence for a long time. Large banks have long had a staff of
"calling officers" who travel the region or the country in search of
business. They can solicit lending business even though the loan
documents may technically have to be signed in the home state of
the bank. Now these bankers can have permanent bases in out-of-
state locations, called "loan production offices."

Edge Act corporations are subsidiaries of banks that are authorized to operate nationwide in the conduct of international banking operations, including the acceptance of deposits and the granting of loans for international trade. The powers of the "Edges" have
recently been liberalized, and major cities around the country are
now host to these subsidiaries of out-of-state banks.

Several large bank holding companies have nonbank subsidiaries operating on a multistate or even national basis. Although the
Bank of America cannot open branches to make consumer loans
outside of California, its FinanceAmerica affiliate can operate
across the country. Some large bank holding companies engage in
mortgage banking, leasing, or commercial financing activities on a
national or regional basis through holding-company subsidiaries.
In many cases, the customer does not know (or care) that he or she
is not dealing with the bank.

[5] The Douglas Amendment allows such interstate acquisitions only if the laws
of the host state specifically allow such activity. Until recently, no states allowed
out-of-state holding-company acquisitions, but South Dakota and Delaware have
enacted laws to allow limited-purpose banks to be established by out-of-state holding
companies. (As a result, Citicorp of New York moved its credit-card operations to
South Dakota.) Several holding companies already had out-of-state subsidiaries
when the Douglas Amendment was enacted; these subsidiaries were "grand-
fathered" (allowed to continue in operation).

Even though these operating units cannot do everything that a bank or bank branch can do, they are effective competitors for many types of business. This activity is growing, and will continue to grow, even without any change in the law in the direction of liberalization of barriers to interstate banking. Many bankers find these devices less than completely satisfactory, however, and have advocated removal of the restrictions on interstate banking.

In many ways, the argument over interstate banking is similar to the argument over branching within a state. Advocates point out that increased competition could result from the entry of large out-of-state banks into local markets, with an improvement in service to customers. Opponents, particularly smaller banks, stress the traditional American concern about concentration of financial power, and warn against the danger of having the U.S. banking system dominated by a few giant New York or Chicago or California banks.

The argument has become more heated in recent years as banks have faced increasing competition from nonbanking firms that are not subject to the geographical restraints applying only to banks and other depository institutions. The giant brokerage firms, insurance companies, and retailers can operate wherever they deem worthwhile. The issue has become more significant as the brokerage firms, such as Merrill Lynch, and the money-market mutual funds have come to offer financial assets that are very competitive with time deposits (and on which checks can be written). Sears, Roebuck has a nationwide network of stores and competes with banks in granting consumer credit. A Sears advertisement proclaims, "You can count on Sears for credit when you need it. Over 60 million Americans carry Sears credit cards."

In addition, until passage of the International Banking Act of 1978, foreign banks had broader interstate banking powers than domestic banks had. The 1978 act removed some but not all of the inequities. In recognition of the problem, Congress called upon the administration to conduct a study of whether there should be a change in the McFadden Act so as to allow banks to branch interstate. That study, completed in 1980, recommended that the Douglas Amendment be eliminated so that bank holding companies could acquire banks across state lines. The recommendation got added support in 1981 when the banking supervisory agencies, concerned about the possibility of large-bank failures, proposed allowing failing banks to be rescued through merger with out-of-state banks. This proposal reflected concern that merger with a local institution might produce an undue level of concentration in the local banking market.

Proposals for interstate banking are controversial and will probably be debated for some time before there is any significant change in the law. It is clear, however, that the trend is in the direction of greater and greater interstate activity. It is a matter of when, not whether, the law will be changed.

BANK MERGERS

Bank mergers have been as important a feature of change in the banking structure as branch banking, and about as controversial. The controversy relates to the advantages of mergers in terms of "banking factors" and the undesirable effects of many mergers on competition.

Bank mergers play an important role in the development of a healthy banking system. Merger is frequently the best means of avoiding a bank failure, and it may also be desirable when a bank is not really failing but is floundering. Some banks in operation are simply not serving their communities' needs adequately, and a merger that allows replacement of these institutions with more vigorous, dynamic banks is often desirable. Furthermore, there are advantages to having larger banks. This is not simply a matter of the economies of scale but a reflection of the fact that there are some specialized banking services that only a large bank can provide.

Of course, not all bank mergers have desirable results. A merger of banks that are or could be significant competitors has the effect of reducing competition. In most banking markets, the number of competing banks is small and the concentration of banking assets is high. Where we already have substantial concentration, it is wise to avoid even small further increases in concentration.

The wave of bank mergers that took place in the early 1950s raised congressional concern with the issue. Lengthy debate over various legislative proposals to regulate bank mergers finally culminated in passage of the Bank Merger Act of 1960. That act gave the three federal banking agencies power to approve or deny proposed bank mergers after giving consideration both to banking factors and to the effect of the merger on competition.

In 1961, the Justice Department sued, under the Clayton and Sherman Acts, to prevent the merger of Philadelphia National Bank (second largest bank in Philadelphia) and Girard Trust Corn Exchange Bank (third largest in the city). The merger had been approved by the Comptroller of the Currency. In 1963, the Supreme

Court ruled that the Clayton Act applied to banking (a surprise to many antitrust experts), and that the proposed merger violated that law (not a surprising conclusion, if the Clayton Act applied). The Court stated that its decision was based solely on the Clayton Act's competitive criteria, and that the banking factors enumerated in the Bank Merger Act of 1960 (earnings prospects, management, capital adequacy, and so on) were irrelevant in the case of a merger that violated the antitrust laws.

In 1964, the Supreme Court ruled that a merger of two banks in Lexington, Kentucky, violated the Sherman Act, and in 1965, a district court in New York found a similar violation in the merger of Manufacturers Trust Company and the Hanover Bank. At the time of the Philadelphia decision, the Justice Department also had a case pending in Chicago, and Clayton Act suits were subsequently brought in St. Louis, San Francisco, and Nashville.

The banks involved were large and not without important friends. Within 30 days of the district-court decision in the Manu-facturers–Hanover case, Senator Robertson of Virginia introduced a bill to exempt banks from the antitrust laws. It soon became clear that this blanket exemption could not muster sufficient support, and a significantly amended version of the bill was finally passed by Congress in 1966.

The Justice Department now has 30 days following approval of a merger by the banking agency to decide whether to file suit. If suit is not filed within the 30 days, the merger becomes forever immune from attack under the antitrust laws. If an antitrust suit is filed, the banks cannot consummate their merger until there is a final court decision on the case (which might take several years). The 1966 law did provide that a merger with significant anticompetitive effects could still be legal if the benefits of the merger to the community "clearly outweigh" the anticompetitive effects. However, the bur-den of proof is on the banks to demonstrate that they do, and this is a burden that is very difficult to sustain.

The 1966 legislation provided that suits against all mergers consummated before the *Philadelphia* decision be dropped. Thus, Manufacturers–Hanover and the banks in Chicago and Lexington were granted relief from their litigation, and all pre-*Philadelphia* mergers that the Justice Department had not yet moved against were granted antitrust immunity.

The Bank Merger Act amendments of 1966 did not bring an end to bank mergers or to antitrust litigation in banking. In recent years, however, there have been very few large *horizontal* mergers— that is, mergers between banks that are already signifi-cant competitors in the same city. The threat of rejection by the supervisory agencies or litigation by the Justice Department has led banks to abandon horizontal mergers in favor of market-extension mergers, those between banks that are not already in competition with one another.

As a result, many of the antitrust cases brought by the Justice Department in the 1970s involved the issue of *potential competition*. These were mergers of banks not currently in competition with one another but that, the Justice Department argued, would come into competition through *de novo* branching if the merger were prevented.

The Justice Department has been unable to convince any district court of the significance of potential competition as a basis for preventing a bank merger. The Supreme Court has acknowledged potential competition as a factor to be taken into consideration in a suit brought under the Bank Merger Act, but it has not yet decided such a case in favor of the Justice Department.

The litigation and legislative problems since the 1960 Bank Merger Act are unfortunate. The 1960 act was a sound piece of legislation. The basic problem with that act was simply that the banking agencies did not give sufficient weight to the competitive factor in evaluating merger proposals and adopted very permissive merger policies. At least partly because of the Supreme Court decisions and the activity of the Justice Department, that situation has changed. Nevertheless, there are still differences among the banking agencies with respect to their attitude toward mergers. The Comptroller of the Currency has tended to be more permissive in approving merger applications than has either the FDIC or the Federal Reserve Board.

Virtually the same competitive standards that apply to bank mergers also apply to acquisitions of banks by bank holding companies. All bank-holding-company acquisitions must be approved by the Federal Reserve, which has taken a relatively strict posture in passing on such applications (particularly those involving "potential-competition" issues). In a few cases, bank holding companies have challenged Federal Reserve denials of their acquisition applications, where the denial has been based on anticompetitive effects that do not rise to the level of a violation of antitrust law. A series of court decisions has held that the banking agencies cannot impose stricter standards than those implied by the antitrust laws.

It is important to realize that only a small fraction of the proposed bank mergers have been denied by the agencies, and only a very small fraction of the approved mergers have resulted in lawsuits by the Justice Department. The vast majority of bank mergers have no significant anticompetitive effects, and warrant approval by any standard.

COMPETITION AMONG FINANCIAL INSTITUTIONS

At one time, each type of financial institution had its own niche in the financial structure of the United States, with little competitive overlap among institutions. Credit unions accepted savings deposits from their members and made installment loans to them. Savings and loan associations and mutual savings banks competed for time deposits and made mortgage loans. Brokerage firms bought and sold stocks and bonds for their customers. Commercial banks specialized in providing service to business firms, and were also the only institutions offering checking accounts to households. The savings institutions could not provide checking accounts, and the banks were not too interested in time deposits. All these institutions have now expanded the range of their services, but one of the most important developments has been the intensified competition for household savings.

As recently as 30 years ago, many commercial banks either did not accept savings accounts or did not pay interest on them. During the postwar years, many new savings and loan associations were established and aggressively promoted this business, advertising higher returns on savings accounts than commercial banks were willing or able to pay. Many banks did not respond to this competitive pressure during the 1950s, feeling that time deposits were not very profitable in any event. As a result, the commercial banks' share of savings accounts and of total financial assets declined steadily after 1945.

By the late 1950s, this competition from savings institutions was beginning to hurt the commercial banks, particularly as demand deposits were increasing at a relatively slow rate. Numerous articles were written in learned journals explaining the reasons that commercial banks were unable to compete with S&Ls for savings-account business. Commercial banks were subject to higher reserve requirements than their competitor institutions. They were subject to more stringent tax regulations and faced restrictions on their holdings of mortgage loans. Mortgage loans were considered to be among the most profitable assets available to banks, and such loans typically made up about 85 percent of the assets of savings and loan associations.

One additional disadvantage faced by commercial banks in their competition with S&Ls in the late 1950s was a regulatory constraint on the maximum interest rates that could be paid on time deposits. The Federal Reserve's Regulation Q sets interest rate ceilings for member banks, and the FDIC has an equivalent regulation applying to insured nonmember banks. From 1957 to 1961, the ceiling was set at 3 percent for savings deposits and other time deposits with a maturity of over six months. The rate ceilings were not applicable to savings and loan associations.

The existence of the interest-rate ceilings was a constraint even on banks that were not paying the maximum allowable interest rates—the ceilings made it clear that the commercial banks could not compete on a rate basis with the S&Ls. Many banks did actively compete for savings deposits during this period by stressing the nonprice aspects of competition. The commercial banks emphasized the advantages of "one-stop banking," for example, since they were the only institutions where a depositor could have both a savings account and a checking account.

The purpose of the interest-rate ceiling was to prevent banks from committing themselves to high interest payments and then reaching for risky assets in order to earn enough to meet the interest commitment. Some bankers have argued that this was at least partly responsible for the banking difficulties of the 1920s and 1930s. A similar argument is made for the existence of the prohibition of interest payments on demand deposits.

The available evidence on bank behavior during the 1920s does not support the view that banks were becoming committed to higher and higher interest payments and that this led them to acquire progressively riskier assets. In fact, it appears that commercial banks actually lowered interest rates paid on time deposits over the decade of the 1920s.

But despite the lack of evidence to support this argument, it has been repeated each time the interest-rate ceiling has been raised. Following the increase in the Regulation Q ceiling on savings deposits to 4 percent in 1962, many bankers expressed fears as to the outcome of the increased rate competition for savings. A former official of the Federal Reserve Bank of New York commented at the time:

> Those who are most alarmed about interest rate competition base their fears on a widely held belief that the banking collapse of the 1930's was in a significant measure the result of competition in rates. In some communities and in some isolated cases, rate competition was probably a contributing factor, but in the country as a whole, and for most banks, history simply does not bear out this contention.[6]

During the 1960s, Regulation Q ceilings were raised whenever they threatened to be a real restraint. A very significant increase in the ceilings took place in December 1965. Maximum rates on time deposits (other than savings accounts) were increased from 4½ to

---

[6] Howard D. Crosse, quoted in *The Wall Street Journal*, March 15, 1962, p. 14.

5½ percent. Up to that time, the dominant form in which consumers held their savings was the ordinary passbook savings account, although commercial banks had been developing consumer-type certificates of deposit that were becoming significant substitutes for regular savings accounts. The new ceilings gave a substantial impetus to this movement and also made it possible for commercial banks to compete fully on a rate basis with savings and loans.

It is interesting to note that increases in interest-rate ceilings in subsequent years left the passbook rate farther and farther behind market rates. This approach was generally supported by the depository institutions, since an increase in the passbook rate would be expensive.[7] The effect of this pattern of rate changes was to weaken the value of this form of deposit. That is an unfortunate result, since the passbook account, with its convenience and immediate availability, could be useful to many consumers. Now the consumer who wants to earn a market return on liquid funds must go to a money-market mutual fund rather than to a depository institution. When deregulation finally comes about, we can expect a re-emergence of the old passbook savings account (perhaps without the passbook).

The problems of the savings institutions seemed almost constant during the 1970s, as interest rates continued to rise to new high ground. Interest-rate ceilings became more pervasive as the agencies sought to plug loopholes devised by imaginative bankers. An attempt by the banking agencies to experiment with elimination of ceilings on long-term deposits in 1973 was promptly halted by Congress. Congressional concern over the position of the savings institutions was also manifested in legislatively mandating that interest-rate ceilings be administered by the supervisory agencies so that savings institutions were allowed to pay at least ¼ percent higher rates than commercial banks. That "differential" in favor of the thrifts became very precious, and many battles were fought over commercial-bank efforts to eliminate it and the thrift institutions' struggle to maintain it. Nearly every attempt to reform the financial structure during the 1970s and early 1980s foundered over this issue. Thrift institutions claimed that they needed this edge because of the broader powers that commercial banks had—the ability to offer checking accounts, and to make installment loans

---

[7] An increase in the rate on, say, two-year certificates has to be paid only to depositors who open new accounts of that type. An increase in the passbook rate has to be paid to *all* such depositors. Moreover, it is generally believed that such depositors are less interest-sensitive (perhaps that means less knowledgeable and easier to take advantage of).

and business loans. Many savings institutions opposed attempts to gain broader powers for themselves out of fear that those powers would be used as an excuse to take away the differential.

The differential was a significant advantage to the thrifts in competing with commercial banks, but to an increasing extent during the 1970s, the competition was with the market, and the problem was disintermediation rather than commercial-bank competition. During the 1970s, the public became increasingly sophisticated about money-market investments. The most important development was clearly the birth and growth of the money-market mutual fund. Well-known, respected firms began to offer a financial instrument that paid rates well above what could be offered by the depository institutions and that was extremely liquid (no penalties for early withdrawal) and convenient (including checking privileges). Although shares in a money-market fund are not insured or guaranteed by the government, the funds are invested in short-term, high-quality assets.

The money-market mutual fund is a potent competitor for the savings institutions and the smaller commercial banks, but it does not drain funds from the large banks. That is because the money-market fund invests a major share of its assets in the large CDs of the large banks. From the point of view of the big bank, the money-market fund is a source of funds, as it shifts funds from the smaller institutions to the big banks. Obviously, the higher interest rates climbed, and the more the spread increased between what the thrifts could pay and open-market rates, the more acute became the problem of the thrifts.

In 1978, the money-market certificate became a major but expensive source of funds for the institutions, as discussed in Chapter 7. Table 16-5 shows how these developments have led to changes in the share of household deposits held by the various institutions.

TABLE 16-5
Shares of Household Savings

Held in:	1950	1960	1970	1976	1980
Commercial Banks	28.4%	32.4%	41.6%	42.7%	39.9%
Mutual Savings Banks	15.4	16.5	14.7	12.2	10.4
Savings and Loan Assoc.	10.8	28.2	29.9	33.6	35.3
Credit Unions	.7	2.3	3.2	3.9	4.2
U.S. Savings Bonds	44.7	20.7	10.6	7.2	5.0
Money-Market Funds	—	—	—	0.4	5.2
Total	100.%	100.0%	100.0%	100.0%	100.0%

We have noted that interest-rate ceilings first came into existence as a means of limiting possibly destructive competition among commercial banks. Their purpose shifted during the 1960s to one of protecting thrift institutions from bank competition, and relatedly one of protecting the housing industry from a shift of funds from the thrifts to commercial banks. It is now generally acknowledged that interest-rate ceilings are an inequitable and inefficient means of protecting the mortgage market and the housing industry, and we are firmly set on a phasing out of such controls. Nevertheless, the problems of the thrift industry are serious and must be taken into account in implementing the phaseout. The Deregulation Act recognized this by accompanying the legislative end of rate-control powers with broadened powers for the thrift industry. One of the most important powers granted was the authority of all depository thrift institutions to offer interest-bearing checking accounts.

Competition in the Payments System

Until the 1970s, only banks could offer checking accounts, and no interest was paid on such accounts. Then a variety of devices were invented to get around the legal prohibition of interest on demand deposits and to allow thrift institutions to offer something like a checking account. NOW accounts were originated in Massachusetts, gradually spread throughout the Northeast, and were legalized on a national basis by the Depository Institutions Deregulation Act.

The result of these developments is a considerable enhancement of competition for household deposits. Savings institutions can offer the same services as a commercial bank and have been aggressively competing for such business. In many markets, the thrifts have offered NOW accounts with lower minimum-balance requirements or lower service charges than the commercial banks. Credit unions have competed for this business through the device of the "share draft" account. Money-market mutual funds and some brokerage firms have set up systems whereby checks can be written against balances on deposit with them.

NOW accounts, like conventional checking accounts, are based on the movement of pieces of paper. Despite the extensive automation of the process, it is still an expensive one. Banks and savings institutions are competing in the development of electronic funds transfer systems (EFTS) to reduce these costs. We have noted the growth of automated teller machines as one part of this process, but there are other devices as well. Point-of-sale terminals in retail outlets will allow payment for goods purchased to be made by electronically moving funds from the customer's account at his or her bank to the store's account. Pay-by-phone systems allow the bank customer to dial the bank (or the bank's computer) and give instructions for payment to be made. As home computers become more prevalent, it will be possible for the customer to pay bills at the computer console without the need to write checks. A less exotic approach to cutting expenses involves a shortcutting or "truncation" of the check-collection process, whereby the bank holds the customer's checks rather than returning them with the monthly statement. This not only saves postage costs; it can save the need for a costly sorting of checks by individual account at the bank. Truncation is universally practiced by credit unions with their share draft accounts, and many savings and loans have opted for truncation as they begin to offer NOW accounts. The ultimate truncation will come when the check is retained by the first bank into which it is deposited, with the information from the check moved on electronically through the collection system.

These electronic systems offer great promise of cost savings and increased convenience to consumers. Before banks paid interest on checking accounts, there was little incentive to develop more efficient payment systems. The spur of increased competition, and the increased costs of interest payments, will lead to a search for improved means of making payments.

QUESTIONS

1 Organizing a new commercial bank requires the permission of a federal or state supervisory agency. Is this restriction on the individual's right to go into business for himself warranted?
2 Who is hurt by a bank failure?
3 What is the name of the present Comptroller of the Currency?
4 What are the principal advantages and disadvantages of branch banking? Do you think branching should be allowed on a nationwide basis?
5 What are the restrictions on branch banking in your state?
6 What is a bank holding company? What agency regulates holding companies?
7 Why have there been so many bank mergers in recent years?
8 What possible advantages created by a merger are important enough to outweigh an unfavorable effect on competition? Which factors do the courts give heavy weight to? Which factors are important to the supervisory agencies?

9 What advantages do commercial banks have in competing with other financial institutions for time deposits? What disadvantages do they face?

10 Do you think that the Regulation Q ceiling should be eliminated immediately?

SELECTED READINGS

Comptroller of the Currency, *Banking Competition and the Banking Structure*. 1966. A collection of articles reprinted from the *National Banking Review*.

Federal Reserve Bank of Chicago, *Proceedings of a Conference on Bank Structure and Competition*. This annual volume provides an excellent discussion of current research on banking structure.

GOODMAN, OSCAR R., "Antitrust and Competitive Issues in United States Banking Structure," *Journal of Finance*, May 1971.

HORVITZ, PAUL M., "Stimulating Bank Competition through Regulatory Action," *Journal of Finance*, March 1965.

———, and BERNARD SHULL, "The Bank Merger Act of 1960: A Decade After," *Antitrust Bulletin*, Winter 1971.

LONGBRAKE, WILLIAM, "Productive Efficiency in Commercial Banking," *Journal of Money, Credit and Banking*, August 1975.

SHULL, BERNARD, "Economic Efficiency, Public Regulation, and Financial Reform," in Murray E. Polakoff, Thomas A. Durkin, et al., *Financial Institutions and Markets*, 2nd ed. Boston: Houghton Mifflin, 1981.

V

CENTRAL BANKING

17

Structure and Operations of the Federal Reserve System

The National Banking Act of 1863 was a considerable improvement over the legislation in force in most states before that time. We have seen in Chapter 14, however, that the national banking system had serious problems of its own. Its most basic deficiency was the lack of a mechanism providing flexibility in the money supply. That is, the money supply was not responsive to changes in the needs of the public for money.

The provisions of the act encouraged banks to keep their reserves in the form of deposits with banks in the large cities, particularly New York and Chicago. The country banks had the right to withdraw these deposits on demand, and when they were in need of funds they did just that. In ordinary times, this did not create any great problems for the city banks, because some country banks would be drawing down their accounts while others would be adding to their accounts. In periods of generally high demand for credit by business and the public, however, the demand on the city banks for funds became strong. Each year this difficulty arose when farmers needed cash to move crops to market. The country banks drew down their accounts with city correspondents, and the city banks had nowhere to turn to replenish their supply of reserves. They were thus forced to call in loans and add to the general monetary tightness. At times, serious financial panics resulted from this forced liquidation of assets by the large commercial banks.

A panic that occurred in 1907 was unusually severe, and there was general agreement that something should be done to prevent the recurrence of financial crises. In 1908, Congress established a National Monetary Commission, under the chairmanship of Senator Aldrich, charged with the task of analyzing the monetary system of the country and recommending changes in the laws relating to banking and currency. The commission did a thoroughgoing research job, turning out several volumes of statistics and information relating to banking and finance. The commission made its report in 1912 and introduced legislation to correct the shortcomings of the banking system. The specific bill proposed by the Aldrich Commission failed to generate widespread support, but Congress did pass a bill, introduced by Carter Glass under the title of the Federal Reserve Act, on December 23, 1913.

The Federal Reserve System has undergone considerable change since 1913, and no attempt will be made here to consider all these changes—our focus will be on the structure as it now exists. Certain basic changes in the Federal Reserve Act will be considered in more detail, however.

THE STRUCTURE
OF THE FEDERAL RESERVE SYSTEM

We examined some of the objectives of the Federal Reserve Act in Chapter 14. These objectives had to do with the needs for a more elastic currency, a more adequate reserve system, and better banking supervision. Over the last 60 years, the conception of the Federal Reserve System has undergone considerable change. Now the fundamental objective of the Federal Reserve is to "help create conditions favorable to sustained high employment, stable values, growth of the country and a rising level of consumption."[1] In other words, the Federal Reserve System is no longer merely providing services for and supervision of the banking system, but is now concerned primarily with economic policy.

This change in the role of the Federal Reserve System did not occur overnight; it has been gradual and arose through both legislative changes and administrative changes in system practices.

---

[1] Federal Reserve Bank of Boston, *Annual Report*, 1958, p. 13.

Congressional actions in regard to the Federal Reserve have almost always involved compromises. Almost any change in the system has provoked controversy, and the resulting compromises have not always been very logical. Thus, there are some aspects of the organization of the Fed that seem illogical or contradictory. Some provisions of the Federal Reserve Act are historical relics, serving no useful purpose in the modern world.

The most fundamental issue involved in the structure of the Federal Reserve had to do with the desirability of a centralized central bank. Most foreign countries had a single, national central bank. To the modern reader it may appear obvious that such a system would be the most efficient solution to the difficulties of the American financial system. However, there was considerable opposition here in the early twentieth century to the idea of a strong, centralized financial authority. This opposition came from many sources and was based on several considerations. Some people argued that a single central bank would be dominated by Wall Street interests. This fear, and the complementary fear of domination by the federal government, led to opposition from liberals and conservatives alike. In addition, many felt that in a large, diversified country like the United States, a system of loosely connected regional central banks would be a better solution.

The Federal Reserve System that emerged from these debates was a typically American resolution of the conflict. By means of an intricate system of checks and balances, the Federal Reserve System struck a delicate balance between central and regional control, between voluntary and compulsory membership, between governmental and private ownership and control. The balance in each of these issues has shifted back and forth over the history of the system, but we will concentrate here on the present state of the issues and on possible shifts in the future.

The Federal Reserve System consists of a Board of Governors, located in Washington, D.C., twelve regional Federal Reserve Banks with twenty-five branches, and several thousand privately owned member banks. In addition, there are several important groups within the Federal Reserve System made up of members of one or more of these basic institutions.

The Board of Governors

The Board of Governors of the Federal Reserve System is the group within the system structure primarily responsible for overall coordination of Federal Reserve policy. It was originally intended as a rather weak agency with limited powers, but it has been granted additional powers over the years. The Board of Governors now represents the real decision-making authority of the system.[2]

The Board of Governors consists of seven members appointed by the president with the consent of the Senate. No two members may come from the same Federal Reserve district—a provision designed to get geographical diversity on the board and to quell the fears of 1912 that Wall Street bankers would dominate the system. The president, in making appointments to the board, must give due regard to "fair representation of financial, agricultural, industrial, and commercial interests."[3]

Board members are appointed for 14-year terms and cannot be reappointed for a second 14-year term. The chairman and vice-chairman of the Board are appointed by the president for four-year terms, but these terms do not necessarily coincide with the term of the president. The purpose of these provisions is to make the board as free as possible from partisan political considerations and independent of the administration. Since only one member's term expires every two years, a president cannot generally appoint a majority to the board until late in his second term of office. Board members presumably can act independently of the wishes of the administration, because they will probably be around after the administration is gone and because they cannot be reappointed anyway. These provisions to ensure a Federal Reserve policy free of political considerations originated at a time when the Board of Governors had substantially less power than is the case today. We will discuss the powers and functions of the Board in a later section of this chapter. The expansion of these powers in recent years has led to some rethinking of the issue of Federal Reserve independence.

---

[2] The strengthening of the Board of Governors was gradual until 1935. The Banking Act of 1935 took a big step in raising the position of the Board. As a symbol of this change, its name was changed to its present "Board of Governors of the Federal Reserve System" from the original "Federal Reserve Board." For obvious reasons, the shorter title is still used.

[3] The geographical restriction is clearly an anachronism—today it is not always possible to determine which district a Governor comes from. Some have argued that representation should be given to labor and consumer interests. If representation is accorded to financial and industrial interests, this seems to be a reasonable position, but the Commission on Money and Credit (1961) had a better solution in recommending that "occupational and geographical qualifications for Board members should be eliminated." They have not been eliminated, but they have been increasingly ignored in recent years.

The Federal Reserve Banks

The Federal Reserve Act provided that the country be divided into between eight and twelve districts, each district to be served by a Federal Reserve Bank. Since every major city in the country wanted to have a Federal Reserve Bank, it is not surprising that the Organization Committee decided on the maximum twelve districts. Figure 17-1 depicts the boundaries of the Federal Reserve districts and the location of the Federal Reserve Banks and branches. These boundaries are essentially those established in 1913, although some slight changes have been made.

Each Federal Reserve Bank has nine directors, three each of three classes. The Class A directors are bankers and are elected by the member banks in each district. Those banks also elect the Class B directors, but the latter must be engaged in commerce, agriculture, or industry and cannot be connected with any commercial bank. For purposes of electing directors, the member banks in each district are classified into three size groups: large, medium, and small. Each size group elects one Class A and one Class B director. The Class C directors are appointed by the Board of Governors, and they are not supposed to be associated with any commercial bank. The Board of Governors also names one of the Class C directors chairman of the board of the Federal Reserve Bank.

Given this complex system for selection of directors, one would assume that the position of director of a Federal Reserve Bank is an extremely important one. We shall see, however, that the directors do not play a very important role in the determination of monetary policy. They do appoint a president and other officers to carry out the day-to-day management of the bank, but the most important officers must be approved by the Board of Governors.

Despite the lack of real power, the position of director of a Federal Reserve Bank is a very prestigious one. The Fed has used its ability to award this title to prominent men and women in a way that has led to a very favorable image of the Federal Reserve among civic leaders.[4]

---

[4] There is nothing sinister in this situation. After all, it is the successful industrialists, newspaper publishers, and community leaders who deserve such recognition. And if a stint as Federal Reserve Bank director makes them lifelong defenders of the Federal Reserve System, why, that may just be a nice by-product of a selection based on merit.

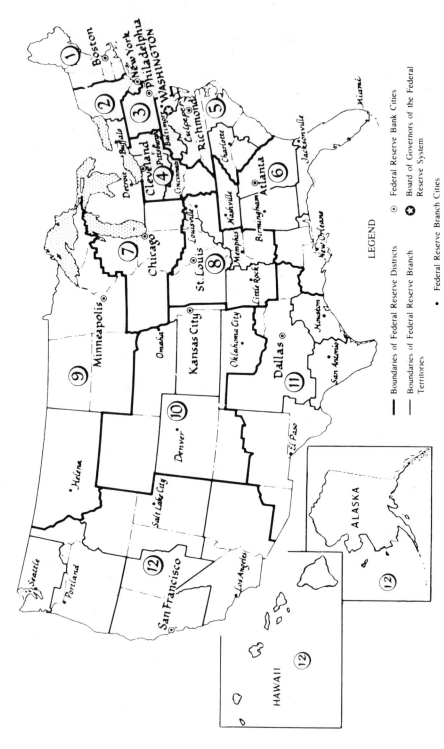

FIGURE 17-1 Boundaries of Federal Reserve Districts and Their Branch Territories

LEGEND

⊙ Federal Reserve Bank Cities

☆ Board of Governors of the Federal Reserve System

● Federal Reserve Branch Cities

— Boundaries of Federal Reserve Districts

— Boundaries of Federal Reserve Branch Territories

Member Banks

All national banks must be members of the Federal Reserve System. Membership is optional for state-chartered banks. The majority of banks in the country are state-chartered, and most of these have consistently chosen to remain outside the Federal Reserve System. Membership is directly related to size, with proportionately fewer members among the smaller banks.

Membership in the system involves certain privileges and obligations. Every member bank must buy stock in its Federal Reserve Bank in an amount equal to 3 percent of the member bank's capital and surplus. The member bank receives an annual dividend of 6 percent on its holdings of that stock.

We have already seen that the member banks can exert some rights of ownership by electing some members of the board of directors of the Federal Reserve Bank. For all practical purposes, however, member-bank ownership of the Federal Reserve System is merely a fiction. The Federal Reserve Banks are not operated for the purpose of earning profits for their stockholders. The Fed does earn substantial profits in the normal course of its operations, but these profits, above the 6 percent statutory dividend, do not belong to the member banks. Net earnings after expenses and dividends are paid to the Treasury. Member bank "ownership" of the Federal Reserve is simply another example of compromise between public and private control of the system.

The principal advantage to a bank in membership is the influence that membership may exert on potential depositors. This may be of some importance in the sale of CDs and the attraction of corporate deposits that are too large to come under deposit insurance. Depositors may feel some additional safety in membership because member-bank lending operations and other matters come under more stringent controls than those imposed by the various states on nonmember banks. These controls, and the related Federal Reserve Bank examination, constitute the most important obstacles to membership now that the 1980 Monetary Control Act has removed reserve requirements from consideration.

The Monetary Control Act, like other significant Federal Reserve changes, was a compromise. Rather than requiring all banks to be members, as some had proposed, the act required all depository institutions to come under the same reserve requirements. One of the many reasons for this compromise was the fact that total membership of banks would still have left uncovered the nonbank depository institutions, and monetary control would still have been incomplete.

Since all banks must now meet the same reserve requirements, membership does not incur any additional cost in this respect. A large number of banks had withdrawn from membership prior to the 1980 act. In 1960, member banks accounted for 80 percent of total deposits, but by 1980, only 65 percent. All depository institutions may now borrow from the Federal Reserve, eliminating this advantage to membership that prevailed prior to 1980. Membership also no longer bestows any advantage with respect to check-clearing services of the Federal Reserve. Formerly these services were free to member banks, but under the 1980 act, they are available to all depository institutions, and a charge is imposed.

In the last several years, a number of state-chartered banks have become members incidental to conversion to national charters. Such conversions have reflected the view of the banks involved that the national charter was advantageous. Considering that these conversions took place despite the reserve-requirement problems imposed, removal of the reserve requirement disadvantage may encourage further such conversions.

Open Market Committee

The most important activity of the Federal Reserve is the purchase and sale of government securities in the open market. These transactions affect the reserves of commercial banks in a manner that we will discuss in the following chapter. These "open market operations" are the major means by which the Fed conducts monetary policy, and determination of open market policy rests with the Open Market Committee.

The Open Market Committee consists of the seven members of the Board of Governors, the president of the Federal Reserve Bank of New York, and four other Reserve Bank presidents. The Reserve Bank presidents serve on the committee on an annual rotating basis. Each year, one from each of the following groups serves on the Committee:

The Federal Reserve Banks of Boston, Philadelphia, and Richmond

The Federal Reserve Banks of Cleveland and Chicago

The Federal Reserve Banks of Atlanta, Dallas, and St. Louis

The Federal Reserve Banks of Minneapolis, Kansas City, and San Francisco

The makeup of the committee, consisting as it does of both members of the Board of Governors and representatives of the regional banks, is another compromise between the desires for centralized and regional control of monetary policy. Chapter 21 will investigate the operations of the Open Market Committee in some detail.

Federal Advisory Council

The Federal Reserve Act provided for a Federal Advisory Council, consisting of one member from each Federal Reserve district. The council member is selected by the board of directors of each Federal Reserve Bank and is almost always a prominent banker. The council is, as the name implies, purely advisory; it has the function of making the views of the banking community known to the Board of Governors.

In 1976, the Federal Reserve established a Consumer Advisory Council, consisting of representatives of consumer groups, to advise the Board on matters related to its responsibilities in this area.

SERVICE FUNCTIONS
OF THE FEDERAL RESERVE SYSTEM

Throughout this book, we are most concerned with the role of the Federal Reserve System in influencing income and prices—that is, in the formulation and execution of monetary policy. But the Federal Reserve System has other functions that greatly facilitate the operations of our monetary system. These "service functions" include check collection, banking supervision, and fiscal functions.

We have already examined the Fed's function in the check-clearing process. This in itself is a massive job, and, in terms of man-hours of work involved, it is the largest Federal Reserve function. In 1980, the Federal Reserve Banks handled over 16 billion checks, amounting to $8.5 trillion, at a cost of $400 million.

Just as an individual or business obtains currency or coin from commercial banks by withdrawing deposits, member banks obtain currency and coin from Reserve Banks by withdrawals from their accounts at those banks. When member banks receive an excess of coin or currency from depositors, it is sent to the Federal Reserve Bank, where it is sorted and counted and the usable money is held for redistribution. Worn-out bills are destroyed in an elaborate procedure.

The Fed provides an efficient system for the rapid transfer of funds by wire. A bank in California may ask the Federal Reserve Bank of San Francisco to transfer $1 million to a bank in New York. Since both banks have deposits with their respective Federal Re-

serve Banks, the Federal Reserve Bank of San Francisco deducts
$1 million from the reserve account of the San Francisco commer-
cial bank and wires the New York Federal Reserve Bank to add $1
million to the reserve account of the New York commercial bank.
This large transaction can be completed almost instantaneously.

The Treasury relies heavily on the Federal Reserve System for
the discharge of many important fiscal duties. The Reserve Banks
handle much of the bookkeeping and routine processing of the various new issues of U.S. government securities. Treasury checks are
drawn on accounts at the Federal Reserve Banks, and much of the
work involved in servicing the federal debt is performed by the
Reserve Banks.

The Federal Reserve has important supervisory powers over
the banking system, although the duties of bank supervision are
shared with other federal and state agencies. Many authorities
have argued that the Federal Reserve's responsibilities for banking
supervision and examination should be taken away so that the
Board of Governors can concentrate on its very important monetary policy responsibilities, but the Bank Holding Company Act
amendments of 1970 gave substantial additional responsibilities in
this area to the Board.[5]

THE FEDERAL RESERVE BALANCE SHEET

Table 17-1 shows the combined balance sheet of the twelve Federal
Reserve Banks as of January 31, 1982. We will first examine the
items in the balance sheet and then see how changes in each of
these items affect the reserve position of the commercial-banking
system.

Gold Certificates. The Federal Reserve Banks do not own gold.
The gold certificates held by the system are issued by the Treasury.
At one time, the Reserve Banks were required to hold gold certificates equal to a stated percentage of the bank's note and deposit
liabilities. As the Treasury issued certificates, based on its gold

[5] The President's Commission on Financial Structure and Regulation (1971)
recommended that the supervisory responsibilities of the Fed be given to the Admin-
istrator of State Banks, an agency to be created as part of the commission's revamp-
ing of the banking supervisory structure. The Fed has long argued officially that
the information it gathers in the bank-examination process is useful in making
monetary-policy decisions. As a matter of fact, there is no regular flow of data from
the bank-examination process to the members of the Board or their staff. It is hard
to see what data needed for monetary-policy purposes would not be available from
other sources than bank examinations conducted by the Federal Reserve.

TABLE 17-1

Consolidated Statement of Condition of all Federal
Reserve Banks, January 31, 1981
(in millions of dollars)

Assets	
Gold certificates	$ 11,159
Cash	468
Loans to depository institutions	1,304
U.S. government securities	125,908
Cash Items in process of collection	7,865
Other assets	12,354
Total assets	**$159,058**

Liabilities and Capital	
Federal Reserve notes	$118,147
Deposits	30,747
Depository institutions	26,621
U.S. Treasury	3,038
Foreign	573
Other	515
Deferred availability cash items	5,585
Other liabilities	1,957
Capital accounts	2,622
Total liabilities and capital	**$159,058**

Source: *Federal Reserve Bulletin*, February 1981.

acquisitions, it received deposit claims on the Federal Reserve. The certificates are carried on the books at $42.22 per ounce of gold, the par value established in 1973 before the suspension of gold convertibility of foreign dollar holdings.

Cash. This is the amount of coin and paper money (other than Federal Reserve notes) held by the Federal Reserve Banks.

Loans. The Federal Reserve Banks have the authority to make loans to depository institutions. Thus, a bank temporarily short of reserves can borrow the needed reserves from its Federal Reserve Bank. This provision of the Federal Reserve Act injects into the monetary system an element of elasticity, the lack of which was one of the defects of the National Banking Act. The Fed is thus the lender of last resort for the financial system: If all other means of raising reserves are unavailable, the Federal Reserve always has the power to provide them. We shall see that the system's ability to control the terms at which such loans are made is one of the tools of the Federal Reserve in influencing the monetary system.

Under the original provisions of the Federal Reserve Act, most of this lending was secured by the promissory notes of the commercial banks' customers. Now it is generally more convenient to borrow by pledging U.S. government securities as collateral for the loan; all banks hold substantial amounts of such securities, and, in fact, some banks leave their government securities with their Federal Reserve Bank for safekeeping and collection of interest. It is thus a simple matter to pledge these securities as collateral for an advance. In the last few years, however, an increasing number of banks have so reduced their holdings of government securities that they do not have enough freely available for securing advances from the Federal Reserve. For these banks, then, there has been a return to the earlier practice of using commercial loans as security for Federal Reserve loans.

Acceptances. One of the early aims of the Federal Reserve System was to aid in the development of an active market in banker's acceptances. To facilitate this development, the Fed has stood ready to buy banker's acceptances at a stated rate. Despite this, the market has never developed to the anticipated extent, and the amount of acceptances held by the Fed is small.

U.S. Government Securities. This is the largest single item in the Federal Reserve balance sheet. We shall see that changes in the Fed's holdings of government securities have important effects on the reserve position of the commercial banks, and that Federal Reserve transactions in the open market are the most important means by which the Fed influences the monetary system.

The Treasury is the original issuer of the securities, as discussed in Chapter 12. The Treasury is not creating money in the process, and thus a government deficit is not necessarily associated with increased money. Only the portion of the government debt bought by the Federal Reserve has the potential for money creation, and this is a policy decision made independently of, and by different authorities than, the decision to incur a deficit.

Cash Items in the Process of Collection. This item represents the volume of checks received by the Federal Reserve Banks but not yet collected. If the Federal Reserve Bank of Atlanta receives a check drawn on a bank in St. Louis, it takes time for that check to be returned to St. Louis and the amount of the check deducted from the reserve account of the St. Louis commercial bank on which it was written. For that period of time—perhaps two or three days— the check appears on the books of the Federal Reserve System as an "uncollected cash item," or "cash item in the process of collection."

Federal Reserve Notes. Federal Reserve notes outstanding represent the largest liability of the Federal Reserve System.

Federal Reserve notes constitute nearly all the currency in circulation; the actual dollar amount varies with the needs of the country. One of the difficulties of the National Banking System, you will remember, was the inelasticity of the currency supply. Now a commercial bank can obtain all the currency it needs from its Federal Reserve Bank, paying for it with a reduction in its reserve account. The Reserve Bank can, in turn, obtain the needed Federal Reserve notes from its Federal Reserve agent, a member of its board of directors appointed by the Board of Governors of the Federal Reserve System. The Federal Reserve agent has custody of all unissued notes.

The Reserve Bank must pledge collateral for all the Federal Reserve notes it issues. This collateral may consist of gold certificates, U.S. government securities, or certain other assets. The only real restriction in the past, that relating to holdings of gold certificates, no longer exists.

Deposits. The other important liability item in the Federal Reserve's balance sheet is deposits. The largest type of deposit is the reserve account of depository institutions, which, along with their vault cash, constitutes the actual working base of the system. Although the Treasury maintains deposits with many commercial banks, its payments are made from deposits with the Federal Reserve. In addition, some foreign central banks or governments maintain deposits with the Fed for the purpose of facilitating international payments or for monetary reserve purposes.

Deferred Availability Cash Items. This item is really the counterpart of the "cash items in the process of collection" account. We have seen that when a check is deposited with the Federal Reserve Bank, it cannot be collected immediately. Since the Fed cannot collect the check instantaneously, it does not give immediate credit to the bank depositing the check. Credit is given to the depositing bank according to an established time schedule. The maximum period for credit to be deferred is two business days. Let us see how this process affects the balance sheet of the Federal Reserve System, through a series of T accounts.

Step 1. First National Bank of Boston deposits check drawn on First National Bank of Seattle.

FEDERAL RESERVE SYSTEM

Assets		Liabilities	
Cash items in process of collection	+ $100	Deferred availability items	+ $100

Step 2. Federal Reserve Bank of Boston starts check-collection process in motion. After one day, the balance sheet remains as above. After two days:

FEDERAL RESERVE SYSTEM

Assets		Liabilities	
Cash items in process of collection	+ $100	Deposits of First National Bank of Boston (reserve account)	+ $100

Step 3. The check is collected by reducing the account of the First National Bank of Seattle.

FEDERAL RESERVE SYSTEM

Assets		Liabilities	
		Deposits of First National Bank of Boston	+ $100
		Deposits of First National Bank of Seattle	− $100

The process usually occurs in the order described—it usually takes longer to collect checks than the time allowed in the schedules. This means that the Federal Reserve is generally giving credit for checks deposited before they are actually collected. The difference between "cash items in the process of collection" and "deferred availability cash items" is called *float*. Float was zero in Steps 1 and 3, but amounted to $100 in Step 2.

Capital Accounts. The capital accounts of the Federal Reserve Banks consist of capital paid in by member banks and retained earnings of the Reserve Banks. When a bank is admitted to membership in the Federal Reserve System, it must purchase stock in its Federal Reserve Bank in an amount equal to 3 percent of its own capital stock and surplus.

QUESTIONS

1 What is meant by the term "inelastic money supply"?
2 What are the advantages of having twelve Federal Reserve Banks?
3 Are the Federal Reserve Banks government institutions? Are they owned by the member banks? Are their officers government officials?
4 What are the advantages and disadvantages of having 14-year terms for Federal Reserve Board Governors?
5 Would you expect that all banks would eventually become Federal Reserve members as a result of the 1980 Monetary Control Act?

6 Is the Federal Reserve System subject to control by Congress? Should it be? Is it subject to control by the Administration? Should it be?

7 The Federal Reserve Banks hold over $100 billion of government securities. Where did the banks get the money to buy these securities?

8 Do the Federal Reserve Banks make a profit? What happens to their earnings?

SELECTED READINGS

Board of Governors of the Federal Reserve System, *The Federal Reserve System: Purposes and Functions.* Washington, D.C., 1974.

PROCHNOW, HERBERT V., ed., *The Federal Reserve System.* New York: Harper & Row, 1960.

REAGAN, MICHAEL D., "The Internal Structure of the Federal Reserve: A Political Analysis," in *Monetary Management.* Commission on Money and Credit. Englewood Cliffs, N.J.: Prentice-Hall, 1963.

WARBURG, PAUL M., *The Federal Reserve System.* 2 vols., 1930. Reprinted by Arno Press, New York.

WILLIS, H. PARKER, *The Federal Reserve System.* New York: Ronald Press, 1923.

YOUNG, RALPH, *Instruments of Monetary Policy in the United States: The Role of the Federal Reserve System.* Washington, D.C.: International Monetary Fund, 1973.

18

The Framework of Federal Reserve Control-I

The Federal Reserve can control the amount of its own money liabilities, but such control does not absolutely determine the nation's money supply if private entities also create assets of a money nature. Use of the term *deposits* for claims on financial institutions gives the misleading impression that the institutions are merely storehouses for currency. This is certainly not the case. In most instances, deposits come into being without currency changing hands. Financial institutions are intermediaries between primary lenders and borrowers. In this process, they create certain claims on themselves that are sufficiently liquid that they deserve consideration for classification as money. If, then, the money supply is to be controlled, the creation of these assets must be controlled.

We are going to illustrate this creation of money-type assets through a commercial bank and its demand deposits. For convenience, we shall use the terms *bank* and *demand deposit*, but the process is not unique to the commercial bank.

Deposits are, of course, a liability of the bank. If we have a $300 deposit in a commercial bank, the bank owes us $300. The deposit itself, however, can arise in various ways. We may have brought $300 in paper money to the bank to deposit in our account. On the balance sheet of the bank, this transaction will simply be reflected as a $300 increase in the bank's holdings of cash and a $300 increase in the bank's deposit liabilities. This transaction is what may be called a *primary deposit*. It should be noted that it does not result in any change in the money supply. We have $300 less in currency and $300 more in the form of a demand deposit; our total holdings of money are unchanged.

Deposits may arise in a different way, however. Let us suppose a business man comes into the bank and wants to borrow $1,000 to cover the costs of some additional inventory he wants to purchase. If the bank approves the loan, the businessman will tell the bank to credit the $1,000 to his deposit account. This will appear on the books of the bank as follows:[1]

Bank Assets		Bank Liabilities	
Loans	+ $1,000	Deposits	+ $1,000

The businessman now has an additional $1,000 demand deposit. No one else's demand deposits have been reduced. This is clearly an increase in the money supply, and it is apparent that the bank created the $1,000.

These *derivative* deposits are very important both quantitatively and theoretically—it is in terms of derivative deposits that banks can be thought of as creators of money. If all deposits arose from primary deposits, banks could not be said to create money.

THE MONOPOLY BANK

There is often confusion between the ability of an individual bank to create deposits and the ability of the banking system as a whole to expand the money supply. We will get around this difficulty by first considering an imaginary economy in which there is only one commercial bank. (This concept is not as artificial as it may seem. What is true of the monopoly bank in this economy is also true of the banking system as a whole in an economy with many banks.) Assume that this bank is required by law to maintain cash reserves equal to 15 percent of its deposit liabilities and that people in this economy do not want to hold currency.

---

[1] This does not pretend to represent the entire balance sheet of the bank. A balance sheet shows the amount of assets and liabilities. This T account shows only the changes produced on the bank's balance sheet by the specific transaction under consideration. We will make frequent use of these abbreviated "balance sheets" to illustrate the effects of the transaction we are discussing.

Our monopoly bank may open for business in the following position:

Bank Assets		Bank Liabilities	
Building and equipment	$1,000	Capital	$1,000

The bank may then advertise for depositors, and perhaps the local miser will decide to take $1,000 in coin out of his mattress and deposit it in the bank. This primary deposit will mean an increase of $1,000 in cash held by the bank and an increase in its deposit liabilities of $1,000. Since the law requires the bank to hold cash reserves of only $150 against its $1,000 of deposits, the bank can consider making a loan. Since the bank has $850 in excess of its required reserves, the manager reacts favorably when Mr. Jones walks into the bank hoping to borrow $850 to buy a used car. The loan is made by setting up a demand deposit of $850 for Mr. Jones. The bank's balance sheet now looks like this:

BALANCE SHEET 1

Bank Assets		Bank Liabilities	
Cash	$1,000	Deposits	$1,850
Loans	850	Capital	1,000
Building and equipment	1,000		
	$2,850		$2,850

Mr. Jones did not borrow $850 simply to have a checking account at the bank. He has plans to spend his money. He may go over to Joe's Used Car Lot and buy a car for $850. He pays for the car by writing Joe a check for $850. Joe takes the check to the bank and asks to have the $850 credited to his account. The bank crosses Mr. Jones off its list of depositors and enters Joe's name instead. Joe now has the $850 deposit instead of Mr. Jones, but there is no change in the total deposits of the bank as a result of Jones's spending his money. Spending the proceeds of a loan does not change the amount of the deposits in existence.

When the bank manager looks his position over again, he notices that he still has excess reserves. Against his $1,850 deposits, he is required to hold only $278 in reserves. At that moment the local economist walks into the bank and requests a loan for $4,817. Since the bank manager knows that the bank has total assets of only $2,850, he is reluctant to consider such a loan. The economist is persuasive and convinces the banker to make the loan. After making the loan and crediting the economist's deposit account, the bank's balance sheet appears as follows:

BALANCE SHEET 2

Bank Assets		Bank Liabilities	
Cash	$1,000	Deposits:	
Loans	5,667	Miser	$1,000
Building and equipment	1,000	Joe	850
		Economist	4,817
			$6,667
		Capital	1,000
	$7,667		$7,667

The bank is now just meeting its legal reserve requirements. Against deposit liabilities of $6,667, it has cash reserves of $1,000 (15 percent). The bank cannot consider any new loan application—it is fully "loaned up." We have seen that spending loan proceeds does not cause any change in the aggregate level of demand deposits, so the economist's spending his $4,817 deposit balance will not disturb the bank's position.

We might wonder how the economist knew how much to borrow to bring about this situation. The basic relationship between reserves and deposits is given by this formula:

$$D = \frac{R}{r}$$

where D is demand deposits, R is reserves, and r is the reserve-requirement percentage. For our example, R is $1,000 and r is 15 percent. This means that D is $1,000/.15, or $6,667. That is, for every new dollar of reserves it receives, the bank can support deposits of $6.67. Our monopoly bank, under the assumptions we have made, can create deposits equal to 6.67 times its excess reserves. If the reserve requirement were 20 percent, the bank could create deposits equal to five times its excess reserves. If the requirement were 25 percent, deposits equal to four times excess reserves could be created. This relationship holds true for the monopoly bank and also for the total of all banks in an economy with many commercial banks.

It is important to recognize the importance of reserves and the reserve requirement in this process. If this bank were not subject to any reserve requirement, or if it had access to an unlimited source of reserves, there would be no limit on its ability to create deposits.

CURRENCY DRAINS
AND OTHER LIMITING FACTORS

One of the unrealistic assumptions we made in this situation was that people did not want to hold their money in the form of currency.

This was important, because if people do want to hold currency, the effect tends to limit the ability of the bank to create money. Let us now assume that people want to hold currency equal to 10 percent of the amount of their demand-deposit balances.

In our last balance sheet, we found that the bank's $1,000 cash could be used to make loans of $5,667 and support total deposits of $6,667. If we assume that people are going to hold $100 in cash for every $1,000 of deposits they hold, the money-creating potential of our bank will be smaller. In this case, the bank will be able to support total deposits of only $4,000. If deposits are $4,000, the public will be holding $400 in currency (10 percent of $4,000). This will leave the bank with only $600 in cash, which is, of course, 15 percent of $4,000. The cash outflow, or "drain," from the bank of $400 prevented a deposit increase of $400/.15, or $2,667. The bank's balance sheet in this situation is:

BALANCE SHEET 3

Bank Assets		Bank Liabilities	
Cash	$ 600	Deposits	$4,000
Loans	3,400	Capital	1,000
Building and equipment	1,000		
	$5,000		$5,000

These figures are the only ones that will satisfy three necessary conditions: First, the balance sheet must balance; that is, assets must equal liabilities and capital. Second, the cash reserves of the bank must equal 15 percent of the deposits. Third, the public must be holding currency equal to 10 percent of the amount of deposits in the bank. All these conditions are met by Balance Sheet 3. Assets of $5,000 equal liabilities and capital of $5,000. Reserves of $600 are 15 percent of deposits of $4,000. The public is holding $400 ($1,000 less the $600 that is still held by the bank), which is 10 percent of the deposits of $4,000.

Since the public now holds $400 of currency, the bank does not have the use of this cash to serve as the basis for further deposit expansion. The relationship between reserves and deposits when there is a cash drain is given by a formula only slightly more complicated than the previous one:

$$\triangle D = \frac{\triangle R}{r + c}$$

where c is the percentage of deposits that the public wants to hold in the form of currency (Δ simply means *change in*). In our example, c is 10 percent. Thus, the maximum amount of deposits that could be supported by the $1,000 in reserves that the bank started with is equal to $1,000/(.15 + .10), or $1,000/.25, or $4,000.

In addition to the limits on the deposit-expansion process imposed by the cash drain, there are other factors operating that tend to reduce, in practice, the bank's ability to create deposits. We have assumed that all the bank's holdings of cash are used as reserves against deposits. That is, we have assumed that a bank would maintain cash reserves equal to the minimum amount prescribed by law.

In practice, a bank would always hold some reserves in excess of the required reserves. These excess reserves serve as protection for the bank against any unexpected withdrawals of cash, or they enable the bank to take advantage of any unexpected investment or loan opportunity that may arise. If the bank, for precautionary reasons, wants to hold excess reserves of, say, 5 percent of its deposits, its deposit-creation powers are significantly lowered. In this situation, $100 of reserves would be adequate to support only $500 of deposits, not the $667 that would be possible with merely the 15 percent legal requirement to be satisfied.

In some cases, the bank may hold excess reserves not because of a desire to do so, but because of a lack of demand for loans. If the bank is unable to find customers who want to borrow, it will be left with excess reserves. The bank could always buy securities, and this would have the same effect on it as making loans—the bank pays for securities by creating a demand deposit. But there may not be an adequate supply of securities available at prices the bank considers reasonable.

Even if there is a large loan demand, the bank may be unwilling to make loans. If the loan applicants are considered poor credit risks, they will not get loans. This situation is characteristic of periods of poor business, when businesspeople are pessimistic and thus unwilling to borrow money; they feel that they will not be able to make enough profit to be able to repay the loans. Since the banks are probably pessimistic also, they may tend to turn down many of those who *are* willing to borrow.

An additional, practical reason for the bank to stop its lending activity short of the theoretical maximum is simply that the banker may not know precisely what the volume of his or her excess reserves is at a particular moment. This has been more true of small banks than large banks, and some have found it easier to operate with large excess reserves than to try to determine accurately what their correct reserve position is.

We can easily incorporate the desire to hold excess reserves in our deposit-expansion formula, adding only a slight complication:

$$\triangle D \ = \ \frac{\triangle R}{r + c + e}$$

where e is the ratio of excess reserves to demand deposits.

CONTRACTION OF DEPOSITS

We have seen that once a deposit is created by the granting of a loan, the borrower's spending his newly created money does not change the total volume of demand deposits. Demand deposits are affected, however, when the borrower repays his loan. Since the borrower will typically repay this loan with a check, the repayment of a $1,000 loan results in the reduction of loans and deposits by $1,000.

Deposits can also be reduced by a withdrawal of cash by a depositor. Should our town miser, who had deposited $1,000 in the bank, decide that he can't sleep without money in his mattress, he may go to the bank and withdraw $100 in cash. If the bank were in the position shown in Balance Sheet 3, it would now have the following balance-sheet situation:

BALANCE SHEET 4

Bank Assets		Bank Liabilities	
Cash	$ 500	Deposits	$3,900
Loans	3,400	Capital	1,000
Building and equipment	1,000		
	$4,900		$4,900

Since the reserve requirement is 15 percent, the bank should hold cash reserves of $585 against deposit liabilities of $3,900. The bank has an $85 reserve deficiency. It may try to correct its position by calling in loans (or by simply refusing to grant new loans when the outstanding ones are repaid). If the bank demands repayment of an $85 loan, the borrower will repay by writing a check on his deposit account. This will leave the bank in this position:

BALANCE SHEET 5

Bank Assets		Bank Liabilities	
Cash	$ 500	Deposits	$3,815
Loans	3,315	Capital	1,000
Building and equipment	1,000		
	$4,815		$4,815

Even after this transaction, however, the bank still has a reserve deficiency. Against deposits of $3,815, it needs cash reserves
of $572. As a matter of fact, the bank will not eliminate its deficiency
until it calls in $567 in loans. At that point, the bank's position
will be:

BALANCE SHEET 6

Bank Assets		Bank Liabilities	
Cash	$ 500	Deposits	$3,333
Loans	2,833	Capital	1,000
Building and equipment	1,000		
	$4,333		$4,333

The point of this exercise is that a loss of reserves by the bank
will have a multiple effect on its deposits in the same way that an
inflow of reserves leads to an expansion of deposits several times
the amount of reserves. The deposit-expansion process works just
as powerfully in reverse, and this illustrates why banks frequently
operate with excess reserves.

DEPOSIT CREATION
AND THE INDIVIDUAL BANK

So far, we have been assuming that there is only one bank in our
economy. It is time now to drop this simplifying assumption and
consider the more realistic situation of a banking system comprising many individual banks. We have noted that even in a system
consisting of only one bank, the bank cannot create deposits indefinitely, since the legal reserve requirement sets a ceiling on its
ability to extend loans. In an economy with many banks, a more
important limitation on the credit-expansion power of the commercial banks is the possibility of adverse clearing balances.

Let us consider the operations of a bank in a multibank system.
Each individual bank has only a small fraction of the total banking
business of the system. We will assume that all banks start from a
position of zero excess reserves. That is, all banks are fully "loaned
up" and cannot make further loans. At this point, the First Bank
receives a primary deposit of $1,000. The result of this transaction
is as follows:[2]

FIRST BANK

Bank Assets		Bank Liabilities	
Cash	+ $1,000	Deposits	+ $1,000

[2] Note that we are back to the use of T accounts here rather than full balance
sheets.

The bank now has excess reserves of $850 (if we assume a 15 percent reserve requirement). If the bank manager is a recent recruit from the monopoly banking system of the previous section of this chapter, he might be tempted to grant a $2,000 loan request. Let us see what happens to the bank's balance sheet if the loan is made:

FIRST BANK

Bank Assets		Bank Liabilities	
Cash	+ $1,000	Deposits	+ $3,000
Loans	+ 2,000		
	+ $3,000		+ $3,000

The bank is satisfying its reserve requirements and appears to be in good shape. However, the person who borrowed $2,000 is paying interest on this loan, and thus it is not likely that he incurred this obligation simply for the prestige of having a deposit in the First Bank—he borrowed money because he plans to spend it. Suppose he buys a car for $2,000. He will pay for the car by writing a check on his account at the First Bank. The automobile dealer will deposit the check in his bank account. It is possible that the automobile dealer by coincidence has his checking account at the First Bank, but this is rather unlikely in an economy with many banks. He may have his account at the Second Bank. His deposit affects the Second Bank's balance sheet as follows:

SECOND BANK

Bank Assets		Bank Liabilities	
Check drawn on First Bank	+ $2,000	Deposits	+ $2,000

The check on the First Bank is of no use to the Second Bank—it cannot serve as part of its legal reserves, and it cannot be used to satisfy depositors desiring to make withdrawals. The Second Bank will try to collect the amount of the check from the First Bank. Since the First Bank does not have $2,000 in cash, it will be unable to meet its obligation to pay its depositors (or their orders) on demand. Apparently, granting the $2,000 loan was a serious mistake.

How large a loan, then, can the First Bank safely make? An individual commercial bank in a multibank system can safely lend only an amount equal to its excess reserves. The First Bank, in the position depicted above, could safely lend only $850. At that point, its balance sheet would be:

FIRST BANK

Bank Assets		Bank Liabilities	
Cash	+ $1,000	Deposits	+ $1,850
Loans	+ 850		
	+ $1,850		+ $1,850

The borrower can normally be expected to use his newly created deposit, and when he does so, the bank's balance sheet will become:

FIRST BANK

Bank Assets		Bank Liabilities	
Cash	+ $ 500	Deposits	+ $1,000
Loans	+ 850		
	+ $1,000		+ $1,000

The First Bank is now just meeting its reserve requirements. If it had made a larger loan, the spending of that loan would have caused the bank some difficulty. By limiting its loans to the amount of its excess reserves, the bank saves itself from facing almost certain embarrassment. It is this fact that leads some bankers to reject the idea that they can create loans equal to several times the amount of their excess reserves. They point out that according to their experience, they can safely lend only the amount of their excess reserves. That is, of course, true as far as the individual bank is concerned, but let us trace the situation a little further.

So far, we have considered only the position of the First Bank. We have seen what happens when it makes a loan and the borrower gives a check for the amount of the loan to a customer of the Second Bank. Let us now examine the results of this for the Second Bank. After collecting the amount of the check from the First Bank, the Second Bank is in the following position:

SECOND BANK

Bank Assets		Bank Liabilities	
Cash	+ $850	Deposits	+ $850

The Second Bank now has excess reserves of $722.50 (required reserves are 15 percent of $850, or $127.50). The Second Bank is now in a position to make a loan equal to its excess reserves. Like the First Bank, it cannot safely lend more than its excess reserves. After granting a loan of $722.50, its position is:

Bank Assets		Bank Liabilities	
Cash	+ $850.00	Deposits	+ $1,572.50
Loans	+ 722.50		

The person who borrowed the rather odd sum of $722.50 is certainly going to spend it. He will write checks against his demand deposit, and the recipient of those checks may deposit them in the Third Bank. The checks will be collected, leaving the Second Bank with cash of $127.50 against deposits of $850 (exactly 15 percent). The Third Bank will now have excess reserves:

THIRD BANK

Bank Assets		Bank Liabilities	
Cash	+ $722.50	Deposits	+ $722.50

Reserves required against $722.50 of deposits amount to $108.38. Thus, the Third Bank has excess reserves of $614.12, which it can safely lend. After granting a loan of $614.12, its balance sheet will show:

THIRD BANK

Bank Assets		Bank Liabilities	
Cash	+ $722.50	Deposits	+ $1,336.62
Loans	+ 614.12		

When the proceeds of this loan are spent (and perhaps deposited in the Fourth Bank), the Third Bank will be left with cash of $108.38, exactly 15 percent of its deposits of $722.50. The Fourth Bank now has excess reserves, and this process can continue for some time. The whole process is summarized in Table 18-1.

As the table indicates, each bank lends out only the amount of its excess reserves. The banking system as a whole, however, has created deposits of $6,667. This is the same figure we arrived at as the limit to the deposit-creating power of a monopoly bank. Likewise, the commercial-banking system ends up with loans of $5,667. Again, this is the same figure as that for the monopoly bank. The explanation of this apparent paradox is relatively simple. An individual bank is limited in its ability to grant loans by the danger of incurring an outflow of cash as borrowers spend their deposits. But this is not an outflow of cash from the banking *system*. One bank's loss of cash is another bank's gain. The banking system as a whole, all through the process described above, has cash reserves of $1,000. A given bank may have a "clearing drain"—that is, may lose de-

TABLE 18-1

Multiple Expansion of Bank Deposits

	Amount Deposited in Checking Account	Amount Loaned by Bank	Amount Kept as Reserves by Bank
First Bank	$1,000.00	$ 850.00	$ 150.00
Second Bank	850.00	722.50	127.50
Third Bank	722.50	614.12	108.38
Fourth Bank	614.12	522.00	92.12
Fifth Bank	522.00	443.70	78.30
Sixth Bank	443.70	377.14	66.56
Seventh Bank	377.14	320.57	56.67
Eighth Bank	320.57	272.48	48.09
Ninth Bank	272.48	231.60	40.88
Tenth Bank	231.60	196.86	34.74
Total of 10 banks	$5,354.11	$4,550.97	$ 803.14
All other banks	1,312.56	1,116.70	196.86
Total for banking system	$6,666.67	$5,666.67	$1,000.00

posits to another bank—but the system as a whole retains the original $1,000 of cash reserves. Table 18-1 also shows the theoretical maximum expansion of commercial-bank loans and deposits with a 15 percent reserve requirement.

As we changed our focus to the individual bank, it emerged that each bank is creating deposits for the system as a whole, not necessarily for itself. This effect becomes even clearer if we assume that the institution buys a security rather than making a loan. The security is bought on the open market and must be paid for with cash (or a check drawn on the bank's Federal Reserve account). The seller of the security then has reserves, which may be deposited in another bank or another institution, creating a deposit for that institution. Now both the security seller and the original depositor in the first bank have money.

In this view, institutions other than banks are also creators of money-type assets (even when their transaction accounts are not involved). Suppose someone makes a deposit in a credit union, obtaining a nontransaction account. The credit union uses the proceeds to buy a security, and the seller of the security now has a bank deposit. Thus the credit union has created a deposit for another institution.

DISTRIBUTION OF RESERVES

The creation of any type of asset can be limited if reserves are required to be held in relation to that asset. In general, the greater the percentage reserve requirement, the greater the degree of control exercised.

Our model was formulated with only one type of deposit, a demand deposit that is transferable; only one type of institution, a commercial bank; and only a single unified reserve requirement for these deposits. Under these circumstances, the control of the level of demand deposits would be rather simple—banks could always be expected to create deposits at a constant multiple of the reserves made available to them. The actual system departs in a number of ways from these assumptions:

It is difficult to predict accurately how much additional currency the public will desire to hold when demand deposits increase.

Depository institutions will maintain some reserves in excess of the amount required; these excess reserves vary according to economic and money-market conditions.

Banks and other institutions create deposits other than demand deposits, and these have varying reserve requirements.

Even for transaction accounts, reserve requirements are not uniform for all the accounts of an institution.

Reserve requirements are not instantly met. There is a lag between an institution's change in deposit liabilities and the time it must meet new reserve requirements.

Under the 1980 Monetary Control Act, reserve requirements apply to all depository institutions. (See Chapter 20 for further discussion.) They were initially set as follows:

Transaction accounts—3 percent of the first $25 million for any institution, and 12 percent on the remaining amount

Savings and time deposits—3 percent for those held by business and government, and no reserve requirement for those held by individuals and nonprofit entities

The Federal Reserve can determine within limits the amount of reserves that the financial institutions have. It cannot, however, determine the distribution of these reserves or the use to which they are put. When deposits of all types are considered, the total amount of deposits that can be created with a given amount of reserves will be much greater if the public chooses nontransaction deposits than if it chooses transaction deposits. If some target level of total deposits is to be maintained, then reserves will have to be reduced if there is a shift toward deposits with low or no reserve requirement.

How the monetary authorities react to a shift of deposits will depend upon the nature of the shift and the targets for control that have been chosen. To illustrate, suppose that a desired level of deposits of all types has been achieved, and then some holders decide to shift from transaction accounts to saving deposits. Let us see the first effect and then consider how authorities might react to it.

Suppose the amount of $1 billion is shifted, and these deposits all had 12 percent reserves against them. The institutions reduce their transaction liabilities by $1 billion and increase savings liabilities by $1 billion. But this is not the end of things, since the savings liabilities require no reserves. The institutions then have $120 million of excess reserves that could be used as the basis of restoring transaction accounts, through loans and securities purchases, back to $1 billion. Thus, the effect of the shift would actually be a net rise in savings deposits by $1 billion. If it is desired that the total of savings and transaction deposits be held constant, then it will be necessary for the authorities to decrease bank reserves by $120 million so that transaction deposits actually fall by the $1 billion.

Now suppose that a $1-billion shift occurs from transaction accounts to time deposits held by business. Again, reserves held by institutions do not change, but institutions must make adjustment in their liabilities because of differential reserve requirements. The $1 billion in transaction deposits had $120 million reserves against them. The $1 billion in time deposits require $30 million of reserves. Thus, the institutions can use $90 million for transaction deposits, enabling them to restore $750 million of the $1 billion lost. To summarize, the net effect of the $1-billion shift is that transaction accounts fall by $250 million and time deposits rise by $1 billion. Again, the authorities can offset this net rise partially or wholly if desired, by a reduction in the reserves available to the institutions.

In the actual conduct of monetary policy, the Federal Reserve sets target growth rates for individual components of the money supply. We shall examine this procedure in considerable detail in Chapter 19.

QUESTIONS

1 Can banks create money? Can savings and loan associations?
2 Would the ability of banks to create deposits be changed if borrowers insisted on receiving currency rather than demand deposits?
3 What is the difference between derivative and primary deposits?
4 What factors limit the banking system's ability to expand deposits?
5 Why do banks sometimes hold excess reserves?
6 Would you rather own a gold mine or a commercial bank?

SELECTED READINGS

CRICK, W.F., "The Genesis of Bank Deposits," *Economica*, 1927. The classic paper on deposit creation.

TOBIN, JAMES, "Commercial Banks as Creators of 'Money,'" in *Banking and Monetary Studies*, Deane Carson, ed. Homewood, Ill.: Richard D. Irwin, Inc., 1963. A provocative challenge to the traditional view of the role of commercial banks in the money-creating process.

19

The Framework of Federal Reserve Control-II

Because of legal reserve requirements, a depository institution cannot have transaction deposits of more than a specified amount for every dollar of reserves. Any single institution may be able to increase its reserves by attracting deposits away from other banks, but in such a case, one bank's gain is another's loss. The reserves of the system as a whole are determined by forces beyond the control of the individual depository institution.

Although many factors affect reserves, the most important for our purposes are discretionary actions of the Federal Reserve. This chapter focuses on the factors affecting reserves, and the relationship between Federal Reserve actions and other forces that affect reserves.

FACTORS AFFECTING RESERVES

We can start by seeing how changes in various factors affect the reserve position of the depository institutions. Let us consider the effects of a change in the amount of *currency in circulation*, one of the most important factors affecting reserves. We define currency in circulation to include the total amount of currency and coin outside the Treasury and the Federal Reserve Banks. It includes currency held by depository institutions as well as by the nonbank public. That is, currency is put "in circulation" when it is issued to banks by the Federal Reserve.

Generally, an increase in currency in circulation reduces reserves. Suppose the public feels a need for more paper money (an event that occurs before every major holiday, for example). As customers withdraw cash from their deposit accounts, the institutions replenish their cash holdings from their Federal Reserve Banks. The net effect is that currency in circulation has increased and reserves have decreased.

It must be noted at this point that holdings of currency by institutions count as part of their required holdings of reserves. An increase in currency in circulation always results in a decrease in reserves held with the Federal Reserve Banks. However, *total* depository institution reserves need not vary inversely with currency in circulation if the change in currency in circulation is accounted for by change in the institutions' holdings of currency. Likewise, if the public increases its holdings of currency by withdrawing deposits from the banks, the immediate effect is a reduction in bank reserves even though total currency in circulation is not changed (the public has more and the banks have less).

It is interesting to compare this last transaction with what occurs when a depositor spends his deposit by writing a check. The check will probably be deposited in a different institution from the one in which he maintains his account, and thus his bank will lose reserves. But the bank in which the check is deposited will experience an equivalent increase in reserves. Thus, writing checks does not affect the reserve position of the financial system as a whole, but withdrawing deposits to add to holdings of currency does reduce reserves.

Treasury Cash Holdings
and Deposits with Federal Reserve Banks

An increase in the Treasury's holdings of currency or deposits with the Fed tends to reduce the reserves of the depository institutions. These transactions can arise in many ways. One such transaction could arise when a taxpayer sends the Treasury a check in payment of taxes. The Treasury may deposit the check in its Federal Reserve account. The Treasury's account will be credited, and the account of the commercial bank on which the check was written will be debited. The same net result arises when the Treasury is paid in currency. The currency must have come ultimately from the Federal Reserve (if it is assumed that there is no overall change in the volume of currency in circulation), and thus, increases in the Treasury's holdings of currency reduce commercial-bank reserves.

Treasury Currency

The comments concerning Treasury cash holdings refer to *assets* of the Treasury. It is important not to confuse this item with changes in Treasury *liabilities* — specifically, Treasury currency outstanding. Although nearly all our paper money now in use is issued by, and a liability of, the Federal Reserve, our coins are minted and issued by the Treasury. Let us assume that there is an increase in Treasury currency (or coin) outstanding. We can imagine this taking place by the unlikely device of the Treasury's paying a government employee with newly minted coin. The employee, we will assume, does not want to increase his holdings of such coins (even more unlikely) and deposits the cash in his checking account. Since holdings of cash are reserves, the reserves of the bank are increased directly by the receipt of the Treasury currency. If the bank does not want to hold the additional currency, it will ship the coins to its Federal Reserve Bank and have its reserve account credited with the amount of the shipment. In either case, reserves are increased with the increase in Treasury currency outstanding.

Other Deposits and Accounts
at Federal Reserve Banks

We have seen that the Federal Reserve Banks hold deposit accounts of some foreign banks and governments and some international financial institutions. It is clear that any transaction that means a shift from institutions' deposits to these accounts tends to reduce their reserves, and any shift in the other direction would increase reserves. Increases in any Federal Reserve Bank liability item then, other than depository reserves, tends to reduce reserves unless it is offset by an equivalent increase in a Federal Reserve Bank asset.

Gold

At one time, Treasury dealings in gold were an important factor affecting bank reserves. Now such transactions are less frequent and less significant, but they provide a good illustration of the relationship between Treasury and Federal Reserve operations and bank reserves. An increase in Treasury holdings of gold increases reserves, regardless of how the gold is acquired. The simplest example of this is to imagine that a gold miner digs up $100 worth of gold and sells it to the Treasury. The Treasury will pay for it by writing a check to the gold miner drawn on the Federal Reserve. The gold miner will deposit this check in his commercial bank, which will send the check to the Federal Reserve, increasing its reserve account and reducing the deposit account of the Treasury. The Treasury can compensate for the reduction in its deposit balance with the Fed by issuing a $100 gold certificate to the Federal Reserve. In terms of T accounts, the entire transaction can be represented as follows:

FEDERAL RESERVE		COMMERCIAL BANK	
Assets	Liabilities	Assets	Liabilities
	2. Deposit of Treasury − $100	1. Treasury check + $100	1. Deposit of miner + $100
	2. Bank reserves + $100	2. Treasury check − $100	
3. Gold certificate + $100	3. Deposit of Treasury + $100	2. Reserves + $100	

In Step 1, the miner deposits his check in a member bank. In Step 2, the bank has the amount of the check credited to its reserve account, which the Federal Reserve does by debiting the account of the Treasury. In Step 3, the Treasury's account is restored to its original level by issuing gold certificates to the Fed. The net result of this transaction is as follows:

FEDERAL RESERVE			
Gold Certificate	+ $100	Bank Reserves	+ $100

COMMERCIAL BANK			
Reserves	+ $100	Deposits	+ $100

TREASURY			
Gold	+ $100	Gold Certificates	+ $100

Thus we can see that the ultimate effect of the increase in our gold stock is an increase in commercial-bank reserves and deposits. It is important to note that the commercial bank now has excess reserves, and that loans and deposits could increase still further. Exactly the same results occur if the new gold comes from abroad rather than out of the ground. In either case, the seller of the gold to the Treasury receives payment that winds up as an increase in commercial-bank reserves.

Federal Reserve Credit

All the factors discussed above directly affect bank reserves, and they also have an effect on the balance sheet of the Federal Reserve System. These results, however, take place without any conscious action on the part of the Federal Reserve. If our gold stock is increased, there is an increase in depository reserves; if Treasury cash holdings increase, there is a decrease in reserves, both without the Fed's taking any action.

We can now consider an important class of transactions in which the initiative is in the hands of the Fed. Federal Reserve credit is an important source of reserves for the depository institutions, and may arise in various ways. The most important, in dollar amount, is through Federal Reserve purchases of U.S. government securities.

The Fed buys securities through a dealer who will have obtained them by purchase from a commercial bank, an individual or nonbank institution, or the Treasury. In analyzing the ultimate effects of Federal Reserve purchases of government securities, we can temporarily ignore the operations of the bond dealer and assume that the Fed buys its securities directly from one of these sources. Such transactions are referred to as "open-market operations."

When the Fed purchases securities in the open market, the reserves of depository institutions are increased by the amount of the purchase. When it sells securities, reserves are decreased by that amount. This is true whether the other party to the transaction is a depository institution or an individual. Let us look at the balance sheet of a commercial bank that sells $1 million of government securities to the Federal Reserve:

FEDERAL RESERVE

Assets		Liabilities	
Government securities	+ 1.0	Bank reserves	+ 1.0

COMMERCIAL BANK

Assets		Liabilities	
Government securities	− 1.0		
Reserves	+ 1.0		

The Fed pays for the securities by crediting the bank's reserve account with $1 million. If the bank is a buyer of securities, the results are reversed—the bank writes a check to the Federal Reserve that is debited to the bank's reserve account.

If the other party to the transaction is an individual or business firm, the accounting is slightly more complex, but the results are similar. An individual buying securities from the Federal Reserve will pay for them with a check drawn on a depository institution. The Federal Reserve collects the check by debiting the account of the institution, as shown in the T accounts. If the individual is a seller of $1 million of securities to the Federal Reserve, he will receive a check that he will deposit. The check will be returned to the Federal Reserve by the institution, and its reserve account will be credited with the $1 million. Thus, the signs of all the entries on these T accounts will simply be reversed:

FEDERAL RESERVE

Assets		Liabilities	
Government securities	− 1.0	Reserves	− 1.0

DEPOSITORY INSTITUTION

Assets		Liabilities	
Reserves	− 1.0	Deposits	− 1.0

One difference between the two sets of T accounts should be noted. When a commercial bank is a party to the transaction, there is no direct and immediate change in the deposits of commercial banks; thus, a $1-million change in reserves means a $1-million change in excess reserves. When an individual is the other party to a transaction with the Federal Reserve, the change in reserves is accompanied by a change in the same direction in deposits; thus, the change in excess reserves is only $1 - r$ times as great as in the first case.[1] This difference is really superficial, however. If the banking system expands or contracts so that excess reserves are zero, then the potential change in deposits for the banking system as a whole is given by the formula introduced in the last chapter: $\Delta D = \Delta R / r$. Thus, if reserve requirements are 20 percent and the Federal Reserve buys $1 million of securities, the potential expansion in de-

---

[1] The reader will recall that r is the symbol we have used for the reserve-requirement percentages. If r is equal to 10 percent, excess reserves will decline by only $900,000 when the Federal Reserve sells $1 million of securities to an individual.

posits is $5 million regardless of whether the seller is a bank or not.

At times, the Federal Reserve may have direct dealings with the Treasury. During World War II, the Fed was given authority to buy securities directly from the Treasury at the latter's initiative. Even though this authority has been used infrequently, we can consider the effect of such transactions on commercial-bank deposits and reserves.

If the Federal Reserve buys $1 million of securities directly from the Treasury, it credits the Treasury's account by the amount of the purchase. There is no immediate effect on bank reserves or deposits. Presumably, however, the Treasury borrowed from the Fed because it needed the funds. When the Treasury uses its newly created deposit, bank reserves and deposits will rise by the amount of the spending. Bank reserves will replace the Treasury's deposit on the books of the Federal Reserve.

The Fed is not apt to sell securities directly to the Treasury, but it may redeem Treasury securities for cash at maturity. The immediate effect of this is simply a reduction in the Federal Reserve's holdings of government securities and an equal reduction in the Treasury's deposit account with the Federal Reserve. However, the Treasury will not passively see its account with the Fed reduced. Since this account represents the Treasury's working balances out of which payments are made, it will attempt to rebuild the account to its desired level. The normal way for the Treasury to do this is to transfer funds from its accounts at commercial banks (the Tax and Loan Accounts) to the Federal Reserve. This will have the effect of reducing commercial-bank reserves by the amount of the transfer.

The ultimate effects, then, of changes in the Federal Reserve's holdings of government securities are the same regardless of whether it deals with individuals, depository institutions, or the Treasury. An increase in Federal Reserve holdings of securities will result in an increase in reserves (and ultimately a multiple expansion of deposits), and a reduction in holdings of government securities will mean a reduction in reserves (and a multiple reduction in deposits).[2]

---

[2] The analytical reader will note that these effects are not limited to changes in the holdings of government securities. In particular, changes in holdings of acceptances will have the same effects, but increases or decreases in the holdings of any asset will have these effects. The Fed could achieve the same effects on depository reserves if open-market operations were conducted in mortgages, wheat, or left-handed monkey wrenches.

Other Federal Reserve Credit

It is easy to see that increases in discounts and advances to depository institutions directly increase reserves. The T accounts corresponding to such a transaction are simply these:

FEDERAL RESERVE

Assets		Liabilities	
Discounts	+ $100	Depository reserves	+ $100

BORROWING INSTITUTION

Assets		Liabilities	
Reserves	+ $100	Due to Federal Reserve	+ $100

Although Federal Reserve lending to depository institutions arises on the initiative of the institution, the Fed exercises considerable control over the volume of such lending. We shall consider the exercise of this control in the following chapter.

We have already seen that float is a form of Federal Reserve credit. The Fed has adopted the policy of giving credit for checks deposited more rapidly, on the average, than such checks can be collected. Any increase in the excess of cash items in the process of collection over deferred availability cash items directly increases depository reserves. In recent years, the Fed has taken steps to reduce the amount of float, and the 1980 Monetary Control Act mandated that the Fed charge banks for float at the Federal-funds rate.

THE RESERVE EQUATION

It is possible to combine the factors affecting reserves in many different ways. The Federal Reserve balance sheet is, in fact, one of them. Since we know that assets equal liabilities plus capital accounts on any balance sheet, we can rearrange the Federal Reserve balance sheet as follows:

$$\text{Assets} = \text{Depository-institution reserves} + \text{Other liabilities} + \text{Capital accounts}$$

We can rewrite this equation as:

$$\text{Reserves} = \text{Assets} - \left\{ \begin{array}{c} \text{Other liabilities} \\ + \\ \text{Capital accounts} \end{array} \right\}$$

We have already seen the meaning of this equation. We noted.
that any increase in Federal Reserve assets tends to increase reserves, whereas an increase in any Federal Reserve liability tends
to decrease reserves.

Although this equation is always true, it is still not in the most
useful form. It does not include some of the factors that influence
the monetary system. Currency in circulation, for example, does not
appear directly in the equation, since it is not an asset or liability of
the Federal Reserve.[3] Neither does gold enter the equation directly.
It is true that gold certificates appear in the equation, but this is not
quite the same as the amount of our gold stock—the Treasury holds
some gold against which it has not issued gold certificates.

We can restate the equation above to give explicit recognition
to the factors it omits. The Fed itself has recognized the desirability
of such a restatement of the system's balance sheet, and thus each
week, issues both a balance sheet, and an additional statement
known as the Reserve Equation.

The Reserve Equation groups together those items in which
an increase results in an increase in reserves and those in which an
increase results in a decrease in reserves. The former are known as
sources of funds, and the latter as *uses of funds*—or sometimes as
competing uses of funds, since reserves themselves are a use of
funds. This leads us to the following equation:

Sources of funds = Uses of funds = Reserves + Competing
uses of funds or, equivalently:

Reserves = Sources of funds − Competing uses of funds

We have already examined the sources and uses of funds, and
we can now simply list the components of the last equation:

Reserves	=	Sources	−	Competing uses
				Currency in circulation
				+
				Treasury cash
		Federal Reserve credit		+
Depository-institution		+		Treasury deposits with
deposits with		Gold stock	−	Federal Reserve
Federal Reserve	=	+		+
		Treasury currency		Other deposits with
		outstanding		Federal Reserve
				+
				Other Federal Reserve
				accounts (net)

[3] Federal Reserve notes, which make up the bulk of currency in circulation, do
appear as a liability of the Federal Reserve.

We began by using the Federal Reserve balance sheet to show that:

$$\text{Reserves} = \text{Federal Reserve assets} - \text{Other Federal Reserve liabilities}$$

We then claimed that:

$$\text{Reserves} = \text{Sources of funds} - \text{Competing uses of funds}$$

If both these equations are to be true, there must be some relation between the items in the first and the items in the second. A close look at the composition of the two equations confirms that this relation does indeed exist. The relations between items in the first equation and items in the second are given by the following equations:

$$\text{Gold stock} - \text{Gold held in Treasury} = \text{Gold certificates}$$
$$\text{(part of Treasury cash)}$$

| Currency in circulation | = | Federal Reserve notes | + | Treasury currency outstanding | − | Cash held by Federal Reserve Banks | − | Treasury cash |

| Other Federal Reserve accounts | = | Capital and surplus | + | Other liabilities | − | Bank premises | − | Other assets |

A few words of warning seem to be in order concerning interpretation of these equations. We have already noted the distinction between Treasury currency outstanding and Treasury cash. Changes in these items have opposite effects on depository reserves. It is also important to remember that reserves with the Federal Reserve Banks are not the total of depository institutions' reserves. Cash held in their vaults also counts towards satisfying reserve requirements.

The Federal Reserve's presentation of the reserve information, using slightly different language, is shown in Table 19-1.

THE MONETARY BASE

The important result of these complex Federal Reserve transactions is the assets remaining in the hands of the private economy. These are the currency holdings of the public and the reserves held by the financial institutions. Currency is a direct component of the

TABLE 19-1

Reserves of Depository Institutions—Amounts Outstanding, December 31, 1981

(in millions of dollars)

Supplying Reserve Funds	
Reserve bank credit outstanding	153,136
U.S. government securities	130,954
Bought outright	127,738
Held under repurchase agreements	3,216
Federal agency securities	9,394
Bought outright	9,125
Held under repurchase agreements	269
Acceptances	195
Loans	1,601
Float	1,762
Other Federal Reserve assets	9,230
Gold stock	11,151
Special drawing rights certificate account	3,318
Treasury currency outstanding	13,687
Absorbing Reserve Funds	
Currency in circulation	144,774
Treasury cash holdings	443
Deposits, other than member bank reserves, with Federal Reserve Banks	
Treasury	4,301
Foreign	505
Other	781
Other Federal Reserve liabilities and capital	5,378
Reserve accounts	25,111

Source: *Federal Reserve Bulletin*, January 1982.

money supply by any definition, and reserve balances support various kinds of deposits that are candidates for inclusion in the money supply. These two assets—currency and reserves—are called the *monetary base*. Some economists have aptly referred to this concept as "high-powered money."

A distinguishing feature of high-powered money is that, from the standpoint of the private economy, it is an asset without a matching liability (also a characteristic of metallic money). For this reason, it is also sometimes called "outside money." Depository types of money arise as financial institutions acquire claims, and thus the private economy also has liabilities matching this "inside money."

The Fed has almost complete control over the monetary base, since it consists of Federal Reserve debt (reserves and nearly all

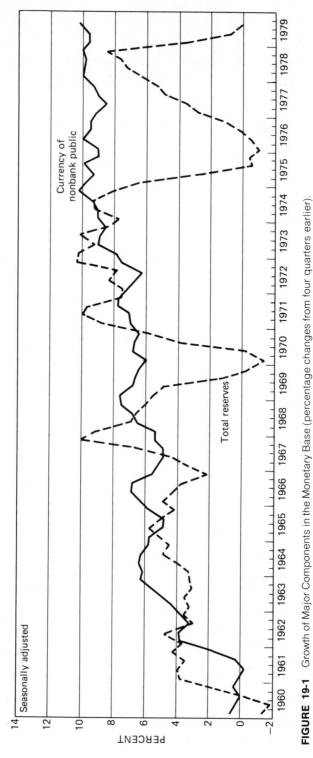

FIGURE 19-1 Growth of Major Components in the Monetary Base (percentage changes from four quarters earlier).

Source: Federal Reserve Bank of New York, *Quarterly Review*, Winter 1979–80.

paper money are liabilities of the Federal Reserve). The Fed need issue no more debt than it wishes.

The base can be calculated from Table 19-1 by selecting the data on reserves with the Federal Reserve ($25.1 billion) and currency in circulation ($144.8 billion). Depending upon the purposes of the analysis, it may be desirable to consider, in a time series, the effects of reserve-requirement changes on the use to which the monetary base can be put. This adjustment would not be made if one were concerned with the significance of the base as "outside money," in which case the data stand on their own. But if one views the significance in terms of a potential deposit expansion, then a reserve requirement reduction, say, would increase the base's potential. The series in Figure 19-1, which is adjusted, shows percentage growth in the monetary base. Because of adjustment, the base could grow either from a rise in the actual levels or from a "release" of reserves by reserve-requirement reductions (or could decline from reserve-requirement increases).

Although control over the monetary base is almost complete, the Federal Reserve actually chooses, as targets for control, broader concepts of the money supply.[4] Because these "monetary

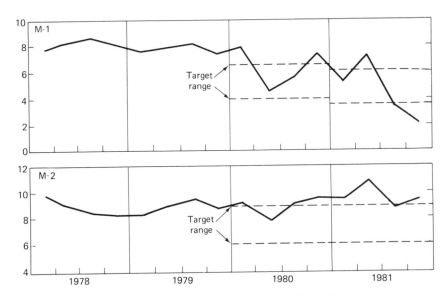

FIGURE 19-2 Monetary Supply—Levels and Targets, 1978–1981.
Source: Federal Reserve Bank of New York, 1981 Annual Report.

[4] Some critics of Federal Reserve policy argue that the Fed should focus on the base, because it is subject to more precise control.

TABLE 19-2
Monetary Aggregates

Component	M1	M2	M3	L
Currency	X	X	X	X
At commercial banks:				
Demand deposits *exclusive* of deposits due to foreign commercial banks and official institutions	X	X	X	X
NOW accounts	X	X	X	X
ATS accounts	X	X	X	X
Overnight RPs		X	X	X
Savings deposits		X	X	X
Small time deposits (< $100,000)		X	X	X
Large time deposits:				
Other than large negotiable CDs			X	X
Including large negotiable CDs			X	X
Term RPs			X	X
At thrift institutions:				
Demand deposits	X	X	X	X
NOW accounts	X	X	X	X
ATS accounts	X	X	X	X
Credit-union share draft balances	X	X	X	X
Savings deposits (mutual savings banks and savings and loan associations)		X	X	X
Small time deposits (< $100,000)		X	X	X
Large time deposits (> $100,000)			X	X
Term RPs (commercial banks and savings and loan associations)			X	X
Other:				
Overnight Eurodollar deposits of U.S. nonbank residents		X	X	X
Money-market mutual funds' shares		X	X	X
Term Eurodollars held by U.S. nonbank residents				X
Banker's acceptances				X
Commercial paper				X
U.S. savings bonds				X
Liquid Treasury securities				X
Totals, Dec., 1981 (billions)	441	1,822	2,188	2,647

Source: Federal Reserve System.

aggregates" include the debt of private institutions, they are less amenable to precise control, but the monetary base clearly influences these aggregates. If the composition of all assets remained static, the precise relation between the money supply (M1) and the base (B) would be:

$$\text{Money stock} = \frac{1+k}{r(1+t+g)+k} \bullet B$$

where k is the currency/deposit ratio, r is the reserves/deposit ratio, t is the time-deposit/demand-deposit ratio, and g is the government-deposit/private-deposit ratio.

M1 and the other monetary aggregates are shown in Table 19-2.[5] For each of the aggregates, the Fed chooses target growth rates and announces these in advance to the public (see Figure 19-2). The targeted growth rate is specified as a range for each of the aggregates rather than a single rate. A range is employed because it gives the Fed some flexibility to respond to unexpected developments, and also because it is impossible to achieve targets precisely. We shall return to the monetary targets in Chapter 21.

QUESTIONS

1 How is the depository reserve position affected if the public decides to hoard currency in mattresses?
2 What is the difference between Treasury cash and Treasury currency?
3 What is the Reserve Equation?
4 Why do banks hold excess reserves?
5 Can the money supply increase without an increase in reserves? Explain.
6 Why doesn't the Treasury simply print dollar bills to pay for expenditures in excess of tax revenue?
7 Show how the economic effect of a given level of federal deficit varies depending on how the deficit is financed.
8 What is the difference between the monetary base and the M1 definition of money?

SELECTED READINGS

BURGER, ALBERT, "Alternative Measures of the Monetary Base," Federal Reserve Bank of St. Louis *Review*, June 1979.
FAIR, DONALD E., "Monetary Control," *Three Banks Review* (Edinburgh, Scotland), March 1981.
GURLEY, JOHN, and EDWARD S. SHAW, *Money in a Theory of Finance*. Washington, D.C.: The Brookings Institution, 1960.
HAFER, R.W., "The New Monetary Aggregates," Federal Reserve Bank of St. Louis *Review*, February 1980.
SIMPSON, THOMAS, "The Redefined Monetary Aggregates," *Federal Reserve Bulletin*, February 1980.

[5] The L in the table is a "liquidity" measure that the Fed reports but does not target for control.

20
Instruments of Monetary Policy: Reserve Requirements and Discount Policy

Monetary policy aims at controlling the supply of money in the economy so as to affect the aggregate level of spending. There are differences among economists as to the means by which changes in the money supply affect spending—differences that we will explore in the following section of this book. Some believe that spending decisions of consumers and businesses are directly influenced by changes in the money supply, and others believe that monetary policy works primarily through its effect on interest rates; however, all agree that basic to monetary policy are actions of the Federal Reserve that affect the reserve position of depository institutions.

In conducting monetary policy, the Fed has several policy instruments at its disposal, the most important of which are reserve requirements, discount policy, and open-market operations. The last two affect the size of the reserve base, and the first determines the deposit volume that can be built upon the reserve base. These policy tools are often referred to as *general* controls, on the grounds that they affect credit markets in general rather than being aimed at specific uses of funds. This is contrasted with such powers as Federal Reserve control over stock-market margin requirements. Policy tools of this latter sort, aimed at particular credit markets, are referred to as *selective* controls. This traditional distinction may not be a very useful one, since even the general controls may have very uneven effects in specific markets.

The Fed also has other powers: some statutory, such as regulations regarding bank assets, and other, rather informal weapons that flow from the power, prestige, and position of the Federal Reserve System as the regulator of the banking system. These informal powers are often referred to as "moral suasion." In addition, the Treasury also has discretionary powers in certain matters that directly affect the monetary system. These will be considered in this and following chapters.

RESERVE REQUIREMENTS

Reserve requirements specify certain types of assets that must be held in some ratio to specified liabilities, primarily deposit-type liabilities. When first enacted, reserves were intended to fulfill a safety function, to ensure that banks maintained some ability to meet depositor demands for withdrawal. In time, the function of reserve requirements has changed to a means of giving the authorities a control mechanism over the money stock. Safety requirements are met in other ways, such as regulation of allowable assets, deposit insurance, and borrowing rights at the Federal Reserve.

Under present law, all institutions offering deposits are subject to the same reserve requirements. The requirements may be met by holdings of currency or by holding reserve deposits at the Fed (either directly or through another institution). The eligible assets are specified in this way so that their total amount—all consisting of Federal Reserve liabilities—can be controlled. If reserves could be held as, say, government securities, then institutions could change the amounts by purchasing more on the open market. The percentage of reserve required depends upon the type of deposit or other liability.

Transaction Accounts

The 1980 Monetary Control Act established the present system of reserve requirements. We will look first at its provisions regarding transaction accounts. Each institution must maintain reserves against these accounts of 3 percent on the first $25 million.[1] Ac-

---

[1] Reserve requirements are actually assessed on net deposits, which are total deposits less cash items in the process of collection and demand balances due from domestic banks. The purpose of assessing reserve requirements against this rather

counts over that amount are subject to a 12 percent requirement. About 40 percent of total transaction accounts are in the 3 percent reserve-requirement category. This means that the effective reserve requirement against all transaction accounts is about 8 percent (40 percent of 3 percent plus 60 percent of 12 percent).

The $25-million cutoff established initially under the act is subject to annual change. It is to be adjusted annually, at midyear, by 80 percent of the change in total transaction accounts over the preceding year. (If transaction accounts increase by 10 percent, then the value of the break point increases by 8 percent.) Thus it is quite possible that as total deposits grow, the proportion subject to each of the two reserve ratios may remain stable.

The act gives the Federal Reserve some discretion to alter rates. The requirement on the first level of accounts remains fixed at 3 percent, but the requirement on remaining accounts can range between 8 and 14 percent. In addition to these regular reserve* requirements, the Fed may also impose a supplemental reserve requirement if five or more members of the Board agree that it is necessary for monetary-policy purposes. This supplemental reserve requirement may go up to 4 percent of total transaction accounts. The institutions would receive interest on the supplemental reserve, with the rate to be based on the average earnings on the Federal Reserve's portfolio.

Nontransaction Liabilities

No reserve requirement may be imposed on savings and time deposits held by individuals and households. The requirement on nonpersonal time deposits is 3 percent, but it applies only to maturities

---

complex concept of net demand deposits is to arrive at an unduplicated total for the demand-deposit liabilities of depository institutions to the public. This can best be seen by considering the deduction of cash items in the process of collection. Suppose a customer deposits a check drawn on Bank A into his account at Bank B. Immediately after the deposit is made, Bank B finds its deposits increased, and the offsetting asset item is the check on Bank A (a "cash item in the process of collection"). Until this check is collected, the account of the customer of Bank A who wrote the check is not reduced. Thus, to the extent of cash items in the process of collection, the balance sheets of the banking system overstate the true amount of deposits owned by the public. The customer of Bank A no longer has his deposit in Bank A. He knows it, but the bank does not until the check is collected. It can certainly be argued that it would be unfair to require both Bank A and Bank B to maintain reserve requirements against what is, in fact, only one deposit. Thus, a bank is not required to maintain reserves against deposits to the extent that the deposits are offset by cash items in the process of collection.

under four years. The Board has the power to set these requirements between 0 and 9 percent, and to vary them according to maturities.

The Federal Reserve has unlimited power to require reserves against institutions' foreign sources of funds, such as Eurocurrency borrowings. This is to prevent banks from favoring overseas borrowing and from using foreign entities, including their own offices, to channel funds and avoid reserve requirements. The reserve requirement against such borrowings is 3 percent.

Emergency powers are granted to the Board to take care of any problems not foreseen in the 1980 act. The Board may impose any level of reserve requirements on any liability of depository institutions for up to 180 days. For this action to be taken, at least five members must concur that it is required because of extraordinary circumstances, and the Board must consult with appropriate congressional committees.

Enforcement

Enforcement of the reserve requirement on depository institutions rests with the individual Reserve Banks in their districts. The Reserve Bank may waive a penalty, may require that the reserve deficiency be made up by the institution's holding additional reserve balances in subsequent periods, or may impose a penalty. The penalty is imposed as an interest rate on the amount and duration of the deficiency, and the rate is 2 percentage points more than the institution would pay if it prevented the deficiency by borrowing from the Fed at its discount rate. With continued violations, the Reserve Bank may enforce the reserve requirement through the courts, with civil money penalties and cease and desist orders.

History of Reserve Requirements

Reserve requirements were established by the Federal Reserve Act at specified levels that remained in force until the 1930s. The Banking Act of 1935 gave the Board of Governors of the Federal Reserve System the power to vary reserve requirements within certain limits to prevent or offset undesirable changes in the money supply.

The Board used this power for the first time in 1936 and has used it a number of times since then. The limits imposed by the Banking Act were wide, and the Board generally found it possible to keep reserve requirements well within the statutory limits. In the inflationary period immediately following World War II, however, the Board felt that reserve requirements higher than those allowed by law would be appropriate, and Congress temporarily raised the requirement ceilings. In recent years, the Fed has felt that some reserve requirements should be lower than the minimums specified in the law.

During the Korean War, reserve requirements were raised for all classes of member banks, but since that time, changes in requirements have generally been downward. The largest banks had their maximum reserve requirements against net demand deposits lowered from 24 percent in 1951 to 16¼ percent in 1978. Small banks enjoyed the largest decrease, from 14 percent in 1951 to 7 percent for the smallest member banks, and to less than 10 percent for the great majority.

In addition to the gradual lowering of reserve requirements over the last 25 years, there have been other changes designed to reduce the burden of reserve requirements on member banks. Until 1960, only reserves held with Federal Reserve Banks counted toward meeting a member bank's reserve requirements. Now currency and coin of the institutions counts as well.

Until 1972, member-bank reserve requirements were based not only on bank size but also on the location of the bank. The Federal Reserve Act carried forward the reserve city classification system of the National Banking Act, described in Chapter 14. Banks in "central reserve cities" had higher reserve requirements than banks located in "reserve cities," which had higher reserve requirements than banks in other cities. Unfortunately, the Fed was never able to develop a reasonable basis for distinguishing between reserve cities and nonreserve cities. Moreover, it did not classify all banks in reserve cities as reserve city banks. Distinctions were made on the basis of bank size, type of business done, and other factors (including how strongly the bank complained).

Prior to the 1980 Monetary Control Act, there had been a gradual downward drift in the ratio of reserves to demand deposits. This came not only from the lowering of reserve requirements by the Federal Reserve, but also from the gradual erosion of membership in the Fed. Reserve requirements applied only to member commercial banks, and membership dropped partly because of these requirements. In the 20-year period, 1959–1979, the proportion of demand deposits held in member banks dropped from 83 to 65 percent. This erosion of monetary control was checked by the 1980 act, which extended requirements to all institutions. As with any bureaucratic institution, the Federal Reserve was concerned about the size of its constituency. Because of the effect of reserve requirements on bank earnings—and banks' willingness to remain in the system—a conflict existed between the requirements of monetary policy and the maintenance of the system. Equity seemed to require that all financial institutions participate in monetary control, an argument that seems unassailable, even if the Federal Reserve System as such were to be abolished.

Reserve-Requirement Reforms

The 1980 Monetary Control Act maintained the Federal Reserve's power, within limits, to alter reserve requirements—a power it has held since 1935. It is not likely to use this power very frequently. The Fed has considered that changes in reserve requirements are a blunt tool for effecting short-run changes in the money stock. Open-market operations have been looked upon as a more flexible instrument. Such operations do not necessarily affect all banks immediately, and they appear to come more from impersonal market forces than from the actions of a few officials.

In contrast to open-market operations, reserve-requirement changes affect all banks. Many banks find it difficult to adjust promptly to increased reserve requirements. Since banks generally maintain only small fractions of reserves as excess, even a small change in reserve requirements may more than wipe out a bank's excess reserves. There are also the "announcement" effects to contend with. Open-market operations can be changed on a day-by-day basis without continued notification to the public. But reserve-requirement changes are announced in advance to forewarn the banks, and such announcements from the central bank may tend to disrupt financial markets.

But some analysts have the view that these alleged disadvantages are actually powerful tools that can be used to advantage. The fact that all banks are affected means that a change is transmitted rapidly throughout the system. The announcement of a change affects the financial markets, but it is in the direction intended. As to the magnitude of effects, it is not necessary that reserve-requirement changes be made in large steps. They can amount to a tenth of a percentage point, a hundredth, or whatever is necessary. Advocates of more flexible use of reserve-requirement changes point to foreign countries, which have used this tool more extensively because of less-developed money markets, making more difficult the use of open-market operations.

More fundamental proposals for change in reserve-requirement policy range all the way from zero reserve requirements to 100 percent. Would deposit expansion be infinite if there were no reserve requirements? Advocates of this reform argue that they would not, that institutions would always have to maintain some ratio of cash to deposit liabilities.[2] The characterization of certain deposits as requiring reserves simply causes institutions to develop alternatives. With zero reserve requirements, open-market operations would still provide reserves to the system, but financial institutions would use them as they wished, to create whatever kind of deposits served the needs of the economy. The monetary base would be the only target of monetary policy.

The 100 percent reserve plan would mean in essence that the public held all its transaction deposits as claims on the Federal Reserve, but did so operating through private institutions. For every $100 of deposit liability, the institution would have $100 of cash or Federal Reserve deposit assets. Since reserves could not be multiplied, open-market operations would have to provide reserves equal to whatever was the desired level of deposits. And since depository institutions could not have loans and securities based on their transaction-account liabilities, they would have to be compensated either by service charges on the accounts or by the payment of interest on their reserves.

Advocates of the 100 percent reserve plan tend to place great weight on the role of money in economic activity. In this analysis, the importance of money requires that it be controlled precisely without any slippage, and that there be no possibility of an institution's defaulting on the monetary obligation. Interest in this plan was aroused by the financial collapse of the Great Depression, but in more recent times, its merits have been regarded as not warranting the extreme disruptions it would cause among financial institutions.

THE DISCOUNT WINDOW

Any institution required to maintain reserves has the privilege of borrowing reserves on a short-term basis from the Federal Reserve. This source of reserves is usually referred to as the "discount window." The borrowing institution may rediscount notes given to it by its customers, or it may borrow on the security of other collateral acceptable to the Reserve Bank (generally U.S. government securities).

---

[2] See Deane Carson, "Is the Federal Reserve System Really Necessary?" *Journal of Finance*, December 1964, p. 652.

Until 1980, the borrowing privilege was limited to member banks. Allowing for the possibility of member-bank borrowing from the Fed was an important safety device in the Federal Reserve Act. The reader will remember that one of the principal difficulties of the National Banking System was that there was no easy way for the banking system as a whole to get additional reserves. Under the Federal Reserve System, the necessary elasticity is injected into the monetary system by making the Reserve Banks, in effect, lenders of last resort to the banking system. In this section we are primarily concerned with discount policy not as a safety factor to the banking system, but as a policy weapon of the Federal Reserve.

When a bank or other institution is short of reserves, it has several possible alternatives to choose from in resolving its problem. It can sell some of its securities; it can call in loans, or at least refuse to make new ones; it can borrow from other banks; or it can borrow from the Federal Reserve. Large banks may be able to pull in funds by raising the rate they are paying on certificates of deposit. Some large banks have foreign branches where they can accept deposits denominated in dollars ("Eurodollars"). The bank's decision will generally be based on considerations of cost—it will raise the funds in the cheapest way possible. If a bank can borrow Federal funds at 10 percent, it will probably do so rather than sell government securities on which it is earning 11 percent. Under normal conditions, it will probably be possible for the institution to obtain the needed funds by borrowing Federal funds or by borrowing from the Fed, without being forced to liquidate loans or investments.

When the Fed is desirous of tightening credit, it can put pressure on reserve positions by raising reserve requirements or, as we shall see, by selling securities in the open market. Under these conditions, the supply of Federal funds will be reduced, and institutions will be forced to the Federal Reserve's discount window. An increase in the discount rate at such a time makes it less profitable for the institutions to raise reserves in this manner, and if the pressure is maintained, they will be forced to contract their loans and investments (and hence deposits). During such a period, the Fed may establish discount rates above the rates prevailing on Treasury bills. This makes it cheaper to obtain the reserves by liquidation of Treasury bills than by borrowing from the Federal Reserve (see Figure 20-1).

In a period of slack business activity, the Fed can make reserves cheaply available to depository institutions by maintaining low discount rates. This ensures that no bank will be forced to turn

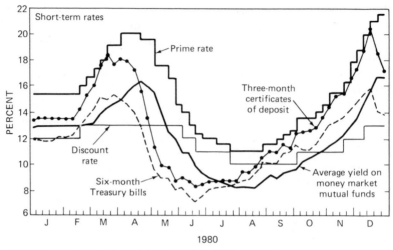

FIGURE 20-1 Short-term Interest Rates, 1980

Source: Federal Reserve Bank of New York.

down loan applications because of lack of funds. It can cheaply obtain the funds it needs from the Federal Reserve.

Setting the Discount Rate

The process by which discount rates are set is somewhat complicated. At least every two weeks, the board of directors of each of the Federal Reserve Banks meets to consider discount rates. At each directors' meeting, the president of the Reserve Bank reports on the latest meeting of the Open Market Committee and on any discussions he or she may have had, concerning monetary policy in general and discount rates in particular, with the Board of Governors. An economist on the staff of the bank may present a review of the current economic situation. After discussing the economic and financial situation, the board of directors votes on whether the discount rate should be changed. A vote on this matter must be taken at every directors' meeting.

According to law, each Federal Reserve Bank establishes its own discount rate, subject to review and determination by the Board of Governors in Washington. The word *determination* is important. Legally, the Board of Governors not only reviews the action taken by the board of directors, but has the right to *set* the bank's rate. This right has been used, and the mere fact that this power exists tends to make the directors more attentive to the views of the Board of Governors than might otherwise be the case.

The president of the bank is in frequent contact with the Board of Governors and knows well the views of the board with respect to discount rates. When these views are presented to the board of directors of the bank, the directors will generally go along without much opposition. At times, of course, the directors may disagree with the view of the Board of Governors. Often they are people with considerable competence in assessing the business situation, and their interpretations of current developments may run counter to those of the Board in Washington. In such cases, the opposition may take the form of a slight delay in making the adjustment desired by the Board.

Such behavior probably makes the directors feel more important in the formulation of monetary policy and, if it does not last long, does the economy no harm. When the Federal Reserve System was established, it was felt that discount rates would be set in accordance with local conditions—another example of the compromise between central and local control of the Fed. During the 1920s, it was common for different Reserve Banks to have substantially different discount rates for long periods of time. Now, however, the money market is truly national in character, and it would be impractical to have different rates prevailing in different parts of the country.

Institutions are to borrow from the Federal Reserve to meet only short-term needs. The discount window is not to be used as a source of funds for re-lending, except to meet temporary, unexpected credit demands. The primary function of borrowing is to meet reserve requirements when there are unexpected deposit outflows. Small institutions may also meet seasonal reserve needs, and institutions with severe financial difficulties may receive emergency credit. The intent of the Federal Reserve is to make the discount window a safety valve for the financial system, not a source of profit for the institutions.

In the past, borrowing privileges were available only to member banks, which seem to have been reluctant to use this source of funds. A Federal Reserve Bank of St. Louis study commented:

> Most member banks do not borrow from the discount window; those few that do so generally borrow infrequently. . . .
>
> The infrequent borrowing of member banks from the Federal Reserve indicates that, in most circumstances, they adjust to reserve losses without resort to the discount window. . . . If borrowing from the discount window were an important means for banks

to adjust their reserve positions to reserve outflows, most member banks would borrow from the discount window. Yet, they do not do so.[3]

Member-bank borrowing has contributed no more than 1–2 percent to the monetary base (reserves and currency). The Fed's approach to administration of the discount mechanism is based on the assumption that banks were "reluctant to be in debt to the central bank in view of its limiting rules and the kind of administrative discipline to which a borrowing bank might be subject." This statement by a Federal Reserve committee suggests that banks do not like to borrow frequently from the Fed because they know the system frowns on continual borrowing, and they fear that frequent borrowing may lead to their being turned down for an advance in a real emergency. Regulation A, which governs borrowing, indicates that the Fed will look carefully at the operations of an institution seeking to borrow funds. Most institutions do not relish the thought of a Federal Reserve official looking closely into their operations and perhaps questioning the judgment of their officers in respect to certain loans or investments.

One additional reason for some banks' reluctance to borrow from the discount window is uncertainty about the ground rules. Regulation A is by no means a clear, straightforward document. There is evidence, in fact, that administration of a discount window varies from one Federal Reserve district to another, despite the fact that all are supposed to be operating under the same rules. The lack of clear ground rules poses a real problem to depository institutions.

Assessment of Discount Policy

The framers of the Federal Reserve Act expected that administration of the discount mechanism would be the most important policy tool of the Federal Reserve System. Discounting was important in the early years of the system, but the large volume of excess reserves held by the banking system during the 1930s and 1940s tended to reduce the importance of the discount rate. With the increasing use of restrictive monetary policy since the 1950s, the discount window has regained some of its earlier importance.

There have been many proposals for change in the discount mechanism, and some serious criticisms regarding its use. It has been argued, for example, that the discount rate is not effective in

[3] E. Alton Gilbert, "Access to the Discount Window for All Commercial Banks: Is It Important for Monetary Policy?" Federal Reserve Bank of St. Louis *Review*, February 1980, p. 16.

counteracting a recession. The Fed can lower the discount rate and seek to make reserves readily available, but it cannot force institutions to make use of these reserves. On the other hand, it has been argued that in an inflationary period, the possibility of discounting allows the system to escape the effects of restrictive monetary policy (see Figure 20-2).

It can be seen that the volume of borrowing from the Fed is indeed larger during periods of high interest rates than during periods of easy money. This does not appear to be a serious problem, however. It is clear that the Fed can take whatever steps are necessary to offset the increase in reserves made available through the discount window. Elimination of the discounting privilege to avoid the reserve expansion that results from its use during periods of credit restraint would eliminate a safety valve that may be necessary sometime in the future.

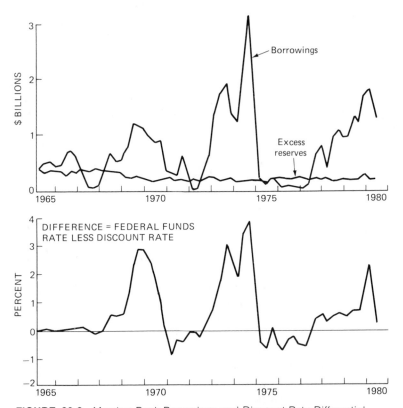

FIGURE 20-2   Member-Bank Borrowings and Discount-Rate Differential

Source: Adrian W. Throop, *Money in the Economy*, Federal Reserve Bank of San Francisco, August 1980, p. 10.

The most notable example of that type of lender-of-last-resort operation was the failure of the Franklin National Bank of New York in 1974. When news of the bank's problems became widely known, Franklin experienced a severe outflow of deposits and found that other banks were unwilling to sell it Federal funds. The bank turned to the Federal Reserve Bank of New York. At the time of the bank's closing, its loan from the Fed exceeded $1.5 billion, by far the largest such loan in the history of the Federal Reserve.

The size of the Franklin loan was such as to have an effect on aggregate monetary-policy operations. The $1.5 billion of reserves injected into the system through the discount-window loan to Franklin had to be offset by open-market operations. Although the Franklin ultimately failed, this largest bank failure in history was handled with no loss to any depositor, no loss to the Federal Reserve on its discount-window loan, and probably no significant loss to the FDIC. Regardless of how one views this effect on monetary policy, or views the usefulness of the discount mechanism as a monetary-policy instrument, it is clear that this source of liquidity is essential as long as we have concern about possible failures of large banks.

Some critics of the discount window believe that it is administered with far more discretion than should reside in a government agency. This discretion has been particularly visible in periods of tight money since the mid-1960s. The restraint on member-bank borrowing during these periods fell very unevenly among banks and led to many complaints concerning administration of the discount window. Some banks took Federal Reserve statements to heart and reduced their lending activity (and probably lost some customers by so doing) in order to keep access to the discount window. Other banks sought loans from the Fed and obtained them accompanied by warnings. Some heeded the warnings, and others ignored them successfully (except to incur more warnings). Some banks stayed away from the discount window completely because of the uncertainty involved. In a sense, the Federal Reserve policy was successful during the period—discounts were kept to relatively moderate levels, while the political problems inherent in an increase of the discount rate were avoided—but the Federal Reserve System lost prestige with member banks that felt unfairly treated by the policy followed.

Opponents of Federal Reserve discretion in lending believe that the discount *rate* should be used to control lending rather than discount *administration*. In some way, a rate should be set that automatically discourages borrowing except as unexpected needs arise. The rate would discourage the institution from remaining continuously in debt to the system or from using borrowed funds to expand loans in a period of credit restraint.[4] This would automatically reduce the problems of administering the discount window. Some authorities have suggested that the discount rate be set automatically with the Treasury-bill rate—say, half a percentage point above it. It is hard to judge, however, just what rate would constitute a penalty rate. To truly be punitive, the rate would have to be higher than the rate the institution could get on any of its assets, including consumer credit and mortgage credit.

One advantage of the automatic discount rate is avoidance of the "announcement effect" of infrequent discretionary changes. Consider the effect of an increase in the discount rate to reduce institutions' borrowing and to restrain credit expansion. Although some institutions may be discouraged from additional borrowing, others may interpret the increase as a sign that the Federal Reserve expects strong business activity, which may encourage them to increase their borrowing while funds are available. This perverse announcement effect of the rate increase may be stimulated even more if the business community makes the same interpretation and increases its demands for bank loans. The opposite perverse announcement effect may prevail in the case of a reduction in the discount rate presumably intended to stimulate institutions' borrowing and lending. A reduction in the rate may be interpreted by institutions and the public to indicate that the Fed is pessimistic about the economic outlook, and this may have adverse effects on business confidence.

Opponents of discretionary discount rates and discretionary administration tend to be those economists who place greatest emphasis on the money stock in explaining economic activity. Others, those who emphasize interest rates as the appropriate target of control, view the setting of the discount rate—the one officially determined interest rate—as a positive function in monetary policy and urge more active use of this tool. One proposal would rename the discount rate the Federal Reserve rate and have it apply to both borrowing from the Fed and "lending to" it, in the form of excess reserves.[5] Thus, every institution with either borrowed reserves or excess reserves would be affected by a change in the rate. A rise in the rate would at the same time discourage borrowing and en-

----

[4] A small step in this direction was taken when the Federal Reserve began in 1980 imposing a surcharge on frequent borrowers from the discount window. The surcharge applies only to larger institutions (over $500 million in deposits) that are in debt more than four weeks in a calendar quarter.

[5] James Tobin, "Towards Improving the Efficiency of the Monetary System," *Review of Economics and Statistics*, August 1960. Interest on demand deposits, not then legally allowed, was a part of the proposal.

courage the institutions to reduce their lending to the public to
maintain excess reserves. Borrowing would be a right, rather than
a privilege.

It is clear that no consensus has yet been reached regarding
the discount window. With open-market operations determining
system reserves, and reserve requirements controlling their use,
the discount mechanism is not an absolute necessity. Yet there is
that lingering feeling that somewhere, sometime, there are institutions that will need help. The problem lies in specifying the ground
rules under which help can be offered without such a source of funds
becoming abused and interfering with the course of monetary
policy.

QUESTIONS

1 Why are depository institutions required to maintain specified
   amounts of reserves?
2 What would happen to the money stock if a 100 percent reserve
   plan were adopted?
3 If the Federal Reserve wants to make money easier, which of the
   policy tools described in this chapter would be most effective?
4 Is the "announcement effect" of discount-rate and reserve-
   requirement changes desirable?
5 Are changes in reserve requirements effective if institutions hold
   excess reserves?
6 When the Federal Reserve makes a change in reserve requirements or the discount rate, what near-term objectives does it have
   in mind?
7 In practice, who makes the decision to change the discount rate of
   the Federal Reserve Bank of Cleveland!?
8 Is it possible for two Federal Reserve Banks to maintain different
   discount rates? Would this be equitable?
9 If the discount rate is below market interest rates, why do institutions not borrow from their Federal Reserve Bank and make a
   profit by investing the proceeds in government securities?
10 Why do banks sometimes borrow money in the Federal-funds
   market at rates higher than the discount rate?

SELECTED READINGS

Board of Governors of the Federal Reserve System, *Reappraisal of the
Federal Reserve Discount Mechanism.* Washington, D.C., 1971. 3 vols.
The publication includes the important documents and studies done
by and for the system committee. The *Report* of the committee, and
Bernard Shull's paper on research done for the committee, are of most
interest.

CACY, J.A., and SCOTT WINNINGHAM, "Reserve Requirements under the Depository Institutions Deregulation and Monetary Control Act of 1980," Federal Reserve Bank of Kansas City *Economic Review*, September–October 1980.

Commission on Money and Credit, *Monetary Management*. Englewood Cliffs, N.J.: Prentice-Hall, 1963.

SMITH, WARREN, "The Instruments of General Monetary Control," *National Banking Review* September, 1963.

WILLIS, H. PARKER, *The Theory and Practice of Central Banking*. New York: Harper & Row, 1936.

21

Instruments of Monetary Policy: Open-Market Operations

Federal Reserve power to change reserve requirements and the discount rate plays an important part in monetary management. In considering changes in these policy instruments, the Federal Reserve must closely follow changes in the economy and in the money market. Uses of these monetary tools, however, are occasional rather than continuous, whereas changes in monetary and economic conditions occur daily. The Fed has long believed that this means that monetary management must be a day-to-day business. It argues that if it is to function effectively, it must act constantly to offset or support changes in money-market conditions.

The purchase and sale of U.S. government securities is the means by which the Federal Reserve exerts its influence over money-market conditions. Although sizable operations in the market for Treasury securities were not contemplated in the original establishment of the Federal Reserve System, such operations have become the most important policy tool of the system. Open-market operations have turned out to be the best means by which the Fed can achieve its objectives.

There are several reasons for this. Open-market operations can be carried out on whatever scale is desired—from very large to very small. The Fed can buy or sell in large enough quantities to determine the desired level of bank reserves. On the other hand, open-market operations can be carried out in very small steps to make rather precise changes in the reserve base. We have noted that reserve-requirement changes do not lend themselves to "fine tuning."

Another advantage of open-market operations is that they are taken at the initiative of the Federal Reserve. This contrasts with discount-window policy, where the Fed can only change the rate or the terms on which member banks can borrow. The effectiveness of discount-window policy depends on the extent to which member banks respond to such changes in rates or conditions. Open-market operations have a direct and predictable effect on bank reserves. Further, any actions that turn out to be inappropriate can be quickly reversed.

We examined in Chapter 19 the means by which Federal Reserve open-market operations affect reserves. When the Fed buys government securities, depository institutions find themselves with additional reserves. Although additional reserves are always welcomed by a depository institution, by themselves they do not add to its earnings. Additional reserves contribute to earnings only to the extent that they are converted into earning assets—loans or investments. The institutions thus have a strong incentive to make prompt use of additional reserves. As we have seen, the acquisition of loans or investments by banks directly increases deposits and the money supply. Exactly the opposite results occur when the Fed sells securities: Depository institutions find their reserves reduced, and they must therefore reduce their holdings of earning assets, which, in turn, means a reduction of deposits.

In general, then, the Federal Reserve buys government securities when it wants to increase the money supply, and sells when it wants to decrease the money supply. Because there are other factors that affect reserves besides open-market operations, and because other things are going on in the economy that affect the money supply, this general statement is somewhat an oversimplification. In this chapter we will examine the way in which the Fed formulates and implements open-market policy, and how open-market operations interact with other developments in the economy.

FORMULATION OF OPEN-MARKET POLICY

The ultimate objectives of monetary policy are measures of general economic well-being—full employment, high and growing GNP, stable prices. The Federal Reserve does not have direct control over any of these general objectives; it hopes to help achieve them by controlling the supply of money in the economy. Monetary policy is useful only if such control can influence the economy in the direction we want—toward higher levels of income and lower rates of inflation.

As we will see in more detail in the chapters discussing monetary theory, there is no full agreement among economists as to the channels by which changes in the money supply affect the economy. Some economists focus on the relation between the money supply and interest rates, and the effect of interest rates on investment spending in the economy. Others, frequently referred to as "monetarists," argue that there are multiple channels by which changes in the money supply affect the economy, in addition to those that work through the interest rate. In either case, there is general agreement that a more rapid rate of growth of the money supply stimulates spending in the economy, whereas a slow rate of growth, or an actual decline, in the money supply tends to restrain spending. The essence of Federal Reserve policy, then, is to influence the economy through control of the rate of growth of the money supply.

Until the last several years, the Fed had always been rather vague about its objectives. It would sometimes characterize its policy as one of "easy money," and talk about moving from a policy of "ease" to one of "active ease" ("active ease" is easier than "easy"). Often, even less precise terminology would be used, such as "leaning against the wind," or "maintaining an even keel." To the extent that one could quantify such statements, they seemed to have more to do with interest rates than with the growth of the money supply. That is, during periods in which the Fed stated that its policy was one of "ease," in the sense that interest rates were low, we often find that monetary growth was slow, indicating a restrictive monetary policy to those who view the rate of growth of the money supply as the primary indicator of monetary policy.

Over time, the Federal Reserve came to give more weight to the "monetary aggregates"—various measures of reserves or of the money supply—as compared with interest rates, particularly during the tenure of Arthur Burns as chairman of the Board. In 1975, Congress passed a resolution, later made a part of the Humphrey-Hawkins Act, calling on the Federal Reserve to disclose its policy objectives for the year ahead. In accord with that mandate, the Fed now announces its goals in terms of money-supply growth rates for the next twelve months. It states these goals as fairly wide ranges of acceptable growth in M1, M2, and M3. For example, in late 1981, the Federal Reserve:

. . . tentatively agreed that for the period from the fourth quarter of 1981 to the fourth quarter of 1982 growth of M-1, M-2, and M-3 within ranges of 2½ to 5¼ percent, 6 to 9 percent, and 6½ to 9½ percent would be appropriate.[1]

These goals or targets are set by the Open Market Committee and reviewed at its monthly meetings. The committee consists, as you will remember, of the seven members of the Board of Governors, the president of the Federal Reserve Bank of New York, and four other Reserve Bank presidents. This is a fairly compact group, but the actual meetings involve much larger participation. Also present are the seven Reserve Bank presidents who are not currently serving on the committee. The manager of the Federal Reserve System Open Market Account (an officer of the Federal Reserve Bank of New York) also attends. In addition, each Reserve Bank president brings an economist from the staff of the bank to act as advisor. When we include several members of the staff of the Board of Governors, we find that the Open Market Committee meetings frequently involve more than 40 participants. Although nonmembers of the committee do not vote at the meetings, they participate in the discussion on the same basis as members.

There are, of course, both advantages and disadvantages in having such a large group determine monetary policy. On balance, however, the system apparently feels that the advantages of having a considerable measure of regional representation, as well as of hearing differing views on monetary conditions and policy, outweigh the danger of having too unwieldy a group.

The Open Market Committee's primary concern is, of course, with open-market policy. Since the meetings of the committee are attended by all Reserve Bank presidents and all members of the Board of Governors, it also presents an excellent opportunity for discussion of other Federal Reserve policy tools.

The discount rate is frequently discussed at Open Market Committee meetings. Various people attending the meeting may present the thought that the discount rates of the Federal Reserve Banks should be changed. According to the Federal Reserve Act, power to establish the discount rate lies with the board of directors for each Reserve Bank. The Reserve Bank presidents attending the meeting can transmit the committee's views to their boards of directors.[2]

[1] *Federal Reserve Bulletin*, September 1981, p. 717.

[2] Although the Board of Governors has the right to set the discount rates of the various Reserve Banks regardless of the views of their directors, obviously it does not like to exercise such power. Generally, the Federal Reserve likes to give the impression—sometimes false—that the system is one big happy family.

The organization of the Federal Reserve System has sometimes been criticized because its three major policy weapons are in
the hands of different groups within the system. Reserve requirements are set by the Board of Governors, discount rates are set by
each Reserve Bank board of directors, and open-market policy is
formulated by a committee consisting of the Board of Governors
and some Reserve Bank presidents.

If policy decisions were made by these various groups independently, this would indeed be a serious criticism. Since, however, all
policy is discussed at the Open Market Committee meetings, which
serve as an open forum in which system officials may present their
views, there is a strong unifying tendency behind all Federal Reserve policy. Changes in reserve requirements, discount rates, and
open-market operations complement rather than offset one
another, although in the short run, two seemingly conflicting actions may be taken to achieve a desired net effect. Thus if, for
example, a 1 percent increase in reserve requirements is considered
too strong a step to take, such an action might be combined with
purchases of securities in the open market. Despite the fact that
different groups are technically responsible for wielding the various
policy tools, a readily discernible basic theme unifies all policy actions at any given moment. The relationships among policy tools
and the structure of the Federal Reserve System are shown in
Figure 21-1.

The meetings of the Open Market Committee, then, involve not
just a review of open-market operations and goals, but rather a
broad review of overall monetary policy. Since the monetary growth
targets are set once a year, it may appear that there is little need
for a monthly meeting (unless, of course, there has been some dramatic change in the economy). Many analysts would agree that the
Open Market Committee need not meet so often. However, a frequent problem that requires resolution by the committee is devia-
tions of money-supply growth from the target path. As we will see,
there are many reasons why the short-run course of monetary
growth may deviate from the Federal Reserve's desired path. When
that happens, the Open Market Committee must consider the optimal route back to the long-run expansion path.

Suppose, for example, that the committee has decided on an
8 percent growth for M2 from fourth quarter to fourth quarter
(2 percent per quarter), but that the actual growth in the first
quarter is 4 percent. There are several options here, assuming that
the 8 percent annual growth is still appropriate: The Federal Reserve could seek an immediate 2 percent decline in M2, or a zero rate
of growth for the next quarter, or a 2 percent rate of growth for the

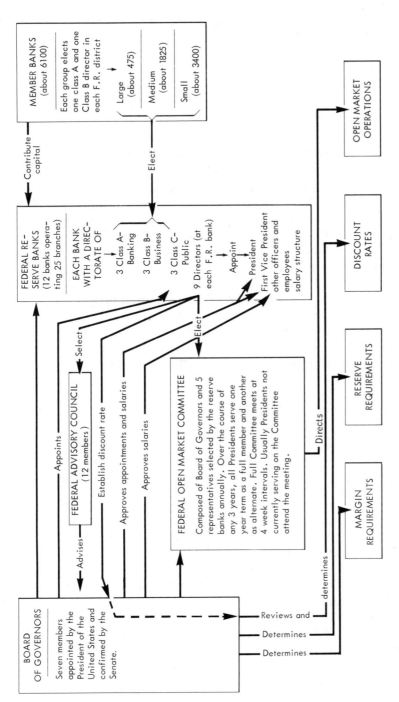

FIGURE 21-1 Organization of Federal Reserve System with Reference to Instruments of Credit Policy

next two quarters. Any of these decisions could lead to 8 percent growth for the year. The committee could even decide that the 4 percent jump in the first quarter was due to some unique event, so that the appropriate policy would be to ignore it and go on with the 8 percent annual growth rate from a new (higher) base. In order to examine this problem, we must consider the Open Market Committee's operating procedures.

OPEN-MARKET OPERATING PROCEDURES

Although Federal Reserve policy objectives are stated in terms of growth rates for various measures of the money supply, the Fed, unfortunately, does not have direct control over the money supply. It would be nice if the Federal Reserve had a sort of monetary thermostat that it could adjust up or down to maintain the desired monetary climate. But no such device exists.

The Fed can buy and sell government securities, and that will affect bank reserves. Of course, as we have seen, a number of other factors affect bank reserves as well (changes in float, in Treasury cash holdings, in currency in circulation, and so on), and the Open Market Committee must take these factors into account in determining the appropriate scale of open-market operations. Because of the difficulty of predicting the change in all these factors, the Fed may fail to hit its desired level of reserves with precision. But even if it does, there are further problems.

The relation between bank reserves and the money supply is not a rigid one. In general, of course, the higher bank reserves are, the higher the money supply, but the precise relationship is affected by a number of factors. Bank reserves of, say, $50 billion may be consistent with an M2 of $500 billion, or with a larger or smaller M2. Some of that $50 billion is going to be required against Treasury deposits, which are not included in M2. Thus, if Treasury deposits are high, that $50 billion of reserves will support a smaller M2 than if Treasury deposits were low.

Some of the $50 billion of reserves will be required against large corporate CDs, which also do not count in M2. More important, different banks are subject to differing reserve requirements, as are different types of deposits. Personal savings accounts are included in M2 but have a zero reserve requirement. Thus, if the public wants to hold large amounts of such deposits, the $50 billion of reserves is consistent with a very large M2.

So far, this example has discussed only M2. But the Fed has objectives in M1 and M3 as well. No Federal Reserve operations apply exclusively to one or another of these money-supply measures. It is possible that developments in the financial system make the three objectives chosen by the Federal Reserve internally inconsistent, so that hitting the M3 target means missing the M1 target.

Even if the Fed could anticipate the day-to-day changes in these factors that affect the relation between Federal Reserve holdings of government securities and bank reserves, and the factors that affect the relation between bank reserves and the money supply, hitting the desired money-supply figure might require large purchases and sales of government securities that could lead to great fluctuations in interest rates in the market. Some analysts believe that unstable interest rates are such a serious matter that the Fed must give attention to the effect of its operations on the money market, and should assure some stability to short-term interest rates.

Traditionally, the FOMC has paid close attention to money-market conditions. Maintaining stability in the money market has been a key objective of the Federal Reserve as far as day-to-day operations are concerned. The principal indicators of money-market conditions relied on by the system are the Federal-funds rate and "free reserves" (excess reserves minus depository institution borrowing from the Fed). The Fed funds rate—the rate banks charge for selling excess reserves to other banks—is probably the most sensitive measure of the demand for, or the supply of, reserves. It is thus one of the best possible measures of the degree of tightness or ease in the money market. But critics have claimed that there is not a particularly close link between the Fed-funds rate and other indicators of money-market conditions, on the one hand, and the money supply and other monetary aggregates on the other. Why then has the Fed always emphasized conditions in the money market? The best explanation has been put forth by a senior Federal Reserve official:

> The chief reason why the FOMC has focused on the money market in its operations has been the feeling that such a focus would lead to less interest rate fluctuation and less danger of liquidity crises than would a focus on a monetary aggregate. The history of central banking, and particularly the genesis of the Federal Reserve System, has had as one of its main themes the need to have an institution that will be able to avert old-fashioned financial panics by providing a source of ultimate liquidity to the economy. Thus, the state of the central money market—where liquidity pressures focus—has historically been a main concern of the Federal Reserve.[3]

[3] Stephen H. Axilrod, "The FOMC Directive as Structured in the Late 1960's: Theory and Appraisal," in *Open Market Policies and Operating Procedures*, Board of Governors of the Federal Reserve System, 1971, p. 15.

When the Federal Reserve viewed its targets as interest rates rather than money supply, it was logical to focus operating procedures on interest rates and conditions in the money market, in which short-term interest rates are determined. As the target has shifted to money-supply growth, the Fed has had to adjust its operating procedures. Because it cannot control the money supply directly, the Fed has recognized that it must operate through an "intermediate target." During the 1970s, it focused on the Federal-funds rate. There is a rather clear relation between short-term interest rates, such as the Fed-funds rate, and the demand for money. The higher the interest rate, the less money the public will want to hold, and the less attractive it is for banks to seek additional Federal funds to expand their assets (and thereby the money supply). When the Federal Reserve buys or sells government securities, the effect on bank reserves affects the Fed-funds rate very quickly.

Under the Federal-funds-rate operating procedure, the Open Market Committee set as an intermediate target the Fed-funds rate that it thought (on the basis of an econometric model) would be consistent with the monetary-growth target that is the committee's real objective. Although this operating procedure could have worked successfully, it required frequent and sizable changes in the Fed-funds rate, which the Federal Reserve was unwilling to adopt. The record of the 1970s shows that the Federal-funds-rate target was hit consistently, but the monetary-growth targets were missed much of the time.

In late 1979, the Federal Reserve adopted a new operating procedure, one focusing on total bank reserves.[4] The open-market operations aim at a level of bank reserves that are believed (again on the basis of a model) to be consistent with the money-supply objective. This approach emphasizes the supply of money directly, rather than attempting to influence it through affecting the demand for money. By adopting the reserve-targeting operating policy, the Fed accepted the fact that interest rates would fluctuate more than they did under a Federal-funds-rate target, and the first few years of experience with the new operating procedure have seen considerable variation in short-term interest rates. This procedure has generally been hailed as an improvement, but it has not solved all the problems that we noted earlier. The Federal Reserve still seeks to hit several monetary-growth targets, and they may not

---

[4] Technically, the intermediate target chosen was "nonborrowed reserves," which excludes reserves obtained by borrowing from the Fed, but this difference is small.

all be consistent. There are still factors that affect the Fed's ability to hit its reserve target and factors that affect the relation between reserves and the money supply. One source of the latter error that we noted earlier is differences in reserve requirements among banks and types of deposits. As the reserve-requirement changes brought about by the Monetary Control Act of 1980 are phased in, these differences will be reduced, and the Fed's ability to hit its targets should be enhanced.

Some analysts are not completely satisfied with the reserves operating policy and argue that a better intermediate target would be the monetary base, which we discussed in Chapter 19. The monetary base consists of bank reserves plus currency held by the public. It includes not only bank reserves, but all assets in existence that are eligible to serve as reserves. Moreover, currency held by the public is part of the money supply. So the monetary base has some characteristics that would make it suitable as an intermediate target.

In the evaluation of a variable to be used as an intermediate target of monetary policy, there are two important criteria: first, that the variable be subject to control by the Federal Reserve; and second, that the intermediate-target variable be related to the real target (money supply). Obviously, a variable is not useful as an operating target if the Federal Reserve does not have the ability to control it. Just as obviously, controlling an intermediate variable is of no value unless that variable is related in a reliable and predictable manner to the money-supply measures. The Federal-funds rate has the advantage of being always observable, so that the Fed can adjust open-market policy in accord with movements of that rate. On the other hand, the link between the Federal-funds rate and the money-supply measures is not as close as the alternative intermediate targets. The monetary base is not as directly controllable as the Fed-funds rate, but the relation between the monetary base and the money supply is rather close. As we saw in Chapter 19, that relation depends on a few key ratios that are reasonably predictable. Although there are some theoretical advantages and disadvantages of the monetary base as compared with other reserve measures, the differences between them seem small as compared with the sizable difference between focusing on money-market conditions or interest rates and on a reserve aggregate.

The importance of this debate over Federal Reserve targets is that although the Fed may be able to control some measure of bank reserves, and may also be able to control some short-term interest rate, it cannot generally control *both* at the same time. Suppose the Fed decides to control the Treasury bill rate at 9 percent. It would do so by buying bills at a 9 percent yield from anyone who wanted to sell, or by selling bills at that yield to anyone who wanted to buy. The Fed would have the ability to peg the bill rate at whatever level it chose (and it did, in fact, do so during World War II and for a while afterward). But while it was doing so, it would lose all control over bank reserves. If individuals or banks chose to sell bills to the Federal Reserve at 9 percent, that would have the effect of increasing bank reserves. The Fed could not limit the growth of reserves except by abandoning its control of the Treasury-bill rate. If, on the other hand, the Federal Reserve decided to focus on a certain growth rate for bank reserves, it could do so by buying or selling the appropriate *amount* of Treasury bills, but it could not simultaneously determine the *price* of Treasury bills.

Our discussion here has dealt with the variable that the Fed should use as a *target* in giving instructions to the Trading Desk. A related but somewhat different question is, Which variable shall observers (in and out of the system) look at as an *indicator* of what the monetary authorities are actually accomplishing through their open-market operations.[5] Different analysts will have different choices, based on their views as to which variable is most closely related to the ultimate goals of monetary policy. These indicators may be the money supply, the monetary base, long-term interest rates, total bank credit, or any of several others.

Even if there were widespread agreement as to the appropriate monetary statistic to control and watch, there would still be very serious practical problems involved in interpretation of the basic statistical data. Monetary variables may be measured in several ways, and each approach may yield different results. For example, the data to be analyzed may be on a daily, weekly, or monthly basis. They may be analyzed on the basis of absolute changes from one period to the next, or on the basis of rates of change. There have frequently been periods in which the rate of growth of the money supply has shown an increase as compared with the growth rate of the previous quarter, but a decline as compared with, say, a year earlier. Does this indicate expansion or slowdown in money-supply growth rates?

There is no easy way to answer this question. The proper evaluation of monetary-policy actions requires knowledge of the policy the Federal Reserve is currently following, as well as calculation of

---

[5] This distinction between targets and indicators was suggested by Karl Brunner and Allan Meltzer. See "The Meaning of Monetary Indicators," in G. Horwich, ed., *Monetary Process and Policy: A Symposium* (Homewood, Ill.: Richard D. Irwin, 1967), pp. 187–217.

the likely effects of such policy on the economy. This task has been made somewhat easier in the last few years as a result of congressional actions intended to promote the availability of better information concerning current and anticipated monetary policy.

IMPLEMENTATION OF OPEN-MARKET POLICY

The Open Market Committee meeting results in a policy directive to the Federal Reserve Bank of New York. All transactions of the Federal Reserve in the government-securities market are executed by the Trading Desk of the Federal Reserve Bank of New York as agent for the system.

The directive includes both short-run and longer-term objectives for monetary growth, and also some proviso concerning Federal-funds rates. Thus, in July 1981, the directive included the following:

> In the short run the Committee seeks behavior of reserve aggregates consistent with growth of M-1 from June to September at an annual rate of 7 percent . . . , provided that growth of M-2 remains around the upper limit of . . . its range for the year. . . . The Chairman may call for Committee consultation if it appears to the Manager for Domestic Operations that pursuit of the monetary objectives and related reserve paths during the period before the next meeting is likely to be associated with a federal funds rate persistently outside a range of 15 to 21 percent.[6]

The specifics of the directive are resolved in a manner calculated to receive general support from the committee. In the past, the wording of the directives was so vague that they could usually be approved unanimously, but now they are specific enough that dissents are more common. At the July 1981 meeting, for example, Mr. Partee dissented from the directive quoted above because "in light of the indications of weakening in economic activity, he preferred . . . a somewhat higher objective for growth of M-1 over the period. . . ."

The manager of the Open Market Account not only reads the directive, he hears the discussion leading up to it. He returns home with a fairly good idea of his objectives for the next month. It is his responsibility, with the aid of the Federal Reserve Board staff, to refine this monetary growth objective into a specific volume of government securities to be bought or sold.

It is important to realize that the duties of the Trading Desk are continuous. Even if there is no change desired in the volume of

---

[6] *Federal Reserve Bulletin*, September 1981, p. 718.

member-bank reserves, the Trading Desk may have to act to offset changes in certain factors that affect reserves. In Chapter 19, we considered how changes in such factors as the gold stock, Treasury operations, currency in circulation, and Federal Reserve credit affect reserves. Most of these factors are outside direct Fed control, so undesirable changes in them must be offset by changes in the one factor that is under the Fed's control—U.S. government securities held by the Federal Reserve System.

The duties of the system in offsetting changes in independent factors to prevent disruption of the monetary system have been referred to as the *defensive* job of the Federal Reserve. Affecting monetary conditions for the purpose of stabilizing the economy has been referred to as the *dynamic* responsibility of the system. The whole history of the Federal Reserve System can be viewed as a movement from the purely defensive conception of system responsibilities at the time it was established to a state today in which dynamic responsibilities are more stressed.

We can best analyze the relation between the defensive and dynamic aspects of open-market operations by considering an annual disruptive force in the banking system—the demand of the public for more currency during the Christmas holiday season. People need more currency because of additional travel during this period, and since retail sales reach a peak at this time, more currency is held in cash registers. As we have seen, an increased demand for currency results in a decrease in bank reserves.

Let us suppose that during the last half of December, the Federal Reserve wants to maintain the level of member-bank reserves that has prevailed in the preceding months. The Fed must buy securities in the open market. If the Federal Open Market Committee decided to expand reserves during this period, the Trading Desk would, of course, buy securities for the system's account. But if, on the other hand, the Fed wants to restrict reserves during the last half of December, it would still buy securities—less than usual for the season, but nevertheless an addition to the system's holdings—even though it is desirous of tightening credit.

The statements made earlier in this chapter, to the effect that the Federal Reserve will buy securities when it wants to ease reserves and sell securities when it wants to reduce reserves, can now be recognized as a simplification of the real situation.

Once the decision is made as to the volume of securities to be bought or sold, the trading staff swings into action. Present Federal Reserve policy calls for open-market transactions to be undertaken mainly in short-term securities, and so most dealings of the Trading Desk in recent years have been in Treasury bills. The Trading Desk will do business with any bond dealer who meets reasonable standards for creditworthiness and who stands ready to shoulder the duties of a dealer. A dealer must set prices and be prepared to sell or buy at that price plus or minus a small spread that constitutes profit. Competition among dealers and other institutions makes these prices consistent and the spreads narrow.

Once the manager has made the decision and briefed the trading staff, all traders begin simultaneously contacting dealers to ask for price quotations on the particular issues of Treasury bills the manager has decided to buy or sell. This process takes very little time, and usually within five minutes after the start of the "go-around," the firm bids and offers of all dealers are assembled. In order to ensure that the Fed's transactions with the dealers are on a freely competitive, nonpreferential basis, the Trading Desk always buys bills at the lowest price offered and sells at the highest bid obtainable.

Most Federal Reserve transactions are outright purchases and sales. In some cases, however, it executes repurchase agreements or "buybacks" with the bond dealers, which means that the Fed buys bills from a dealer, but the dealer agrees to buy them back at a specified time and price. This arrangement makes it possible for the Fed to inject reserves into the banking system temporarily and avoid the necessity of buying securities in the market one day and selling the next day. This type of transaction, although often a convenience for the Trading Desk, is in effect a short-term loan to the bond dealer, helping him to finance his inventory of securities.

DISCLOSING MONETARY POLICY

Central bankers have traditionally been a close-mouthed lot. In keeping with this tradition, the Federal Reserve has always been reluctant to indicate publicly what its current policy directive is, what it is thinking about future monetary-policy actions, or even what its forecasts are with respect to general economic conditions or interest rates.

The Fed has always provided a plethora of data showing what monetary policy has been. The monthly *Federal Reserve Bulletin* and the periodic publications of several of the Federal Reserve Banks (particularly New York) include detailed analyses of what monetary policy has been in the preceding month. The *Annual Report* of the Board of Governors presents a complete picture of what monetary policy has been in the preceding year. It is only with respect to current or future policy that the Fed prefers silence.

There are several reasons for this preference for not disclosing the reasons behind a particular policy action.[7] The Federal Reserve, and other central banks, have argued that explaining their actions might simply lead to profits for speculators. They fear that announcement of a change in policy could lead to a considerable disruption in the government-securities market and impair the Treasury's ability to handle its financing problems. The Fed has also argued that the authorities might be hesitant to take action or to change policy if they knew they would be expected to explain publicly and defend their actions before they had a chance to see how these actions were working. The Federal Reserve adds that the uncertainty engendered by this no-explanation rule actually works to reinforce its policy actions.

These arguments do not seem adequate to convince everyone. As Prof. Colin Campbell has pointed out:

> By letting people interpret for themselves—and quite possibly misinterpret—the Fed often makes it easy for them to do precisely what it wants them not to, often with very disturbing results for the securities markets. And when people realize they have made a mistake, they are likely to react too far in the opposite direction, again causing undesirable, and perhaps quite violent, shifts in securities prices and interest rates.[8]

The "Freedom of Information Act" required the Federal Reserve to release the summary of its Open Market Committee meetings more promptly than it had in the past. Even so, it allowed a lag of 90 days between a committee meeting and the release of the summary minutes of it. (Of course, this did represent a tremendous improvement from the policy of not disclosing the record of policy actions taken by the FOMC until the publication of the Board's *Annual Report* in March of the following year.) Now current policy is to publish a summary of the meeting and the policy actions taken, including the policy directive, about one month after the meeting. In many cases, this means that the policy directive is public information while it is still in effect.

A more significant change in the publicizing of current monetary policy occurred as a result of a congressional resolution passed

---

[7] For a good presentation of the Federal Reserve's case, see the statement by Alfred Hayes, president of the Federal Reserve Bank of New York, before the Joint Economic Committee, June 2, 1961. The statement was reprinted in the *Monthly Review* of the Federal Reserve Bank of New York in July 1961.

[8] Colin D. Campbell, "The Federal Reserve and the Business Cycle," *Tuck Bulletin 26*, Amos Tuck School, Hanover, N.H., 1961, p. 13.

in 1975. In response to that resolution, the chairman of the Federal Reserve Board now announces projected growth ranges in the monetary aggregates for the next year. These announcements are made in quarterly presentations to the Senate and House Banking Committees. This provides a convenient forum in which the Federal Reserve's analysis is made available to the public, and in which congressional views as to the appropriate direction of monetary policy can be conveyed to the Fed.

This procedure has generally been successful despite some problems—the Federal Reserve is obviously entitled to change its mind after the public statement, congressional quizzing of the chairman on reasons for the policy plans has not been very enlightening, and the Fed has not always managed to hit the targets spelled out in the congressional presentations. Nevertheless, some useful information has been conveyed, and the sessions have not seemed harmful even by those who originally feared that they would infringe upon the "independence" of the Federal Reserve.

Former Federal Reserve Chairman Burns is not happy with this trend toward greater disclosure of Federal Reserve policy. He recently told an interviewer:

Nowadays, there appears to be great currency to the notion that public confidence in our government will be enhanced, and the quality of decision-making may itself be improved, by exposing to public scrutiny nearly every detail of the governmental decision-making process. . . . We do not share this view.[9]

Even with the information available on past, and now on projected future, policy actions, reaching an accurate determination of the current state of monetary policy and its implications for the economy and for financial markets is still a difficult task. Some years ago, a leading Federal Reserve spokesman pointed out, "The interpretation of central bank action, and the evaluation of its influence, has become, like many other things in this modern day, a zone reserved largely for the specialists."[10] There is a good deal of truth in this statement, but the informed layman who is willing to spend the time necessary to analyze the published data now has a better opportunity to interpret and understand Federal Reserve policy and actions.

[9] *The Washington Star*, November 25, 1977.

[10] Robert V. Roosa, *Federal Reserve Operations in the Money and Government Securities Markets* (New York: Federal Reserve Bank of New York, 1956), p. 104.

QUESTIONS

1 What economic indicators does the Open Market Committee consider in reaching monetary-policy decisions? Which should be most important?
2 Do you think better decisions would result if there were fewer members of the Open Market Committee? more members?
3 How many members of the Open Market Committee are professional economists? Do you think better decisions would result if more of the members were economists? How many are bankers? Should there be more bankers on the committee?
4 Should the Secretary of the Treasury participate in Open Market Committee meetings?
5 If the Federal Reserve adds to its holdings of government securities, does this mean that the system is moving toward easier or tighter money?
6 Should Open Market Committee meetings be open to the public?
7 From currently available statistics, how would you determine whether the Fed is moving toward easier or tighter money?
8 What is the difference between a target and an indicator?
9 What is the division of responsibility between the Open Market Committee and the Trading Desk? Which do you think is more important in determining monetary policy?
10 Under what circumstances will open-market operations be ineffective in accomplishing their objectives?

SELECTED READINGS

ANDERSEN, LEONALL C., and JERRY L. JORDAN, "The Monetary Base—Explanation and Analytical Use," Federal Reserve Bank of St. Louis *Review*, August 1968.

Federal Reserve Bank of Boston, *Controlling Monetary Aggregates*, June 1969. *Controlling Monetary Aggregates II: The Implementation*, September 1972. Proceedings of conferences.

GILBERT, R. ALTON, and MICHAEL E. TREBING, "The FOMC in 1980: A Year of Reserve Targeting," Federal Reserve Bank of St. Louis *Review*, August 1981.

KEIR, PETER, and HENRY WALLICH, "The Role of Operating Guides in U.S. Monetary Policy," *Federal Reserve Bulletin*, September 1979. A good survey of Federal Reserve operating procedures up to the 1979 change.

MAISEL, SHERMAN, *Managing the Dollar*. New York: W.W. Norton, 1973. The author is a former member of the Board of Governors.

ROOSA, ROBERT V., *Federal Reserve Operations in the Money and Government Securities Markets*. Federal Reserve Bank of New York, 1956.

22

Instruments of Monetary Policy: Other Controls

Open-market operations and changes in reserve requirements and the discount rate affect the availability and cost of reserves to the banking system. They do not attempt, however, to affect the use to which banks put their funds. By using these powers, the Federal Reserve seeks to control the total supply of money and credit and the general level of interest rates. It does not seek to control the amount of credit flowing into different uses and the interest rates prevailing for specific types of loans or securities. This problem of allocation of the credit supply to the demand is left to the functioning of the market system.[1]

SELECTIVE CONTROLS

There are some people who feel that certain types of credit need more specific control than the general credit-control tools can exercise. Some of these selective controls are advocated on a perma-

[1] We shall discuss later the extent to which this characterization of "general" credit-control measures is accurate. It will suffice to note at this point that our previous discussion of discount-rate policy raised the issue that administration of the discount rate may be uneven and discriminatory.

nent basis, and others are considered necessary only under certain conditions.

Selective controls have been used in three important areas: stock-market credit, consumer credit, and real estate credit. At the present time, the only selective control of the Federal Reserve is over stock-market credit.

Margin Requirements

The Board of Governors was given control of stock margin requirements under the Securities Exchange Act of 1934. The reason for use of this selective tool goes back to the Federal Reserve's inability to cope with the flow of credit into the stock market in the late 1920s. Much of the increase in prices of stocks during this period was supported by large amounts of borrowed funds. The Fed recognized that this was unsound, but there was little that it could do about it. The economy as a whole was not booming, and prices were stable. The use of general credit controls would have unnecessarily depressed the economy. The Fed tried to use persuasion, but this was unsuccessful. Feeling forced to use general credit restriction, it saw business activity decline more than stock speculation. In fact, it is very likely that the Federal Reserve's restrictive policies were at least partly responsible for the severity of the ensuing depression.

Control over margin requirements means, in effect, control over down payments that must be made in buying securities on credit. A margin requirement of 60 percent means that the buyer must put up 60 percent of the purchase price in cash and can borrow the remaining 40 percent. A margin requirement of 80 percent would allow borrowing of only 20 percent of the purchase price, and a margin requirement of 100 percent means that purchasers of securities must pay cash. The Fed actually did raise margin requirements to 100 percent in 1946, as shown in Table 22-1.

The margin requirements apply to all loans for the purpose of purchasing and carrying securities listed on national securities exchanges, as well as some unlisted securities. The requirements, unlike most Federal Reserve controls, apply to all lenders, not just depository institutions.

The Federal Reserve is concerned with the flow of credit into the stock market; it does not attempt to control stock prices. Variation in the availability of credit with which to purchase stocks certainly does affect stock prices, but the relation is not a simple one.

TABLE 22-1

Margin Requirements on Stocks

Date of Change	Percentage Requirement
November 1, 1937	40%
February 5, 1945	50
July 5, 1945	75
January 21, 1946	100
February 1, 1947	75
March 30, 1949	50
January 17, 1951	75
February 20, 1953	50
January 4, 1955	60
April 23, 1955	70
January 16, 1958	50
August 5, 1958	70
October 16, 1958	90
July 28, 1960	70
July 10, 1962	50
November 6, 1963	70
June 8, 1968	80
May 6, 1970	65
December 6, 1971	55
November 24, 1972	65
January 3, 1974	50

Source: *Federal Reserve Bulletin.*

There have been periods in which stock prices have gone up in the face of substantial increases in margin requirements.[2] Former Federal Reserve Chairman William McChesney Martin stated that the purpose of the regulation is to prevent "excessive" use of stock-market credit. Imposition of margin requirements "helps to minimize the danger of pyramiding credit in a rising market, and also reduces the danger of forced sales of securities from undermargined accounts in a falling market."[3]

In this view, then, the purpose of regulation of margin requirements is to aid in producing more stable stock prices. It is probably true that in falling stock markets, some forced selling by owners of

[2] One reason for a perverse response of stock prices to changes in margin requirements may be the effect of the announcement itself. The Federal Reserve announces an increase in margin requirements and the investor thinks to himself, "The Fed must think stock prices are going up; they must know, so now is a good time to buy."

[3] Senate Committee on Banking and Currency, *Stock Market Study*, 84th Cong., 1st sess., 1955, p. 550.

stock bought on margin can aggravate the slide in prices. On the other hand, low margin requirements facilitate speculation. It is not clear, however, whether speculation by margin buyers is stabilizing or destabilizing in the short run.[4]

Even if margin requirements are desirable, it does not follow that it is desirable for the Federal Reserve Board to have the authority to vary margin requirements within very wide limits. Professor Moore has pointed out that changes in margin requirements:

> . . . do give the Federal Reserve a way of expressing its concern with movements of the stock market. But statements by the Federal Reserve setting forth its view might be substituted for changes in margin requirements, if the Federal Reserve feels a need to voice its view of stock market activity.[5]

Most authorities have felt that Federal Reserve control over margin requirements is a useful addition to the arsenal of economic-policy weapons. In fact, some economists who are opposed on philosophical grounds to almost all types of government intervention in specific markets do support regulation of margin requirements. Despite such support, evidence of the usefulness of the power to change margin requirements is not overwhelming. The spur to imposition of margin requirements was, of course, the crash of 1929 and the feeling that this in some way was responsible for the Great Depression of the 1930s. This view of the depression has generally fallen into disfavor in recent years, but support for margin requirements is still widespread among both the academic and financial communities.

Mortgage Credit Controls

During the Korean emergency period, the Board of Governors was given control over down-payment and maturity terms for certain types of real estate loans. The board's regulations (Regulation X)

---

[4] For a good analysis of the data on the effect of margin requirements, see Thomas G. Moore, "Stock Market Margin Requirements," *Journal of Political Economy*, April 1966, p. 158. Moore's data do not indicate that margin requirements have had a significant effect in achieving the presumed objectives of the regulation. It should also be noted that evasion of the margin requirements is not difficult. Margin requirements apply only to loans for the purpose of purchasing or carrying securities. There is no restriction on the amount that a bank can lend on the basis of stock-market collateral for other purposes. Borrowers have been known to misrepresent the purpose of their loans.

[5] *Ibid.*, p. 167.

applied to all lenders, not just member banks. There has not been much debate since that time about the desirability of mortgage credit controls. The arguments in favor of selective controls are generally based on the premise that the type of credit involved is not significantly affected by general credit controls. This argument does not hold up when it comes to mortgage credit, however. Mortgage credit is quite sensitive to changes in general credit conditions.

Some parallels with the stock market of the 1920s began to emerge in the late 1970s as real estate speculation drove prices to high ratios relative to rental income. Although the speculation was mortgage-financed, there were no strong sentiments toward mortgage credit controls. To some extent, lending institutions themselves used down payments as a rationing device, requiring smaller down payments for owner-occupants.

In wartime conditions, mortgage controls did not affect new construction, which was severely restricted in any event. In the more recent housing market, construction has been well below potential, and credit controls might further worsen this situation. It thus seems that reimposition of Regulation X is highly unlikely. If controls were to be imposed, attempts would probably be made to exempt new construction and owner-occupants, but such selectivity offers difficult enforcement problems.

Consumer Credit Control

The Board of Governors does not now have any control over the extension of consumer credit. It had such control during the inflationary periods of World War II, the postwar era, and again during the Korean War. During these periods, it was felt that increases in consumer credit would mean increased consumer expenditures and, hence, add to inflationary pressures in the economy.

The board administered control over consumer credit under its Regulation W, which prescribed minimum down payments for various consumer durable goods and also set maximum maturities for borrowing to finance purchase of these goods. Thus, the regulation might provide that washing machines could be purchased only with a minimum down payment of one-third and a maximum term for the loan of 18 months.

Since many consumer goods are purchased on installments, regulation of credit terms can significantly affect the volume of sales of such goods. There is little doubt, for example, that imposition of stiff credit terms on purchases of automobiles would have the effect of considerably lowering the volume of car sales.

There is very little support for consumer credit control on a permanent basis. Advocates of such controls generally do not favor continuous regulation, but rather argue for the existence of standby controls so that when it becomes necessary, the Federal Reserve could step in with regulations without having to wait for congressional action. It is possible that there will be no need for such controls, but, they argue, it is desirable that the Fed have the power to impose them when the need arises rather than having to begin convincing Congress that such controls are needed at that time.

The Case for Consumer Credit Control.   The case for direct regulation of consumer credit terms is relatively straightforward. The output of durable consumer goods fluctuates greatly during business cycles, and much of this output is purchased on an installment basis.[6] Therefore, if we can control installment buying, we can control total spending on durable consumer goods. Installment credit is not sensitive to general credit controls. Therefore, to affect the use of credit to purchase durable goods, we must control the credit directly.

The means by which such controls are expected to work is also simple. In a period of inflation spurred by "excessive" use of credit to purchase durable goods, the Federal Reserve would set minimum down payments and maximum maturities for installment loans to purchase various goods. If the terms for purchase of a new car, for example, should require a one-third down payment and a maximum of 18 months to pay, some potential customers would be forced out of the market. The new-car shopper with $2,000 cash will find his Oldsmobile dealer's door shut to him (although he may still be welcome at a Honda dealer). Other potential customers may have the required down payment but would not be able to handle the monthly payments necessary to pay off the debt in 18 months. Thus, the total spending in the economy for new cars, as well as other customer durables, would be decreased, and one source of inflationary pressure reduced.

If the inflationary period were followed by a recession, the controls would be removed, dealers would tend to liberalize their

---

[6] Furthermore, after installment credit has expanded during a period of prosperity, consumers are unwilling to spend heavily in the next recession, because much of their income is committed to paying off their existing installment obligations.

terms, and buyers forced out of the market during the control period would now be able to buy the goods they wanted. This buying power would help to cushion or reverse the downturn.

The Case Against Consumer Credit Control. The opponents of direct controls challenge virtually every argument of the advocates of such controls and add some arguments of their own. They doubt that purchases of consumer durables add substantially to the degree of business fluctuations. They argue that consumer credit is sensitive to general credit controls. They argue also that our previous experience with direct controls is not relevant—during World War II, the decline in installment credit was due not to credit controls but to the lack of durable goods. Further, our problems with inflation in the 1970s and 1980s have not been due to excessive consumer spending on durable goods.

One of the strongest arguments against controls over consumer credit concerns the problem of administration and enforcement. This was, of course, a serious problem during previous experiments with such controls, but enforcement during peacetime would no doubt be much more difficult. When Regulation W was in force, people cooperated, much as they did with price controls, because this was recognized as a wartime emergency measure, and thus patriotic motives were involved. The difficulties in enforcing retail price controls during 1971–1973 are instructive.

It has been estimated that there are nearly a quarter of a million firms (most of them not financial institutions) that would be subject to the proposed regulation of consumer credit. Proponents point out that this would not be a continual problem—they advocate such controls on a standby basis, to be used only rarely. Furthermore, they argue, even the possession of such standby powers by the Federal Reserve may be a force making for restraint in consumer credit expansion. Thus, the existence of the power may make its use unnecessary.

The principal reason that many people are opposed to direct controls is their discriminatory effect. Direct controls work on specific industries and individuals. If a consumer wants to buy an Oldsmobile by making a $900 down payment and taking 30 months to pay the balance, and if a dealer is willing to sell it to him on these terms, is it fair for some outside agency to prohibit this arrangement? Is it fair to force this person to turn to a bus, while the consumer with $10,000 in cash can buy a new Oldsmobile? Many economists see an important issue of economic freedom involved in this problem. One of the foremost defenders of economic freedom in this country has summed up the question of direct controls as follows:

Government is essential to the maintenance of a free society. But Government can also be a threat to freedom. Every extension of Government activity encroaches on the freedom of some individuals, and threatens further encroachment. This does not mean that we should never use Government. Far from it. What it does mean is that any proposed act of Government intervention . . . has this indirect effect . . . of expanding the area of Government action and reducing the area of individual action. In casting up the balance sheet of advantages and disadvantages of any particular action, this . . . should be listed among the disadvantages. The action is not worth taking to the believer in freedom unless there is a reasonably clear and reasonably significant balance of direct advantages over direct disadvantages; a marginal difference is not enough. . . .

As I evaluate the balance sheet, the advantages of . . . consumer credit control . . . seem dubious and minor; the disadvantages, clear and significant. There is nothing like that clear balance of direct advantages over direct disadvantages that the believer in freedom should demand before supporting any proposed act of Government intervention.[7]

Advocates of direct controls over consumer credit argue that Professor Friedman's concern with freedom and the discriminatory effects of direct controls is a phony issue. They concede that direct controls have discriminatory effects and that this is bad, but they go on to argue that even so-called general credit controls have discriminatory effects.

We have already seen that the general tools of monetary policy do not fall equally on the whole economy and that residential construction is sensitive to changes in interest rates, whereas large corporations are not deterred in their investment plans by tight money. Warren Smith, in a study for the Joint Economic Committee, wrote:

Recent experience suggests that general credit controls have different effects on different classes of borrowers. . . . Instead of distinguishing between general and selective controls on the basis of principle, it seems better to admit that each policy instrument—general as well as selective and monetary as well as fiscal—has its own peculiar incidence on the economy.[8]

Professor Smith went on to detail the incidence of monetary policy during the postwar period:

It is clear that by far the greatest impact on monetary policy in the past few years has been on residential construction. . . . Aside from this sector, the effects of monetary policy have probably been greatest on State and local government construction

---

[7] Milton Friedman, "Consumer Credit Control as an Instrument of Stabilization Policy," *Consumer Installment Credit* (Washington, D.C.: Federal Reserve System, 1957), Part II, Vol. 2, 101–3.

[8] Joint Economic Committee, "Employment, Growth, and Price Levels," *Staff Report*, 86th Cong., 1st sess., 1959, p. 363.

expenditures and on capital outlays by smaller businesses, although the evidence in these cases is far from definitive. The effects on plant and equipment expenditures of larger business concerns appear to have been very slight. . . .[9]

If we are concerned with questions of equity and economic freedom, is it fair that the potential home buyer should be affected by our stabilization policies and not the large manufacturing firm? Questions of fairness in the results of stabilization policies are not exclusively in the realm of selective controls.

The problem of enforcement is a powerful argument for not adopting a continuous program of direct controls over consumer credit. The question of standby powers for the Federal Reserve is not as clear-cut, and this subject will probably be debated in the future if we ever experience an inflation that appears to be fueled by a rapid increase in consumer credit.

Selective Reserve Requirements

When an institution is required to hold reserves, the effect on earnings is similar to a tax. For example, suppose that an asset yields 15 percent, but that 10 percent of the holdings of such an asset must be placed in non-interest-bearing reserves. The effective rate of interest on the asset then would be only 13.5 percent (15 percent of 90 percent). This is the effect no matter what the base of the reserve requirement might be—certain types of liabilities or certain types of assets.

Just as selective taxation can be used to reduce certain types of spending, selective reserve requirements can be used to reduce certain types of borrowing or lending. Here is a potential vehicle by which the Federal Reserve can selectively influence credit flows— higher reserve requirements, say, on stock-market loans than on loans to students. Although reserve requirements have usually applied to liabilities, they can also be applied to assets.

In 1980, the Federal Reserve imposed reserve requirements on any institution's increase in certain consumer credit. Only unsecured credit was involved, and the principal target was credit-card borrowing. It was a "marginal" requirement, in that it applied only to additions to such credit made after the announcement date of March 14. In addition, the same marginal requirement was im-

---

[9] *Ibid.*, p. 393. This study by Professor Smith was made before our experience with the credit crunches of the last two decades. That is, even without those rather special cases, monetary policy was found to have its greatest impact on the housing market.

posed on increases in assets of money-market mutual-fund shares. Both requirements terminated July 28, 1980. The actions were announced as means to restrain credit growth and were a part of broader antiinflation efforts.

History cannot tell us how successful the control was. It is true that consumer credit growth was negligible in 1980 compared to about $40 billion in each of the two preceding years, but the economy went into recession about the time of the new policy action, and consumer credit always slows down in recessions. The Federal Reserve Bank of New York presented a mixed view on the success of the program. Noting that cutbacks were not confined to the credit covered by the program, the bank stated:

> Indirectly, however, the program did change the behavior of both borrowers and lenders and had an important psychological effect on household willingness to finance purchases with credit.
>
> Nevertheless, it would be wrong to exaggerate the effects of the credit restraint program in dampening consumption. Although on a quarterly basis the collapse in consumption spending appears to have coincided with the program, monthly data suggest that personal consumption spending had begun to decline in advance of the program.[10]

The unlikelihood of frequent use of such controls is revealed in testimony by Federal Reserve Board Vice-Chairman Frederick Schultz before the House Small Business Committee, April 7, 1981:

> It . . . would be extremely unwise for the Federal Reserve to get into the business of setting guidelines or reserve allocation schemes designed to channel credit flows to specific sectors. Our experience with the credit restraint program last year reinforces our reluctance in this regard. I can assure you that administering these controls proved to be a task filled with intractable problems.

MORAL SUASION

Although Federal Reserve officials do not deem it desirable to explain all their actions, they frequently do give some indication, in speeches or other public statements, of the type of policy they would like banks to follow. There is, of course, no legal obligation for the member banks to go along with all the expressed wishes of the Federal Reserve, but certainly statements by system officials carry some weight.

Suppose, for example, that the Board of Governors feels that too much bank credit is being extended in the form of term loans. A

---

[10] Federal Reserve Bank of New York, *1980 Annual Report*, pp. 6–7.

member of the Board of Governors may make a speech indicating concern over the volume of term lending by commercial banks. A bank that may already be concerned about the volume of its term lending might give future loan applications a closer look.

In many countries, there are only a small number of commercial banks, and in these countries there is no question but that moral suasion can be an important tool of the central bank. If the central bank wants to slow down the expansion of term lending, it might be possible to get an informal agreement from all the banks involved. In the United States, with thousands of independent banks, most of them not even members of the Federal Reserve System, those banks that voluntarily comply with the desires of the Fed may place themselves at a competitive disadvantage.

But even though these considerations alone would lead one to doubt the efficacy of moral suasion as a monetary-policy device, there have been cases in the past in which it has been moderately successful. During the 1960s, the Fed administered a voluntary foreign-credit-restraint program aimed at reducing the outflow of dollars from the United States. The Federal Reserve, at least officially, considers this program to have been a success.

Some calls for cooperation were backed up with the threat, implied or explicit, that lack of cooperation will be taken into account at the discount window or in other ways. In September 1966, for example, the Federal Reserve Board sent a letter to all member banks calling for restraint in granting business loans, particularly loans for "nonproductive" purposes. The letter indicated that banks that failed to cooperate could not expect the increase in their loan portfolios to be considered an adequate reason for the extension of Federal Reserve credit through the discount window.

Another example can be found in the administration's 1971 "New Economic Policy," which included a program of "voluntary" restraint on interest rates, administered by the Committee on Interest and Dividends (CID). The CID, dominated by Federal Reserve Chairman Burns, attempted to "talk interest rates down." Cooperation seemed fine as long as interest rates were going down anyway, but when market rates turned upward in 1972, many banks raised the rates they charged on loans. The threat employed by the CID in this case was the possibility of mandatory interest-rate controls if banks raised their charges in the face of Federal Reserve moral suasion to hold them down.

This situation became more dramatic in early 1973, when the large commercial banks, in the face of a rapidly rising demand for business credit, attempted to raise their prime rates. In view of the prevailing level of interest rates on securities, the international financial situation following the devaluation of the dollar, and the need to combat the growing inflationary pressures in the economy, an increase in rates on loans to large businesses seemed very appropriate. Nevertheless, Chairman Burns harshly criticized the increases and urged restraint out of concern that Congress would take action to control interest rates if they rose too rapidly. Although the actions that Burns was urging on the banks made no economic sense, his use of moral suasion was relatively successful for a time. Part of the reason for this success lay in another role of the Federal Reserve—its power to pass on applications for expanded activities by bank holding companies. Many of the banks involved in the prime-rate controversy feared that any applications they might bring before the Federal Reserve Board might be adversely viewed if they defied the Board's chairman.

It appears, in fact, that the Fed's control over holding-company activities and acquisitions has represented a substantial increase in the Board's ability to "jawbone" bankers into taking actions deemed appropriate by the Federal Reserve. Nearly all the very large banks in the country can expect that at some time they will be appearing before the Board, asking for approval of one sort or another. Bankers feel, probably correctly, that their chances are better if they do not have the image of being uncooperative with the Federal Reserve.

Use of moral suasion has many of the same disadvantages as selective controls. Indeed, the possibilities of discriminatory treatment are even greater, since the banks do not really know where they stand after a speech or phone call by a Federal Reserve official. Unless the penalties and rewards associated with compliance are clearly spelled out, there is no way for the banker to know what losses he may suffer by cooperating or not cooperating. Unfortunately, with programs of this sort, the "good guys" who cooperate find their profits squeezed, while the uncooperative reap large gains. It is not surprising that such programs lead to large evasions and ultimately break down.

MONETARY POWERS OF THE TREASURY

The basic responsibility for control over the monetary system lies with the Federal Reserve System. We have examined the various weapons the Fed uses to carry out its responsibilities in this area. But the Treasury also has powers that affect the monetary system. In most cases, these powers are more or less side-products of various Treasury functions, such as managing its cash balance and borrowing money when necessary. The Treasury is not continuously operating to control the monetary system, but ideally its actions should be such that they do not conflict with the operations of the Federal Reserve. The most important Treasury operations in terms of effects on the economy are those relating to taxes and expenditures. We will consider fiscal policy later on; here, we will examine the purely monetary powers of the Treasury.

We saw in Chapter 19 how variations in Treasury holdings of cash and deposits affect bank reserves. These variations form a very powerful tool of Treasury monetary control. Actually, Treasury cash management is planned not to control the monetary system but simply to minimize conflict with Federal Reserve policy and the disruptive effects on the banking system of variations in Treasury expenditures and tax receipts. The Tax and Loan Accounts at commercial banks are managed with these ends in view.

If there were no Tax and Loan Accounts, then at certain times of the year when tax collections are at a high level—at quarterly corporate income tax dates, for example—there would be a substantial drain on the reserves of the banking system. In terms of T accounts, the payment of a billion dollars in taxes would have the following effects:

FEDERAL RESERVE (billions)			COMMERCIAL BANKS (billions)			
	Treasury deposit	+1.0	Reserves	−1.0	Deposits	−1.0
	Bank reserves	−1.0				

When the Treasury sent checks received from taxpayers to the Federal Reserve, the depository institutions would lose a billion dollars in reserves in a very short period of time. This obviously would have substantial disruptive effects on the system. Conversely, a period in which Treasury expenditures exceeded tax collections would flood the system with excess reserves.

Through the device of the Tax and Loan Accounts, these disruptive effects are minimized. Now the result of a high rate of tax collections is simply an increase in the size of the Tax and Loan Accounts. The banks do not suffer a loss of reserves or deposits—only the ownership of the deposits shifts from taxpayers to the Treasury. The bank knows that the Treasury will ultimately transfer the account to the Federal Reserve, thus causing a loss of reserves, but the bank has time to plan for this and adjust its portfolio accordingly.

The Treasury tries to maintain its balance at the Federal Reserve at a level appropriate to its expenditures in the period ahead.

If expenditures are expected to be heavy, "calls" will be made on the Tax and Loan Accounts and they will be transferred to the Federal Reserve. Banks are divided into three classes, based on the amount of Treasury deposits they hold. Those banks with the largest amounts are subject to call most frequently. A call may be made by authorizing the Federal Reserve Banks to transfer a certain percentage of each bank's Tax and Loan Account to the account of the Treasury. The result is exactly the same as if the Treasury had written a check on its account at a commercial bank and deposited the check with the Federal Reserve. This latter method would be much more cumbersome, however, since the Treasury maintains thousands of Tax and Loan Accounts.

QUESTIONS

1 If margin requirements existed during the 1920s, could the Great Depression have been avoided?
2 What is the objective of an increase in margin requirements?
3 "Selective credit controls have discriminatory effects on different borrowers, whereas general credit controls affect everyone equally." Do you agree?
4 Why is it generally agreed that direct controls over real estate credit are unnecessary?
5 During a period of general monetary restriction, which borrowers are most affected?
6 "Much of the beneficial impact of monetary-policy actions could be achieved much more simply by means of a letter or phone call from the Federal Reserve to the banks." Do you agree? Would this be desirable?
7 What are the monetary-policy powers of the Treasury?
8 Which monetary-policy weapon would be most effective in combating inflation? depression?

SELECTED READINGS

BARTELS, ROBERT, "Justification for Direct Regulation of Consumer Credit Reappraised." *Journal of Finance*, May 1953.
Board of Governors of the Federal Reserve System, *Consumer and Community Affairs Handbook.* 1981.
———, *Securities Credit Transactions Handbook.* 1981.
———, the Federal Reserve, and the Treasury Department, *Answers to Inquiries of the Commission.* Commission on Money and Credit. Englewood Cliffs, N.J.: Prentice-Hall, 1963.
CHANDLER, LESTER V., *Selective Credit Control.* Washington: Board of Governors of the Federal Reserve System, 1967.

HORVITZ, PAUL M., "The Committee on Interest and Dividends: An Assessment," *Policy Analysis*, Winter 1977.

KAMINOW, IRA, and JAMES M. O'BRIEN, eds., *Studies in Selective Credit Policies*. Federal Reserve Bank of Philadelphia, 1975. An excellent group of papers on various aspects of the controversy over selective credit controls.

MOORE, THOMAS G., "Stock Market Margin Requirements," *Journal of Political Economy*, April 1966.

Report of the National Commission on Consumer Finance. Washington, D.C.: U.S. Government Printing Office, 1973.

VI

MONETARY THEORY

23

Quantity-Theory Approaches to a Theory of Money

Now that we have described the financial system and the mechanisms of money and credit policy, the time has come to inquire into the effects of the financial system on the economy.

Finance is not an end in itself; it is a part of the mechanism by which the economy determines the production of goods and the distribution of income. In looking at the interaction of finance and the economy, we are in the realm of theory. Cause-and-effect relationships cannot be proved; they can only be theorized, and the theory in this regard is far from settled.[1] In theory construction, we can make certain assumptions about relationships and then draw

[1] The uncertain state of monetary theory can be illustrated by two quotations from Federal Reserve publications, issued about the same time at opposite sides of the country. From the Federal Reserve Bank of New York: "There is little evidence that tighter month-to-month (or even quarter-to-quarter) control of money growth would result in a smoother course for income growth since, even on a quarterly basis, the relationship of money to GNP has been unstable and unpredictable." (*1980 Annual Report*, p. 19.) From the Federal Reserve Bank of San Francisco: "The Federal Reserve has adopted the monetary aggregates as the primary targets for monetary policy because of their strong empirical association with the variables related to ultimate policy goals—stable growth in output, full employment, stable prices, and a stable exchange value of the dollar." (Adrian W. Throop, *Money in the Economy*, August 1980, p. 12.)

397

conclusions about outcomes. But the validity of the conclusions depends upon the reality of the assumptions.

Monetary theory concerns the effect of changes in money on the economy. The money stock is usually taken to be an exogenous variable. This means that it is not itself a product of the economy but is determined independently. Various theorists use different definitions of money (the correct definition being one of the many points of dispute), but for simplicity, the reader may think of the transaction definition of money in the expositions that follow, unless it is specifically stated to the contrary.

The question theory asks is, How will a change in money affect the economy? We approach this problem from something of a historical standpoint, starting in this chapter with the central theory that emerged prior to the Great Depression of the 1930s. We then cover the challenge to this theory (the Keynesian revolution) and then the counterrevolution (the monetarist approach). Neither the Keynesian (more precisely, neo-Keynesian) nor monetarist position is easily stratified, and it must be recognized that we are presenting our interpretation of these positions.

THE QUANTITY THEORY: A FIRST APPROXIMATION

The earliest type of monetary theory postulated some sort of direct relation between the quantity of money and the price level. A fairly well-developed statement of this "quantity theory," whose origins lie in antiquity, can be found in David Hume's essay, "Of Money," published in 1752.

In its purest and most rigid form, the quantity theory asserts that there is a precise, proportional relation between the quantity of money and the level of prices. According to this theory, a doubling of the money supply would mean a doubling of prices; an increase of 38¼ percent in the money supply would result in an increase of 38¼ percent in the price level. Although hardly anyone has ever held to the theory in this rigid form, it is possible to find statements to this effect in the literature—a result, generally, of the author's failing to make clear the assumptions or qualifications he or she had in mind.

This crude type of quantity theory focuses on money as a medium of exchange. It assumes that money is desired not for its own sake or as a store of value but simply for its purchasing power. Many early writers were not very explicit about the mechanism by which prices would change. Since the latter part of the eighteenth century, however, economists have rejected the notion that there is a fixed, automatic relationship between the quantity of money and its value. It has been recognized that changes in the money supply affect prices only by first affecting demand. John Stuart Mill wrote, "Money acts upon prices in no other way than by being tendered in exchange for commodities."[2] Once it is recognized that increases in the money supply increase prices only by increasing demand, it can be seen that a given increase in the money supply may not result in a proportionate increase in prices. If everyone in the economy should wake up one morning and find his holdings of money doubled, then prices might also double. But if, for example, we wake up one morning and find the total money supply doubled but all the increase held by one person, not all prices would double. This one very rich person would increase his demand for many goods, but demand for all goods in the economy would not be doubled.

We can represent symbolically the type of quantity theory that holds that an increase in the money supply will result in a proportionate increase in prices:

$$\frac{\triangle M}{M} = \frac{\triangle P}{P}$$

where M represents the money supply and P is the general price level. This equation states that a 10 percent increase in M will mean a 10 percent increase in prices.

THE EQUATION OF EXCHANGE

To carry the analysis somewhat further than the theory described above, monetary theorists have added two more factors that involve supply and demand considerations. If money affects the economy through its effect on spending, a logical variable to include in the analysis would be some measure of the amount of spending that a given unit of money accounts for during the period under consideration. The quantity theorists did this by considering velocity, or V. The velocity of money is simply the average number of times a unit of money is spent during a unit time period. MV thus represents the total amount of spending in the economy. If $M = \$200$ and $V = 3$ (each dollar, on the average, is spent three times during a year), then the total amount of spending in the economy (MV) is \$600.

[2] Mill, *Principles of Political Economy*, p. 65. Don Patinkin has a note entitled, "The Mechanism of the Quantity Theory in the Early Literature," in his *Money, Interest, and Prices*, 2nd ed. (New York: Harper & Row, 1965).

The following anecdote by Dennis Robertson illustrates the relations among velocity, money supply, and total spending:

On Derby Day two men, Bob and Joe, invested in a barrel of beer, and set off to Epsom with the intention of selling it retail on the racecourse at 6d. a pint, the proceeds to be shared equally between them. On the way Bob, who had one threepenny-bit left in the world, began to feel a great thirst, and drank a pint of the beer, paying Joe 3d. as his share of the market price. A little later Joe yielded to the same desire, and drank a pint of beer, returning the 3d. to Bob. The day was hot, and before long Bob was thirsty again, and so, a little later, was Joe. When they arrived at Epsom, the 3d. was back in Bob's pocket, and each had discharged in full his debts to the other: but the beer was all gone. One single threepenny-bit had performed a volume of transactions which would have required many shillings if the beer had been sold to the public in accordance with the original intention.

The total amount of spending must be equal to the total value of goods purchased in the same period. It is obvious that if people are spending $600 during the year, they are buying $600 worth of goods. Spending and buying actually mean the same thing. The total dollar amount of goods bought during the year is equal to the number of goods bought times their average price. If P represents the average price level and T the number of transactions or purchases during the year, then total purchases are equal to PT.

If we put both sides of this expenditure equation together, we arrive at the so-called *equation of exchange:*

$$MV = PT$$

The considerations of the last few paragraphs make it clear that the equation of exchange is a truism—it is always correct. The two sides of the equation are simply two ways of looking at the same thing. The total value of the money given in exchange for goods, MV, must always equal the total value of the goods given in exchange for money, PT. The equation states that any change in spending can be attributed to a change in the amount of money involved or to a change in the speed with which an average unit of money is spent. This is analogous to the situation in value theory whereby any change in price can be attributed to a change in either supply or demand.

The fact that the equation is a trusim—true by definition— does not mean that it is not useful for economic analysis. The equation is useful because it includes consideration of the price level and of the three immediate determinants of the price level. It will be realized, of course, that M, V, and T are not elemental, or basic, economic factors. Each of these factors is determined by a whole host of other factors. The value of the equation of exchange is that it provides a neat system for analyzing all these ultimate determinants of the price level. Let us examine the components of the equation of exchange in somewhat more detail.

The definition of M, the stock of money, has long been the subject of debate. Since the equation focuses on exchange, it seems appropriate to define money in terms of its function as the medium of exchange. In earlier days, under specie standards, the stock of money was considered to include gold (and/or silver) bullion and metallic currency. Debate centered on whether to include paper money and, later, demand deposits. Now we include paper money and demand deposits without question, but there is debate about inclusion of time deposits at commercial banks and savings accounts at other financial institutions.

V, the average number of times a unit of money "turns over" during a year, is not an observable entity. We do have data on debits to checking accounts—that is, the amount of checks written against demand deposits. This allows us to make some estimates of the velocity of demand deposits, but we have no way of knowing how many times per year the average dollar bill is spent. V, then, is arbitrarily defined so as to make the equation of exchange correct.

P is the average price involved in all transactions that take place in the economy during the year. This includes purchases of all goods (shoes, ships, sealing wax) as well as financial transactions (purchases of bonds, stocks, and so on) and gifts. There is no way of calculating such an average price, even though price indexes of varying degrees of coverage are calculated and published for the economy.

T represents the physical volume of transactions taking place during the year. If we were to list the factors determining T, we might come up with the factors given in Table 23-1.

TABLE 23-1
Factors Determining the Volume of Transactions, T

1. Resources of the economy
   a. Population: size, skills, philosophy
   b. Land: quantity, fertility, natural resources
   c. Capital
   d. State of technology
2. Extent to which resources are utilized
3. Business structure and practice
   a. Extent of specialization
   b. Degree of vertical integration
   c. Extent of barter
4. Volume of goods already in existence

All these factors have some influence on the total volume of transactions. Clearly, the greater the resources of the economy and the greater the extent to which these resources are used, the greater will be the volume of transactions. Somewhat less obvious are the effects of vertical integration. If automobile manufacturers are vertically integrated, so that each firm makes its own steel, glass, tires, and so forth, there will be fewer transactions in this economy than in one in which the auto manufacturers buy steel from steel companies, which, in turn, buy iron ore from mining companies and coal from coal-mining firms.

As can be seen from the sort of factors involved in a determination of T, they are quite different from those involved in the other components of the equation of exchange. Economists have found the equation of exchange useful because it sets up a useful classification of the ultimate factors at work in the economy. The classification is useful because each category contains factors that are largely independent of those in the other categories.

It is important to stress that the equation of exchange is *not* a theory. MV equals PT always and under any circumstances because of the way in which we have defined the various terms. It is possible to build a theory around the equation by making hypotheses about the behavior of M, V, P, and T, but all the equation of exchange tells us is that if any one of these variables changes, at least one other must also change. The equation by itself does not tell us which other factor will change.

If, for example, the quantity of money is doubled, the equation of exchange tells us that velocity must fall by one-half, the volume of transactions must double, the price level must double, or some combination of increases in some factors and decreases in others must occur so as to leave $MV = PT$. Put another way:

> A doubling in the velocity of circulation of money will double the level of prices, *provided the quantity of money in circulation and the quantities of goods exchanged for money remain as before.* . . . We must distinctly recognize that the quantity of money is only one of three factors, all equally important in determining the price level.[3]

THE QUANTITY THEORY: THE TRANSACTION APPROACH

A more refined version of the quantity theory builds on the basic framework of the equation of exchange. By making assumptions

---

[3] Irving Fisher, *The Purchasing Power of Money* (New York: Macmillan, 1911), pp. 20–21.

about the behavior of the various factors in the equation, however, it attempts to explain the determination of the general price level. The general conclusion of the quantity theorists, after analyzing the equation of exchange and the behavior of the variables involved, was not very different from the conclusion of earlier writers, but the later quantity theorists made explicit some of the assumptions involved in their analysis. As Irving Fisher, the economist most closely associated with this theoretical approach, put it:

> We may now restate, then, in what causal sense the quantity theory is true. It is true in the sense that *one of the normal effects of an increase in quantity of money is an exactly proportional increase in the general level of prices.*[4]

In order to arrive at this result, three assumptions are necessary. The validity of the quantity theory really rests upon the validity of these assumptions. First, the quantity theorist holds that changes in the quantity of money do not affect velocity. Fisher argues:

> No reason has been, or, so far as it is apparent, can be assigned, to show why the velocity of circulation of money . . . should be different, when the quantity of money . . . is great, from what it is when the quantity is small.[5]

The second assumption is that changes in the quantity of money do not affect the volume of transactions. Fisher justifies this assumption on these grounds:

> An inflation of the currency cannot increase the product of farms and factories, nor the speed of freight trains or ships. The stream of business depends on natural resources and technical conditions, not on the quantity of money. The whole machinery of production, transportation, and sale is a matter of physical capacities and technique, none of which depend on the quantity of money. . . . We conclude, therefore, that a change in the quantity of money will not appreciably affect the quantity of goods sold for money.[6]

The third assumption is that the chain of causation runs from money to prices and not in the other direction. That is, changes in the quantity of money affect the price level, but changes in the price level do not affect M, V, or T. Fisher puts this assumption as follows: *"The price level is normally the one absolutely passive element in the equation of exchange.* It is controlled solely by the other elements and the causes antecedent to them, but exerts no control over them."[7]

[4] *Ibid.*, p. 157.
[5] *Ibid.*, p. 154.
[6] *Ibid.*, pp. 155–156.
[7] *Ibid.*, p. 172.

In presenting Fisher's position in regard to the behavior of V and T in response to changes in M, we have not been quite fair. Fisher was primarily interested in the long-run effects of monetary changes, and he believed that his assumptions were valid *in the long run*. He readily conceded that V and/or T might change in response to changes in M during transition periods. Fisher points out, "We have emphasized the fact that the strictly proportional effect on prices of an increase in M is only the *normal* or *ultimate* effect after transition periods are over."[8]

The statement is somewhat akin to Mill's view that money has significant effects on the economy only when it gets "out of order." Part of the reason for the diminishing popularity of the quantity theory in the postdepression years was the fact that economists became more interested in those "periods of transition" in which money is "out of order." The modern economist is interested in answering such questions as these: In a recession, will an increase in the money supply increase T (which is probably a good indicator of general business conditions), or will it simply result in an offsetting decrease in V? In an inflationary period, will a decrease in M restrain increases in the price level, or will it decrease T and perhaps lead to recession, or will it perhaps be offset by a corresponding increase in V? These questions concern the transition periods, in which Fisher concedes that his analysis does not apply.

THE QUANTITY THEORY: INCOME FORM

The quantity theory in the form we have explored it poses serious empirical difficulties. There simply are no data with which to analyze the concepts of "transactions" or "general price level." Moreover, much of what is included in the transactions concept is of limited economic significance. Many of the transactions are simply a transfer of existing goods. Much of the expenditure measured by MV does not result in the creation of real income. The difference can perhaps be illustrated by the situation of a person buying a house. The effect on the economy is different if she buys an existing house than if she hires an architect, builder, and construction workers to build a new house. In the latter case, all the people hired now have higher incomes. In the former case, there was simply an exchange of existing assets—the home buyer has a house but less money, and the seller has more money but no house.

Both of these transactions would be included in the T of the quantity theorists. The economist often wants to narrow down

[8] *Ibid.*, p. 159.

the scope of the analysis to those transactions that directly involve the production of goods and services.

It is, of course, possible to restrict ourselves to income-generating transactions and still use the equation-of-exchange framework. The equation then becomes:

$$MV_y = P_yT_y$$

where M = the money supply (exactly as before)
P_y = the price index for all final goods produced in the period
T_y = the physical volume of final goods produced in the period
V_y = the *income* velocity of money

The equation in this form is just as valid and just as much a truism as the familiar $MV = PT$. It may be more useful, in that it brings income into the picture and eliminates consideration of purely financial transactions that do not affect income. One difficulty of this formulation is that V_y does not have as simple an interpretation as V. Since most payments in this country are made by check (an estimated 90 percent), and since bank records show how often deposits are spent, we could, perhaps, make reasonable estimates of V. It is impossible from existing data to determine V_y or the number of times, on the average, that a dollar is spent for final goods or services produced during the time period.

V_y is calculated in a sort of backhanded manner in practice. We know what M is, and from national income accounting, we know what P_yT_y is. V_y is then simply calculated as (P_yT_y/M). If we use GNP for P_yT_y, V_y has risen, with fluctuations, since mid-century, and the quantity theorist is on no sounder empirical grounds in holding that V_y is constant over time than in assuming that V is constant. Since the volume of purely financial transactions varies from year to year, there is no fixed relationship between V and V_y. However, empirical studies of the behavior of these two variables indicate that over the long run, they do tend to move together.[9]

THE QUANTITY THEORY:
THE CASH-BALANCES APPROACH

The transaction type of monetary theory has in the past been most popular in the United States, owing primarily to the work of Irving

[9] For an excellent theoretical and empirical analysis of velocity concepts, see George Garvy and Martin R. Blyn, *The Velocity of Money*, Federal Reserve Bank of New York, 1969.

Fisher. In Europe, and particularly in England, a somewhat different approach has been used in expounding the same basic theory. This latter type of analysis has become known as the cash-balances approach to the quantity theory.

As in the transaction approach, the cash-balances theorists start with the equation of exchange, $MV = PT$. A simple algebraic manipulation of this equation brings us to the point of view of the cash-balances approach. If $MV = PT$, then $M = 1/V \times PT$. The Cambridge economists (Marshall, Pigou, Keynes, Robertson) who expounded this approach used the letter k to represent $1/V$. Thus the equation becomes $M = kPT$. M, P, and T have exactly the same definitions as in our earlier discussions, but it is necessary to say a few words about the meaning of k.

If V is the number of times a dollar is *spent* during the year, then $k(= 1/V)$ is the length of time in which the dollar is *held*, on the average, before being spent. If a dollar is spent three times a year ($V = 3$), then the dollar is held, on the average, one-third of a year. We can look on k as the proportion of people's annual expenditures over which they want to have command by holding money. If the public wants to hold money equal to one-fourth of their annual expenditures, then $k = 1/4$. This is, of course, the same as saying that each dollar will be turned over four times during the year ($V = 4$).

The two approaches are just two views of the same phenomenon. The transaction approach focuses on the spending of money, or "money on the wing," as one writer has put it. The cash-balances approach focuses on the holding of money, or "money sitting."[10] This difference in point of view, however, has some important implications for the development of monetary theory.

With the use of the cash-balances approach, and particularly in the income form, the equation of exchange can be interpreted in terms of supply and demand, concepts with which economists are accustomed to dealing. In the equation $M = kP_yT_y$, kP_yT_y can be viewed as the demand for money. The equation shows the amount of money that people want to hold. The desired amount of cash balances is a proportion, k, of their total income, P_yT_y.

Even more important is the fact that the cash-balances approach relates the determination of the value of money to the motives and decisions of individuals. The cash-balances-approach

---

[10] See Dennis H. Robertson, *Money*, 4th ed. (New York: Harcourt, Brace & World, 1948), p. 28.

theorist is brought face to face with the question of why people want to hold money. Instead of analyzing the mechanical concept of velocity (determined by such factors as frequency of payments, speed of transportation, and check-clearing facilities), we must look into the motivation of people who decide that their cash balances should be, say, 10 percent or 15 percent of their annual expenditures. In attempting to explain the behavior of k, economists have been led into investigation of speculation, interest rates, problems of uncertainty, and other areas that the transaction approach had not considered. These avenues of exploration have proved very valuable in the development of economic theory.

We can put this difference in terms of the functions of money. The transaction approach focuses on money simply as a medium of exchange. The velocity concept relates money to the amount of spending that can be carried out with the given money supply. Analysis of k involves the same factors—if people are paid very frequently, for example, they need on the average to hold less cash than if they are paid once a year—but it also brings up some other questions. Are there other reasons for holding money besides the need to make payments? Clearly, there are. We have discussed the fact that money serves as a store of value. People may decide to hold money not to make expenditures now but to preserve it for some future contingency.

This brings us back to the question of a definition of the money supply. The transaction approach makes it natural to define money in terms of the medium of exchange. The cash-balances approach, focusing on money as a temporary store of purchasing power, makes it seem appropriate to include such stores of value as time and savings accounts, which do not function as a means of payment (although they are readily convertible into the medium of exchange).

It is a logical extension of the cash-balances approach to ask why people want to hold money in excess of their needs for transaction purposes, when by so doing they are forgoing the interest that could be earned by investing their surplus funds. The extent to which people are willing to forgo the possibilities of earning interest will depend upon, among other things, the level of interest rates. We will discuss the details of this relationship later on, but it is important to note here that consideration of the rate of interest is now involved in monetary theory. Earlier economists had thought that interest theory and monetary theory were quite separate compartments of economic theory. It is not a coincidence that the *General Theory of Employment, Interest, and Money* was written by one of the foremost theorists of the cash-balances school.[11]

The mechanism of the cash-balances approach is similar to that of the transaction approach, but with the former it may be somewhat easier to see what happens in "transition" periods. Suppose we start from a period of equilibrium in which the supply of money is equal to the demand for money—that is, the amount of money that people want to hold is just equal to the amount that exists. Suppose there is then a decrease in the supply of money. The public, collectively, will want to hold more money than there is to be held. An individual can increase his holdings of money only by cutting down on his expenditures. But if everyone reacts in this way, and if T is constant, the result of the decline in M will be a decline in P. If the original equilibrium position is disturbed by an increase in M, people will find that they are holding more money in relation to their expenditures than they think desirable. The only way they can restore balance between their money holdings and their expenditures is to increase their expenditures, and this will result in an increase in P. These results are exactly the same as those postulated by the transaction approach, which should not be surprising, since we have indicated that the two approaches amount to the same thing.

It should be kept in mind, then, that the transaction approach and the cash-balances approach give similar results. It cannot be said that one is more correct than the other. It is a historical fact, however, that the cash-balances approach has led economists down more fruitful paths of exploration.

Interest in the quantity-theory approach to money declined in the decades following publication of Keynes's *General Theory*. It did not completely die, however, and there are claims that during the 1930s and 1940s, the quantity theory was alive and living in Chicago. In any case, it reemerged during the 1950s, although in a form that its early sponsors might find difficult to recognize. We shall examine the modern reformulation of the quantity theory in Chapter 26.

[11] John M. Keynes, *General Theory of Employment, Interest, and Money* (New York: Harcourt, Brace & World, 1936). This point has given rise to an interesting debate on the history of the quantity theory. Milton Friedman has written, "Fisher and other earlier quantity theorists explicitly recognized that velocity would be affected by . . . the rate of interest." ("Money—II: Quantity Theory," *The International Encyclopedia of the Social Sciences*, Vol. 10, 436.) On the other hand, Franco Modigliani writes that Fisher "makes no mention of interest rates in his list of factors affecting velocity." ("Liquidity Preference," *Ibid.*, Vol. 9, 395.)

QUESTIONS

1 What does it mean to speak of money as a "veil"?
2 Does $MV = PT$ during a severe depression? if V is unstable?
3 Trace the mechanism by which an increase in the money supply affects the price level.
4 Why do people hold money?
5 In assessing the validity of the quantity theory, does it make any difference how the money supply is defined?
6 Did Keynes believe that the quantity theory was valid?
7 Discuss the similarities and differences in the quantity theories of Fisher and the Cambridge economists.
8 What do you do if you find yourself holding more money than you need?

SELECTED READINGS

BOORMAN, JOHN T., and THOMAS HAVRILESKY, *Money Supply, Money Demand, and Macroeconomic Models*. Boston: Allyn & Bacon, 1972. An excellent combination of text and readings.

FISHER, IRVING, *The Purchasing Power of Money*. New York: Macmillan, 1911.

FRIEDMAN, MILTON, "Money—II: Quantity Theory," *The International Encyclopedia of the Social Sciences*. New York: Macmillan and Free Press, 1968.

KEYNES, JOHN M., *A Treatise on Money*. New York: Harcourt, Brace & World, 1930.

PATINKIN, DON, *Money, Interest and Prices*, 2nd ed. New York: Harper & Row, 1965.

ROBERTSON, DENNIS H., *Money*, 4th ed. New York: Harcourt, Brace & World, 1948.

ROUSSEAS, STEPHEN W., *Monetary Theory*. New York: Knopf, 1972. Chapters 2 and 3 are particularly relevant to the discussion in this chapter.

24
The
Income-Expenditure
Approach
to Monetary Theory

The earlier versions of the quantity theory aimed at explaining variations in the price level. In the last few decades, economists have also been concerned with the problem of explaining changes in the level of employment and real income. This has been true of economists using the quantity theory as well as the income-expenditure approach.

There are two major reasons for the increased interest of economic theorists in problems of employment. First, the depression of the 1930s was so serious and so long that it was impossible to argue, as economists had in the past, that times of high unemployment were simply short periods of transition and would go away by themselves. Monetary theorists had argued previously that, in the long run, the economy would operate at full employment. The classical economists felt that general overproduction or a "general glut of the market" was impossible.[1] The Great Depression proved that this position was not valid.

The second reason for the increased interest in problems of unemployment was the publication in 1936 of John Maynard

[1] This argument rested on "Say's Law." J.B. Say, a French economist of the early nineteenth century, postulated that "supply creates its own demand," in that the production of any good results in income to its producers, and this income provides demand for other goods.

Keynes's *General Theory of Employment, Interest, and Money*. Keynes presented a theoretical framework within the classical tradition in which he argued the economy could be in equilibrium with less than full employment. The book stirred up tremendous controversy concerning both the theory and its policy implications. Many of Keynes's propositions have been amended somewhat, owing to later empirical and theoretical research on the concepts he introduced. It is impossible here to cover even the barest outline of the historical development of the "Keynesian Revolution"; we will concentrate on the outcome of the controversy that developed from Keynes's work, particularly on its implications for the theory of money and monetary policy.

NATIONAL-INCOME CONCEPTS

The income-expenditure approach focuses on the determinants of aggregate income. Loosely put, national income is simply the total income earned by everyone in the economy. The national-income concept does not treat all expenditures in the economy equally—it considers only those that mean income to the recipient. We noted in the preceding chapter the need to separate transactions involving newly produced goods and services from those involving financial transactions or sales of existing goods. Once the conceptual decision is made to concentrate attention on expenditures for goods and services produced by the economy in a given period of time, there still remains the problem of refining this definition to fit actual transactions. Economists have devised several measures of national income, each with a separate viewpoint and emphasis.

The most widely used measure of national income is known as *gross national product*, or GNP. Gross national product is defined as the market value of all final goods and services produced by an economy during a year, before the deduction of depreciation and other allowances for the consumption of capital. The word *final* is inserted in the definition to eliminate double counting. If the output of an economy during a year consisted of three automobiles sold at a market price of $10,000 each, we would say that the GNP of that economy is $30,000. It would clearly be misleading in an enumeration of the income produced by the economy to include also the value of the steel and glass used in producing the automobiles and the value of the coal and iron produced to make the steel. In fact, what our measure of GNP does, in effect, is to conceive of the economy as being one huge production unit turning out goods for sale to consumers, business firms, and the government. GNP is the market value of the goods produced by this one "firm."

When we consider GNP in this manner, it can be seen that it has another interpretation. GNP can be viewed as the total income earned by members of the economy. All of the $30,000 of gross national product of our simplified economy is income to someone. Much of it will accrue to workers as wages and salaries for their efforts in manufacturing the cars. Some of the $30,000 will probably be paid as interest to banks and other institutions that have lent the funds needed to finance production of the automobiles. Some of it may be paid to owners of buildings rented to carry on production of the cars. Some of the sales revenue will accrue to the "firm" in the form of depreciation to compensate for capital equipment used up or worn out in production. Some of the $30,000 will probably have to be paid in taxes to the government, and if anything is left over, it belongs to the stockholders who own the "firm."

The claims on the $30,000 revenues of the economy are exhaustive—every penny is part of the income of someone in the economy. When we analyze it in this manner, we may speak of the output of the economy as "gross national income." The important point is that in any year, gross national product and gross national income are exactly the same.

Gross national product in the United States in 1981 was $2.9 trillion. This can be looked at as the sum of the expenditures for final goods and services by consumers, by business firms, and by the government, and net expenditures for our goods by foreigners.[2] The breakdown of GNP in this manner is shown in the left-hand side of Table 24-1. We can also look at this total of $2.9 trillion as the total of income accruing to various types of income recipients. This is shown in the right-hand side of Table 24-1.

Because gross national product includes allowances for depreciation, it does not give us a good measure of the net output of the economy; some of the output as measured by GNP must be used to replace equipment that is wearing out. In order to obtain some measure of the net gain to the economy during the year, it may be desirable to exclude depreciation allowances from our measure of output. The resulting figure is called *net national product* (NNP = GNP − Capital consumption allowances).

It is often desirable to analyze national output in terms of returns to the basic factors of production: land, labor, and capital. This measure of national output is called *national income*; it consists of wage and salary income, profits of unincorporated enterprises, corporate profits, rental income received, and net interest

---

[2] Net in the sense that we must subtract the amount of expenditures by Americans for foreign goods and services.

TABLE 24-1
Gross National Product and Income 1981
(in billions of dollars)

Personal consumption expenditures	1,858	Compensation of employees	1,772
Gross private domestic investment	451	Income of unincorporated businesses	134
Net exports of goods and services	24	Rental income of persons	32
Government purchases of goods and services	589	Corporate profits	189
		Net interest received	215
		Indirect business taxes and business transfer payments	257
		Capital consumption allowances	321
Gross national product	2,922	Gross national income	2,922

Note: Indirect business taxes are all tax payments made by business firms except taxes on net income (which are included in corporate profits). Excise taxes, for example, are included in consumer expenditures, but are then paid to the government without becoming part of anyone's income. Deficits of government enterprises and subsidies paid by the government are treated as deductions from indirect business taxes. Business transfer payments consist mainly of gifts of business firms to charitable institutions. The figures for corporate profits include an adjustment to eliminate inventory profits.

Source: Department of Commerce, Office of Business Economics.

received. Alternatively, it can be defined in this way:

$$NI = NNP - (\text{Indirect business taxes} + \text{Business transfer payments} + \text{Statistical discrepancy})$$

National income thus is the income earned (before income taxes) by the factors of production in turning out net additions to the goods and services of the economy during the year. *Personal income* is the current income received by people from all sources, inclusive of transfer payments from government and business but exclusive of transfers among people. It excludes income earned but not received during the year. An example of the difference between national income and personal income can be seen in the treatment of corporate profits. The total of corporate profits is included in national income. Personal income includes only that part of corporate profits that the stockholder actually receives—that is, dividends paid. The part of corporate profits paid to the government in the form of income taxes and the amount retained by the corporation are not included in personal income. In addition, that portion of wages withheld for Social Security taxes is not included in personal income but is part of national income.

On the other hand, certain income receipts that have not been earned during the current year are included in personal income (although not in national income). Social Security benefits, unemployment compensation, and veterans' benefits are examples of the latter category. In formal terms:

Personal income = NI + Transfer payments − (Corporate profits not paid out to stockholders + Contributions for social insurance)

One further national-income concept is frequently useful in analyzing consumer expenditures. Personal income measures the income that people receive, but this does not tell us how much they have available to spend, because personal taxes must be paid out of this income. *Disposable income* is a measure of the amount received that is available to be disposed of after payment of taxes. Thus:

Disposable income = Personal income − Personal taxes

Disposable income is clearly the concept most closely related to consumer expenditure decisions. In terms of the overall level of business activity, GNP is probably the best measure. In any case, all these measures of national output vary from year to year in roughly the same way.

Although the actual measurement and reporting of output involves many detailed adjustments, for analytical purposes the important thing to grasp is the fundamental identity between a nation's output and its factor income. The value of factors' income is totally derived from the value of what they produce. Net of depreciation on existing capital, this is called *net national product* and is the same as the nation's income.

NOMINAL AND REAL OUTPUT

In comparing movements of national output over time, we must recognize that those movements can come from both changes in the amounts of goods and services produced and changes in the prices at which they are sold. It is desirable to separate these two components so that we can know what is happening to the physical output of goods and service. When output is stated in terms of the prices that prevailed at the time, this is called the "nominal" measure. When movements in output, as distinct from price changes, are reported, these are called "real" measures.

If money were serving its unit-of-accounting function ideally, we would not have to concern ourselves with this adjustment. But the inflation of the last decade has rendered the dollar a rather imperfect unit of account. It has become increasingly important to distinguish nominal from real, and the techniques that are available for doing this are far from perfect.

When output data are gathered, they are in terms of expenditures at prices prevailing at the time, $P \times Q$, where P stands for price and Q for quantity. If we wish to compare GNP in two separate years, we would like to standardize the measure for a single price. For this purpose, price data are separately gathered on a sample basis, and later-year data are "deflated" to earlier-year prices, with 1972 currently used as the reference year. Thus, "constant-dollar GNP" series are reported in terms of 1972 prices. For any component of GNP, the calculation is as follows:

$$\frac{1980 \text{ expenditures}_{1980 \text{ prices}}}{\text{Price index}_{1980/1972}} = 1980 \text{ expenditure in } 1972 \text{ prices}$$

Suppose expenditures are 500 and prices have risen 80 percent. Then expenditures in 1972 prices are 500 divided by 1.80, or 278.

In nominal terms, GNP went from \$2.41 trillion in 1979 to \$2.63 trillion in 1980. But in real terms, it was essentially unchanged. Expressed in 1972 dollars, GNP was \$1.48 trillion in both years.

Separate price indexes are used for different categories of goods in GNP. A composite of all these indexes is called the *GNP deflator*. Since this composite index includes all goods purchased in the economy, it differs from the more widely used Consumer Price Index, which better serves the purpose of measuring the effect of price changes on consumer purchasing power.

Although the deflation technique gives us a way of estimating real movements, we must recognize that it is an estimation only. As rates of inflation have increased, our ability to measure the economy and its changes has lessened.

DETERMINANTS OF NATIONAL INCOME

The expenditure approach to gross national product is summarized in this definition:

$$Y = C + I + G + F$$

where Y = Gross national product
$\quad C$ = Personal consumption expenditure
$\quad I$ = Gross private investment
$\quad G$ = Government expenditures on goods and services
$\quad F$ = Net foreign investment (roughly, the excess of our exports over our imports)

For the present, we will not consider F, analysis of which will wait for Chapter 31. The omission at this point is not serious, since, for the United States, net foreign investment is a very small part of gross national product. This omission does not affect the analysis, even though international considerations play an important role in monetary-policy deliberations. We will concentrate then on analysis of C, I, and G.

Consumption

Probably the most important factor influencing the level of a person's consumption expenditures is the level of that person's income. Many complications set in when we try to spell out this relationship precisely, but it is clear that on the average, the person with an annual income of $20,000 will spend more on consumer goods during the year than a person with a $10,000 income. This relationship between income and consumption is called the *consumption function*. It can be generalized to apply to an economy as well as to an individual. Again, if a country has a high national income, we would expect consumption to be higher than if income were low. Probably the most logical income concept to connect with consumption is disposable income, but since disposable income and gross national product vary over time in a very similar manner, it is possible to look at the relationship between consumption and GNP. In recent years, consumption has averaged about 63 percent of GNP and about 92 percent of disposable income.

It would be very helpful if the economic analyst could count on the fact that consumption would be 92 percent of disposable income. Thus, if we could forecast accurately the level of income at a given time, we would have a good estimate of consumption expenditures in the months ahead. Unfortunately, factors other than current income affect consumption.

People's expectations about future prices (inflation expectations) clearly play a role in the consumption decision. In the 1960s and early 1970s, inflation seemed to cause people to consume less so that they would have funds to buffer themselves against future prices rises. This was the attitude expressed in household surveys and was confirmed by aggregate data. With the acceleration of inflation in the mid-1970s, attitudes changed; people increased their purchases of goods in order to buy them before prices rose still further. This has been the historical reaction to hyperinflation in other countries.

The size of liquid-asset holdings also exerts some influence on consumption expenditures. If I had $20,000 in the bank and $200,000 in securities, I could spend my entire current income (or even more than my income) without being greatly concerned. If I have no liquid assets, I must manage to keep consumption expenditures equal to or less than my income.

This factor became significant at the end of World War II, when many economists incorrectly forecast a depression on the basis of the decline in defense expenditures. Part of their mistake lay in ignoring the effect on consumer expenditures of the huge amount of liquid assets (cash, savings deposits, and government bonds) that people had built up during the war period, in which earnings were high and many consumer goods were unobtainable.

Apart from this unusual situation, it is difficult to assess the practical importance of this "wealth effect." It has played an important role in economic theory, however, particularly in monetary theory. The concept entered the economic literature as part of the debate over the Keynesian argument that the economy could remain in equilibrium with less than full employment. Professor Pigou had argued that in a world with fully flexible prices, unemployment would result in price decreases. This would mean that the real value of money held by consumers would increase; they would respond to this increase in their real wealth by spending more, and this increased spending would restore the economy to full employment.

This effect plays a major role in modern versions of the quantity theory and in the portfolio approach to monetary theory. In the modern quantity theory, an increase in the money supply exerts its effects by increasing consumers' cash balances above the amount they desire to hold. They restore the desired balance in their portfolios of assets by spending some of the excess cash balances. This spending stimulates the economy (and not just prices, as in the early versions of the quantity theory).[3]

Past income may in many cases be as important a factor in determining the level of consumption expenditures as current income. The family whose income has suddenly jumped from $9,000 per year to $15,000 will probably spend less than the family whose income has fallen from $20,000 to $15,000.[4] In other words, the consumer's view of his "normal" income may be more important in a given period than his actual income. Several economists in recent

---

[3] It should be noted that Keynes was not unaware of this concept. In this analysis, however, a consumer finding himself with cash balances beyond what he planned to hold would put the excess in bonds or other securities. Thus the whole effect would be felt in the bond market, not in the market for goods and services.

[4] Eventually, of course, it is expected that both families would adjust to their new level of income.

years have devoted considerable attention to this concept of "permanent income" in attempting to explain consumer behavior.

Because the relation between income and consumption is rather clear, for the remainder of these chapters we will assume that consumption depends only upon the current level of income. The reader should keep in mind that this is an oversimplification, and that the consumption function does depend in part on the other factors discussed in the preceding paragraphs.

The Propensity to Consume. The concept of average propensity to consume (APC) refers to the percentage of income spent on consumer goods and services. Although the concept of *average* propensity to consume is a useful one, it has been found that the *marginal* propensity to consume is the analytically more important concept. The marginal propensity to consume is the ratio between a change in income and the associated change in consumption. Symbolically, the marginal propensity to consume, MPC, is equal to $\Delta C / \Delta Y$. Thus, from 1980 to 1981, disposable income increased from \$1,821.7 billion to \$2,015.8 billion, while consumption increased from \$1,672.8 billion to \$1,857.9 billion, and we could calculate MPC as 185/194, or 95 percent.

Related to these concepts are those concerning average and marginal propensity to *save*. Actually, the only alternatives available to a person with respect to his disposable income are either to spend it (consumption) or to save it. Thus, the percentage of income spent (APC) plus the percentage of income saved (APS) must equal 1. Likewise, out of any addition to one's disposable income, the only alternatives are consumption or saving. Thus, the marginal propensity to save and the marginal propensity to consume must also total 1: MPS + MPC = 1. These concepts can be examined geometrically in Figure 24-1.

The line OA, which forms a 45° angle with the base of the diagram, has a particular economic significance. At any point along that line, consumption and income are the same. In other words, OA is the consumption function that would exist if people always spent exactly 100 percent of their income. The line CC' shows an example of a more realistic consumption function. At very low levels of income, CC' is above OA, which means that people are spending more than their incomes. At higher levels of income, CC' is below OA, meaning that people are saving (not spending) some of their income. With the consumption function CC', income level OB can be called the consumer breakeven point. At this level of income, consumers are spending all their income—saving is zero.

The marginal propensity to consume is shown as the ratio of

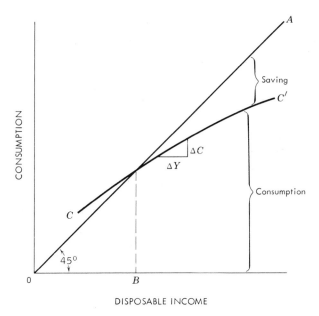

FIGURE 24-1 The Propensity to Consume

the increase in consumption to an increase in income. Geometrically, this amounts to saying that MPC is measured by the *slope* of the consumption function—that is, by $\Delta C / \Delta Y$. There is no reason to assume that MPC is constant at all levels of income. A lower income person is apt to spend a higher proportion of any additional income than a millionaire is. This is shown in Figure 24-1 as a "flattening out" of CC' at high levels of income.[5]

Investment

Investment spending is the second major component of GNP. We have discussed investments of commercial banks and other financial institutions in terms of purchases of securities. In analyzing national income, however, this sort of financial investment is not of direct concern. The type of investment expenditures we are concerned with here is spending for new capital goods. We are concerned with increases in our stock of plant and equipment, inventories, and housing. For purposes of national-income analysis, not

[5] It might be noted that for the country as a whole, this "flattening out" does not occur. Consumption represents about the same proportion of disposable income now as in earlier years. Either the consumption function is a straight line, or, more probably, it has shifted over time.

only are purchases of stocks and bonds omitted from consideration but also purchases of existing capital goods. The sale of a ten-year-old steel mill for $5 million may be an important transaction worthy of considerable space on the financial page, but it does not create as much income and employment as the construction of a new poolroom. The latter transaction will mean increased income for construction workers while the facility is being built; it will mean increased income for producers of cues, billiard balls, felt, chalk, and so forth. It will provide increased employment opportunities for people who want to work in a poolroom. It is hard to think of increased income resulting from transfer of ownership of the steel mill, except possibly for the broker arranging the sale.

Investment expenditures represent a much smaller portion of gross national product than does consumption. Nevertheless, probably more attention has been given to the behavior of investment expenditures than to the theory of consumption. There are two major reasons for this: First, investment is quite unstable. Domestic private investment expenditures fluctuate greatly from year to year. Second, some policy weapons are aimed at investment expenditures with a view to influencing the total amount of such expenditures.

In periods of severe depression, investment can fall to virtually zero. From 1929 to 1932, for example, consumption fell from $77.2 billion to $48.6 billion (a drop of 37 percent), while investment fell from $16.2 billion to $1 billion (a drop of 94 percent). The recessions of the last 25 years can be found in the investment statistics. In all of them, consumption expenditures actually increased from the preceding year, while investment spending declined.

This instability does not arise because of frivolous or erratic decisions on investment expenditures. The business firm considering purchase of a new $50,000 widget-forming machine is going to give careful analysis to the profitability of the purchase. The decision will be based on cold economic calculation, and the firm will probably not be swayed by the fact that the new machine comes in a wide choice of colors or has bigger tailfins than previous models.

A considerable literature has grown up on the proper technique to be followed by a firm in making investment decisions. This is not the place to analyze these techniques, but we can summarize part of the process briefly. First the firm must estimate the savings or additional income that will result from the new investment. These savings must be adjusted to allow for the fact that they will not all be garnered now but will accrue over a period of years. A dollar to be earned five years from now is not as valuable as a dollar in the hand now. These adjusted (or discounted) savings are then related to the purchase price of the machine or plant. Keynes has called the rate of return on the proposed investment the "marginal efficiency" of investment.[6]

The managers of the firm may find some investment projects on which they expect to earn a rate of return of 50 percent. There may be other proposed investments that may yield 20 percent, or 15 percent. There will probably be a great many projects that can reasonably be expected to yield 5 to 10 percent. We may represent the investment problem facing the firm graphically, as in Figure 24-2.

The schedule indicates that the firm has a small volume of potential investment expenditures that will yield relatively high rates of return. A large volume of investments will yield 5 percent or more, and a very large volume will yield 1 percent or more. The firm will have to decide on some cutoff point in its investment program, and this cutoff point will be related to the cost to the firm of capital to finance the proposed investment expenditures. If the firm can arrange financing at a cost of 5 percent, it is clearly desirable to go ahead with a project that is expected to yield a return of 25

[6] More precisely, the marginal efficiency of investment is that rate of discount that makes the present value of the net expected revenue from an investment equal to the cost of the investment.

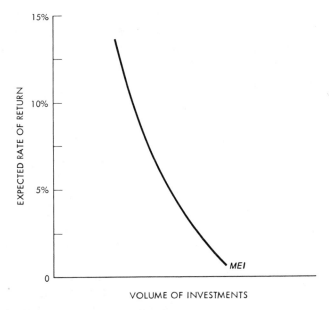

FIGURE 24-2 Marginal Efficiency of Investment

percent. It is clearly unprofitable to borrow at 5 percent for a project that is expected to have a yield of 3 percent. Thus, it is possible to relate the firm's investment expenditures to its marginal-efficiency-of-investment schedule and to the interest rate. By summing up investment plans for all firms in the economy, we can arrive at a national investment schedule that is a function of the interest rate. Thus, Figure 24-2 can be considered as an investment schedule for the economy as a whole.

Although the general outlines of this analysis are widely accepted, there is, as in the case of consumption expenditures, considerable dispute over the details. If the investment schedule is relatively "elastic" or sensitive to changes in interest rates, it implies that monetary policy affecting interest rates can have a considerable effect on investment expenditures. There are, of course, several different types of investment, with differing degrees of sensitivity to variations in interest rates. In general, long-lived projects tend to have high interest elasticities, in part because interest becomes a large portion of the total cost of such projects. We have already seen that interest costs are important in residential housing construction. On the other hand, interest costs may not play such an important role in decisions regarding investment in inventories.

Some analysts argue that since the investment schedule is based on *expected* returns, investment expenditures are more sensitive to changes in expectations than to changes in interest rates. In terms of Figure 24-2, this amounts to saying that it is not movements along the investment schedule that are important but shifts in the position of the curve itself.

Clearly, expectations are important in investment considerations, and businesspeople may at times be unduly optimistic or pessimistic. Thus, investment expenditures will fluctuate over a wider range than underlying economic conditions may warrant. To some extent, though, large investment projects (by public utilities, for example) are increasingly subjected to careful planning and analysis in which long-run considerations are paramount. To the extent that this is so, the possibilities of stabilization of investment expenditures through monetary-policy actions become more feasible.

Inflation and Investment. Inflation has greatly complicated long-run planning, and the uncertainties it introduces have probably made more uncertain the effect of any monetary policy on investment demand. It is sometimes thought that inflation encourages investment, because rising prices will increase the return on the investment by increasing the cash flow in future years. This kind of thinking involves money illusion, because the money flows in the future will have less purchasing power. Economic calculations should always be made in units of constant purchasing power.

But this is clearly difficult to do, since one does not know what inflation will be in future years. One way or another, however, inflation estimates are built into the investment decision because they enter into the market's determination of the rate of discount.[7] To further complicate the investment decision, price uncertainty has greatly reduced the willingness of lenders to extend credit at a fixed interest rate. Bank loans, commercial mortgages, and even some corporate bonds are now generally placed at variable rates. Until recent years, the entrepreneur knew with certainty the supply cost of the capital goods and the interest to be paid. Now only the supply cost is known. Both the future cash flows and the rate of interest must be estimated.

In addition to the problems of *expected* inflation, *realized* inflation may have a separate and distinct effect. The new investment project will carry a much higher supply cost of the capital goods than was paid by similar projects already in existence. If prices of the output of such investment projects have not caught up with replacement costs, the new project will be at a cost disadvantage. This seems to have been the case with, for example, rental housing units, where rental rates have not kept up with construction cost. Inflation may offer a possible encouragement to investment if it is felt that the market value of the capital good in question may rise more than the general price level. As inflation expectations mount, the public tends to flee financial assets and acquire real assets, driving up their price. Ultimately, a rising nominal rate of interest will bring equilibrium if monetary policy permits such rises.

On balance it would seem that inflation, with the necessarily high nominal interest rates it brings, would be a negative influence on investment. Certainly investment has not fared well in the inflation of the last decade, when its growth is analyzed in real terms. Other factors may have been responsible, but we ought minimally to be able to conclude that inflation gives no positive fillip to investment.

EQUILIBRIUM ANALYSIS

How will expenditures in one period compare with the income received in the preceding period? That is, will the level of national

---

[7]James Van Horne has pointed out that calculations will be biased against a proposed investment if expected price increases are embodied in the discount rate but are omitted from the cash-flow estimates. Van Horne, *Fundamentals of Financial Management*, 4th ed. (Englewood Cliffs, N.J.: Prentice-Hall, 1980), Chap. 14.

income remain constant, or will it increase or decrease? Is the current level of national income an optimal one—does it provide jobs for everyone who wants to work, while prices remain stable? The classical economists assumed that the economy would operate as if guided by an "invisible hand" so as to provide optimal levels of income, prices, and employment. Keynes, however, argued that free-market forces could not be depended upon to keep the economy in equilibrium at these levels.

To answer these questions, we must analyze the process by which the economy reaches an "equilibrium" level of income—a level that can be maintained if nothing happens to disrupt it. For our present purposes, it is probably adequate to consider this process only in its bare outlines. Our interest in this book is in money and monetary policy and their influence on the economy. Our analysis of the determination of the level of national income will only go far enough to enable us to trace the means by which monetary policy affects the economy. We will do this by making several assumptions that will simplify the analysis without greatly distorting it—at least in terms of the role of monetary policy. The interested reader can pursue the analysis in more advanced treatments that do without these assumptions.[8] One such simplification (which we will later do without) is that there are no taxes and no government expenditures. We will also assume that there are no foreign transactions in the economy. We can represent such a simplified economy by Figure 24-3.

In this simplified view of the economy, consumers receive income from business firms in the form of wages, interest, rent, and dividends. They spend most of this income on consumer goods, and whatever is spent reenters the income stream and is received by business firms that, in turn, pass it back to income recipients. There are two breaks in this otherwise closed system. First, consumers need not spend all their income. Saving is seen in the diagram as a drain from the spending stream. The higher saving is, the lower the income of business firms, and thus the less they have to pass on to income recipients in the next period. Another break in the circular flow occurs when business firms make investment expenditures. A firm may not only pay out to income recipients its sales receipts (after making payments for goods purchased), but may perhaps build a new factory. People working on construction of the factory will receive wage and salary income. The firm will pay interest on money borrowed to finance the construction, and the construction

---

[8] See the list of selected references at the end of this chapter.

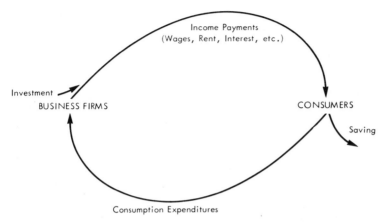

FIGURE 24-3 The Circular Flow of Income

firm will probably make a profit that accrues to its stockholders. All this additional income tends to enlarge the income stream.

This illustrates how saving tends to reduce the size of the income stream while investment tends to increase the level of national income. As long as these two forces are equal, the level of national income will remain unchanged. If investment is greater than saving, income will tend to rise. If saving is greater than investment, income will tend to fall.

We are using the terms *saving* and *investment* in the sense of *desired* or *planned* saving and investment. These plans may not be carried out. I may plan to save $1,000 next year out of an income of $20,000, but if my income turns out to be less than $20,000, I will probably save less than I planned. The owner of a small clothing store may plan to invest $10,000 in increased inventory during the year, but if his sales are less than expected, he may find that his inventory has increased by more than $10,000. Obviously this is not an equilibrium situation—he will compensate for this by planning to invest less in the following period. Equilibrium can result only when *planned saving* is equal to *planned investment*.

It is worth noting that *actual* investment and *actual* saving are always equal. This simply follows from the definitions of saving and investment we have adopted. Omitting consideration of government operations and net foreign investment, we have defined national income as $Y = C + I$. This means that $I = Y - C$. We have also defined savings as that part of income that is not spent; that is, $S = Y - C$. Since investment and saving are equal to the same thing $(Y - C)$, they are equal to each other. In an accounting sense, then, saving and investment are always equal. That is, if we examine the national income accounts of the United States for 1935 or 1985, we will always find that saving and investment are equal. The level of national income is in equilibrium, however, only when *planned* saving and investment are equal.

The relation between saving and investment in the determination of the level of national income can be seen in Figure 24-4. *OA* is drawn at a 45° angle to the base of the figure to represent the locus of all points at which income, measured on the horizontal axis, is equal to expenditures, measured on the vertical axis. Any point on *OA* is equidistant from the horizontal and vertical axes. We know that in equilibrium, total expenditures will be equal to total income. If total expenditures are greater than total income, income will be higher in the following period. If expenditures are less than income, income will be lower in the following period.[9] Thus we know that the equilibrium position must lie somewhere on this 45° line, *OA*.

The consumption line *CC'* shows the amount of consumption at various levels of income. In general, of course, we expect this line to rise to the right—consumption is higher at higher levels of income.

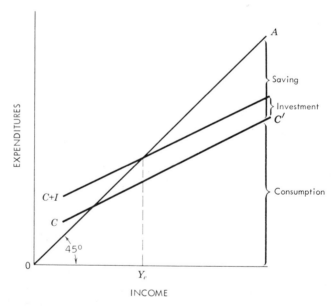

FIGURE 24-4   Determination of the Level of National Income

[9] This can easily be seen in the circular-flow diagram, Figure 24-3. If the total of consumption and investment expenditures is greater than income, then income will be higher in the next "round."

The distance between the consumption line and the 45° line shows the amount of saving.[10] CC' has been drawn so that saving increases as income increases—the result we would consider normal.

We introduce investment into this diagram by simply adding the amount of investment expenditures planned at each level of income to the amount of consumption expenditure. The distance between the $C + I$ line and the consumption schedule is drawn as a constant amount, indicating that the same amount of investment will be undertaken at all levels of income. This may not be realistic, but no harm is done to the theory by making this assumption.

The equilibrium level of national income is Y_e, the level corresponding to the point where the $C + I$ schedule crosses the 45° line. This point has particular economic significance. It is the only point at which saving and investment are equal. Investment is the difference between the consumption line and the $C + I$ line. Saving is the difference between the consumption line and the 45° guide line. Thus, saving and investment are equal only when the $C + I$ line is the same as the 45° line. The only point at which they are the same is at the income level Y_e. Thus the equilibrium level of income is Y_e, the only level of income at which saving and investment are equal. Once the economy is at that level of income, unless there are disrupting factors, the level of national income will tend to remain there.

DISEQUILIBRIUM

Our analysis of the determination of the equilibrium level of national income has made no mention of the level of employment. Keynes's analysis, he said, showed that the economy could be in equilibrium at a level of income that might correspond to much less than full employment. In Figure 24-5, the full-employment level of national income might be Y_f, although the equilibrium level is Y_e. It is clearly desirable that some action be taken that would tend to raise the level of income in the economy. To put the policy problem in geometric terms, we must raise the $C + I$ line so that it crosses the guide line at the full-employment level of income, Y_f. This could be done by increasing investment expenditures or by increasing consumption expenditures. Since consumption is relatively stable, it may be more feasible to think about the possibilities of raising

[10] See Figure 24-1.

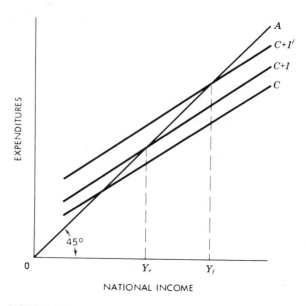

FIGURE 24-5 The Deflationary Gap

investment expenditures.[11] Our analysis of investment and the MEI schedule has indicated that a lowering of interest rates may tend to increase investment, thus wiping out the "deflationary gap."

It is just possible that our equilibrium level of national income may be above the full-employment level of income. Obviously, we cannot have more goods and services produced in the economy than the amount that can be produced at full employment. If income is higher than the full-employment level of income, it can only be higher in a monetary sense—that is, through higher prices. Since inflation is undesirable, our policy problem now is the lowering of total expenditures (consumption plus investment) so as to lower the equilibrium level of income to the full-employment level. Again, one way of doing this is by affecting interest rates, but this time we want to raise interest rates so as to lower investment.

[11] In a more complete situation, where we allow for government taxes and expenditures, our policy possibilities are greatly increased. We could raise the level of expenditures directly by having the government spend more, or we could reduce taxes so as to encourage business investment or to make consumption expenditures rise in response to the higher level of disposable income. These measures are a part of fiscal policy.

THE MULTIPLIER

If it is desired to change the level of investment expenditures so as to bring the equilibrium level of income up to (or down to) the full-employment level, it is important to know how great a change in investment is necessary. Suppose, for example, the full-employment level of income is $20 billion higher than the equilibrium level. How great an increase in investment is desired in this case? At first glance it may appear that a $20 billion increase is in order. The concept of the *investment multiplier* shows that this large an increase is not necessary.

The effect of an increase in investment expenditures can be seen easily if we turn back to our circular-flow diagram (Figure 24-3). If investment expenditures increase, this will mean a direct increase in income. We have already noted how a decision to build a new factory means increased income to construction workers, suppliers of building materials, and so forth. These people will spend some of their increased income. The amount they spend will be determined by their MPC. Thus, an increase in investment expenditures of $10 million means an immediate $10 million increase in income. But perhaps $7 million of this additional income will be spent on additional consumption goods (if an MPC of 70 percent is assumed). This means that in the next period, incomes will be $7 million higher (if investment expenditures are maintained at their new level). In the next period, an additional $4.9 million will be spent on consumer goods (70 percent of $7 million), and thus incomes will be increased by another $4.9 million.

Income will continue to increase for many periods, but this process does not go on without limit. We have already seen that the additional consumption expenditures induced by the original investment expenditure become smaller and smaller as time goes on. The first increase in consumption was $7 million. In the next period, it was $4.9 million. In the third, it would be $3.43 million (70 percent of $4.9 million), and by the tenth period, it would be a very small amount.

The multiplier is the relation between an increase in investment expenditures and the increase in income resulting from this increase in investment. Symbolically, then, the multiplier equals $\Delta Y / \Delta I$. Clearly, the value of the multiplier depends upon the marginal propensity to consume. If the MPC is low, increased income resulting from the increase in investment will have little effect on consumption, and thus the total increase in income will be small. If the MPC is high, the initial increase in income will be nearly all spent, and thus the total increase in income will be large. It turns out that the multiplier, m, is equal to 1/MPS.[12] Thus, if the MPC is ¾, the MPS is ¼, and m = 1/¼, or 4.

The multiplier process is shown graphically in Figure 24-6. A small increase in investment raises the $C + I$ line to $C + I'$. The increase in investment is simply the distance between these two lines. Income increases by a much larger amount—the distance from Y_1 to Y_2. The reason for this greater increase is seen in the effect on total expenditures. The total increase in expenditures is the distance BA. Only BI represents the increase in investment, and the remainder, AI, represents the increase in consumption induced by the increase in investment.

Economists of the 1930s seized upon the multiplier concept with much enthusiasm. It was hoped that the multiplier could be used with precision to solve the difficult problems of economic policy. That is, if the level of national income is $30 billion less than the full-employment level, and we know through empirical research that the multiplier is 3, then all we have to do is increase investment (or government expenditures) by $10 billion, and our recession is over. Unfortunately, the real world is more complex than our simple economic model.

---

[12] We can derive the formula for the multiplier as follows:
Since

$$Y = C + I, \qquad \Delta Y = \Delta C + \Delta I$$

Dividing both sides of the equation by ΔI, we get:

$$\frac{\Delta Y}{\Delta I} = \frac{\Delta C}{\Delta I} + 1$$

$\Delta C / \Delta I$ can be rewritten without changing its values as:

$$\frac{\Delta C}{\Delta Y} \frac{\Delta Y}{\Delta I}$$

Substituting this back in the previous equation, we get:

$$\frac{\Delta Y}{\Delta I} = \frac{\Delta C}{\Delta Y} \frac{\Delta Y}{\Delta I} = 1$$

Rearranging the equation, we get:

$$\frac{\Delta Y}{\Delta I} - \frac{\Delta C}{\Delta Y} \frac{\Delta Y}{\Delta I} = 1, \quad \text{or} \quad \frac{\Delta Y}{\Delta I} \left(1 - \frac{\Delta C}{\Delta Y}\right) = 1$$

Dividing by $1 - (\Delta C / \Delta Y)$, we get:

$$m = \frac{\Delta Y}{\Delta I} = \frac{1}{1 - \Delta C / \Delta Y}$$

But $\Delta C / \Delta Y$ is the MPC, and $1 - \text{MPC} = \text{MPS}$. Therefore:

$$m = \frac{1}{1 - \text{MPC}}, \quad \text{or} \quad m = \frac{1}{\text{MPS}}$$

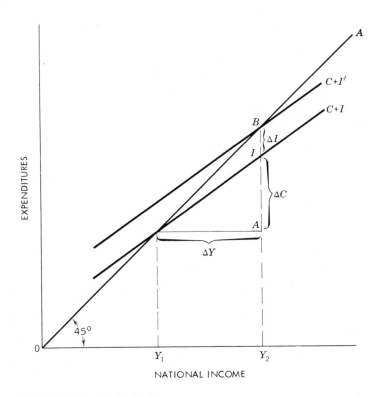

FIGURE 24-6 The Multiplier

Probably every sentence in our exposition of the workings of the multiplier should have been qualified with the statement, "other things remaining the same." This is fine for the purpose of explaining the multiplier concept, but in the actual operations of the economic system, conditions have a habit of not remaining the same. The MPC is certainly not a constant figure; it varies not only over time but among different groups in the economy. Thus, it becomes very difficult to attempt to apply the multiplier concept literally to problems of economic policy. Nevertheless, it is clear that the multiplier concept is still useful. It helps point out relationships that are significant and indicates at least the direction of response that is likely to follow various actions, even if it cannot be used to predict accurately.

FISCAL POLICY

The complete determination of equilibrium output must also incorporate the activities of government in its spending and taxation.

Governments—federal, state, and local—purchase goods and services, and these purchases are a part of national product, as shown in Table 24-1. Government purchases usually account for a little more than 20 percent of GNP. Like consumption and investment, output of goods and services for governments also leads to a flow of income exactly equal to the value of the output.

In addition to spending for output, governments also make *transfer* payments to the private economy. Nearly one-half of federal-government outlays are transfers, such as payments for Social Security, unemployment compensation, aid to farmers, and interest on the national debt. Although these payments are not a part of GNP, indirectly they will affect GNP because they are treated as income by the recipients, whose spending will be affected accordingly.

In analyzing equilibrium output, government expenditures can be treated in much the same manner as investment. We could, in fact, draw a diagram similar to Figure 24-4, with another line above the $C + I$ line, to be labeled $C + I + G$. The distance between the $C + I$ line and the $C + I + G$ line would represent government expenditures, and the equilibrium level of income would be determined by the intersection of the $C + I + G$ line and the 45° line.

It is apparent from the nature of government expenditures that an increase in such expenditures, other things being equal, will tend to raise the level of national income, whereas a decrease in government spending will cause a decrease in national income. The effect will not be on a one-to-one basis; government expenditures have multiplier effects also.

Taxes do not directly enter into GNP, but like transfer payments, they effect the expenditures of those who pay them. A rise in tax rates will tend to lower the consumption curve, because people will have less disposable income out of which to make their consumption decisions. Taxes may also lower the investment curve, as they reduce the after-tax cash flow from the investment.

Fiscal policy refers to the use of government expenditures and taxation to affect economic activity. Although fiscal effects are similar for all government units, it is almost exclusively the federal government that employs fiscal policy for the purpose of its national economic effects. Thorough discussion of fiscal policy is beyond the scope of this volume, and the brief space devoted to it is not to be taken as an indication of the relative merits or importance of fiscal versus monetary policy as stabilization techniques.

Economists have long been intrigued with the possibilities of varying government expenditures from one period to the next in a countercyclical manner. In a period of severe unemployment, the government would increase its expenditures; in a period of inflation, the government would decrease its expenditures. To some extent, this happens automatically. When we are in a recession with large numbers of unemployed, government expenditures to aid the unemployed naturally increase. It is when we try to push counter-cyclical spending beyond these automatic actions, however, that we encounter difficulties.

One important problem relates to time lags.[13] Once we are in a recession, or heading into one, it takes time to recognize the situation. Time is required to plan government projects that would call for additional spending. Time elapses while Congress approves the new program and while the program is put into effect. By the time all steps have been taken, the recession may be over, and, in fact, we may now be in a period of inflation in which sound policy actually calls for a decrease in government spending. It is true also that once a project is started, it becomes very difficult to stop. It would not be very feasible to stop construction of a huge dam because the recession was over.

It has been suggested that Congress approve certain projects in advance. Then, in time of recession, administrative action (perhaps initiated by the president) would be all that is required to get the program under way. Congress, however, has not been willing to go along with proposals that involve giving up some of its control over spending programs.

Another difficulty with the idea of timing government expenditures to increase during periods of poor business is that this policy might mean postponing some immediately desirable programs until a period of recession that may be years in the future. If we need new schools, hospitals, and highways now, it is not desirable to wait for a time in which the demands of the private sector of the economy on our resources are reduced. It is not logical that the public needs of the economy must always be subordinated to private demands.

Since there are shortcomings in the policy of using variations in government expenditures to stabilize the economy, another type of fiscal policy would involve variation in tax policy as a stabilization device. Again, the basic idea is simple enough. If taxes are reduced, people will have more disposable income out of a given level of national income, and thus consumption expenditures should rise. If business taxes rather than personal taxes are reduced, this may have an upward effect on business investment expenditures. In a period of inflation, the opposite steps could be taken—an in-

---

[13] Monetary policy also involves lags, which are discussed in Chapter 26.

crease in taxes would tend to reduce consumer, and perhaps business, spending.

Because of the framework of our present tax structure, some of these desirable steps occur automatically. Since most people pay taxes on a withholding basis, any drop in incomes and employment automatically means a decrease in taxes paid. This is true not only of income taxes but Social Security taxes as well. Moreover, since we have a progressive income tax system (higher-income earners pay taxes at higher rates than low-income earners), the reduction in taxes paid is more than proportional to the drop in income. Thus, for example, if I suffer a 20 percent drop in my income, my tax payments may drop 30 percent. These built-in stabilizing effects of personal taxes also apply to corporate taxes. As corporate income fluctuates, so do corporate tax payments. The corporation that suffers a loss pays no taxes, and thus may be as willing and as able to undertake an investment program as a firm that operated at a profit.

These automatic stabilizers are important to the economy. One study indicated that in the period 1966–1969, when the economy was at full employment and in a state of excess demand, automatic fiscal policy held back 55–78 percent of the rise in aggregate demand that would otherwise have taken place.[14] In the 1973–1975 recession, these stabilizers prevented 33–39 percent of the decline in real output that would otherwise have occurred. The stabilizers are less effective in an inflation-recession combination, because rising money incomes continue to bring in increased taxation.

Everyone agrees that these built-in stabilizers are a desirable aspect of fiscal policy. It is when discussion turns to discretionary aspects of taxation policy that disputes arise. The U.S. record with respect to use of discretionary fiscal policy as a countercyclical device has not been very impressive. Until the Kennedy administration, American presidents had always paid at least lip service to the desirability of having a balanced federal budget. Obviously, if the budget is to be balanced each year, the scope of fiscal policy is not very great. President Kennedy's strong support for a tax cut during the early 1960s—despite the budget deficit—was a significant breakthrough in economic policy. The tax cut of 1964 was an economic success, despite the failure of the Johnson administration to follow up with a tax increase as Vietnam costs increased.

Fiscal policy was overexpansionary in the later 1960s and has been blamed by many as the origin of the inflation of the last decade

[14] Ansel M. Sharp and Mohammad Khan, "Automatic Fiscal Policy, 1966–1975," *Nebraska Journal of Economics and Business*, Summer 1980.

(see Chapter 30). Regardless of the blame for the inflation, fiscal policy aimed at aggregate demand is ill-equipped to deal with an existing inflation when it is coupled with relatively high levels of unemployment. Thus, the Reagan administration emphasized fiscal measures for long-run "supply-side" responses—tax reductions to increase capital formation and work incentives (see Chapter 26). On the demand side, the call was for a return to a balanced budget at a lower level of spending and taxing. Thus there was no fiscal policy response to the 1981–1982 recession, other than some built-in tax reductions enacted before knowledge of the recession's onset.

QUESTIONS

1 What happens to the GNP if an automobile manufacturer merges with a steel company? What happens when a person retires on Social Security benefits?
2 What factors determine the amount of your consumption expenditures?
3 What is Say's Law? Is it valid in our economy? Would it be valid in a barter economy?
4 Why is the average propensity to consume generally higher than the marginal propensity to consume?
5 What is the "deflationary gap"?
6 "Velocity is impressively stable over cycles by comparison with the multiplier." Is this true? If so, what are the implications of this fact for the merits of the quantity theory relative to the income-expenditure approach?
7 "Since consumption is the largest part of national product, policy measures aimed at stabilizing the economy should focus on consumption expenditures rather than investment or government spending." Do you agree?
8 Is saving the same thing as investing? Is it correct to say that the function of financial institutions is to make investment equal to savings in the economy?

SELECTED READINGS

BIERMAN, HAROLD, JR., and SEYMOUR SMIDT, *The Capital Budgeting Decision*, 4th ed. New York: Macmillan, 1975. Recommended for a detailed exposition of the investment planning process. See especially Chapter 16, "Capital Budgeting and Inflation."
BOORMAN, JOHN T., and THOMAS HAVRILESKY, *Money Supply, Money Demand, and Macroeconomic Models*. Boston: Allyn & Bacon, 1972. An excellent combination of text and readings.

FRIEDMAN, MILTON, *A Theory of the Consumption Function*. New York: National Bureau of Economic Research, Inc., 1957.

KEYNES, JOHN M., *The General Theory of Employment, Interest, and Money*. New York: Harcourt, Brace & World, 1936.

MUSGRAVE, RICHARD, and PEGGY MUSGRAVE, *Public Finance in Theory and Practice*, 3rd ed. New York: McGraw-Hill, 1980.

PETERSON, WALLACE, *Income, Employment, and Economic Growth*, 4th ed. New York: W.W. Norton, 1978.

ROBINSON, JOAN, *Introduction to the Theory of Employment*. London: Macmillan, 1956. A very clear, simple analysis of national income theory.

ROUSSEAS, STEPHEN, *Monetary Theory*. New York: Knopf, 1972.

25

The Rate of Interest

The analysis in the preceding chapter did not give a complete theory of the determination of the level of national income. We can summarize the previous analysis symbolically as follows:

$$Y \longleftarrow \begin{cases} C \\ + \\ I \end{cases} \longleftarrow \begin{cases} MEI \\ \\ i \end{cases}$$

The level of national income is determined by consumption and investment. Consumption itself depends upon income, and investment is a function of the MEI schedule and the rate of interest. The next step in our analysis is to investigate the determination of the rate of interest.

In our discussion of the financial markets, we indicated that there are actually many interest rates in the economy. Economists generally find it convenient to speak of "the" interest rate, which can be conceived as a rough representation of the whole interest-rate structure. In this chapter, we will use this device of analyzing "the" interest rate—the typical or average interest rate.[1] The

[1] The interest rate is entirely separate from a compensation for risk. In order to measure a "pure" interest rate, the rate on federal-government securities is

reader should recognize that this is not thoroughly accurate; in later analysis of monetary policy, we will consider the more realistic situation in which there are many interest rates that may not all respond in the same way to a specific policy action.

The interest rate is the price of borrowing. It is the premium that must be paid by the borrower, who wants current purchasing power, to the lender, who surrenders current purchasing power. The interest rate quantifies society's time preference. Goods in the present are preferred over goods in the future. The rate of interest is the discount that is applied to future values to convert them to present values.

As with all economic calculations, a stable unit of account is needed. Ideally, the rate of interest should reflect the society's preference for real values in the present over some given real value in the future. But loans are made in money units of accounting, and the goods value of money changes. The *nominal* rate of interest expresses the society's time preference between future and present money without regard to the changing real value of money. There is no satisfactory method for converting the nominal rate to the real rate, although there is clearly such a concept. When inflation has become the expected course of events, it can be assumed that borrowers and lenders build such expectations into their loan contracts. Past price changes cannot be used as deflators because the interest rate links present values with the future, not the past. Lacking knowledge of people's expectations, we have no deflator to apply to the nominal rate.[2] Our discussion of the theory of interest is in terms of the nominal rate, but we shall consider how inflation may affect it.

CLASSICAL THEORY

In the classical system, the interest rate was determined by the supply of, and demand for, capital. This has been called a *real* theory of interest, because the interest rate does not depend in any way on monetary considerations. The supply of capital in this scheme is the

---

usually used as an indicator of rates in the economy. Government obligations are devoid of risk of repayment in money terms, since the government is the creator of legal-tender money.

[2] In fact, a reverse calculation is sometimes made. Assuming some "normal" real interest rate, a departure of existing rates from this normal rate is the measure of inflation expectations.

same thing as savings. People make capital available by abstention from consumption—by saving. The demand for capital consists basically of the demand by business firms for investment. Both saving and investment were considered to depend on the interest rate. The interest rate was the price of capital and the factor that made saving and investment equal in the classical system.

The investment schedule, as we have seen, slopes downward. At lower interest rates, business firms desire to invest more. The saving schedule in the classical system was generally described as rising with higher interest rates. The classical economists felt that if interest rates were high, people would save more than if they were low. I might indeed save a larger proportion of my income if I could obtain 15 percent return on my savings. However, the opposite result is also possible. Suppose I am saving to provide funds for a trip to Europe in five years. I will save a certain amount each year, so that with the accumulated interest on this fund, I will have enough to pay for the trip in five years. If interest rates should rise, I would now be able to accumulate the same amount by saving *less* each year (because the interest would amount to more). Thus, higher interest rates do not necessarily mean higher saving. Empirical studies that have been made of consumer behavior indicate that consumer saving is not very sensitive to changes in interest rates. That is, the saving schedule should probably be drawn as nearly vertical.

Figure 25-1 shows the determination of the rate of interest under the classical system and also shows what happens when there is a shift in one of the determinants of interest. The intersection of the S and I curves determines the interest rate, i. This is the equilibrium rate of interest because this is the only rate at which saving is equal to investment. Suppose now that people become more thrifty and decide to save a larger amount at every rate of interest. This downward (or rightward) shift of the savings schedule means that the interest rate will fall to i'. This is now the rate of interest at which investment is equal to saving (as shown by the new savings schedule). This is, of course, a reasonable result. We would normally expect that an increased desire to save would result in lower interest rates.

The classical theory of interest was very much a part of the whole classical scheme by which the economy was assumed to equilibrate at full employment. According to Say's law, supply creates its own demand. Whatever a full-employment economy produces, it generates just the purchasing power to buy this output. But what about those who choose to produce but not to

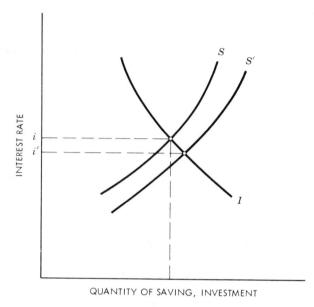

FIGURE 25-1 Classical Interest Theory

consume—to save? Here was where the theory of interest came in. Both saving and investment were considered highly responsive to the interest rate, and the rate of interest equilibrated investment with full-employment saving.[3]

The classical interest theory has a certain appeal. The society as a whole can substitute future value for present value only by capital formation. The true rate of interest obtained by a lender must ultimately relate to the rate of return for the substitution of capital goods for consumer goods. But still, interest rates fluctuate in loan markets, and there is really no such thing as a market for savings. The rate of interest is not the price for saving, but is more realistically thought of as the price for loans or credit. To tidy up this theory, the neoclassical economists developed the loanable-funds approach.

[3] Some reservations concerning the classical theory involve matters of definition rather than substance. How about interest on consumer credit and government borrowing? These borrowers are units in the economy that can be netted out to arrive at the society's desired excess of current income (including the portion paid in taxes) over current expenditures (including those of government). Consumer lending and consumer borrowing cancel out in the total. The loanable funds presentation below retains this netting-out procedure, although it is desirable for some purposes to put government borrowing and lending and consumer borrowing and lending separately in the demand and supply schedules.

THE LOANABLE-FUNDS THEORY

The neoclassical economists started with the classical formulation of interest theory and added additional factors to the analysis to make it better correspond with the actual operations of the economy. Their analysis focused on the concept of *loanable funds*. Interest is the price paid for the use of loanable funds. As in the classical system, the basic demand for loanable funds comes from businesses that want to invest; the basic supply of loanable funds comes from people who are saving some of their income. Other factors affecting interest equilibrium are hoarding and changes in the money supply. The government and the financial system can provide loanable funds without anyone in the economy increasing saving. This creation of money (ΔM) during the period is shown in Figure 25-2 as an addition to the supply of loanable funds. The money-supply definition must be confined to assets that are immediately spendable, because these are the only assets a borrower will accept. In the present system, these would consist of currency and transaction accounts. As in all supply–demand analysis, all other variables must be taken as given—prices, incomes, tastes, and so on.

Hoarding and dishoarding occur as money holders change their willingness to lend. This decision is distinct from saving and

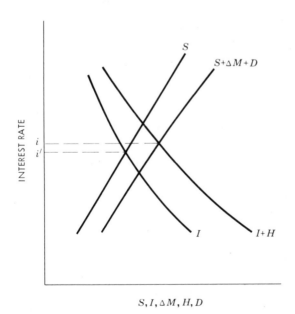

FIGURE 25-2 Loanable-Funds Theory

new-money creation. Hoarding is a desire to increase money balances. Dishoarding is a desire to decrease money holdings. Loanable funds is a flow concept, and thus in all cases we are looking at
desired changes, at each given interest rate, in a period of time.[4]
Figure 25-3 looks only at the hoarding-dishoarding component of
loanable funds. At any interest rate below 12 percent, the public
would choose to increase money balances. The lower the rate, the
greater this desire. The desired increases constitute hoarding, and
this is shown on the negative side of the axis in the sense that it
represents a reduction from the supply of loanable funds. At 12
percent, there would be no hoarding or dishoarding. At any rate
above 12, the public would choose to draw down money balances,
and this dishoarding would add to the supply of loanable funds.

In any given period, not everyone will behave the same with
respect to hoarding, even at the same interest rate. Hoarding-
dishoarding can be netted out, or they can be shown separately. We
have chosen to show them separately in Figure 25-3. All desired
dishoarding is added to the supply of loanable funds. All desired
hoarding is added to the demand. The equilibrium interest rate that
emerges is i. In the classical theory, without consideration of hoarding and money creation, the equilibrium would have been at i'.

LIQUIDITY PREFERENCE

Whereas the neoclassical loanable-funds theory built on the classical "real" theory, Keynes took a significantly different approach
to interest theory. Instead of analyzing interest as the price for
savings or for loanable funds, he considered interest as payment for
the use of *money*.

Keynes argued that consideration of saving and investment as
determinants of the interest rate not only was empirically unjusti-

---

[4] Hoarding is a case where confusion is often encountered between stocks and
flows, as discussed in the flow-of-funds analysis of Chapter 4. As in that chapter,
hoarding is here defined in terms of flows, because it is a desired change in holdings,
and hoarding-dishoarding cannot be inferred solely from the existence of stocks. If
you keep currency under the proverbial mattress and do not disturb it through the
1980s, you have neither hoarded nor dishoarded. If you increase your credit-union
transaction account tomorrow, you have hoarded, because you have chosen to increase your immediate purchasing power. Some analysts prefer to define hoarding
as a change in stock relative to a usual flow (e.g., increased holdings of sugar relative
to its usual consumption). The loanable-funds analysis is consistent with that definition. Any rise in desired money holding as shown on the graph is with income and
expenditures held constant. Thus, the ratio of desired money to income would rise in
desired money holdings.

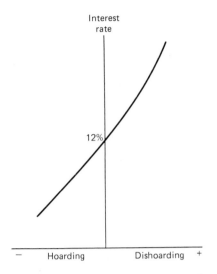

FIGURE 25-3 Hoarding and Dishoarding

fied but also involved a logical error. The classical and, to some extent, the loanable-funds economists treated saving and investment as two independent factors whose interaction determined the rate of interest. But, by means of the type of income analysis presented in the preceding chapter, Keynes argued that saving depends basically on income, and income in turn depends largely on investment. Thus, saving is very closely connected to investment, so we cannot treat these as two separate independent variables sufficient to determine the interest rate.

In Keynes' "liquidity-preference" analysis, interest was determined by two factors: the supply of money and the desire to hold money. Thus, while loanable funds is a *flow* analysis, Keynes's liquidity-preference theory is a *stock* analysis. As will be discussed later, most economists now believe this choice of stock versus flow is not of critical importance in the analysis. The primary difference among theorists lies in the importance they assign to each of the variables in the determination of the equilibrium rate.

The stock of money is largely taken as independent of the rate of interest and in our diagrams is drawn as a straight line up from the horizontal axis. The Federal Reserve sets targets for money growth, and in doing so, it is not responding to given interest rates. The money supply that is drawn is therefore the targeted money supply, independent of the rate of interest. Even though financial institutions pay interest on their transaction accounts, it is as-

sumed that because of the spread between interest paid and interest received, they have the incentive to acquire all they can. Even
if they are inclined to acquire more at higher rates of interest, the
Fed can compensate by supplying less reserves. It is on this basis
that we assume a money stock independent of the interest rate,
even though clearly, under other institutional arrangements, the
supply of money might very well have a positive slope.

Money Demand

With a given money stock, it is the interest rate that will equilibrate
to bring equality between the amount of money supplied and the
amount the economy demands. Let us look more carefully at the
demand for money. As always, the demand function is viewed with
reference to one variable (the market interest rate) with all other
variables given, including in this case the rate of interest on transaction deposits. When interest was not allowed on such deposits, the
deposit rate was implicitly assumed at zero. With interest allowed,
the deposit rate is assumed to be at some given positive level. (At a
more advanced level, we could assume that the deposit rate bore
some given relation to the market interest rate, but this more
complicated assumption would not change the basic thrust of the
analysis.)

At one level, the demand for money seems easy to explain.
After all, everyone would like to have more money. But is it really
more money that we want? Most people (other than misers) want
money for the sake of what they can buy with it. Aside from the
desire to have money to spend, money seems to be a rather unprofitable asset to hold. If, instead of money, a person holds government
bonds, the interest on the bonds will exceed the interest on money.
On the other hand, there is some risk involved in holding securities
rather than money. We have already seen that even very high-
quality securities (U.S. government bonds, for example) can fluctuate in price, and thus losses are possible. The problem of why
people want to hold money is more complicated than it appears at
first glance.

Keynes attacked the problem by distinguishing three different
reasons or motives for the holding of money. These are the "transactions," "precautionary," and "speculative" motives. The transactions motive for holding cash refers to the need of individuals and
business firms to hold cash for the sake of making payments. I carry
money in my pocket because I expect to buy a newspaper and lunch.
I maintain a checking account because I have monthly bills that

must be paid. A business firm needs currency in its cash register to make change and a balance in its checking account to pay for goods purchased, salaries, and so forth. We must hold cash because we continually make expenditures, whereas income is received only at specified intervals.

The amount of money people hold for transactions purposes depends on the dollar amount of expenditures they expect to make and on such factors as were mentioned in our discussion of velocity. Since the dollar amount of expenditures is closely related to our concept of national income, we can say that for the economy as a whole, the transactions demand for money depends upon the level of income.

The precautionary motive is the desire to hold money for emergencies that may or may not arise. Thus, when I leave my house in the morning I carry not only enough money to pay for my newspaper and my lunch, but also an additional amount to provide for unforeseen expenditures. It is difficult to express the precautionary motive as a function of any single variable, but it is certainly related in some way to income (the higher one's income, the more cash he may keep "for a rainy day"), and in some way to interest rates (if interest rates are very high, one may hold less cash for precautionary purposes and more earning assets).

At least part of the motive for holding money arises from expectations about the future course of interest rates. Suppose a man has some money not needed for transactions purposes. He may use this money to purchase government securities. If he does so, however, he takes the chance that bond prices will fall (interest rates will rise) and that he will suffer a capital loss. Someone who feels that a rise in interest rates is likely will prefer to hold cash rather than purchase securities. He is, in effect, speculating on bond prices.

This can be an expensive form of speculation. If interest rates are high, the holder of cash is forgoing substantial interest income in order to maintain his cash position. Thus, when interest rates are high, it is likely that the demand for money for speculative purposes will be small. When interest rates are low, however, this sort of operation looks more attractive. For one thing, if interest rates are low, the holder of cash is not losing much interest income. Second, and perhaps more important, if interest rates are low, they are apt to rise in the future, and thus holding cash is better than holding bonds, which are likely to decline in price. This demand for money, then, is a function of the interest rate, and therefore, the demand for money in Figure 25-4 is drawn as increasing with decreases in the interest rate.

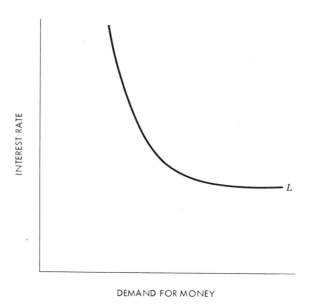

INTEREST RATE

DEMAND FOR MONEY

FIGURE 25-4 The Speculative Motive for Holding Money

Keynes suggested that at some very low level of interest rates, the demand for money could become "infinitely elastic"—horizontal in Figure 25-4.[5] This view is based on the belief that at some very low rate of interest, people would feel that it is preferable to hold money rather than securities because the risk of capital loss (through increase in interest rates) would outweigh the small amount of interest to be obtained from securities. Keynes called this flat section of the demand curve the "liquidity trap." As we shall see, the question of the existence of a "liquidity trap" has important implications for monetary policy.

The demand for money consists then of two basic parts: the transactions demand for money, which is a function of the level of income, and the speculative demand for money, which is a function of the interest rate. Each of these demands includes part of what Keynes called the precautionary demand. We can represent the former demand by the symbol L_t and the latter by L_L. The total demand for money, L, is equal to the sum of these two demands: $L = L_t + L_L$.

[5] Keynes was always careful to stress that this was a theoretical possibility only, and not a realistic description of the economy, even during the 1930s. In *The General Theory* (p. 207), he stated that "whilst this limiting case might become practically important in the future, I know of no example of it hitherto."

This analysis brings us very close to the loanable-funds theory. In this formulation of liquidity preference, the interest rate depends upon the supply of money and the demand for money. The demand for money is made up, in part, of the transactions demand, which depends upon income. Income, of course, depends upon saving and investment, and thus, even in the Keynesian approach to interest-rate theory, saving and investment are at least indirectly involved. Figure 25-5 shows the determination of the interest rate with this modified liquidity-preference theory.

In Figure 25-5 (A), L_t is shown as a vertical line. That is, the transactions demand for money does not depend upon the interest rate. The speculative demand for money, L_L, is added to the L_t curve to obtain the L curve. This curve intersects the supply of money M at interest rate i', which is the equilibrium rate of interest in this analysis.

In Figure 25-5 (B), we assume that the money supply remains unchanged, but the level of income is higher than in 25-5 (A). This means that the transactions demand for money is higher at all levels of the interest rate. When the same L_L curve is added to this higher L_t curve, we have a higher L curve. This new demand-for-money schedule (L') intersects the M schedule at a new higher rate of interest, i'. Thus, an increase in income (through increased investment expenditures), results in a higher rate of interest. This is exactly the same result we would obtain through the loanable-funds analysis.

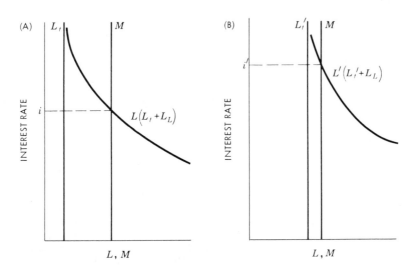

FIGURE 25-5 Liquidity Preference and Income

An increase in the desire to save would have just the opposite effect on interest rates. The increased desire to save would result in lower income, which would lower the demand for money for transactions purposes. This lower demand for money would mean that L and M would be equal at a lower rate of interest. Thus, as in loanable-funds theory, an increase in the desire to save results in a lowering of the interest rate.

Both loanable-funds theory and liquidity preference would lead us to expect that an increase in the money supply would result in a decrease in the rate of interest. In loanable funds, this would shift the supply curve to the right. How about a rise in the speculative demand for money?[6] By this we mean that at all interest rates, the public prefers to hold more money because of expectations that interest rates will rise. But an increased desire to hold money is hoarding, and the amount of the increase (the flow) would add to the demand for loanable funds.

As a result of a lengthy debate, most economists are now satisfied that, provided the terms are defined precisely and the time period specified, the loanable-funds theory and the liquidity-preference theory amount to exactly the same thing. By this we mean simply that they give the same result, although the process by which interest rates are thought to be determined may differ in the two approaches. If we gave a loanable-funds theorist all the information he desired regarding saving, investment, new-money creation, hoarding, and so forth, he could tell us what the interest rate would be. If we gave a liquidity-preference theorist all the information he desired regarding the money supply, demands for money, and income, he could also tell us what the rate of interest would be, and the result would be exactly the same as that of the loanable-funds theorist.

One advantage of liquidity preference is that it is more likely than loanable funds to force a complete analysis. Take the case of a

---

[6] Changes in the speculative demand (the hoarding function) can also be brought about by Federal Reserve action. As the Fed announces discount-rate changes or reserve-requirement changes, the market reassesses the future course of interest rates by its interpretation of the Fed action. This "announcement effect" may cause the speculative demand curve to shift and move interest rates in the desired direction even before the actual policy measure takes place. Similar results occur from the market's interpretation of money-supply changes, but these may not always be in the desired direction. Often the market interprets money-supply changes as being undesired by the Federal Reserve. If a rise is interpreted as undesired, the speculative demand is increased on the assumption that Fed will be taking subsequent action to reverse the money-stock rise. Thus, the announcement of the money rise becomes associated with a rise in interest rates, contrary to the result that would be expected from the money-stock rise alone.

government deficit. A loanable-funds approach might coax the analyst to a quick conclusion of higher interest rates from the increased government borrowing. A liquidity-preference theorist—and a more careful loanable-funds theorist—would have to inquire what caused the deficit and consider what other effects may be associated with it. Will saving rise because of reduced tax rates (if this was the cause of the deficit)? Will the transactions demand for money rise if the cause was increased government spending? Or did the deficit come from decreased investment spending (a negative effect on interest rates) that lowered national income and thus tax collections? In short, a deficit *per se* cannot be analyzed, and this is readily apparent in liquidity preference but not in loanable funds.

Nonmoney Intermediation

In both the loanable-funds and liquidity-preference theories, we defined money in terms of an immediately spendable asset, and under current conditions, the public's holdings of only currency and transaction accounts in financial institutions meet these conditions. This definition seems justified, particularly in the loanable-funds theory, on the grounds that borrowers require immediate purchasing power. But the difference between these narrowly defined money assets and a wide variety of other liquid assets, sometimes called "near money," is very small, and we must not conclude that other liquid assets have no effect on the rate of interest.

In general, we can conclude that the effect of near-money assets, other things being equal, will be to lower interest rates. An asset such as a savings deposit at a financial institution is a very close substitute for money, since it can, very quickly and with little inconvenience, be transformed into a transaction account. The same can be said for money-market mutual funds, which the holder can liquidate by writing a check. Since near-money is a close substitute for money, the more near-money there is, the less will be the demand for money. Thus, through the liquidity-preference theory, with an unchanged money stock (narrowly defined), the lower the demand for money, the lower the interest rate.

A similar conclusion is reached through the loanable-funds theory. If the public has a substitute for money that is preferred, usually because of its higher interest rate, then dishoarding will take place. Desired money balances will fall as the public reduces money and acquires the substitute. The intermediary has issued a liability of the form the public wants and has used the proceeds to acquire assets of the form that borrowers want. A lender who would be unwilling to lend to a mortgage borrower or a car buyer on credit is willing to lend to a financial institution, which in turn will make the loan. Intermediation, then, tends to lower interest rates, and any impediment to that process will tend to make interest rates higher than they would otherwise be. The continuing rise of near-money assets, and the continued creation of new kinds of such assets, has been a prominent feature of the American economy in the past three decades. Shortly after World War II, money by the narrow definition was about one-half of GNP. In 1980, it was less than one-sixth of GNP.

The Term Structure of Interest Rates

Our discussion of the speculative motive for holding money and, hence, of the crucial role of expectations in interest theory suggests the need to add to the discussion of yield curves introduced in Chapter 4. There we considered briefly some possible explanations of various shapes of yield curves. There are two major alternative approaches to the problem of accounting for differing yields on short- and long-term securities: the *expectations theory* and the *segmented-markets theory*.

The view that expectations regarding future interest rates are the principal determinant of the present structure of rates has long been popular among economists. It dates back at least to the work of Irving Fisher around the turn of the century. The theory holds that the long-term interest rate at any time represents the average of expected short-term interest rates. That is, the rate on five-year bonds is equal to the average of the present rate on one-year bonds plus the expected rate on one-year bonds one year hence, two years hence, and so on.

If this view is correct, the investor will receive the same net yield if he buys the five-year bond or if he buys a one-year bond and, when it matures, buys another one-year bond, and repeats the process for five years. This is easy to see, for example, if the current rate on bonds of all maturities is, say, 14 percent and is expected to remain at that level. If the expectations are correct, it is clear that an investor will earn 14 percent whether he buys short- or long-term securities. If, on the other hand, rates on different maturities are different, the yield differential represents a market prediction that interest rates will change in the future.

Consider the investor who can buy bonds with either one or two years to maturity that are selling at yields of 14 percent and 15 percent, respectively. He can buy the two-year bond and receive an average yield of 15 percent, or he can buy the one-year bond, earning 14 percent for the first year, and then reinvest the funds at maturity for another year. According to the expectations theory, the market must be expecting the yield on a one-year loan to be 16 percent one year in the future. This would be necessary to provide the investor with an average return of 15 percent (14 percent the first year, 16 percent the second). Alternatively, the market is predicting a 1 percent decline in the price of the two-year bond during the year. This would mean a yield to the investor of 15 percent regardless of whether he bought the one-year bond (yield 15 percent) or the two-year bond (yield 16 percent minus a capital loss of 1 percent).

In summary, the expectations theory holds that differences in yields on securities of differing maturities are established not because the market expects an investor to receive a higher return on one security than on another, but because the market expects the rates of return on the two securities to be the same over an equal period of time. If this relationship were not the case, the investor would shift to the maturity of bonds that he expected would provide the highest returns. It is this arbitrage procedure (buying one maturity and selling another) that provides the mechanism by which expected returns of the different maturities are brought into equality. According to the expectations theory, the up-sloping yield curve indicates that the market is expecting yields to rise in the future. The down-sloping yield curve reflects the expectation that yields will fall over time. These conclusions are similar to those we reached in Chapter 4.

The liquidity-preference analysis has added an important qualification to some treatments of the expectations theory. We have noted earlier the fact that the prices of short-term securities vary less with changes in market interest rates than do the prices of long-term securities. The investor in short-term securities is taking less risk of adverse market developments than the holder of long-term securities. In view of this factor, some investors are willing to forgo some expected return in order to hold short-term securities. Even though the investor may make decisions primarily on the basis of his expectations about the course of interest rates, he is aware that his expectations may not be realized. It is surely not irrational for a cautious investor to prefer a return of 6¼ percent on short-term securities to a return of 6½ percent on long-term securities that will be earned only if his expectations are realized. If this version of the theory is correct, the level of short-term rates would always be lower than it might have been if the structure of interest rates had been determined solely by expectations.

The principal alternative to the expectations theory holds that interest rates are determined in several more or less separated or segmented markets. Some investors prefer short-term securities (commercial banks, for example), and others prefer long-term securities (life insurance companies). Bonds of differing maturities are imperfect substitutes for individual investors and hence for the market as a whole. According to the segmented-markets theory, the yield curve results from the interplay of several supply and demand functions for different securities. An increase in the supply of long-term securities will tend to depress their prices, and hence raise their yield, without significantly affecting the interest rate on short-term securities.

There is no question but that the type of institutional practices the segmented-markets theory relies upon do exist. In addition to the commercial-bank and insurance-company examples, it is also true that borrowers' demands for funds are segmented; for example, purchases of houses are financed with long-term mortgages, and inventories are generally financed with short-term loans. But it is not clear that the segmentation is as complete as the theory requires. Even if individual investors are not indifferent between three-month and 50-year bonds, it is possible that the markets in which different investors or institutions function overlap substantially. That is, the commercial bank may not consider purchasing a 30-year bond but may be willing to consider any maturity up to ten years. The mutual savings bank may not need many short-term securities but may be interested in the best expected yield available in the five- to 20-year maturity range. The life insurance company may not want to hold anything under ten years but may be active in any longer maturities. The degree of overlap may be large enough so that the market as a whole will approximate the results expected under the expectations approach.

Several empirical investigations have been carried out in recent years to determine which approach provides a better explanation of the interest-rate structure. Some studies have focused on the prediction aspect of the expectations theory to see whether the predictions inherent in the yield curve under that theory have turned out to be correct. This is not a fair test of the theory, however, because all the expectations theory claims is that yield differentials exist because the market expects interest rates to change. The theory does not necessarily claim that the predictions will be correct.

Other studies have examined the related conclusions that under the expectations theory, on the one hand, variations in the supply of securities of various maturities should have no effect on the yield curve, whereas under the segmented theory, on the other hand, the maturity composition of outstanding debt will affect the term structure of rates.

The results of the various studies, although perhaps not providing a definitive answer, have tended to give strong support to the expectations approach (perhaps modified to accept the existence of a "liquidity premium" on long-term bonds). Several studies have found that changes in the maturity composition of debt have little, if any, effect on the maturity structure of yields.

The questions of how the yield curve is determined and how easily it can be affected by monetary and debt-management policies is an important one for monetary authorities. We shall return to this issue in our later discussions of monetary policy.

MONEY, INTEREST, AND INCOME

The beginning of this chapter presented a schematic representation of the determination of the level of national income. We are now in a position to add to that diagram the other factors necessary to present a more complete picture of the interrelationships of money and the real factors in the economy.

The arrows in Figure 25-6 indicate the direction in which the causal relationships operate. Income consists of consumption expenditures and investment expenditures. Consumption is determined by the propensity to consume and the level of income. Investment is determined by the interest rate and the marginal efficiency of investment. The interest rate, in turn, is determined by the supply of money and the demand for money. The supply of money is determined by the operations of the central bank and the financial

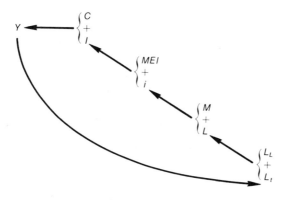

FIGURE 25-6 Money, Interest, and Income

system. The demand for money is made up of the transactions demand and the speculative demand, with the transactions demand dependent upon the level of income.

This approach seems to involve circular reasoning—we start out by trying to discover the level of income and find that in order to determine that, we must know the transactions demand for money, but in order to determine the transactions demand for money, we must know the level of income. This is not really a circular process. What it does show, in fact, is that all these variables (Y, C, I, i) are mutually interdependent. The economic system determines the value of all of them simultaneously.

Let us look at this process a little more closely. Figure 25-5 shows us that, given the money supply, M, the demand for money, L, can equal the supply at a high interest rate (if income, and hence L_t, is high as in Figure 25-5 [B]) or at a low interest rate (if income, and hence L_t, is low as in Figure 25-5 [A]). This relationship can be seen more clearly in Figure 25-7, which shows several demand-for-money curves, each representing the demand for money at a different level of income. Points A through E each represent combinations of interest rate and income at which the demand for money is

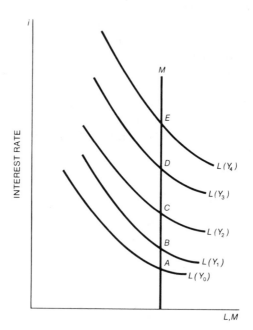

FIGURE 25-7 Money Demand and Supply

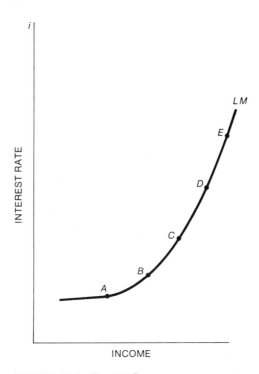

FIGURE 25-8 The *LM* Curve

equal to the supply of money. There will be a different such point corresponding to each possible level of income. The locus of all such points, shown in Figure 25-8 and called *LM*, represents combinations of interest rate and income where *L* (the demand for money) is equal to *M* (the supply of money).

Exactly the same analysis can be made of the saving–investment relationship. If interest rates are high (so that investment is low), desired saving and investment can be equal at a low level of income. If interest rates are low, thus encouraging a high level of investment, income will also be high, and therefore saving and investment can be equated.

Figure 25-9 shows the investment schedule *I* and several savings schedules, each one representing a different level of income. They are drawn nearly vertical on the assumption that saving does not vary significantly with the interest rate. Y_4 represents a higher level of income than Y_0, since higher savings is associated with higher income. Points *A* through *E* represent combinations of income and interest rates at which saving and investment are equal.

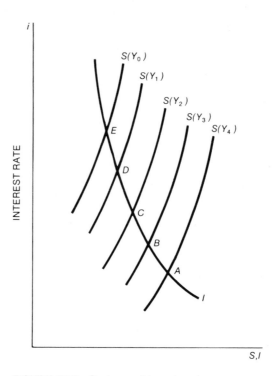

FIGURE 25-9 Saving and Investment

These points are shown in Figure 25-10 as the IS curve, representing all such combinations of interest rate and income at which I (investment) is equal to S (saving).

The LM curve and the IS curve can be put together in the same diagram, as shown in Figure 25-11. The intersection of the two curves has special significance (as such intersections usually do in economics). It represents the only combination of a rate of interest i and a level of income Y at which the demand for money is equal to the supply of money, and savings equals investment. This diagram, then, shows how the equilibrium levels of income and interest rates are determined together, given the variables shown in Figure 25-6: the liquidity-preference schedule, the stock of money, the marginal-efficiency-of-investment schedule, and the consumption function (or the saving function).

The system we have described is the simultaneous solution to two equations. In previous analyses, where we have always used only one equation, either the interest rate or income had to be given. Now they are assumed to be determined by the operations of

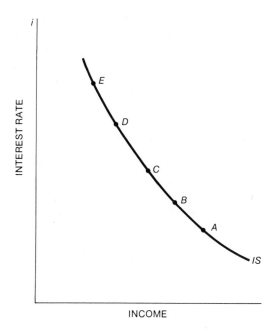

FIGURE 25-10 The *IS* Curve

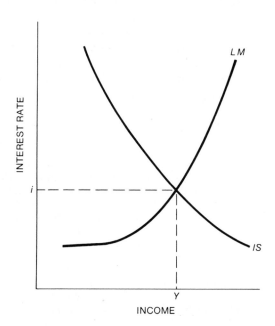

FIGURE 25-11 *IS* and *LM* Curves

the system. The two equations that must be satisfied are (1) desired saving out of income equals desired investment, and (2) money demand must equal the money stock. We illustrate with a simple hypothetical example.[7] Assume:

Desired saving $(S) = -70 + .2$ income (Y)

Investment $(I) = 260 - 200 \times$ the interest rate (i)

Transaction money demand $(L_t) = .3Y$

Speculative money demand $(L_L) = 90 - 500i$

Money stock $(M) = 465$

In equilibrium, $S = I$ and $M_t = L_t + L_L$.

$$-70 + .2Y = 260 - 200i$$
$$465 = .3Y + 90 - 500i$$

The values that will satisfy both these equations are:

$$Y = 1,500$$
$$i = .15$$

The model can be used to demonstrate the ultimate outcome of any number of changes. The reader can work through on LM a rise in the money stock, and it will be seen that the entire LM curve shifts to the right. The new intersection with IS shows that the increased money stock causes some fall in interest rates and some rise in equilibrium demand for output. If interest rates have little effect on investment, the IS curve will be relatively steep, and most of the effect of the money increase will be on interest rates rather than output. This is one of the assumptions of Keynesian

---

[7] The system sketched here also captures some of the spirit of econometric models used to predict the course of the economy and to simulate the effects on the economy of certain assumed changes, such as the money stock or the tax rate. Where our presentation has two equations, econometric models have hundreds, so they became feasible only after development of computer technology. The equations in these models incorporate the effects of variables in previous periods, such as last year's income, and these variables are among the givens when the next period is calculated. Examples of other givens are tax rates, the stock of durable goods, the government budget (which is enacted in advance), and the population. The model most relevant in financial analysis is one operated jointly by the Federal Reserve Board and the Massachusetts Institute of Technology (FRB-MIT model). See F. de Leeuw and E.M. Gramlich, "The Federal Reserve–MIT Econometric Model," *Federal Reserve Bulletin*, January 1968.

analysis. Another Keynesian assumption is that if *IS* intercepts *LM* at relatively low interest rates, *LM* is flat, and increases in the money stock are ineffective. This is the liquidity trap.

A rise in the marginal efficiency of investment is a shift to the right in the *IS* curve. The effect is to raise equilibrium output, but some of the rise is checked by a rise in interest rates, assuming that the money stock is unchanged. A rise in the consumption function is a fall in the saving function. This too will increase both the equilibrium output and interest rate.

A rise in the speculative demand for money (increased money hoarding) will, with a given money stock, shift *LM* to the left. Thus the increased demand for money will increase interest-rate equilibrium and lower output.

Effects of Inflation

Any *IS-LM* formulation is necessarily at a given price level, since both output and income, as well as all the variables relating to them, require price information. Suppose now that an equilibrium is struck—say, *Y* in Figure 25-11—but the maximum potential output (full employment) lies to the left of it. Although an equilibrium is reached, it is necessarily temporary because of the inflationary gap. This level of output can be accommodated only at a higher price level, and when prices rise, a new equilibrium must be struck.

Higher prices have the potential of affecting many of the underlying variables. Speculative money demand may change because of expectations of higher interest rates. The distribution of income may change as price changes affect different incomes differently. The consumption–saving function may change as consumers anticipate further price changes. Let us assume away all these possibilities, however, allowing only higher prices and the higher money incomes that flow from these prices. In nominal terms, then, it is clear that *IS* will shift to the right because of the higher supply prices that must be paid for investment goods and the higher money income that flows to the factors making them. This effect occurs even if the consumption function itself remains unchanged. The *LM* curve, however, stays put, because it looks at money demand and money stock in nominal terms; no real values are embodied in it. The maximum potential output shifts to the right, since that maximum real output must now be valued at the higher price level.

It can be concluded that as the inflation takes place, potential output and *IS* continually shift to the right, but *IS* intersections move along an *LM* curve.[8] Consequently, interest rates will tend to rise, and this in time will check the further advance of the equilibrium output. This is the operation of the real balance effect; that is, the real value of the given money stock is falling. Of course, this effect can be stopped if the money stock is allowed to rise along with the rate of inflation. The analysis above can also be applied if the inflation arises from some cause other than excess demand (see Chapter 30). The *IS* curve shifts out, *LM* stays put. The only difference is that the original equilibrium is not struck with an inflationary gap.

Our simplified analysis has ruled out many of the things that are apt to accompany inflation, and these must be analyzed individually. Inflation, for example, brings expectations of still higher prices, and this may have the effect of raising the consumption function. Thus, *IS* shifts out by even more than the realized inflation. In a similar way, inflation brings expectations of still higher interest rates. If interest rates are expected to rise, the speculative demand for money increases (at all interest rates), and *LM* shifts to the left. Thus, the rate of interest rises by even more than would result from the realized inflation operating alone.

The problems of inflation occupy a prominent place in more recent controversies in monetary and economic theory. We deal with these more fully in the chapter to follow, on the monetarist approach, and in Chapter 30.

QUESTIONS

1 What role does money play in the classical interest-rate theory?
2 Distinguish between the loanable-funds and liquidity-preference theories of interest.
3 Why do people hold money?
4 What is the "liquidity trap"? Do you believe that such a phenomenon exists?
5 Show that investment equals saving everywhere on the *IS* curve.
6 What is the "yield curve"?
7 Explain the downward-sloping yield curve in terms of the expectations theory.
8 From the point of view of an investor, does it matter which interest theory is correct?

---

[8] Alternatively, each period's *IS-LM* could be formulated in terms of the beginning period's prices. In this case, *IS* would stay put by the assumption that goods demand in real terms is unaffected. Money demand is also unaffected, but *LM* would shift to the left because the deflated value of the given nominal money stock would fall.

SELECTED READINGS

BOORMAN, JOHN T., and THOMAS M. HAVRILESKY, *Money Supply, Money Demand, and Macroeconomic Models*. Boston: Allyn & Bacon, 1972.

CONARD, JOSEPH W., *An Introduction to the Theory of Interest*. Berkeley: University of California Press, 1959.

HICKS, JOHN R., "Mr. Keynes and the 'Classics'; A Suggested Interpretation," *Econometrica*, April 1937. The original formulation of the *IS-LM* model.

KEYNES, JOHN M., *The General Theory of Employment, Interest, and Money*. New York: Harcourt, Brace & World, 1936.

LUTZ, FRIEDRICH A., "The Structure of Interest Rates," *Quarterly Journal of Economics*, November 1940. The classic exposition of the expectations theory.

MALKIEL, BURTON G., *The Term Structure of Interest Rates: Theory, Empirical Evidence, and Application*. Morristown, N.J.: General Learning Press, 1970.

MODIGLIANI, FRANCO, and RICHARD SUTCH, "Debt Management and the Term Structure of Interest Rates: An Empirical Analysis of Recent Experience," *Journal of Political Economy*, November 1967.

PATINKIN, DON, *Money, Interest and Prices*, 2nd ed. New York: Harper & Row, 1965. Chaps. 14, 15.

26

The Modern
Monetarist Approach

The quantity theory, in one form or another, was the generally held explanation of changes in money income until the development of the income–expenditure approach pioneered by Keynes. Keynes attacked the quantity-theory approach on a theoretical basis and also attacked some of the institutional assumptions on which it was based. It is common now to speak of conflict between Keynesians and quantity theorists or "monetarists." One label or the other is frequently pinned on both economists and institutions. In fact, these labels are misleading. The modern monetarists accept much of the Keynesian analysis, and many of the contributions of the monetarists are accepted by those labeled as Keynesians.[1] It can be argued that the monetarist reformulation of the quantity theory owes more to Keynes than to the earlier quantity theorists.[2]

---

[1] An example would be the emphasis the monetarists place on the role of price expectations in determining the interest rate. Although ignored by Keynes, who was concerned with a world of generally inflexible prices, it has been incorporated into Keynesian approaches to economic analysis.

[2] Thus, Don Patinkin has shown that Milton Friedman's basic model of monetarist thought is really a sophisticated version of Keynesian liquidity-preference theory. See "The Chicago Tradition, the Quantity Theory, and Friedman," *Journal of Money, Credit and Banking*, February 1969, p. 46.

THE NEW QUANTITY THEORY

In this chapter we will examine the essential differences between the Keynesian and monetarist approaches, with special emphasis on the implications of the alternative theoretical frameworks for monetary policy. We shall see that it is on the level of policy prescriptions, rather than pure theory, that the differences are most significant. And even many monetarists insist that the differences between themselves and the Keynesians are empirical rather than theoretical.

One of the developments that has fostered the monetarist point of view is the inflation of the 1970s and 1980s in association with high rates of unemployment and sluggish economic growth. The traditional Keynesian analysis cannot be used to explain this phenomenon, but it is easily incorporated in the monetarist scheme. The policy proposals that follow from differing interpretations of the inflation show the striking way in which Keynesian and monetarist solutions differ. The monetarist says that the route to inflation control is monetary restraint and that the long-run effect of this restraint will be on prices and not on real income. The Keynesian approach holds that if money affects prices at all, it will be through reduced aggregate demand, further aggravating unemployment.

Contrary to what might be expected by the label, the monetarists do not hold that money has any great effect on the real performance of the economy in the long run. Money affects only nominal values (that is, as measured in money prices); its effects on real output are only transient. Real interest rates, real output, and employment are essentially unaffected by money except in a transient sense. Thus, fluctuations in money engineered by policy makers are more apt to cause disturbances than to correct them.

One area where the differences and similarities can best be seen is the matter of the demand for money. Its importance can be found in Milton Friedman's statement that "the quantity theory is . . . a theory of the demand for money." David Fand, agreeing on the importance of the demand-for-money concept, has pointed out the differing role of the money-demand function in the two theories:

> The modern quantity theory and income expenditure theory thus differ sharply in their analysis of the money demand function. In the modern quantity theory it serves as a velocity function relating . . . money and money income . . . ; in the income-expenditure theory, it serves as a liquidity preference theory of interest rates. . . .[3]

[3] David Fand, "Some Issues in Monetary Economics," Federal Reserve Bank of St. Louis *Review*, January 1970, p. 17.

In the earlier versions of the quantity theory, the demand for money was viewed as determined largely by income. That is, k (or V) was considered to be a constant. Keynes attacked that view, arguing that k is highly unstable, particularly in periods of substantial unemployment. In such a period, changes in the money supply would not affect spending. Thus, an increase in M would simply result in an offsetting increase in k, leaving money income unchanged.

Keynes's analysis led to his emphasis on liquidity preference as the basic factor in the demand for money. The earlier quantity theorists generally did not consider the interest rate as a significant factor in explaining the demand for money.

The quantity theorists consider it inaccurate to accuse them of believing that k or V is constant. Friedman claimed that "hardly anyone has ever held the theory in that form" and emphasized that:

> [The] quantity theorist need not, and generally does not, mean that . . . the velocity of circulation of money is to be regarded as numerically constant over time. . . . [T]he stability he expects is in the functional relations between the quantity of money demanded and the variables that determine it.[4]

The liquidity-preference theory treats the demand for money as a function of interest rates and the level of income. The monetarist demand function has some similarities but quite different emphases. Interest rates are included in the monetarist function but they are considered relatively weak. Income enters the monetarist formulation in a different way also. The public is assumed to want to hold money as some portion of its total wealth. Income in the future has value in the present, and this is what wealth is—the discounted value of future income. Thus, a change in income affects the demand for money through the effect of the change on wealth. The more permanent a change is expected to be, the greater is the effect on the public's perception of its wealth, rendering a strong expectational element to the influence of income on money demand. Expected price movements also enter the demand function, since price changes affect different forms of wealth in different ways. Money demand is a negative function of anticipated price rises, since the rise in prices will erode the real value of money holdings.

It can be seen that the monetarists use income only in the sense that it affects wealth. Income is thus much more prominent

---

[4] "The Quantity Theory of Money—A Restatement," in *Studies in the Quantity Theory of Money* (Chicago: University of Chicago Press, 1956), pp. 16–17.

than it is in the liquidity-preference theory, where it is a measure of the need for an asset for transactions purposes.[5]

An aspect of the demand for money emphasized by the monetarists is that, in their view, the demand for money is a demand for *real*, not *nominal*, balances. Keynes treated the demand for money in terms of nominal balances on the assumption that prices are relatively rigid (at least in a period of depression), and that hence there is no need to distinguish between nominal and real quantities.

This distinction is important to the monetarists and carries over into the distinction between nominal and real income. The classical economists viewed money as the primary factor affecting the price level, whereas the level of real income was determined solely by real factors. Thus, Milton Friedman states:

> We have accepted the quantity-theory presumption, and have thought it supported by the evidence we examined, that changes in the quantity of money as such *in the long run* have a negligible effect on real income, so that nonmonetary forces are "all that matter" for changes in real income over the decades. . . . On the other hand, we have regarded the quantity of money, plus the other variables . . . that affect *k* as essentially "all that matter" for the long-run determination of nominal income.[6]

This brings us to a theoretical issue that is important for monetary policy. Everyone agrees that an increase in the money supply will lead to an increase in nominal income—that is, income measured in terms of current dollars. But there is no agreement as to how much of that increase in money income will represent an increase in *real income*, and how much will reflect an increase in prices. Friedman believes that, in the long run, only prices, and not real income, will be affected by changes in the money supply. Keynes believed that, if we start from a point of slack in the economy, stimulus to income would produce an increase in *real income* rather than in prices. Once we reach the point of full employment, or the capacity of the economy, then again all agree that further stimulus can raise only prices and not real income. This is an issue to which we shall return in our discussion of monetary policy.

---

[5] In Milton Friedman's view, "The emphasis on income as a surrogate for wealth, rather than as a measure of the 'work' to be done by money, is conceptually perhaps the basic difference between more recent work and the earlier versions of the quantity theory." "A Theoretical Framework for Monetary Analysis," *Journal of Political Economy*, March 1970, p. 203. It should be noted that the origin of this emphasis on money as one asset in a portfolio of a wealthholder lies with Keynes, not the earlier or the recent quantity theorists.

[6] Friedman, "A Theoretical Framework for Monetary Analysis," p. 216.

The monetarists are frequently accused of not having a comprehensive theory of just how changes in the supply of money exert their effect on income. The Keynesians have the neat, if somewhat complex, mechanism described in the preceding chapter to explain the means by which an increase in the money supply results in an increase in income. The monetarists rely on empirical evidence showing a close connection between changes in the money supply and changes in income. Critics charge that the monetarists have a "black box" theory of the transmission mechanism—an increase in money goes in and an increase in income comes out, but the mechanism is concealed within the black box.

Within the last several years, the monetarists have attempted to spell out their views of the linkages between money and income in answer to the critics.[7] Basically, the path of adjustment to an increase in the money supply for the monetarists begins with individuals or firms finding themselves with more of their assets in the form of money than they consider desirable. They react by buying other assets, both financial assets like bonds and real assets like automobiles and consumer goods. This spending will affect the prices of assets (which means changes in interest rates on securities) and the quantities supplied. These changes in prices affect the real value of money balances and hence react again through the demand-for-money function. Although the monetarists see this mechanism as a very rich and complex one, since they view the demand for money function as very stable, the *results* of a change in the money supply are predictable even if the precise steps in the process cannot be spelled out.

Actually, this view of the linkage between money and the economy would be acceptable to many economists who do not consider themselves to be monetarists. In an interesting article analyzing the differences between Keynesian and monetarist thought, Ronald Teigen pointed out:

> [T]here is nothing inherent in the Keynesian system which is inconsistent with the introduction of a general portfolio adjustment transmission mechanism; and, indeed,

---

[7] This raises the interesting question of whether a theory is needed or not. Some monetarists would argue that since their empirical work has demonstrated a close link between changes in money and changes in income, for monetary policy purposes all we need to know is that an x percent increase in the money supply will produce a y percent increase in income within z months. As a practical matter, I can plant a seed and expect a flower to grow without any real knowledge of biology, botany, or biochemistry. Mother Nature (or the invisible hand, or the black box) takes care of the problem for us. The detailed means by which monetary policy works may be of interest to the theoretician, but is not, they may argue, of concern to the monetary-policy maker or the banker.

there has been a substantial development in this direction in Keynesian thinking and practice during the last several years. On the theoretical side, the work of Tobin and others may be cited, while at the operational level, the developers of the Federal Reserve Board–MIT econometric model of the U.S. economy have attempted to incorporate such a mechanism into their model.[8]

The relation between changes in the money supply and interest rates is a very important one in modern monetarist thought. The monetarist would expect the immediate effect of an increase in the money supply to be a decrease in interest rates. But the increased money supply will generate an increase in money income that, in turn, will generate an increased demand for money. The increased demand for money will eventually offset and overcome the effect of the initial increase in the supply of money so that interest rates will rise, perhaps above their initial value. Although it may take six months or more for the immediate decline in interest rates to be eliminated, the monetarist holds that an increase in the money supply cannot produce a permanent decrease in the interest rate.

Another aspect of monetarist interest theory comes into play here. We noted in the preceding chapter the distinction between the *nominal* rate of interest quoted in the market and the *real* rate—the nominal rate corrected for changes in the price level. This effect has been particularly important to monetarist thought. It reinforces the analysis of the preceding paragraph. That is, the increased money supply that temporarily depresses interest rates also pushes up prices. The higher prices, by affecting the demand and supply of loanable funds, lead to higher nominal interest rates. Again, the monetarists conclude that the increase in the money supply cannot affect the real rate of interest and will tend to increase, rather than decrease, the nominal rate of interest (at least once the immediate effect of the increased money supply is past).

It is important to realize that this is not merely an abstract debate among theorists; it has significant implications for the financial markets. Consider the problem that the Federal Reserve has faced for much of the last several years: a higher rate of inflation than we consider comfortable, a relatively slow rate of economic expansion, and a high unemployment rate. Further, the financial markets seem to have accepted the monetarist analysis sketched above. That is, if the Fed takes steps to increase the rate of growth of the money supply, the market immediately reacts as though the higher monetary growth will produce higher prices and

[8] Ronald L. Teigen, "A Critical Look at Monetarist Economics," Federal Reserve Bank of St. Louis *Review*, January 1972, p. 18.

higher interest rates. This does produce an immediate *increase* in interest rates following the increase in the money supply. The market's perception and expectations may be wrong, but the result is that a stimulative effect of monetary policy may be blocked. In Keynesian terms, expansionary monetary policy requires a decline in interest rates to be effective, and monetary policy may be unable to produce that decline.

MONETARISTS AND INFLATION

Regardless of the state of output or employment, the monetarist approach to inflation control is a reduced rate of growth of the money supply. In the monetarist analysis, there is a "natural rate of interest" and a "natural rate of unemployment," and changes in the money supply cannot affect these.

The natural rate of interest is the premium the economy assigns to present as opposed to future values, and the productivity of capital primarily determines it. If the money stock declines, the immediate effect may be a rise in the market rate of interest. But then prices fall, and the real rate of interest returns to its natural rate. The adjustment of the nominal rate of interest to the natural (real) rate is not exact, because the public does not know what prices will do in the future. It is possible that in the absence of monetary restraint, nominal interest rates may overadjust to inflation. In this situation, to bring down nominal interest rates, inflation expectations must be reduced, and monetary restraint may accomplish this. Thus, reductions in the money stock are associated with falling interest rates, contrary to the usual assumptions of rising interest rates with money-stock reductions.

The natural rate of unemployment is the monetarists' replacement for the classical assumption that the economy always tends toward "full" employment. Employment (unemployment) is determined in the market for labor services. With any given labor productivity, the real wage that workers receive will fall short of that which some workers will demand. This natural rate of unemployment will not be disturbed by monetary forces, which affect prices. A reduction in money may reduce employment temporarily by affecting demand for goods, but then price reductions increase the real wage, and the economy reverts to its natural rate of unemployment.

In the Keynesian tradition, whether or not a decrease in money affects prices would have to be considered along with movements in money velocity. If the Federal Reserve is successful in reducing the money supply, it may fail to affect total spending because V may increase so as to compensate for the decline in M. One writer presented this view as follows:

> When credit conditions are tightened and the creation of new money through the banking system is restricted, the financial machinery of the country automatically begins to work in such a way as to mobilize the existing supply of money more effectively, thus permitting it to do most of the work that would have been done by newly created money had credit conditions been easier.[9]

There is considerable validity in these arguments, and a thorough analysis of this position requires careful examination of the factors determining V. In an article aimed at refuting the arguments presented above, Lawrence Ritter, after conceding that during the early stages of monetary restraint there may be considerable "offset" of the effects of credit restriction through increase in V, concludes that eventually, "velocity is likely to encounter an upper limit, a rough and perhaps flexible ceiling, but a ceiling nevertheless."[10]

Because of the mechanical factors behind V, it is reasonable to assume that at any given time, with a given set of institutional arrangements, there is indeed some limit to V. V may increase somewhat, as indeed it has in the last 30 years, but there is some limit on the extent to which V can increase so as to offset the effects of decreases in M. If the Federal Reserve takes into account the probable effects of its policy actions on V, it can still achieve the desired degree of restraint on total expenditures, MV, by acting solely on M. Remember, the modern quantity theorists do not argue that V is a constant, only that there is a stable relationshp between V and other variables in the economy.

MONETARISTS AND FISCAL POLICY

Given their views on natural rates of employment and interest rates, it is not surprising to find that the monetarists do not hold that fiscal policy has much potency in influencing real variables in the economy. Certainly fiscal policy influences the *allocation* of output between the public and private sectors, but it does not influence the *size* of output.

[9] Warren L. Smith, "On the Effectiveness of Monetary Policy," *American Economic Review*, September 1956.

[10] Lawrence S. Ritter, "Income Velocity and Anti-Inflationary Monetary Policy," *American Economic Review*, March 1959.

An expansionary fiscal policy results in what is called "crowding out," a situation in which the public sector takes resources from the private sector. As government finances its spending by the sale of bonds, private lending is reduced, and there is a reduction in private demand for a wide category of interest-sensitive purchases. In an inflationary situation, conventional fiscal policy would normally take the form of increased tax rates, on the assumption that reduced disposable income would reduce demand. But in the monetarist analysis, the increased taxes reduce government borrowing that would otherwise take place. Funds (equal to the increased tax revenues) that would otherwise be lent to government flow directly or indirectly into spending.

Associated with the monetarist view is a new emphasis on "supply-side" economics. In this view, stabilization policy has placed too much emphasis on influencing aggregate demand and has paid too little attention to aggregate supply. In fact, demand-manipulating tax policies, by their discouragement of capital formation and work incentive, have actually tended to reduce productivity below what would otherwise have been achieved. Taxes drive a wedge between income earned and income received. This lesser income is part of the reason for the high natural rate of unemployment. Tax-induced reductions on the return to capital have lessened capital formation.

Supply-side economists advocate reductions in tax rates as a way to actually increase government tax revenues. Tax revenues are the result of the application of a tax rate to the nation's income. If incomes rise more than enough to offset tax-rate reductions, then revenue can actually rise. One proponent of this view, Arthur Laffer, depicts a curve with tax rates on the horizontal and tax revenues on the vertical axis. At zero rates, no revenue; at 100 percent, no revenue (because no one chooses to produce income). In between is an inverted U-shaped curve (which John Kenneth Galbraith calls "terribly freehand"). Reduced tax rates are then the means to increase employment, to increase tax revenue, and to increase capital formation and productivity. At the same time, transfer payments (such as unemployment compensation) are to be minimized because they cause "voluntary unemployment." The antiinflation aspect of this supply-side program is through the price-moderating effect of increased supplies in the economy.

Such painless (even pleasurable) remedies for inflation and unemployment were highly appealing in the presidential campaign of 1980, and President Reagan's three-year tax reduction passed Congress in August 1981. The concept of a built-in tax reduction over three years—regardless of the state of the economy when the reductions become effective—was greatly abhorrent to disciples of flexible fiscal policy. Although there is nothing novel in questioning the effects of taxation on incentives, such questioning had never heretofore been so strong as to suggest that the means to fight inflation was actually to increase the public's purchasing power.

AUTOMATIC MONETARY POLICY

Statistical studies show a strong association between changes in the money supply and GNP. The cornerstone of monetarist theory is that it is the changes in the money supply that *cause* the changes in nominal GNP. A nonmonetarist is not surprised at the relation between money supply and GNP but disagrees regarding the direction of causation, saying that it is the increase in GNP that generates an increase in the demand for money. The increased demand for money bids up interest rates and stimulates an increase in the money supply from the banking system.

Statistical studies cannot easily resolve this debate, since both sides expect a high correlation between money supply and GNP. In monetarist thought, this relationship is a very stable one—more stable, in particular, than the marginal propensity to consume, which plays the key role in the Keynesian model of GNP determination. The important issue then becomes the question of the precise means by which changes in the money supply affect GNP.

For the Keynesians, people make choices between holding money and holding securities, and changes in the money supply thus have an effect on the price of securities (interest rates). For the monetarist, the individual chooses among all assets, including real goods and services. A person holding more money than he or she thinks necessary may spend the excess on new clothing or a new car as well as on financial assets. Thus, an increase in the money supply can *directly* stimulate spending in the economy without first influencing interest rates.

Although monetarists are specific in assigning the ultimate effect of money to prices, the effects are long delayed because of the time required to complete the transmission mechanism. Many investigators have studied this lag problem, and most find that indeed the length of the lag does raise questions about the usefulness of monetary policy for short-term purposes. Historically, the money stock has changed direction prior to a change in direction of the economy as a whole. Demand deposits and currency make up one of the "leading indicators," statistical series used for forecasting purposes because of their tendency to precede changes in the economy.

The Department of Commerce uses demand deposits and currency as one of twelve indicators that are put together as an "index of leading indicators." Generally, a drop in the leading indicators for three consecutive months is interpreted as a rather clear sign of impending recession, but even a fall of this long a duration has not always been an accurate forecaster.

Using a money-supply definition that included commercial-bank time deposits, Milton Friedman and Anna Schwartz found that in 18 business cycles, the cycle peak occurred 16 months after monetary conditions tightened.[11] An econometric model operated by the Federal Reserve and the Massachusetts Institute of Technology generated an estimate that ". . . a once-and-for-all increase in the money supply of $1 billion in a given quarter has almost no effect on GNP in that quarter and, even after four quarters, the level of GNP is only about $400 million higher than it otherwise would be."[12] This is one of a number of "structural" econometric models—models that structure the economy by sector and by output—all of which find long lags associated with changes in monetary conditions.

In addition to the lag problem, monetarists tend to recoil from active monetary policy because of its imposition of government values on the society. Although a libertarian philosophy is not a necessary corollary to being a monetarist, the movement's intellectual strength is from scholars who tend to favor rules over discretion in the exercise of the state's powers. Friedman and his followers favor a monetary policy in which the money stock is set to grow at a predetermined rate, this rate to be chosen roughly in accord with the long-term growth in real output. With this rule, monetary policy would always be "right" in that it was pointing in the direction of the economy's potential. If aggregate demand grew at a greater rate, then demand would tend to be inflationary, and the failure of the money stock to grow commensurately would in time check the inflation.

The increased emphasis on the monetary aggregates by the Federal Reserve and other central banks is a move in the direction advocated by Friedman, since it places less emphasis on interest rates as control targets, with resulting fluctuations in the money stock. The Humphrey-Hawkins Act requires that the Fed announce

---

[11] Friedman and Schwartz, *A Monetary History of the United States, 1867–1960* (Princeton, N.J.: Princeton University Press, 1963).

[12] Michael J. Hamburger, "The Lag in the Effect of Monetary Policy: A Survey of Recent Literature," Federal Reserve Bank of New York *Monthly Review*, December 1971. (Money-stock changes were calculated on the basis of changes in non-borrowed reserves and reserve-requirement changes.)

its monetary targets semiannually, and even though this is far from a predetermined rule, such announcements do reduce some of the Fed's discretion. Central banks entered the 1980s with a rather strong inclination toward monetarism, backed by a public mandate to do something about inflation.

In recent years . . . Keynesian ideas have come under heavy attack and are widely, though not universally, held to be discredited. Indeed, restrictive policies of the kind so long denounced as absurdly inappropriate to the needs of the early thirties are again being followed at a time of recession. . . . Unfortunately, the monetarist theories that have so largely superseded the Keynesian ones are much more explicit about the measures needed to check an inflation than about those appropriate for fostering a recovery.[13]

QUESTIONS

1 How would a quantity theorist expect a restrictive monetary policy to restrain inflation?
2 Why do people hold money?
3 Which provides the better mechanism for analyzing monetary policy—the quantity theory or the income-expenditure approach?
4 Is it important that the Open Market Committee have a good understanding of how monetary policy works?
5 Do monetarists believe that V is constant? If not, how can they forecast the effect of an increase in the money supply?

SELECTED READINGS

BOORMAN, JOHN T., and THOMAS HAVRILESKY, *Money Supply, Money Demand, and Macroeconomic Models*. Boston: Allyn & Bacon, 1972. An excellent combination of text and readings.
FRIEDMAN, MILTON, "A Theoretical Framework for Monetary Analysis," *Journal of Political Economy*, March 1970. The best presentation of Friedman's view of monetary theory. This article led to an important series of articles that provide an excellent summary of the debate between monetarists and Keynesians: "Symposium on Friedman's Theoretical Framework," *Journal of Political Economy*, 1972, pp. 133–67.
GORDON, ROBERT J., ed., *Milton Friedman's Monetary Framework: A Debate with His Critics*. Chicago: University of Chicago Press, 1974.
MAYER, THOMAS, *The Structure of Monetarism*. New York: W.W. Norton, 1978.

[13] Thomas Wilson, "1929–33—Could It Happen Again?" *Three Banks Review* (Edinburgh, Scotland), December 1980, p. 4.

ROUSSEAS, STEPHEN, *Monetary Theory*. New York: Knopf, 1972.

SPRINKEL, BERYL W., *Money and Markets: A Monetarist View*. Homewood, Ill.: Richard D. Irwin, 1971.

TEIGEN, RONALD L., "A Critical Look at Monetarist Economics," Federal Reserve Bank of St. Louis *Review*, January 1972.

WILSON, THOMAS, "Crowding Out: the Real Issues," Banca Nazionale del Lavoro *Quarterly Review* (Rome, Italy), September 1979.

VII

MONETARY POLICY

27

The Goals of Monetary Policy

During the late 19th and early 20th centuries, the problems of the day were of a kind that led economists to concentrate on the allocation of resources and, to a lesser extent, economic growth, and to pay little attention to short-run fluctuations of a cyclical character. Since the Great Depression of the 1930s, this emphasis has been reversed. Economists now tend to concentrate on cyclical movements, to act and talk as if any improvement, however slight, in control of the cycle justified any sacrifice, however large, in the long-run efficiency, or prospects for growth, of the economic system.[1]

Government arises because of the belief that people can do collectively certain things that they cannot do acting individually. There is some loss of freedom in collective action, and only if the collective gain exceeds that loss is government intervention desirable. As a form of government intervention, monetary policy has goals that are not distinct from those of other government instrumentalities, but it is better equipped for some of those goals than for others. And sometimes, in concentrating on these objectives, others are forgotten, as Friedman reminds us so well in the quotation above.

Many targets of government often thought of as goals are not really ultimate objectives. We do not care about interest rates *per*

---

[1] Milton Friedman, "A Monetary and Fiscal Framework for Economic Stability," *American Economic Review*, June 1948, p. 245.

se, the balance of payments, the money stock, or even the price level, except as they are intermediate targets to more fundamental objectives. The intermediate targets must not be allowed to replace the more fundamental objectives; if they are, this would make the manipulation of policy instruments an end in itself.

Government serves an economic purpose only if it can make the utility (satisfaction from economic goods) of the society higher than it would be in its absence. Therefore we can state that maximizing output is an ultimate objective, provided that it is not done in a way that otherwise reduces satisfaction (forced labor, for example). Even this objective cannot be accepted without qualification, since the question arises, Over what time period? We might then change our statement to "maximizing output *and* economic growth," but recognizing that there is some tradeoff between the two. Students exemplify this tradeoff. The learners of today sacrifice current employment so that they will be more productive in the future.

There is a still further and more important qualification in the utility-maximization goal, and that is, Maximize utility for whom? Government has never allowed the marketplace to be the final arbiter of the allocation of proportionate shares of national output among the population. This concern about the distribution of income shows up in many government programs—graduated income taxes, welfare payments, unemployment compensation, free public schooling, subsidized housing, subsidized medical care, and so on and on. Government thereby reduces some of the inequality in the distribution of income.

In seeking to maximize utility, government aims to keep output within its potential—that is, to prevent economic contractions. This is called the *stabilization* goal. It also changes the composition of output by substituting some collective (government) goods for private goods that would otherwise be produced, and by influencing the composition of private demand (for example, by taxing some goods). This is the *allocative* goal, and it assumes that more utility is derived from the composition of goods so determined than if this decision were left entirely to the market.

The economic goals of government, then, can be classified as (1) stabilization, (2) economic growth, (3) distributional equity, and (4) allocative efficiency.[2] Many specific actions of government overlap

---

[2] This discussion owes much to Richard Musgrave, *The Theory of Public Finance* (New York: McGraw-Hill, 1959). The attempt to identify and classify these goals is not meant to imply that there is a consensus on their desirability, or that they should be the same in all times and places. Less-developed countries necessarily

in their goals, and there are many subgoals within these classifications.

Monetary policy can be judged successful only if it is compatible with all these goals. Note the choice of an ambiguous word, "compatible," because monetary policy certainly cannot *achieve* all goals. And all policy, including monetary, inevitably involves some tradeoff. Economic growth, for example, requires capital formation and maximization of reward to promote incentive—measures that fly in the face of equity in income distribution. Allocative goals require sacrifice of private goods, which in time may reduce incentive to maximize output. Policy makers must transform these ultimate goals into more immediate targets. These immediate targets, which overlap in the ultimate goals they affect, are considered in more detail below.

STABLE PRICES

Stability in the overall price level is the only goal that many people associate with central banking, doubtless owing to the persistent influence of the quantity theory—more money, higher prices.[3] In-

---

place greater emphasis on growth than does the United States, which may pay more attention to allocative efficiency. The present authors favor active intervention for all these goals. Milton Friedman favors tax policy to redistribute income (the negative income tax) but opposes the growth goal:

> There is no way a free society to say in advance that one or another numerical rate of change is needed or desirable, or that a higher rate of change is better than a lower. . . . Whatever rate of change in the statistical aggregate results from the efforts of free men to promote their own aspirations is the right rate.

From U.S. Joint Economic Committee, "Employment, Growth, and Price Levels," *Hearings*, Part 9A, 86th Cong., 1st sess. (Washington, D.C.: U.S. Government Printing Office, 1959), pp. 3019–20.

[3] It is important to make a distinction between the two types of price increases that may take place in the economy. First, we can consider changes in the price of one good in relation to the prices of all other goods. Such changes are a basic characteristic of the operation of a competitive, free-enterprise economy. If the demand for a particular commodity rises, its price will tend to rise, and the price increase will provide an incentive for an increase in production of the commodity. The normal operation of the free-enterprise economy provides for an increase in supply to meet the increased demand, and the price system is the mechanism that automatically carries out this function.

Obviously, some people in the economy will benefit from such price changes and others will suffer from them, but such changes do no harm to the economy as a whole. In fact, by tending to produce a more efficient allocation of resources, they increase the level of welfare in the economy.

flation, a general advance in money prices, threatens more than one economic goal. These were well identified in a statement by the prestigious Committee for Economic Development:

> A high inflation rate disrupts the economy and divides the society. Increasing prices erode the real purchasing power of savings and of invested capital. An inflationary surge interferes with rational output and investment decisions, contributes to social and industrial strife, and diverts an undue share of the nation's productive energies into efforts to beat the inflation spiral. It distorts and undermines financial market processes. Inflation is also highly inequitable. It redistributes incomes in a capricious fashion, usually hitting hard at the weakest in the society.[4]

Allocative efficiency is threatened because people become more concerned about purchases to beat inflation than about the intrinsic utility from the purchases. Economic growth and current output are threatened as inflation renders almost impossible the calculations needed to plan and invest for the future. To the extent that inflation reduces output through its disincentive effect, the whole of society loses. These aggregate losses are not nearly as great as commonly stated, however, because of confusion over the relation between money income and prices. Many people tend to take the size of their money income as given, and then blame inflation for all the erosion of its purchasing power. In the aggregate, this is not the case at all. Income arises from real output times its price; as money prices rise, so do incomes. As John Kenneth Galbraith states, the public tends to attribute income to its own enterprise and blame government for the price rise that erodes that income. In the aggregate, the public does not lose in real terms from inflation, except for the unknown extent to which it introduces inefficiencies in the economy and lessens real output.

But the inequity of inflation is a major concern. Some people are hurt more than others by it, whereas some may actually gain from inflation.

Low-income people keep a larger proportion of their total assets in the form of savings deposits and insurance. Because of inflation, these assets have, of course, depreciated in real value. Higher-income people hold a larger proportion of their assets in stocks and real property, which may tend to increase in value during periods of inflation. There have been several studies of the effects of inflation on different income groups. The general conclusion is that wealthy people have been able to protect themselves from the encroachment

---

[4]*Fighting Inflation and Promoting Growth* (New York: Committee for Economic Development, 1976), p. 11.

of rising prices and even to gain from inflation, a gain made at the expense of the less wealthy.[5]

The different effects of inflation on incomes are perhaps more important. Some groups in the economy may be able to increase their incomes to keep pace with any increase in prices. The businessman may find his profits increasing with inflation. Some labor groups may be able to secure wage increases in step with price increases or may be protected by "escalator clauses" in their contracts providing for automatic wage increases as prices rise.

For many people, however, increases in their earnings may not keep up with price increases. The salaries received by some workers have been slow to respond to a rising cost of living. Retired people living on private pensions or annuities have fixed incomes—no matter how much prices go up, their incomes remain the same. People living on Social Security payments have fared better because benefits have been automatically increased as prices rose.

The intent of monetary policy in counterinflationary moves is that the distributional effect of the policy measures will be superior to the distributional effect of inflation. Although the assumption is probably valid, we cannot really verify it, because the distributional effect of monetary policy poses an unanswerable question. We simply cannot know what the distribution of income would have been under alternative combinations of monetary policy, fiscal policy, and inflation. The picture is not clear even if consideration is limited to the effect on various income classes as determined by debtor-creditor positions of each class. There are both data limitation problems and difficult conceptual issues.[6] Where distributional effect is concerned, fiscal policy has the advantage. Because taxes are based specifically on income, the incidence of fiscal policy is more easily managed than is the incidence of monetary policy.

Despite our concern with price stability, this objective has not been spelled out in any legislation. Definitions of "reasonable price stability" may vary,[7] but it is clear that the Federal Reserve and

[5] See, for example, Albert E. Burger, "Effects of Inflation, 1960–1968," Federal Reserve Bank of St. Louis Review, November 1969; and George Bach, "Inflation: Who Gains and Who Loses?" Challenge, July/August 1974.

[6] For example, interest on the public debt rises with a restrictive monetary policy, and the burden of such interest is borne in accord with the distribution of taxes. Should such an effect be treated as monetary policy or fiscal policy?

[7] These definitions may vary over time also. In the second edition of Professor Samuelson's elementary economics textbook, he indicated that a 5 percent annual rate of increase in prices was an acceptable performance. In the third edition, he stated, "If price increases could be held down to, say 3 percent per year, such a mild steady inflation need not cause too great concern." In the fourth edition, the figure was down to 2 percent, and in the fifth, he spoke of holding price increases "below 2 percent." No comment on acceptable performance can be found in recent editions.

every administration are dedicated to containing inflationary price movements to a minimum consistent with other economic goals.

Price Movements in the United States

In view of the importance attached to the goal of price stability in the economy, it is important to review the actual behavior of prices over the years. Figure 27-1 provides a convenient picture of price changes in this country during the last century and a half. The price data used in constructing this chart are not too reliable for the earlier years but are adequate to illustrate major shifts in the price level. The first impression the chart gives is that the price level has increased substantially over this period. On the other hand, there have been prolonged periods of price stability, and many years of price declines.

A closer examination shows that much of the price increase has occurred during wars. There were sharp increases in prices during the Civil War, World War I, World War II, the Korean War, and the Vietnam War. Prices rose in nearly all the war years. But for most of our roughly 135 years of peace, prices on the average were virtually unchanged. Table 27-1 shows movements in consumer prices in several selected periods chosen to isolate the war

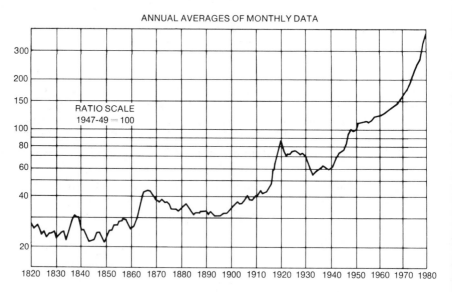

FIGURE 27-1 Index of Consumer Prices

TABLE 27-1
Consumer Price Movements in the United States

Periods	Annual Average Rate of Change
1820–1861	− 0.1%
1861–1866 (Civil War)	+ 12.6
1866–1915	0.0
1915–1920 (World War I)	+ 20.0
1920–1940	− 1.5
1940–1947 (World War II)	+ 8.6
1947–1950	+ 2.3
1951–1953 (Korean War)	+ 3.7
1953–1964	+ 1.4
1964–1972 (Vietnam War)	+ 4.0
1972–1981	+ 8.8

periods. It is clear from this table that with one major exception, all the periods of large price increases were war years.

A major war is almost certain to be accompanied by some degree of inflation. A substantial portion of the country's resources must be devoted to the production of war goods, and thus incomes rise without a corresponding increase in the quantity of goods available to consumers. This additional purchasing power can be siphoned off by higher taxes, but there are limits to the level of taxes. There is always the danger that too high a level of taxation may reduce incentives and thereby reduce production.

In the periods following the Civil War and the First World War, there were substantial declines in prices.[8] Following World War II, however, we have had almost uninterrupted increases in consumer prices. There is sharp controversy over why this has happened, and we shall explore these theories in detail in Chapter 30.

FULL EMPLOYMENT

Full employment has long been an objective of national economic policy, but it formally became a responsibility of the government with passage of the Employment Act of 1946, which states:

[8] Data on wholesale prices going back to 1779 indicate that there were also large price declines following the Revolutionary War and the War of 1812. The Mexican and Spanish-American Wars did not have significant effects on the general price level.

It is the continuing policy and responsibility of the Federal Government to use all practicable means consistent with its needs and obligations and other essential considerations of national policy, with the assistance and cooperation of industry, agriculture, labor and state and local governments, to coordinate and utilize all its plans, functions and resources for the purpose of creating and maintaining, in a manner calculated to foster and promote free competitive enterprise and the general welfare, conditions under which there will be afforded useful employment opportunities, including self-employment, for those able, willing, and seeking to work, and to promote maximum employment, production, and purchasing power.[9]

It is more meaningful to speak in terms of the rate of unemployment than of the level of employment, since unemployment is really the principal concern. As the labor force grows, we may have an increased rate of unemployment at the same time that there is a higher level of employment. For this reason, we will discuss the employment objective in this chapter in terms of the proportion of the labor force that is unemployed. Figure 27-2 shows how the rate of unemployment has varied for the last fifty years.

We are concerned about unemployment because of its effect on the unemployed and its effects on the economy as a whole. These concerns relate, respectively, to the distributional-equity goal and

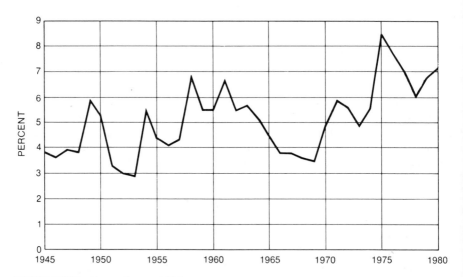

FIGURE 27-2 Unemployment Rate

[9] It might be noted that Congress has never defined precisely what is meant by the term "maximum ... purchasing power." The Federal Reserve has apparently interpreted this as having something to do with price stability, but there is no evidence that this was the intent of Congress. Note also that the title of the act is the Employment Act, not the *Full* Employment Act.

the stabilization goal. Unemployment is not simply an economic problem. For the unemployed, it not only means a loss of income, and thus hardship for themselves and their families; it may also mean a loss of self-respect and a sense of personal failure. A father's unemployment may mean the end of a child's hopes for further education. In the aggregate, unemployment is a waste of productive resources and means that the goal of maximum economic growth is not being achieved.

It is surprisingly difficult to pin down a precise definition of unemployment. Certainly not everyone who is not working should be classified as unemployed. The definition currently in use by the Bureau of Labor Statistics (BLS) is a reasonable one: A person is classified as unemployed if he or she is over 16 years of age, has done no work for pay or profit during the week, and is actively seeking work.[10]

The Bureau of the Census conducts a monthly survey of employment and unemployment on a sample basis. Although it is possible to argue about the definition of unemployment, the statistical work of the bureau is as good as our present knowledge can make it. The monthly figure on unemployment as a percentage of the labor force is reasonably accurate. Moreover, statistics are available on various segments of the labor force so that analysts can use the measure that they think is most appropriate. For example, unemployment figures are calculated for experienced wage and salary workers so as to exclude the effect on the unemployment rate of persons just entering the labor force. Data are also published on the percentage of labor-force time lost as a result of both total unemployment and involuntary part-time work.

There are some disturbing aspects of our postwar employment experience. We know that unemployment increases during recessions, and we obviously want to moderate the frequency and severity of economic recessions. But even in expansion, low unemployment rates have been infrequently achieved. Following recessions, unemployment rates have failed to return to their prerecession lows, except for the long expansion of the 1960s, when it finally dipped below 4 percent. In the severe recession of the mid-1970s, unemployment hit 9 percent, and it never fell much below 6 percent thereafter. It came close to 8 percent in the 1980 recession and was back to 9 percent by 1982. Part of the problem in the 1970s was a rise in labor-force participation rates, the portion of the population

[10] In some cases, however, people are counted as unemployed even though they are not active jobseekers. This includes people who would be looking for work except for temporary illness, those waiting to start a new job, and those who have been laid off and are waiting to be called back to work.

entering the labor market. This rise is explained by the increasing portion of the population entering their working years and by increased participation of women in the work force.

It is important to realize that unemployment (at least as the BLS defines it) can never be completely eliminated. Even if there is a perfect balance between the number of jobs and the number of workers, some firms will be expanding employment while other firms are laying off workers. It simply takes time for the process of switching jobs to be accomplished, and during this time the worker is unemployed. Many workers quit jobs each month without having another job, and until they find or select another job, they are unemployed. Thousands of high school and college graduates enter the labor force each June. Until they find jobs, they are classified as unemployed. This type of unemployment is called "frictional unemployment," and regardless of the overall needs of the economy for workers, some frictional unemployment will always exist. As a matter of fact, even during World War II, when defense plants and consumer-goods firms were urgently in need of additional manpower, unemployment was around 2 percent of the labor force.

When we speak of full employment, then, what we really mean is a low level of unemployment, not zero unemployment. One reasonable definition of a "full-employment unemployment rate" is the lowest rate of unemployment attainable under the existing institutional structure that will not result in accelerating inflation. In 1962, the Council of Economic Advisers proposed 4 percent as a goal for unemployment. That was approximately the rate that prevailed in the stable full-employment year of 1956. There is reason to believe, however, that a comparable figure for our present institutional environment would be somewhat higher, since the composition of the labor force has changed. Teenagers now make up a larger proportion of the labor force than they did 20 years ago, reflecting the effect of the postwar baby boom. Women aged 20 and over have increased as a percentage of the labor force from 28 percent to over 35 percent over the past 20 years. Both these groups tend to be in and out of the labor force more frequently, with resulting periods of unemployment.

There have also been changes in the economic aspects of employment and unemployment that affect the rate. Unemployment compensation coverage has been broadened over the years. For many families, the financial burden of unemployment has been lessened because there are now two wage earners. On the margin, these factors make it possible for the unemployed to be more selective in accepting potential jobs and tend, other things being equal, to raise the unemployment rate. In view of these complications, the 1973 unemployment rate of 4.9 percent may represent a reasonably satis-factory situation, but that was the last time unemployment on an annual basis was under 5.5 percent.

ECONOMIC GROWTH

Born during the Industrial Revolution, the United States has throughout its history experienced remarkable economic growth. It is remarkable because, through most of recorded history, economic output has been essentially stagnant. In the long-term perspective, the experience of the last two centuries is more the exception than the rule.

The performance of the economy can be measured in a number of ways, none entirely satisfactory. One widely used measure is real GNP, gross national product adjusted for price changes. By this measure, output grew at an annual rate of 3.2 percent in the period 1972–1980. In the two decades 1960–1980, the growth rate was 3.5 percent. A study by the Congressional Joint Economic Committee estimated that in the preceding 120 years, 1839–1959, the growth rate was 3.7 percent.[11] Although the economy largely maintained its growth rate in the 1970s, an increasing work force was required to do this, so that output per worker has not done so well.[12]

Another measure of growth available in the post–World War II period is the index of industrial production, compiled by the Federal Reserve Board. The monthly index measures movements in phys-ical output in manufacturing, mining, and utilities. Together these account for about 40 percent of gross national product by value (although the output is not measured in value terms). In the period 1967–1980, industrial production grew at about 3.1 percent a year.

Always suspicious of central planning, the United States, un-like many countries, does not set long-run economic-growth targets. Growth is a policy concern, but targets are not specified. Short-term targets are implied in the attempt to reach full-employment output, quantified in the "full-employment GNP."

In the 1970s, continued economic growth and its desirability began to be questioned—a radical departure from the nearly unani-mous desire for growth as we entered the 1960s. For one thing, concern arose over continued depletion of natural resources and

---

[11] *Staff Report on Employment, Growth and Price Levels*, 1960.

[12] To further complicate matters, real GNP per capita has performed well, increasing 2½ percent per year 1960–1980, compared to 1⅔ percent in 1839–1959. The explanation lies in the rapid braking in the rate of population rise.

fear that resource exhaustion would soon bring an end to growth.[13] The desirability of continued growth was questioned because of its negative effect on the environment.[14] Does the increased utility from output compensate for the increased disutility from environmental pollution? Because of a rising population, a cessation of growth would entail continued reductions in per capita income. If growth is not available to absorb a rising work force, programs would be needed to spread the available work. A nation that has relied on growth for two centuries will not adapt quickly to doing without it.

Monetary policy has far-reaching implications for growth. Although there is a current belief that it may have been overemphasized in the past, capital formation is nevertheless important in contributing to productivity. Given the role of the interest rate in influencing investment demand, monetary policy influences the allocation of output between current consumption and capital formation. At times this is one of the more powerful arguments against the use of restrictive monetary policy as opposed to tax policy. The thrust of restrictive monetary policy is in the purchase of capital goods, whereas taxation can be more specifically directed at consumption. This is also an argument against frequent reversals of policy direction, because of the uncertainties they create in investment planning.

CONFLICTS AMONG OBJECTIVES

The major problem in achieving all our economic goals is that the policy action necessary to move toward one goal may conflict with the action required to move toward some other goal. The relation between price stability and full employment is a case in point. If there is excessive unemployment, easing credit is an appropriate policy action to stimulate demand. This increased demand, however, may have an inflationary effect on some segments of the economy.

It is generally agreed that if unemployment is very severe, increases in demand will not be inflationary. On the other hand, if unemployment is down to, say, 5 percent of the labor force, trying to reduce unemployment still further may result in substantial inflationary pressures. Unfortunately, there is no general agreement as

[13] See Dennis L. Meadows, *The Limits to Growth* (New York: New American Library, 1972).

[14] See E.J. Mishan, "Growth and Antigrowth: What Are the Issues?" *Challenge*, May–June 1973.

to how high unemployment must rise before inflationary tendencies are completely eliminated. During the 1960s, it was generally believed that a rather attractive set of tradeoff possibilities existed between unemployment and inflation, but the tradeoff seemed to worsen as the decade of the 1960s came to an end. Some structural changes have been suggested to reduce the tradeoffs. These include such things as improved training programs to make the unemployed better qualified for whatever jobs are available. Dissemination of better information about job openings may help reduce unemployment without affecting inflation. More vigorous antitrust action may be used to break up business firms (or even unions) that have market power to raise prices (or wages) even in periods of slack demand. Such changes may be desirable, but they are unlikely to yield great improvements in the tradeoffs available.

The inevitability of a tradeoff at one time led to serious suggestions that we should simply accept the inflation. A former member of President Nixon's Council of Economic Advisers argued:

> We may just have to live with inflation. The many calculations that have been made indicate that inflation does not seriously hurt any major group. Our economy is well adjusted to it.[15]

A decade later, with a 12 percent inflation rate, it was no longer argued that the economy had adjusted to it. When inflation is mild, some protection against its redistributive effects can be enjoyed by indexing wages to the price index and by interest rates that keep up with inflation.[16] By these and other measures, an *anticipated* inflation will have less undesirable redistributive effects than an unanticipated one. But even then, people have varying abilities to defend themselves against the coming higher prices, and adverse effects cannot be wholly eliminated. And if anticipated, the inflation will tend to accelerate as more and more groups seek built-in protection.

Inflation and Economic Growth

There seem to be no serious conflicts between the goals of increasing our rate of growth and maintaining low levels of unemployment.

---

[15] Hendrik Houthakker, "Thoughts on Phase II," *Brookings Papers on Economic Activity*, 1972, p. 197.

[16] The pros and cons of "indexation" and its history are set forth in two excellent articles in the November 1974 issue of the *Economic Review* of the Federal Reserve Bank of Richmond: Thomas M. Humphrey, "The Concept of Indexation in the History of Economic Thought"; and James F. Tucker and Warren E. Weber, "Indexation as a Response to Inflation: An Examination."

These two goals are really mutually reinforcing: We are certainly not achieving maximum growth if unemployment is high, and low unemployment is probably an encouragement to business firms to introduce labor-saving equipment that will improve productivity.

The relation between growth and price stability is a more controversial one. There are some who contend that sustained long-term growth cannot be achieved unless we maintain price stability; some who argue that inflation is actually a stimulus to growth; and still others who take the middle ground that inflation, while not an aid in achieving more rapid growth, is an inevitable concomitant of growth.

Inflation as a spur to growth may act by making borrowing more profitable (loans will be repaid in depreciated dollars) and reducing the financial risks of investment. On the other hand, inflation may hinder growth by encouraging wasteful, speculative activity, rather than growth-producing investment. The view that inflation must accompany growth is based on the fact that full employment is a prerequisite for maximum growth, and full employment may mean inflation. Empirical studies of economic growth in many countries do not reveal an appreciable relationship one way or the other between rates of increase in output and in prices, indicating that inflation is not a necessary growth stimulus.

Conflicts with External Balance

Disequilibrium in economic flows between the United States and the rest of the world manifests itself as a change in the exchange rate between the dollar and other currencies. A stable exchange rate is one of the intermediate targets of policy. Wide fluctuations in exchange rates render inefficiencies in international trade—and ultimately in the available goods to satisfy our wants—and a depreciating exchange rate puts inflationary pressures on the domestic economy.

Maintenance of external equilibrium often involves conflict with domestic targets. To reverse capital flows, a restrictive monetary policy may be called for. If this occurs during a period of economic contraction, the restrictive monetary policy goes in the wrong direction from the standpoint of the domestic stabilization goal. Although relative interest rates are the most immediate of the effects of monetary policy on external balance, there are many other interrelationships. To the extent that monetary policy alleviates inflation, relative goods prices between the United States and the rest of the world are affected. To the extent that domestic stabilization is achieved, the nation becomes attractive for foreign investment. Improvements in productivity will manifest themselves in favorable price comparisons with the rest of the world.

ENDS AND MEANS

The Machiavellian maxim that "the end justifies the means" is not widely accepted in the United States. When we seek to achieve certain ends, the means involved must be consistent with certain standards and beliefs. Thus, our attempts to seek more rapid growth, stable prices, and full employment must be made in the context of our desires for economic freedom and maintenance of the basic form of our economic system.

This does not mean that economic freedom is an absolute. We are willing to give up some economic freedom to gain other objectives. There is, of course, a very wide area of disagreement as to how much economic freedom we should give up to achieve other ends. We have a progressive income tax to aid in achieving an equitable distribution of income, even though any tax is a restriction on economic freedom. We have a compulsory Social Security system because we think the result is worth the loss of economic freedom involved. (There are, of course, still some people who oppose the progressive income tax and compulsory Social Security.)

It has long been recognized that we could hold down the price indexes if we had a law forbidding labor unions from striking or a law prohibiting the raising of prices by business firms. Until recently, we have had such laws only during wartime periods of emergency. The reluctance to use direct controls has reflected concern for economic freedom and the view that the price system in a free, competitive economy is an efficient means of allocating resources. Actually, of course, our economy is not perfectly competitive. We have unions and business firms with the power to significantly influence, if not set, prices and wages. Breaking up such concentrations of economic power is not easy. In such a situation, resorting to direct controls may seem attractive when unemployment and prices do not react appropriately to aggregate economic-policy measures. The mandatory price and wage controls of the Nixon administration were unprecedented in peacetime, but they differed only in degree from the less formal wage-price "guideposts" of the Kennedy, Johnson, and Carter administrations.

Price and wage controls obviously have great implications for economic freedom and considerations of equity, but such issues also exist in normal monetary-policy operations. Any policy action is going to have effects on various people or groups within the economy. A tight-money policy that results in higher home-mortgage interest rates may prevent a family from buying a new house. Their effective freedom to own a home has been reduced by this policy action. Is the overall effect of this policy on the economy worth this loss in effective economic freedom that it causes? Is it "fair" that this family is unable to borrow money to buy a home of their own when the oil man finds no difficulty in obtaining financing for his ventures even during a period of tight money? Is it reasonable to put the power to make such decisions in the hands of a board or committee?

RULES VERSUS AUTHORITIES

This last question has given rise to a long-lived debate over "rules versus authorities." The issue in this debate is whether monetary policy should be determined by a board with a wide range of discretionary powers, as we have at present, or whether it would be preferable to have policy actions taken in accord with a predetermined rule.

The classic statement in favor of a rule rather than discretionary actions is by Professor Henry Simons, a liberal in a somewhat different sense from the one the term is used in today. Simons's position was that having monetary policy determined by a board was incompatible with economic freedom.[17] The preference for a rule is also based on the belief that authorities tend to make poor decisions, and, even if they should make a decision that is right at the time it is made, the policy action may be inappropriate by the time it takes effect on the economy.

A positive advantage of the "rule system" is that the public would know what monetary-policy actions will be. That is, not only do we avoid conscious wrong decisions, but also we eliminate uncertainty and guesswork about those decisions. A considerable amount of effort is expended by people dealing in securities and credit in trying to "outguess the Federal Reserve." Under our present system, there are large rewards for those who are able to predict correctly what the Fed is going to do. A definite rule for monetary policy would minimize uncertainty, and uncertainty is a cost.

The major difficulty with the rule approach, of course, is finding a good rule—a rule so good, in fact, that it will be appropriate

---

[17] See his "Rules versus Authorities in Monetary Policy," *Journal of Political Economy*, February 1936, p. 3.

for all circumstances that might arise. If we can find such a rule, then we do not even have to enact it into law, because the authorities would presumably be sensible enough to use it. The question still remains, however, Do we have such a rule?

Professor Simons's rule was that a "federal authority endowed with large administrative powers" would act so as to stabilize a price index, "preferably an index of prices of competitively produced commodities." This authority, with fiscal as well as monetary powers, would take deflationary actions when the price index was rising and inflationary actions when the price index was falling. It should be noted that this does not remove discretionary powers from the monetary authority; it simply pins down the objective that is to be their single goal. Price stability is taken as the only goal of national economy—full employment and growth are not given any weight in the determination of policy.

Most people today would not be willing to accept Simons's rule, and the present advocates of a rule have gone back to modify an earlier suggestion of Simons. At one time, he proposed that the monetary authority simply maintain a constant supply of money. He later rejected this because of the fuzziness concerning the definition of money—the monetary authority might have difficulty in determining which concept of the money supply they were supposed to stabilize. The current proposal by the rule proponents is that the Federal Reserve increase the money supply at a steady rate—say, 3 percent per year.

Adoption of this sort of rule means, in effect, that we would make no attempt at all to smooth out economic fluctuations through monetary policy. Despite the fact that the record of monetary-policy actions to combat fluctuations has not been a terribly good one, it seems premature to give up the effort completely. Furthermore, the record of recent years has been better than that of the more distant past.

QUESTIONS

1 What is meant by "full employment"?
2 What is meant by "stable prices"?
3 What is meant by "a high rate of economic growth"?
4 If it were necessary to set priorities for the various economic objectives, how would you rank the importance of the goals discussed in this chapter?
5 Why does inflation generally occur during wars?
6 "Most of the unemployed do not really want to work anyway." Do you agree?

7 Would you prefer 7 percent unemployment and stable prices, 5 percent unemployment and a 3 percent annual rate of price increases, or 3 percent unemployment and a 5 percent annual rate of price increases?

8 If government price and wage controls could successfully keep prices stable, would you favor their permanent use?

9 What policy objectives does the Federal Reserve consider most important?

SELECTED READINGS

BACH, GEORGE L., *Making Monetary and Fiscal Policy*. Washington, D.C.: The Brookings Institution, 1971.

Board of Governors of the Federal Reserve, *Public Policy and Capital Formation*. Washington, D.C., 1981.

DEWALD, WILLIAM G., and HARRY G. JOHNSON, "An Objective Analysis of the Objectives of American Monetary Policy, 1952–1961." In *Banking and Monetary Studies*, Deane Carson, ed. Homewood, Ill.: Richard D. Irwin, 1963.

FRIEDMAN, MILTON, *A Program for Monetary Stability*. New York: Fordham University Press, 1959.

GINZBERG, ELI, "The Job Problem," *Scientific American*, November 1977, p. 43.

MAYER, THOMAS, *Monetary Policy in the United States*. New York: Random House, 1968.

REES, JIM E., "The New Inflation," *Journal of Economic Issues*, June 1977.

YEAGER, LELAND, ed., *In Search of a Monetary Constitution*. Cambridge, Mass.: Harvard University Press, 1962.

28

Federal Reserve Policy: The First Fifty Years

The Federal Reserve System came into being amid considerable controversy over its purposes and functions. As Professor Chandler has put it, "The nature of the Federal Reserve Act practically assured a maximum of conflict and controversy within the new System."[1] The Federal Reserve Act itself was not very precise about many of the functions and operations of the new system. To some extent, of course, this was intentional and desirable—Congress was creating a system that, it was hoped, would be flexible and adaptable to changes in economic and financial circumstances. The Federal Reserve Act, however, shared some of the shortcomings of much legislation that arises from the work of a committee. Some provisions may be compromises with which no one is wholly satisfied, and others may purposely be stated in ambiguous terms so that people with differing views may feel that, properly interpreted, the legislation supports their view. It is possible that if the Federal Reserve Act had clearly stated provisions dealing with all aspects of system structure, operations, and functions, no legislation at all would have passed Congress. And clearly, the Federal Reserve Act as enacted by Congress was better than no legislation at all.

[1] L.V. Chandler, *Benjamin Strong, Central Banker* (Washington, D.C.: The Brookings Institution, 1958), p. 6.

Part of the controversy over the operations of the Federal Reserve System in its formative years arose because it was not clear what the major functions and purposes of the system should be. The direct stimulus to the establishment of a central bank in the United States (which had been without one since the demise of the Second Bank of the United States in 1836) was the panic of 1907. Therefore, some viewed the sole purpose of the new Federal Reserve System as preventing a recurrence of such financial crises. But even this is not a clear mandate to action. It could be interpreted to mean that the system should act only during periods of actual or imminent financial crisis; but it could also be interpreted to mean that the system should act continuously, if need be, to prevent the development of conditions that could lead to financial crisis.

The Federal Reserve Act states its purposes thus: "To furnish an elastic currency, to afford means of discounting commercial paper, to establish a more effective supervision of the banking in the United States, and for other purposes." The only elaboration of these purposes is the statement that the system should use its powers "to accommodate commerce and business."

It is the purpose of this chapter to describe the change in Federal Reserve operations from concentration on the rather narrow objectives listed above to the major responsibility the Fed now has of formulation and execution of monetary policy for the purpose of economic stabilization.

WORLD WAR I

The Federal Reserve Banks opened for business in November 1914, under most inauspicious conditions. War had broken out a few months earlier, bringing with it both financial panic and economic crisis. Shipping in the Atlantic was severely disrupted, and in 1914 and early 1915, considerable domestic unemployment resulted from the drop in American exports.

Conditions improved rapidly, and by 1916, business activity was booming. Gold poured into the country, providing the banking system with ample reserves to expand loans. Demand deposits were up by 19 percent at the end of 1916 as compared with the end of 1914, and wholesale prices were up by 26 percent.

Despite the inflationary situation, the Federal Reserve was helpless to prevent monetary expansion. Raising the discount rate would not have done any good, since banks had ample reserves and thus had no need to borrow from the Federal Reserve. The Fed did not have the power to raise reserve requirements, and the system could not sell securities in the open market because it had no securities. In fact, the Reserve Banks actually bought some securities during this period to provide themselves with adequate earnings to meet their expenses.

The Federal Reserve System faced its first major task as an important cog in the vast financial machinery necessary to finance the United States' role in World War I. During 1918–1919, the Treasury spent over $30 billion. For the sake of comparison, it might be noted that total government expenditures in 1916 were less than $750 million.

Nearly three-fourths of the government expenditures during World War I were financed through borrowing rather than by taxation. It was clear that the primary objective of Federal Reserve activity during this period was to facilitate the Treasury's financing of its huge deficits. The Federal Reserve Banks performed many services as fiscal agent for the Treasury, and the mechanics of Treasury financing ran very smoothly. The system contributed to the financial success of Treasury operations by maintaining low discount rates and encouraging banks to borrow from the Federal Reserve Banks in order to buy government securities. The rates were set below the coupon rate on government bonds, and thus banks could profit by buying government securities and then pledging these securities as collateral for loans from their Federal Reserve Bank.

During the period of war financing, member-bank borrowing from the Reserve Banks increased by about $2 billion. Open-market operations, on the other hand, were quite limited. Total system holdings of government securities remained below $300 million all during this period in which the Fed was encouraging banks and individuals to invest heavily in government securities. Benjamin Strong, governor of the Federal Reserve Bank of New York, felt that the use of discount policy to encourage purchase of government securities was less inflationary than direct purchase of securities by the Fed.[2]

Inflation continued unchecked during the war. Although the Fed was concerned about the inflation, it was certainly of secondary importance as compared with the need to aid in Treasury financing.

---

[2] The structure of the Federal Reserve System at this time was such that the powers of the Federal Reserve Board were relatively weak as compared with those of the Reserve Banks. The New York Bank, by virtue of its size, was clearly the most powerful bank, and Strong, by virtue of his ability, was clearly the most powerful figure within the system. Throughout much of the history of the Fed, the balance of power between the Board in Washington and the New York Bank was a frequent cause of friction.

Substantial but unsuccessful attempts were made to use moral suasion to restrain credit expansion.

Although the Federal Reserve and the Treasury had worked together smoothly during the war, the armistice brought an end to these peaceful relations. The Federal Reserve was greatly concerned about inflation. Unfortunately, Treasury spending and borrowing continued at high levels immediately after the war, and although the Fed was anxious to tighten credit to fight inflation, it was not until late 1919 that the first modest step in that direction was taken.

The lack of action by the Federal Reserve during 1919 may be counted as the first major mistake of the system in monetary policy. Friedman and Schwartz comment:

> The reason for Federal Reserve inaction was not, as in the earlier period . . . , the absence of technical power to control monetary expansion. On the one hand, there was a gold outflow rather than inflow; on the other, the System had acquired a substantial portfolio. By raising discount rates and selling securities on the open market, the System was clearly in a position to keep down the growth of the stock of money to any desired rate. Nor was the reason, at least after the Spring of 1919, Treasury deficit financing.[3]

Governor Strong and others within the system urged that restrictive steps be taken during the year. In spite of these suggestions and a widespread concern with inflationary developments, the Federal Reserve:

> . . . restricted itself to moral suasion, urging banks to discriminate between "essential and non-essential credits"—a formula that successive use from that time to this has rendered neither less appealing to the Reserve System as a means of shifting responsibility nor more effective as a means of controlling monetary expansion.[4]

The Fed finally took stronger action—an increase in discount rates by all twelve banks to 6 percent in January 1920, with some banks subsequently going as high as 7 percent. The timing of the restrictive actions was extremely unfortunate. The inflationary bubble, which had been growing since 1915 with only a slight interruption in 1918, burst in early 1920. Despite the sharp drop in prices and production that took place in 1920 and early 1921, the Fed maintained its policy of monetary stringency until May 1921.

[3] Milton Friedman and Anna Schwartz, *A Monetary History of the United States* (Princeton, N.J.: Princeton University Press, 1963), p. 223.

[4] *Ibid.* It might be noted that this comment still seems to be valid, even though the Fed made exactly the same exhortations to banks in the late 1960s.

Much well-deserved criticism has been leveled at the Fed for its handling of the post–World War I period. It clearly would have been desirable if the Fed had taken more vigorous action in 1919, but since it had not, it would have been better if it had acted less vigorously in 1920. More difficult to understand, however, is the steadfastness of the system in not reversing itself earlier once the inflation was clearly over. Part of the reason is to be found in the gold position of the Federal Reserve Banks. An embargo on gold exports imposed during the war was lifted in 1919, and gold flowed out of the country. The Federal Reserve Banks at this time were required to hold gold equal to 40 percent and 35 percent against Federal Reserve notes and deposits respectively. The reserve ratio fell to around 40 percent in 1920 for the system as a whole because of the gold outflow and an expansion in note and deposit liabilities. The Federal Reserve Bank of New York ran several reserve deficiencies on which it paid penalties. However, the Federal Reserve did have the power to suspend the gold reserve requirement.

In a narrow sense, the tight-money policies of 1920–1921 were a success—there was no financial panic such as occurred in 1907, and the monetary system weathered the threat to our gold position without being forced to abandon the gold standard. It is true that we suffered a severe business recession, but at the time it was not clear that preventing such recessions was the responsibility of the Federal Reserve System. Partly as a result of this experience, it became clear that preventing or moderating business recession was the real mission of the Federal Reserve.

One side effect of the tight-money policy of 1920–1921 deserves notice. Banks and individuals pressed for cash sold large quantities of government securities at falling prices. People who had patriotically followed the exhortations of their government to buy government securities during the war found that they suffered severe monetary losses from having done so. Many people, including Governor Strong, had doubts as to the equity of such a monetary policy. This issue returned to plague the Fed after World War II.

THE 1920s: BOOM AND BUST

The United States came out of World War I as the leading industrial country of the world. Recovery from the postwar depression was rapid. England and other European countries had suffered heavily during the war, and most foreign countries had abandoned the gold

standard.[5] New York was now the principal financial center of the
world.

It was with this situation as background that the Federal Reserve began anew its considerations of the appropriate role of a
central bank in the American economy. During this period, the Fed
accepted the view that monetary policy must be concerned with
maintenance of price-level stability and a high level of economic
activity. Several developments in Federal Reserve techniques took
place during the early 1920s. Open-market operations had been a
function of the individual Reserve Banks, but in 1923, the system
established an Open Market Committee consisting of five Reserve
Bank presidents. Whereas in the past, open-market operations had
frequently been undertaken for the sake of improving Reserve
Bank earnings, it was now recognized that they had important
effects on bank reserves and that such operations should be conducted with a view toward their effect on the general credit situation.

One of the principal factors complicating Federal Reserve
policymaking during the 1920s (as during the 1960s) was our gold
position. Gold flowed into the United States during the early 1920s,
and it was clear that the old "rules of the gold-standard game" could
no longer be applied. Under these "rules," it was the duty of a
country receiving an inflow of gold to allow this gold to expand the
domestic money supply, drive up prices, and hence lead to an import
surplus. This would mean a gold outflow that would return the
system to equilibrium. A country experiencing a gold outflow was to
allow the loss of gold to cause a domestic deflation, which would lead
to an export surplus, which in turn would mean a return flow of
gold. Even by the 1920s, it was clear that few countries were willing
to suffer alternating periods of inflation and deflation for the sake
of preserving the "gold-standard game."

The inflow of gold to the United States during the 1920s meant,
obviously, that other countries were losing gold, and their gold
losses were disrupting their attempts at economic recovery. The
United States was not willing to suffer a serious domestic inflation

---

[5] The United States remained on the gold standard throughout the war and
was legally obliged to redeem U.S. currency for gold on demand, but the Treasury
discouraged people from requesting gold. As Secretary of the Treasury Houston put
it, "The United States call the attention of persons requesting gold to the Treasury's
attitude . . . and invite them to accept other currency instead, but gold . . . will not
be refused to persons who demand it." Professor Chandler suggests that "Secretary
Houston might have added that those who tried to get gold usually gave up after a
long runaround." See Chandler, *Benjamin Strong*, pp. 103ff.

as a means of reversing this flow, but the Federal Reserve did want to aid foreign countries in the restoration of their gold standard.

During the 1920s, the Fed varied its policy actions in general accord with economic conditions. The 1920s were generally prosperous, and thus high discount rates and sales of securities in the open market were called for and carried out. Relatively minor recessions occurred in 1924 and 1927, and in both cases, the Fed reacted promptly with lowered rates and open-market purchases.

It is important to realize that these two goals of Federal Reserve policy could conflict. Aiding foreign countries with their gold problems calls for an easy-money policy. If interest rates in this country are lower than interest rates abroad, a sizable amount of investable funds, seeking the highest attainable return, would flow abroad. Low interest rates in this country would also tend to stimulate business investment and hence national income, and with a higher level of national income, our demand for foreign goods would be higher. It is clear, then, that if the Fed wanted to aid in the restoration and maintenance of gold standards abroad, an easy-money policy was called for.

On the other hand, the generally prosperous domestic business situation would call for a relatively tight monetary policy. Federal Reserve statements consistently held that domestic goals would not be sacrificed to international ones, but the policy actions were not always in accord with this position. During the years of high-level business activity, monetary policy was perhaps not as restrictive as it could have been, and during the years of recession, it appears that the Fed took a much more vigorously easy policy than the domestic situation called for.

Restoration of the gold standard in England was one of the leading economic issues of the 1920s. It was more or less taken for granted that the British goal was a return to a gold standard under which the pound would be valued at $4.87, its prewar price. This was not accomplished until 1925, but Strong and Montagu Norman, the governor of the Bank of England, had discussed the problem for several years. The recession of 1924 gave the Fed the opportunity it had been looking for. Now both domestic and international considerations called for a policy of ease, and the system undertook its most aggressive easy-money policy since World War I.

In April 1925, Britain returned to the gold standard with the pound pegged at $4.87. In retrospect, this was a mistake. The high price of the pound made British goods expensive in world markets. England became an unattractive place to buy and a good place in which to sell. British exports dropped far below imports, and, as Professor Galbraith has put it, "In 1925 began the long series of exchange crises which, like the lions in Trafalgar Square and the street walkers in Piccadilly, are now an established part of the British scene."[6]

The easy-money policy of 1924 had important domestic effects as well. It certainly contributed to the very vigorous recovery from the recession. It also made funds available for stock-market speculation, which was becoming a serious problem.

The following years, 1925 and 1926, were years of general prosperity. The Federal Reserve became increasingly concerned about stock-market speculation but took no strong action. In the first place, many system officials believed that regulating speculation was not the duty of the Fed. Second, there were no inflationary tendencies in the economy as a whole, and there was the danger that any restrictive action taken to restrain speculation might disturb the high level of business activity.

A modest decline in business activity during 1927 was the occasion for a reduction in Federal Reserve Bank discount rates and expansive open-market operations, to some extent at the urging of foreign central bankers. There has been much criticism of the 1927 actions. Much of the newly created credit found its way into the stock market and contributed to the speculative excesses of 1928 and 1929. One economist has said that "from that date, according to all the evidence, the situation got completely out of control."[7]

There was some opposition within the Federal Reserve System to the easing of credit in 1927. When the Federal Reserve Board and Governor Strong urged the Reserve Banks to reduce their discount rates from 4 percent to 3½ percent, the Chicago Bank refused. The board then ordered the Chicago Bank to reduce its rate, and controversy arose over the board's authority to take such action.

The original philosophy of the Federal Reserve Act contemplated different discount rates in the various districts, determined on the basis of local conditions. By the late 1920s, however, it was clear that the money market is a national one, and the trend was toward uniformity of rates. The board won its case, and since then, "the Board's right to change discount rates on its own initiative has not been seriously questioned."[8]

The chief concern of the Federal Reserve during the next two years was the stock market. Until 1928, it was quite possible to argue that the level of stock prices was reasonable considering the

---

[6] John K. Galbraith, *The Great Crash* (Boston: Houghton Mifflin, 1954), p. 14.

[7] Lionel Robbins, *The Great Depression* (New York: Macmillan, 1934), p. 53.

[8] E.A. Goldenweiser, *American Monetary Policy* (New York: McGraw-Hill, 1951), p. 148.

growth in corporate earnings, the prospects for the future, the peaceful world outlook, and prospects for reelection of a sympathetic Republican administration. In 1928, however:

> The nature of the boom changed. The mass escape into make-believe, so much a part of the true speculative orgy, started in earnest. . . . [T]he market began to rise, not by slow, steady steps, but by great vaulting leaps.[9]

Much of the stock-market activity was financed by credit. Loans to brokers quadrupled from 1924 to 1929. Eager speculators were willing to pay very high interest rates to obtain the funds needed for their purchases of stock. By the end of 1928, the call loan rate reached 12 percent. These loans were repayable on demand and secured by readily salable stocks. They were thus a virtually riskless investment, and from all over the country and abroad, funds poured into Wall Street to earn this attractive rate.

Combatting the speculation posed a difficult problem for the Federal Reserve. The Fed did not have the power to set margin requirements in 1928. It was only in the aftermath of the crash that it acquired this tool. Restrictive actions by the Fed ran the risk of interfering with legitimate business activity.

The Federal Reserve met with considerable criticism for even the relatively mild steps that were taken. It faced a puzzling problem. Speculation was out of hand, but business activity was not really booming. Price inflation was not a problem; in fact, prices had been falling throughout the 1920s. A majority of the Federal Reserve Board believed that "stock-market speculation was none of the System's business . . . and that it would be wrong to penalize legitimate business by high rates imposed to curb speculation."[10]

Once the turning point arrived, the Federal Reserve Bank of New York acted vigorously to offset the effects of the stock-market collapse. The bank's efforts were not universally supported within the Federal Reserve System, and several attempts by the New York Bank to lower its discount rate were vetoed by the Federal Reserve Board.

THE GREAT DEPRESSION

The business downturn that began in the summer of 1929 turned into the most disastrous depression in American history. Unemployment reached 25 percent of the labor force in 1933. Industrial

[9] Galbraith, *The Great Crash*, pp. 16–17.
[10] Goldenweiser, *American Monetary Policy*, p. 153.

production fell by over 50 percent and did not recover to its 1929 level for eight years. The Great Depression was not only deep but long as well. Business firms failed by the tens of thousands, and the financial system virtually collapsed. The international gold standard, which the world's central bankers had toiled so hard to reconstruct during the 1920s, disintegrated in the face of world economic depression. The United States had experienced recessions in 1927 and 1924, as well as a serious depression in 1920–1921; but these declines were short-lived, and recovery from them was rapid. Why did the depression of the 1930s deepen and intensify rather than lose its force and turn upward?

It is sometimes assumed that the stock-market crash caused the depression. This is not the case—the business downturn began well before the market decline. On the other hand, the effect of the crash on confidence was serious, as well as its effect on people's spending. The reasons for the severity of the depression, though, must be sought in other factors.

The concepts of the multiplier and the accelerator are helpful in understanding the depression. Capital expenditures were on a high level during the 1920s. The price stability of the 1920s may indicate that throughout the decade, despite general prosperity and high levels of demand, capacity was more than adequate. The investment boom ended as capacity had gotten considerably ahead of demand.

As incomes dropped, there was little incentive for firms to add to their physical assets. Even when plant and equipment wore out, the remaining capacity was ample to handle the reduced volume of business. This situation is typical of business cycles, of course. If the structure of the economy had been basically sound and appropriate policy steps had been taken, it is probable that the depression that began in 1929 would have run its course in a short period of time.

Unfortunately, the economy was not basically sound. The banking system was in bad shape. Its structure consisted of thousands of small unit banks. The decline in real estate prices generated large losses on real estate loans, and widespread business failures led to losses on business loans. Many banks that were basically solvent were illiquid, and "runs" forced many to close their doors. The failure of one small local bank led to fears for the safety of others, and the problems of one bank spread to another in a chain reaction.

The corporate structure also suffered from serious structural flaws. Holding companies controlled large segments of the electric-utility and railroad industries. Dividends from the operating companies were necessary to pay interest on bonds of the holding companies, and this led to pressure to cut capital expenditures to provide cash for dividend payments lest the whole structure collapse.

The international financial structure was also in a precarious state. Despite the rebuilding effort of the 1920s, the balance-of-payments positions of many countries, particularly the raw-material suppliers, were vulnerable. Many of these countries had achieved balance only by borrowing heavily from the United States. The stock-market crash and the onset of the depression weakened confidence and reduced the willingness of financial institutions to extend loans to foreign countries. The international panic began in earnest with the failure of the Credit-Anstalt, Austria's largest bank, in 1931. Many creditors reacted by demanding gold (large amounts of the international lending of the time were repayable on demand or on short notice), and Austria and then Germany suspended gold payments. England abandoned the gold standard late in 1931, and by the middle of 1932, most of the leading countries of the world had left the gold standard. The United States was also subject to drains of gold in 1931, and this had a significant effect on Federal Reserve policy.

Federal Reserve actions during the first two years of the depression were pitifully weak, despite the push toward stronger action by the Federal Reserve Bank of New York. Discount rates were reduced in several steps, with the rate at the New York Bank lowered to 1½ percent in 1931. About $500 million of government securities were bought by the Fed in the two years following the onset of the depression. Although this amount was fairly sizable by the standards of the day, it was less than the reductions in member-bank borrowing from the Federal Reserve Banks. The net effect, then, was an absolute reduction in the volume of Federal Reserve credit. As a result, the money stock dropped sharply during this period. From the point of view of monetarist economic historians, it was the decline of the money supply that was responsible for the length and severity of the depression.

That problem was aggravated by the gold outflows that resulted from the breakdown of the gold standard in 1931. As in 1920, the gold outflows induced the Fed to adopt the traditional policy of a central bank faced with gold losses—raise interest rates! This policy has been rationalized on the basis of collateral requirements against Federal Reserve notes outstanding. But once that requirement was lifted by the Glass-Steagall Act in 1932, the Federal Reserve, after a brief period of vigorous open-market operations, again allowed the money supply to continue its decrease in 1933.

Many banks were in a critical position at this time owing to defaults on loans, and bank failures were frequent. On March 4, 1933, the day of his inauguration, President Roosevelt urged state governors to declare banking holidays in their states, and nearly all complied. A four-day national banking holiday was declared immediately thereafter. The immediate problem facing the new president was the reopening of the banks, and steps were taken promptly to achieve this purpose.

The supervisory authorities examined all the banks and divided them into three classes. Those in good condition were permitted to resume business. Those that appeared to be permanently insolvent were permanently closed. Steps were then taken to aid the middle class of banks—banks not sound enough to be immediately reopened but not in a hopeless condition. Funds were advanced to some banks through the device of purchases of preferred stock by the Reconstruction Finance Corporation, a government credit agency. As a result of these actions, most banks reopened successfully. The depression was not over by any means, but the financial panic was ended.

In the period following the banking crisis, banks held large amounts of excess reserves. This was not the result of direct Federal reserve actions, but rather resulted from the huge gold inflow that the Fed did not offset. The country's gold stock, which totaled about $3 billion in 1929, amounted to over $10 billion in 1936. As a result, member banks had excess reserves of $3 billion.

At this time, unemployment was still serious, consumer prices were just barely above the 1933 lows, and industrial production was still below 1929. Yet the Fed became concerned about the large amount of excess reserves—not that there was any immediate or foreseeable danger of inflation, but because of the fact that these excess reserves insulated the banking system from Federal Reserve action. It was felt that if it ever became desirable in the future to adopt a restrictive monetary policy, the system would be helpless. An increase in discount rates would be meaningless, since banks were not borrowing from the Fed. Sales of securities in the open market could not seriously affect the reserve position of the banks when excess reserves were so large. In 1936, and again in 1937, the Board of Governors raised reserve requirements (a power they had just been given) so as to regain control of the monetary system and to "bring the System in closer touch with the market." The Board stated, by way of explanation for its action:

> By the present action excess reserves will be reduced to within the amount that could be absorbed through open-market operations, should such action become desirable. . . . It is far better to sterilize a part of these superfluous reserves while they are still unused, than to permit a credit structure to be erected upon them and then to withdraw the foundation of the structure.[11]

[11] Quoted in Goldenweiser, *American Monetary Policy*, p. 176.

Excess reserves fell substantially, dropping below $1 billion during May 1937. The Federal Reserve did not act adequately through open-market operations to offset part of the restrictive impact of the reserve-requirement changes. Regardless of the merits of the Fed's desire to regain control of the monetary system, the action taken was most unfortunate. The recovery had been rather steady during the mid-1930s, but incomplete—unemployment was still about 15 percent of the labor force in 1937. The economy turned down in 1937, and the recession, though short-lived, was sharp.

The cause of the Federal Reserve's errors in raising reserve requirements in 1936 and 1937 lay in the view of excess reserves as representing idle and unneeded funds. In the Fed's view, the increase in reserve requirements, leaving member banks with substantial excess reserves anyway, would have no immediate adverse effect on monetary conditions. But bankers in 1936, not unreasonably, *wanted* to hold excess reserves. Federal Reserve actions to reduce excess reserves led to actions by the banks to restore their holdings of excess reserves. Such actions produced a drop in the money supply and the 1937 recession.

It is easy to be critical of the Fed for its policies or lack of them during the Great Depression. It is somewhat more difficult to assess what would have happened if monetary-policy decisions were optimal. A Federal Reserve official has answered this question with the conclusion that "the difference in the effect of what was actually done and what could conceivably have been considered by the authorities is not great."[12]

Friedman and Schwartz come to the opposite conclusion in their monumental *Monetary History of the United States*. There is, of course, no way to be certain about questions of "what might have been," or "what would have happened if . . . ?" The view of most economists today seems to be that even with optimal decision making by the Federal Reserve System, there would have been an economic downturn in 1929. It is reasonable to believe that this downturn would have been a relatively serious recession, but it is quite clear that it need not have developed into the long-lived, deep depression that actually took place.

BANKING AND MONETARY REFORMS: 1933–1935

The financial collapse after 1929 led to a substantial amount of new banking and monetary legislation. The most important for our pur-

---

[12] Goldenweiser, *American Monetary Policy*, p. 159.

poses are the Banking Acts of 1933 and 1935. Other important financial legislation of this period included the Securities Act of 1933 and
the Securities Exchange Act of 1934. Although the provisions of all
this legislation cannot be discussed here in full, it is desirable to
indicate some of the significant changes in the structure and operations of the financial system introduced during this period.

One prominent aspect of these legal changes was a major reorganization of the structure of the Federal Reserve System. The
Federal Reserve Board was replaced by a new Board of Governors.
More than a mere change of title was involved: The terms of office
for members of the Board were lengthened, and the ex officio mem-
berships on the Board of the secretary of the Treasury and the
Comptroller of the Currency were eliminated. The aim of these
moves was to strengthen the authority of the board relative to the
Reserve Banks. In addition, the position of the Federal Open Market Committee was written into the law. The Banking Act of 1935
also set the membership of the committee, giving the Board a
majority of the membership.

The powers of the Federal Reserve System were also broadened by this legislation. The Board was given authority to vary
reserve requirements for member banks up to twice the levels specified in the Federal Reserve Act. It was also given the power to set
minimum margin requirements on securities loans, and these applied to all lenders, not just member banks. This is a power that
might have been useful in 1928 and 1929.

The Board was authorized to set maximum interest rates that
could be paid by member banks on time deposits. The Banking Act
of 1933 carried a provision prohibiting the payment of interest on
demand deposits. In addition, the supremacy of the Board in disputes with the Reserve Banks over discount rates was made explicit.

Not only was the Federal Deposit Insurance Corporation
established to protect depositors in commercial and mutual savings
banks, but also the Federal Savings and Loan Insurance Corporation was set up to provide protection for S&L depositors. The Securities and Exchange Commission was given broad powers over
corporations issuing securities and over the operations of organized
stock exchanges. It had become clear that the federal government
has an obligation to prevent recurrence of the economic disaster of
the 1930s.

WORLD WAR II AND AFTERWARD

The outbreak of World War II necessitated large government expenditures for war goods, and they were intensified following

United States entry into the war in 1941. The Treasury tried to finance as large a proportion of the deficit as possible by borrowing from individuals and nonbank institutions. This has a less inflationary effect than borrowing from banks or the Federal Reserve. Sales of War (savings) Bonds to individuals were pushed aggressively. Since this technique could not provide all the funds needed, bank financing was necessary. Various devices were used to encourage banks to buy government securities. The most important of these had to do with the rate structure.

The Treasury adopted a structure of rates to be paid on securities of varying maturities, ranging from ⅜ percent to be paid on bills to 2½ percent on long-term bonds. The Fed stood behind this rate structure by supporting the price of government securities at par. This "pegging" of government-security prices made such securities perfectly liquid—no one need fear taking a loss on a purchase of government bonds, since the Fed was willing to buy them at par. And since long-term government bonds were perfectly liquid, there was no incentive to buy shorter-term securities with lower yields. In particular, commercial banks did not have to hold Treasury bills for liquidity purposes at a rate of ⅜ percent; long-term bonds providing a return of 2½ percent were just as liquid. The net result of this attempt to fix the rate structure was that the Federal Reserve System ended up holding all the Treasury bills outstanding.[13]

The effect of the wartime economic pressures and the tax and financing policies adopted was a strong inflationary pressure in the economy. The direct effects of this pressure were constrained by a whole raft of direct controls on the economy. Price and wage ceilings were established, many goods were rationed, and "black-market" trading in such goods was illegal. Probably because of a strong patriotic urge to comply with the laws, the direct controls worked fairly well—better than most economists would have predicted, and probably better than similar controls can work in peacetime.

The combination of fiscal and monetary inflation with direct controls was not a happy one. Professor Shaw has characterized the policy as follows: "The money accelerator was pushed to the floorboard, and policemen were employed in droves to keep the public out of the way of the money juggernaut."[14]

Regardless of the merits of the financing program adopted for the war, once the decision was made, the Federal Reserve was obli-

[13] Some attempt was made to deal with this situation. Commercial banks were not allowed to purchase new bond issues with a maturity of over ten years.

[14] Edward S. Shaw, "Money Supply and Stable Economic Growth," in *United States Monetary Policy*, American Assembly (New York: Columbia University Press, 1958), p. 58.

gated to support it wholeheartedly. As in the post–World War I period, the return to peacetime economic activity posed problems for the monetary authorities.

In the immediate postwar period, there was agreement between the Treasury and the Federal Reserve System that the low-interest-rate policy, involving Federal Reserve pegging of government-bond prices, should be continued. Forecasts of serious postwar depression were common, based on the prospects for a sharp cut in federal-government spending. It was this presumption that inflation would not pose a problem after the war that led to early elimination of direct price and wage controls.

The postwar depression did not develop. Indeed, inflation was the serious economic problem of the period. It seems clear what monetary policy should be in such a situation—steps should be taken to tighten credit conditions. These steps must include substantial sales of government securities by the Federal Reserve. In fact, however, such actions were not taken. The Fed was concerned about inflation, and many statements were issued proclaiming that it would be nice if prices would stop rising. Unfortunately, but not surprisingly, prices did not stop rising. Several reasons were advanced by the Fed and the Treasury for maintaining the easy-money policy of the war years.

The most obvious reason for the low-interest-rate policy was the minimization of the interest costs of the federal debt. The debt had increased tremendously during the war, and interest costs made up a substantial portion of the federal budget. Low and stable interest rates facilitate the problems of Treasury finance. Even though the Treasury had surpluses during much of this period, refunding operations were carried out on a large scale. It was feared that a decline in government-bond prices, which would accompany a restrictive monetary policy, would weaken confidence in the credit standing of the U.S. government, and also that confidence in some financial institutions suffering large capital losses on their bond holdings might be impaired.

Many people were concerned with the equity of an end to Federal Reserve support of government bond prices. It was argued that it would be unfair to inflict losses on citizens who had invested heavily to support their government. Thus, President Truman pledged continuation of the support program, declaring that "the investment market will not be subjected to the demoralization which swept over it in 1920 when the unsupported market for Government bonds fell about 20 percent below par."[15] The situations

---

[15]*Economic Report of the President*, 1948, p. 86.

were not quite analogous. In 1920, many relatively small investors suffered capital losses. After World War II, the small investors were protected from declines in market price, since most of their holdings were in the form of nonmarketable savings bonds.

Some people favored retention of the Fed's easy-money policies because of the fear that tight money would lead to depression. Others (and sometimes the same people) argued that support should be retained because tight money would be ineffective in fighting inflation.

The outbreak of the Korean conflict in mid-1950 accelerated the forces of inflation. Consumers and business alike, fearing the return of wartime shortages, rushed to buy. The Consumer Price Index increased by 8 percent from 1950 to 1951. Some restraint was achieved by a very successful fiscal policy involving substantial tax increases. Monetary policy, however, made no contribution to price stability. The money supply increased rapidly during 1950, and the Fed added about $3 billion to its holdings of government securities during the last half of 1950.

Federal Reserve officials had generally favored the easy-money policy during the immediate postwar years, although some of its officials were unhappy with the policy that was actually followed. In 1950, the Fed became even more unhappy with the Treasury's view, and attempts were made to compromise. The Treasury refused, and the conflict broke into the open. After considerable controversy, the Fed and the Treasury reached an "accord" on March 4, 1951. A joint Federal Reserve–Treasury statement issued at that time announced:

> The Treasury and the Federal Reserve System have reached full accord with respect to debt-management and monetary policies to be pursued in furthering their common purpose to assure the successful financing of the Government's requirements and, at the same time, to minimize monetization of the public debt.

Several steps were taken in direct response to the accord, but the major result was the announcement that a 2¾ percent bond would be offered by the Treasury. Long-term government-bond prices promptly dropped below par, for the first time since 1937. The accord was a clear-cut victory for the Federal Reserve and meant a return to discretionary monetary policy.

AFTER THE ACCORD

The Fed used its regained authority very cautiously in the months following the accord. It sold some government securities during 1951, but the amounts involved were not large. Inflationary pressures had subsided. The economy was operating at a high level of activity, spurred by large defense expenditures.

Economic activity continued strong through early 1953, and then it began to weaken. The recession began in the summer of 1953 and reached its low point in the second quarter of 1954. The most important factor contributing to the decline was a sizable cut in federal-government expenditures, and business inventories also declined significantly. The Fed took vigorous action to combat the downturn—all three Federal Reserve weapons were used during 1953 and 1954. Reserve requirements were cut in 1953 and again in 1954. Large amounts of government securities were purchased, and discount rates were cut. The yield on Treasury bills was under 1 percent for much of 1954.

Recovery from the 1954 recession was rapid and vigorous. Gross national product, which amounted to $360 billion in 1954, was running at an annual rate of over $400 billion at the end of 1955. The principal factor in the boom was the rise of capital outlays by business firms. Corporate profits reflected the state of business conditions, rising by 30 percent from 1954 to 1956.

Unfortunately, this period of prosperity was accompanied by inflationary tendencies in the economy. The Consumer Price Index was quite stable during 1955 but began to rise rapidly in 1956 after a four-year period of general price stability. From mid-1952 to early 1956, there had been virtually no change in the price index. From February 1956 to the end of 1956, prices rose by nearly 3 percent, and 1957 saw another 3 percent increase. A 3 percent inflation rate seems modest by recent standards, but at the time, it was considered a serious problem.

As the boom proceeded through 1955 and early 1956, the Federal Reserve took actions to restrain the inflationary tendencies of the economy. Securities were sold in the open market, and discount rates were raised in several small steps. The discount rate stood at 2¾ percent in the spring of 1956. In retrospect, these actions do not seem particularly strong in view of the underlying economic factors. The Fed, however, was sensitive about criticism that tight-money policies had caused the 1954 recession, and thus it moved very cautiously in handling the boom.

Business activity was proceeding at a high level in early 1957. The Federal Reserve sold large amounts of securities, and the level of interest rates substantially exceeded that of 1956.

This more vigorous policy of credit restraint was followed despite uncertainties as to the business outlook. The Open Market Committee officially recognized the danger of a downturn in its March directive, but actions taken by the Fed continued to be strongly restrictive. The end of the boom did occur in August 1957, but there were signs before then that the strength of the boom was waning. Some economic indicators had turned down several months earlier.

The Fed acted strongly once it became convinced that the downturn was genuine, but it was not until March 1958 (after the decline in business activity had been going on for about seven months) that the Open Market Committee actually adopted a policy of "monetary ease."

Recovery from the 1958 recession came quickly. The recession was a sharp one, with industrial production declining 14 percent from its peak and GNP declining by nearly 4 percent, in contrast to respective declines of 10 percent and less than 3 percent in 1954. The trough was reached only two quarters after the peak, and the economy had bounced back to record levels of production less than a year after the bottom. The vigorous credit-easing measures taken by the Fed during the recession certainly deserve some of the credit for the speed of the recovery, but monetary policy in this case was substantially aided from the fiscal side.

Much of the cushioning by fiscal policy during the recession came from the effect of automatic stabilizers. There was no fortuitous tax cut as had occurred during the 1954 recession, but nevertheless the federal government moved from a budgetary surplus in 1957 to a deficit of $12 billion in the fiscal year beginning July 1958.

The movement of the economy into record high ground in 1959 was accompanied by renewed upward movement of consumer prices. The Federal Reserve moved to counteract the inflation. Credit conditions became extremely tight by mid-1959, and interest rates reached the highest levels since the early 1930s, exceeding by substantial amounts the rates of 1957.

THE "SOARING SIXTIES"

A high note of optimism marked the start of 1960. Most business publications carried very rosy economic forecasts for the 1960s. It soon became apparent, however, that the rapid expansion that took place during much of 1959 was missing, even though economic activity continued at record levels during the first quarter. As the year wore on, however, this "high-level stagnation" was followed by a definite but mild recession.

The policy of the Federal Reserve became one of active ease as the year wore on—reserve requirements were lowered, discount rates were lowered, and member banks were allowed to include more, and finally all, of their vault cash as part of their legal reserves. Interest rates fell sharply from the very high levels of late 1959 as it became apparent that a business boom was not in the cards for 1960.

During 1960, the United States experienced a substantial gold outflow. Although the fundamental causes of the outflow lay outside the direct control of the Federal Reserve, the policy of monetary ease and the associated low interest rates tended to encourage short-term funds to seek higher returns in other countries. Combatting these outflows would require higher interest rates, but this would conflict with the desire to maintain an easy-money policy for purposes of facilitating domestic economic recovery. The Fed had followed the situation closely during the year, and at the Open Market Committee meeting of October 25, the existing directive was amended to recommend a policy of "encouraging monetary expansion, while taking into consideration current international developments."

The implication of this decision was that the Fed would continue to make reserves freely available to the banking system but would try to keep short-term rates from falling too steeply. This appears to involve contradictory policies, but the Federal Reserve managed during the latter half of 1960 to maintain measures of reserves at a high level while interest rates did not decline to the low levels of 1954 or 1958. Thus, the rate on Treasury bills fell below 1 percent in 1954 and 1958 but not below 2 percent during 1960. Of course, the 1960 recession was not as severe as the earlier ones and perhaps did not call for such strong measures.

The recession of 1960 and the general question of economic growth became important issues during the presidential campaign of 1960. Democrats pointed to the current recession, as well as to the two previous recessions during the Eisenhower administration, as proof of Republican failure in the area of economic policy making. Although it is never clear how many votes are swayed by a particular issue, the 1960 election results were so close that the economic issue was obviously an important factor in the election of President Kennedy. This lesson was not lost on his opponent in the 1960 campaign. Richard Nixon had argued within the Eisenhower administration in favor of a tax cut to fight the recession and later showed his willingness to incur huge federal budget deficits to counter high unemployment during his first term as president.

The decline in business activity ended in early 1961, and the recovery was rapid, bringing the economy to record levels during the year. The recession turned out to be the mildest of our postwar recessions by any measure and the return to previous peaks the most rapid. Personal income had declined only slightly, and consumer expenditures on nondurable goods actually rose all through the recession.

Following the recession of 1960, the economy embarked on its longest uninterrupted period of economic growth. From 1961 to 1969, GNP grew at a rate of over 5 percent per year in real terms. Over the same period, industrial production grew at an annual rate of 6.5 percent. Until the acceleration of the Vietnam War in 1965, prices were relatively stable. The Consumer Price Index increased at an average rate of only 1.2 percent from 1961 to 1964. Wholesale prices were actually lower in 1964 than they had been in 1960.

The performance of the economy in absorbing increases into the labor force was not fully satisfactory during this period, however. Recovery from the 1960 recession was not complete, and unemployment averaged an unsatisfactorily high 5.7 percent in 1963.

Monetary policy was easier in the early 1960s than it had been in the late 1950s. The money supply grew at an annual rate of about 3 percent from 1961 through 1964, as compared with a rate of increase of under 1 percent from 1956 to 1960. Even though the course of the economy during this period was relatively satisfactory, there was considerable controversy concerning the appropriate role of monetary policy.

In view of the substantial unemployment and the stability of the price level, many urged a more expansionary policy. The Fed resisted calls for easier money on two grounds: First, the balance-of-payments deficit was a persistent problem, and it was argued that lower interest rates would lead to larger outflows of funds; second, Federal Reserve officials argued that, to a considerable extent, the unemployment problem was structural in nature and hence not amenable to monetary-policy actions. They said that technological developments in the economy put greater stress on the need for skilled workers, whereas the unemployed were mostly unskilled and hence "unemployable." Easier money or greater aggregate demand for goods would not, in their view, have much of an effect on this unemployment.

In any case, the major effort at reducing unemployment and stimulating the economy at this time was through fiscal rather than monetary policy. As the first 50 years of the Federal Reserve System's existence ended, it was being asked simply to accommodate actions taken by the administration rather than being faced with the responsibility for the major role in economic policy.

QUESTIONS

1 What were the objectives of monetary policy during the 1920s?
2 What factors were responsible for the relatively high number of bank failures during the 1920s? What factors were responsible for bank failures during the 1930s? Were bank failures the cause or the result of the depression?
3 Describe the relative power of the Federal Reserve Board and the Federal Reserve Bank presidents during the 1920s.
4 What was the relation between the level of stock prices, monetary policy, and the depression?
5 "The Great Depression resulted from the unwise actions of the Federal Reserve System." Do you agree? If the Federal Reserve had acted differently after the onset of the depression, would recovery have been more rapid?
6 Why do banks hold excess reserves?
7 Compare Federal Reserve policy during and after World War II with that of World War I.
8 What was the "accord"?
9 Appraise the correctness of the *actions* taken by the Federal Reserve during the 1950s, and of the *timing* of Federal Reserve actions during this period.
10 Which economic policy goals were most important to the Federal Reserve during the 1950s? the 1960s?

SELECTED READINGS

AHEARN, DANIEL S., *Federal Reserve Policy Reappraised, 1951–1959*. New York: Columbia University Press, 1963.
BACH, GEORGE L., *Making Monetary and Fiscal Policy*, Chap. 4. Washington, D.C.: The Brookings Institution, 1971.
CHANDLER, LESTER V., *Benjamin Strong, Central Banker*. Washington, D.C.: The Brookings Institution, 1958.
FRIEDMAN, MILTON and ANNA SCHWARTZ, *A Monetary History of the United States, 1867–1960*. Princeton, N.J.: Princeton University Press, 1963.
GALBRAITH, JOHN K., *The Great Crash*. Boston: Houghton Mifflin, 1954. A fascinating account of the stock-market crash of 1929 and the events leading up to it.
GOLDENWEISER, E.A., *American Monetary Policy*. New York: McGraw-Hill, 1951.
WILLIS, H. PARKER, *The Theory and Practice of Central Banking*. New York: Harper & Row, 1936.

29

Federal Reserve Policy: The Recent Experience

The monetary policy of the last 20 years or so is the most interesting to analyze. In recent history we have the advantage of being able to remember at least some of the events that took place. You do not remember the slight recession of 1924 or the more serious panic of 1907, but you may have been personally affected by the recessions of 1980 and 1981.

The period since the middle 1960s is worth investigating for other reasons as well. The Federal Reserve has had all its monetary-policy tools at its disposal, and the freedom to use them in combatting recession and inflation—a situation that has existed only since 1951. During this period, monetarist thought has had an increasing influence on the Federal Reserve and on participants in the financial markets. This has produced interesting debate over the theory of monetary policy as well as over specific policy actions. The last 20 years have also included our worst peacetime inflation ever, and the sharpest recession since the Great Depression.

THE CREDIT CRUNCHES

The tax cut proposed early in the Kennedy administration finally went into effect in 1964 and did much to bring the economy close to its potential. Coming at a time when the federal budget was already in deficit, it was a great victory for Keynesian analysis and policy. The tax cut so stimulated the economy that we had a budget surplus in 1965. This achievement also swelled the confidence of economists. We began to hear about the ability of modern economic analysis to "fine-tune" the economy so as to produce full employment and stable prices. Unfortunately, the economic problems since 1965 have not proved as susceptible to such fine-tuning.

Unemployment did get down close to 4 percent in 1965, and, perhaps in response, prices rose somewhat more rapidly than they had in the preceding years. Spending by all sectors of the economy—government, consumers, business—accelerated during the year. Monetary expansion continued at a relatively high rate through 1965, but by the end of the year, the Federal Reserve felt that some monetary or fiscal restraint was necessary. The fiscal situation became more difficult as spending for Vietnam War needs increased rapidly.

Interest rates moved up rapidly to record levels in 1966, and became still higher as the money supply began to decline in the spring. Although the Federal Reserve had raised deposit interest-rate ceilings in December 1965, by mid-1966, rates on short-term money-market instruments exceeded the rates banks could pay on deposits. Time deposits stopped flowing into financial institutions, and some experienced significant outflows, as we moved into our first period of disintermediation. The high interest rates and the lack of funds in savings institutions had a very severe effect on the housing market. Housing construction dropped to nearly its lowest level since the end of World War II.

Early 1967 could not properly be considered a recession period, but the pace of business activity was distinctly lower than in the previous year. Monetary policy was easier during most of 1967 in response to the slowdown in business activity. Most analysts forecast a pickup in the second half of the year, and President Johnson called for a 10 percent tax increase to reduce some of the potential inflationary pressure. Prices rose at a more rapid rate in 1967 than in the previous years. The Federal Reserve Board was unanimous in calling for swift passage of the proposed tax increase—in their view, the burden of combatting inflationary pressure without the tax increase would fall solely on monetary policy. The Fed feared the repercussions of a return to the high interest rates of 1966. When it became clear in late 1967 that a tax increase would not be voted by Congress in that year, the Fed moved more vigorously to tighten credit. Interest rates rose sharply.

The problem of inflation accelerated during 1968. Consumer prices increased at an annual rate of over 5 percent during 1968 and

1969, and unemployment averaged below 4 percent. Interpretation of monetary policy is rather difficult for this period. Interest rates rose to record levels in 1968 and 1969, but the money supply grew at a rate of over 7 percent from early 1967 to mid-1969.

Growth of the money supply slowed in 1969, growing at an annual rate of under 2 percent in the latter part of the year. Total spending in the economy did respond to the high interest rates and slower monetary growth. The hope of the policy maker in this sort of situation is that the restrictive policy will slow the pace of the inflation without greatly affecting the course of real growth. Unfortunately, the policy makers were due to be disappointed.

The restrictive monetary policy of 1969, combined with a restrictive fiscal policy, did produce a significant slowing down of the economy. However, the inflationary forces in the economy responded only slightly to the slowdown.

During the 1968–1969 period of monetary restraint, the Federal Reserve used virtually all the tools at its command. In addition to open-market operations, reserve requirements were increased, and Federal Reserve Bank discount rates were raised several times, remaining for much of 1969 and 1970 at the post-depression record high of 6 percent. The Fed made heavy use of moral suasion, frequently calling on banks to follow policies not in their own interest, and also used interest-rate ceilings on deposits (Regulation Q) as a major tool of policy. During 1968, 1969, and much of 1970, interest rates prevailing in the open market were higher than those that could legally be paid by commercial banks.

The policy adopted provided considerable help to the savings and loan industry. It also proved to be of considerable benefit to most of the commercial banks. Although disintermediation did result, meaning a loss of deposits for many commercial banks, a more important effect was that the interest costs of commercial banks were held down. The net effect was that most banks found their earnings were higher than they would have been in the absence of interest ceilings.[1]

If the policy benefited savings and loans and also benefited commercial banks, who lost by this restriction of free competition? The answer is simple and not surprising—the losers were savers. Bank customers received lower interest payments than they would have obtained in a free market. The policy was particularly unfair to small depositors. Large depositors, after all, could invest directly in Treasury bills or other open-market instruments. This

[1] See Stanley C. Silverberg, "Deposit Costs and Bank Portfolio Policy," *Journal of Finance*, September 1973.

was so obvious, even to the Federal Reserve, that the pattern of interest-rate ceilings allowed banks to pay higher rates on large deposits than on small, so as to enable banks to hold onto their large depositors.

The high interest rates that prevailed during 1968–1970 and the problems of the savings and loan industry had serious repercussions on the housing market. The housing market suffers during such a period for several reasons: Savings institutions do not have the inflow of funds that enables them to expand mortgage lending, commercial banks will probably have more attractive alternative uses of funds, and, on the demand side, some potential home buyers lose interest at the high prevailing mortgage rates.

Because of our commitment to improved housing as a social and economic goal, or perhaps because of the political clout of various segments of the housing industry, such periods always give rise to pressure for means of insulating the housing market from the effects of tight money. During 1968–1969, several steps were taken to achieve this end. These included liberal lending policies by Federal Home Loan Banks to S&Ls and increased operations by FNMA and GNMA in the secondary market.

The year of 1970 was not a good one for the economy. As the Federal Reserve Board summarized it in its *Annual Report* for the year:

> Real output was stagnant and unemployment was rising, and at the same time prices continued upward under continued cost pressures. Meanwhile, the balance of payments was affected by adverse shifts in capital flows. . . .

As business activity slowed, interest rates fell, and the rate of growth of the money supply was stepped up. As the president saw it in his *Economic Report*, "1970 was the year in which we paid for the excesses of 1966, 1967, and 1968."

The rapid growth of the money supply in the first half of 1971, together with the disappointing performance of prices, led to concern—both at home and abroad—about the adequacy of American economic policies to restrain inflation. This concern manifested itself in large shifts out of dollar assets and into other currencies by international investors and speculators. The problem, as the Fed saw it, was that "the slack in the domestic economy made it clear that monetary policy needed to remain expansive."[2]

---

[2] Board of Governors of the Federal Reserve System, *Annual Report*, 1971, p. 6.

THE NIXON ECONOMIC PROGRAM

It was against this background that President Nixon made his dramatic switch in August to a program that included a freeze of prices and wages, increased tariffs, and suspension of convertibility of the dollar into gold.[3]

The freeze of prices had, obviously, an immediate effect on the rise of consumer prices. In addition, interest rates fell rather sharply. Monetary policy was not as expansive following the president's announcement as it had been before, but the Federal Reserve argued that the dramatic change in policy had restored confidence and lowered the demand for money; hence a reduction in the rate of increase of the supply of money did not represent a shift away from a basically expansive-policy posture.

Business activity was at a high level in 1973. Despite the controls program, this became the most inflationary peacetime year in our history. In January, the administration moved into Phase III, which involved an easing of controls over prices and wages. Before the end of the first quarter of the year, it was clear that inflation not only was still with us, but was becoming a worsening problem. There was some stiffening of the Phase III program in the spring, and, following an increase in the Consumer Price Index at an 8 percent rate for the first five months of the year, a new freeze was imposed in June. It was followed in August by a new set of controls, Phase IV, which was in some ways tougher than Phase II.

The sharp escalation in the inflation rate during 1973 was the result of a combination of factors. A worldwide economic boom stimulated demand for U.S. products and bid up prices of many goods and services. This was particularly the case with respect to agricultural goods, for which foreign demand shot up in response to an unfortunate set of crop failures around the world. The problems ranged from failure of the wheat crop in Russia, leading to huge purchases from the United States, to the disappearance of Peruvian anchovies, an important feed stock for cattle. On top of these natural disasters, we faced the oil embargo and then the tremendous increase in the price of oil posted by the Organization of Petroleum Exporting Countries.

Monetary policy was restrictive throughout the year. Interest rates rose to record levels. The money supply increased at a rate of

[3] For a detailed and provocative review and evaluation of the program, see Roger L. Miller and Raburn M. Williams, *The New Economics of Richard Nixon: Feezes, Floats, and Fiscal Policy* (New York: Harper & Row, 1972).

about 5 percent, which, in the light of the increase in prices during the period, meant a significant reduction in the real value of the money supply.

The increase in the price of oil in 1973 was the major source of economic difficulties in the following year. President Nixon stressed this problem in his 1974 *Economic Report:*

> The higher prices will cause dislocations and impose burdens on all consuming coun-
> tries; they do not have to cause a spreading recession if we manage our affairs co-
> operatively and wisely.[4]

Unfortunately, we did not manage our affairs wisely in the aftermath of the oil price increase, in part because the effects of the higher prices were not correctly perceived. It was easy to see that the price increase led to inflationary pressures throughout the economy as the costs of nearly all goods were affected by the higher fuel, transportation, and raw-material costs resulting from the higher oil prices. Not so obvious was the fact that the higher price of imported oil had the effect of a tax in draining spending power out of the economy, since consumers had less income available to buy all other goods and services. Thus, the higher oil prices could simulta-neously lead to inflation and recession.

During most of 1974, the attention of the Ford administration and the Federal Reserve was riveted on the inflation problem. It deserved attention, since the inflation rate was higher than the 1973 pace, but the restrictive monetary policy followed during the year was not what the weakening economy needed. Interest rates, which had hit record levels in 1973, rose to new record levels in mid-1974. The Federal-funds rate exceeded 13 percent and the bank prime rate hit 12 percent, before falling with the decline in the economy.

The recession that began in 1974 was the most severe in our postwar experience. Real GNP declined in 1974 and 1975. Unemploy-ment reached 9 percent in May 1975, and averaged 8.5 percent for the year. Housing starts fell from 2.4 million in 1973 to 1.2 million in 1975. Financial problems accompanied the recession. In 1974, the Franklin National Bank became the largest bank failure in our history, and the recession also saw the virtual collapse of the REIT industry and the financial problems of New York City.

Monetary policy attempted to walk a fine line in stimulating the economy during the recession, but with attention still paid to the inflationary potential of the economic situation.

---

[4]*Economic Report of the President*, February 1974, p. 7.

THE LATE 1970s

Recovery began in 1975 and continued at a strong pace through 1976. Real GNP rose by over 6 percent in 1976, but this rate of growth was only sufficient to reduce the average rate of unemployment to 7.7 percent, still extremely high by historical standards. The Consumer Price Index rose by about 5 percent, a considerable improvement over the double-digit rate of 1974–1975. Interest rates tended to fall during the year, something rather unusual for a year of strong recovery, but the major factor here was probably a reduction in the inflation premium built into interest rates during the rapid inflation of 1974 and 1975.

During the year, the Fed tended to reduce slightly its indicated ranges for the monetary aggregates. This did not represent significant tightening of monetary policy from the preceding year, since actual growth rates had been on the low side of the proposed ranges.

The recovery continued in 1977, despite the uncertainties of one sort or another that cropped up all during the year. The economy seemed strong early in the year, although an unusually harsh winter with fuel shortages confused the figures. The real growth rate exceeded 6 percent in the second quarter but slowed in the last half. Still, real growth was substantial enough to absorb the growth in the labor force and eat slightly into the still-high unemployment figures. Unemployment dropped significantly late in the year and was 6.4 percent at year's end.

Concern began to be expressed over the accelerated rate of increase in the money supply during the second and third quarters, in which $M1$ (slightly different from the present $M1$) increased at annual rates of 8.4 and 9.3 percent as compared with an average of about 5½ percent for 1976 and early 1977. Short-term interest rates did increase during this period, partly, it seemed, in response to market fears that the rapid rate of money growth would lead to more rapid inflation.

This situation led to a vigorous debate on monetary policy based on ideological grounds. Monetarists saw a danger of increased inflation as a result of what they saw as the Fed's *easy*-money policy (as measured by rapid money growth). Keynesians saw the risk of recession increase as a result of what they saw as the Fed's *tight*-money policy (as measured by the higher interest rates). They would concentrate on the unemployment problem, because they saw the inflation problem as essentially structural and built into the economy as a result of the past inflation and a wage-price spiral as business and labor sought to catch up with past increases in prices and costs. The Keynesians did not see monetary policy as having much possible influence on this problem. The monetarists, on the other hand, see inflation as essentially a monetary phenomenon, to be attacked by monetary policy, whereas they view the unemployment problem as largely structural (due to changes in the composition of the labor force, the minimum wage, unemployment benefits, and so on), and not susceptible to improvement by monetary-policy actions.

The Federal Reserve attempted, in late 1977 and early 1978, to give weight to the arguments of both camps. In a way, the Fed had been lucky during the first two years of the recovery, in that interest rates tended to decline—an unusual situation for a recovery period. This fact held off the sharp Keynesian-monetarist clash that finally broke out in 1977 when rates turned upward. As the recovery matured in 1978 (and actually became a rather long business expansion), the Fed's problem became more difficult. Inflation accelerated, reaching double-digit rates in mid-1978, as unemployment dropped to the lowest levels in several years. Since 1975, the U.S. economy had recovered much more rapidly than those of most other leading countries, which meant that our imports grew more rapidly than our exports. The step-up in the U.S. inflation rate aggravated that problem, and the U.S. dollar dropped substantially on world currency markets. All these factors would justify a more restrictive monetary policy, and the Fed clearly shifted in that direction— interest rates rose to the highest levels since 1974. But the Fed was hit with criticisms from both sides: Some were afraid that a tight-money policy would bring about a recession in 1979 (and forecasts of such a recession for late 1978–1979 became common); others felt that the growth of the money supply during 1978 was too rapid in view of the high rate of inflation.

Real economic growth took place in 1978–1979, but at a gradually slowing pace and with rising unemployment. Food prices rose 12 percent in 1978, and in 1979, the overall inflation rate approached 13 percent.

With a relatively strong economy and a high rate of inflation, the U.S. external position deteriorated. All signs—domestic demand, inflation, and a depreciating exchange rate—pointed toward a need for monetary tightness. The focus in 1978 was on the exchange rate, and in 1979 somewhat more on domestic demand. The Federal Reserve used discount-rate and reserve-requirement changes conspicuously to convince foreigners that something was being done and to offer an interest-rate incentive to turn capital flows in favor of the United States. On November 1, 1979, the discount rate rose a full percentage point as part of an overall international package to improve the exchange rate. The discount rate started 1979 at 6 percent and ended at 9½ percent.

In mid-1978, depository institutions received approval for issuing six-month money-market certificates that they could offer depositors at a rate pegged to Treasury securities. The Fed hoped the move would help take some of the burden of monetary tightness off the housing market as the certificates attracted funds to mortgage-lending institutions. By 1979, these certificates, along with money-market mutual funds, were rising at a rate that caused concern about the possible effects of the increased liquidity on inflation. In October 1979, the Fed shifted its operating procedures to place much greater weight on control of the monetary aggregates. More precise control over the aggregates meant that interest rates would be left more to market forces, and the Fed-funds rate immediately responded to the announcement of the new procedures.

RECENT EXPERIENCE AND CURRENT PROBLEMS

Going into 1980, consumers were picking up their credit-financed spending, and in March, increments in consumer credit became subject to special reserve requirements to slow down the pace of borrowing. The program was short-lived, because by the time it was imposed, the long-awaited recession had come. Its duration was only until the middle half of 1980. The first and last quarters produced essentially the same real GNP, with the slump in between. Output expansion in the first quarter of 1981 was vigorous, but another recession set in in the second quarter. During most of the year, the Federal Reserve was maintaining tighter control over the monetary aggregates with the powers granted it under the 1980 Monetary Control Act. Monetary policy remained relatively tight because of inflationary fears, and critics of such policy blamed the Fed for the recession.

By 1982 the unemployment rate matched the postwar high of 9 percent. The federal deficit moved into the $100 billion—plus range. Critics of the deficit, holding it partly responsible for continuing high interest rates, called for tax rate increases and reduced government spending—the opposite of the remedies the economy had learned to expect from Keynesian economics of the post-depression era. The alternative—monetization of the deficit—was steadfastly opposed by the Federal Reserve. Inflation was begin-

ning to moderate, but the cost, in terms of unemployment and foregone output, was high. We examine this dilemma in more detail in
the following chapter.

QUESTIONS

1 Did Regulation Q become a tool of general credit control during the
   1960s?
2 Was the control program that began in August 1971 effective in
   combatting inflation?
3 In terms of the quantity theory, why was there inflation during the
   Vietnam War?
4 Compare the performance of the economy with regard to
   employment, price stability, and growth under the Eisenhower
   administration (1953–60), the Kennedy-Johnson administrations
   (1961–68), the the Nixon administration (1969–74).
5 Why did the Federal Reserve change its operating procedures in
   1979?
6 Was monetary policy easy or tight in the last half of 1977? How do
   you know? What evidence can you cite?

SELECTED READINGS

MEIGS, A. JAMES, *Monetary Matters.* New York: Harper & Row, 1972.
MILLER, ROGER L., and RABURN M. WILLIAMS, *The New Economics
   of Richard Nixon: Freezes, Floats, and Fiscal Policy.* New York:
   Harper & Row, 1972.
OKUN, ARTHUR M., *The Political Economy of Prosperity.* Washington,
   D.C.: The Brookings Institution, 1970.
WILSON, THOMAS, "1929–33—Could it Happen Again?" *Three Banks
   Review* (Edinburgh, Scotland), December 1980.
WOODWORTH, G. WALTER, *The Money Market and Monetary
   Management,* 2nd ed., Chaps. 22–24. New York: Harper & Row, 1972.

30

Inflation, Unemployment, and Monetary Policy

As the nation entered the 1980s, opinion polls showed that the public viewed inflation as the number 1 economic problem. In 1979 and 1980, prices as measured by the Consumer Price Index increased more than 12 percent each year. In one decade, the purchasing power of the dollar had been cut in half. The relentless course of inflation continued through both economic expansion and contraction. The combination of inflation and unemployment of 6 percent or more gave rise to the term *stagflation*, a concept that did not fit well with conventional economic theory.

EXCESS-DEMAND INFLATION

Economists have traditionally viewed inflation in terms of excess demand. That is, prices rise when total spending by consumers, by business firms, and by government exceeds the value (at existing prices) of the total output of the economy. In terms of the quantity-theory approach, if T is constant, P changes as total demand MV changes. Schematically, this can be viewed as similar to the determination of the price of a single good with inelastic supply, as shown in Figure 30-1.

The level of demand is determined by all the variables that relate to equilibrium, such as consumption propensities, govern-

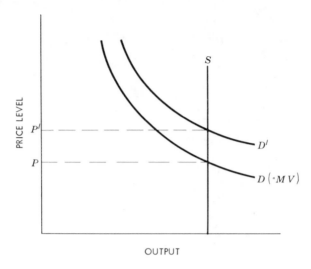

FIGURE 30-1 Output and Price Levels

ment purchases, and the investment function. It is not related to the price level in the same way that demand responds to the price of a single good when all other variables are held constant, particularly incomes and the prices of other goods. The aggregate price level means that all other prices are moving too. And incomes fluctuate with the price level, since income is derived from the price and quantity of goods sold. We can, however, assume a negatively sloped demand curve if the nominal money stock is unchanged.

Compare two prices, one "high" and one "low." As prices move from high to low, the real value of the money stock rises. With a higher real money stock, interest rates fall, and the equilibrium output level is thus higher at the lower price. It is by this mechanism that, with other variables given, an aggregate demand curve is negatively related to the price level.

Assume now a shift in demand.

As demand increases from D to D', the price level increases from P to P'. This analysis of inflation fits the frequently heard expression about the cause of inflation—"too much money chasing too few goods."

Of course, this picture is much too simple. For one thing, the supply of output is not very well described by the vertical line in our diagram. Early Keynesian analysis viewed the supply schedule of the economy as shaped like the S curve in Figure 30-2.

Figure 30-2 allows for unemployment as well as for inflation. If total demand in the economy could be represented by D, the level of output would be O_u and the price level would be P. Since we are at a position of unemployment, in the Keynesian analysis any increase in demand would make itself felt by an increase in output (and employment) without any increase in prices. Thus, if demand increased to D', we would move to the full employment output, O_f, and the price level would remain at P. Once we are at the bend in the supply curve (the full-employment level of output), any further increases in demand will have quite different effects. An increase in demand to D'', for example, will succeed only in increasing prices. Obviously, output, in real terms, cannot increase beyond the full-employment level, and thus the increase in spending can be accomplished only at higher prices (P_i).

If the supply curve of total output in the economy had the shape described in Figure 30-2, economic policy would be relatively simple. Total demand should be increased or constricted so that it intersects with the supply curve at point F. Here we achieve full-employment output with stable prices. If demand is less than D', we will have unemployment; if demand is greater than D', we will have inflation. The demand curve can be affected by variations in government spending and taxation (fiscal policy) or by variations in monetary factors so as to affect business investment spending.

Unfortunately, the problem is somewhat more complex. The

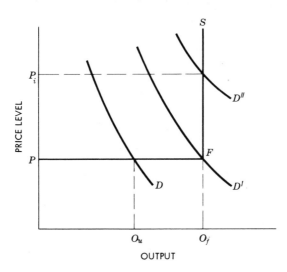

FIGURE 30-2 Shifts in Demand

supply curve for the economy may look somewhat more like the
schedule pictured in Figure 30-3 than that of Figure 30-2. Point *F*
corresponds to full employment, and thus, this is the desired level of
output. As production rises toward that level of output, however,
costs begin to rise. As capacity is approached in one industry after
another, it become more and more expensive to expand output.
Machines must be used overtime, shortages of material begin to
slow up production, and one factor after another becomes a bottle-
neck, holding up production (and raising costs) all down the line.

In the situation pictured in Figure 30-3, it is not so easy to
determine the appropriate monetary and fiscal policies. A policy of
credit ease designed to raise demand to the full-employment level of
output will also allow for some increase in the price level. A policy
of monetary restraint designed to prevent inflation will necessitate
some unemployment. The question, then, is, How important are
supply factors in causing inflation? Does the supply curve of total
output in the economy look like the curve in Figure 30-3?

THE PHILLIPS CURVE:
THE INFLATION–UNEMPLOYMENT
TRADEOFF OF THE U.S. ECONOMY

A more meaningful way to view the supply curve for inflation analysis is not in absolute amounts but in relation to potential supply.

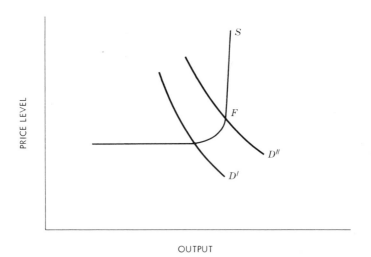

FIGURE 30-3 Supply and Inflation

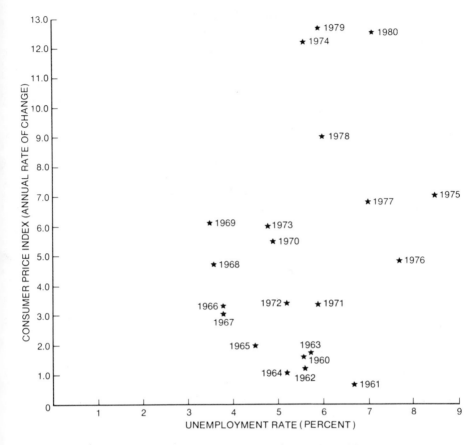

FIGURE 30-4 Unemployment and Price Changes (U.S. 1960–1980)

At full employment, the potential is reached, and the rate of unemployment is a measure of the slack. The closer the economy is to full employment, the greater the pull of demand on supply. By relating prices to employment-unemployment, we can view the achievement of two goals—price stability and full employment. Figure 30-4 depicts this relationship, plotting for each year shown, price increases of the year against the rate of unemployment. The plots look almost randomly distributed. In fact, a vertical line drawn upward from 5½ percent unemployment would seem to be about as good a fit as any. Is it possible that there is no relation at all between the tautness of demand and the price level?

The relationship we have plotted has been the subject of considerable controversy following a pioneering study of historical data in England by A.W. Phillips. For the years 1851–1957, Phillips found a rather smooth inverse relation between the rate of change of money wages and the level of unemployment, giving rise to the name *Phillips curve*. Following the publication of this work in 1958, economists in the United States quickly seized on the technique, and in the 1960s, a predictable relation between unemployment and inflation was thought to prevail. Figure 30-5 is the same as 30-4, except that the 1960s data are shown separately as dots and a free-hand curve is fitted to them. This curve was viewed as a representation of the short-run tradeoff that was available to policy makers. The cost of less unemployment was more inflation, but at least the extent of that inflation could be predicted.

As the U.S. Phillips curve of the 1960s broke down, economists began to realize that there was a flaw in the concept; perhaps the failure to recognize the flaw earlier arose from acceptance of a

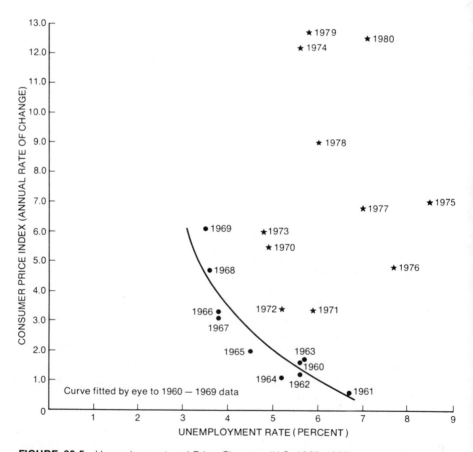

FIGURE 30-5 Unemployment and Price Changes (U.S. 1960–1980)

statistical relationship without adequate consideration of a theory to explain it. Phillips's original formulation used money wages, not prices, and concentrated on labor markets. This focus was lost as later economists substituted goods prices.

Wage bargains are struck in labor markets as laborers offer their services at various prices (a supply curve) in conjunction with employers' negatively sloped demand curve. Now suppose that a wage equilibrium is struck when inflation is at 7 percent a year. Surely this is an unstable equilibrium: If workers remain content with the same money wage, they would in time experience a 7 percent decline in real wages. If they have what have been called *rational expectations* regarding price rises, then the required equilibrium wage will drift upward at the same unemployment rate.

It was the monetarists who pointed out this rational-expectations explanation. Remember, the monetarists believe that money and prices are independent of real variables in the economy —that there is a natural rate of unemployment, which is affected by such things as productivity, capital formation, discrimination in hiring, inefficiency of job-information flows, and minimum wage laws. According to the monetarists, then, the economy determines its natural rate of unemployment. If monetary policy seeks to override this by increasing the money supply, the result will be higher prices. Workers will incorporate the higher prices in their wage decisions, and if unemployment is to be temporily reduced again, inflation will have to exceed their expectations. In time, this higher rate of inflation will be anticipated, and then a still higher rate of inflation is needed. Obviously this exercise could not continue indefinitely without a total monetary collapse. This necessity of a rising rate of inflation to overcome inflation expectations has been called the *accelerationist* principle.

COST-PUSH INFLATION

The neo-Keynesian analysis of aggregate prices starts with factor prices as the origin of costs, and goods prices flowing from these costs. Factor prices are determined by a host of social and economic considerations that are rather far removed from the conventional price equilibrium of supply–demand equations. Arthur Okun, a former member of the President's Council of Economic Advisers, stated:

> In a small and shrinking sector of the U.S. economy, products are traded in organized auction markets in which prices vary from day to day to keep supply and demand in balance. . . .

Most of our economy is dominated by cost-oriented prices and equity-oriented wages. Most prices are set by sellers whose principal concern is to maintain customers and market share over the long run. . . .

Similarly, the key to wage decisions in both union and non-union areas is the common long-run interest of skilled workers and employers in maintaining their job relationships. . . .

The customer and career relationships that desensitize wages and prices from excess supplies and demands in the short run have a genuine social function. They are not creations of evil business monopolies or unduly powerful labor unions, but rather efficient arrangements for a complex interdependent economy in which customers and suppliers, workers and employers benefit greatly from lasting relationships.[1]

The concept of cost-push is that owners of factors—labor and capital—may seek to increase their remuneration independently of demand. This is the area of "administered" prices and wages, and it is inconsistent with an assumption of competition. Samuelson and Solow wrote in 1960:

. . . the Keynes model, which assumes stickiness of wages even in the face of under-employment equilibrium, rests on various assumptions of imperfect competition. And when we recognize that, considerably before full employment of labor and plants has been reached, modern prices and wages seem to show a tendency to drift upward irreversibly, we see that the simple Keynesian system must be modified even further in the direction of an imperfect competition model. . . . But to explain possible cost-push inflation, it would seem more economical from the very beginning to recognize that imperfect competition is the essence of the problem and to drop the perfect competition assumptions.[2]

American industry is characterized by markets in which a few firms dominate. Across industry lines in manufacturing, on the average the top four firms in an industry account for more than 40 percent of the industry's sales. Firms in these industries find it difficult to arrive at the profit-maximizing price, because each firm does not know how its rivals will react to a price change. Given a rise in costs facing all firms, they are better able to act in concert to raise prices, and this is what happens when the industry arrives at a higher wage settlement with its unions.

This process can give rise to an inflationary spiral. If a union succeeds in raising wages, the firm may decide to raise prices in order to maintain its profits. Then unions will seek additional wage increases, because the price rises have contributed to an increase in the cost of living. This justifies a further increase in prices, and so on. It really makes little difference, once the spiral is under way,

[1] Arthur Okun, "An Efficient Strategy to Combat Inflation," *The Brookings Bulletin*, Spring 1979, p. 2.

[2] Paul Samuelson and Robert Solow, "Analytical Aspects of Anti-Inflation Policy," *American Economic Review*, May 1960, p. 180.

whether the initial impetus came from union wage push or from business firms' raising administered prices.

In terms of our analysis through aggregate demand and supply, the wage push can be thought of as an upward shift in the supply function. It might be thought that this would create unemployment and a fall in demand, and thereby be self-correcting, but it is not. The reason is that the demand curve does not stay put. Remember that we are dealing with aggregate demand, and as wage and profit incomes rise in the aggregate, so does aggregate demand. Thus the demand curve also shifts upward.

> Suppose wages rise. We are led to expect a decrease in output. But in the modern world, all or most wages are increasing. Nor is this the first time they have done so. And in the past, general wage and price increases have not resulted in any decrease in aggregate real demand—perhaps the contrary. So that even in a single industry supply and demand curves may not be independent. The shift in costs is accompanied by, indeed may bring about, a compensating shift in the subjectively viewed demand curve facing the industry. And so prices may rise with no decline and possibly an increase in output. If there is anything in this line of thought, it may be that one of the important causes of inflation is—inflation.[3]

There may be some self-correcting forces, however, among them the declining real value of money and liquid assets, if these are held fixed while prices are rising. If the central bank fails to let the money stock keep up with the rising money value of output, then the effect will be to increase interest rates, with the resulting effect on demand. This is the way the central bank may be led into money-stock increases that accompany the inflation, since to do otherwise might create unemployment. The observer viewing a rise in both money and prices might be inclined to infer a causal relationship.

Since monetary policy is aimed at demand restraint, it is rather powerless in the face of cost-push inflation. Because interest is a cost, to some extent higher interest rates even contribute to the inflation. This is why the public is so puzzled at the direction of policy as to be even skeptical of motives. People see monthly mortgage payments climb with interest rates and wonder if the authorities have lost their senses in proclaiming such moves to be deflationary. The intent of such policy is that the effects in suppressing demand far outweigh price effects of higher interest costs, but this case is difficult to prove and not very convincing to an angry mob. A Federal Reserve official made the case as follows:

> The general cost-raising, the inflationary, effect of higher interest rates is relatively small. For nonfinancial corporations as a whole, interest payments come to about

---

[3] Samuelson and Solow, "Analytical Aspects," p. 182.

3 percent of total costs. . . . Estimates for the period since 1975 show that business costs have been raised by less than 1 percent, cumulative, over this period as a result of higher interest rates. Over the same period the cost of living has gone up by 38 percent.

In contrast, in evaluating the anti-inflationary effect of a jump in interest rates, it is the higher cost of new projects that becomes relevant. The increase in the cost of financing new projects reduces their profitability, and this tends to tip the balance in favor of postponing them. If that happens, total demands in the economy are reduced.[4]

PRODUCTIVITY AND INFLATION

It is probable that, as with many economic problems, there is no single answer to the causes of all inflations. Some element of both cost-push and excess demand may be involved in any inflationary period, and it is impossible to distinguish between the two. If excess demand causes prices to rise in some sectors, this in turn generates cost-push as labor and other factors attempt to restore their real incomes.

A common interpretation of the inflationary spiral of the last two decades is that it started with the excess demand generated by the Vietnam War. Cost-push then exacerbated the problem, and going into the 1970s, two problems arose. One was the rise in oil and energy prices (administered prices abroad), and the other was the failure of productivity to rise as it had in the past.

In the period 1948–1967, output per employee grew at an average annual rate of 3.2 percent. From 1967 to 1978, the growth rate was down to 1.7 percent. The problem became increasingly severe in 1974, and for two years there was an actual decline in national income per person employed. In 1978, this measure was only 1 percent higher than it had been in 1973.[5]

In a climate of no growth, it is impossible for real incomes to rise. Any increase in real income to one group is at the expense of another group. In the past, if workers received higher money wages, it was not necessary for these to be fully passed on as higher prices because of productivity advances. When output per employee is stagnant, money-wage rises in the aggregate cannot bring up real wages. Thus it has frequently been argued that if wage increases are geared to changes in the average productivity of labor, we will not be subject to cost-push inflation.

[4] Peter Fousek, senior vice-president of the Federal Reserve Bank of New York, "Monetary Restraint, Interest Rates, and Inflation," in the Bank's Quarterly Review, Autumn 1979, p. 11.

[5] Edward Denison, Accounting for Slower Economic Growth: The United States in the 1970s (Washington, D.C.: The Brookings Institution, 1979).

The proposal that wage increases be limited to productivity increases rests on the fact that such wage increases leave labor costs *per unit of output* unchanged, and thus will not exert upward pressure on prices. A simple example may help make this point clear. Suppose a worker produces 100 widgets in one eight-hour day and is paid at the rate of $5.00 per hour. Labor cost per widget amounts to 40 cents. Now suppose that productivity increases so that the worker can turn out 10 percent more widgets per day—a total of 110 per eight-hour day. If his hourly wage is increased by 10 percent (the amount of the increase in productivity), the labor cost per unit will remain at 40 cents. That is, his total output will be 110 widgets, and his total daily earnings will be $44.00 ($40.00 plus 10 percent), resulting in a per-unit labor cost of 40 cents (4,400¢/110).

One frequently heard objection to the proposal that wage increases be geared to changes in productivity is that it would give labor the full benefit on any increases in productivity even though they may be due to improved equipment or improved management. This objection does not hold up under close examination. Making wage increases equal in percentage terms to increases in productivity does *not* mean that labor gets the entire gain from increased output per man-hour. Again, a simple example may help make the point clear.

Suppose a firm produces $100 million worth of widgets each year and has total labor costs of $60 million. This leaves a gross profit of $40 million. Now let us assume a 10 percent productivity gain accompanied by a 10 percent wage increase. Total output will amount to $110 million (if there is no price change), and wages will amount to $66 million, leaving a gross profit of $44 million—an increase of 10 percent also. Labor received a 60 percent share of total output before the productivity and wage increase and a 60 percent share afterward.

Under the circumstances described, the average productivity guide to wage adjustments is neutral with respect to relative shares of total income. The position sometimes taken that the proposal involves distributing all of the gains to labor is incorrect.[6]

Another difficulty of the proposal concerns the concept of *average* productivity for the economy. If the proposal is to be successful in its aim of preventing upward pressure from wages on prices, wage increases must be limited to the average productivity increase in the economy, rather than to productivity increases in

[6] "Average Labor Productivity as a Guide to Wage Adjustments," Federal Reserve Bank of Kansas City *Monthly Review*, (March–April 1962, p. 11. This article is an excellent discussion of the relation between wages, productivity, and prices.

the particular industry in which wage negotiations are taking place. Productivity increases do not occur in all industries at an equal pace. One year there may be substantial productivity gains in the steel industry, the next year in the textile industry, and the following year in the copper industry. The proposal we have been analyzing would require that a year that witnessed a sizable productivity gain in the steel industry, wage increases in that industry be limited to the average gains in productivity in the economy as a whole.

This requirement is necessary not to prevent upward pressure on prices but to preserve equity in the labor market and to ensure that it will function effectively in allocating labor to industries in which it is needed. The alternative, which would tie wage increases in particular industries to productivity increases in those specific industries, would destroy the functioning of the labor market and lead to considerable inequities in the wage structure.

If productivity in the steel industry increases by 6 percent per year but by only 1 percent in the aluminum industry, wage increases equal to the productivity increases would lead to wide and unjustified differences in earnings of workers in the two industries. The higher wages would tend to attract workers to the steel industry, where, because of the productivity increases, fewer workers might be needed.

GUIDELINES AND CONTROLS

The concept of tying wage increases to increases in productivity became an integral part of American economic policy in 1962. The annual report of the Council of Economic Advisers for that year concluded that the long-run rate of productivity gain in the U.S. economy was 3.2 percent, and urged that annual wage increases be kept to a rate no higher than that. Also associated with this call for restraint in wage demands was the view that price increases would be unjustified as long as wage increases were within the bounds of productivity increases in particular industries. Industries with higher rates of productivity increase would be expected to lower their prices.

These wage-price "guideposts" were set out with a plea for voluntary compliance. No legal sanctions or enforcement powers were lodged with the council or with any other agency. It was expected, of course, that the administration would use its powers of persuasion to enforce the guideposts, with the possibility of unfavorable publicity and adverse public opinion facing potential violators. Also, the federal government, as a very large consumer of many industrial products, was in the position to put economic pressure on some industries should they seek "unjustified" price increases.

The basic objection to guidelines is that they are out of place in a free-enterprise, profit-based economy. Workers and businesses in our economy are supposed to try to maximize their incomes. The price system is an efficient allocator of resources only if such maximization takes place. Why should workers take less for their services or businesspeople less for their products than the market price determined by supply and demand?

The answer given to this criticism is simply that the efficiency of the price system is based on the assumption of competitive markets. If labor unions have the power to obtain wages higher than would prevail in a perfectly competitive market, or if business firms have the power to set prices, the theoretical advantages of relying on the market as an allocator of resources are subject to question.

Many supporters of the guideposts argue that many unions and large corporations have too much market power for the price system to provide optimal results. The guideposts, in effect, urge that unions and firms act as if they did not have such market power. In reply, it may be argued that antitrust policy provides a more direct means of solving this problem.

Mandatory controls were tried in the early 1970s. Although President Nixon and his economic advisors started out with strong objections to the use of price and wage controls, the combination of inflation and unemployment proved to be more than the administration's "game plan" could handle. The wage-price freeze announced by the president in August 1971, and the system of controls that became known as Phase II of the New Economic Program, represent a conclusion that general monetary and fiscal policies were unable to cope with the situation.

Evaluation of the effect of the wage and price controls on inflation is difficult. There is no doubt that the rate of increase of prices slowed during the price freeze of 1971. It also seems likely that the rate of inflation was less in 1972 and 1973 than it would have been without controls, but many observers believe that some of the inflationary pressure was just shifted forward into 1974 and 1975. That is, they argue that the inflation rate was greater than it otherwise would have been in 1974 and 1975, so that the general price level in 1978 (or 1984) was just about what it would have been with or without the controls program.

President Carter disavowed any interest in mandatory price and wage controls but did find the guidelines approach appealing.

Although the bases for determining of acceptable wage and price increases were similar under both the guideposts program and the New Economic Program (considerations such as productivity increases, profit margins, and so on), the two programs differed as to the legal force behind the determinations. The guideposts of the 1960s and of the Carter administration were "voluntary," whereas the rulings of the Price Commission and the Pay Board of the New Economic Program had the force of law.

In October 1978, the Carter administration introduced a program of voluntary guidelines to hold wage increases to 7 percent annually and price increases to 5¾ percent. A tax incentive to laborers to limit increases was proposed but never enacted. Some activities were exempt from the guidelines, such as food, interest rates, and energy costs originating abroad. Price increases were especially strong in these areas in the period following the guidelines, and it is impossible to determine whether the 12 percent inflation that ensued in the first year of the guidelines would have been any worse without them.[7]

Programs relying on "jawboning" or voluntary compliance have a built-in inequity. Those who cooperate with such a program lose in relation to those who do not. The union that accepts a 3 percent wage increase in accordance with voluntary guideposts finds that its members end up worse off than members of the union that insists on a 6 percent settlement.

It may be desirable, from the point of view of the economy as a whole, for a given union to accept a lower wage offer than it could get. It may even be in the interests of the union members to do so if they can be sure that restraint on their part will be followed by similar restraint on the part of other unions and business firms, thus ensuring price stability. Since there is no way they can be given this assurance (as long as the guidepost program is a voluntary one), it is clearly not in their interest to accept a smaller settlement than their bargaining power warrants. The mandatory controls of the Phase II (or even Phase III) type allow all to seek what is in their own best interests—but what they can get is limited by law. The reliance on law rather than conscience may be more appropriate to a free-enterprise economy.

The rationale for price control is the imposition of an outside arbiter to stop a process that has no internal forces of resistance.

---

[7] At least one analysis concluded that the program did cause some moderation in wage increases in the sectors covered, particularly among nonunion workers. Paul Bennett and Ellen Greene, "Effectiveness of the First Year Pay and Price Standards," Federal Reserve Bank of New York *Quarterly Review*, Winter 1979–80.

Inflation is a race in which everyone must run just to keep up. Even if an individual union believes that higher wages in general will mean higher prices, it still pays that particular union to get its wage increase. The effect of that increase is more important to the union members than the price increases directly caused by it. That is, even if a union is fully aware of the undesirable effects of a wage-price spiral, it still pays to be first in the race.

It is possible, of course, that if union leaders were convinced that the Federal Reserve would take no steps to ease credit when faced with unemployment caused by wage increases, they would not make excessive wage demands. It would be very difficult, however, to convince labor and management that the Fed would stick to its anti-inflationary guns regardless of unemployment.

But price controls, having the force of law, are more believable and perhaps could succeed in reducing expectations of inflation. One proposal has been made to use price controls as a short-run device while adjusting monetary policy to a money growth in accord with real-output growth.[8] The controls could be lifted once they had succeeded in eliminating inflation expectations. Both monetarists and neo-Keynesians accept the fact that elimination of inflation requires elimination of inflation expectations. This goal provides both a rationale for price controls and a criterion by which they could eventually be lifted.

A proposal that lies between mandatory controls and voluntary guidelines is the tax-based incomes policy (TIP), which would subject corporations to higher corporate tax rates if they give pay increases higher than a guideline set by the government. The aim is to curb inflation, but also to minimize interference with the functioning of the market. The guideline would not be voluntary, but violation of it would not be illegal either. It would simply mean a higher tax bill for the offending corporation—using the tax-collection system as the means of enforcement. TIP is based on the assumption that the inflation problem is of the cost-push variety, and that business is unable or unwilling to resist union pressures for higher wages. It is easier to simply pass them on in the form of higher prices.

The novelty of the plan begins to fade if one replaces the word "tax" with "fine." If the tax is high enough, it is the equivalent of a fine for noncompliance with price controls. If it is low, it reduces the gain from price-wage increases but does not eliminate it, and all that is accomplished is a cumbersome means of higher tax collec-

[8] Robert R. Keller, "Inflation, Monetarism, and Price Controls," *Nebraska Journal of Economics and Business*, Winter 1980.

tions from some corporations. One highly significant feature of the plan, however, is that it penalizes corporations for higher prices but not unions for higher wages.

President Reagan eschewed both legal and voluntary ceilings and guidelines for wages and prices. His program relied heavily on elimination of inflationary expectations, with the hope that the change in expectations would lead to reduction of price pressures. Expectations were to be eliminated by reductions in federal spending, control over the monetary aggregates, and eventual elimination of the federal deficit. Tax rates were reduced in 1981 legislation, but it was hoped that increased incentives from lower taxes would actually increase output and, as a consequence, federal tax revenues. Although it was not realized at the time, a recession had begun when the tax program was enacted, blocking any hope for an early end to the federal deficit. The recession itself took some of the force out of the inflation, and in some hard-hit firms, workers were accepting wage reductions.

QUESTIONS

1 What is meant by "guns or butter"?
2 How can monetary policy be used to stimulate economic growth? Would these measures conflict with the achievement of other economic goals?
3 Can monetary policy be effective in combatting inflation that is due to cost-push factors?
4 If wage increases equal the average rate of productivity increases, will all prices remain stable? Will the average price level remain stable?
5 If you could choose any point on the Phillips curve shown in this chapter, which point do you believe is preferable?
6 If we are going to have some kind of control over prices and wages, which do you believe is preferable: voluntary guideposts or mandatory ceilings?
7 "If everyone is protected against inflation, no one will care to fight it. Runaway inflation is the only possible result." Do you agree?

SELECTED READINGS

DOUGHERTY, THOMAS, *Controlling the New Inflation*. Lexington, Mass.: Lexington Books, 1981.
HUMPHREY, THOMAS M., "Some Recent Developments in Phillips Curve Analysis," Federal Reserve Bank of Richmond *Economic Review*, January 1978.

LAIDLER, DAVID, ed., *Essays on Money and Inflation*. Chicago: University of Chicago Press, 1975.
————, and MICHAEL PARKIN, "Inflation: a Survey," *The Economic Journal*, December 1975.
PHELPS, E.S., *Inflation Policy and Unemployment Theory*. New York: W. W. Norton, 1972.
————, ed., *Microeconomic Foundations of Employment and Inflation Theory*. New York: W.W. Norton, 1970.
WEINTRAUB, SIDNEY, *Our Stagflation Malaise*. Westport, Conn.: Greenwood Press, 1981.

31

Monetary Policy in an International Economy

The goals of monetary policy are not changed when the economy is viewed in an international context, but the forces that must be considered in seeking the goals are widened. Americans buy, sell, invest, and borrow abroad, yet monetary measures do not directly reach the rest of the world. Monetary policy must pay attention to these spillovers as it sets its targets.

In addition to the domestic economy, the United States is concerned about long-run international stability. The American dollar, an international money, is widely held and used all over the world. Any threat to the stability of the dollar is a threat to the world order. Monetary-policy makers consider the effects of their actions on world currency markets and on worldwide holders of dollars.

DOLLAR EXCHANGE RATE

The variable that most directly links the American economy with the outside world is the dollar exchange rate. Changes in the U.S. economy and policy actions affect that rate, and in turn, changes in the exchange rate reverberate back to the economy. Movements in both goods and capital affect the exchange rate. The dollar will tend to depreciate from increases in imports and increased lending abroad (capital outflows). It will tend to appreciate from increases in exports and increased borrowing from abroad (capital inflows). The external effects from a particular policy move are not always in the direction desired for domestic stability. A move to expand the economy, for example, may increase imports and thereby depreciate the dollar.

Exchange-rate depreciation may at times occur without demonstrable internal explanation. Like domestic stock markets, foreign-exchange markets often overreact to short-run developments.[1] In a two-year period, 1977–1978, the dollar lost 12 percent of its value when measured against the currencies of our ten major trading partners. There were no fundamental reasons for this decline, as the subsequent recovery verified. In November 1978, President Carter announced major policy actions, with the assistance of other industrial countries, to halt the dollar's decline. These included support for the dollar on the exchanges and a tightening of monetary policy. The discount rate was raised by a full percentage point as a part of the move.

In addition to the effects of dollar depreciation on the world monetary order, another problem is its effect on domestic inflation. The prices of imported goods (a component of domestic prices) tend to rise, exerting an upward push on the price level in two ways: Demand is diverted from imported to domestic goods, increasing their prices; and the rising price of imports increases demands for compensatory wage increases. Countries all over the world have found that they must consider the exchange rate in combatting domestic inflation, and in the United States' case, depreciation has worldwide repercussions. They come about when holders of dollars all over the world become concerned about the real value of their holdings. Since there is no currency that significantly rivals the dollar, a flight from the dollar is apt to mean a flight from currency into gold and other commodities, driving up their prices.

A Federal Reserve study has attempted to quantify some of the effects on domestic prices of the 1977–1978 depreciation.[2] It estimated that the 12 percent depreciation raises U.S. consumer prices

[1] A Federal Reserve official told an audience in 1980, "I would share with you my concern as to the role rumors play in the foreign exchange and commodities markets, and with some growing spillover into the government bond market. . . . I get troubled by the fact that the markets are so responsive to rumor. I get more troubled by the impression that market participants start the process." Thomas Timlen, First Vice-President, Federal Reserve Bank of New York, published in the bank's *Quarterly Review*, Spring 1980, p. 4.

[2] Joel Prakken, "The Exchange Rate and Domestic Inflation," Federal Reserve Bank of New York *Quarterly Review*, Summer 1979, pp. 49–55.

by 2½ percent. This rise is spread over a three-year period, reaching 1.7 percent within two years. The estimate assumed no relation between the depreciation and subsequent oil-price rises. If the oil price increases that took place are assumed a part of the response, then the ultimate effect on consumer prices is 2.8 percent.

Given the conflicts that exist between exchange-rate fluctuation and the goals of the domestic economy, the reader may very well think that the best course of action would be to control the exchange-rate movements by exchange-market intervention and then use economic policy for domestic purposes. We shall examine the history of such an attempt.

Before the Great Depression, most industrialized countries were part of an international gold-standard system, which, at least in theory, provided an automatic mechanism for correction of balance-of-payments problems. Not only was the mechanism automatic, the "rules of the game" prohibited active monetary-policy measures by any country seeking to intervene and interfere with the mechanism. A brief examination of the traditional gold-flow system may help put our present problems with the international payments system in perspective.

THE GOLD-FLOW MECHANISM

We examined the characteristics of the gold standard in Chapter 2. Basically, it involves each country's defining its monetary unit in terms of gold and standing ready to redeem its money in gold on demand. If two countries are on the gold standard, the exchange rate between their currencies is automatically fixed. If the dollar were defined as 1/40 ounce of gold and the pound as 3/40 ounce of gold, then the pound would be worth $3. The basic element of the gold standard as far as foreign exchange is concerned is the ability and willingness of a country to redeem its currency in gold at a stated rate. Under the gold standard, a country's balance of payments could be in "deficit" or "surplus." A deficit occurs as foreigners accumulate money claims on the country and redeem these monetary claims in gold, and thus the country with a balance-of-payments deficit has a gold outflow.

Since the eighteenth century, economists have been concerned about this outflow of gold following a balance-of-payments deficit. Is there any limit to this process, or will it continue until the deficit country runs out of gold? The classical and neoclassical economists analyzed this problem in terms of the relation between gold and the domestic monetary systems of the countries concerned. The theory of the *gold-flow mechanism* was devised to explain the smoothness with which the gold standard worked during the nineteenth century.

Suppose country A has a deficit in its balance of payments and country B has a surplus. Gold will flow out of A and into B. If it is assumed that both countries are on a full gold standard, the loss of gold will mean a reduction in the money supply of A and an increase in the money supply of B. Through the workings of the quantity theory, the increased money supply in B will result in an increase in prices, whereas prices fall in A because of its reduced money supply. But if prices fall in A, it will find it easier to increase its exports, and imports will be discouraged—domestic goods are now cheaper. The higher prices in B will tend to reduce B's exports and increase its imports. The net effect of this whole chain of causation will be the elimination of A's balance-of-payments deficit and of B's surplus.

Although the theory seemed very neat, the gold-flow mechanism seemed to work even more smoothly than could be accounted for by the theory. Modern income analysis proved to be the missing part of the explanation for the gold-flow mechansm. An inflow of gold (increase in the money supply) tends not only to raise prices but also to raise incomes. We have already discussed the means by which an increase in the money supply can affect the level of national income. The increased level of income results in an increased demand for all types of goods, including imports.[3] The opposite takes place in the country losing gold. The decline in the domestic money supply tends to raise interest rates and to lower investment and income. The lowered income results in a reduced demand for imports. Again, these changes are in the direction of reducing the balance-of-payments deficit of the gold-losing country and reducing the surplus of the gold-gaining country.

The role of the monetary authorities under such a gold standard is very clear. The central bank of a country experiencing a gold inflow should allow the inflow to raise the domestic money supply. Likewise, the country losing gold should not attempt to offset the gold outflow, but should aid in reducing the domestic money supply.

The mechanism has several advantages. Exchange rates are stable and there is an automatic preventive of domestic inflation. Some people feel that governments have a strong bias in favor of inflation and cannot be trusted to manage the monetary system. Under the full gold standard, the country's money supply is deter-

---

[3] If the surplus is from the trade account, exports generate domestic income directly, and the rising income increases imports.

mined by the gold supply. If a country inflates, it will run a balance-of-payments deficit and will have its money supply automatically deflated. Furthermore, the mechanism is relatively simple—it requires no international institutions such as the International Monetary Fund to keep it working smoothly.

In view of these advantages, why is it that we do not consider returning to this system? The system has several disadvantages, but one is predominant. No modern country is likely to be willing to follow the "rules of the gold-standard game." The rules of the game require that a country losing gold should suffer deflation and unemployment in order to reduce its demand for foreign goods and thus eliminate its international deficit. Balance-of-payments stability is, of course, an important economic objective. But full employment and economic growth are at least equally important. We will not suffer unemployment to solve the problem of a gold outflow if other measures can be used instead.

A country receiving a gold inflow is equally unlikely to abide by the rules of the game and inflate its money supply. It is hard to imagine a country anxious to endure the inequities and distortions of inflation just to help solve other countries' balance-of-payments problems. Basically, then, the gold-flow mechanism can work well when there are no serious strains put upon it. If balances of payments are generally in equilibrium and very little gold flow occurs, the system works fine. If there are large-scale deficits or surpluses, the system is apt to break down. Under serious strain, countries abandon the gold standard.

Interest Rates and Monetary Policy

The classical gold-flow mechanism was framed in terms of changes in gold (or money) affecting price levels. Account should also be taken of the effect of the gold flows on interest rates. Suppose again that country A has a balance-of-payments deficit and country B has a surplus. The increase in the money supply in B, resulting from the gold outflow, may tend to reduce interest rates in B. The opposite developments may be occurring in A, producing higher interest rates in A than in B. This interest-rate differential will tend to induce a flow of funds from B to A. Investors in either country (or in other countries, for that matter) will find that the higher interest rates make purchases of securities or deposits in banks more attractive in A. This will tend to offset or reverse the initial gold flow from

A to B. This effect, like the price effect, tends to stabilize gold flows and balance-of-payments positions.[4]

In terms of the balance of payments, the decision of an American investor to purchase, for example, German Treasury bills rather than U.S. Treasury bills shows up as an outflow in our balance of payments. If interest rates are higher in Germany than in the United States, this type of outflow is encouraged.

It may appear that this makes a balance-of-payments deficit a very simple problem to solve. All we have to do is raise interest rates in this country to a level high enough to discourage the outflow of capital seeking higher rates abroad. In fact, by raising interest rates high enough here, we could encourage a flow of foreign short-term capital into this country. The catch to this approach is that the high-interest-rate policy desired for international reasons may not be the policy that is best suited for the state of the domestic economy. During a recession, sound monetary policy calls for *low* interest rates. During a period of balance-of-payments deficits, sound monetary policy calls for *high* interest rates. The conflict between domestic and international goals exists under any kind of international monetary system. As countries have more aggressively pursued discretionary economic policies, it has been at the cost of stability of exchange rates.

THE BRETTON WOODS SYSTEM

During World War II, the international payments mechanism was, of course, completely disrupted. Governments were exercising control over many aspects of trade, including, in many cases, determination of the type and quantities of goods that could be exported and imported. Many countries found their productive facilities destroyed by war and their gold and foreign-exchange reserves depleted. The United States, on the other hand, ended the war with its productive capacity increased over the prewar level. No one could tell how balances of payments would be affected if each country returned to the exchange rates that had prevailed before the war.

---

[4] This interest-rate effect is based on the assumption that an increased money supply will tend to reduce interest rates in the country experiencing the gold inflow. We have already discussed the argument by some economists, principally the monetarists, that increases in the money supply eventually produce increases in interest rates. If that position is correct, the interest-rate changes generated by gold flows cannot be counted on to help stabilize the situation and, in fact, will tend to increase the flows.

After World War I, many countries did attempt to return to their former gold standard. The attempts were unsuccessful, and it was clear that after World War II, some sort of international cooperation would be necessary to speed restoration of a multilateral system of international payments without need to resort to direct exchange controls. In 1944, experts from 44 countries met at Bretton Woods, New Hampshire, to consider postwar monetary plans. One result of the Bretton Woods conference was the establishment of the International Monetary Fund.

The IMF was formed based on the premise that countries with a basically sound economic position and fixed exchange rates may, from time to time, be faced with temporary balance-of-payments difficulties. In the absence of the fund, these countries might attempt to correct their problems by resorting to direct exchange controls or bartering arrangements that would be injurious to the multilateral nature of world trade. The fund has resources that are made available to members to allow them to weather a stormy period without being forced to impose restrictions on current transactions. The IMF was not intended to balance the accounts of countries with basic, chronic balance-of-payments deficits.

When the fund was established, the member countries agreed upon the par values of their currencies in terms of gold or the dollar. Each country was obligated to limit exchange-rate fluctuations to 1 percent on either side of the par value. Most countries chose to stabilize the value of their currency by using the dollar to intervene in the spot foreign-exchange market. The United States, on the other hand, met its exchange-stability obligations by standing ready to buy or sell gold at $35 an ounce.[5]

If a member country found that its par value resulted in a fundamental balance-of-payments disequilibrium, it could change the par value, although sizable changes required the approval of the fund. Most such changes in the postwar period were devalua-

---

[5] The reader will recall that the United States had already gone off the full gold standard in 1933. U.S. residents could not convert dollars to gold, nor were they allowed to hold gold. Gold was reserved for international purposes. Foreign governments and central banks that acquired dollars did have the right to exchange them for gold at a fixed rate. The acquisition of dollars was considered a balance-of-payments deficit for the United States, whether or not gold conversion took place. In the period 1933–71, the United States was the only nation that maintained any kind of gold convertibility whatsoever. A few nations have struck gold coins and sold them for numismatic purposes, but this bit of enterprise in no sense constitutes a gold standard. A presidential commission in 1982 recommended such a coin for the United States.

tions,[6] but a few countries whose currencies were in strong demand revalued their currencies upward.

The International Monetary System
after Bretton Woods

The international financial system worked reasonably well for about 25 years after the Bretton Woods agreements, but not quite along the lines anticipated by those arrangements. The Bretton Woods system was based heavily on gold, which was the only asset possessing the general acceptability necessary to serve as reserves for the international financial system. Gold supplies are limited, however, and gold reserves did not grow sufficiently in the postwar years to provide an adequate base for the increased volume of world trade.

Fortunately (or unfortunately, as it may have turned out), the dollar became an international currency with sufficient acceptability to serve as the reserve asset behind many foreign currencies. The United States ran substantial balance-of-payments deficits, and the resulting outflows of dollars provided the necessary increase in the world volume of reserves. The gradual accumulation of dollars by foreigners was at first welcomed, but then resented. Question arose as to how many dollars foreigners would want to hold. If the United States had taken steps to halt its balance-of-payments deficits, the increase in the world supply of liquidity would have been halted. On the other hand, the deficits left the United States in the position of increasing its purchases of foreign goods and acquisition of foreign assets while foreigners became increasingly unwilling holders of dollar assets. Some critics (President DeGaulle of France may have been the most prominent, but there were others, both foreign and domestic) claimed that this system served only to finance American enterprise and military adventures abroad.

Another problem with the Bretton Woods system is that it anticipated relatively frequent changes in par values for currencies. In fact, however, countries were very reluctant to change the value of their currency, and they have also been reluctant to take economic-policy measures to improve their international balance at the expense of domestic economic objectives. Tariffs, quotas, and

---

[6] A *devaluation* is a reduction in the foreign-exchange value of a currency from a change in its official par value. A *depreciation* is a reduction that results from market forces on the exchanges.

other restrictions were resorted to as a means of insulating domestic economies from the discipline of the international trading
arena. This became a more serious problem as economic inter-
dependence among countries became more developed and the whole
system became more susceptible to destabilizing speculation and
large-scale flows of short-term capital.

There are several reasons for the shift from a surplus position
for the United States in the early postwar years to deficits. The
most important, of course, was the economic recovery of Western
Europe and Japan. During the late 1940s, the United States was
exporting consumer goods to these areas, since local production was
inadequate. In addition, the United States was exporting machinery and equipment necessary to rebuild productive capacity abroad.
As recovery proceeded in the industrialized countries of Europe and
Asia, these countries became able to satisfy a greater proportion of
their domestic needs with domestic production. In addition, their
production included goods that became attractive to American consumers during the 1950s. The boom in imported automobiles in the
late 1950s is the most striking example, but other imported products, such as transistor radios, portable typewriters, and cameras,
became popular and sold well in this country.

There has been some tendency to blame the decline in our
favorable balance of trade on United States goods' "pricing themselves out of the market." It has been argued that wage increases
in this country have led to price increases that have reduced the
ability of American goods to compete in world markets. Some
analysts have pointed to the great difference between the wage
rates in this country and in foreign countries and indicated that
differences in productivity no longer justify this differential. The
issue of productivity is an interesting one, because the productive
facilities of Europe and Japan have been mostly rebuilt since 1945,
and thus in many respects are more modern than U.S. plant and
equipment. The slow pace of investment spending by American
business firms in recent years has aggravated this situation. The
reasons for that are complex, but certainly the high and uncertain
rate of inflation is partly responsible.

Although inflation in the United States has been serious, in
many periods foreign wage rates and prices rose more rapidly than
those here. It may not be accurate to attribute primary importance
to inflationary pressures in the United States as a cause of weakness of the dollar, and yet it is true that the long-standing differences between U.S. and foreign wage rates have become more important as the ability of foreign countries to produce a wide range
of goods efficiently has grown. And it is certainly true that if our

wages and prices had increased less, our ability to compete would have been that much better.

Part of the reason for the deficit can be found in the behavior of investment capital. During the postwar years, the government encouraged the flow of private capital to investment opportunities in foreign countries, and the outflow of private long-term capital was sizable. During the early postwar years, this outflow did not really have an adverse effect on the balance of payments. If an American firm decided to build a plant abroad, it had to import American equipment to build the plant and American machinery to operate it. Foreign investment by American firms, whether in Europe or Africa, meant an increase in U.S. exports.

The present situation is somewhat different. When an American firm builds a plant in a developed country—say, in Western Europe—there is not necessarily an immediate increase in U.S. exports. The plant can be built and equipped with machinery produced in the foreign country. Moreover, the plant, when completed, may turn out goods that replace goods previously exported from the United States. Much of the increased investment by American firms abroad in recent years has been in the industrialized countries and thus does not lead to an increase in U.S. exports.

THE DOLLAR AND INTERNATIONAL RESERVES

With the recognition that the United States could not indefinitely accumulate foreign liquid liabilities against a falling gold stock, much effort and discussion went on during the 1950s and 1960s to develop some other means for the creation of international reserves. It was in this framework that the International Monetary Fund's SDR was created, as a way by which countries of the world could collectively increase reserves, periodically, by whatever amounts were desired. By the time the SDR was established in 1970, the link between the dollar and gold had already begun to crack, providing an unreceptive environment for an untried experimental plan.

Concern over the ability of the United States to maintain gold convertibility of the dollar arose in 1960 and was reflected in a speculative increase in the price of gold in the free market. That problem was handled for a while by several countries' selling gold in the free market in sufficient amounts to push the price down. But as U.S. deficits continued during the 1960s, doubts about the U.S. dollar grew, and operations of this "Gold Pool" proved unable to prevent an increase in the price of gold. In 1968 the Gold Pool was disbanded, and the monetary authorities replaced it with a "two-tier" gold system.

The two-tier system allowed gold transactions on two levels, an official market and a free market. On the official tier, monetary authorities agreed to buy from and sell to each other gold at the official price and not to buy newly mined gold or sell to private buyers. The free-market tier consisted of all other transactions in gold, with the price being determined by supply and demand. This arrangement, in effect, made a distinction between the monetary and the private uses of gold.

These changes in the gold market did not affect the U.S. balance-of-payments position, which weakened even more in the very late 1960s. The weakening was partially concealed by large inflows of short-term capital from abroad, because of the very high interest rates that prevailed in this country. As U.S. monetary policy shifted toward ease in 1970 in response to the weakening of the domestic economy, these funds flowed back in large amounts.

Moreover, the underlying U.S. balance-of-trade surplus, the strength of our balance of payments for many years, began to deteriorate during the late 1960s because of accelerating inflation in this country. The balance of trade became very weak in late 1970 and into 1971. Currency speculation and hedging transactions against possible devaluation of the dollar or upward revaluation of the German mark and other currencies were commonplace. It became increasingly clear that the 1971 U.S. balance-of-payments deficit would far exceed any deficit on record. It was against this background that President Nixon acted in August 1971.

The Smithsonian Agreement

The international aspects of the administration's program included the suspension of convertibility of the dollar into gold and imposition of a 10 percent surcharge on most imports. These measures were aimed partly at improving the U.S. balance of payments directly, and partly at encouraging other countries to increase the value of their currencies with respect to the dollar. Other countries, when they experience a fundamental deficit in their balance of payments, may devalue their currencies. Many currencies have been devalued, some several times, since the establishment of the International Monetary Fund. Under the existing rules of the international financial system, however, the United States did not have the ability to devalue the dollar in terms of other currencies. It had the power to change the value of the dollar with respect to gold, but if other countries maintain their parities with the dollar, nothing is really accomplished by such a step.

In the immediate aftermath of the suspension of convertibility, several countries allowed their currencies to appreciate against the dollar on the foreign-exchange market. Some imposed restrictions on the inflow of funds. Increasing use of exchange restrictions posed a real threat to the expansion of world trade, as well as increasing political tensions.

Efforts among the Group of Ten major industrial countries to resolve the problem culminated in an agreement reached at a December 1971 meeting at the Smithsonian Institution. The agreement set new parities for each country's currency, and also enlarged the band within which currency values could fluctuate from 1 percent to 2¼ percent on each side of the central rate. The United States removed the 10 percent import surcharge, and negotiations were carried out to reduce foreign discrimination against imports of American products. Part of the agreement required a devaluation of the dollar by means of an increase in the price of gold, from $35 per ounce to $38. Although the new parities involved a significant devaluation of the dollar relative to other leading currencies, the increase in the price of gold had no practical effect. The reasons for the devaluation in terms of gold were political and not economic: In the mythology of international finance, a change in the value of a currency is viewed as a sign of failure, and other countries were anxious to have the United States make the public confession of error that a devaluation seems to imply. The increase in the price of gold is the equivalent of having the secretary of the Treasury don sackcloth and ashes, and has about as much effect. After all, since we are not selling gold, it makes no difference whether we refuse to sell at $38 per ounce or at $35 per ounce.

The Smithsonian Agreement represented only a temporary solution to the international currency crisis (although President Nixon, with characteristic hyperbole, hailed it as "the most significant monetary agreement in the history of the world"). It was clear, however, that the old monetary system had broken down and could not simply be put together again to function just as it had before. Foreign governments and central banks held huge amounts of dollars—greatly exceeding U.S. reserve assets—thus precluding a prompt return to convertibility of the dollar. Doubts about the stability of the system led to speculative flurries in foreign-exchange markets, but, with the exception of the pound, major currencies held through 1972 within the ranges set at the Smithsonian.

Floating Rates

A major wave of currency speculation against the dollar broke out in early 1973. Fear of further devaluation of the dollar led businessmen, bankers, and speculators to shift dollar holdings to German marks, Japanese yen, and other strong currencies. The fears were based on continued U.S. balance-of-payments deficits, an increased rate of inflation in the United States, and doubt as to the Federal Reserve's determination to fight inflation with high interest rates and monetary restraint. The United States made very little effort to defend the value of the dollar and seemed willing to negotiate a further devaluation in terms of gold, this time to $42.22 an ounce.

Most other countries were unable to settle on exchange rates vis-à-vis the dollar that they would commit themselves to maintain, so most currencies were allowed to float on the exchange markets. Although many economists believe that a system of freely or "cleanly" floating rates is a desirable one, the 1973 float was a relatively "dirty" one. That is, governments intervened in foreign-exchange markets to affect (if not control) the price of their currency.

Some smaller countries decided to peg their currencies to that of their principal trading partner. The European Community tried unsuccessfully during this period to link its currencies for a common float against the dollar and other currencies. This European Monetary Union existed only in 1972–1973, but in 1979 another attempt was begun, this time called the European Monetary System, with seven members. Currencies within this system are allowed to float only within a 2¼ percent band. The system's future will depend upon the ability of its members to deal with the problem of divergent rates of inflation—varying from 3 to 13 percent—among them.

Many had hoped that the floating-currency regime that began in 1973 was to be only temporary, but the world was buffeted soon after by the OPEC cartel's massive increase in oil prices and by explosive rates of inflation in most major countries. International negotiations have taken place on a regular basis, and agreements of greater or lesser significance have been arrived at. The last decade has not been propitious for arranging a new world monetary order. It seems clear that floating exchange rates are going to be with us for some time. Table 31-1 shows exchange rates for selected dates, before and after the suspension of the par value system.

The move to floating exchange rates did not mean that the

TABLE 31-1

Selected Exchange Rates

	January 1971 Par Values	Average 1978 Market Prices	January 1982 Market Prices
Australia (dollar)	$1.12	$1.14	$1.11
Belgium (franc)	.020	.032	.026
France (franc)	.181	.222	.172
Germany (mark)	.275	.499	.436
Italy (lira)	.0016	.0012	.0008
Japan (yen)	.0028	.0048	.0044
Mexico (peso)	.08	.044	.038
Netherlands (guilder)	.278	.463	.398
Spain (peseta)	.014	.013	.010
Sweden (krona)	.194	.221	.178
United Kingdom (pound)	2.44	1.92	1.89
U.S. dollar against 10 major currencies (index)[a]		92.4	107.0

[a] March 1973 = 100. Average exchange value of dollar against the currencies, weighted by the global trade of the 10 countries, 1972–76.

Source: Federal Reserve System.

International Monetary Fund was dismantled. Countries still borrow and use reserves to moderate fluctuations in exchange rates. The reserves needed are not nearly as great as would be the case with absolutely fixed exchange rates, and thus a great expansion of reserves through SDR creation does not seem likely. Countries' reserves consist primarily of their holdings of dollars, plus small amounts of other currencies.

A proposal has been offered within the IMF to establish "Substitution Accounts" that countries would exchange for their dollar holdings. The country would take an SDR-denominated claim on the IMF, and in turn the IMF would acquire the U.S. Treasury securities now held by the country. The United States would pay interest to the IMF, which would pay interest to holders of the SDRs. This system is designed to enhance the status of the SDR as a unit of account and to take some of the pressure off the dollar as a reserve currency. It cannot be expected that countries will easily forgo their holdings of dollars. In the past, they have shown a strong preference for holding claims on a nation of vast resources and a stable government over an international institution without an economy or government.

The role of the dollar in the Bretton Woods system had some

advantages to the United States. It was possible for the United States to run balance-of-payments deficits and find that other countries were willing to simply hold the extra dollars they received. Other countries in a deficit position found themselves hard put to defend the value of their currencies, as they were obligated to do, when the holders of the currency sought to convert it to stronger currencies. In essence, the United States was less subject to the discipline of the balance of payments than other countries were.

We also enjoyed the benefits that go with an overvalued currency—foreign goods were cheaper than they would be if the dollar had a lower price in foreign-exchange markets. This was a benefit to American consumers, even though it made it more difficult for American producers to meet foreign competition. Currency values now more nearly represent relative real costs of production.

Foreign trade represents a relatively small portion of economic activity in the United States. Although we do want to bring our international flows into at least rough balance, we do not want to take steps that will hurt the 90 percent of the economy that is not dependent on international trade. Nevertheless, U.S. monetary policy must now be formulated in an international framework. During the 1950s, a monetary policy based solely on domestic considerations may have been feasible, but coming up with the right answers on monetary policy in the future will prove a more difficult task, because at least some weight has to be given to possible implications for the balance of payments and the value of the dollar.

QUESTIONS

1 How does the gold-flow mechanism work?
2 Would high interest rates in this country improve or intensify our balance-of-payments problem?
3 In what way could an improvement in our balance-of-payments situation create liquidity problems in other countries?
4 What are the "rules of the gold-standard game"?
5 What are the principal differences between our balance of payments of 1980 and 1963? To what do you attribute the changes?
6 Does it make any great difference whether or not the United States is willing to convert dollars to gold at a fixed price?
7 "Since foreign trade is such a small part of the U.S. economy, monetary policy should be based on domestic economic needs, with virtually no weight given to international considerations." Do you agree?

SELECTED READINGS

ARGY, VICTOR, *The Post War International Money Crisis*. Winchester, Mass.: Allen & Unwin, 1981.

KRAUSE, LAWRENCE B., *Sequel to Bretton Woods*. Washington, D.C.: The Brookings Institution, 1972.

PONIACHEK, HARVEY, *Monetary Independence under Flexible Exchange Rates*. Lexington, Mass.: Lexington Books, 1979.

SOBOL, DOROTHY, "A Substitution Account: Precedents and Issues," Federal Reserve Bank of New York *Quarterly Review*, Summer 1979.

TREZISE, PHILIP, ed., *The European Monetary System: Its Promise and Prospects*. Washington, D.C.: The Brookings Institution, 1979.

WARD, RICHARD A., *International Finance*. Englewood Cliffs, N.J.: Prentice-Hall, 1965.

ZOLOTAS, XENOPHON, *International Monetary Issues and Development Policies*. New York: New York University Press, 1977.

32

Monetary Policy: A Concluding Look

Throughout history, people have always thought that money is extremely important. Economists have not always shared this view, as we have seen. The role of money in economic theory has waxed and waned. The mercantilists of the sixteenth, seventeenth, and eighteenth centuries stressed that money was the most desirable form of wealth and that nations should adopt policies that would ensure the inflow and accumulation of large hoards of gold.

This preoccupation with gold was not just a harmless form of miserliness. Acceptance of the mercantilist philosophy led (and still leads) countries to adopt policies that may have hindered their long-term development. Restrictions on trade and the policies adopted in relation to treatment of colonies are examples of this.

The classical economists, beginning with Adam Smith, revolted against this overemphasis on money. They were concerned with goods that could satisfy consumer needs. In their view, then, the "wealth of nations" consisted not in hoards of gold and silver but in productive capacity. Money was desirable for what it could buy, not for its own sake. The classical economists treated money as a useful device for facilitating exchange and thus increasing opportunities for division of labor. They recognized that barter was inefficient, that it was easier for the baker to sell his bread for money and use the money to buy shoes from the shoemaker than for the

baker and shoemaker to attempt to trade bread for shoes. Nevertheless, they viewed the real transaction as being the exchange of
bread for shoes—the money transaction simply made the real
transaction more convenient.

The classical economists recognized that changes in the
amount of money in circulation would affect the level of money
prices (that is, the price in dollars or pounds of a pair of shoes or a
loaf of bread), but they argued that the amount of money had no
effect on the level of output of shoes or bread or the price ratio
between bread and shoes (that is, the number of loaves of bread that
would equal one pair of shoes).

The treatment of money as purely a means of exchange was
provided with its logical foundation by the work of Jean-Baptiste
Say, which we noted in Chapter 1. He argued that there could be no
such thing as general overproduction or depression. Say came up
with this conclusion in spite of the fact that periodic depressions
were occurring while he was studying the behavior of the economy.
Keynes demonstrated that "Say's Law" is valid only in a barter
economy, not in a money economy in which people can hoard money.
The money that is hoarded is not a part of the demand for goods, nor
is it available for investment. Keynes showed that hoarding may be
a rational activity and that the extent of hoarding can affect interest rates and thus the real aspects of the economy—production,
distribution, and income.

The classical economists, including Say, were willing to admit
that money can cause distortions in the economy when it gets "out
of order." But they considered this to be merely a short-run phenomenon. Keynes' approach stressed the short run ("In the long
run we are all dead") and the view that money is always "out of
order."

This is not necessarily a pessimistic view of money. If money
can cause economic difficulties, this means that proper management of money can help the economy. The Keynesian analysis leads
to the view that monetary policy can affect interest rates, and hence
investment, and thus can have a stabilizing effect on the economy.
This is so even though Keynes himself was not a strong advocate of
using monetary policy in handling the depression of the 1930s,
because he felt that its expansionary effects would be slight in such
a deep, prolonged depression.

Money and monetary policy thus recovered substantially in
their standing among economists from the low repute in which the
classical economists had held them. World War II once again made
monetary policy a relatively unimportant subject. The Federal

Reserve was committed to a policy of facilitating Treasury financing of war expenditures. There was no debate about the wisdom of the policy during the war period. However, the policy of subordinating monetary policy to the desires of the Treasury was continued after the war—a more questionable decision.

THE STRUCTURE OF POLICY MAKING

It was not until the Treasury–Federal Reserve accord of 1951 that monetary policy in this country was free to demonstrate its capabilities and its limitations. In fact, it became *too* free. We have been excessively dependent upon monetary policy for economic stabilization since the accord. Built-in automatic fiscal stabilizers are powerful, but discretionary fiscal policy was used little to help stabilize the economy.[1] Even most strong believers in the efficacy of monetary measures to restrain inflation and contain recession feel that in such periods, some use of fiscal policy is necessary.

In many countries, the central bank is a government department. This is not formally the case in the United States, but obviously there must be close coordination between the activities of the Federal Reserve and the government. The concept of Federal Reserve independence has been widely discussed, but clearly the Fed must be subject to some political control. The long, staggered terms of members of the Board of Governors are designed to free the board from political pressures and to prevent the president, even in the course of two terms, from completely dominating the Board with his appointees. Some attempt at coordination is achieved by giving the president the power to designate the chairman of the Board, but the four-year term is not coterminous with the presidency.[2]

The structure of the Federal Reserve System is such that even within the system, authority is widely diffused. The Board of Governors consists of seven people; there are also twelve Reserve Bank presidents and 108 Reserve Bank directors. Not all these 127 individuals have equal influence. The directors tend to go along with

[1] A notable exception when proposed was the tax cut of 1964, but it came later than it should have for its intended purpose. The surcharge of 1968 also came late, and its announced temporary nature blunted the effect on consumer spending.

[2] The Commission on Money and Credit, a prestigious privately sponsored study, in 1961 recommended establishment of an advisory board with representation from the Council of Economic Advisers, the Federal Reserve Board, the Office of Management and Budget, and the Departments of State, Treasury, Agriculture, Commerce, Labor, Housing, and Health, Education and Welfare. The size of this list gives some indication of the problems of coordination.

the views of their president. Frequently, Governors have been people with little knowledge of monetary policy, who have been willing to follow the lead of the chairman. During the 1960s, most appointees to the Board of Governors were professional economists. Even though a Ph.D. in economics should not be a requirement for a seat on the board, it does seem reasonable to expect a Governor to have some knowledge of or experience with monetary policy or with the functioning of the financial system. The chairman, however, may have an interest in not having a Board consisting of six other competent, well-trained independent thinkers.

Suggestions have been made to improve the prestige and attractiveness of appointment to the Board of Governors. Board members now receive lower salaries than Reserve Bank presidents, although their position is (or should be) more important. An increase in salary might help attract extremely well-qualified people to serve on the Board.

Other suggestions for change in the Board of Governors usually include a reduction in the size of the Board.

The relationship between the Board of Governors and the Reserve Bank presidents also causes some concern. Reserve Bank presidents account for five of the twelve members of the Open Market Committee. Many authorities have been concerned about the fact that a considerable amount of influence and power has been delegated to people who are not responsible to the electorate for their actions. Some think this is a desirable situation—that people who are concerned with the political implications of their acts and with their chances for reelection or reappointment would find it difficult to take unpopular actions when they were necessary. This, of course, is an indictment of the democratic system as a whole and does not apply just to Federal Reserve policy.

There is no evidence that the lack of political responsibility has resulted in undesirable actions by the Reserve Bank presidents. They seem to consider their function that of representing the general interest rather than the interests of the banking community. In recent years, Federal Reserve Bank presidents have frequently been drawn from the ranks of professional economists. Although there would seem to be a basis, on theoretical grounds, for having policy decisions within the Fed made by elected officials or those responsible to elected officials, it would be undesirable to eliminate the useful advice that can flow from the presidents to the board. Two of the most outstanding men in the system's history have been presidents of the Federal Reserve Bank of New York: Benjamin Strong and Alan Sproul. Officers and staff of the Federal Reserve Bank of St. Louis have played a key role over the years in advocating the monetarist approach to monetary policy, even when that view was not accepted by the Board of Governors.

THE DIRECTION OF MONETARY POLICY

In the coming years, monetary policy must pay more attention to the preservation of financial intermediation than to the shorter-term problems of economic stabilization. Inflation has undermined the public's confidence in financial saving. In time, this could threaten the saving–investment flows so important to a growing economy.

American personal saving took a plunge beginning in 1976. In 1975, the ratio of financial saving to disposable personal income was 6.6 percent. By 1979, it was down to 1.9 percent, but back to 3.6 percent in 1980. Total personal saving also fell in relation to income, but not as much as financial saving because of a rise in saving through net investment in housing. Financial assets relative to GNP have shown a slight drop. In 1970, financial assets of individuals were two times GNP; in 1980, they were 1.7 times GNP. (Table 32-1 shows the composition of assets in the two periods.)

In an inflationary environment, the financial saver runs the risk that savings will be worth less over time. A higher interest rate is needed to compensate for this risk, but until the 1980s, interest-rate ceilings made this impossible, although the position of many institutions, locked into low-yielding assets, would have limited their ability in any event to offer attractive deposit rates. It is hoped that the long-term effect of the 1980 reforms, in liberalizing portfolios and freeing deposit interest, will maintain the ability of financial intermediaries to service the economy.

To some extent, the economy has taken measures to protect itself from wide swings in interest rates. Long-term fixed-interest-rate contracts are becoming less and less available. When loans are made and securities sold at floating rates, both borrowers and lenders become less sensitive to changes in rates. A rise in rates, for example, will have less power to reduce borrowing, since borrowers will still benefit from any subsequent fall in rates. And as interest changes are applied to old contracts, these contracts are subjected to less change in market value than they would with fixed interest payments. These changes mean that monetary policy will have less effect on the economy than in the past—fluctuations in the long-term interest rate are a less potent factor as a stabilization device.

Higher interest rates, without wide swings, may serve the economy better than countercyclical fluctuations in rates. In the

TABLE 32-1
Household Financial Assets, 1970 and 1980[a]

	Billions of Dollars	
	1970	1980
Demand deposits & currency	136.8	263.0
Savings accounts	426.7	1307.2
Money-market fund shares	—	74.4
U.S. government and agency securities	107.2	292.6
State and local obligations	46.0	69.7
Corporate & foreign bonds	34.3	80.0
Open-market paper	11.7	28.5
Investment-company shares	47.6	55.5
Other corporate equities	681.8	1088.6
Private life insurance reserves	123.1	214.6
Private pension reserves	151.6	444.8
Govt. ins. & pension reserves	95.2	294.0
Misc. financial assets	105.2	282.4
Total	1967.2	4495.2

[a] Includes farms and noncorporate business.

Source: Federal Reserve Flow-of-Funds Accounts.

longer-term perspective, higher interest rates are not necessarily wholly negative in their effects on capital formation. Investment can be accommodated only if the public is willing to forgo consumption. An equilibrium must be struck between the interest rate that savers require and one that will justify investment.[3]

A policy of allowing realistic interest rates for the long-term perspective does not necessarily mean an active countercyclical monetary policy. It is easy to become convinced that it is unwise to conduct a monetary policy of starts and stops aimed at offsetting cyclical instability in the economy. There are two principal problems: implementation and incidence.

With respect to implementation, it seems impossible to time monetary-policy changes so that the effects are felt when needed. First, there are problems in knowing when to initiate action. Lags in collection of data and uncertainties in their interpretation mean that we are never sure at any one moment just where the economy is or where it is headed. Once monetary policy has changed course, time is required for spending units in the economy to adjust their

[3] Some less-developed countries have found national savings rates to be surprisingly responsive to changes in national policy lifting interest-rate ceilings that had been kept articifically low. See Edward Shaw, *Financial Deepening in Economic Development* (New York: Oxford University Press, 1973). For an informative case study, see Gilbert T. Brown, *Korean Pricing Policies and Economic Development in the 1960's* (Baltimore: Johns Hopkins University Press, 1973).

plans. The principal thrust of monetary policy would seem to be on interest-sensitive expenditures, and these are long-term investment projects, both private and public. Once planned and initiated, investment outlays continue on such projects for many months. In the other direction, an easy-money policy that stimulates such expenditures will require many months before the maximum effect on the economy is felt.

With respect to the incidence of monetary-policy changes, the most demonstrable result occurs in residential construction. Plant and equipment spending is doubtless affected, but the lags involved and the complex interaction with other variables in the economy make this difficult to assess. We can also assume that when business is restrained in spending, the least likely to be affected are the large entrenched corporations with internally generated funds and ready access to capital markets—hardly the measure needed to foster competition in the marketplace.

Although supply-side economists have overemphasized the disincentive effect of taxation and transfer payments, it is to their credit that they have brought attention to the possible negative effect on supply of an undue concentration on demand manipulation. An attack on investment spending has short-term deflationary effects, but repeated attacks, cycle after cycle, will take their toll in productive capacity.

An active countercyclical monetary policy seems to assign housing and plant and equipment to a low-priority expenditure that can be sacrificed as needed to consumption expenditures. This approach is inconsistent with the overall goals of economic policy. Both the distributional goal (in the case of housing) and the growth goal (in the case of plant and equipment) are sacrificed, and for this reason, government often takes action elsewhere to undo the effects of monetary policy. Examples are subsidized mortgages, grants to state and local governments, investment-tax credit, accelerated depreciation allowances, small-business loans, export credit, and farm loans.

But these powerful arguments against an aggressive monetary policy with frequent reversals in direction do not constitute a case against *any* monetary policy. As long as government provides the ultimate payments media—legal-tender money and clearing balances at the Federal Reserve—some kind of policy necessarily results from the decision at any time as to how much of such media to provide. What therefore constitutes a "neutral" policy, one that neither restrains the economy nor pushes it? If we could ever devise means to pursue an active fiscal policy, a neutral monetary policy might very well be in order, but no one so far has been able to satisfactorily define such neutrality. A stable interest rate has been suggested, but since desires for borrowing and lending necessarily shift, a constant interest rate would have a variable effect. And with rising prices, the concept of a "stable" interest rate is undefinable — a stable real rate, or a stable nominal rate?

Milton Friedman's proposal for a stable money-growth rate (Chapter 26) comes close to a neutral monetary policy, but only if prices remain stable. Even in this unlikely circumstance, the dynamic nature of financial markets is apt to render obsolete in time whatever group of assets is initially targeted for control.

Thus we are left with discretionary monetary policy, with the hope that the authorities will pay more attention to the goals than to the game.

QUESTIONS

1 Which of the goals of economic policy do you think will be most important in the year 2000?
2 Would frequent changes in controls on consumer credit serve the economy better than frequent interest-rate changes?
3 Should monetary policy be conducted any differently if we had price controls?
4 How much information should the Federal Reserve be required to give the public concerning its policy and the reasons for it? And when should this information be given?
5 Would you favor a rule of a constant growth rate in the money stock? Which money stock?

SELECTED READINGS

BACH, GEORGE L., *Making Monetary and Fiscal Policy*, Chaps. 2–4. Washington, D.C.: The Brookings Institution, 1972.

Commission on Money and Credit, *Money and Credit*. Englewood Cliffs, N.J.: Prentice-Hall, 1961.

Committee on Financial Institutions, *Report of the Committee*. Washington, D.C.: U.S. Government Printing Office, 1963.

MAISEL, SHERMAN J., *Managing the Dollar*. New York: W.W. Norton, 1973.

MINTS, LLOYD W., *Monetary Policy for a Competitive Society*. New York: McGraw-Hill, 1950.

SMITH, ADAM, *The Wealth of Nations*, Vol. I, Book 2, Chap. 11. London, 1776.

The Report of the President's Commission on Financial Structure and Regulation. Washington, D.C.: U.S. Government Printing Office, 1971.

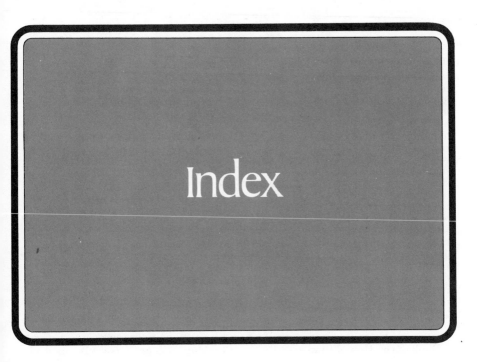

Index